The Acts of the Apostles

by

Charles W. Carter, M.A., Th.M., D.D.

and

Ralph Earle, Th.D.

Schmul

First published 1959

Published by Schmul Publishing Co.
PO Box 776
Nicholasville, KY 40340

Printed in the United States of America

ISBN 10: 0-88019-050-7
ISBN 13: 978-0-88019-050-3

DEDICATION

In recognition of the verity of a popular American philosopher's words, "The road to success is crowded with men who are being pushed along by their faithful wives," the authors appreciatively and affectionately dedicate this work to their companions.

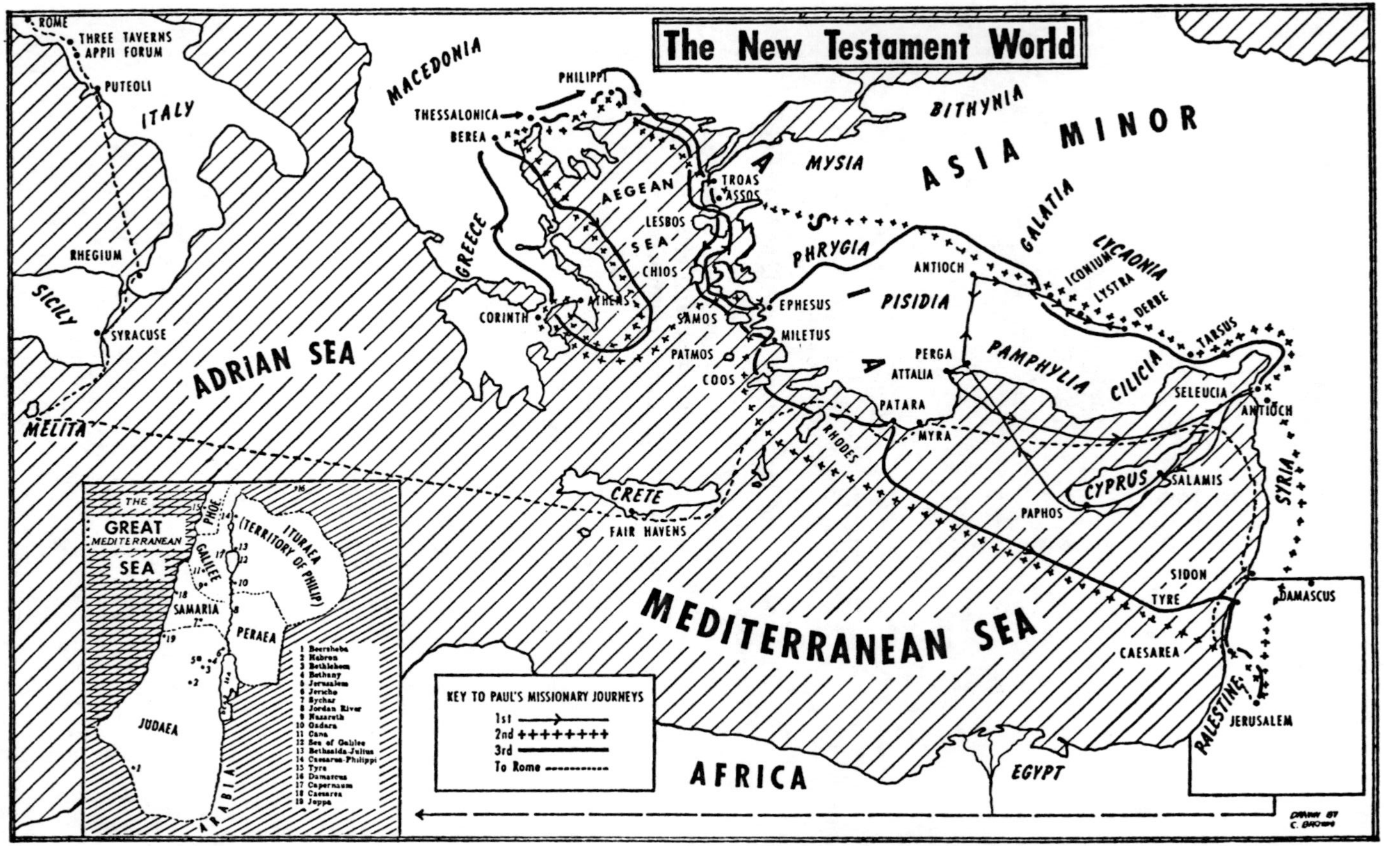
The New Testament World
ROME
THREE TAVERNS
APPII FORUM
PUTEOLI
ITALY
RHEGIUM
SICILY
SYRACUSE
MELITA
ADRIAN SEA
MACEDONIA
PHILIPPI
THESSALONICA
BEREA
GREECE
CORINTH
ATHENS
AEGEAN
SEA
LESBOS
CHIOS
SAMOS
PATMOS
COOS
TROAS
ASSOS
MYSIA
BITHYNIA
ASIA MINOR
GALATIA
PHRYGIA
ANTIOCH
PISIDIA
EPHESUS
MILETUS
LYCAONIA
ICONIUM
LYSTRA
DERBE
TARSUS
PERGA
ATTALIA
PAMPHYLIA
CILICIA
PATARA
MYRA
RHODES
SELEUCIA
ANTIOCH
SYRIA
CYPRUS
SALAMIS
PAPHOS
CRETE
FAIR HAVENS
SIDON
TYRE
CAESAREA
DAMASCUS
PALESTINE
JERUSALEM
MEDITERRANEAN SEA
AFRICA
EGYPT
KEY TO PAUL'S MISSIONARY JOURNEYS
1st
2nd
3rd
To Rome
THE GREAT MEDITERRANEAN SEA
PHOE.
GALILEE
ITURAEA (TERRITORY OF PHILIP)
SAMARIA
PERAEA
JUDAEA
ARABIA
1 Beersheba
2 Hebron
3 Bethlehem
4 Bethany
5 Jerusalem
6 Jericho
7 Sychar
8 Jordan River
9 Nazareth
10 Gadara
11 Cana
12 Sea of Galilee
13 Bethsaida-Julius
14 Caesarea-Philippi
15 Tyre
16 Damascus
17 Capernaum
18 Caesarea
19 Joppa

ABBREVIATIONS

I. Versions:

KJV — King James Version (1611).
ASV — American Standard Version (1901).
RSV — Revised Standard Version (1946–52).
RV — Revised Versions.

II. Commentaries:

CGT — Cambridge Greek Testament.
EGT — Expositor's Greek Testament.
IB — Interpreter's Bible.
ICC — International Critical Commentary.
JFB — Jamieson, Fausset, and Brown.
MC — Moffatt Commentary.
NBC — New Bible Commentary (1 vol.).
NIC — New International Commentary on the New Testament.
WC — Westminster Commentaries.

III. Miscellaneous:

HDAC — Hastings Dictionary of the Apostolic Church.
HDB — Hastings Dictionary of the Bible (5 vols).
HDCG — Hastings Dictionary of Christ and the Gospels.
ISBE — International Standard Bible Encyclopedia.
LXX — Septuagint.
MS — manuscript (MSS — manuscripts).
MT — Massoretic Text (of O.T.).
VGT — Vocabulary of the Greek Testament (Moulton and Milligan).
WDB — Westminster Dictionary of the Bible.

PREFACE

The authorship of *The Acts of the Apostles: A Commentary* represents the combined scholarship of two men whose theological positions and practical purposes bear a high degree of similarity, if indeed not identity. Dr. Charles W. Carter is the author of the Analytical Outlines, the Expositions of the text and the Additional Notes on special subjects at the close of certain chapters. Dr. Ralph Earle is the author of the Introduction and the Exegesis of the text. This dual authorship of the work finds its justification in the respective qualifications and specialized interests of the authors.

Dr. Carter's special interest in the message of the Book of Acts results in considerable measure from his many years of missionary experience in West Africa, plus his extensive teaching and lecturing service with missionaries, national church leaders, and in theological colleges and seminaries in many lands. These include the Caribbean Islands, South America, Mexico, Japan, the Philippines, Taiwan and India. In addition to eleven years as Chairman of the Division of Philosophy and Religion at Marion College, and twelve years in the same position at Taylor University, the Expositor has taught at Union Biblical Seminary in Medillen, Colombia, the Caribbean Wesleyan Bible College on Barbados, Union Biblical Seminary at Yeotmal, India, and Central Taiwan Theological College in Taiwan. For a number of years he was Principal and Professor of the Clarke Memorial Biblical Seminary in Sierra Leone, Africa. He is presently Visiting Professor of Theology and Ethics at China Evangelical Seminary in Taipei, Taiwan.

Dr. Carter holds the Th.B. and B.A. degrees from Marion College, the M.A. in Theology from Winona Lake School of Theology, the M.A. and Th.M. from Butler University, and the B.D. and D.D. degrees from Asbury Theological Seminary. He has also studied at Ohio State University and has done graduate work at Chicago Lutheran Theological Seminary. He is a member of the National Honor Society *Phi Kappa Phi* and the International Honor Society *Theta Phi*. He holds membership in the Evangelical Theological Society, and is Editor and Promotional Secretary of the Wesleyan Theological Society. He is cited for his achievements in several works of national recognition.

In addition to the General Editorship of the seven-volume *Wesleyan Bible Commentary* (Eerdmans, 1964-69), plus the commentaries on Acts, Ephesians, I Corinthians, Hebrews and Job, the Expositor has published a number of widely read books and scholarly articles. His many years of teaching the Book of Acts, plus his extensive practical service in the ministry and missionary work will be reflected in his interpretation of the message of the Book of Acts.

Dr. Ralph Earle, the writer responsible for the exegesis of the text of Acts in the present work, is Professor of New Testament at Nazarene Theological Seminary. Dr. Earle is widely recognized as a competent New Testament scholar and lecturer. He has lectured at many colleges and seminaries throughout America and abroad. These include institutions in Europe, South America, the Near East and several countries of the Far East. Dr. Earle holds degrees from Eastern Nazarene College, Boston University, and the doctorate from Gordon Theological Seminary. He has also done graduate study at Harvard and Edinburgh Universities.

Among Dr. Earle's published works are *The Quest of the Spirit; The Story of the New Testament; Know Your New Testament;* and *Meet the Minor Prophets.* Dr. Earle is also New Testament Editor of the *Wesleyan Bible Commentary* and contributor of the commentaries on the Synoptic Gospels in Vol. IV of that series.

The present work, *The Acts of the Apostles: A Commentary,* which now constitutes the volume on the Acts of the Apostles in the new *Zondervan Commentary Series*, was originally prepared and published in 1959 as the volume on Acts in the projected, but unrealized forty-volume *Evangelical Bible Commentary* series. The Acts volume was soon sold out and has now been out of print for several years. The volume received high acclaim from many leading reviewers, scholars and ministers both in America and abroad.

With certain revisions, but minus the exegetical sections, the materials contained in the original volume were incorporated into Volume IV of the *Wesleyan Bible Commentary* published and copyrighted by the Wm. B. Eerdmans Publishing Company. Grateful acknowledgment is here expressed to the Wm. B. Eerdmans Company for permission to republish in the present volume the materials incorporated into Volume IV of the WBC. The materials in *The Acts of the Apostles: A Commentary*, now published as a volume in the *Zondervan Commentary Series*, remain essentially as they appeared in the original work, *The Evangelical Commentary: The Acts of the Apostles* with certain exceptions. In this volume the Introduction has been enlarged and extended, the Bibliography has likewise been extended to include certain works of importance which have appeared since the original volume was published in 1959, and the Preface has been rewritten.

While the original assignment for the production of this commentary on Acts was given to the Expositor, he was most fortunate to engage the efficient collaboration of Dr. Ralph Earle for the exegetical portion of this commentary. Without Dr. Earle's contribution this work could not have attained its intended value. This volume represents many years of preparation and applied scholarship on the part of both the Expositor and the Exegete. The combined bibliography reflects the scholarly and practical works consulted and sometimes quoted or cited by the authors in the preparation of this commentary.

The American Standard Version of the Bible is the basic text of the Scriptures used and incorporated into the present commentary. However, many parallel versions, as also the original languages of the Bible, have been consulted, and on occasion cited or quoted for the additional light which they might throw upon the text.

While the authors have aimed at a high level of accuracy and scholarship, the commentary is slanted toward the practical rather than a highly technical production. However, it is sincerely hoped that the scholarship underlying even the more practical interpretations will be evident to the discerning reader. The commentary is designed to serve the interests and needs of the students of the Book of Acts both on the lay and ministerial levels, as well as more specialized scholars, and especially students in formal preparation for Christian service in Christian colleges and seminaries.

The authors have sought diligently to recover the spirit and purpose of the writer of the Book of Acts, and to interpret accurately and convey that spirit and purpose to the readers of this commentary. That Luke's prime purpose in writing the Book of Acts was to present Jesus Christ as the risen and victorious "Lord of man and the universe" is evident from the recurrence of the title LORD assigned to Him no less than 110 times in the Book of Acts. This title, as applied to the risen Christ, occurs more often than any other important word in the Book of Acts. The Holy Spirit working in and through Christ's first century disciples is represented as witnessing to the universal Lordship of Jesus Christ. This is made evident from Christ's words in the "key verse" of the Book of Acts: *But ye shall receive power, when the Holy Spirit is come upon you: and ye shall be my witness* (Acts 1:8a); as also in Christ's words to His disciples as recorded in the Great Commission in the Gospel according to Matthew. Here Christ says, *All authority hath been given unto me in heaven and on earth, Go ye therefore, and make disciples of all nations* (Matt. 28:18b, 19a). All else in the Book of Acts is incident to this prime purpose. Luke never loses sight of this divine objective in his Acts record from the opening to the closing words of the book.

The authors have followed the natural divisions of the Book of Acts in the development of the commentary. The first seven chapters are devoted to the witness to Christ's Lordship in Jerusalem and Judea. Chapters eight through twelve are devoted to the witness to Christ's Lordship in transition from the Jewish to the Gentile world. Chapters thirteen through twenty-eight are concerned with the witness to Christ's Lordship to all the world of the first century, with implications of the significance of this witness to the entire world of every succeeding generation of the human race. The Analytical Outlines, printed at the opening of each chapter of the commentary, and also incorporated into the expositions, have served to direct the authors' efforts in attempting more clearly and systematically to present the meaning and purpose of the author of the Book of Acts. Again, the authors have sought to bring to light and life the spirit and meaning of first century Christianity with their relevance for the twentieth century, as these are revealed in the Book of Acts.

The Acts of the Apostles: A Commentary is presented to all who seek for the true meaning of Christianity at its source, with the earnest prayer and sincere desire that it may prove to be a safe and accurate guide to the readers' realization of that desired objective.

The authors would express their most sincere appreciation to their faithful and efficient typists, Alta F. Slater and Rachael Enyart, typists for Dr. Charles W. Carter, and Marion Snyder, typist for Dr. Ralph Earle. Their painstaking and untiring service in typing and retyping the manuscripts for this commentary can only receive its due reward in the contribution which this commentary may make to the cause of Christ. Acknowledgment of indebtedness to all authors and publishers of works consulted or quoted in this commentary is hereby gratefully rendered. Due credit is given to these sources in the footnote documentations and the Bibliography. The authors would also express their most sincere gratitude to the Zondervan Publishing House for its decision to honor this work with a place in the publication of their *Commentary* series.

Taipei, Taiwan
September 20, 1972

CHARLES W. CARTER

INTRODUCTION

I. AUTHORSHIP

A. External Evidence

The earliest testimony to Luke as the author of Acts is found in the Anti-Marcionite Prologue to St. Luke's Gospel (ca. A.D. 150–180). There it is stated: "Moreover, the same Luke afterwards wrote the Acts of the Apostles." [1]

The Muratorian Fragment (ca. A.D. 170–200) says:

> But the Acts of the Apostles [a strangely exaggerated title!] were written in one volume. Luke compiled for 'most excellent Theophilus' what things were done in detail in his presence, as he plainly shows by omitting both the death of Peter and also the departure of Paul from the city, when he departed for Spain.[2]

Likewise coming from the latter part of the second century is the witness of Irenaeus[3] and Clement of Alexandria[4] that Acts was written by Luke. Eusebius speaks of "the testimony of Luke in the book of Acts."[5] Clement writes: "Luke in the Acts of the Apostles records that Paul said, 'Men of Athens, I see in all things that you are very religious.'" He also declares: "It is acknowledged that Luke wrote with his pen the Acts of the Apostles." There appears not to have been raised in the early church any question about the Lukan authorship of Acts. Zahn says: "No other position concerning its authorship had been expressed in any quarter."[6]

B. Internal Evidence

One of the most certain results of modern New Testament study is that *the Third Gospel and Acts were written by the same author.* This is definitely implied by the reference in the first verse of Acts to "the former treatise" and the fact that both books are addressed to Theophilus. There is also a great similarity of style and vocabulary. Moffatt notes that there are no less than 57 words which in the New Testament are found only in both the Third Gospel and Acts.[7] Windisch admits: "Lexical, stylistic, and material points of contact between the two prove that both documents derive from the same author."[8] A. C. Clark has sought to deny this.[9] But his arguments have been answered in careful detail by W. L. Knox.[10] Henry J. Cadbury, who rejects Lukan authorship, subscribes strongly to the unity of the two books, as reflected in the title of his volume, *The Making of Luke–Acts* (1927).

In the second place, *the one who wrote the "we" sections*[11] *also wrote the rest of the book,* so that the author of Acts was *a companion of Paul.* Again Windisch, who is opposed to Lukan authorship, writes: "Attention must be called to the pervasive lexical, stylistic, and redactional *unity* of Acts as it has been demonstrated by the representatives of the most varied points of view, and, what is especially important, with the inclusion of the 'we' sections.[12] Har-

1 H. D. A. Major, T. W. Manson, and C. J. Wright, *The Mission and Message of Jesus* (New York: E. P. Dutton and Co., 1938), p. 253.
2 Kirsopp Lake and Silva Lake, *An Introduction to the New Testament* (New York: Harper & Brothers, 1937), p. 280.
3 *Against Heresies,* III. 14, 1.
4 *Stromata,* V. 12.
5 Pamphilus Eusebius, *Ecclesiastical History.* Trans. Frederick Cruse. (Grand Rapids: Baker Book House, 1955 reprint), III, 4.
6 Theodor Zahn, *Introduction to the New Testament,* Trans. John Trout, *et al.* (Grand Rapids: Kregel Publications, 1953 reprint), III, 3.
7 James Moffatt, *An Introduction to the Literature of the New Testament.* (3rd. ed.; New York: Charles Scribner's Sons, 1918), p. 297.
8 H. Windisch, "The Case Against the Tradition," *The Beginnings of Christianity* (London: MacMillan & Co., 1920-33), II, 306.
9 A. C. Clark, *The Acts of the Apostles* (Oxford: University Press, 1933), pp. 393 ff.
10 Wilfrid L. Knox, *The Acts of the Apostles* (Cambridge: University Press, 1948). See especially pp. 2-15, 100-109.
11 Acts 16:10-17; 20:5-21:18; 27:1-28:16.
12 *Op. cit.,* p. 305.

nack emphasizes in strongest terms the unity of the "we" sections with the rest of the book.[13] Plummer writes:

That the "we" sections are by the same hand as the rest of the book is shown by the simple and natural way in which they fit into the narrative, by the references in them to other parts of the narrative, and by the marked identity of style. The expressions which are so characteristic of this writer run right through the whole book. They are as frequent inside as outside the "we" sections, and no change of style can be noted between them and the rest of the treatise.[14]

In the third place, *the author was a physician*. Without doubt Hobart overstated the case in his book, *The Medical Language of St. Luke*.[15] But Harnack gave weighty support to the thesis. Not only did he examine the evidence offered by Hobart, but he made a fresh investigation of the subject.[16] His final conclusion was: "The evidence is of overwhelming force; so that it seems to me that no doubt can exist *that the third gospel and the Acts of the Apostles were composed by a physician*."[17] Zahn accepted this view. He writes: "W. K. Hobart has proved to the satisfaction of anyone open to conviction, that the author of the Lucan work was familiar with the technical language of Greek medicine, and hence was a *Greek physician*."[18] Moffatt asserts that Harnack's study "has proved this pretty conclusively."[19]

In his commentary on Acts in *The Expositor's Greek Testament,* R. J. Knowling writes:

The evidence in favour of this position must be cumulative, but it depends not merely upon the occurrence of technical terms in St. Luke's writings, but also upon his *tendency* to employ medical language more frequently than the other evangelists, upon the passages in his Gospel in which we come across medical terms which are wanting in the parallel passages in St. Matthew and St. Mark, upon the account which he gives of miracles of healing not only in comparison with the other Evangelists, but also of the miracles peculiar to his own narratives; upon the way in which he *abstains from using* in a medical sense words which medical writers abstain from so using.[20]

More recently Cadbury claims to have demolished Hobart's theory. He says: "It is doubtful whether his [Luke's] interest in disease and healing exceeds that of his fellow evangelists or other contemporaries who were not doctors, while the words that he shares with the medical writers are found too widely in other kinds of Greek literature for us to suppose that they point to any professional vocabulary."[21]

It would seem that Cadbury's claim is as far exaggerated one way as Hobart's case is the other. More reasonable is the statement of H. D. A. Major: "Nevertheless, there are passages in the Lucan writings, which although they cannot be said to prove, yet do support the hypothesis, that the author was a physician."[22] Bruce has stated the case very fairly: "We shall probably be right in concluding that while the presence of medical diction in Luke-Acts cannot by itself prove anything about authorship, the more striking instances may properly be used to illustrate, and perhaps even to support, the conclusion reached on other grounds, that the author of the twofold history was Luke the physician."[23]

In Colossians 4:14, Paul refers to "Luke, the beloved physician." The only other places in the New Testament where Luke is named are II Timothy 4:11 and Philemon 24.

One other argument for the Lukan authorship of Acts may be mentioned. That is the fact that such a relatively obscure person as Luke—as far as the New Testament record goes—should be named unanimous-

13 Adolph Harnack, *Luke the Physician*. Trans. J. R. Wilkinson; ed. W. D. Morrison (London: Williams & Norgate, 1907), pp. 52f.
14 Alfred Plummer, *A Critical and Exegetical Commentary on the Gospel According to S. Luke* (3rd ed.) "International Critical Commentary" (Edinburgh: T. & T. Clark, 1900), p. xiii.
15 W. K. Hobart, *The Medical Language of St. Luke* (Grand Rapids: Baker Book House, 1954 [original edition, 1882]).
16 Harnack, *op cit.*, pp. 175-198.
17 *Ibid.*, p. 198.
18 Zahn, *op. cit.*, III, 146.
19 EGT, II, p. 10.
20 Moffatt, *op. cit.*, p. 298.
21 Henry J. Cadbury, *The Making of Luke-Acts* (New York: Macmillan Co., 1927), p. 358.
22 Major, *loc. cit.*
23 F. F. Bruce, *The Acts of the Apostles* (Greek text; 2nd ed.; Grand Rapids: Wm. B. Eerdmans Publishing Co., 1952), p. 5. Notice should also be taken of the Early Church tradition that the writer of Acts was a physician (Eusebius, *Ecclesiastical History,* III, 4).

ly by the Early Church as author. Creed states the case well: "If the Gospel and Acts did not already pass under his name there is no obvious reason why tradition should have associated them with him."[24]

II. DATE

John Knox thinks that "Luke-Acts as a finished work belongs to the middle of the second century."[25] That is because he feels that it did not appear until after Marcion had appropriated an earlier, shorter version of Luke's Gospel. Overbeck would place the writing of Acts in "the second and third decades of the second century."[26] Moffatt prefers a date around A.D. 100.[27] Goodspeed[28] and Scott[29] suggest A.D. 90. It should be noted that the last three named hold that Luke wrote Acts. Dibelius a bit more generously chooses "the last ten to thirty years of the first century."[30] Zahn says: "It may be assumed with practical certainty that Luke wrote his work about the year 75."[31]

Harnack has been the outstanding exponent of a date before A.D. 70. He declared that Luke wrote "perhaps even so early as the beginning of the seventh decade of the first century."[32] A little later he expressed himself thus: "The concluding verses of the Acts of the Apostles, taken in conjunction with the absence of any reference in the book to the result of the trial of St. Paul and to his martyrdom, make it in the highest degree probable that the work was written at a time when St. Paul's trial in Rome had not yet come to an end."[33] This quotation indicates the main reason for holding to an early date for Acts.

C. C. Torrey thinks that "the Third Gospel was written before the year 61, probably in the year 60" and that Acts was written soon after.[34] This is the commonly accepted view of conservative scholars today: that Luke probably wrote his Gospel during Paul's two years' imprisonment at Caesarea and Acts during the apostle's two years' imprisonment at Rome. Bruce gives a very clear and convincing presentation of the reasons for holding to this date. Some of the reasons are as follows:

> (1) Luke betrays surprisingly little acquaintance with the Pauline epistles. . . . (2) The abrupt manner in which Acts closes can best be explained thus. . . . (3) There is no certain hint in advance of Paul's death. . . . (4) The attitude to the Roman power throughout the book makes it difficult to believe that the Neronian persecution of A.D. 64 had begun. . . . (5) There is no hint throughout the book of the Jewish War of A.D. 66–70. . . . (6) Prominence is given to subjects which were of interest in the Church before the Fall of Jerusalem, but which soon lost their practical importance afterward. . . . (7) Both in conception and in terminology the theology of Acts gives an impression of primitiveness.[35]

III. PURPOSE

Probably the preface to Luke's Gospel (Luke 1:1–4) was intended to serve as a statement of the purpose for writing the two-volume work, Luke-Acts. Luke desired to give Theophilus an authoritative history of the beginnings of Christianity, in order that he might "know the certainty concerning the things wherein thou wast instructed."

More specifically, the purpose of Acts is suggested in its first verse, where it is stated that the "former treatise" gave what Jesus *began* to do. Here, then, we are to read what He *continued* to do through His apostles and prophets (see Exegesis of 1:1).

Kirsopp Lake and Silva Lake give a three-fold purpose for the book as follows: "a. A desire to prove the supernatural in-

24 J. M. Creed, *The Gospel According to St. Luke* (London: Macmillan Co., 1930), p. xiii.
25 John Knox, *Marcion and the New Testament* (Chicago: University of Chicago Press, 1942), p. 121.
26 See Edward Zeller, *The Contents and Origin of the Acts of the Apostles*, to which is prefixed Dr. F. Overbeck's Introduction to the Acts, trans. Joseph Dare (London: Williams and Norgate, 1875), I, 71.
27 *Op. cit.*, p. 312.
28 Edgar J. Goodspeed, *An Introduction to the New Testament* (Chicago: University of Chicago Press, 1937), p. 196.
29 E. F. Scott, *The Literature of the New Testament* (New York: Columbia University Press, 1936), p. 94.
30 Martin Dibelius, *A Fresh Approach to the New Testament and Early Christian Literature* (New York: Charles Scribner's Sons, 1936), p. 264.
31 *Op. cit.*, III, 159.
32 Adolph Harnack, *The Acts of the Apostles*. Trans. J. R. Wilkinson (New York: G. P. Putnam's Sons, 1909), p. 297.
33 Adolph Harnack, *The Date of the Acts and of the Synoptic Gospels*, trans. J. R. Wilkinson (New York: G. P. Putnam's Sons, 1911), p. 99.
34 C. C. Torrey, *The Composition and Date of Acts* (Cambridge: Harvard University Press, 1916), p. 68.
35 *Op. cit.*, pp. 11-12.

spiration and guidance given to the Church on the day of Pentecost . . . b. A desire to show that the best Roman magistrates never decided against the Christians . . . c. A more purely historical desire to show how the Church ceased to be Jewish and became Greek."[36]

The apologetic purpose of Acts seems unquestionable.[37] There is every evidence to indicate that Luke wanted Theophilus to know that Christianity was not officially persecuted by Roman rulers in the first generation of its history.

The Tübingen school of criticism in Germany, as is well known, subordinated this apologetic emphasis to an irenic purpose. Acts was written primarily as an effort to harmonize and reconcile the Petrine and Pauline parties in the church.[38] Consequently it was claimed that Acts is unreliable; it gives an intentionally distorted view of the primitive Church. The Epistles of Paul give the true picture: Paul rebuking Peter publicly (Gal. 2:11-14), Pauline and Petrine parties in Corinth in mutual opposition (I Cor. 1:12), etc., etc. But this Tübingen theory has been largely discredited in this century, so that it is no longer widely held. Henshaw says that "the Tübingen school launched an attack on the authenticity of the history presented in 'Acts,' by representing it as a second-century work, written to cover up a controversy between Jewish and Pauline Christianity, which, it was alleged, divided the whole of the early Church," and then adds: "Investigation has now completely refuted the theory."[39]

The highest purpose for Luke's writing is perhaps expressed in these words of Barnett: "To put Christianity in its true light, therefore, the author of Luke-Acts described the life and message of Jesus and showed how He remained the determining influence in the Christian movement through the person of the Spirit."[40] Clogg thinks that Acts 1:8 gives the twofold aim of the book; namely, the emphasis on the power of the Holy Spirit and on the rapid expansion, numerically and geographically, of the Church.[41]

In seeking to sum up the theological purpose of the book, Cadbury notes that three important convictions of the Early Church are presented therein: (1) the resurrection of Jesus; (2) His return from heaven; (3) the coming of the Holy Spirit into the hearts of His disciples.[42]

IV. TRUSTWORTHINESS

The Tübingen school of German criticism in the nineteenth century dismissed the Book of Acts as historically unreliable.[43] But as early as 1896 Ramsay could assert that Acts "was written by a great historian, a writer who set himself to record the facts as they occurred."[44] In 1911 he stated even more emphatically: "The present writer takes the view that Luke's history is unsurpassed in respect of its trustworthiness."[45]

These statements take on added significance when it is remembered that Sir William Ramsay began his notable career with a strong bias in favor of negative criticism, holding that the Book of Acts was written in the middle of the second century and was historically unreliable. Then he went to the Middle East. For thirty years he made an intensive study of the geography and ancient history of Asia Minor, until he became the leading authority in this field. Over and over again he found that Luke was precisely correct. With regard to the titles of various officials and frequently changing status of many Roman provinces, Luke never makes a mistake. Only one who

36 *Op. cit.*, p. 66.
37 Streeter calls it "the first of the Apologies" (B. H. Streeter, *The Four Gospels* [London: Macmillan Co., 1936]), p. 539.
38 See Zeller, *op. cit.*, II, 111-160.
39 T. Henshaw, *New Testament Literature* (London: George Allen and Unwin, 1952), p. 185.
40 Albert E. Barnett, *The New Testament* (New York: Abingdon-Cokesbury Press, 1946), p. 174.
41 F. B. Clogg, *An Introduction to the New Testament* (New York: Charles Scribner's Sons, 1937), p. 247.
42 Henry J. Cadbury, "Acts and Eschatology," *The Background of the New Testament and Its Eschatology* (Cambridge: University Press, 1956), p. 300.
43 Cf. Zeller, *op. cit.*, II, 111ff.
44 W. M. Ramsay, *St. Paul the Traveller and the Roman Citizen* (New York: G. P. Putnam's Sons, 1896), p. 14.
45 W. M. Ramsay, *The Bearing of Recent Discovery on the Trustworthiness of the New Testament* (Grand Rapids: Baker Book House, 1953 reprint), p. 81.

lived in the first century and had current knowledge of the situation could have written with such complete accuracy.

In the meantime F. H. Chase had taken up the gauntlet against the extreme radical criticism. In 1902 he wrote: "Thus the 'traditional' view of the Book, which we know to have been that of the Christian society since the time of Irenaeus, stands the test of careful and thorough investigation, and may claim to be accounted the 'critical' view."[46]

Since the epochal work of Ramsay and Harnack, the Book of Acts has been held in higher respect. The main point at which some scholars today would question its complete trustworthiness is in the matter of the speeches. For instance, one of the most recent writers of a text in New Testament introduction says: "The speeches of Acts . . . look like deliberate compositions of the writer himself, following the methods of Greek historians, in which he seeks to give the essential items in the earliest proclamation of the Gospel."[47] That is, the speeches do not give us what Paul or Peter or Stephen actually said but only a sample of the apostolic *kerygma.*

Knowling has a good discussion of the speeches in Acts. He shows that these speeches give evidence of authenticity. For instance, "The speech to the Ephesian elders at Miletus, xx.18–35, is constantly marked by St. Paul's characteristic words and phrases, and its teaching is strikingly connected with that of the Ephesian Epistle."[48] A strong case could also be made for the reliability of other discourses of Paul recorded in Acts. E. G. Selwyn, in his outstanding commentary on the Greek text of I Peter, points out the striking affinities between Peter's First Epistle and his speeches presented in the opening chapters of Acts. The time has passed for a cavalier dismissal of the speeches in Acts as having been invented by the author of that book.

The confirmation of the Acts record at so many points by archaeological discovery (see commentary, *passim*) ought to make the honest student slow to doubt the reliability of Acts as a trustworthy account of what actually happened in the first generation of the Christian Church. F. F. Bruce wisely concludes: "Luke's accuracy betokens not only contemporary knowledge but a natural accuracy of mind, and if his trustworthiness is vindicated in points where it can be checked, we should not assume that he is less trustworthy where we cannot test his accuracy."[49] This is certainly a reasonable position for the honest student of Acts to take.

46 Frederick H. Chase, *The Credibility of the Book of the Acts of the Apostles* (London: Macmillan Co., 1902), p. 296.
47 Donald T. Rowlingson, *Introduction to New Testament Study* (New York: Macmillan Co., 1956), pp. 108f.
48 EGT, II, 20. For a further discussion of the speeches in Acts see the Exegesis, on 2:14-36, where the writer accepts a middle view—that what is given is "a faithful reproduction of the thought, spirit, and main content of each of the speeches."
49 *Op. cit.*, p. 17.

CHAPTER I

The former treatise I made, O Theophilus, concerning all that Jesus began both to do and to teach,

---

EXEGESIS *

1 The Greek word for **former** is *prōton*, which means "first." In classical Greek "former" would be expressed by *proteron*. But in the Koine Greek of New Testament times the strict classical meaning of *prōton* had broken down somewhat. It is generally acknowledged by scholars today that the use of *prōton* here does not necessarily indicate that Luke planned to write a third volume, following the Third Gospel and Acts.[1] F. F. Bruce, in his excellent commentary on the Greek text of Acts, says: "Just as we loosely use 'first' for 'former' even when only two things are in question, so in Hellenistic Gk. *proteros* was largely superseded by *prōtos*."[2]

Treatise is *logos* in the Greek. The most common meaning of this term, of course, is "word" (cf. John 1:1); that is, "a word as embodying a conception or idea."[3] But it

---

EXPOSITION

THE CHURCH IN PREPARATION

- I. THE AUTHOR'S PROLOGUE, Acts 1:1–5.
  - A. The Author's Purpose, vs. 1.
  - B. The Lord's Confirmation, vss. 2, 3.
  - C. The Lord's Command, vs. 4a.
  - D. The Lord's Promise, vss. 4b, 5.
- II. THE LORD'S PLAN, Acts 1:6–11.
  - A. The Disciples' Misapprehension of the Plan, vs. 6.
  - B. The Divine Revelation of the Plan, vss. 7, 8.
  - C. The Divine Attestation of the Plan, vss. 9–11.
- III. THE DISCIPLES' PRAYER, Acts 1:12–14.
  - A. The Place of the Prayer, vss. 12, 13a.
  - B. The Personnel of the Prayer, vss. 13b, 14b.
  - C. The Persistence of the Prayer, vs. 14a.
- IV. THE DISCIPLES' PURPOSE, Acts 1:15–26.
  - A. A Purpose to Realize the Fulfillment of Prophecy, vss. 15–20.
  - B. A Purpose to Fulfill the Apostolate, vss. 21–26.

I. THE AUTHOR'S PROLOGUE (1:1-5)

The prologue to the *Book of Acts* links the authorship of this later work to that of the *Third Gospel.* It also links the acts and instructions of the Lord Jesus which were begun in Luke with their continuance by the Holy Spirit in His disciples in the Acts record. Further, it confirms these works and teachings by reference to Christ's appearances to His disciples subsequent to His death and resurrection. It records His command to His disciples to remain in Jerusalem until the Father's promise had been fulfilled to them, and it concludes with a promise of their not far distant baptism with the Holy Spirit.

A. THE AUTHOR'S PURPOSE (1:1)

The former treatise I made, O Theophilus, concerning all that Jesus began both to do and to teach.

The former treatise (a systematic presentation of facts and principles) unquestionably refers to the *Third Gospel* written by the same author as *Acts*. Says Cadbury:

* In the Exegesis, when a word quoted from the text is put in parentheses after a Greek word, or vice versa, it is usually because the lexical form of the Greek word is given, rather than that appearing in the passage.

[1] This view, however, was held by Ramsay and Zahn. See W. M. Ramsay, *St. Paul the Traveller and the Roman Citizen* (New York: G. P. Putnam's Sons, 1896), p. 23; Theodor Zahn, *Introduction to the New Testament* (Kregel Publications, 1953), III, 60f.
[2] F. F. Bruce, *The Acts of the Apostles* (Chicago: Inter-Varsity Christian Fellowship, 1952), p. 65. See also Foakes Jackson and Kirsopp Lake (eds.), *The Beginnings of Christianity*, Part I, Vol. IV (London: Macmillan Co., 1933), p. 2, where it is noted that *proteron* is rare in the papyri. (This work is hereafter referred to as *Beginnings*.)
[3] G. Abbott-Smith, *A Manual Greek Lexicon of the New Testament* (2nd ed.; Edinburgh: T. & T. Clark, 1923), p. 270f.

2 until the day in which he was received up, after that he had given commandment through the Holy Spirit unto the apostles whom he had chosen:

---

may also mean "a story, tale, narrative."[4] That is its use here. Cadbury and Lake declare: "*Logos* was a customary name for a division of a work which covered more than one roll of papyrus."[5]

Made is perhaps better translated "wrote."[6]

Theophilus (found only here and in Luke 1:3) means "friend of God." The name may have been given to him at his Christian baptism,[7] although Lenski thinks the omission of "most excellent" here indicates that the man had been converted since the writing of Acts.[8] But the idea that such a title of respect would not be used in addressing a fellow Christian seems a bit strained. Bruce points out the very striking parallel in the opening lines of the two parts of Josephus' work, *Against Apion*, in which the author addresses his patron, Epaphroditus, in words very similar to those used by Luke in his Gospel and here—a further confirmation of the idea that the Third Gospel and Acts were intended to be two parts of one great work.[9] Streeter's suggestion that "Theophilus" may have been a secret Christian name for Flavius Clemens, joint consul of the Emperor Domitian (A.D. 95),[10] has not gained wide acceptance.

The force of the word **began** has been a matter of dispute. Cadbury and Lake say that "there is probably no emphasis on the 'began.'"[11] Macgregor, following Blass, says:

> It is necessary once more to remind the reader that it was the custom in antiquity, on account of the purely physical conditions of writing, to divide works into volumes, to prefix to the first a preface for the whole, and to add secondary prefaces to the beginning of each later one.... The book of Acts is no afterthought. The word "treatise" implies a more complete work than does *logos*. . . . Luke 1:1-4 . . . is the real preface to Acts as well as to the Gospel, written by the author when he contemplated not merely one but both volumes. . . . It is as necessary to apply the phraseology of the preface [to Luke] to Acts as to the Gospel.[a]

The continuity of Acts with Luke is suggested in the identity of *authorship*, Luke; the *reader*, Theophilus; and the *subject*, Jesus Christ, though He is now in the person of the Holy Spirit working in and through His disciples. What Jesus began to do in the days of His flesh He planned and prepared to continue in a larger measure by His Spirit indwelling His disciples. Said Jesus to His disciples, "Verily, verily, I say unto you, He that believeth on me, the works that I do shall he do also; and greater works than these shall he do; because I go unto the Father" (John 14:12). Thus Luke's purpose in writing Acts is clearly to supplement his Gospel narrative of Jesus' earthly life and works with an historical record of the works of the ascended Christ through the Holy Spirit with whose personality and power His followers were soon to be endued. Acts is Luke's history of the infant Church. The word "began" suggests the continued activity of the Church indefinitely.

Theophilus is an enigmatical character. History can help us but little in knowing who or what he was. Tradition is for the most part unreliable. The latter links Theophilus with Antioch of Syria, and thus some think him to have been a Greek or Roman official of governmental rank at that city. Dummelow[b] considers him more likely a distinguished Roman citizen residing at Rome, since the title "most excellent" was applied to high-ranking Romans, and especially was a technical title in the second century, designating equestrian (knighthood) rank. This title was applied to both Felix and Festus in Acts 23:26; 24:3, and 26:25. However, it was sometimes used solely to designate friendship. The tradition contained in the *Clementine Recognitions* (X. 71), about the middle of the second century, holds that Theophilus was a superior-ranking governmental officer at

---

[4] *Ibid.*, p. 271. [5] *Beginnings*, IV, 2. [6] *Ibid.* [7] Ramsay, *op. cit.*, p. 388.

[8] R. C. H. Lenski, *The Interpretation of the Acts of the Apostles* (Columbus, Ohio: Wartburg Press, 1944), p. 21.

[9] Bruce, *op. cit.*, p. 66.

[10] B. H. Streeter, *The Four Gospels* (rev. ed.; London: Macmillan and Co., 1936), p. 539. [11] *Beginnings*, IV, 3.

[a] Henry J. Cadbury, "Commentary on the Preface of Luke," *The Beginnings of Christianity* (London: Macmillan & Co., Limited, 1922), Part one, II, 491, 492.

[b] J. R. Dummelow, ed. *A Commentary on the Holy Bible* (New York: Macmillan Company, 1936, rep. 1951), p. 737.

3 to whom he also showed himself alive after his passion by many proofs, appearing unto them by the space of forty days, and speaking the things concerning the kingdom of God:

"**Began to do** in Semitic idiom means little more than 'did.'"[12] Bruce, however, declares: "*Erxato* is emphatic here, and should not be regarded merely as a Semitizing auxiliary."[13] Many good commentators in the past (e.g., Rackham, Hackett, Lechler [in Lange's commentary], Olshausen, and others) have emphasized "began" as suggesting that Acts tells what Jesus *continued* to do through His disciples.

The phrase **to do and to teach** summarizes the contents of Luke's Gospel, which gives us the *works* and *words* of Jesus.

2 The terminal point of the Gospel of Luke is the Ascension. This is indicated in the phrase **until the day in which he was received up.** Luke is the only Evangelist who actually records the story of the Ascension—at the end of his Gospel and at the beginning of Acts.[14]

The Greek word for **he was received up** (*anelēmphthē*) is used of Elijah's translation (II Kings 2:9-11, LXX).

The adverbial phrase **through the Holy Spirit** has given trouble to some commentators. In what sense could it be said that Jesus commanded the disciples through the Holy Spirit? Lenski comments: "All the acts of Jesus were done in connection with the Spirit who had been bestowed upon the human nature of Jesus."[15] Most authorities are agreed that this phrase should be taken with "commanded." Macgregor writes: "The order of the Greek words shows that **through the Holy Spirit** should be taken with **given commandment** rather than with **had chosen.**"[16]

3 The verb **showed** is literally "presented" *(parestēsen)*—used thirteen times in Acts. Jesus "placed himself beside them" in such a definite way that they knew it was He.

The word for **proofs** is *tekmēriois*, found only here in the New Testament. It means, in the singular, "a sure sign, a positive proof."[17] Thayer defines it as "that from which something is surely and plainly known; an indubitable evidence, a proof."[18]

Antioch, and that he consecrated the palace in which he resided (the great basilica), under the name of a church.

In any event, the name Theophilus applies to a Gentile of rank and honor who had likely been converted to Christianity by Luke or Paul. He may have been a Christian of wealth who financed the publication of Luke and Acts, which fact may account for Luke's having dedicated these works to him.

That Theophilus was a real person, and not a fictitious name for all the Christians or "friends of God" as some suppose, is attested by the fact that the singular number is used, and the title "most excellent" could not apply to all the Christians as with an individual. Cadbury holds that, when the form of this preface is considered in the light of contemporary Hellinistic literature,

> its adoption at once suggests a certain flavour of conventionality on the part of the author as consciously presenting his book to the publir. The dedication to Theophilus means this, rathec than that the book is intended for a limited circle.[c]

B. THE LORD'S CONFIRMATION (1:2, 3)

to whom he also showed himself alive after his passion by many proofs, appearing unto them by the space of forty days. vs. 3a.

The incarnation, life and work, death, resurrection, appearances, commission of His disciples, ascension to the Father, and the descent of the Holy Spirit are all continuous and integrated factors in the divine plan of human redemption. No one factor may be intelligibly considered apart from the whole divine process. Thus the personal work of Christ continued on earth until His ascension; **the day he was received up.**

Christ's ascension did not occur until He had made provision for the continuance of His redemptive work by giving **commandment**

---

[12] *Interpreter's Bible*, ed. G. A. Buttrick, *et. al.* (New York: Abingdon-Cokesbury Press, 1954), IX, 24.
[13] *Op. cit.*, p. 66.
[14] Mark 16:19 is probably not genuine (cf. the author's *The Gospel According to Mark* (Grand Rapids: Zondervan Publishing House, 1957), p. 22.
[15] *Op. cit.*, p. 22. [16] IB, IX, 25. [17] Abbott-Smith, *Lexicon*, p. 441.
[18] J. H. Thayer, *A Greek-English Lexicon of the New Testament* (New York: American Book Co., 1889), p. 617.

[c] Cadbury, *op. cit.*, p. 490.

Aristotle explained it as meaning "a compelling sign."[19] Hobart asserts: "Galen expressly speaks of the medical distinction between *tekmērion*—demonstrative evidence —and *sēmeion,* stating that rhetoricians, as well as physicians, had examined the question."[20] It meant, medically, "a clear symptom."[21] That there was no question in the minds of the disciples about the reality of Jesus' resurrection is shown by the way they preached it so constantly, fearlessly, and at the risk of their lives, as recorded in the opening chapters of the Book of Acts.

Appearing is the present middle participle *optanomenos.* The verb occurs only here in the New Testament and is accurately translated "being seen" in the King James Version. Cadbury and Lake render it "being visible."[22] It is found in the Septuagint in Numbers 14:14, where it is used of God's

---

through the Holy Spirit unto the apostles whom He had chosen for that purpose. This "Commandment," or "Great Commission," as it is popularly designated, has its fullest and most specific record in Matthew 28: 18–20. Here, following His death and resurrection and just prior to His ascension, on the occasion of His appearance to the disciples on a mountain in Galilee, Jesus issued His kingdom command. "All authority hath been given unto me in heaven and on earth. Go ye therefore, and make disciples of all nations, baptizing them into the name of the Father and of the Son and of the Holy Spirit: teaching them to observe all things whatsoever I commanded you: and lo, I am with you always, even unto the end of the world." Corresponding but less detailed accounts of this commission occur in Mark 16:14–18; Luke 24:45–49; and John 20:23; and finally, in its epitomized form in Acts 1:8. Matthew's account sets forth: *First,* the "resource and authority" of the commission as vested in Christ's victory over death and His consequent universal Lordship; "All authority hath been given unto me in heaven and on earth." This is a claim which Christ nowhere makes for Himself until after His death and resurrection (see also Rev. 1:17b, 18). *Second,* the "objective" of the commission is defined as twofold: "make disciples," and "teaching them to observe all things whatsoever I commanded you." *Third,* the "extent" of the commission is suggested in the words, "Go ye therefore "[unto]". . .all the nations." These words should be understood to imply all nations of every generation from that day until the close of the Gospel Age. Finally, Christ presents the divine "assurance" of the commission. "Lo, I am with you always, even unto the end of the world" [or the consummation of the age].

Let the universality of this commission be carefully noted as indicated by the word "all": "All authority. . .all the nations. . .all things. . .always" [all-ways].

Christ's issuance of the commandment **through the Holy Spirit** unto the apostles is clear testimony to the inseparableness of the third person of the Holy Trinity from any communication of divinity to humanity.

A. T. Robertson takes note of eleven appearances of Christ. They are as follows: *first,* Mary Magdalene (Mark 16:9 and John 20:11–18); *second,* other women (Matt. 28:9, 10); *third,* two disciples including Cleopas, enroute to Emmaus (Mark 16:12, 13 and Luke 24:13–32); *fourth,* Simon Peter (Luke 24:33, 34 and I Cor. 15:5); *fifth,* the disciples, Thomas being absent (Mark 16:14; Luke 24:36–43; and John 20:19–25); *sixth,* to the disciples including Thomas (John 20:26–31 and I Cor. 15:5); *seventh,* the seven disciples by the Sea of Galilee (John 21:1, 2); *eighth,* the eleven on a mountain in Galilee (Mark 16:14–18; Matt. 28:16–20) and above 500 (I Cor. 15:6); *ninth,* James the brother of Jesus (I Cor. 15:7); *tenth,* the disciples at Jerusalem with another commission (Luke 24:44–49 and Acts 1:3–8); *eleventh,* the last appearance to the disciples on Mount Olivet between Jerusalem and Bethany (Mark 16:19, 20; Luke 24:50–53; and Acts 1:9–12).[d] If included, the post-ascension appearance to

[19] Bruce, *op. cit.,* p. 67.
[20] W. K. Hobart, *The Medical Language of St. Luke* (Grand Rapids: Baker Book House, 1954), p. 184.
[21] *Beginnings,* IV, 4.
[22] *Ibid.* They also suggest that this should be regarded as a deponent verb with the active meaning "appear." For a discussion of the nature of Jesus' body which "appeared" to the disciples see the editorial note of Alvah Hovey in H. B. Hackett, *A Commentary on the Acts of the Apostles* (Philadelphia: American Baptist Publication Society, 1882), p. 31.

[d] A. T. Robertson, *A Harmony of the Gospels* (New York: George H. Doran Co., 1922), pp. 242–252.

appearing to His people in the wilderness.

By the space of forty days is literally "through forty days"—*dia* with the genitive. Bruce asserts that this indicates that Jesus appeared at intervals, whereas the accusative without a preposition would mean "continuously." [23] In this he follows the great fourth-century preacher, Chrysostom. Cadbury and Lake take issue with this interpretation, but it cannot be dismissed lightly. It should be noted that this is the only place in the New Testament which gives the length of Jesus' post-resurrection ministry.

The kingdom of God is a phrase used often in the Gospels—thirty-three times in Luke, fifteen in Mark, four in Matthew, and once in John. Luke also uses it six times in Acts. Matthew's phrase "kingdom of heaven" (literally, "the kingdom of the heavens"), occurring thirty-three times in that Gospel (and nowhere else), means exactly the same thing as "kingdom of God." The central idea of the term "kingdom" is *reign* rather than *realm.*

Paul (I Cor. 15:8) on the Damascus road would make twelve. Christ's appearance to Stephen in his hour of martyrdom (Acts 7:55, 56) and to John the Revelator on the Isle of Patmos (Rev. 1:9–18) are also noteworthy. Except for the last three mentioned, these appearances of Christ occurred within the forty days between His resurrection in His glorified form and His ascension. Thus the appearances of Christ to Stephen, Paul, and the Revelator were not different from His appearances to His disciples before His ascension. This fact supports Paul's argument that his apostleship was validated by Christ's appearance to him on the Damascus road.

The many [infallible] **proofs** attesting Christ's resurrection from the dead included: (1) the carefully guarded but empty tomb (Luke 24:5, 6); (2) the declaration of the angels (Luke 24:4–7); (3) the testimony of the Roman guards (Matt. 28:11–15); (4) the post-resurrection appearances, above enumerated (see notes on previous verse); (5) the release of the saints from their graves following Christ's resurrection (Matt. 27:51–53); (6) the occurrence of Pentecost in fulfillment of the promise of the Holy Spirit to His disciples (Acts 1:8; 2:1–4); (7) the arrest of, and appearance to, the persecutor Saul on the Damascus road (Acts 9:1–18); (8) the appearance to Stephen in the hour of his death (Acts 7:55, 56); (9) the appearance to John on Patmos (Rev. 1:9–18); (10) His eating and drinking with the disciples (Luke 24:39–43); (11) His important instructions and commission to His disciples (Matt. 28:18–20); (12) the forty days of ministration during which time His claims could be adequately investigated and substantiated or denied by His friends or foes; (13) His fulfillment of Old Testament prophecy; and (14) His fulfillment of His own predictions. Finally, perhaps the greatest evidence of Christ's resurrection has been His influence upon the lives of men and nations throughout the subsequent ages. The "Good News" of Christ's atoning death and victorious resurrection has ever borne the evidence of **many** [infallible] **proofs** (see Romans 1:16, 17 and I Thess. 1:5).

The things concerning the kingdom of God, about which Jesus spoke to His disciples, pertained to the spiritual nature of that kingdom which He came to establish. This spiritual kingdom was to be wrought in, and outworked through, the lives of His disciples by the personal operation of the Holy Spirit: the doctrines that would mould it, the discipline that would direct and preserve it, and the spirit and methods that would propagate it.

C. The Lord's Command (1:4a)

He charged them not to depart from Jerusalem, but to wait for the promise of the Father.

The **being assembled together with them** on the occasion of this command may refer to the meeting with the more than 500 disciples on a mountain in Galilee (I Cor. 15:6), since the promise of the Holy Spirit to be fulfilled at Pentecost was for all believers and not just the apostles. Luke's gospel record of this event would rather appear to locate the place and time of Christ's command on the Mount of Ascension; however, the actual time of the command and the promise that follows may have preceded the ascension.

Luke's earlier recorded command, "But

[23] *Op. cit.*, p. 67.

4 and, being assembled together with them, he charged them not to depart from Jerusalem, but to wait for the promise of the Father, which, *said he*, ye heard from me:

---

4 One of the most puzzling words in the Book of Acts is the single Greek term rendered **being assembled together with them**—*sunalizomenos*. The standard English versions seem to assume that it is from *sunalizein*, "to gather together." But, "The difficulty is that the word is nowhere found in the middle voice, and can scarcely mean 'being gathered together with them.' "[24] Some have suggested that it is derived from *halizein*, "to salt," and so means "eating salt together with them"; or, more simply, "eating with them." A third suggestion is that the term is a variant spelling of *sunaulizomenos*, which would mean "passing the night, lodging." This is the reading found in Eusebius, and is favored as correct by Cadbury and Lake[25] and Macgregor,[26] in spite of the overwhelming manuscript evidence against it. Probably the best view is the second one, translating the word as "eating with them."[27] This is the marginal reading of the King James, American Standard, and Revised Standard versions.

The command **not to depart** suggests that the disciples were already thinking of returning to Galilee. Indeed, Mark and Matthew both record the instructions given the women at the tomb that the disciples were to meet Jesus in Galilee (Matt. 28:7; Mark 16:7), and Matthew (28:16–20) describes such a meeting. John also (21:1–14) records the appearance of Jesus to the seven disciples by the Lake of Galilee. But that does not give justification for the suggestion of some[28] that Luke is contradicting the "Galilean tradition" of the other Gospels by implying that the disciples had stayed near Jerusalem. There is no reason to question the trip to Galilee and then the return to Jerusalem for the Ascension and Pentecost. If Jesus appeared to different ones several times during the first eight days after His resurrection—as the Gospels indicate—and then these appearances in the Jerusalem area ceased, it is only natural that the disciples would return to their old home territory.

Wait is literally "remain around" *(perimenein)*. The **promise** was **of the Father**; that is, given by the Father (subjective genitive). Rackham writes: "The title *the Father* is very Johannine, and its occurrence here and in verse 7 is a sign of the genuineness of the narrative, just as the sudden change from indirect to direct speech (**said he** is not in the Greek) is characteristic of the dramatic style of St. Luke."[29] The phrase ye **heard** refers to Luke 24:49, where the same command is given as here. It could also be a reference to Jesus' last discourse with the disciples (John 14–16).

---

tarry ye in the city, until ye be clothed with power from on high" (Luke 24:49b), agrees with the later Acts account concerning **the promise of the Father** (Acts 1:4); and here, as always, is conditioned for its fulfillment upon the obedience of the disciples to the divine command to "tarry" or "wait" in Jerusalem. Christ's supreme authority qualified Him to issue the command. Obedience to that command assured the fulfillment of the promise. Had they in impatience failed to wait in obedience, there would have been no Christian Pentecost, and had there been no Pentecost, there would have been no Church for the evangelization of the first-century world. There is no substitute for obedience, and there is no spiritual Pentecost without obedience. The Church signs her own spiritual death warrant when she fails to obey the divine command to wait for her spiritual Pentecost. Dr. Edwin S. Johnson has quoted D. L. Moody as having said, "You might as well try to see without eyes, hear without ears, or breathe without lungs, as to try to live the Christian life without the Holy Spirit."

[24] *Beginnings*, IV, 4 f. [25] *Ibid*, p. 5. [26] IB, IX, 27.

[27] So C. R. Bowen, *Studies in the New Testament* (ed. R. J. Hutcheson; Chicago: University of Chicago Press, 1936), pp. 89–109. Cf. T. D. Woolsey, *Bibliotheca Sacra*, XXXIX (Oct., 1882), 602–618; also Lenski, *op. cit.*, p. 26.

[28] E.g., *Beginnings*, IV, 6; IB, IX, 27.

[29] Richard B. Rackham, *The Acts of the Apostles* (8th ed.; London: Methuen & Co., 1919), p. 5.

5 for John indeed baptized with water; but ye shall be baptized in the Holy Spirit not many days hence.

6 They therefore, when they were come together, asked him, saying, Lord, dost thou at this time restore the kingdom to Israel?

---

5 The language of this verse is most closely paralleled in Matthew 3:11, Mark 1:8 and Luke 3:16. In all three places the words are attributed to John the Baptist. But that certainly does not justify the assertion: "Luke, like many after him, is not incapable of ascribing quotations to the wrong source." [30] Why could not Jesus have echoed the words of the Baptist?

Jesus declared that they would be baptized **in the Holy Spirit**. Bruce thinks the Greek word *en* is instrumental.[31] The Holy Spirit would baptize them. But the account of Pentecost in chapter two indicates that they were also filled with the Holy Spirit in the act of being baptized by the Spirit. The last phrase of this verse, **not many days hence,** is idiomatic Greek—*ou meta pollas tautas hēmeras*. Robertson says, "The litotes, *ou meta pollas*, does not have the usual order," and adds: "The free translation 'not many days hence' is essentially correct. It is literally 'after not many days these' as a starting-point (from these)." [32]

6 After the introduction, consisting of the first five verses, Luke begins a new section with his favorite connective formula—*hoi men oun*. It literally means "they indeed

---

D. The Lord's Promise (1:4b, 5)

Ye shall be baptized in the Holy Spirit not many days hence.

Just as the whole of the Jewish economy looked forward to, and found its fulfillment and meaning in, Christ the Messiah crucified, dead, buried, and victoriously resurrected, so the New Testament economy finds its fulfillment and significance in the Father's verification of His promise to every believer through the baptism with the Holy Spirit. He, the Holy Spirit, is the Father's promise to all believers by His holy prophets (Acts 2:16–21), by John the Baptist (Matt. 3:11, 12), by Christ Himself (John 16:7), and finally as directly given by the Father. Nor was this promise restricted to the apostles or immediate disciples of Jesus. Peter applies Joel's prophecy concerning Pentecost to the assembled multitudes at Jerusalem thus: "Ye shall receive the gift of the Holy Spirit. For to you is the promise,...and to all that are afar off, even as many as the Lord our God shall call unto him" (Acts 2:38b, 39).

John's baptism was with water unto repentance, but Christ's baptism was with the Holy Spirit unto purification, animation, and power. Says Clarke:

> Christ baptizes with the Holy Ghost, for the destruction of sin, the illumination of the mind, and the consolation of the heart.... Christ's baptism *established* and *maintained* the kingdom.[e]

This promise most evidently refers to the communication of the Holy Spirit on the following Pentecost "to *illuminate*, *regenerate*, *refine*, and *purify* the heart. With this, sprinkling or immersion are equally efficient: without this, both are worth nothing."[f]

In Luke 12:49 and 50, Christ declared that He "came to cast fire upon the earth.... But," said He, "I have a baptism to be baptized with; and how am I straitened till it be accomplished." His casting of fire, in the Pentecostal effusion, could not be realized until the accomplishment of His baptism of suffering and death. His baptism is now past and He is about to cast Himself upon earth in the unrestrained and unlimited fiery baptism of His disciples by the Holy Spirit.

II. THE LORD'S PLAN (1:6–11)

In this paragraph is recorded the disciples' continued misapprehension of the divine plan for the kingdom; Christ's revelation of His plan to His disciples, and the Father's attestation of that plan.

[30] *Beginnings*, IV, 7. [31] *Op. cit.*, p. 69.
[32] A. T. Robertson, *A Grammar of the Greek New Testament in the Light of Historical Research* (5th ed.; New York: Harper & Brothers, 1931), p. 702.

[e] Adam Clarke, *The New Testament of our Lord and Saviour Jesus Christ* (New York: Abingdon-Cokesbury Press, n.d.), V, 683.
[f] *Ibid.*

therefore." Bruce suggests that *men oun* is best translated "so, then." [33] The complete phrase occurs at least eight times in Acts (1:6; 2:41; 8:4, 25; 11:19; 15:3, 30), while the latter two words also occur, with another pronoun, five times (1:18; 9:31; 11:5; 13:4; 16:5). The phrase here introduces the story of the Ascension (vss. 6–11), which forms a distinct paragraph, connected closely, nevertheless, with what precedes and what follows. This is probably a different occasion from that mentioned in verse four.

The verb **asked** is imperfect *(ērōtōn)*. This perhaps suggests that the disciples asked the question repeatedly.[34] But Knowling, while allowing that it may indicate that "the same question was put by one inquirer after another" notes that the imperfect may also mean that "the act of questioning is always imperfect until an answer is given." [35]

The present tense of the question, **dost thou?**, strengthens the force of **at this time** and emphasizes the fact that the disciples were looking for Jesus to set up an earthly kingdom immediately. They had not yet understood His teaching on the kingdom of God.

A. The Disciples' Misapprehension of the Plan (1:6)

Lord, dost thou at this time restore the kingdom to Israel? How reminiscent are these words of the remark of one of the disciples on the road to Emmaus, after Christ's death: "But we hoped that it was he who should redeem Israel" (Luke 24:21a).

These Jewish disciples of Christ had been so thoroughly imbued with the age-old, Jewish materialistic concept of the Messianic kingdom that, until the hour of Christ's ascension, they were unable to grasp the spiritual significance of the kingdom Christ came to establish. They, like the Pharisees, had not yet learned that "The kingdom of God cometh not with observation:...for lo, the kingdom of God is within you" (Luke 17:20b, 21b); or, as Paul later voiced it, "The kingdom of God is not eating and drinking, but righteousness and peace and joy in the Holy Spirit" (Rom. 14:17; see also Matt. 20:21 and Heb. 12:16, 17).

The Romans, not the Israelites, wielded the scepter of government. The Jews hoped and prayed for deliverance from this galling foreign yoke. Even Christ's disciples shared, in a measure, this materialistic hope. Pentecost was necessary to disillusion Christ's disciples of the false notion of the kingdom. Pentecost is ever a necessity to clarify and establish spiritual realities. With Pentecost spiritual values will be clarified; without Pentecost they will become obscured and confused. No Spirit baptized and directed ministry will ever lose its way doctrinally or otherwise.

B. The Divine Revelation of the Plan (1:7, 8)

But ye shall receive power, when the Holy Spirit is come upon you: and ye shall be my witnesses . . . unto the uttermost part of the earth.

Christ mildly rebukes the disciples' query concerning the restoration of the kingdom. He does not deny that He has a kingdom to restore. In fact He admits that His plan provides for a universal kingdom over the souls of men (vs. 8), though that plan is not for a narrow, limited, material kingdom such as His Jewish disciples had conceived.

In His rebuke, **It is not for you to know the times or seasons, which the Father hath set within his own authority** (vs. 7), Christ implies that God is never the agent of a fatalistic determinism. Says Clarke:

> Infinite, eternal liberty to act or not to act, to create or not to create, to destroy or not to destroy, belongs to God alone, and we must take care how we imagine decrees, formed even by His own prescience, in reference to futurity, which power is from the moment of their conception laid under the *necessity* of performing. In every point of time and eternity, God must be free to act or not to act, as may seem best to His godly wisdom.[g]

It must ever be remembered that God's respect for the intelligent moral freedom with which He has endowed man influences

[33] *Op. cit.*, p. 70.
[34] So A. T. Robertson, *Word Pictures in the New Testament* (New York: Richard R. Smith, 1930), III, 9.
[35] R. J. Knowling, "The Acts of the Apostles," *The Expositor's Greek Testament* (Grand Rapids: Wm. B. Eerdmans Publishing Co., n.d.), II, 56.

[g] *Ibid.* V ,684.

7 And he said unto them, It is not for you to know times or seasons, which the Father hath set within his own authority.

8 But ye shall receive power, when the Holy Spirit is come upon you: and ye shall be my witnesses both in Jerusalem, and in all Judaea and Samaria and unto the uttermost part of the earth.

---

7 The two terms, **times** and **seasons,** are probably distinct in meaning here. The first, *chronoi*, is the usual word for mere passage of time. The second, *kairoi*, is used of "Time in the sense of a fixed and definite period." [36] Some writers make these two terms synonymous. "But here *chronous* may well be taken to mean space of time as such, the duration of the Church's history, and *kairous* the critical periods in that history." [37] This distinction is borne out by Trench.[38]

All date-setting is in the Father's **authority** *(exousia)*. The King James Version's confusion of *exousia* and *dynamis*, translating them both as "power," is unfortunate. This is especially true in this passage. The average reader is not aware that "power" in verse eight is something far different from "power" in verse seven. In the eighth verse it is *dynamic* power; in the seventh verse it is *authority.* While the term "power" is used in English for both ideas, the clear distinction in meaning between the two Greek words should be brought out in translation.

His prevision of, and decisions in, human events (see Jonah).

On the positive side it was *power*, or *divine energy*, not the divine *authority* of verse seven, that the disciples were to receive through their enduement with the Holy Spirit. Nor was the divine energy a gift to be received apart from the personal Lordship of Christ through the Holy Spirit in their lives. An interesting and helpful reading of verse eight is found in the margin of the Authorized Version. "Ye shall receive the power of the Holy Spirit coming upon you." This rendering directly relates the "power" to the "person" of the Holy Spirit. His power is never disassociated from His personality. God does not parcel out His power. This promise became a reality on the day of Pentecost when "they were all filled with the Holy Spirit" (Acts 2:4a), which Holy Spirit Chadwick designates as the "Other Self of the Christ." [h]

The geographic, national, and temporal plan of the universal spiritual kingdom is then outlined by Christ for His disciples in this passage, as well as the whole plan of the Book of Acts. This passage which reveals the divine plan for the Christian witness to Christ's finished work to the world may be viewed thus:

I. *The enduement of the disciples with the Spirit for the world witness:* **But ye shall receive power, when the Holy Spirit is come upon you.**

II. *The divine commission of the disciples to the world witness:* **And ye shall be my witnesses.**

III. *The universal scope of the world witness:* **In Jerusalem, and in all Judaea and Samaria, and unto the uttermost part of the earth.**

Otherwise considered this key verse to the Book of Acts (Acts 1:8) may be analyzed as follows:

I. *The Pentecostal promise:* **ye "shall receive."**

II. *The Pentecostal power:* **ye shall receive "power."**

III. *The Pentecostal person:* **the "Holy Spirit."**

IV. *The Pentecostal purpose:* **Ye shall be "my witnesses."**

V. *The Pentecostal plan:* **in "Jerusalem," and in all "Judaea" and "Samaria," and unto "the uttermost part of the earth."**

The divine commission of the disciples was to witness to Christ. A witness is one who gives testimony to that which he has seen or experienced, and of which he conse-

---

[36] Abbott-Smith, *Lexicon*, p. 226. [37] Knowling, EGT, II, 56.

[38] R. C. Trench, *Synonyms of the New Testament* (Grand Rapids: Wm. B. Eerdmans Publishing Co., 1947), p. 211.

[h] Samuel Chadwick, *The Way To Pentecost* (Berne, Ind.: Light and Hope Publications, 1939), p. 21.

8 Acts 1:8 is the key verse of the book. It gives us both the *power* and *program* of the church of Jesus Christ. The *power* is the Holy Spirit. The *program* is world evangelization.

This verse also suggests a threefold outline for the book. [39] (See Exposition).

---

quently has personal firsthand knowledge; and the witness given is an attestation of a known fact or event. Now in the realm of personal subjective experience, religious or otherwise, the individual is the final authority. From his experience and testimony there is no further human appeal, since he only can know what transpires within his subjective self, or between that self and God. Such knowledge of personal experience is a matter of personal faith. In fact, all knowledge of whatever kind is finally based upon personal faith. This principle was grasped and expressed by the great apostle Paul: "For who among men knoweth the things of a man, save the spirit of the man, which is in him?" (I Cor. 2:11). Now, the knowledge of the person, work, teachings, death, and resurrection of Jesus Christ was a matter of personal experience with these disciples. Peter implies that one of the requirements for a first-century Christian apostle was that he must have known Christ in the flesh (Acts 1:21, 22; also I John 1:1–4). Having reiterated the accomplishments of His suffering, death, and resurrection, Jesus declared to His disciples: "Ye are witnesses of these things" (Luke 24:48). Nor was their witness to consist of the mere historical fact of Christ's death and resurrection, of which they had certain knowledge, but theirs was to be a living witness to the personal, ever living presence of Christ who was to indwell and abide with them forever through the Holy Spirit with whom they were to be endued on the day of Pentecost. This was the commission of the first-century Christian disciples, and this is the abiding commission to the disciples of Christ in every age and for all time. (For O.T. parallel see Isa. 6).

The universal scope of the divine plan of witnessing arrests our attention: **In Jerusalem, and in all Judaea and Samaria, and unto the uttermost part of the earth.** What a Herculean task Jesus assigns to this little flock of first-century Christians!

That the universal scope of the Christian world witness is geographic, racial, and temporal appears evident from the words of this commission, as well as those of Matthew 28:18–20. The apostles themselves were Jewish Christians, and the Holy Spirit first descended on them in Jerusalem. This effusion of the Spirit next influenced the Jews residing in, or assembled at, Jerusalem for the Jewish Pentecost, resulting in the conversion of 3,000 souls. The Gospel was declared to be first for the Jews, and the early Christian disciples and apostles consistently practiced witnessing first to the Jews wherever they went. Jerusalem was the religious capital of the Jews. Christ and Christianity were the fruit of the faith of the Jews, the end product of the Jewish economy. Saint Augustine is reported as having said that "the Old Testament is the New Testament infolded; the New Testament is the Old Testament unfolded. The New is in the Old concealed; the Old is in the New revealed. The Old Testament is the New Testament in bud; the New Testament is the Old Testament in full bloom."

The scope of the commission broadens both geographically and racially with the mention of Judaea and Samaria. While primarily a geographic province of southern Palestine throughout which Jews for the most part resided, the term Judaea also embraced the Gentile administrative capital of Caesarea. The country of Samaria to the north of geographic Judaea, on the other hand, consisted of a despised, mongrel people, half Jew, half Gentile, both racially and religiously. They, together with the Jews of the Dispersion, formed the bridge of transition for the Christian witness from the Jerusalem Jews to the Gentile nations and the uttermost part of the earth. (See ADDITIONAL NOTE I, *Samaria and the Samaritans* at end of Chap. VIII).

The last division of this scope of the Christian witness is all-inclusive of peoples, geography, and ages or generations, to the close of the Gospel Age.

The foregoing analysis of the scope of the Christian witness clearly underlies Luke's

[39] It should be noted that the Greek puts Judaea and Samaria together by omitting the article before the latter.

Jesus said, **Ye shall be my witnesses.** This translation is based on the better text *mou*, as found in the older Greek manuscripts (Aleph A B C D), instead of *moi* ("to me") which has only late support. It emphasizes the fact that Christians are to be Christ's personal witnesses. The word **witnesses** is found thirteen times in Acts (singular and plural). The idea of witnessing is very prominent in this book.[40]

Chapters 13–28 tell of the spreading of the Gospel to **the uttermost part of the earth** *(eschatou tēs gēs)*. This exact phrase is used in *Psalms of Solomon* 8:16 (first century B.C.), where it clearly refers to Rome. It seems more than coincidental that the Book of Acts ends with Paul in Rome, though clearly the scope of Jesus' prediction reaches beyond that to the farthest corners of the globe.

---

plan in setting forth the history of the Christian witness in the Book of Acts. In outline it would be as follows:

I. *The witness in Jerusalem*, Acts 1–7.
II. *The witness in transition*, Acts 8–12.
III. *The witness in all the world*, Acts 13–28.

The principal characters in the first division are Peter and Stephen; in the second, Peter, Philip, and Barnabas; and in the third, Paul. In Paul is found a combination of the characteristics of all the foregoing, and the task he began continues unfinished in our day. However, that the first-century disciples of Christ realized in large measure the fulfillment of the scope of this commission for their generation is the clear testimony of Paul in his epistles. To the church at Rome, Paul could write within 30 years of Pentecost: "First, I thank my God through Jesus Christ for you all, that your faith is proclaimed throughout the whole world" (Romans 1:8). And again in the Colossian letter, written during his first Roman imprisonment about A. D. 60, Paul made a like declaration: "The gospel . . . is come unto you; even as it is also in all the world bearing fruit and increasing, as it doth in you also, since the day ye heard and knew the grace of God in truth" (Col. 1:5b, 6).

Nor does Paul stand alone in his testimony to the early wide spread of the Christian Gospel. Justin Martyr (100?–165?), writing in the second Christian century, is reported by Harnack to have said:

> There is not a single race of human beings, barbarians, Greeks, or whatever name you please to call them, nomads or vagrants or herdsmen living in tents, where prayers in the name of Jesus the crucified are not offered up. . . .
>
> Through all the members of the body is the soul spread; so are Christians throughout the cities of the world.[i]

While Tertullian lived and wrote at a slightly later date (160–230 A. D.), yet his memorable tribute to the far-reaching influences of the Christian religion reflects, according to Harnack, the success of the first-century Christian evangel.

> We [the Christians] are but of yesterday. Yet we have filled all the places you frequent — cities, lodging houses, villages, townships, markets, the camp itself, the tribes, town councils, the palace, the senate, and the forum. All we have left you is your temples. . . . Behold, every corner of the universe has experienced the gospel, and the whole ends and bounds of the world are occupied with the gospel.[j]

Writing of the rapid spread of the Gospel in the days of the cruel emperor Nero, a contemporary of the Apostle Paul, Lactantius observes, according to Harnack, "Nero noticed that not only at Rome but everywhere a large multitude were daily falling away from idolatry and coming over to the new religion."[k]

Adolf Harnack takes note of these reports of the universal proclamation of the Gospel within the Apostolic Age as follows:

> This belief, that the original apostles had already preached the gospel to the whole world, is therefore extremely old. . . . The belief would never have arisen unless some definite knowledge of the apostles' labours and whereabouts (i.e., in the majority of cases) had been current. Both Clemons Romanus and Ignatius assume that the gospel had already been diffused all over the world. . . . Finally, as the conception emerges in Hermas, it is exceptionally clear and definite; and this evidence of Hermas is all the more weighty, as he may invariably be assumed to voice opinions which were widely spread and commonly received. On earth, as he puts it, there are twelve great peoples, and the gospel

[40] For an extended discussion of the meaning and use of the term see *Beginnings*, V, 30–37.

[i] Adolf von Harnack, *The Mission and Expansion of Christianity in the First Three Centuries* (New York: G. P. Putnam's Sons, 1908), II, 4, 5.
[j] *Ibid.*, pp. 7, 16. [k] *Ibid* ,p. 16.

9 And when he had said these things, as they were looking, he was taken up; and a cloud received him out of their sight.

10 And while they were looking stedfastly into heaven as he went, behold two men stood by them in white apparel;

---

9 The **cloud** that **received him out of their sight** was a symbol of God's glory. All three Synoptics mention a cloud in connection with the Transfiguration (Matt. 17:5; Mark 9:7; Luke 9:34).

10 The disciples were **looking stedfastly** heavenward as Jesus disappeared from their gaze. The Greek verb *atenizō* is a strong word, used only by Luke and Paul in the New Testament. It occurs twice in Luke's Gospel, ten times in Acts, and twice in II Corinthians. It indicates "a fixed, steadfast, protracted gaze."[41] Hobart says: "It is employed by the medical writers to denote a peculiar fixed look."[42]

The angels—for such they obviously were—are described as wearing **white apparel.** This is elsewhere spoken of as the clothing of angels (cf. Matt. 28:3; John 20:12).

---

has already been preached to them all by the apostles.[l]

Many more testimonies, of Biblical and extra-Biblical writers, could be added as evidence that these disciples of Jesus Christ at Pentecost caught a vision under the powerful illumination of God as revealed in the person of the Holy Ghost that irresistibly impelled them to proclaim the glorious Gospel of Jesus Christ to the ends of the earth. Pentecost then, as ever, set on fire the hearts of these first-century Christians. They were inflamed with a passion that could not be satisfied as long as a creature remained who had not heard of Christ and His saving provisions.

C. The Divine Attestation of the Plan (1:9–11)

While they were looking stedfastly into heaven . . . two men stood by them . . . who also said . . . why stand ye looking into heaven?

The ascension of Jesus Christ to the Father in the sight of His disciples at the completion of His instructions to them was conclusive evidence of the Father's approval of His plans. Following the Resurrection, He had more than once appeared and vanished from their sight only to reappear again. This ninth verse, however, records His final departure in physical form. The heaven into which He disappeared was primarily the cloud-enshrouded physical atmosphere. These clouds swallowed His physical presence from their sight, but His spiritual presence was to remain with them forever, though the fuller revelation and realization of that presence must await the day of Pentecost.

Amazed and dazed by the final bodily disappearance of their Lord, these disciples were suddenly shocked to the realization of their responsibility to Christ's last command by the question of two messengers. These messengers are here designated "men," but they are, when correctly understood, angels in the physical form of men, who were fresh from the throne of God, to the right hand of which Christ had just ascended. These messengers seem to say: "Why further concern yourselves about your Lord's person? His work is completed; you have His blueprint for the construction of His universal spiritual kingdom in the hearts of men on earth. This same incarnate God-man, who by reason of the Father's acceptance of His person and work in the Ascension, is made Lord of the universe and will indeed **so come in like manner as ye beheld Him going into heaven.** However, His return **in like manner** as He departed will depend upon your faithfulness in executing the command. He will personally return to receive and rule over the spiritual kingdom which you, His disciples, prepare for Him through the power of His Spirit working through you in witnessing to all the world. To Pentecost, and from thence to the challenge of a world witness!" This is the message of the two heaven-sent messengers to the "heavenward gazing" disciples on the Mount of Ascension.

[41] Knowling, EGT, II, 57.

[42] *Op. cit.*, p. 76.

[l] *Ibid.*, 24.

11 who also said, Ye men of Galilee, why stand ye looking into heaven? this Jesus, who was received up from you into heaven, shall so come in like manner as ye beheld him going into heaven.
12 Then returned they unto Jerusalem from the mount called Olivet, which is nigh unto Jerusalem, a sabbath day's journey off.

---

11 Angels announced the birth of Jesus (Matt. 1:20; Luke 1:26–35), His resurrection (Matt. 28:5–7; Mark 16:5–7; Luke 24:4–7), and here at His ascension they predict His second coming.

12 The mount of the Ascension is here called **Olivet**. This form comes from the Latin. The Greek word *elaiōn* literally means "oliveyard." The more common name is "Mount of Olives," found eleven times. **Olivet** [43] occurs only here in the New Testament, though found in the papyri and Josephus.

The Mount of Olives was **a sabbath day's journey** from Jerusalem. This distance was a little more than half a mile. The Rabbinical

---

How much like the disciples on the Mount of Transfiguration they were (see Matt. 17:4 and Mark 9:9, 17–29).

The kingdom of Christ has ever suffered from two fatal deficiencies on the part of its servants: a heavenward gaze, on the one hand, without a sense of manward responsibility; and, on the other hand, a disproportionate sense of manward responsibility without the heavenward gaze. The true religion of Jesus Christ places redeemed man in a position of ambassadorial mediatorship (II Cor. 5:20). Christ's promise, "and lo, I am with you alway, even unto the end of the world" [the consummation of the age], is forever conditioned upon the disciples' obedience to the Master's command, "Go ye" (Matt. 28:20b and 19a). Morgan's observation on this passage is unusually pertinent.

> The realization of the promise of His abiding presence is entirely dependent upon the church's willingness to fulfill her responsibility. She has no right to apply this gracious word to herself save as she fulfills the conditions imposed. If we have no passion in our hearts for the discipling of the nations, we have no warrant for believing that He remains in fellowship with us.[m]

The religion of the Lord Jesus Christ is like a carpenter's square, one arm of which points Godward, and the other manward; the first is religious or spiritual and the second, social (see Matt. 22:37–40). "Adventism" has overemphasized the first, while the "social gospel" has overemphasized the second (cf. I Thess. 1:9, 10). These messengers' words, **this Jesus**—denoting His human nature, and **as ye beheld him going into heaven**—denoting His identity, distinguishes Christ's second coming from the Holy Spirit's manifestation at Pentecost, as well as exposes the mistaken notion of some that it refers to Christ's coming for His saints at death. There is no more certain scriptural fact than the personal Second Coming of Jesus Christ at the end of the Gospel Age. While it was clearly the purpose of Luke in the Acts to portray the universal Lordship of Jesus Christ, the Second Coming of Christ is a dominant concern in the epistles.

III. THE DISCIPLES' PRAYER (1:12–14)

Following the account of Christ's ascension, Luke records the place, personnel, and nature of the disciples' prayer in preparation for Pentecost.

A. The Place of the Prayer (1:12, 13a)

Then returned they unto Jerusalem. . . . And when they were come in, they went up into the upper chamber.

At last disillusioned of their mistaken materialistic concept of Christ's kingdom and fully committed to His spiritual program of world evangelization, the disciples returned to Jerusalem, which was **a sabbath day's journey off. A sabbath day's journey** is generally regarded as 2,000 cubits, and a cubit, according to Josephus, was approximately $1^1/_2$ feet; thus a distance of approximately 3,000 feet seems to be indicated. This distance was established by

[43] For discussion of the variations in the Greek words used see Knowling, EGT, II, 59.

[m] G. Campbell Morgan, *The Missionary Manifesto* (New York: Fleming H. Revell Co., 1909), p. 56.

13 And when they were come in, they went up into the upper chamber, where they were abiding; both Peter and John and James and Andrew, Philip and Thomas, Bartholomew and Matthew, James *the son* of Alphaeus, and Simon the Zealot, and Judas *the son* of James.

---

regulation on this point was arrived at by combining Exodus 16:29—"Let no man go out of his place on the seventh day"—with Numbers 35:5, which indicates that the suburbs of the cities were to be counted as extending two thousand cubits (about 3,000 feet) from the walls.[44] The top of the Mount of Olives is about one-half mile east of the Temple Area and some two hundred feet above it. In Luke 24:50 it is stated that Jesus led the disciples "out as far as to Bethany" (KJV). This has sometimes been cited as a contradiction of the account here, since Bethany was nearly two miles from Jerusalem. But the American Standard Version gives the translation "over against Bethany," which would resolve the conflict.[45]

13 When the disciples had returned to Jerusalem, they went up into **the upper chamber**. The definite article suggests that it was a well-known room. This would point most naturally to the upper room of the last supper, which was perhaps the place of Jesus' first post-resurrection appearance to the apostles (Luke 24:36). It has also commonly been identified with a room in the home of John Mark's mother (cf. Acts 12:12).[46]

Some have held that this upper room was in the temple. But Luke 24:53 does not imply anything more than that the disciples were daily in the temple, especially at the hours of prayer. Most scholars today would agree with Knowling's verdict: "A meeting in a private house...is far more likely." [47]

The Greek word for abiding, *katamenontes*, has been taken by many [48] as indicating a permanent place of abode. But Moulton and Milligan give examples from the papyri of the word being used for temporary residence. They say: "Various passages from our sources show that this verb has not necessarily the meaning of 'remain permanently.'"[49] Probably the best interpretation is that of Lenski, who writes: " 'They were abiding' means that the apostles and other disciples were making this room their headquarters while they were in Jerusalem." [50]

The list of eleven apostles given in this verse is in close agreement with those found in the three Synoptic Gospels (Matt. 10:2-4; Mark 3:16-20; Luke 6:14-16). The slight differences may be seen by comparing them.

MATTHEW	MARK	LUKE	ACTS
Peter	**Peter**	**Peter**	**Peter**
Andrew	James	Andrew	John
James	John	James	James
John	Andrew	John	Andrew
Philip	**Philip**	**Philip**	**Philip**
Bartholomew	Bartholomew	Bartholomew	Thomas
Thomas	Matthew	Matthew	Bartholomew
Matthew	Thomas	Thomas	Matthew
James	**James**	**James**	**James**
(of Alphaeus)	(of Alphaeus)	(of Alphaeus)	(of Alphaeus)
Thaddaeus	Thaddaeus	Simon	Simon
		(the Zealot)	(the Zealot)
Simon	Simon	Judas	Judas
(the Cananaean)	(the Cananaean)	(of James)	(of James)
Judas Iscariot	Judas Iscariot	Judas Iscariot	

44 For another suggested explanation of the origin of this phrase see the Exposition.
45 This translation is based on the reading *pros*, found in Aleph B C D L 33, instead of *eis* (Textus Receptus).
46 Cf. Zahn, *op. cit.*, II, 429; *Beginnings*, IV, 10.
47 EGT, II, 60.
48 E.g., A. T. Robertson, *Word Pictures*, III, 13; Abbott-Smith, *op. cit.*, p. 236 — "to remain permanently."
49 VGT, p. 329.
50 *Op. cit.*, p. 39.

14 These all with one accord continued stedfastly in prayer, with the women, and Mary the mother of Jesus, and with his brethren.

Several interesting observations appear from this comparison: (1) In every list Peter heads the first group of four, Philip the second, and James the third; [51] (2) the same four names occur in the same group in every list, with the one exception of the substitution of Judas of James (Luke and Acts) for Thaddaeus (Matthew and Mark); (3) there is considerable variation in the order of the names within each group; [52] (4) every list begins with Peter and ends with Judas Iscariot (except Acts, after Judas' death).

Only three of the eleven apostles are mentioned again in Acts. The prominent places in the narrative are taken by others, such as Stephen, Philip, Barnabas, and Paul.

The first **James** was the son of Zebedee. The identity of **Alphaeus,** father of the other James, is unknown. The fact that Luke (both in his Gospel and Acts) calls the second Simon **the Zealot** *(zēlōtēs)* has provoked some complaint. It is alleged that the party called "the Zealots" did not appear until the beginning of the revolt against Rome in A.D. 66. But that there were zealous opponents of Roman rule at this time, who might have been called Zealots, cannot be denied.[53] Then, too, this might be simply a reference to Simon's zealous disposition.

The father [54] of **Judas**—identified as "not Iscariot" in John 14:22—should not be confused with any other James mentioned in the New Testament. In view of the close parallelism of the four lists, it seems altogether reasonable to identify this Judas with the Thaddaeus named by Matthew and Mark.

14 It is stated that the eleven apostles were praying **with one accord** *(homothymadon)*. This favorite adverb of Luke occurs ten

---

Mosaic law as the spacing between the ark and the people. When the ark halted in its course at sundown Friday, the people were allowed to traverse the intervening distance of 2,000 cubits for worship on the sabbath, hence the origin of this "sabbath day" measurement.[n]

The exact location of the disciples' ten-day prayer meeting, between Christ's Ascension and Pentecost, is a disputed question among scholars. Some hold that **the upper chamber** to which they resorted for prayer was the identical location of the "last supper." Some have thought that they were in a compartment of the temple, which view seems to find support in Luke 24:53. However, upper rooms of private houses were not uncommonly used for religious purposes. It would be a pleasant thought that they were guests in the evidently well-to-do and commodious home of the disciple Mary, the mother of John Mark, where Christian disciples later assembled for prayer (see Acts 12:12–16). Certainly such a private dwelling is more fitting to the Acts statement, **where they were abiding** [or residing], for a period of ten days, than would be a room in the temple. Further, Luke's statement descriptive of the Pentecostal effusion, "it filled all the 'house' where they were sitting" (Acts 2:2), lends weight to this position.

B. The Personnel of the Prayer (1:13b, 14b)

These all with one accord continued stedfastly . . . with the women, and Mary the mother of Jesus, and with his brethren.

With two exceptions, consisting of a slight difference in the order of listing and the omission of Judas from the Acts record, Luke's record of the apostles in Acts 1:13 agrees with his earlier record in Luke 6:12–16. The priority given to Peter here and in the following early chapters of Acts indicates Luke's purpose in presenting Peter as the divinely chosen leader of the infant Judaeo-Christian church. Luke is careful to make special note of **Mary the mother of Jesus,** of

---

[51] This is emphasized above by the use of boldface type.

[52] For an explanation of points (2) and (3), see the author's *The Gospel According to Mark*, pp. 54, 55. The most interesting change here is that of John to a position right after Peter, due to the fact that in the early chapters of Acts Peter and John are closely associated.

[53] *Ibid.*, p. 55. See also William R. Farmer, *Maccabees, Zealots, and Josephus* (New York: Columbia University Press, 1956), p. 189.

[54] The idea of "brother of," held by some, is very unlikely (see Knowling, EGT, II, 60).

[n] James Hastings, ed., *Dictionary of the Bible* (New York: Charles Scribner's Sons, 1909, rep. 1921), p. 968.

times in Acts and only once elsewhere in the New Testament (Rom. 15:6).[55] It comes from *homos*, "same," and *thymos*, "mind or spirit." So it means "with the same mind or spirit."

It is also declared that the apostles **continued stedfastly** *(proskarterountes)*. This verb is used only by Luke (six times in Acts) and Paul (Rom. 12:12; 13:6; Col. 4:2), with the exception of one passage (Mark 3:9). It is a forceful word, compounded with the adjective *karteros*, "strong, stedfast." It means "attend constantly, continue stedfastly."

The expression **in prayer** [56] is literally "in the prayer" *(tēi proseuchēi)*. Bruce says: "The article probably indicates the appointed service of prayer." [57] A. T. Robertson comments: "They 'stuck to' the praying . . . for the promise of the Father till the answer came." [58] Knowling explains the force of the definite article by saying that it "seems to point to a definite custom of common prayer as a bond of Christian fellowship." [59] In addition to the common interpretations of this expression as referring to public prayers in the temple or private prayer in the upper room, Cadbury and Lake suggest a third explanation. Calling attention to the fact that *proseuchē* was sometimes used for synagogue [60] they prefer the translation "Place of prayer," meaning synagogue.[61] Jackson and Lake hold it "probable that the Christians were also recognized as a synagogue or Keneseth, for according to the Mishna, ten Jews could at any time form one, and there was nothing schismatic in such action." [62]

There were also **women** in the group. Since the article is missing, it might be better to adopt the marginal reading "with certain women," rather than **with the women**. The Western text has "with their wives and children."

After **women** the expression **and Mary** seems a bit odd. Bruce suggests that *kai* here should be translated "including," or "in particular." [63]

The mention of **his brethren** is somewhat surprising, since it is stated in John 7:5 that they did not believe in Him. But after His resurrection Jesus appeared specifically to James (I Cor. 15:7)—generally identified as the Lord's brother and the one who became

---

whom this is the last mention in the Bible, and **his brethren** who had not believed in His Messiahship before His death and resurrection (Matt. 12:46–50). **The women** mentioned must have included those who remained with Him at the Cross and were present at the Resurrection, and certainly included Mary Magdalene from whom Christ had cast seven demons. Likely the wives of some of the apostles, including Peter's (Matt. 8:14) and those wives and other relatives of devout men, were present. Most probably Joanna the wife of Herod's steward, Susanna and other women who had been cured of illness or demon possession and who in grateful loyalty had followed and ministered to him (Luke 8:2, 3), were there. Mary, the mother of James and Joses, Salome the wife of Zebedee (Mark 15:40), Mary and Martha of Bethany and certainly Mark's mother Mary, who was probably hostess to the company, were all most likely present. The total company consisted of approximately 120 persons (vs. 15). A deep sense of sadness settles over the soul at the deathly silence concerning Judas.

C. The Persistence of the Prayer (1:14a)

These all with one accord continued stedfastly in prayer; or, as it appears in Williams' translation, "with one mind they were all continuing to devote themselves to prayer."[6]

What a diversity of persons constituted this praying assembly, and yet what unity of spirit and purpose those words, "with one mind," suggest to the serious reader! *Unity* is the keynote of the sacred occasion—"with one mind." They were characterized by: *first*, unity of plan to assemble *en masse* at a

[55] According to Moulton and Geden, *Concordance to the Greek Testament* (Edinburgh: T. & T. Clark, 1926) pp. 693, 694
[56] "and supplication" (KJV) is not in Aleph A B C D E, and so should be omitted.
[57] *Op. cit.*, p. 74. [58] *Word Pictures*, III, 14. [59] EGT, II, 61.
[60] See full evidence for this in Emil Schürer, *A History of the Jewish People in the Time of Jesus Christ* (Edinburgh: T. & T. Clark, 1885), II, ii, 69.
[61] *Beginnings*, IV, 11. [62] *Ibid.*, I, 304. [63] *Op. cit.*, p. 74.

[6] See Additional Note I on *Homothumadon = One Accord*, by J. A. Huffman, at end of chapter I.

15 And in these days Peter stood up in the midst of the brethren, and said (and there was a multitude of persons *gathered* together, about a hundred and twenty),

16 Brethren, it was needful that the scripture should be fulfilled, which the Holy Spirit spake before by the mouth of David concerning Judas, who was guide to them that took Jesus.

---

leader of the church in Jerusalem (Acts 12:17; 15:13; 21:18.

Who were these **brethren**? The endless discussion of this question has produced three answers. In the fourth century Epiphanius taught that they were stepbrothers, sons of Joseph by a previous marriage. In opposition to this emphasis on celibacy, Helvidius (ca. A.D. 380) held that they were the children of both Mary and Joseph. In reply Jerome (A.D. 382 or 383) set forth a new view—that they were really the cousins of Jesus. This is the Catholic view today. But the author would agree that the burden of proof lies on those who would deny that the word should be taken in its natural meaning of blood relationship.[64]

15 **Peter,** having been forgiven by Jesus for his threefold denial (cf. Mark 16:7—"and Peter"; Luke 24:34) and restored to apostleship (John 21:15–17), now takes his place again as the natural leader of the group.

The expression **stood up** is the second aorist participle in Greek, *anastas*. This form is found seventeen times in Luke's Gospel, nineteen times in Acts, twice in Matthew and five times in Mark (besides 16:9). Knowling comments: "It is very characteristic of St. Luke to add a participle to a finite verb indicating the posture or position of the speaker." [65]

The word **brethren** is "disciples" in the King James Version. But the former reading *(adelphōn)* has by far the best support (Aleph A B C). Probably *mathētōn* ("disciples") was substituted in the later manuscripts to avoid confusion with the **brethren** of Jesus mentioned at the end of verse 14.

Parenthetically it is stated that **there was a multitude of persons**. The King James Version has "the number of names." In this case the American Standard Version gives

---

designated location in Jerusalem and pray and wait in faith for the fulfillment of the Father's promise (Luke 24:49); *second,* unity of place where physical proximity would lend strength and faith to their vigil (see Matt. 18:20); *third,* unity of purpose which gave direction and focus to their praying (see Mark 11:24); *fourth,* unity of persistence which afforded drive to their praying (see James 5:16b); and *fifth,* unity of prayer which integrated their desires with their objective and thus sealed to them by faith the fulfillment of the Father's promise to endue them with power from on high.

IV. THE DISCIPLES' PURPOSE (1:15–26)

The purpose of the disciples in preparation for Pentecost appears to have been twofold: *first,* to realize the fulfillment of Jewish prophecy in relation to the betrayer Judas; and *second,* to supply the vacancy left in the apostolate by Judas' failure.

A. A PURPOSE TO REALIZE THE FULFILLMENT OF PROPHECY, VSS. 15–20.

Brethren, it was needful that the scripture should be fulfilled.

The inauguration or dedication (not the birthday as some suppose—see **Additional Note I,** Chap. II, *The Practical Significance of Pentecost*) of the Christian Church was about to occur with the Pentecostal effusion. Peter having been restored to the grace of his Lord and his appointed office, which he had temporarily forfeited by his triple apostasy (Luke 22:54–62 and John 21:15–19), now resumed his former role as the apostolic chairman and called the assembly to order for the business of electing an apostolic successor to replace the fallen Judas.

The assumption of this initiative and

---

[64] For extended discussions of this controversial question, see the following: Samuel Andrews, *The Life of Our Lord Upon the Earth* (Grand Rapids: Zondervan Publishing House, 1954), pp. 111–123; J. B. Lightfoot, *St. Paul's Epistle to the Galatians* (Zondervan, n.d.), pp. 88–128; Joseph B. Mayor, *The Epistle of St. James* (Zondervan Publishing House, 1954), pp. v-lxv. Lightfoot held the Epiphanian view, as did Westcott. Lange and Ellicott held the view of Jerome. But the majority of Protestants hold the view of Helvidius, that these were blood brothers. This position is defended exhaustively by Mayor (see reference above).

[65] EGT II, 62.

a literal translation of the first noun, the King James Version of the second. Since 120 would not now be thought of as a **multitude,** the Revised Standard Version has "company."[66] There is ample evidence from the papyri that *onomatōn* (lit., "of names") was commonly used for **persons;**[67] hence the Revised rendering. This usage is also found in the Septuagint (Num. 1:2, 18, 20; 3:40, 43, etc.).

Different explanations have been given of *epi to auto*, **gathered together**. Cadbury and Lake translate it "amounting to" and state: "This is a customary meaning of *epi to auto* in papyri."[68] Bruce comments: "The phrase seems to have acquired a quasi-technical sense not unlike *en ekklēsia* ('in church fellowship') in the New Testament ... and the Apostolic Fathers."[69] Knowling thinks the expression may suggest the unity of the early believers.[70]

Bruce finds no significance in the number **a hundred and twenty.**[71] But Cadbury and Lake think it "can scarcely be an accident" that this is ten times the number of apostles. More important is their statement: "It is remarkable that *Sanhedr* 1:6 enacts that the number of officers in a community shall be a tenth of the whole, and that 120 is the smallest number which can hold a 'small Sanhedrin.' "[72]

16 **Brethren** is literally "men, brethren," *andres adelphoi*. This is a classical Greek idiom, but since Peter spoke in Aramaic the translation **brethren** is adequate and correct.

The scripture is singular *(hē graphē)* and so refers to a passage of Scripture. The reference is to Psalms 69:25 and 109:8, quoted in verse 20.

---

office by Peter (**Peter stood up in the midst of the brethren**, vs. 15; cf. 2:14) is clearly personal and not official, as the church of Rome assumes. In support of this position are the following evidences. *First*, Peter's understanding and confession of Christ's divinity, not Peter's character, was to be the foundation of the Church (Matt. 16:18). *Second*, Christ committed the apostolic authority to all the apostles and not to Peter exclusively, nor even primarily (see John 20:19-23). *Third*, the whole New Testament regards the twelve apostles, and not Peter alone, as the Church's foundation (see Matt. 19:28; Eph. 2:19-22; Rev. 21:14). *Fourth*, the Church called Peter into question for having preached the Gospel to the household of the Gentile Cornelius (Acts 11:1-3). *Fifth*, Peter assumed a role subordinate to James at the first general church council in Jerusalem (Acts 15). *Sixth*, Paul regarded his apostleship equal to, and independent of, that of Peter and the other apostles (II Cor. 11:5; Gal. 2:6-9). *Seventh*, Paul rebuked and reprimanded Peter for his divisive conduct at Antioch (Gal. 2:11-18). *Eighth*, Peter himself assumed a position of equality with, and not superiority to, his fellows (I Peter 5:1). And *Ninth*, Luke made no further mention of Peter in the Acts record after his appearances at the Jerusalem conference (Acts 15).

Thus Peter's primacy on this occasion, as well as elsewhere, was the natural expression of his personal character and ability, rather than of divine appointment. His characteristic zeal, courage, readiness, even venturesomeness and audacious faith, naturally brought him into prominence as the leader of the apostles.

Peter recognizes and asserts that the Church of Christ is to be built upon the divinity of Christ. The revelation of that divinity was given to and through the twelve apostles. The apostolate is now incomplete in Judas' absence, and thus an inadequate foundation for the Church is afforded. It is therefore necessary to choose an apostolic successor to Judas.

The number of brethren assembled for this occasion, **about a hundred and twenty,** fulfilled the Jewish requirement for the number of a council in any city, and thus was the election of an apostle to be made both official and legal.

The meaning of Peter's statement, **Brethren, it was needful that the scripture should be fulfilled,** is best understood in the light of the last part of verse 20, **his office let another take.** There are no scriptural or logical

[66] Incidentally, this shows that *ochlos*, frequent in the Gospels (49 times in Matt., 38 in Mark, 40 in Luke, 20 in John) and Acts (22 times) does not *by itself* necessarily indicate thousands of people.
[67] VGT, p. 451.
[68] *Beginnings*, IV, 12.
[69] *Op. cit.*, p. 75.
[70] EGT, II, 62.
[71] *Op. cit.*, p. 76.
[72] *Beginnings*, IV, 12.

17 For he was numbered among us, and received his portion in this ministry.
18 (Now this man obtained a field with the reward of his iniquity; and falling headlong,
he burst asunder in the midst, and all his bowels gushed out.

---

17 **Numbered** is in Greek the compound verb *katarithmeō*, found only here in the New Testament. Perhaps it adds a bit of emphasis that he was actually **counted among** the apostles.

Portion is literally "lot" *(klēron)*. However, the original meaning had weakened to "portion." Cadbury and Lake translate the phrase as "obtained the rank." [73] The word has come by way of the Latin *clerici* into English as "clergy"—those who are chosen.

18 Two problems present themselves in this verse. The first relates to the purchase of the **field**. The second has reference to the manner of Judas' death.

With regard to the first, there seems on the surface to be a contradiction of the statement in Matthew 27:7 that the chief priests bought the field. Perhaps the best explanation is that given by Edersheim: "By a fiction of law the money was still considered to be Judas', and to have been applied by him in the purchase of the well-known 'potter's field.' " [74]

---

grounds for a conclusion that Judas' betrayal and fall was made necessary to fulfill a divine decree. In consideration of the fact of Judas' apostasy, it was necessary to choose an apostolic successor in order to fulfill the divine prophecy, as well as the divine plan for the Christian Church. Indeed Judas' fall and the related events recorded in verses 15 through 20 are the fulfillments of the divine prophecy, but as consequences of Judas' decisions and conduct, and not of necessity to the fulfillment of a divine prediction. Dummelow offers a pertinent observation on Peter's words, **it was needful that the scripture should be fulfilled.** Says this authority:

> Just as the scandal and stumbling block of the death of Jesus was diminished by the discovery that it was foretold in the O. T., and was part of the determinate council of God (Luke 24:26, 46; Acts 2:23; 3:17, 18, etc.), so the scandal of the fall of an Apostle was relieved by the discovery that David had foretold it in the Psalms: cp. Jn. 13:18; Mt. 26:24. Peter quotes Pss. 69:25 and 109:8. David really spoke of his own enemies, perhaps (in Ps. 109) of Ahithophel, but Peter regards the words as a typical prophecy of the treachery of Judas.[p]

That Judas had been a genuinely regenerated member of the body of Christ is suggested: *first*, by the words of Peter, **he was numbered among us** (vs. 17; see also John 13:18); and *second*, by his divine election to the apostleship, having **received his portion in this ministry** (vs. 17b). Certainly Judas could not be thought to have actually received his apostolic appointment by the authority of Christ had he not first become partaker of the divine nature. Such a sacred commission could not have been given to an enemy of the kingdom of grace by the omniscient king Himself. Further, that Judas fell from both his divine relationship and his apostolic office by a deliberate choice of material gain at the expense of his loyalty to Christ is made clear by Peter's continued address: **Now this man obtained a field with the reward of his iniquity; and falling headlong, he burst asunder in the midst, and all his bowels gushed out.**

This passage may be better understood in relation to the words in verse 25, which read: **this ministry and apostleship from which Judas fell away, that he might go to his own place.** On this latter passage Dummelow remarks: "St. Peter speaks with merciful reserve, but probably means Hell ('Gehenna'). The same euphemism is found in rabbinical writings." [q]

The most likely explanation of this whole matter concerning Judas Iscariot seems to be as follows. *First*, he was chosen a disciple and elected an apostle by Jesus Christ (John 14:12; 17:11, 12; and Acts 1:17). *Second*, he neglected or otherwise failed to grasp the spiritual significance of Christ's kingdom and his own personal discipleship and ministry and consequently became covetous of material gain and betrayed his sacred trust as treasurer of the apostolic

[73] *Ibid.*
[74] Alfred Edersheim, *The Life and Times of Jesus the Messiah* (8th ed.; New York. Longmans, Green & Co., 1903), II, 575.

[p] Dummelow, *op. cit.*, p. 819. [q] *Ibid.*

The second problem is more complicated. In Matthew 27:5, it is stated that Judas hanged himself. But here we read that **falling headlong, he burst asunder in the midst, and all his bowels gushed out**. There is general agreement that *prēnēs genomenos* means "falling flat" (lit., "having become prone"). Many modern commentators have followed Augustine's suggestion of combining the hanging and the falling. Knowling, for instance, says: "If the rope broke, or a branch gave way under the weight of Judas, St. Luke's narrative might easily be supplementary to that of St. Matthew." [75] Hackett describes his reactions when he stood in the Valley of Hinnom, just south of Jerusalem, and looked at the steep cliffs with their overhanging trees at the top and jagged rocks at the bottom, where Judas' body might easily have broken open.[76]

In recent times considerable attention has been given to the Papias tradition that the body of Judas became so swollen that it burst open.[77] So *prēnēs genomenos* has been translated "swelling up." But there does not appear to be any sufficient evidence that *prēnēs*, found only here in the New Testament, carries that meaning. The best solution of the problem is probably that given above.

---

group (John 12:3–6). *Third*, he became deceptively hypocritical (Matt. 26:25, 48; Luke 22:47, 48). *Fourth*, he spurned every overture of divine mercy designed to restore him to grace and save him from his ultimate tragedy, both when he was made the honored guest of the last supper by the Lord (John 13:26), and when Jesus tenderly addressed him as "friend" on the occasion of His arrest in the garden (Matt. 26:50). *Fifth*, he transferred his will, devotion, and obedience from Christ to Satan (John 13:27). *Sixth*, he deliberately took his leave of the Master to execute his evil purpose (John 13:30). *Seventh*, he purposefully and calculatingly bargained with the enemies of the Lord for Christ's betrayal into their hands (Matt. 26:14–16; Luke 22:3–6). *Eighth*, he deliberately and calculatingly executed his evil intention of Christ's betrayal by identifying himself with and directing the Sanhedrin's servants to the place of Christ's arrest (Mark 14:11; Matt. 26:16, 47–49). *Ninth*, upon his awakening to the shocking consequences of his deed, at the condemnation of Christ to death, Judas' repentance and confession (Matt. 27:3, 4) were the self-imposed result of the remorseful "sorrow of the world [which] worketh death," and not that "godly sorrow [which] worketh repentance unto salvation, a repentance which bringeth no regret" (II Cor. 7:10). *Tenth*, he consequently went out and committed suicide by hanging himself (Matt. 27:5), from which position he likely fell on a rocky cliff by reason of the rope having broken, and thus his abdomen was ruptured on the jagged rocks and his intestines were forcefully ejected from their body cavity (Acts 1:18b). *Eleventh* and finally, his career terminated in final and awful separation from God as the natural consequences of the willful choices which he made and the evil course that he deliberately followed; as Peter who knew Judas so well phrases his awful doom: **that he might go to his own place** (Acts 1:25b), or the place of his own choosing, the end and state for which he had conditioned himself by rejection of all that he knew to be right, and deliberate conformity to that which he knew to be wrong. Satan promises much but affords little. Somewhere Ethymius is reported as having said, "Before we sin, he [Satan] suffers us not to see the end of it, lest we repent. But after the sin is committed he suffers us to see it to cause us remorse and to drive us to despair."

That Judas could have sincerely repented and experienced restoration to God at any moment prior to his fatal suicide there can be no reasonable doubt (cf. Luke 23:39–43); but that he did so there lacks scriptural evidence. Thus the eternal fate of his soul will best remain in the determinate council of an all-wise and just God.

The problem of the reconciliation of Luke's parenthetical statement concerning Judas' obtaining **a field with the reward of his iniquity** (Acts 1:18, 19), with Matthew's account (Matt. 27:3–10) is not without a

[75] EGT, II, 65.

[76] H. B. Hackett, *A Commentary on the Acts of the Apostles* (Philadelphia: American Baptist Publication Society, 1882), p. 37, n. 3.

[77] For the various forms of this tradition see Kirsopp Lake, "The Death of Judas," *Beginnings*, V, 22–30.

19 And it became known to all the dwellers at Jerusalem; insomuch that in their language
that field was called Akeldama, that is, The field of blood.)
20 For it is written in the book of Psalms, Let his habitation be made desolate, And
let no man dwell therein: and, His office let another take.

---

19 **Their language** was Aramaic, spoken by the Jews in Palestine after the Babylonian captivity. The word *dialektos* ("language") is used only in Acts, where it occurs six times. This phrase suggests that verses 18 and 19 are a parenthetical explanation by the author. Luke, who was probably a Gentile, would speak of Aramaic as "their language."

In addition to the two problems noted in verse 18, a third occurs in this verse. It is stated that the field purchased with the betrayal money was called **Akeldama, that is, The field of blood** because of the gory nature of Judas' death. Quite another explanation is found in Matthew 27:6–8, where the reason given for the name is that it was bought with "the price of blood." But, as Knowling says, "Why should there not be two reasons?" [78] Both of these current traditions of that day could easily be true.

20 **Habitation** is *epaulis*, found only here in the New Testament. It means a country house or cottage. The usual meaning in the papyri is "homestead." [79]

Office is the translation of *episkopē*, from which comes "episcopal." This word occurs four times in the New Testament and in the King James Version is translated three different ways: "visitation" [80] in Luke 19:44 and I Peter 2:12, "bishoprick" here, and "office of a bishop" in I Timothy 3:1. The word literally means "overseership." The King James rendering is open to the objection that the word did not at this time have the later "episcopal" connotation.

---

likely resolution. It is possible that Judas was motivated by economic interest in his betrayal of Jesus for thirty pieces of silver, which money he intended to invest in a parcel of land containing soil especially valuable for pottery-making. Thus he may have bargained with the owners for this field, but may not as yet have paid the money for it before his remorseful awakening at the sight of Jesus' condemnation, and his consequent suicide. His return of this money to the chief priests may have eventuated in their use of it to consummate the deal begun by Judas, with a view to its use as a cemetery in which to bury poor strangers who came to Jerusalem and died there away from home and friends, since it was unlawful to put such money into the temple treasury. Thus in this sense it could be said that Judas **obtained a field with the reward of his iniquity.** On the other hand, it may be simply meant to imply that the purchase of this field by the priests was a consequence of Judas' monetary betrayal of Christ, though no part of his intelligent purpose. Either view leaves no particular problem in the reconciliation of Luke's account with that of Matthew.

That this parcel of land was called **The field of blood** by the inhabitants of Jerusalem (vs. 19), may be accounted for by either one of two factors, or even a possible combination of both. *First*, it may have been so called by reason of the fact that it was purchased with "blood money," the thirty pieces of silver for which Christ was betrayed unto death. *Second*, it is possible that it was so called because Judas may have committed suicide in the field and was buried in this very field from which he had intended to enrich himself by material gain. In either event **this man obtained .... The field of blood .... with the reward of his iniquity.** Ill-gotten gain can never procure spiritual security. That is obtained solely by giving, and never by getting. Judas won a dismal burying ground as a reward. His fellow apostles won an eternal spiritual kingdom for their loyalty to Christ.

B. A Purpose to Fulfill the Apostolate (1:21–26)

Of these must one become a witness with us of his resurrection .... to take the place in this ministry and apostleship from which Judas fell away, vss. 22b and 25a.

Peter presents three specific requirements

[78] EGT, II, 65. [79] *Beginnings*, IV, 13.
[80] From the idea of a visit of inspection made by an overseer.

21 Of the men therefore that have companied with us all the time that the Lord Jesus went in and went out among us,

22 beginning from the baptism of John, unto the day that he was received up from us, of these must one become a witness with us of his resurrection.

23 And they put forward two, Joseph called Barsabbas, who was surnamed Justus, and Matthias.

---

21 **Went in and went out** *(eisēlthe kai exēlthen)* is described by Knowling as "a Hebraistic formula expressing the whole course of a man's daily life." [81]

22 The candidate for apostleship must be one who had firsthand acquaintance with the entire public ministry of Jesus, **from the baptism of John, unto the day that he was received up from us**. Peter and the other earliest apostles had been disciples of John the Baptist and then had followed Jesus throughout His ministry and right up to the time of His ascension. The primary function of this newly appointed apostle was to be **a witness . . . of his resurrection.**

23 **Put forward** is better than "appointed" (KJV), since the appointment had not yet taken place. This was a nomination of two candidates for the office.

Barsabbas is Aramaic for "son of the sabbath." He was probably called that because born on a sabbath day. **Justus** was his Gentile name (cf. Saul Paul; John Mark).

Matthias is identified by Eusebius as one of the seventy disciples sent out by Jesus.[82] The name means "gift of Jah" (Jehovah).

---

to be met by the apostolic successor of Judas. These conditions are, as implied in the address of Peter: *first*, a true discipleship to Jesus Christ: **beginning from the baptism of John,** the baptism of repentance and saving faith in Christ (vs. 22a); *second*, faithful and loyal membership in the Christian disciple family (vss. 21, 22a); *third*, a living witness to the personal resurrection of Jesus Christ from the dead (vs. 22b). These requirements advanced by Peter as qualifications for Christian apostleship placed Paul under necessity of defending his apostleship before his enemies as being directly from God, and not of men, as witness the introductions of most of his epistles.

Though the eleven apostles might have selected a successor for Judas without reference to the lay disciples, they rather consulted the assembly and thus set a precedent by introducing a popular element into the policy of the infant Church's government. This precedent is followed through the Church in the Acts record (cf. Acts 5:3–6). The organizational weakness of the Church at this juncture is evidenced by the following facts: *first*, that two candidates were advanced for the apostolic position clearly indicated the disciples' uncertainty of the divine will in the matter; *second*, that the disciples' choice was made from among the disciples and their candidates presented to God before prayer was offered for divine direction; *third*, that they employed the **lot** (Urim), a sacred device used under the law to ascertain the divine will, but here for the first and last time employed by the followers of Christ. Dummelow[r] thinks it may have consisted in the writing of the names of the candidates on tablets and then shaking them up until one fell out. In any event, there is no evidence that it was ordered or approved of God on this occasion.

Joseph, called Barsabbas, not to be confused with Barnabas of later date, and **Matthias** were the disciples' choice. Their prayer for God's choice between the candidates is the first recorded "post-ascension" Christian prayer, and it was directed to the **Lord** Jesus Himself. Such became the accepted practice of the apostolic church (see Acts 9:14). It is natural that they should have petitioned Christ in the choice of this apostle, since He had chosen the original twelve.

That neither Joseph nor Matthias was Christ's choice of a successor for Judas seems evident from the fact that, though the lot fell on Matthias, he is not heard of again in the New Testament and evidently did not fill the

81 EGT, II, 66.
82 *Ecclesiastical History*, II, 12.
r *Ibid.*

24 And they prayed, and said, Thou, Lord, who knowest the hearts of all men, show of these two the one whom thou hast chosen,

25 to take the place in this ministry and apostleship from which Judas fell away, that he might go to his own place.

26 And they gave lots for them; and the lot fell upon Matthias; and he was numbered with the eleven apostles.

---

24 **Lord** probably means Jesus.[83] The same Greek word *exelexō*, **chosen,** is used here as in verse two (for Jesus' choice of His disciples).

Who knowest the hearts is all one word in the Greek, *kardiognōsta* (lit., "heart-knower"). It is "found chiefly in Christian liturgical use."[84]

25 **Place** *(topon)* is the reading of A B C D, against *klēron*, "part" (KJV; lit., "lot"), found in Aleph E. This suggests a contrast with **his own place,** to which he went.

Fell away is literally "transgressed" *(parebē)*.

26 **Gave lots** is the literal Greek *(edōkan klērous)*. We should rather have expected "cast [*ebalon*] lots." This was the common Jewish way of ascertaining the divine will (cf. Prov. 16:33). "The method employed by the Jews was to put the names written on stones into a vessel and shake it until one fell out."[85] But there is no indication that the disciples ever did this after Pentecost.[86]

---

office, though, of course, "silence" is not conclusive evidence. All subsequent evidence seems to point to Paul as the divine selection to complete the apostolate.

Morgan, while acknowledging that it is a debated question in Biblical interpretation, nevertheless unhesitatingly asserts that the disciples were mistaken in their choice of Matthias to succeed Judas.

"...my own conviction is that we have a revelation of their inefficiency for organization; that the election of Matthias was wrong. Their idea of what was necessary as a witness to the resurrection was wrong. They said that a witness must have been with them from the baptism of John. They thought a witness must be one who had seen Jesus prior to His ascension. As a matter of fact the most powerful incentive to witness was the seeing of Christ after resurrection, as when He arrested Saul of Tarsus on his way to Damascus. So their principle of selection was wrong. Their method of selection was also wrong. The method of casting lots was no longer necessary. Thus we have the wrong appointment of Matthias. He was a good man, but the wrong man for this position, and he passed out of sight; and when presently we come to the final glory of the city of God, we see twelve foundation stones, and twelve apostles' names, and I am not prepared to omit Paul from the twelve, believing that he was God's man for the filling of the gap.

These men were perfectly sincere, proceeding on the lines of revealed truth, but they were ignorant of God's best method; unable to bear their witness; unable to organize themselves for the doing of the work; and consequently needing the coming of the Paraclete."[s]

Additional Note I

HOMOTHUMADON = ONE ACCORD[t]

"Through The Book Of Acts With Homothumadon"

This... word [homothumadon]... occurs only eleven times in the Westcott and Hort Greek New Testament and all these instances, with one exception only, in the Book of the Acts... The one exception is found in Rom. 15:6.

Homothumadon is compounded of the Greek words, *homos*, which means *together* or in *unison*, and *thumos*, which primarily means to *rush along*, or to *breathe violently*. The best English phrase with which *homothumadon* can be translated is, *with one accord*. In the pronunciation of the word *homothumadon*, the letter u of the third syllable is pronounced like the English e with a macron over it.

[83] So Bruce (p. 80), Knowling ("may well have been" — p. 68), Hackett (p. 39), and allowed by Cadbury and Lake (*Beginnings*, IV, 15).
[84] *Beginnings*, IV, 15. [85] *Ibid*. For another explanation see Exposition.
[86] For a discussion of whether or not the disciples acted in divine order in this election, see the editorial note of Alvah Hovey in Hackett, pp. 40f.

[s] G. Campbell Morgan, *The Acts of the Apostles* (New York: Fleming H. Revell Company, 1924), p. 21.
[t] From *Golden Treasures from the Greek New Testament for English Readers*, by Jasper Abraham Huffmann (Butler, Indiana: The Highly Press, 1951), pp. 155–160. Used by permission.

The Greek word itself cannot be said to be a musical term, but the best English word with which to translate it, *accord*, is decidedly musical. It means, among other things, to *agree in pitch and tone*. The other uses of this word in the Book of Acts are varied, even including the united opposition of the people to the preaching of the Gospel in 18:12; but it is in relation to the Church that we wish to examine the use of *homothumadon*.

Here is a picture: As Chairman of the Music-Lecture Course Committee of the College with which he has been connected, this writer, two or three times, secured the services of one of America's best-known and greatly loved harpists. Before beginning her program, and always as she began a new series of selections, this harpist would run her nimble fingers across the strings of the harp, and then, with her delicately trained ear, would listen intently for some discordant sound. Sometimes she must have heard some sound not in perfect accord, though the audience would not have been able to detect it; for she would take the large key which lay beside her, put it on the particular post of the instrument to which the string of the harp was attached, and adjust it. This she continued to do until there was no longer heard the least sound of disharmony. The music which then came from that great golden harp was well-nigh heavenly. There was no discord, but accord. This is *homothumadon*.

I. *Homothumadon as the Pentecostal Pre-Requisite*.

The first use of *homothumadon* in the Book of Acts is in 1:14, where the setting is that of the upper room, during the ten days intervening between the ascension of Jesus and the day of Pentecost. "These all *with one accord* continued stedfastly in prayer, with the women, and Mary the mother of Jesus, and with his brethren."

"These all" refers to the twelve apostles (now eleven, Judas counted out) and the other persons mentioned. Keeping the apostles particularly in mind, there had not always been *homothumadon*. There had been wrangling, jealousy, and strife. But these existed no longer. Confessions had been made, apologies offered, old scores, whatever they were, settled; and now pre-Pentecostally, they were *with one accord*: there was *homothumadon*. The exact details of the procedure we are not told, but we are apprised of the fact of the absence of all discord.

Why ten days? God who knows the end from the beginning, and all the contingencies of the way, knew how to schedule this period between the Ascension and Pentecost. It was not how long it would take God, but how much time His people needed to meet the Pentecostal prerequisite—*homothumadon*.

II. *Homothumadon as a Pentecostal Requisite*.

The American Standard Version reads: "And when the day of Pentecost was now come, they were all together in one place." The King James reads: "And when the day of Pentecost was fully come, they were all with one accord in one place." The difference is that the phrase, "with one accord," is omitted in the American Standard Version. The reason that this phrase is not found in the American Standard Version is that this version is an accurate translation here of the Westcott and Hort Greek New Testament, and the word *homothumadon* is not in this verse of that Greek Manuscript where variations are found. Westcott and Hort spent 27 years in the examination of the Greek Manuscripts and found the preponderance of evidence in favor of the text which they produced.

Since however *homothumadon* is found pre-Pentecostally, and also post-Pentecostally, even if the word itself were not found in Acts 2:1 in the Greek Manuscripts, the King James translators were justified in inferring that the Pentecostal prerequisite and the post-Pentecostal requisite must have obtained Pentecostally. The logic of this is sound, and the conclusion inescapable.

That the Pentecostal participants should be in one place is easy to comprehend. That it is possible for a group of people to be in *one place* without being with *one accord* is as readily understood, as most people have seen such situations. But that the Pentecostal participants should be both in one place and with one accord as an absolute necessity cannot be disputed. What obtained in Acts 1:14 must have equally obtained in Acts 2:1.

III. *Homothumadon in Post-Pentecostal Fellowship.*

The next appearance of this interesting word in the Book of Acts is in 2:46, where the verse reads as follows: "And they, continuing daily with one accord [*homothumadon*] in the temple, and breaking bread from house to house, did eat their meat with gladness and singleness of heart."

Here is one of the references which shows that even post-Pentecostally the Christian religion was a movement within Judaism, and the temple continued to be generally recognized as their regular place of service. The break which caused the Christians to abandon the temple for private houses for worshiping places, and later chapels, came more or less gradually.

Here, however, the Christians are depicted as living with one accord, even in the midst of the temporary Christian communion of goods which was made necessary by the unusual circumstances under which they found themselves. The acid test of Christianity is not in the temple or church services, but in the daily grind of the commonplace. These early Christians stood the test of *homothumadon*, even under the irregularities of that day and situation.

IV. *Homothumadon in Post-Pentecostal Prayer and Worship.*

Perhaps the secret of *homothumadon* in Acts 2:46 is found in Acts 4:24, where the word is used in relation to prayer and worship of the early Church. It reads as follows: "And when they heard that, they lifted up their voice to God with one accord..."

This is the reaction of the early Christians to the arrest of Peter and John when they had healed the lame man at the temple gate. They had preached, had been arrested, had been imprisoned, preached some more, had been threatened, and commanded to preach no more in the name of Jesus. They had placed God first, and refused to become subject to the decrees of the magistrates. Being let go, they returned to their own company of believers and reported. Immediately the above statement is made by the writer of the sacred narrative, in which *homothumadon* is employed in relation to their praying.

Here the baptism with the Holy Spirit and *homothumadon* are linked together in a post-Pentecostal way, as it was in chapters one and two, pre-Pentecostally and Pentecostally. Those persons who had been previously filled with the Spirit on this prayer meeting occasion were *homothumadon*.

V. *Homothumadon in Relation to Christianity's Difficult Problem.*

No general body of the Christian Church ever met a more difficult problem than that first gathering of the Christians held in Jerusalem about 50 A.D. James the brother of our Lord was chairman and, besides others representing the two extreme oppositions, Paul and Peter were present as expert witnesses.

The extremely difficult problem before this conference was the relation of Jew and Gentile in the Christian body: Must Gentile become Jew to become Christian?

The detailed minutes of this gathering would have made a volume of interesting and exciting reading. God has seen fit, however, to hand down this report in the small compass of verses 1–35 in chapter 15 of the Acts.

There was testimony, disputation, a recourse to prophecy, and evidently much prayer and patience, and finally the "Great Magna Charta of Christian Liberty" was agreed upon, emerged, and was written down.

It was a magnificient technique which was employed, resulting in a document with fundamental applications to all problems for all times.

The whole account of this conference merits very close and prayerful study by all charged with the solution of the doctrinal and practical problems of the Christian Church. But couched among the things written down is found again our interesting Greek word, *homothumadon*. Here it is: "It seemed good unto us, being assembled with one accord (*homothumadon*)...," (verse 25, KJV). No, it is not strange, but significant that in the same document are also found these words: "It seemed good to the Holy Ghost, and to us," (verse 28, KJV).

Where there is *homothumadon* among

Christians, there the Holy Spirit is present. What men think in the *homothumadon* way, the Holy Spirit can think with them and inspire their difficult problem solutions.

In our first *homothumadon* reference, Acts 1:14, the Twelve were involved. In the second reference, Acts 2:1, the one hundred and twenty were involved. In the subsequent references, and particularly the last one, the interests of the whole Church are at stake. Why not give *homothumadon* a chance in our churches and conferences today? [u]

[u] Unless otherwise stated, all Scripture quotations in this chapter were taken from the American Standard Version.

CHAPTER II

And when the day of Pentecost was now come, they were all together in one place.

EXEGESIS

1 The great event described here is said to have taken place **when the day of Pentecost was now come.** The words *en tōi sunplēr-ousthai* literally mean "when it was being fulfilled." Exactly the same phrase occurs in Luke 9:51.[1] There "day" (*hēmera*) is in the plural and the reference clearly is to the fulfillment of the period of forty days before the Ascension. Many commentators [2] give the same meaning to the phrase here. Bruce adds that "the Hebrew name of the festival, *shābū'ōth* ('weeks'), includes the 7 weeks." [3]

But the problem is that "day" here is in the singular. Perhaps the best solution is to recall the fact that the Jewish day began at sunset, and so the next morning could be described as "when the day of Pentecost was being fulfilled." Lenski prefers to make the time element secondary and emphasize the fact that God's appointed time for the outpouring of the Spirit had fully come.[4]

Pentecost is called in the Old Testament the Feast of Weeks (Ex. 34:22; Deut. 16:10), because it was celebrated seven weeks after the offering of the barley-sheaf during the passover season (Lev. 23:15). The Greek-speaking Jews called it "Pentecost"[5] (Gr. "fiftieth") because it came on the fiftieth day from the feast of first fruits (Lev. 23:16), which was celebrated in connection with the feast of unleavened bread.

EXPOSITION

THE CHURCH'S FIRST PENTECOST

I. The Fact of Pentecost, Acts 2:1–11.
   A. The Preparation for Pentecost, vs. 1.
   B. The Occurrence of Pentecost, vss. 2–4.
   C. The Effects of Pentecost, vss. 5–8.
   D. The Nations at Pentecost, vss. 9–11.

II. The Explanation of Pentecost, Acts 2:12–21.
   A. The Pentecostal Question, vss. 12, 13.
   B. The Pentecostal Spokesman, vs. 14.
   C. The Misapprehension of Pentecost, vs. 15.
   D. The Truth Concerning Pentecost, vss. 16–20.
      1. Fulfillment of the Divine Plan, vs. 16.
      2. Universal Divine Manifestation, vss. 17–20.
   E. The Purpose of Pentecost, vs. 21.

III. The Declaration of Pentecost, (or Peter's Pentecostal Sermon), Acts 2:22–40.
   A. The Son of God Crucified, vss. 22, 23.
   B. The Son of God Resurrected, vss. 24–32.
   C. The Son of God Ascended, vss. 33a, 34.
   D. The Holy Spirit Descended, vs. 33b.
   E. The Christ of God Declared Lord of All, vss. 35, 36.
   F. The Door of Salvation Opened to All, vss. 37–40.

IV. The Church of Pentecost, Acts 2:41–47.
   A. The Converts of the Church, vs. 41.
   B. The Communion of the Church, vs. 42.
   C. The Influence of the Church, vs. 43.
   D. The Liberality of the Church, vss. 44, 45.
   E. The Service of the Church, vs. 46.
   F. The Prosperity of the Church, vs. 47.

[1] The verb *sunplEroB* is used only by Luke, in these two passages and Luke 8:23.
[2] E.g., Hackett, p. 41; Cadbury and Lake, *Beginnings*, IV, 16; Bruce, p. 81.
[3] *Acts*, p. 81.
[4] *Op. cit.*, p. 56.
[5] This name first appears in the intertestamental period, in Tobit 2:1 and II Macc. 12:32 (LXX).

2 And suddenly there came from heaven a sound as of the rushing of a mighty wind, and it filled all the house where they were sitting.

It was the second of the three great annual feasts which every male Israelite was required to attend (Deut. 16:16). Because the Passover came early in the sailing season on the Mediterranean, Jews from a distance usually preferred to attend the feast of Pentecost. In many ways it was the most popular feast of the Jewish year.[6]

Whether or not the Jews of Jesus' day connected **Pentecost** with the giving of the law at Sinai is a matter of dispute. Purves, after noting that there is no mention of such a view in the Old Testament, Josephus, or Philo, makes this statement: "It was probably after the fall of Jerusalem that this view originated." [7] Dosker goes a step further and says: "It originated with the great Jewish rabbi Maimonides and has been copied by Christian writers." [8] But Foakes-Jackson asserts: "There is reason to suppose that Pentecost was already the festival commemorating the giving of the Law." [9] Kirsopp Lake simply says of this view that it "cannot be proved to be as early as Acts." [10]

The disciples were **all**—probably still the 120, though not so stated—**together.** The King James Version says "of one accord." But *homothymadon*, while genuine in Acts 1:14 and 2:46 (and in eight other passages in Acts), is not found here in the oldest manuscripts. Instead they have *homou*, **together.**[11]

2 **Suddenly** (*aphnō*, found only in Acts, three times) there came a **sound.** The Greek word is *ēchos* (English "echo"). It is used in Luke 4:37 of a rumor or report and in Luke 21:25 of the roar of the sea. The narrative does not say that they heard a wind, but the noise **as of** a roaring wind. This **sound,** not wind, **filled all the house.** Probably this was a private house, not the temple. "If the Temple were meant... it would have been specified." [12] It should be noted that they were **sitting.** Evidently they had finished their praying and were waiting.

"As of a rushing mighty wind" (KJV) is better translated **as of the rushing of a mighty wind** (ASV) and still more smoothly "like the rush of a mighty wind" (RSV). The Greek,

I. THE FACT OF PENTECOST (2:1–11)

The Pentecost of Acts 2 occurred at Jerusalem during the annual Jewish feast which, in the opinion of some scholars, commemorated the giving of the Law on Mount Sinai. At the Jewish Pentecost God wrote His Law on tables of stone for Israel's moral government. At the Christian Pentecost He wrote His moral laws on hearts of flesh for the moral government of mankind. The former was external; the latter was internal. The former was legal; the latter was spiritual.

A. The Preparation for Pentecost (2:1)

And when the day of Pentecost was now come. The allusion here is primarily to the first day of the week when the Jewish Pentecost was held at Jerusalem (Lev. 23:15). However, in reference to the outpouring of the Holy Spirit, it bespeaks the culmination of the divine plan of redemption and the full preparation of the Christian disciples to receive the special effusion and dispensation of the Holy Spirit, and to begin the world-wide witness to which Christ had commissioned them (see Matt. 28:18–20 and Acts 1:8). It was that "fulness of time" to which Paul later referred (Gal. 4:4). The disciples' unity of spirit,[a] purpose, plan, and place made possible the divine effusion of the Holy Spirit. Whether Christ's disciples were in a compartment of the temple or in the upper room of a private home where they

[6] For full discussion of this feast and its relation to the New Testament and the Early Church, see the article "Pentecost" in each of the following: Hasting's *Dictionary of the Bible*, III, 739–742; Hasting's *Dictionary of the Apostolic Church*, II, 160–164; *The International Standard Bible Encyclopaedia* (rev. ed.), IV, 2318 f.

[7] G. T. Purves, "Pentecost," HDB, III, 742.

[8] Henry E. Dosker, "Pentecost," ISBE, IV, 2318.

[9] F. J. Foakes-Jackson, *The Acts of the Apostles*, "The Moffatt New Testament Commentary" (New York: Harper and Brothers, 1931) p. 10.

[10] Kirsopp Lake, "The Gift of the Spirit on the Day of Pentecost," *Beginnings*, V, 115.

[11] So Aleph A B C.

[12] Knowling, EGT, II, 72. So also Lenski, *op. cit.*, p. 58.

[a] See Additional Note I, *One Accord*, at end of Chapter I.

3 And there appeared unto them tongues parting asunder, like as of fire; and it sat upon each one of them.

4 And they were all filled with the Holy Spirit, and began to speak with other tongues, as the Spirit gave them utterance.

---

hōsper pheromenēs pnoēs biaias, is literally "as of a violent wind being borne along"; that is, "like the whirr of a tornado." [13] It was a sudden blast or roar.[14] The adjective *biaios*, found only here in the New Testament, means "violent." The noun *pnoē* is found only here and in Acts 17:25, where it is translated "breath." It means "a blowing, blast, wind." [15]

3 After the tornado-like roar **there appeared unto them tongues parting asunder;** literally, "being distributed" *(diamerizomenai)*. The King James translation "cloven tongues" misses the point. Lenski writes: "Perhaps we may say that the flamelike tongues appeared in a great cluster and then divided until a tongue settled on the head of each one of the disciples." [16]

The experience was not for the group as a whole but for every single individual—**and it** (a tongue) **sat upon each one of them.** They were all, every one, to be filled with the Spirit and to use their tongues in giving witness.

4 **They were all filled with the Holy Spirit**—that was the central thing at Pentecost. All else was merely accompaniment.

But why all this spectacular display, these startling phenomena of a roaring sound and tongues of fire? One answer may be found in a comparison with the giving of the law at Sinai. Then "there were thunders and lightnings, and a thick cloud upon the mount, and the voice of a trumpet exceeding loud... And mount Sinai, the whole of it, smoked, because Jehovah descended upon it in fire... and the whole mount quaked greatly" (Ex. 19:16–18). Why all this divine display? Because God wanted His people to realize the importance of this epochal event when He was making a covenant with the new nation. These phenomena produced awe and reverence in their hearts (cf. Heb. 12:18–21).

Similar was the case at Pentecost. A new era was being inaugurated—the dispensation of the Holy Spirit. The supreme importance of this event must be recognized. The rushing roar alerted the disciples; perhaps they were a bit drowsy after a week or ten days of waiting and praying for the Holy Spirit. But now all were wide awake. With open eyes they saw the flames of fire and were fully conscious of being filled with the Holy Spirit.

Another accompaniment of this epochal outpouring of the Spirit was that the recipients **began to speak with other tongues.** This phenomenon is mentioned only twice more in Acts (10:46; 19:6). Elsewhere in the New Testament speaking in tongues is mentioned in only one book, I Corinthians. There, in chapters 12–14, Paul seeks to correct its abuse in the church at Corinth. The members of that congregation were glorying in the abundance of ecstatic utterances, but it led only to confusion.

---

may have eaten the last supper with the Lord, when Pentecost occurred, is not known for certain. The latter seems likely (Acts 1:12–14). That they were in Jerusalem appears certain (Luke 24:49).

B. The Occurrence of Pentecost[b] (2:2–4)

And suddenly... they were all filled with the Holy Spirit. The suddenness of the Pentecostal effusion was resultant from fourteen and a half centuries (Lightfoot) of preparation, from the giving of the Law on Mount Sinai. God may take long to prepare, but when His plans are completed and the time is propitious, He moves suddenly and significantly. Four words may summarize the significance of this first Christian Pentecost: namely, *power*, **the rushing of a mighty wind;** *purity*, **tongues parting asunder, like**

[13] A. T. Robertson, *Word Pictures*, III, 20.
[14] Lenski suggests: "The volume of the sound denotes vast, supernatural power" (p. 58).
[15] The word *pneuma*, occurring 111 times in the New Testament and usually rendered "Spirit" (or "Ghost" in KJV), is once translated "wind" (John 3:8—"The wind bloweth where it will"). It is evidently not used here so as to avoid confusion with the Holy Spirit (vs. 4).
[16] *Op. cit.* p. 59.

[b] See Additional Note I, *The Practical Significance of Pentecost*, at the end of Chapter II.

5 Now there were dwelling at Jerusalem Jews, devout men, from every nation under heaven.
6 And when this sound was heard, the multitude came together, and were confounded, because that every man heard them speaking in his own language.

The Spirit-filled disciples spoke **as the Spirit gave them utterance;** literally, "to be uttering" *(apophthengesthai)*. This verb occurs only in Acts (cf. vs. 14 and 26:25). It means to "speak forth" and is so rendered in Acts 26:25. It is used of weighty or oracular utterance.

5 The word for **dwelling,** *katoikountes,* properly relates to living regularly in a place. Moulton and Milligan state: "More technically used, the verb refers to the permanent 'residents' of a town or village, as distinguished from those 'dwelling as strangers' or 'sojourners' *(paroikountes)*." [17] But here the context seems to indicate both those residing permanently in Jerusalem and also those who had come as pilgrims to the Feast of Pentecost.

Most commentators [18] agree that **devout** *(eulabeis)* **men** refers to Jews rather than to Gentile "God-fearers" (see on 10:2 and its footnote). The word is used in the New Testament only by Luke, and in its other three occurrences (Luke 2:25; Acts 8:2; 22:12) it clearly describes Jews.

6 The people of Jerusalem heard a **sound** *(phōnēs)*. The King James rendering, "now when this was noised abroad" suggests that a report was spreading concerning what had taken place. But most recent commentators and translators agree that "sound" is the correct rendering.

But what was the sound which was heard? Cadbury and Lake say: "The sound mentioned here is *phōnē*, the voice of the inspired speakers rather than the *ēchos* of the second verse." [19] But Hackett prefers the reference to the mighty sound of verse two.[20] Alford, in fact, suggests that this was so loud as to be heard "probably over all Jerusalem." [21] Perhaps the best conclusion is that of Bruce: "The latter (vs. 4) seems more likely, but we need not exclude the former (vs. 2)." [22]

The **multitude** gathered. Luke uses *plēthos*, "a great number." It is a favorite word of his, occurring twenty-five times in his Gospel and Acts and only seven times elsewhere in the New Testament.

Every man heard them speaking in his own **language.** Again the word is *dialektos* (cf. 1:19). It is found only in Acts, where it occurs six times. Parthians, Medes, and Elamites may have spoken different Persian dialects.

---

as of fire, . . . sat upon each one of them; *possession,* **they were all filled with the Holy Spirit;** and *proclamation,* they **began to speak with other tongues, as the Spirit gave them utterance.** Christ had promised divine power as a concomitant of Pentecost (Acts 1:8; Luke 24:49). John the Baptist had likewise promised the divine purifying fire (Matt. 3:11; see also Heb. 12:29). Christ's plan for the full and abiding possession of His disciples by the Holy Spirit at Pentecost was made explicit to them by Him while He was still with them (John 14:16, 25, 26; 15:26; 16:7). That immediate effective proclamation of the Gospel was the purpose of the miracle of **other tongues** is evident from prophecy (Isa. 66:18), and the need arising out of the occasion and opportunity where **there were dwelling at Jerusalem Jews, devout men, from every nation under heaven** who, when they heard the Spirit-animated disciples proclaiming Christ, **were confounded, because that every man heard them speaking in his own language** (see also vss. 7–11).[c]

C. The Effects of Pentecost (2:5–8)

The multitude came together, and were confounded. Pentecost was a threefold miracle of interpretation, clarification, and conviction. The assembled multitude heard these disciples proclaim **the mighty works of God** in their own languages and were deeply

[17] VGT, p. 338.
[18] E.g., *Beginnings*, IV, 18; Knowling, EGT, II, 73; Bruce, p. 83; Hackett, p. 43; Lenski, p. 64; A. C. Hervey, "The Acts of the Apostles" (Exposition), *The Pulpit Commentary*, ed. Joseph S. Exell, I, 50.
[19] *Beginnings*, IV, 18.
[20] *Op. cit.*, pp. 43 f. So also Lechler, *op. cit.*, p. 33.
[21] Henry Alford, *The Greek Testament* (6th ed.; London: Rivingtons, 1871), II, 17, 18.
[22] *Op. cit.*, p. 83.

[c] See Additional Note II, *The Bible Gift of Tongues*, at close of Chapter II.

7 And they were all amazed and marvelled, saying, Behold, are not all these that speak
Galilaeans?
8 And how hear we, every man in our own language wherein we were born?
9 Parthians and Medes and Elamites, and the dwellers in Mesopotamia, in Judaea and
Cappadocia, in Pontus and Asia,
10 in Phrygia and Pamphylia, in Egypt and the parts of Libya about Cyrene, and sojourners from Rome, both Jews and proselytes,

---

7 **Amazed** and **marvelled** are both strong words, indicating shocked surprise. The first, *existanto*, literally means, "they were standing out of themselves" with astonishment. Both verbs are in the imperfect tense, indicating a continuing amazement and wonder.

Galilæans were noted as narrow provincialists. It was doubly remarkable, therefore, that they were speaking many different languages.[23]

8 **Our own language** is literally "our very own dialect." While these were evidently all Jews, they had been **born** and brought up in different lands, and the language of their own locality constituted their mother tongue.

9, 10 **Parthians and Medes and Elamites** were three groups living east of the Tigris River. These, with **the dwellers in Mesopotamia,** would cover the general area of the Tigris-Euphrates valley and beyond.

Judaea is the most problematical item in this list of place names. It is given here as if it filled in the gap between Mesopotamia and Asia Minor. More surprising still is the omission of Syria, where very many Jews lived. Cadbury and Lake suggest one helpful solution of the problem. They write: "If Judaea be taken in the prophetic sense as the country 'from Euphrates to the river of Egypt' this covers in fairly methodical order all the districts round the east of the Mediterranean." [24] ("This" refers to the list from Parthians to Cyrenian Libya.) [25]

Cappadocia, Pontus, Asia, Phrygia, and **Pamphylia** were all districts of Asia Minor. **Phrygia** was not a province, but a racial territory. In the New Testament **Asia** never means the continent but usually refers to the Roman province of Asia at the west end of Asia Minor. (See on 16:8 and its footnote 16.)

---

convicted in their hearts of the truthfulness of that message. Said Christ: "And when he [the Holy Spirit] is come, he will reprove [convict] the world of sin, and of righteousness, and of judgment" (John 16:8).

D. The Nations at Pentecost (2:9–11)

Fifteen different nations are listed in this passage. They consisted of Gentile proselytes to the Jewish faith, *God-fearers* (Gentiles who worshiped the God of the Jews but who did not subscribe to the Jewish ceremonials), Jews of the *Diaspora*, and the Judean Jews. Here it may be noted that the first phase of the *Diaspora* occurred in 722 B.C. when the ten Northern Tribes were carried away into captivity at the hands of the cruel Assyrians, while the second phase occurred in 586 B.C. when the Southern Kingdom was taken to Babylonia under the conquest of Nebuchadnezzar. While there is no record of the restoration of the Northern Kingdom, the Southern Kingdom, after some 70 years, was in part returned to its native land under the benevolent Cyrus. However, the greater percentage of these later captives was widely distributed throughout the Persian Empire which followed in political succession the Babylonian. During the height of the Persian Empire, there occurred the incidents recorded in the Book of Esther. It is of particular interest that the author of this book notes that there were 127 provinces in the Persian Empire, ranging from India to Ethiopia, whatever the significance of these placenames may be to history, and further that there were Jews dwelling in all of these Persian provinces (see Esther 1:1; 3:8). In

[23] For evidence that the Galilean accent was easily recognizable, see Matt. 26:73; Mark 14:70; Luke 22:59.
[24] *Beginnings*, IV, 19.
[25] It is interesting to note that Lenski (p. 66) adopts Zahn's emendation of *Ioudaian* into *Ioudaioi* ("Jews") and thus reduces the number of nations to fourteen. But Metzger holds that this List was apparently "lifted from a standard geographical chart current in antiquity" and indicates "comprehensiveness." See Bruce Metzger, *Interpretation*, XI (Jan., 1957), 95.

11 Cretans and Arabians, we hear them speaking in our tongues the mighty works of God.

Egypt and the parts of Libya about Cyrene designates North Africa. It is claimed that a million Jews lived in Egypt at this time. Josephus quotes a striking passage from Strabo:

Now these Jews are already gotten into all cities; and it is hard to find a place in the habitable earth that hath not admitted this tribe of men, and is not possessed by them; and it hath come to pass that Egypt and Cyrene... maintain great bodies of these Jews.[26]

Sojourners from Rome probably refers to Jews who lived temporarily at Rome. The verb *epidemountes* is used in Acts 17:21 of "strangers sojourning" at Athens who are distinguished from the regular "Athenians." Some, however, would make the sojourning refer to Jerusalem and interpret it as describing Roman Jews who were living temporarily there. Cadbury and Lake state that "*Rōmaios* regularly means a citizen of the Roman empire, not an inhabitant of the city of Rome." [27]

Bruce makes **both Jews and proselytes** refer only to those from Rome.[28] But Hackett and Rackham, with many others, would apply the twofold designation to the entire preceding list. That is the view of the author. There seems to be little doubt that there would be representatives of both groups from every nation.

For Gentile **proselytes** to Judaism there were four requirements: (1) instruction, (2) circumcision, (3) baptism, (4) sacrifice.[29] After the destruction of the temple in A.D. 70, the fourth had to be suspended. Because the second was most inconvenient, there were many more women than men proselytes. The first and third were taken over by the Christian church.

Kirsopp Lake has made a strong case against identifying the "God-fearers" in Acts with the medieval Jewish phrase "proselytes of the gate," as has often been done by older writers. He asserts that there was actually only one class of "proselytes", those who joined the synagogue.[30]

11 **Cretans** [31] **and Arabians** "seem to have been added to the list as an afterthought." [32] Knowling uses this as an argument for the authenticity of the passage. This is no artificial list made up by the author of Acts. He has recorded what was reported to him by one who was there (cf. Luke 1:1–4). Perhaps the reporter momentarily forgot these two names and added them at the end, and the inspiring Spirit has permitted this form to remain. The narrative breathes the spontaneity that is a mark of sincerity and genuineness.

The island of Crete lies near Greece. The Epistle to Titus shows that there were many Jews there (cf. Titus 1:10, 14). Bruce says

addition to the *Diaspora* there were, according to Benjamin Robinson,[d] three other major dispersions. The first of these latter occurred in the third century B.C. during the control of Palestine by Egypt, when the Jews migrated in large numbers to the city of Alexandria where they formed a sizable colony, adopted the Greek language, imbibed much of the Greco-Egyptian culture, and translated the Old Testament into the Greek, giving to the world the version known as the Septuagint.

In the second century B.C., when Palestine fell under the power of Syria, the Jews migrated in large numbers northward and settled in and about Antioch, from which place they further penetrated into Cilicia, and from thence scattered into the cities of Asia Minor and crossed over into Macedonia and Greece, establishing colonies and synagogues wherever they went.

The third stage of this latter migration occurred after the Roman conquest of Palestine under Pompey in the first century

26 Ant. XIV, 7, 2.
27 *Beginnings*, IV, 20.
28 F. F. Bruce, *Commentary on the Book of Acts*, "The New International Commentary on the New Testament" (Grand Rapids: Wm. B. Eerdmans Publishing Co., 1954), p. 63. (Hereafter referred to as NIC.)
29 Kirsopp Lake, "Proselytes and God-Fearers," *Beginnings*, V, 77–79.
30 *Ibid.*, pp. 80–88.
31 By a strange quirk KJV translates the Greek *Kretes* as "Cretians" in Tit. 1:12 but "Cretes" here. The latter is incorrect, as the word has two syllables. The Revised "Cretans" is the correct form.
32 Knowling, EGT, II, 76.

d Benjamin Willard Robinson, *The Life of Paul* (Chicago: University of Chicago Press, 1928), p. 9 f.

12 And they were all amazed, and were perplexed, saying one to another, What meaneth this?
13 But others mocking said, They are filled with new wine.

that "Arabia in Graeco-Roman usage generally meant the kingdom of the Nabatean Arabs, then at the height of its power under Aretas IV (9 B.C.—A.D. 40)." [33] So these names suggest territories to the west and east of Palestine.

The **speaking in our tongues** at Pentecost suggests a reversal of what took place at the Tower of Babel—at least for the moment.

Mighty works is *megaleia*.[34] It is an adjective meaning "magnificent, splendid." Outstanding among these magnificent works would be the resurrection of Jesus Christ.

12 Once more it is stated that the people were **amazed** *(existanto)*, this time with the addition: **were perplexed** *(diēporounto)*. It is a strong compound, meaning "to be quite at a loss, be in great perplexity." The word is used only by Luke in the New Testament.

13 Another reaction soon set in. Some were **mocking,** *(diachleuazontes*, only here in N.T.), accusing the disciples of being **filled** (*mestoō*, only here in N.T.: "tanked up" [35]) with **new wine** *(gleukos*, likewise only here in N.T.). Since the earliest grape harvest was in August—some two months yet ahead—it is perhaps best to render this "sweet wine"; that is, wine that was not completely fermented. Writers of that day

B.C. At this time there occurred a general dispersion of the Jews throughout the whole Roman Empire and even into lands beyond Rome's domain. Robinson holds that there were at least 150 Jewish colonies throughout the Empire of Rome by the time of Christ's appearance. In most of these Jewish communities there were synagogues which were in close relationship with the temple at Jerusalem and paid revenue to the Temple. Though these synagogues were much more simple and modest in their architecture and forms of worship than was the Temple, as well as more liberal in their attitude toward the Gentile world, they were at the same time an integral part of the Jewish religious system. It was from these Jewish settlements out in the Roman Empire, and even beyond, that the Jewish representation at Pentecost, as recorded in Acts 2, had come. The latter probably constituted by far the greater percentage of the foreign population present for the Jewish Pentecost.

II. THE EXPLANATION OF PENTECOST (2:12–21)

The new spiritual dispensation inaugurated by the Pentecostal descent of the Holy Spirit required a divinely inspired explanation. God's Word properly understood and expounded always clarifies His acts.

A. The Pentecostal Question (2:12, 13)

They were all amazed, and were perplexed, saying one to another, What meaneth this? Those who heard the preaching of the **mighty works of God** in their own languages by the Spirit-filled disciples felt the mighty influence of that Spirit and found themselves in a state of spiritual ecstacy, for such is the meaning of the word **amazed,** beyond their ability to understand. That something supernatural had happened certain of the multitude were well aware, but what it signified they could not tell. The manifestations of God always arrest attention, awaken interest, and provoke inquiries concerning spiritual truth. Nothing produces moral sanity and spiritual inquiry like mighty divine manifestations. When man begins to inquire, God stands ready to inform. One has said that it is only at the point of man's recognized need that God can help him.

But while some were moved to honest, reverent inquiry, under the Spirit's influence, others sceptically mocked and scoffed at the divine manifestation, giving the sacred a secular and profane interpretation, saying **They are filled with new wine.** A lump of moist clay and a block of ice placed together in the sun react differently, with quite opposite results. The one is melted, the other hardened. So by the same divine manifest-

[33] Bruce, *Acts* (Greek text), p. 86.
[34] Found only here in the New Testament (not genuine in Luke 1:49).
[35] A. T. Robertson, *Word Pictures*, III, 25.

14 But Peter, standing up with the eleven, lifted up his voice, and spake forth unto them, *saying*, Ye men of Judaea, and all ye that dwell at Jerusalem, be this known unto you, and give ear unto my words.
15 For these are not drunken, as ye suppose; seeing it is *but* the third hour of the day;
16 but this is that which hath been spoken through the prophet Joel:

---

give instructions on how to keep new wine sweet for many months.[36]

14–36 There has been a great deal of discussion about the speeches in Acts. Many liberal scholars today take the view that they are inventions on the part of the author or editor of the book, putting into the mouth of each speaker words that are considered appropriate to the occasion. At the other extreme are those who would treat the speeches as verbatim reports of exactly what was said. Probably a middle view would be most correct—that they are a faithful reproduction of the thought, spirit, and main content of each of the speeches, under the guiding inspiration of the Holy Spirit. Bruce describes them as "summaries giving at least the gist of what was really said on the various occasions." [37] Selwyn suggests a further thought: "At the same time we cannot rule out the possibility that some of the speeches in Acts are dependent on written sources or oral information; and the rough Semitic style and the primitive doctrine which mark parts of St. Peter's speeches... suggest that this is so in their case." [38]

In this speech there are striking parallels with the language and thought of I Peter, which will be noted at the appropriate places. They tend to give mutual support to the authenticity of this speech and the genuineness of I Peter.

14 The phrase **lifted up his voice** is found only in Luke's Gospel (17:13) and Acts (cf. 14:11; 22:22). It has often been pointed out that **standing up, lifted up his voice,** and **spake forth** (*apephthenxato*, inspired utterance) are three things that should always characterize the preacher in the pulpit.

Men of Judaea is literally "men, Jews." Bruce suggests the translation, "Fellow Jews.[39] The word *enōtisasthe*, **give ear**, is found only here in the Testament, but frequently in the Septuagint.

15 **The third hour** was 9:00 A.M., the morning hour of prayer. The devout Jew would not eat before this hour.[40]

16 The preposition **through** *(dia)* suggests that Joel was just the mouthpiece for the Holy Spirit. The quotation that follows in verses 17–21 is from Joel 2:28–32.

17, 18 **In the last days** ("afterward" in

---

ation, one person may be melted into submission to the divine will, while another may reject that manifestation and become spiritually calloused.

B. The Pentecostal Spokesman (2:14)

But Peter, standing up with the eleven, lifted up his voice. Peter, ever the ready and gifted spokesman, once having ignominiously failed his Lord, but now fully restored, answers the charge of the scoffers by standing erect before the multitude to prove that he was not drunk, to which the other disciples add their support by standing also. Peter **lifted up his voice** in full confidence and conviction of the divine origin of the phenomenon, ready to courageously witness to the risen Christ in the face of violent opposition.

C. The Misapprehension of Pentecost (2:15)

These are not drunken, as ye suppose. Very evidently there was a sharp division of the people, as well as of opinions concerning the spiritual manifestations. While the Jews of the dispersion inclined to the influence of the Spirit, the Judaean Jews who had been responsible for the rejection and crucifixion of Jesus Christ and did not wish to hear that He was alive again, labelled the whole affair irrational intoxication. It is to this latter class of Judaean Jews that Peter addresses his great Pentecostal sermon, and that in

[36] See Bruce, NIC, p. 65, n. 37, for an interesting quotation from Cato.
[37] *Acts* (Gk.), p. 21. See his excellent discussion of the subject in *Acts*, pp. 18–21; also Knowling in EGT, II, 119–122.
[38] E. G. Selwyn, *The First Epistle of Peter* (2nd ed.; London: Macmillan & Co., 1947), p. 33.
[39] *Acts*, p. 89.
[40] *Beginnings*, IV, 21.

17 And it shall be in the last days, saith God,
I will pour forth of my Spirit upon all flesh:
And your sons and your daughters shall prophesy,
And your young men shall see visions,
And your old men shall dream dreams:
18 Yea and on my servants and on my handmaidens in those days
Will I pour forth of my Spirit; and they shall prophesy.
19 And I will show wonders in the heaven above,
And signs on the earth beneath;
Blood, and fire, and vapor of smoke:
20 The sun shall be turned into darkness,
And the moon into blood,
Before the day of the Lord come,
That great and notable *day*:

Joel 2:28 in both MT and LXX) evidently takes in the entire Christian age, after the Jews had rejected Jesus as Messiah. The common custom nowadays of applying the expression only to the end of this age is ruled out by its use here. Probably it is equivalent to the Jewish phrase, "the day of the Messiah."[41]

All flesh in Joel's mind doubtless meant all classes of Jews—**sons** and **daughters, young men** and **old men, servants** and **handmaidens.** In the mind of the Spirit who inspired Joel it took in all humanity, potentially. What it signified in the mind of Peter is a debatable point. In the light of his later hesitation about extending the privileges of salvation to the Gentiles (cf. chap. 10), it may well be assumed that for him, as for Joel, it meant "all Jews."

19, 20 The interpretation of apocalyptic language always poses a real problem. It is obvious that only in a very figurative way could the language of these verses be applied to the Passion and Pentecost. Will they find a more complete and more literal fulfillment at the end of this age? This is a point where extreme dogmatism is out of order. It should be said, however, that the atomic age has made a literal application seem far less fantastic than heretofore.

---

their common language, as witness his words, **Ye men of Judaea, and all ye that dwell at Jerusalem.** Doubtless the other disciples witnessed to Christ likewise in the various languages of those present and less prejudiced than the former. The third hour (nine o'clock in the morning) would in itself rule out the charge of drunkeness. "They that are drunken are drunken in the night" (I Thess. 5:7).

D. The Truth Concerning Pentecost (2:16–20)

This is that which hath been spoken through the prophet Joel. Peter makes the Spirit's manifestation the fulfillment of the Jewish prophecy by Joel, with which they were familiar and which they readily accepted. Pentecost was the fulfillment of their own prophecies.

In verses 17 through 20, Peter quotes Joel's prediction of Pentecost and interprets it as an impartial and universal, divine, evangelical visitation. Joel's prophecy of Pentecost reflects four major constituents: namely, (1) *the Holy Spirit's universal effusion,* **I will pour forth of my Spirit upon all flesh;** (2) *the universal proclamation of the Gospel,* **your sons and your daughters shall prophesy . . . my servants and . . . my handmaidens . . . shall prophesy** (preach); (3) *spiritual illumination,* **your young men shall see visions** (the illuminating and animating *forward look* (see Isaiah 6:1–8), **and your old men shall dream dreams** (the clarified and rewarding *retrospect* of advanced age); and (4) *arresting and confirmatory miracles,* **I will show wonders in the heaven above, and signs on the earth beneath** (see I Thess. 1:5, 6).

E. The Purpose of Pentecost (2:21)

Purpose, or what the philosophers call teleology – that is, plan or design directed

[41] Cf. S. Mowinckel, *He That Cometh.* Trans. G. W. Anderson (New York: Abingdon Press, n. d.), pp. 302 ff.

21 And it shall be, that whosoever shall call on the name of the Lord shall be saved.
22 Ye men of Israel, hear these words: Jesus of Nazareth, a man approved of God unto
you by mighty works and wonders and signs which God did by him in the midst of you,
even as ye yourselves know;
23 him, being delivered up by the determinate counsel and foreknowledge of God, ye by
the hand of lawless men did crucify and slay:

---

21 This is one of the great texts of the Old Testament and definitely anticipates the gospel message of the New Testament.

22 **Approved** *(apodedeigmenon)* is perhaps better "appointed" or "demonstrated." The Revised Standard Version translates it "attested"; that is, as Messiah. The verb is used frequently in the contemporary papyri in the sense of "proclaiming" an appointment to public office.[42] The miracles which Jesus performed proclaimed Him to be God's appointed Messiah.

The three words commonly used to describe the miracles of Jesus all occur here together[43]—*dunameis, terata, sēmeia.* The first, **mighty works,** is literally "powers."[44] The second, **wonders,** is never used in the New Testament without the third, **signs.**[45] Knowling comments: "God's *terata* are always sēmeia to those who have eyes to see."[46]

23 This verse combines in a remarkable way two inescapable phenomena of life—divine sovereignty and human freedom. It was by **the determinate counsel**[47] **and foreknowledge of God** that Christ died to become the Saviour of men, and yet it is also true that **him . . . ye . . . did crucify and slay.** The fact that God had foreknown and predestined the death of His Son did not in any way mitigate the guilt of those who, with free wills, voluntarily chose to condemn Him and bring about His execution. This is the constant paradox of life.

The Greek word for **foreknowledge** is *prognōsis*, which has been taken over bodily into English. (A large proportion of medical terms come from the Greek.) The word is used only here and in I Peter 1:2. This is one of the many significant parallels between Peter's speeches in Acts and his First Epistle.

Lawless men *(anomōn)* in the Jewish mind would mean Romans;[48] that is, "men without the Law" (of Moses).

Prospēgnymi, **crucify,** literally means "fasten to"; that is, to a cross. The word is found only here in the New Testament. The regular word for "crucify" is *stauroō*, which occurs 46 times.

---

to a given end – characterizes all of the acts of God from His creative work to the final restoration of all creation (sinfully rebellious man excepted) through the redemptive plan and provision. Pentecost was the culmination of a long process of divine planning for human redemption. Here Peter openly declares to the Jewish opponents of Christ, as well as those favorably inclined, that the threefold Pentecostal purpose is: (1) a *universal evangelical invitation,* **whosoever;** (2) a *universal evangelical condition,* **call on the name of the Lord;** and (3) a *universal evangelical provision,* **shall be saved** (see Matt. 11:28–30 and John 7:37–39).

III. THE DECLARATION OF PENTECOST (or Peter's Pentecostal Sermon) (2:22–40)

Having prefaced his sermon by the confirmatory prophecy of Joel, Peter proceeds directly to an assertion of Jesus Christ's divine approval and redemptive mission, and then openly charges the Judaean Jews with His rejection and crucifixion (vss. 22, 23). The divine irony, and the Jews' resultant burning shame and consternation, is scathingly depicted by Peter in God's miraculous resurrection of His Son from the dead, confirmed by their illustrious father David's

[42] VGT, p. 60.
[43] As also in Rom. 15:19; II Cor. 12:12; II Thess. 2:9; and Heb. 2:4. The second and third occur together eight times in Acts.
[44] The KJV rendering "miracles" obscures this.
[45] Translated "miracles" 13 times in KJV in John's Gospel.
[46] EGT, II, 80 (on vs. 19).
[47] *Boulē* is perhaps better translated "purpose." Luke alone in the New Testament uses the phrase *boulē tou theou,* "purpose of God." (Cf. Luke 7:30; Acts 13:36; 20:27).
[48] Cf. *Beginnings,* IV, 23—"often used in Jewish literature of the Romans."

24 whom God raised up, having loosed the pangs of death: because it was not possible
that he should be holden of it.
25 For David saith concerning him,
I beheld the Lord always before my face;
For he is on my right hand, that I should not be moved:
26 Therefore my heart was glad, and my tongue rejoiced;
Moreover my flesh also shall dwell in hope:
27 Because thou wilt not leave my soul unto Hades,
Neither wilt thou give thy Holy One to see corruption.
28 Thou madest known unto me the ways of life;
Thou shalt make me full of gladness with thy countenance.
29 Brethren, I may say unto you freely of the patriarch David, that he both died and was
buried, and his tomb is with us unto this day.

---

24 **Whom God raised up**—This is "God's Great Reversal" of the crucifixion. Here is the first public proclamation of the Resurrection, and it was made at a time when the truth of that claim could be checked.

Pangs is better than "pains" (KJV), since *ōdines* literally means "birth-pangs." It is used in this literal sense in I Thessalonians 5:3—"as travail upon a woman with child." It is also used metaphorically for extreme suffering (Matt. 24:8; Mark 13:8). But here, as in Matthew and Mark, it may suggest the birth-pangs of a new age.

25–28 The quotation is from Psalm 16 (LXX, 15):8–11. The Psalmist rejoices that Jehovah will preserve him alive and not abandon his soul to **Hades** (vs. 27). This word, the equivalent of the Hebrew *Sheol*, was first used for the god of the nether world and then for the abode of the spirits of all the dead. It should not be translated "hell."

29 Peter started his speech by saying, "Men, Jews" (vs. 14). After his lengthy quotation from Joel, he resumed with, "Men, Israelites" (vs. 22), reminding them perhaps of their covenant relationship to God. Now he says, **"Men, brethren."** [49] By these courteous forms of address, he sought to hold both the attention and good will of his audience.

Peter's argument in verse 29 is that the words quoted from Psalm 16 could not apply fully to David, since he did see corruption—**he both died and was buried.** Furthermore, **his tomb is with us unto this day,** so that the presence of his body in the place of death could be checked and proved. Not so with Christ, whose tomb was empty.

Guides today point out the tomb of David on Mount Zion, the southwest hill of Jerusalem, just outside the walls of the Old City. But this tradition only goes as far back as the crusades.[50] The more probable location is on the south side of the southeast hill, near the pool of Siloam.[51] Josephus says that "Hyrcanus opened the sepulchre of David... and took out of it three thousand talents." [52] He also declares that Herod the Great, having heard that Hyrcanus had robbed David's tomb of 3000 talents of silver, entered it at night and took away the gold furniture. But when two of his guards investigated farther they were slain by a

---

own testimony (vss. 24–32). Christ's acceptance with the Father in His ascension, supported likewise by David's testimony, is presented next in order (vss. 33a, 34). All of this, Peter reasons, adds up to the incontrovertible deity and universal Lordship of Jesus Christ (vss. 34, 36; see also Matt. 28, esp. vss. 18–20). It is noteworthy that the burden of the message of Acts may be summed up in six phrases: namely, (1) *Christ crucified*; (2) *Christ resurrected* (the word with its cognates occurs at least 22 times in Acts); (3) *Christ ascended*; (4) *the Holy Spirit descended*; (5) *Christ Jesus declared Lord of all* (Lord occurs at least 110 times in Acts); (6) *the door of salvation opened to all.*

In response to the inquiry, **What shall**

[49] Found also in 1:16 and 2:37. "Men, Galileans" occurs in 1:11.
[50] *Beginnings*, IV, 24.
[51] At the present time this is in Jordan, whereas Mount Zion is in Israel. Both are south of the present city walls.
[52] *Ant.* XIII, 8, 4.

30 Being therefore a prophet, and knowing that God had sworn with an oath to him, that
of the fruit of his loins he would set *one* upon his throne;
31 he foreseeing *this* spake of the resurrection of the Christ, that neither was he left unto
Hades, nor did his flesh see corruption.
32 This Jesus did God raise up, whereof we all are witnesses.
33 Being therefore by the right hand of God exalted, and having received of the Father
the promise of the Holy Spirit, he hath poured forth this, which ye see and hear.
34 For David ascended not into the heavens: but he saith himself,
The Lord said unto my Lord, Sit thou on my right hand,
35 Till I make thine enemies the footstool of thy feet.
36 Let all the house of Israel therefore know assuredly, that God hath made him both
Lord and Christ, this Jesus whom ye crucified.
37 Now when they heard *this*, they were pricked in their heart, and said unto Peter and
the rest of the apostles, Brethren, what shall we do?

---

sudden burst of flame. This caused Herod to build a white marble monument as an act of propitiation. Josephus gives it as his opinion that Herod's family troubles were in part caused by his desecrating David's tomb.[53]

30 The construction of this verse is a bit difficult. Probably *kathisai* should be taken as transitive, to **set**, rather than "to sit" (KJV).[54] But what is the object of this infinitive? The American Standard Version supplies **one.** Bruce has suggested the best explanation: "The phrase *ek karpou* (of fruit) is treated as a noun and made the object of *kathisai*, 'God had sworn to him with an oath to set *of the fruit of his loins* (i.e. one of his descendants) upon his throne.'"[55]

31 Too much should not be read into the word **foreseeing.** Peter himself declares (I Pet. 1:10–12) that the prophets did not understand the full meaning of what they wrote. What this verse suggests is that David was conscious of prophetic inspiration, that he realized his words had a significance that reached beyond himself and his day.

32 *Hou*, **whereof,** could be translated "of whom." But the context rather suggests "of which"—that is, the Resurrection.

33 The Ascension was a necessary postlude to the Resurrection[56] and prelude to Pentecost.

Poured forth is preferable to "shed forth" (KJV). The verb, *ekcheō*, is used in the Septuagint of Joel 2:28, 29, quoted above in verses 17 and 18. It is also used similarly in Zechariah 12:10.

34 The chapter of the Old Testament most often quoted in the New is Psalm 110. Just a few weeks before this Jesus had used the same words of the first verse of this Psalm in confounding the scribes (Matt. 22:44; Mark 12:35; Luke 20:41). Even the Jews held this Psalm to be Messianic. They said that the Messiah would **sit on my right hand,** while Abraham would sit on the left.[57] It should be noted that the first **Lord** here stands for the Hebrew Jehovah (or Yahweh) while the second **Lord** stands for *adoni* (or *adon*).

35 **The footstool of thy feet** represents the ancient custom of conquerors placing their feet on the necks of the conquered (cf. Josh. 10:24).

36 The climax of Peter's sermon was the declaration that God had made **this Jesus whom ye crucified** to be **both Lord and Christ** (Messiah).[58] To the Jews the shocking thing was that Peter dared to equate Jesus with the great Old Testament name Jehovah (Yahweh).[59]

37 The effect of Peter's preaching was that the people were **pricked in their heart.** The

---

we do?, made by those of his audience who were convicted by the Spirit, Peter opens wide the door of universal salvation through Christ's finished redemptive work and invites all to enter by the way of repentance, remission of sins, and the gift of the Holy Spirit (vss. 37–40).

[53] *Ant.* XVI, 7, 1, 2.
[54] The preceding phrase, "he would raise up Christ" (KJV), is not found in Aleph A B C.
[55] *Acts*, p. 94. [56] See parallel in I Pet. 3:21, 22. [57] Edersheim, *Life and Times*, II, 721.
[58] Cf. the striking passage in I Pet. 3:15—"But sanctify in your hearts Christ as Lord."
[59] This he had already done by implication in vs. 21, where *Kurios*, originally used for Jehovah, is transferred to Christ (see Knowling, EGT, II, 81).

38 And Peter *said* unto them, Repent ye, and be baptized every one of you in the name of Jesus Christ unto the remission of your sins; and ye shall receive the gift of the Holy Spirit.

39 For to you is the promise, and to your children, and to all that are afar off, *even* as many as the Lord our God shall call unto him.

40 And with many other words he testified, and exhorted them, saying, Save yourselves from this crooked generation.

---

verb *katanyssō* is a strong term, occurring only here in the New Testament. It means "to pierce, to sting sharply, to stun, to smite." [60] Homer uses it of horses pawing the ground with their hoofs.[61] It is a striking description of the Holy Spirit's conviction of a human heart. It caused the listeners to cry, "What shall we do?"

38 Peter's reply was twofold. First, they were to **repent.** The verb *metanoeō* signifies a change of mind *(meta + nous)*. This is more than mere emotionalism, although true repentance is almost always accompanied by deep emotion. It involves a change of attitude toward God, sin, the world, oneself.

Secondly, they were to **be baptized.**[62] Repentance and baptism were connected in the ministry of John the Baptist (Mark 1:4). John had baptized those who came to him confessing their sins. The Jews required Gentile proselytes to Judaism to be baptized. Today on the mission field converts are baptized as a sign that they have accepted Christ as Saviour. That is the meaning here.

That is suggested by the phrase that follows, **in the name of Jesus Christ.** Peter had challenged his hearers to accept Jesus as Messiah and Lord. By their baptism they would acknowledge publicly that they had done this.[63] **Unto the remission of your sins** may be translated "on the basis of the remission of your sins." The same preposition, *eis*, is used in Matthew 12:41, where it is stated that the Ninevites repented "at" *(eis)*—or because of, on the basis of—the preaching of Jonah. Robertson says that Peter was urging baptism on those who repented, "and for it to be done in the name of Jesus Christ on the basis of the forgiveness of sins which they had already received." [64] In doing so they became candidates to **receive the gift** (*dōrean* = free gift) **of the Holy Spirit.**[65]

39 The promise of the Holy Spirit was not only to them, but **to all that are afar off.** This probably signifies distance both chronologically and geographically; that is, to the Gentiles. The latter is suggested in Isaiah 57:19.

As many as the Lord our God shall call should be interpreted in the light of verse 21—"Whosoever shall call on the name of the Lord shall be saved."

40 **Testified** *(diemartyrato)* is "solemnly protested." It refers to "solemn and emphatic utterance." [66] It may also carry the

---

IV. THE CHURCH OF PENTECOST (2:41-47)

The Pentecostal Church has remained a model for Christians of all subsequent ages. Briefly characterized: (1) *its converts* joyfully received the Gospel, were baptized, and identified themselves with the Church (vs. 41); (2) *its sacred communion* consisted in steadfastness of purpose, doctrinal instruction, Christian fellowship, observance of the Lord's Supper (Lange), and prayers (vs. 42); (3) *its moral and spiritual influence* profoundly affected the community, and frequent miracles confirmed its divine mission (vs. 43); (4) *its liberality* abounded toward the needs of the entire body of Christ[e] (vss. 44, 45); (5) *its service* reflected constancy, unity,[f] fellowship, joy, and guileless sincerity (vs. 46); and (6) *its spiritual prosperity* is reflected in its victorious praises, its confidence of and favor with the community, and its evangelical fervor and success (vs. 47).

[60] Robertson, *Word Pictures*, III, 34. [61] *ibid.*

[62] Literally "and let each one of you be baptized." The command to "repent" is more direct and forceful, as being the more important of the two.

[63] "As a primitive baptismal formula the invocation of the name implies primarily recognition of Jesus as 'Lord and Christ.'" (IB, IX, 49).

[64] *Word Pictures*, III, 36.

[65] Robertson calls this the "genitive of identification," the gift which *is* the Holy Spirit (*ibid.*). [66] VGT, p. 152.

[e] See Additional Note I, *Christian Communism*, at end of Chapter IV.

[f] See Additional Note I, *Homothumadon, or One Accord*, at end of Chapter I.

41 They then that received his word were baptized: and there were added *unto them* in that day about three thousand souls.

42 And they continued stedfastly in the apostles' teaching and fellowship, in the breaking of bread and the prayers.

43 And fear came upon every soul: and many wonders and signs were done through the apostles.

44 And all that believed were together, and had all things common;

45 and they sold their possessions and goods, and parted them to all, according as any man had need.

46 And day by day, continuing stedfastly with one accord in the temple, and breaking bread at home, they took their food with gladness and singleness of heart,

47 praising God, and having favor with all the people. And the Lord added to them day by day those that were saved.

---

meaning "testified by argument."[67] For **crooked generation** see Deuteronomy 32:5 and Psalm 78:8; also Philippians 2:15.

41 Peter[68] and the apostles won more converts on the day of Pentecost—**about three thousand souls**—than had Jesus during the three years of His ministry. One is reminded of Jesus' words in John 14:12—"Greater works than these shall he do; because I go unto the Father." **Souls** here means "persons" (cf. 27:37).

42 **Continued stedfastly** is the verb *proskartareō*, already found in 1:14 and occurring again in verse 46. The new Christian community was giving steadfast adherence to **the apostles' teaching and fellowship** *(didachē* and *koinōnia)*. There was a unity of belief and of spirit. The **breaking of bread**[69] seems to indicate that the Lord's Supper was observed regularly and frequently. **Prayers** may refer both to private prayers in the home and public prayers in the temple (cf. vs. 46).

43 The use of the imperfect tense in verses 43–47 must be noted carefully if one is to find a correct interpretation of this passage. This tense occurs no less than eight times in the five verses.

The words **came** and **were done** are translations of exactly the same Greek form, *egineto*, the imperfect of *ginomai*. It shows that fear was steadily settling down **upon every soul** as the **apostles** were continuing to perform many **wonders and signs.**

44, 45 More significant is the use of the imperfect tense in these two verses. It has often been assumed that in the early church in Jerusalem there was a full-fledged community of goods. But the Greek does not bear this out. "The usual translation 'sold' rather implies one great sale, but the meaning of the Greek rather is that they sold things as they had need of more money."[70]

Verse 45 might accurately be paraphrased thus: "And from time to time they were selling their possessions and goods, and were parting them to all, according as from time to time any man had need."

46 The early disciples continued to worship daily **in the temple,** as would naturally be expected. The break with Judaism would come only later and gradually and would be precipitated by Jewish persecution.

But they were also breaking their bread **at home** *(kat'oikon)*. The meaning of the Greek phrase is not altogether clear. The King James Version translates it, "from house to house." Moffatt has "in their own homes." Goodspeed has "in their homes." In the papyri it has the meaning "by households."[71] Just what its exact meaning is here we cannot be sure. But one thing is clear: it indicates Christian fellowship in private homes.

47 The King James translation of the last words of this verse, "such as should be saved" is one of the most reprehensible in that version. The Greek says very clearly and simply: "The Lord added together[72] daily *those that were being saved*" *(tous sōzomenous)*. There is no hint here of foreordination.

[67] *Beginnings,* IV, 27.
[68] The *hoi men oun* at the beginning of this verse indicates that the new paragraph should commence at this point.
[69] The exact Greek phrase is found only here and in Luke 24:35. For a full discussion of this expression, as also of the others in this verse, see Rackham, *op. cit.*, pp. 32–41. He holds that the term may indicate the Agape alone, the Eucharist alone, or a combination of the two (p. 39).
[70] *Beginnings,* IV, 29. [71] *Ibid.* [72] *Epi to auto.* "The church" (KJV) is not in the oldest MSS (Aleph A B C).

Additional Note I

The Practical Significance of Pentecost

I. PENTECOST SIGNIFIES DIVINE POWER

And suddenly there came from heaven a sound as of the rushing of a mighty wind, and it filled all the house where they were sitting, Acts 2:2.

There appears to have been a twofold purpose in this divine phenomenon described by Luke as, **a sound as of the rushing of a mighty wind.** *First*, it was intended to stimulate the faith of the disciples for all that was to follow. *Second*, its purpose was to arrest the attention of the masses of people assembled in Jerusalem for the Jewish Pentecost and thus provide audience for that inspired apostolic preaching which was to result in the initial conversion of 3,000 people.

Power has ever been the passion of man. Nor does the acquisition and exercise of power appear to have been absent from God's plan and purpose for man. Immediately following creation we read the divine commission to man: "Be fruitful, and multiply, and replenish the earth, and subdue it; and have dominion over the fish of the sea, and over the birds of the heavens, and over every living thing that moveth upon the earth" (Gen. 1:28b). A review of man's material and intellectual achievements through the centuries would bear near conclusive testimony to the fulfillment of that commission. But there are two important realms in which man, devoid of the grace of God, has ever failed to fulfill the commission to "subdue . . . and have dominion," namely, the realms of the spiritual and the moral. Solomon grasped this truth when he said, "He that ruleth his spirit [is greater], than he that taketh a city" (Prov. 16:32). Man has, through the exercise of his native abilities, become a giant, but in the absence of divine grace he is a morally insane giant, a giant who will inevitably destroy himself by his own powers, unless he places himself under the control of God. It is an inner divine power that man requires if he is to fulfill God's purpose in his existence.

The application of the divine power to the personal indwelling presence of the Holy Spirit in the life of the Spirit-baptized Christian believer is multifold. A few examples of these practical applications will be helpful.

First, Pentecostal power is the assurance of the sanctified Christian's victory over temptation and sin. It was this provisional assurance that the Apostle John had in mind when he wrote, "Ye are of God, *my* little children, and have overcome them: because greater is he that is in you than he that is in the world" (I John 4:4). And again, the Apostle Paul set forth the assurance of this spiritual victory through the indwelling presence of the Holy Spirit most forcibly and beautifully in the eighth chapter of the letter to the Romans, especially verses 11, 31–39.

Second, the Pentecostal power is an effective enablement to the execution of the Christian witness. Said Jesus, "But ye shall receive power, when the Holy Spirit is come upon you: and ye shall be my witnesses both in Jerusalem, and in all Judaea and Samaria, and unto the uttermost part of the earth" (Acts 1:8). Again, of the early disciples subsequent to Pentecost, Luke wrote, "with great power gave the apostles their witness of the resurrection of the Lord Jesus" (Acts 4:33a). The indwelling presence of the Holy Spirit is quite as much an enabling to witness by a consistent, righteous, exemplary life as by oral testimony. Each validates the other.

Third, the efficacy of Pentecostal power for the endurance of persecution is well exemplified by the first Christian martyr, Stephen. Repeatedly in the early chapters of the Acts of the Apostles, we read of the spiritual victories of the apostles through the energizing presence of the Holy Spirit in the experiences of most extreme and severe persecution.

Fourth, the practice of demon expulsion by the Spirit-filled apostles dots the pages of the first-century Christian history. A notable failure of such an attempt in the name of Jesus, but in the absence of the indwelling presence of the Holy Spirit, is that of the sons of Sceva at Ephesus (Acts 19:14–17).

Fifth, Pentecostal power for Christian healing in the first-century Church is quite as much in evidence as is demon expulsion. The Acts of the Apostles is replete with such divine healings at the hands of the Spirit-filled apostles.

Sixth and finally, death itself was made to give up its victim at the command of these Spirit-filled servants of God. The restoration of Dorcas to life at the hands of Peter is a familiar example. Paul would seem to be thinking of both the healing of the body and of the final resurrection of the body when he uttered those words: "But if the Spirit of him that raised up Jesus from the dead dwelleth in you, he that raised up Christ Jesus from the dead shall give life also to your mortal bodies through his Spirit that dwelleth in you" (Rom. 8:11).

II. PENTECOST SIGNIFIES DIVINE PURIFICATION

And there appeared unto them tongues parting asunder [parting among them or, distributing themselves], **like as of fire; and it sat upon each of them** (Acts 2:3).

John Baptist's prophetic words concerning Christ are here fulfilled:

> "I indeed baptize you with water unto repentance: but he that cometh after me is mightier than I, whose shoes I am not worthy to bear: he shall baptize you in [or with], the Holy Spirit and *in* fire: whose fan is in his hand, and he will thoroughly cleanse his threshing-floor; and he will gather his wheat into the garner, but the chaff he will burn up with unquenchable fire" (Matt. 3:11).

The meaning of the phenomenon of fire on the day of Pentecost is not far to seek. It must be borne in mind that in the Pentecostal effusion God was manifesting or revealing Himself primarily to the believing disciples of Jesus Christ, who on the day of Pentecost **were all together in one place.** They had given up the world and had dedicated themselves in faith to the pursuit and execution of the will of God in Christ. At last their hopes of an earthly kingdom were forever gone (See Acts 1:6, 7). They were now in earnest and desperate pursuit of the inner spiritual kingdom which Christ had promised to them. Before the inner reign of Christ could be fully realized in their lives, there must be an inner purification, a consuming of the inner nature of self and sin, a renovation of every secret chamber of the soul, that nothing foreign or opposed to the nature of God might remain within. It was God's purpose that His disciples should be so inwardly pure that they might declare their independence of the domain of sin and the devil, as did Christ when He said, "The prince of the world [Satan] cometh: and he hath nothing in me" (John 14:30). There was to be no claim foreign to the claim of Christ upon, or within, the lives of these disciples of Jesus.

For the purpose of this inner purification, God revealed Himself to the waiting disciples under the symbol of **tongues parting asunder, like as of fire.** Consistently throughout the Scriptures, "fire" is employed as a symbol of divine purification. Fire has ever been a symbol of the holiness and justice of God. Thus God revealed Himself to His servants in ancient times (Deut. 4:24; Exod. 3:2; 19:18; Isa. 6:4; Ezek. 1:4; Dan. 7:10).

Malachi predicted the coming and the work of Christ under the symbol of fire.

> "The Lord, whom ye seek, will suddenly come to his temple; and the messenger of the covenant, whom ye desire, behold, he cometh, saith Jehovah of hosts. But who can abide the day of his coming? and who shall stand when he appeareth? for he is like a refiner's fire, and like fullers' soap: and he will sit as a refiner and purifier of silver, and he will purify the sons of Levi, and refine them as gold and silver; and they shall offer unto Jehovah offerings in righteousness" (Mal. 3:1–3).

Likewise in His post-ascension and second coming appearances, Jesus is represented under the symbol of fire (Rev. 1:12–18). Even the Word of God is likened unto fire: "Is not my word like fire? saith Jehovah" (Jer. 23:29a).

Finally, God Himself is represented by the author of the letter to the Hebrews under the symbol of fire: "Our God is a consuming fire" (Heb. 12:29). Thus it was God the Holy Spirit in consuming fire who manifested Himself in **tongues like as of fire** to the disciples on the day of Pentecost, purifying, sanctifying their inner natures (cf. Acts 15:8, 9).

At the first great general Christian council held at Jerusalem Peter, speaking in defence of the Gospel for the Gentiles, declared that their purification was on the same basis as that of the disciples at Pentecost. Said Peter: "And God, who knoweth the heart, bare them witness, giving them the Holy Spirit, even as He did unto us; and he made no distinction between us and them, cleansing their hearts by faith" (Acts 15:8, 9). At this juncture the testimony of Adam Clarke is significant: "Christ baptizes with the Holy Ghost, for the destruction of sin, the illumination of the mind, and the consolation of the heart."[a]

Finally, the tongues of fire were the manifestation of God's personal purifying presence to the inner impure natures of the disciples, making them inwardly clean in preparation for complete and uncontested possession and dominion by His Spirit. In the midst of the general manifestation of God's presence there was an individualization, or "personal" manifestation, providing for the personal conditions and needs of each disciple. Thus, while this purification or sanctification of the disciples' inner natures was primarily negative, it was a necessary and adequate provision of God for the positive work which was to immediately follow; namely, the complete possession of their inner beings by the personal presence of the Holy Spirit, giving them power over sin, the world, and the devil, and energizing them with a dynamic spiritual fervor for the proclamation of the Gospel of Christ to all men throughout the world of their day.

III. PENTECOST SIGNIFIES DIVINE POSSESSION

And they were all filled with the Holy Spirit (Acts 2:4a).

It was God's evident purpose in the creation of man to personally indwell him by His spirit. The "Fall" evicted the Spirit of God from the heart of man. Redemption through Christ provided a means of reconciliation between an offended God and offending man. However, reconciliation, important and essential as it is, is not enough to satisfy the heart of God. He longs to indwell the soul of man. Before such an unrivalled establishment of God in the soul of man could be realized, the inner nature of pollution and enmity against God must be cleansed away. For this purpose "Jesus also, that he might sanctify the people through his own blood, suffered without the gate" (Heb. 13:12). God's purpose in this great cleansing work, provided for the soul of converted man by Christ, is set forth by Paul in his first letter to the Thessalonian Christian converts thus: "This is the will of God, *even* your sanctification" (I Thess. 4:3).

But, the question may be fairly asked, was not the Spirit of God in these disciples from the time of their conversion before Pentecost? That such was the case no careful student of the Word of God would attempt to deny. The regenerative work of God in the lives of penitent sinners is the work of the Holy Spirit in the inner nature of man. Indeed, Jesus declared to Nicodemus on this subject: "Verily, verily, I say unto thee, Except one be born of water and the Spirit, he cannot enter into the kingdom of God. That which is born of the flesh is flesh; and that which is born of the Spirit is spirit" (John 3:5, 6). And Paul declared, "But ye are not in the flesh but in the Spirit, if so be that the Spirit of God dwelleth in you. But if any man have not the Spirit of Christ, he is none of his (Rom. 8:9). There is, in fact, no stage or part of the redemptive work that can be divorced from the direct operation of the Spirit of God. Jesus declared that even the work of conviction for sin on the world was to be the work of the Holy Spirit (see John 16:7–11). According to Jesus there can be no true worship apart from the Holy Spirit: "God is a Spirit, and they that worship him must worship him in spirit and truth" (John 4:24).

It will be noted that it was after His death and resurrection, and in conjunction with the Great Commission, which was not to be carried out until after Pentecost, that Jesus "breathed on them [His disciples], and saith unto them, "Receive ye the Holy Spirit" (John 20:22). That this was a prophetic act and word of the Master to be fulfilled on the day of Pentecost is evident from the prophetic commission of the preceding and following verses. In fact, the divine outpouring of the Holy Spirit on the day of Pentecost cannot be separated from the Great Commission. "But ye shall receive power, when the Holy Spirit is come upon you: and ye shall be my witnesses" (Acts 1:8). If the witnessing could not begin until Pentecost was a reality in the lives of the disciples, Pentecost could not become a reality in their lives until the outpouring of the Holy Spirit on the day of Pentecost. So likewise it is in the prophetic sense of this

[a] Adam Clarke *op. cit.*, V, 683.

Pentecostal fullness that Christ's words in John 4:17 must be understood. There is no indication in Christ's words, "for he abideth with you, and shall be in you," that the Holy Spirit had not become the vital principle of their new lives in Christ. Rather the utterance is a prediction of that fullness of the Spirit which they were to experience on the day of Pentecost. Says Samuel Chadwick: "the change from *with* to *in* marks the transition from one dispensation to another." It is indeed the difference between the personal, physical presence of Christ with His disciples, and what His spiritual inner abiding presence through the Holy Spirit would be as a result of Pentecost.

Again Chadwick remarks:

> There is often some confusion in the interchange of terms, and the elimination of the middle factor. The Son comes in the coming of the Spirit, and abides in the soul in the presence of the Spirit; and in the coming of the Son through the Spirit the Father comes and abides also. "He will come . . . I will come . . . We will come" all refer to the coming of the Spirit as promised in our Lord's farewell talk with His disciples (John 14:16–23). "In their relation to the human soul the Father and the Son act through and are represented by the Holy Spirit. And yet the Spirit is not merged in either the Father or in the Son." This is absolute unity with perfect distinction of persons in the Trinity. They are never confused in the unity nor divided in the distinction. Each is Divine and all are one.[b]

IV. PENTECOST SIGNIFIES UNIVERSAL PROCLAMATION

And [they] **began to speak with other tongues, as the Spirit gave them utterance** (Acts 2:4b).

Pentecost was a miracle of **other tongues.** Someone has said that any purported miracle must possess a moral value to validate itself. If the moral value validates a miracle, the miracle of **other tongues** on the day of Pentecost was well established.

Peter, taking advantage of the arrested attention and interest of the assembled multitude, consequent upon this miracle of proclamation in their diverse languages, arose and interpreted the meaning of the Pentecostal phenomena with such effectiveness as to result in the conversion of 3,000 souls (Acts 2:41).

Thus the miracle of **other tongues, as the Spirit gave them utterance,** was not only the direct means in the hands of God for the confounding and conversion of this multitude on the day of Pentecost, but there was also precipitated that great world-wide missionary movement that was to follow the inauguration of the Church on the day of Pentecost. As there were present there at Jerusalem representatives **from every nation under heaven,** so this Gospel of Jesus Christ was to be carried to "every nation under heaven" by fire-baptized and Holy Spirit-possessed men and women. The **other tongues** were necessary vehicles for the expression of **the mighty works of God,** and the result was the conversion of the multitude. This phenomenon was an intelligent and intelligible proclamation of the **wonderful works of God** (the Gospel of Christ) to a people who otherwise could not have understood it. It was the work of the Holy Spirit in the lives of the sanctified disciples. It marked the beginning and made possible the great missionary evangelistic program to which Christ commissioned His disciples when He said, "Go ye therefore, and make disciples of all nations" (Matt. 28:19); and again, "Ye shall receive power, when the Holy Spirit is come upon you; and ye shall be my witnesses . . . unto the uttermost part of the earth" (Acts 1:8).

Additional Note II

The Bible Gift of Tongues

And they . . . began to speak with other tongues, as the Spirit gave them utterance (Acts 2:4b).

Among the accompanying miracles of Pentecost was the gift of languages. It is logical that any purported miracle must demonstrate a moral value to validate its claims. On the basis of this principle, the miracle of **other tongues** given on the day of Pentecost was amply validated. The Gospel was thus proclaimed, and they witnessed the conversion of about 3,000 souls (Acts 2:41).

It should be noted from the very outset that the word *unknown,* in relation to "the Bible gift of tongues," does not occur in the original Greek of the New Testament. Nor is it found in the *American Revised Version.*

b Chadwick, *op. cit.*, p. 44.

The word *unknown* occurs only in italics in the KJV of the New Testament (and that misleadingly) in an attempt to clarify the meaning of the word **tongues.** Thus, properly speaking, there is no *unknown tongue* in the language of the New Testament. The Greek word *glossa*, meaning a tongue, or a language (Acts 2:11), or a nation of people distinguished by their language (Rev. 5:9; 7:9), is consistently used in its various forms throughout the New Testament, except where the word *dialektos*, meaning speech, dialect, or language, is used (Acts 1:19; 2:6, 8; 21:40; 22:2; 26:14).

Webster defines the word "tongue" as "The power of communication through speech . . . Act of speaking; esp., a spoken language." Hence a tongue, in this sense, is an articulate, intelligible speech or language used for the purpose of communicating ideas from one person to another. *That the foregoing definition of "tongues" accords with the Biblical use of the word throughout the New Testament it is the purpose of this study to show.*

Let it be noted that, with the occurrence of the divine miracle of tongues at Pentecost, the disciples **began to speak with other tongues, as the Spirit gave them utterance** (Acts 2:4b), and the multitude exclaimed, **How hear we, every man in our own language wherein we were born? . . . we hear them speaking in our tongues the mighty works of God** (Acts 2:8, 11). Again, in the case of Cornelius' household, it is said that the Jews who accompanied Peter **heard them speak with tongues, and magnify God** (Acts 10:46). Matthew Henry remarks on this passage:

> *They spoke with tongues* which they never learned . . . that they might communicate the doctrine of Christ to the hearers . . . Or being enabled to speak with tongues intimated that they were all designated for ministers, and by this first descent of the Spirit upon them were qualified to preach the gospel to others, which they did but now receive themselves . . . when they spoke with tongues, they *magnified* God, they spoke of Christ and the benefits of redemption, which Peter had been preaching to the glory of God.[c]

Likewise when this phenomenon occurred at Ephesus, it is stated that **they spake with tongues, and prophesied** (Acts 19:6). Both Clarke and Matthew Henry take the position that this **prophesying** was preaching in the miraculously given tongues (languages), to people who could not otherwise have heard the gospel message.

As to the significance of "tongues," as Paul deals with that problem in the church at Corinth, due consideration will be given elsewhere.

I. THE NECESSITY OF THE BIBLE GIFT OF TONGUES

The Acts record informs us that,

There were dwelling at Jerusalem Jews, devout men, from every nation under heaven. And when this sound [the sound as of the rushing of a mighty wind] **was heard, the multitude came together, and were confounded, because that every man heard them speaking in his own language. And they were all amazed and marvelled, saying, Behold, are not all these that speak Galileans? And how hear we, every man in our own language wherein we were born?** (Acts 2:5–8).

There then follows a list of fifteen different nations which were represented at the Jerusalem Pentecost, into the countries of which Jews of the *Diaspora* had been born, whose language these representative Jewish people spoke and understood.

In order to comprehend the fuller significance of this necessity for the miracle of other tongues on the day of Pentecost, it is necessary to briefly examine the character of the hearers of the Pentecostal message. The record states that **there were dwelling at Jerusalem Jews, devout men, from every nation under heaven** (Acts 2:5). Whether these devout men were proselytes (Gentile converts to the Jewish faith and practice), or Gentile worshipers of Jehovah but not full proselytes, or whether the expression is meant to characterize the Jewish dwellers at Jerusalem, seems uncertain. In any event, they represented the dwellers at Jerusalem, who for the most part had been attracted there by the temple worship, from the lands of the *Diaspora*. However, there is also another class of people concerned in the Pentecostal effusion. They are represented by Luke thus: **And when this sound was heard, "the multitude" came together, and**

[c] *Matthew Henry's Commentary on the Whole Bible* (New York: Fleming H. Revell, n.d.), VI, Comment on Acts 10:46.

were confounded, because that every man heard them speaking in his own language (Acts 2:6). Very evidently this multitude comprised not only the dwellers at Jerusalem, but also those who had gathered from the various lands to keep the feast of Pentecost, which was one of the principal annual Jewish feasts to which Jewish worshipers were expected, if at all possible, to come.

The linguistic problem at Pentecost, presented by this multitude, is suggested by the presence of **Parthians, Medes,** and **Elamites,** nations beyond the Roman Empire and the influence of Rome where the Ten Tribes of the Northern Kingdom were supposed to have settled after their captivity in 722 B.C. (see II Kings 17:6). **Mesopotamia,** the chief Jewish center of which Babylon, famed for its rabbinical schools and formerly the point of the "confusion of tongues" at the construction of the Tower of Babel, had its representatives present at Pentecost. **Judaea,** probably as distinguished from Galilee, the home of Christ's disciples, was naturally represented. **Cappadocia, Pontus, Asia, Phrygia** and **Pamphylia** represented the countries of Asia Minor from which foreign-born Jews and proselytes had come to Pentecost. **Egypt** where according to Philo, the famed Greco-Jewish philosopher of Alexandria, a million Jews resided and formed a large part of the population of Alexandria and imbibed much of the Hellenic[d] culture, including language—had sent its representatives to Jerusalem. North African **Libya** and the North African Greek city of **Cyrene,** a quarter of the great population of which consisted of Jews with full citizenship rights, also sent representatives to the Jerusalem feast of Pentecost. It is of special interest that it was Simon of *Cyrene* who bore the cross of Christ en route to Calvary (Matt. 27:32). There were those of the synagogue of the Cyrenians who disputed with Stephen on the occasion of his martyrdom (Acts 6:9). There were Christian representatives of Cyrene who first bore the Gospel to the Greek population of Antioch of Syria (Acts 11:20); and there was a Christian prophet, Lucius of Cyrene, in the Antioch church who played an important part in instigating the first Christian missionary journey of Paul and Barnabas (Acts 13:1). **Sojourners from Rome, both Jews and proselytes** (vs. 10b), were present. And finally, inhabitants of the large Mediterranean island of Crete and of the Arabian peninsula are named as present at Pentecost.

These dwellers at Jerusalem, sojourners, Hellenistic Jews, Gentile proselytes, and "God-fearers" exclaimed, **we hear them speaking in our tongues the mighty works of God** (Acts 2:11b).

A. J. Maclean[e] observes that the languages enumerated in Acts 2, in which the disciples spoke on the day of Pentecost, may have been in large part but varied dialects of the Greek and the Aramaic,[f] especially the latter, since the Jews of the *Diaspora* may have spoken principally Greek or Aramic. However, thus allowing, it is nevertheless necessary to consider that dialects may and often do vary so greatly that they practically amount to different languages as far as speaking communication is concerned. Therefore, a miracle of speaking would be necessary to cover these varied dialects at Pentecost, to say nothing of the distinct languages that may have been represented. It is also necessary to note that, beside the Jerusalem and Hellenic Jews present at Pentecost, there were many "proselytes" and "God-fearers" present. The latter were a people who were not of the Jewish nationality, but were nevertheless worshipers of Jehovah in the more liberal fashion of the Jewish synagogues out in the countries of the Roman Empire and beyond. These Jewish communities, Benjamin Robinson thinks, may have reached 150 by the time of Paul.[g] In addition, there were those synagogues that were established in Jerusalem, which are supposed to have numbered about 250. It is hardly logical to assume that all of these latter people understood and spoke either Greek or Aramaic, but they did hear the disciples preaching Jesus and His resurrection: **the mighty works of God, . . . every man in . . . his own language wherein . . .** [he was] **born** (Acts 2:8b).

[d] Hellenic—A term characterizing the classical Greek culture. Thus, a Hellenist is "one who affiliates with Greeks or imitates Greek manners; esp., a Jew who used the Greek language as his mother tongue" (Webster).

[e] A. J. Maclean, "Gift of Tongues," *Dictionary of the Bible*, Ed. James Hastings (New York: Charles Scribner's Sons, 1909, rep. 1921), pp. 943, 944.

[f] Aramaic: the Semitic-Hebrew vernacular in use in Palestine at this time.

[g] Robinson, *op. cit.*, pp. 9–12.

From the foregoing considerations it becomes evident that this initial occurrence of the miraculous gift of languages is to be understood as the use of the *bona fide* languages of people present who otherwise would have been incapable of hearing the Gospel of Jesus Christ, and that by men who themselves were unfamiliar with the languages which they were using.

Adam Clarke's comment is interesting at this juncture.

> At the beginning of Babel the *language* of the people was *confounded;* and, in consequence of this, they became scattered over the face of the earth; at this *foundation* of the *Christian Church*, the gift of various languages was given to the apostles, that the scattered nations might be *gathered;* and united under one shepherd and superintendent (episkopos) of all souls.[h]

That this Pentecostal miracle may have been in part a miracle of the interpretation of the speech of the disciples into the language of the hearers by the Holy Spirit was suggested by Gregory of Nyssa and others, but from Acts 2:6 this appears extremely unlikely. Thus it is impossible to deny that the **others tongues,** with which these Spirit-filled disciples spoke, were divine miraculous gifts of speech to the disciples for the purpose of evangelizing the representative multitude present at Pentecost.

The miracle of the proclamation of the Gospel in the different languages of those present for the Jewish Pentecost, and which resulted in the great Pentecostal awakening, seems to anticipate the fulfillment of the "Great Commission" of Christ (Matt. 28: 18–20 and Acts 1:8). This is further suggested by the universal representation of redeemed humanity as depicted in Revelation (see Rev. 5:9, 10; 7:9, 10).

II. THE PURPOSE OF THE BIBLE GIFT OF TONGUES

Maclean holds that "Tertullian apparently judged the gift [of tongues] to be an ecstatic utterance of praise."[i] This position seems impossible to defend when all of the Scriptural facts are considered. Nevertheless, he admits that most of the Church Fathers, including Origen (A.D. 185?–A.D. 254?), Chrysostom (A.D. 347–A.D. 407), Theodoret (A.D. 396–A.D. 457), Gregory of Nyssa (A.D. 331–A.D. 394), and Gregory of Nazianzus (A.D. 329–A.D. 390), understood the miraculous gift of tongues, as recorded in Acts, to be for the purpose of evangelizing the nations. The preaching of **the mighty works of God** (the resurrection of Jesus Christ from the dead) was made intelligible to the people of the nations enumerated in the second chapter of Acts by reason of the miracle of tongues, with the result that some 3,000 were initially converted to Christ and added to the Church. This event in itself is sufficient to establish the fact that the divine gift of tongues was for evangelization purposes.

In perfect accord with the evangelistic purpose of the gift of tongues on the day of Pentecost is the prediction of Isaiah, which prediction looks ultimately to the Gospel Age, and possibly embodies Pentecost itself. Says the prophet: "The time cometh, that I will gather all nations and tongues; and they shall come, and shall see my glory. And I will set a sign among them, . . . and they shall declare my glory among the nations" (Isa. 66:18, 19). And it is in conjunction with the Great Commission that Mark records Christ's prediction of the phenomenon of "new tongues" (Mark 16:15–17).

But the evangelistic purpose of the divine gift of tongues does not rest exclusively upon the Pentecostal incident. There are three other distinct occurrences of this phenomenon recorded in the New Testament; indeed some think they see even a fourth, in the incident of the outpouring of the Holy Spirit on the Samaritan Christians when they were visited by Peter and John from Jerusalem, as recorded in Acts 8:14–24. However, there is no mention made, in this account concerning Samaria, of the gift of tongues accompanying the bestowment of the Holy Spirit, and there appears to have been no need for it in the presence of a common language spoken by these people. To the other three instances of the gift of tongues at Caesarea, Ephesus, and Corinth consideration will be given in "Additional Notes" on Chapters 10 and 19.

[h] Clarke, *op. cit.*, p. 693.
[i] A. J. Maclean, *op. cit.*, p. 943.

CHAPTER III

Now Peter and John were going up into the temple at the hour of prayer, *being* the ninth *hour*.

EXEGESIS

1 **Peter and John** are not "paired off" in the Gospels, with one exception. They were sent to prepare the passover meal the night before Jesus' crucifixion (Luke 22:8). But in the first part of Acts they are described as working together (cf. 8:14). John is undoubtedly the son of Zebedee,[1] one of the three apostles of the inner circle in the Gospels.

The two apostles **were going up into the temple** (*hieron* = Temple Area) **at the hour of prayer, being the ninth hour** (i.e., 3:00 P.M.).[2] Josephus states that the priests, even during the siege by the Romans, "did still twice a day, in the morning and about the ninth hour, offer their sacrifices on the altar."[3] Schürer describes the morning and evening sacrifices and says that incense was offered on the golden altar before the burnt offering

EXPOSITION

THE CHURCH'S FIRST RECORDED PHYSICAL MIRACLE

I. A Notable Miracle, Acts 3:1–11.
   A. The Power of Prayer, vs. 1.
   B. The Opportunity for Service, vs. 2.
   C. The Appeal of Helplessness, vs. 3.
   D. The Stimulus to Faith, vss. 4, 5.
   E. The Healing Virtue in the Name, vss. 6–8a.
   F. The Spiritual Transformation, vs. 8b.
   G. The Salutary Results, vss. 9–11.
II. A Powerful Sermon, Acts 3:12–18.
   A. The Human Disclaim to Power, vs. 12.
   B. The Correct Ascription of Power, vs. 13a.
   C. The Charge Against Israel, vss. 13b–15a.
   D. The Divine Victory over Death, vs. 15b.
   E. The Power of Christ's Name, vs. 16.
   F. The Irony of Opposition, vss. 17, 18.
III. A Fervent Exhortation, Acts 3:19–26.
   A. The Necessity of Repentance, vs. 19.
   B. The Inescapable Lordship of Christ, vss. 20–22.
   C. The Certainty of Divine Judgment, vs. 23.
   D. The Ancient Promise of Salvation, vss. 24, 25.
   E. The Present Offer of Salvation, vs. 26.

I. A NOTABLE MIRACLE (3:1–11)

Luke evidently singled out this one notable miracle from among the "many wonders and signs... done through the apostles" (Acts 2:43b) for the purpose of depicting the mighty onmoving power of the Holy Spirit through the Pentecostal Church. It is the first recorded miracle of divine healing, following Pentecost, and it is fully validated by its salutary moral and spiritual results. The Pentecostal power of the Holy Spirit indwelling and working through the Apostles (Acts 1:8) here becomes effective in removing opposition and unbelief and in paving the way for the preaching of salvation through Christ to the Jews and the pagan world beyond.

A. The Power of Prayer (3:1)

Peter and John were going up into the temple at the hour of prayer. As yet the disciples of Christ and the apostles constituted but a new, spiritual life movement

[1] The suggestion of Lake and Cadbury that this might be John Mark (*Beginnings*, IV, 31) is too farfetched to need refutation.
[2] There is some question as to whether the other two hours of prayer were third and sixth, or early in the morning and at sunset (cf. EGT, II, 102 f.).
[3] *Ant.* XIV, 4, 3.

2 And a certain man that was lame from his mother's womb was carried, whom they laid daily at the door of the temple which is called Beautiful, to ask alms of them that entered into the temple;

---

on the brazen altar in the morning and after it in the evening, "so that the daily burnt offering was, as it were, girt round with the offering of incense."[4] He further says: "While this was going on the people were also assembled in the temple for prayer."[5]

2 The **Beautiful** Gate of the temple is usually identified with the gate of Nicanor, which was exceedingly beautiful (see Exposition). In medieval times the Shushan gate was called the "Golden Gate," and that name is still applied to a gate—blocked in with building stones—in the east wall of the Temple Area, which is part of the east wall of the city of Jerusalem. The Nicanor gate was inside the Temple Area, opening from the outer Court of the Gentiles into the Court of the Women, which only Jews could enter. This is the more likely identification, though the matter is not settled conclusively.[6]

At the Beautiful Gate was laid a man crippled from birth **to ask alms.** Someone has said, perhaps facetiously, that "he asked for alms and got legs!"

---

within the Jewish communion. It remained for Stephen to gain the larger vision of the mission of Christianity to the Gentile world, which vision cost him his life, but which also produced the great apostle to the Gentiles, Paul. The disciples were not even called Christians until later at Antioch (Acts 11:26). They worshipped Christ, but as yet after the Jewish pattern. They observed the three, daily, stated Jewish periods of prayer in the temple (Acts 2:42, 46): namely, "the third hour" (Acts 2:15), about nine o'clock in the morning; "the sixth hour" (Acts 10:9), about noon; and "the ninth hour" (Acts 3:1; 10:3), about three o'clock in the afternoon (cf. Ps. 55:17). Vitalized by the Holy Spirit, their communion with God became a prime source of sweet fellowship and spiritual power for life and service. Prayer was a prized privilege and a chief practice of the Apostolic Church (Acts 6:4), and accounted for many mighty miracles and victories (Acts 12:3–17). The habit and engagement of prayer is ever the secret of Christian victory (see Dan. 6:10 and Ps. 55:17). Lange[a] holds that Christian custom had firmly established the observance of these three hours of prayer by later apostolic times. A prayerless church is a powerless church. A praying church is an invincible church. The miracle of healing that followed was resultant from the united prayers of these Spirit-filled, Christian brother apostles.

B. The Opportunity for Service (3:2)

And a certain man that was lame from his mother's womb was carried. God often selects the apparently hopeless cases for the demonstration of His power. It was no recent or temporary affliction which might be remedied by time or natural means, from which this man suffered. Rather, from birth he had been unable to walk and must be carried on a litter if he went about at all. He was a common spectacle **whom they laid daily at the door of the temple which is called Beautiful.** What a contradiction! A poor, ragged, wretched, helpless, and hopelessly deformed beggar lying dejectedly, with his beggar's cup feebly extended to passers-by. There he lay framed in the most ornate and expensive gate, **called Beautiful,** of the great Jewish temple, **to ask alms of them that entered into the temple** in selfish, hypocritical, ceremonial, religious masquerade.

Dummelow[b] holds that the gate referred to here was the *Gate of Nicanor* and that it was constructed of fine Corinthian brass. He regards it as having been far more expensive than the other gates of the temple which were overlaid with silver and gold. The *Gate of Nicanor* opened to the east by the "gate of the holy house" itself. Josephus

---

[4] Emil Schürer, *A history of the Jewish People in the Time of Jesus Christ* (Edinburgh: T. & T. Clark, 1934), II, i, 290.
[5] *Ibid.*
[6] For full discussion of the location of the Beautiful Gate see *Beginnings*, IV, 32 f.; V, 479–486.

[a] John Peter Lange, *Commentary on the Holy Scriptures* (Grand Rapids: Zondervan Publishing House, n.d.), p. 62.
[b] Dummelow, *op. cit.*, p. 822.

3 who seeing Peter and John about to go into the temple, asked to receive an alms.
4 And Peter, fastening his eyes upon him, with John, said, Look on us.
5 And he gave heed unto them, expecting to receive something from them.
6 But Peter said, Silver and gold have I none; but what I have, that give I thee. In the name of Jesus Christ of Nazareth, walk.

---

3 The beggar **asked**—*ērōta*, imperfect, was asking repeatedly—**to receive.** This last phrase *(labein)* is in the best manuscripts.[7]

4 **Fastening his eyes** is all one word in the Greek, *atenisas* (cf. vs. 12). The verb indicates a fixed looking or gazing. In Acts 1:10 it describes the disciples "looking stedfastly" into heaven as Jesus ascended.

5 **Gave heed** is literally "was holding"; [8] that is, his mind, or eyes. He turned all his attention toward the apostles.

6 **Silver and gold have I none**—*ouch hyparchei moi*, literally, "does not belong to me"—**but what I have** *(echo)*—the eternal, spiritual power which I really possess—**that I give to thee.** Peter did not have what the man wanted, but he gave him what he needed.

---

says, concerning this gate: "its height was fifty cubits, and its doors were forty cubits, and it was adorned after a most costly manner, as having much richer and thicker plates of silver and gold upon them than the others."[c] It may be that Peter got his text from this gold-and-silver-plated brass gate when he said, **Silver and gold have I none.**

The cripple had got no nearer to God than the gate of the temple, and he got no more from the religionists that passed through the gate than their scornful glances and pitiful pittances. Nor will morally and spiritually injured and helpless society ever receive more from the church than this man received, until the latter experiences a new Pentecostal revival. So long as the church "fares sumptuously every day" (see Luke 12:16–21 and Rev. 3:14–22), the beggars, "full of sores," will lie at her gate. So long as priests and Levites "pass by on the other side," the robbed, beaten, and bleeding world will lie "half dead" at the side of the road (Luke 10:25–37).

C. The Appeal of Helplessness (3:3)

Who seeing Peter and John about to go into the temple, asked to receive an alms. Long exposed to the spiritual deadness and compassionlessness of formal religion, the crippled beggar could conceive of religion only in the terms of materiality. No more than a pittance could he hope for from the temple. He was there for what he could get, and he got little indeed. Meager will be the benefits to society from the Church when she loses her spiritual power and mission.

D. The Stimulus to Faith (3:4, 5)

Peter, fastening his eyes upon him, with John, said, Look on us. The apostles, moved by his sad condition and pitiful plea for alms, conceived, under divine inspiration, a better and a permanent way of alleviating the wretched man's plight. Physical healing would not only restore him to normality, independence, and self-respect, but it would also demonstrate to the world God's compassion for the suffering and His miraculous power to restore the afflicted. There radiated from the Spirit-filled apostles' countenances a confidence and faith born of communion with the living God which, as he looked expectantly on them, inspired renewed hope and challenged him to believe. Faith is contagious. Faith in the Christian begets faith in the unbelieving world. Faith, like love, comes to birth under the influence of another in whom it is manifested. Thus John could say, "We love [him], because he first loved us" (I John 4:19). The world will believe little and the Church's influence will remain sadly limited until Christians renew their faith in the goodness and power of God. Faith flourishes in the soil of spiritual manifestations. Prayer produces such manifestations. Likewise Christ's faith in man begets man's faith in Christ (see Gal. 2:20).

[7] Aleph A B C.
[8] The frequent use of the imperfect tense (five times in the first five verses) should be noted.

[c] Flavius Josephus, *The Works of Flavius Josephus* (Philadelphia: David McKay, Publishers, n.d.), "Wars" V.V. 3.

7 And he took him by the right hand, and raised him up: and immediately his feet and his ankle-bones received strength.

8 And leaping up, he stood, and began to walk; and he entered with them into the temple, walking, and leaping, and praising God.

9 And all the people saw him walking and praising God:

10 and they took knowledge of him, that it was he that sat for alms at the Beautiful Gate of the temple; and they were filled with wonder and amazement at that which had happened unto him.

In the name of Jesus Christ means by the authority of Jesus Christ. **Walk,** *peripatei,* is present tense: start walking, and keep on walking.[9]

7 Hobart emphasized the idea that *baseis* **(feet),** *sphydra* **(ankle-bones),** and *estereōthēsan* **(received strength)** were all medical terms.[10] This has been challenged by Cadbury, who calls attention to the use of these words in classical poetry.[11] But since the first two are found only here in the New Testament and the third is found elsewhere only in verse 16 and 16:5, and all three are frequent in Greek medical writings, it would seem that *some* significance should be attached to the fact that Luke uses medical terms more frequently than any other writer in the New Testament, even though many of these words are found in non-medical literature. It seems to us that there is a residuum of valid evidence here.[12]

8 **Leaping up**[13] suggests that the man responded with alacrity. This would seem to indicate faith on his part. **Stood** *(estē)* is aorist, **began to walk** *(periepatei)* imperfect (inchoative). The latter could also mean "continued walking about."

10 **Took knowledge of** *(epeginōskon,* im-

E. The Healing Virtue in the Name (3:6–8a)

In the name of Jesus Christ of Nazareth, walk. Obedience to the apostle's command was a human impossibility, but inspired by the sheer confidence and authority of that command, **in the name of Jesus Christ of Nazareth,** and supported by Peter's extended hand, the cripple forthwith sprang up, **stood, and began to walk.** He suddenly realized himself to have been made every whit whole. A divine healing current surged through his twisted and deformed body, straightening, restoring, healing, and animating it throughout, **and immediately his feet and his ankle-bones received strength.** The suddenness with which his feet and ankle-bones received strength was proof of a miraculous cure, and that cure was evidenced by his standing, **walking, and leaping, and praising God**[d]. The miracle was more than a physical healing. Here a man immediately stands, walks, and leaps who, crippled from birth, had never learned to stand, not to mention walking or leaping. Divine animation often restores unavoidably lost opportunities and facilitates progress in the life of the restored one.

While Peter and John possessed and exercised the authority to command the cure of the cripple in the name of Jesus, his responsive cooperation was required to effect the cure. Though devoid of money, either for the church treasury or alms for the crippled beggar, these apostles had access to a far richer treasure with which none else could compare (Phil. 4:19), and which they stood ready to dispense where worthy needs existed. **Silver and gold have I none,** said Peter, **but what I have that give I thee.** Thomas Aquinas is reported by Clarke[e] to have once appeared in the chamber of Pope Innocent IV, where vast sums of church money were being counted. The Pope remarked to Thomas: "You see that the church is no longer in an age in which she can say, *Silver and gold have I none?*" "It is true, holy father," replied the angelical doctor, "nor can she now say to the lame man, '*Rise up and walk!*'" (cf. Rev. 3:14–22).

[9] The preceding phrase, "rise up and" (KJV), is not found in Aleph B D.
[10] *Op. cit.*, pp. 34–36.
[11] Cf. *Beginnings*, IV, 33 f.
[12] Cf. Knowling, EGT, II, 106—"has been justly held to point to the technical description of a medical man."
[13] *Exallomenos*, found only here in N.T.

[d] Clarke, *op. cit.*, V, 705. [e] *Ibid.*

11 And as he held Peter and John, all the people ran together unto them in the porch that is called Solomon's, greatly wondering.

12 And when Peter saw it, he answered unto the people, Ye men of Israel, why marvel ye at this man? or why fasten ye your eyes on us, as though by our own power or godliness we had made him to walk?

13 The God of Abraham, and of Isaac, and of Jacob, the God of our fathers, hath glorified his Servant Jesus; whom ye delivered up, and denied before the face of Pilate, when he had determined to release him.

---

perfect) is better translated "recognized." **Amazement**, *ekstasis*, "ecstasy," is literally "a standing out." They were "standing out of themselves" with astonishment.

11 **Porch,** *stoa*, is better rendered "portico" or "colonnade." This Colonnade of Solomon was probably on the east side of the Court of the Gentiles,[14] against the outside wall of the Temple Area—a sort of arched way or covered walk. Such a colonnaded walk may be seen today against the *inside* (west) wall of the Temple Area. Josephus writes: "And when they had built walls on three sides of the temple round about... they then encompassed their upper courts with cloisters." [15] He also says of the eastern cloisters (or their foundation): "This was the work of King Solomon, who first of all built the entire temple." [16] He thus reflects the view of his day that the eastern foundations of the Temple Area dated back to the days of Solomon.

12 When Peter saw the crowd gathering, **he answered**; "i.e., to their looks of astonishment and inquiry." [17] **This man** is perhaps better "this" (KJV and RSV); that is, this miracle. However, the Greek could be either masculine or neuter. **Power or godliness** is better "power or piety" (RSV).

13 **God . . . hath glorified his Servant Jesus.** This change from "his Son Jesus" (KJV) has been interpreted by some as an effort to discount the deity of Jesus. But all the best conservative commentators are agreed that "Servant" [18] is the better translation. The reason is that the background of this term appears to be the "Servant Songs" of Isaiah, which refer to the Messiah. Knowling writes: "The rendering 'Servant' is undoubtedly most appropriate; cf. var. 26, and

---

F. The Spiritual Transformation (3:8b)

And he entered with them into the temple, walking, and leaping, and praising God. A purported divine cure that produces no spiritual or moral change in the patient is subject to legitimate suspicion. With the affliction at last removed, that had all his lifetime barred him from the temple worship and service, the well and normal man now enters the temple with the apostles to worship God. A faith healing that does not lead to the worship and service of God is worse than useless. A cure had been effected in this man that made him a joyful worshipper of God and brought new life and interest into the temple service. When divine healing leads the soul to God in Christ and spiritually animates the Church it is creditable indeed.

G. The Salutary Results (3:9–11)

And all the people saw him . . . and they were filled with wonder and amazement . . . and ran together unto them in the porch that is called Solomon's, greatly wondering. The lifelong impotency of the cripple and his normally dejected spirits, as he lay at the *Gate Beautiful* begging, were well known by the citizens, and especially the temple patrons. Thus their attention was arrested, and **wonder** and **amazement** gripped them at his sudden restoration to normal physique and activity. His animated spirit and action, as was evidenced by his **walking, leaping, and praising God** in the temple, were sufficient evidence of his cure. This miraculous cure not only afforded Peter a text from which to preach, but also an interested and expectant audience to hear his powerful sermon which followed. Pews will not long

[14] Cf. *Beginnings*, V, 485 f.
[15] *War*, V, 5, 1. Cf. also *Ant.* XV, 11, 5.
[16] *Ant.* XX, 9, 7.
[17] Knowling, EGT, II, 109.
[18] *Pais* is translated "servant" in KJV in ten out of its twenty-four occurrences in N.T. and "son" only three times, two of them here in vss. 13 and 26 (cf. John 4:51).

14 But ye denied the Holy and Righteous One, and asked for a murderer to be granted unto you,
15 and killed the Prince of life; whom God raised from the dead; whereof we are witnesses.
16 And by faith in his name hath his name made this man strong, whom ye behold and know: yea, the faith which is through him hath given him this perfect soundness in the presence of you all.
17 And now, brethren, I know that in ignorance ye did it, as did also your rulers.

---

iv. 27, 30 (employed in the Messianic sense of Isa. xlii. 1, lii. 13, liii. 11) where the LXX has *pais*."[19] Bruce agrees with this interpretation and notes further that "Our Lord himself explicitly interpreted His Messiahship in terms of the Isaianic Servant... and so do the NT writers generally."[20]

Pilate was procurator of Judea, A.D. 26–36. Josephus describes Pilate as despotic and cruel and one whose reign was very offensive to the Jews[21].

14 **The Holy and Righteous One** *(ton hagion kai dikaion)* are both Messianic titles (cf. Isa. 53:11). In I Enoch 38:2; 53:6, the Messiah is called the Righteous One. This is a favorite designation in the New Testament (cf. Acts 7:52; 22:14; I Pet. 3:18; I John 2:1).

15 Note the tremendous contrast: **asked for a murderer to be granted unto you** (vs. 14) **and killed the Prince of life.** The word *archēgos* has two distinct meanings: (1) founder, author; (2) prince, leader. It is found four times in the New Testament (cf. 5:31; Heb. 2:10; 12:2). Bruce writes: "Here and in Heb. ii. 10 it denotes Christ as the *Source* of life and salvation; in v. 31 the meaning 'Prince' or 'Leader' is uppermost; in Heb. xii. 2, the meaning 'Leader,' 'Exemplar.'"[22] Perhaps "Author of life" is the best translation here.

16 This verse reads awkwardly in the Greek. But probably both the King James and the American Standard versions give essentially the correct idea.

17 In a conciliatory and kindly tone Peter now addresses them as **brethren** and declares that it was **in ignorance** *(kata agnoian)* that they had killed Jesus; that is, they did not realize fully that He was the Messiah. Paul wrote to Timothy: "I was before a blasphemer, and a persecutor, and injurious:

---

remain empty when hearts are Spirit-filled and God's wonder-working power is in evidence. God revealed insures transforming results (see Luke 7:19–23 and Acts 16:18).

II. A POWERFUL SERMON (3:12–18)

There is much in this second recorded sermon of Peter's that is reminiscent of his Pentecostal Day sermon (Acts 2:22–40). The occasion, like the first, was produced by a divine miracle; there the gift of languages, here the healing of a cripple. Both arrested the attention and heightened the interest and expectations of the multitudes, and Peter was thus given audience. Here Peter and John, like Paul and Barnabas later at Lystra under very similar circumstances (Acts 14:8–18), disclaimed any human, miracle-working power (vs. 12). Rightfully, Peter ascribes the power and the glory to God in the vindication of His Son Jesus Christ (vs. 13a). How unlike so many modern professed faith healers and miracle workers was Peter's response to this miracle. Taking advantage of the occasion, Peter delivered a direct, penetrating indictment of the Jews, in which he made them responsible for the rejection, condemnation, and cruel execution of God's Son and their Messiah. They had counted Him less than the murderer Barabbas (vss. 13b–15a). This charge was immediately followed by a declaration of God's victory, through Christ's resurrection, over their wicked designs, to which victory the apostles joyfully gave witness (vs. 15b). The validity of Christ's resurrection from the dead was attested by the miracle of healing through faith in His Name, which they had just witnessed (vs. 16). The irony of the situation, Peter pointed out, was that the Jews ignorrantly served the end against which they fought (vss. 17, 18).

[19] EGT, II, 109. [20] *Acts*, p. 108. [21] *Ant.* XVIII, 3, 1, 2; 4, 1, 2.
[22] *Acts*, p. 109. This variety of meanings can also be found in the LXX. Macgregor would use "orginator" or "author" for Acts 3:15; Heb. 2:10; 12:2 and "captain" for Acts 5:31 (IB, IX, 58).

18 But the things which God foreshowed by the mouth of all the prophets, that his Christ should suffer, he thus fulfilled.

19 Repent ye therefore, and turn again, that your sins may be blotted out, that so there may come seasons of refreshing from the presence of the Lord;

20 and that he may send the Christ who hath been appointed for you, *even* Jesus:

21 whom the heaven must receive until the times of restoration of all things, whereof God spake by the mouth of his holy prophets that have been from of old.

---

howbeit I obtained mercy, because I did it ignorantly in unbelief" (I Tim. 1:13).

18 **His Christ** is perhaps better rendered "His Messiah." Lake and Cadbury comment: "This is a more primitive usage than 'the Messiah' without qualification." [23] That the Messiah **should suffer** [24] is shown especially in Isaiah 53 and Psalm 22, though these passages were not generally interpreted messianically by the Jews.

19 As in his first sermon, Peter sounds the evangelistic note: **Repent. Turn again** *(epistrepsate)* is the same as "be converted" (KJV). The word is used in the Septuagint in the sense of "return," which means "turn again." In Joel 2:14 (LXX) these same two words are found together.

The result of **sins** being **blotted out** would be **seasons of refreshing.** This translation accords with the only occurrence of *anapsyxis* in the Septuagint (Ex. 8:15). Lake and Cadbury assert: "This phrase does not appear to be used in Rabbinical or other literature as a synonym for the Messianic period." [25] They translate it "times of revival."

20 The Jews had rejected Jesus at His first coming. Now Peter exhorts them to repent and turn again that they might not only have times of revival but also that God **may send the Christ.** The primary reference seems to be to the Second Advent.[26]

21 The expression, **the times of restoration of all things,** has been seized upon by those who hold to a final universal salvation. But they forget the qualifying phrase, **whereof God spake by the mouth of his holy prophets.** Only such a restoration as is taught in the Old Testament scriptures is here intended.

Apokatastasis **(restoration)** is a double compound, meaning literally "a placing down away from." It occurs only here in the New Testament and is not found in the Septuagint. In the papyri it is used of repairs and restorations of temples.[27] In Josephus it is used of the restoration of the Jews to their own land.[28] Philo uses it of the restoration of family inheritances in the year of Jubilee.[29] Lake and Cadbury prefer "establishment." [30] Bruce writes: "*Apokatastasis*, may here be rendered 'establishment,' 'fulfilment,' referring to the fulfilment of all OT prophecy, culminating in the establishment of God's kingdom on earth." [31]

III. A FERVENT EXHORTATION (3:19–26)

Having convincingly presented his argument and having made his charge against the Jews, Peter observed the convicting effect of the truth on his hearers and proceeded directly to exhort them to repent and turn from the wickedness of their thoughts and deeds, that they might receive forgiveness of sins and the favor of God (vs. 19). But the preacher warns that they must now be willing to receive Christ as their Saviour and the personal Lord of their lives, though formerly having rejected Him, if they are to be saved (vss. 20–22). Personal divine judgment is inescapable if they again reject Christ in the light of this convincing truth and the miracle of healing which they have witnessed (vs. 23). His hearers are the heirs of the promises, given through the prophets, of free universal salvation and blessing in this Pentecostal dispensation (2:23, 25). Peter's exhortation closes with the solemn reminder that Christ was first raised for, and that salvation is first offered to, the Jews. There is evidence that this sermon and exhortation bore immediate fruit unto salvation in Peter's hearers and precipitated the first apostolic persecution.

[23] *Beginnings*, IV, 37. (But cf. Rev. 11:15; 12:10).
[24] Compare the same point of view expressed by Peter in his First Epistle (1:11): "Searching what time or what manner of time the Spirit of Christ which was in them did point unto, when it testified beforehand the sufferings of Christ."
[25] *Beginnings*, IV, 37. [26] So Bruce, p. 111. [27] Abbott-Smith, *Lexicon*, p. 51.
[28] *Ant*. XI, 3, 8. [29] *Decalogue*, 30. [30] *Beginnings*, IV, 38. [31] *Acts*, p. 112.

22 Moses indeed said, A prophet shall the Lord God raise up unto you from among your brethren, like unto me; to him shall ye hearken in all things whatsoever he shall speak unto you.

23 And it shall be, that every soul that shall not hearken to that prophet, shall be utterly destroyed from among the people.

24 Yea and all the prophets from Samuel and them that followed after, as many as have spoken, they also told of these days.

25 Ye are the sons of the prophets, and of the covenant which God made with your fathers, saying unto Abraham, And in thy seed shall all the families of the earth be blessed.

26 Unto you first God, having raised up his Servant, sent him to bless you, in turning away every one of you from your iniquities.

22, 23 The quotation in these two verses is a combination of Deuteronomy 18:15 with perhaps the last part of Leviticus 23:29. This verse in Deuteronomy was also quoted by Stephen (7:37). The primary application in Moses' day was to Joshua, who would be Moses' successor. But the prophecy also looked forward to Christ. Bruce thinks that there was a collection of "Testimonies" from which this passage was taken.[32]

24 **Samuel** is here named as the founder of the great succession of prophets. It is asserted that all **told of these days;** that is, there were Messianic elements in their prophecies.

25 Peter further declared that his hearers were **the sons of the prophets;** that is, they were heirs of the promises of God which were proclaimed by the prophets.

26 **Unto you first** is the order throughout the Book of Acts. Paul, the main figure, made it his regular practice to preach to the Jews first. Only when they rejected his message did he turn to the Gentiles.

Having raised up his Servant perhaps refers primarily to the Incarnation rather than the Resurrection, although the use of *anastēsas* in connection with the latter and the statement in 4:2 (cf. also 26:22, 23) suggest that the Resurrection may be the main reference here.[33]

[32] *Ibid.*, p. 113. For an extensive discussion of these *testimonia*, see C. H. Dodd, *According to the Scriptures* (New York: Charles Scribner's Sons, 1953).

[33] Cf. IB, IX, 61.

CHAPTER IV

And as they spake unto the people, the priests and the captain of the temple and the Sadducees came upon them,

2 being sore troubled because they taught the people, and proclaimed in Jesus the resurrection from the dead.

EXEGESIS

The style here changes to smoother Greek. This is evidently due to the fact that Luke had an Aramaic report of Peter's speech (3:12–26), which of course was delivered in Aramaic. Now he writes in his own free style.

1 The use of the present participle *(lalountōn)*, **as they spake**—better, "as they were speaking" (RSV)—indicates that the speech of Peter and his associates was interrupted. This phenomenon is rather common in Acts (cf. 7:54; 10:44; 17:32; 22:22).

Priests *(hiereis)* is "chief priests" *(archiereis)* in Vaticanus and Ephraemi. The latter reading was adopted by Westcott and Hort, but probably the former is preferable (Nestle). These priests may have been part of the temple guard.

The captain of the temple *(stratēgos tou hierou)* was probably the Sagan, or captain of the priesthood, whose duty it was to keep order in the temple precincts.[1]

The **Sadducees** are mentioned only fourteen times in the New Testament—seven times in Matthew, once each in Mark and Luke, and five times in Acts. In contrast, the Pharisees are named 100 times. About the origin of the Sadducees nothing definite is known.[2] It has commonly been held that they were named after Zadok, perhaps the one mentioned in Ezekiel 44:15; 48:11. At any rate, they were prominent in the priesthood of Jesus' day. Their policy was that of coöperation with the Roman rulers, which made them less popular with the people than were the more nationalistic Pharisees.

2 **Sore troubled** is better than "grieved" (KJV), which suggests today a commendable attitude. But the 1901 rendering is also out-of-date English. The verb *diaponeō*[3] means "worked up, indignant."[4] It is rendered "annoyed" in the Revised Standard Version. Moulton and Milligan translate it "upset" in a papyrus.[5]

In Jesus means "in the case of Jesus."[6] They proved by the resurrection of Jesus that the Sadducean denial of any resurrection was wrong.

EXPOSITION

THE CHURCH'S FIRST PERSECUTION

I. The Apostles' Arrest, Acts 4:1–4.
   A. The Occasion of the Arrest, vss. 1, 2.
   B. The Time of the Arrest, vs. 3.
   C. The Failure of the Arrest, vs. 4.
II. The Apostles' Trial, Acts 4:5–12.
   A. The Personnel of the Court, vss. 5, 6.
   B. The Question of the Court, vs. 7.
   C. The Answer to the Court, vss. 8–12.
III. The Apostles' Victory, Acts 4:13–22.
   A. The Apostles' Secret, vs. 13.
   B. The Apostles' Evidence, vs. 14.
   C. The Court's Consternation, vss. 15, 16.
   D. The Court's Decision, vss. 17, 18.
   E. The Apostles' Reply, vss. 19, 20.
   F. The Apostles' Release, vss. 21, 22.
IV. The Church's Prayer, Acts 4:23–31.
   A. The Apostles' Report, vs. 23.
   B. The Church's Petition, vss. 24–30.
   C. The Lord's Answer, vs. 31.
V. The Church's Prosperity, Acts 4:32–37.
   A. The Unity of the Church, vs. 32a.
   B. The Generosity of the Church, vss. 32b; 34–37.
   C. The Witness of the Church, vs. 33a.
   D. The Grace of the Church, vs. 33b.

1 Schürer, *op. cit.*, II, i, 257 ff. See also the discussion in *Beginnings*, IV, 40.
2 Cf. Schürer, *op. cit.*, II, ii, 31–34.
3 Found only here and in 16:18 in N.T. (cf. Mark 14:4, WH mg.).
4 Robertson, *Word Pictures*, III, 49.
5 VGT, p. 153.
6 Robertson, *Word Pictures*, III, 49.

3 And they laid hands on them, and put them in ward unto the morrow: for it was now eventide.

4 But many of them that heard the word believed; and the number of the men came to be about five thousand.

5 And it came to pass on the morrow, that their rulers and elders and scribes were gathered together in Jerusalem;

---

3 The **ward** (KJV, "hold") was a place where prisoners were kept under guard. The Revised Standard Version translates it "in custody."

4 The American Standard rendering, **came to be,** is much preferable to the King James "was." The latter has led many to assert that 5,000 more converts were added to the church at this time. But the Greek *(egenēthē)* clearly indicates that the total number of believers at this point reached **about five thousand.**

5 **Rulers and elders and scribes** comprised the Sanhedrin at Jerusalem. This consisted of seventy-one members, representing Moses and the seventy elders.[7] They sat in a semicircle, "like half a round threshing-floor," so that all the judges might see each other's faces.[8]

Rulers is evidently equivalent to "chief priests" (cf. Mark 14:53). They are named first, since they were the leading members of the Sanhedrin.

Elders *(presbyteroi)* is a general word for members of the Sanhedrin, which is sometimes designated as the *presbyterion* (cf. 22:5; Luke 22:66). They "owed their position not to office but to blood or wealth or religious prestige." [9]

The **scribes** *(grammateis)* were "a class of learned Jews who devoted themselves to a scientific study of the Law, and made its exposition their professional occupation." [10] They were mainly, but not exclusively, Pharisees.[11]

The Sanhedrin met **in Jerusalem.** The exact meeting place is a subject of dispute. According to Josephus it was just outside

---

I. THE APOSTLES' ARREST (4:1–4)

Those most adversely affected by the healing of the crippled man and the Apostles' preaching in the name of the risen Christ were: *first,* **the priests.** They were the prime and most bitter enemies of Christ from the beginning. The *second* was **the captain of the temple,** a superior priest next in rank to the high priest, who supervised a body of temple orderlies, consisting of lesser priests and Levites. And the *third* consisted of the **Sadducees,** who rejected the oral traditions, the existence of spirits and angels, predestination and fatalism, immortality and the bodily resurrection (see Acts 5:17; 23:6; and Matt. 3:7; 16:1). The Pharisees evidently took no part in the arrest, for reasons that will appear later.

The cause of the arrest appears to have been fourfold: *first,* jealousy of the apostles' influence over the multitude (vs. 2); *second,* the apostles' assumption of teaching authority without formal education or rabbinical ordination (vs. 13a); *third,* possibly a fear that the enthusiasm of the multitude would precipitate trouble with the Roman authorities.[a] But chiefly, Sadducean objection to the doctrine of the resurrection seems to have motivated their arrest. The Pharisees believed in the resurrection; many were favorably disposed to Christianity (Acts 5:34; 23:6); and some believed on Christ (Acts 15:5).

Since the arrest of the apostles was at evening and Jewish trials at night were illegal, the apostles were incarcerated in the public prison until the next day (vs. 3). The utter failure of the opposition's purpose is evidenced by the fact that **many of them that heard the word believed,** and the Church thus increased until **the number of the men came to be about five thousand,** probably meaning the total male Christian communion to that date (exclusive of women and children; cf. Matt. 14:21; Luke 9:14; Acts 5:14).[b]

[7] *Beginnings,* I, 34. There were 70 members plus the president.
[8] *Ibid.* For full discussion of the history and constitution of the Sanhedrin, see HDB, IV, 397–402; HDCG II, 566–569; HDAC, II, 454–457; ISBE, IV, 2688–2690; Schürer, *op. cit.,* II, i, 163–195.
[9] IB, IX, 61. [10] HDCG, II, 582. [11] *Ibid.*

[a] Dummelow, *op. cit.,* p. 823. [b] Lange, *op. cit.,* p. 7–

6 and Annas the high priest *was there*, and Caiaphas, and John, and Alexander, and as many as were of the kindred of the high priest.

---

the Temple Area, on the west side.[12] The Talmud, however, places it inside the Temple Area, at the southern end. Schürer has sought to harmonize these apparently conflicting witnesses.[13] Since the testimony of Josephus is definitely earlier, it should probably be accepted.[14]

6 **And** is rendered by Bruce "including in particular," [15] since the ones named in this verse were members of the Sanhedrin. They are singled out as dominant leaders in that group.

Annas is designated as **high priest.** Actually he held that office from A.D. 6 to A.D. 14 [16] or 15.[17] But he continued to exercise a powerful influence over the ruling high priests. That may easily be inferred from the fact that five of his sons (Eleazar, A.D. 16–17; Jonathan, A.D. 36–37; Theophilus, A.D. 37–41; Matthias, A.D. 43; Ananus II, A.D. 62) were high priests, as well as one son-in-law.[18]

Caiaphas (A.D. 18–36) actually held the office of high priest at this time. He was the son-in-law of Annas (cf. John 18:13). Josephus gives his name as Joseph Caiaphas.[19] Luke 3:2 speaks of the "high-priesthood of Annas and Caiaphas." Annas held the power, Caiaphas the position. Since the time of Ptolemy IV (182–146 B.C.), the Old Testament regulation for the succession of the sons of Aaron had ceased to function. From then on the appointment of high priests was in the control of the Seleucid kings, the Hasmoneans, the Herods, and the Romans.[20] During the New Testament period the office of high priest was the pawn of politicians. Caiaphas held the position longer than anyone else in the first century.

John appears as "Jonathan" in the Western text (D). It is possible that he is to be identified with the son of Annas who followed Caiaphas as high priest in A.D. 36. About **Alexander** we know nothing beyond the statement here that he was **of the kindred of the high priest.** The Greek adjective *archieratikos* (high-priestly) is found only here in the New Testament but occurs in Josephus [21] and an inscription from the time of Augustus.[22]

II. THE APOSTLES' TRIAL (4:5–12)

This is the Christians' first appearance before an ecclesiastical or civil court after Pentecost. Here begins the Christian heritage of persecution, promised by Christ (Mark 10:28–30; John 15:20, 21), and which was to play such an important part in the Church's subsequent history. The Church began by giving a good account of herself before the ruling authorities.

A. The Personnel of the Court (4:5, 6)

And it came to pass on the morrow. Seldom has anyone been honored by trial before such an imposing tribunal. The importance of the case is evidenced by the assemblage of the full Sanhedrin, or Grand Council of the Jews, the national Jewish council of seventy members (possibly seventy-one including the high priest), which consisted of **their rulers,** or the chief priests; the **scribes,** or rabbis, professional teachers; and the **elders,** or those members who were neither scribes nor rabbis, but who with the **rulers** came to judge the apostles. Present with the council was **Annas,** not actually the high priest, but who had been for nine years, and still retained the office in his family and excercised the supreme authority as president of the Sanhedrin (see John 18:13); **Caiaphas,** the nominal high priest and son-in-law to Annas, who had condemned Christ to death; **John,** possibly the son of Annas;[c] **Alexander,** a brother to the famous Greco-Jewish philosopher Philo Judaeus and one of the richest men of his day, according to Josephus;[d] **and the kindred of the high priest,** who probably came to add the weight of their votes to his decision. What a formidable foe the infant Church faced!

The forerunner of the Jewish Sanhedrin

[12] *War*, V. 4. 2. [13] *Op. cit.*, II. i. 191. [14] *Beginnings*, V, 478. [15] *Acts*, p. 118.
[16] *Beginnings*, IV, 41. [17] Bruce, *Acts*, p. 118; also WDB, p. 29. [18] *Beginnings*, IV, 41.
[19] *Ant.* XVIII. 2. 2. [20] *Beginnings*, IV, 42; also I, 30. [21] *Ant.* IV. 4. 7; etc. [22] See VGT, p. 82.

[c] Matthew Henry, *op. cit.*, VI, comment on Acts 4:5, 6.
[d] Flavius Josephus, *op. cit.*, "Antiquities," XIX.V.1.

7 And when they had set them in the midst, they inquired, By what power, or in what name, have ye done this?

8 Then Peter, filled with the Holy Spirit, said unto them, Ye rulers of the people, and elders,

---

7 **Ye** *(humeis)* occurs at the very end of the Greek sentence and expresses the contempt of the questioners. They ask: **By what power** [*dynamis*, might], **or in what name, have ye done this?** The question implies that the Jewish leaders assumed some magical power or name to have been invoked in the healing of the lame man.

8 Normally prisoners before the Sanhedrin were very submissive. Josephus quotes a member of that court as saying that a defendant usually appeared "with his hair dishevelled, and in a black and mourning garment."[23] But Peter was **filled with the Holy Spirit.** This is the key phrase of the Book of Acts (cf. 2:4; 4:31; 9:17; 13:9—exactly the same in Greek as here), together with "full of the Holy Spirit" (6:5; 7:55; 11:24). The term "Holy Spirit" is used some forty times in Acts. The verb **filled** *(pimplēmi)* is found thirteen times in Luke's Gospel and nine times in Acts, and only twice elsewhere in the New Testament (Matt. 22:10; 27:48).

---

was the Gerousia or Senate of Jerusalem, the exact origin of which is in doubt, though it may have emerged from the assembly of 150 chief citizens under Nehemiah (Neh. 5:17). The Gerousia was designed to provide limitations upon the high priest who was supreme in politics and religion in Judea during the Egyptian subjugation in the third century B.C. Its effectiveness was doubtful, however.

In the first Christian century there were local Sanhedrins in eleven toparchies of Judea which were responsible, under the Roman procurator, for the collection of taxes. Further, it appears that those local Sanhedrins were empowered to handle such civil and criminal cases as involved Jews only, or they might refer them to the Jerusalem national Sanhedrin. The appointment and removal of the Jewish high priests were in the power of the Roman procurator or governor, except by concession to the Herods.

Concerning the national Sanhedrin in the first Christian century, Mould remarks:

> The Jerusalem Sanhedrin administered Jewish law covering civil, criminal, moral, and religious questions. Its civil authority was limited to Judea. It could make arrests and its authority over Jews, provided they did not possess Roman citizenship, was practically unlimited except in the matter of capital punishment, which required the procurator's approval. However, the Jews did have the right to kill on the spot any gentile who entered the sacred courts of the temple beyond the Court of the Gentiles. The Jerusalem Sanhedrin consisted of seventy members. The high priest was its head. Apparently it was a self-perpetuating body, filling its own vacancies by members chosen from the ranks of the high-priestly families, the scribes, and the elders. The religious prestige of this body extended wherever there were Jews.[e]

With the destruction of Jerusalem in A.D. 70 the Sanhedrin disappeared, though the synagogue survived.

B. The Question of the Court (4:7)

By what power, or in what name, have ye done this? Note the similarity of this question to the one asked Christ by the chief priests and elders (Matt. 21:23b). The question itself is twofold. *First*, it implies illegality and was intended to incriminate the apostles: "Where are your credentials for the performance of miracles and teaching the people?" **By what power...have ye done this?** The Sanhedrin claimed the exclusive right to authorize religious healers and teachers, and they had given no such rights to the apostles. *Second*, the question hints at magical practices for which, if convicted, the apostles could be condemned to death by the Sanhedrin, if the sentence were approved by the Roman procurator. Such practices were not uncommon, and even the name of Jesus was later used by magicians (see Acts 19:13–20).

C. The Answer to the Court (4:8–12)

Then Peter . . . said unto them. Peter, who cringed before a maid's question and denied Christ in Pilate's judgment hall, now, **filled**

[23] *Ant.* XIV. 9. 4.

[e] Elmer W. K. Mould, *Essentials of Bible History* (New York: Ronald Press Co., rev. ed. 1951), pp. 467, 468.

9 if we this day are examined concerning a good deed done to an impotent man, by what means this man is made whole;
10 be it known unto you all, and to all the people of Israel, that in the name of Jesus Christ of Nazareth, whom ye crucified, whom God raised from the dead, *even* in him doth this man stand here before you whole.
11 He is the stone which was set at nought of you the builders, which was made the head of the corner.
12 And in none other is there salvation: for neither is there any other name under heaven, that is given among men, wherein we must be saved.

---

9 **By what means** *(en tini)* could be rendered "in whom," as the Greek does not indicate whether it is neuter or masculine. Older commentators often held to the latter interpretation, but most modern authorities prefer the former.[24]

Is made whole is *sesōstai.* The same verb, *sōzō,* is translated "saved" in verse 12. Occurring some 111 times in the New Testament, it is translated "save" 94 times in the King James Version. It is found some 56 times in the Gospels and 14 times in Acts. In the Gospels it usually carries the idea of *physical healing.* In Acts the dominant emphasis is on *spiritual salvation.* Verses 9 and 12 of this passage illustrate the transition from the former to the latter. In the Epistles, as would be expected, the regular meaning is the latter.[25]

10 As in his sermon on the day of Pentecost, Peter charged the Jewish leaders with the death of Jesus—**whom ye crucified** (cf. the same phrase in 2:36). But God reversed their action—**whom God raised from the dead.** The Greek phrase *en toutō* may be translated **in him** (masculine; literally, "in this one") or "in this [name]" (neuter). **Whole** is *hygiēs,* from which comes "hygiene."

11 The reference is to Psalm 118:22. The same passage is cited in Mark 12:10 (= Matt. 21:42; Luke 20:17) and I Peter 2:7.[26] **The head of the corner** would seem to suggest a stone at the top of the corner.[27] Knowling, however, writes: "Probably . . . the expression here refers to a foundation-stone at the base of the corner."[28] The same double interpretation attaches to Mark 12:10 and parallels.

12 This verse contains one of the great declarations of the Book of Acts. The utter uniqueness of salvation through Jesus Christ is stated in the very strongest of terms. It should be noted that the immediate context in Psalm 118 (vs. 21) contains the assertion: "thou hast answered me, and art become my salvation."

---

with the Holy Spirit, boldly makes answer to the Sanhedrin (see Luke 12:11, 12). Pentecost makes courageous men out of cowards and witnesses out of moral weaklings. Peter's defense before the court is fourfold. *First,* the miracle of healing was beneficial to the cripple and injurious to no one; **a good deed done** (vs. 9). *Second,* **in the name of Jesus Christ of Nazareth** the impotent man had been made **whole,** and his presence bore undeniable testimony (vs. 10). *Third,* God has outwitted the rulers of the Jews through victory over death: **He is the stone** [Christ] **which was set at nought** [rejected] **of you the builders** [rulers of the Jews], **which was made the head of the corner** [raised up in power] (vs. 11). *Fourth,* Christ is unique in that **neither is there any other name under heaven, that is given among men, wherein we must be saved** (vs. 12). Peter leaves no place for the modern liberal view of "other ways of salvation."

III. THE APOSTLES' VICTORY (4:13–22)

There were three insurmountable obstacles to the designs of the Jewish court on the lives of the apostles: namely, (1) the boldness of the apostles (vs. 13); (2) the evidence of the man made whole (vs. 16); and (3) their fear of the people already convicted of the validity of the risen Christ (vs. 21b).

[24] E.g., Bruce, *Acts,* p. 120; Hackett, *op. cit.,* p. 68; Lenski, *op. cit.,* p. 162.
[25] For exceptions, however, see I Tim. 2:15; James 5:15; Jude 5.
[26] Also in the Epistle of Barnabas 6:4. [27] So IB, IX, 67. [28] EGT, II, 127.

13 Now when they beheld the boldness of Peter and John, and had perceived that they were unlearned and ignorant men, they marvelled; and they took knowledge of them, that they had been with Jesus.

14 And seeing the man that was healed standing with them, they could say nothing against it.

13 The word for **boldness,** *parrēsia,* means "freedom of speech, plainness, openness." It is used again in verses 29 and 31.

The members of the Sanhedrin recognized that Peter and John were **unlearned and ignorant men.** The first adjective, *agrammatoi,* literally means "unlettered." But this does not indicate that the apostles were illiterate. Rather, they were "without technical training in the professional rabbinical schools." [29] However, in the papyri the word does commonly signify one who cannot write. Moulton and Milligan observe: "The great frequency of *agrammatos,* invariably in this sense, suggests that the sneer in Acts 4:13 is intended to picture the Apostles as 'illiterate,' and not merely 'unversed in the learning of the Jewish schools' (Grimm)." [30]

The other adjective, *idiōtai,* is derived from *idios,* "one's own." Knowling comments: "The word properly signifies a private person . . . as opposed to any one who holds office in the State, but as the Greeks held that without political life there was no true education of a man, it was not unnatural that *idiōtēs* should acquire a somewhat contemptuous meaning." [31] A good translation for *idiōtai* would be "laymen." The modern use of "idiot" suggests a "private" person who cannot function properly in public; or, perhaps more particularly, "one who has nothing but his idiosyncracy." [32]

They took knowledge of them, that they had been with Jesus. Perhaps a better translation would be "recognized" (RSV). It has been objected that the rulers already knew this (cf. vs. 2). But Ramsay offers a good solution of the problem by noting that this is just one of a series of things stated here. The Jewish leaders heard "the bold and fluent speech of Peter and John; and yet they observed from their dress and style of utterance that they were not trained scholars; . . . and they further took cognisance of the fact that they were disciples of Jesus." [33]

14 The healed man, no longer a helpless cripple, was **standing with them.** How he happened to be there before the council —whether he had been imprisoned with the apostles or not—we are not told. But his grateful loyalty is seen in his standing by their side, a living testimony to the power of God through His servants.

A. The Apostles' Secret (4:13)

When they beheld the boldness of Peter and John. Courage born of confidence is the most disarming weapon known to man. Here there was no anticipation of objections met by subtile arguments of logic. Rather, the apostles believed so certainly and witnessed so definitely that their faith became contagious, even in testimony to the unbelieving Sanhedrin. The rulers discerned that they were but unschooled laymen, as far as literary education went. Then, however, they learned, from the apostles or elsewhere, that they had been disciples of Jesus Christ, and they seemed to grasp the reason for their superhuman wisdom. That the secret of their power was in Christ at last dawned upon the Sanhedrin.

B. The Apostles' Evidence (4:14)

And seeing the man . . . they could say nothing against it. There is an inescapable logic in the situation before the Sanhedrin. If the apostles' doctrine of the resurrected Christ were false, then the man could not have been healed in Christ's Name. If the man, whom they all knew to have been a cripple for more than forty years (vs. 22), is healed through the Name of Christ, then the doctrine must necessarily be true. The man stands in their midst perfectly whole, through the Name of Christ. Therefore the doctrine of the apostles is true, and consequently, they could say nothing against it. One demonstration of divine power is worth ten thousand theological or philosophical arguments. Christ commissioned His dis-

[29] Robertson, *Word Pictures,* III, 52. [30] VGT, p. 6. [31] EGT, II, 128 f. [32] Robertson *Word Pictures,* III, 52.
[33] W. M. Ramsay, *St. Paul the Traveller and the Roman Citizen* (New York: G. P. Putnam's Sons, 1896), p. 371.

15 But when they had commanded them to go aside out of the council, they conferred among themselves,
16 saying, What shall we do to these men? for that indeed a notable miracle hath been wrought through them, is manifest to all that dwell in Jerusalem; and we cannot deny it.
17 But that it spread no further among the people, let us threaten them, that they speak henceforth to no man in this name.
18 And they called them, and charged them not to speak at all nor teach in the name of Jesus.

---

15 The Greek word for **council** is *synedrion.* This was transliterated in Hebrew and Aramaic in the form *sanhedrin,* which has been taken over into English.[34] It was the supreme court of the Jewish people and was often identified with the council of seventy elders (Num. 11:16). The first mention of it seems to be in Josephus in connection with an incident that took place in 198 B.C.[35] Here it is called the "senate" *(gerousia);* the first occurrence of the name *synedrion* for it is apparently related to the time of Antipater (ca. 47 B.C.).[36] The word occurs twenty-two times in the New Testament—three each in Matthew and Mark, one each in Luke and John, and fourteen in Acts.

16, 17 The question is sometimes raised as to the source of information for this conversation. It is altogether possible that Paul was present. For even if he was too young to be a member of this august body, he may have been one of the younger disciples of the rabbis, who "sat in front of them [in] three rows." [37]

Notable miracle is literally "known sign" *(gnōston sēmeion).* But *gnōston* came to be used in the sense of "notable"; that is, something that is a matter of knowledge. It is a favorite word with Luke, who uses it twice in his Gospel and ten times in Acts (only three times elsewhere in N.T.).

18 The apostles were charged **not to speak . . . nor teach in the name of Jesus.** The two present infinitives indicate that they were to *stop* speaking and teaching. The verb **speak** *(phthengesthai)* is found only here and in II Peter 2:16, 18. The apostles were not to "utter a sound" concerning Jesus.

---

ciples to witness (Acts 1:8), and here is a convincing testimony.

C. The Court's Consternation (4:15, 16)

What shall we do to these men? Having put the apostles out of the court room, the Sanhedrin went into a huddle. They were convinced by the miracle of healing, by the witness of the apostles, by the capitulation of the multitudes to Christ, and by their own consciences, that the doctrine of Christ's resurrection was true. They should have asked: "What shall we do about our relation to Christ's claims upon our lives?" But they hardened their hearts and refused to believe, even though the evidence was undeniable. They only sought to know how they might keep the fame of the miracle, and consequently the name of the risen Christ, from spreading further. It was already **manifest to all that dwell in Jerusalem.** How could they keep it from spreading beyond Jerusalem?[f]

D. The Court's Decision (4:17, 18)

Let us threaten them . . . And they . . . charged them not to speak at all nor teach in the name of Jesus. The court's decision involved three serious considerations: *first,* it was based on no previous apostolic offense: they **let them go, finding nothing how they might punish them** (vs. 21); *second,* it included an official and authoritative command to cease all witnessing, preaching, or teaching in Christ's name, whether to individual, congregation, or multitude, in private or in public (vss. 17b and 18b); and *third,* the command was enforced by an illegal threat of the severest punishment, perhaps even death, should they resume their testimony for Christ, though that testimony had brought only good (vs. 9). Thus the court's decision was groundless, unreasonable, and unjust.

[34] The spelling "Sanhedrim," found in many older works, is incorrect. It was wrongly assumed that it is a Hebrew plural noun.
[35] *Ant.* XII. 3. 3.
[36] See *Ant.* XIV. 9. 3-5, where the word occurs frequently.
[37] Schürer, *op. cit.*, II, i, 193 f.

[f] See notes concerning Sanhedrin on Acts 4:5, 6, relative to the limitations of Jewish authority.

19 But Peter and John answered and said unto them, Whether it is right in the sight of God to hearken unto you rather than unto God, judge ye:
20 for we cannot but speak the things which we saw and heard.
21 And they, when they had further threatened them, let them go, finding nothing how they might punish them, because of the people; for all men glorified God for that which was done.
22 For the man was more than forty years old, on whom this miracle of healing was wrought.
23 And being let go, they came to their own company, and reported all that the chief priests and the elders had said unto them.

---

19 Peter and John presented the issue in such a way that the Jewish leaders had no answer. They could not deny that God's will was supreme.

20 The apostles expressed their dilemma thus: **we cannot but speak;** literally, "we are not able not to go on talking." The message burned in their hearts, as with the prophet Jeremiah (20:9).

21 The members of the Sanhedrin had only one more recourse: **when they had further threatened them**—all one word in the Greek, *prosapeilēsamenoi,* found only here in the New Testament. Threatening is a cheap substitute for reasonable argument.

Glorified God is a favorite Lukan expression. While it is found twice in Matthew and once in Mark, Luke uses it eight times in his Gospel and twice in Acts (cf. 11:18).

22 The cripple had been lame from birth (3:2). Now he was **more than forty years old.** This made the miracle of healing all the more remarkable. His case would normally have been considered absolutely hopeless.

23 **Being let go, they came to their own company.** It is not what one does under compulsion but what one does in his leisure hours that both demonstrates and determines his character. Thomas Macaulay is credited with this wise observation: "The measure of a man's real character is what he would do if he knew he would never be found out."

The chief priests and elders is another way of designating the Sanhedrin. The **chief priests** would consist first of ex-high priests, of which several would still be living. In the three years between the administrations of Annas and Caiaphas (i.e., A.D. 15–18) there were three high priests in office. During the lifetime of Jesus (ca. 5 B.C.—A.D. 30) there were eleven high priests. From the death of Jesus to the destruction of the temple (A.D. 30–70) there were fourteen more. This meant an average term of three years during the first century—twenty-five high priests in seventy-five years—in an office that was supposed to be held for life! [38]

In the second place the **chief priests** would include members of the high-priestly families.[39] It should be noted that the Greek for **chief priests** is *archiereis,* the plural of *archiereus,* which is regularly translated "high priest." But there was only one high priest at a time.[40]

E. The Apostles' Reply (4:19, 20)

Peter and John answered. . . . we cannot but speak the things which we saw and heard. The apostles' answer was resolute, appealing to the consciences and the judgment of the judges (Lange). They clearly placed the responsibility for the continuance of their testimony on the Sanhedrin. You, our judges, profess to serve the same God whom we serve, and since He has commanded us to witness, and has honored our witness as you behold by the evidence before you, should we place your prohibitive command above His positive command? Judge ye. The assumed reply is negative. They are silenced. We must and will continue to witness to Christ's resurrection, was the audacious apostolic reply to the court. They would obey the higher authority.

F. The Apostles' Release (4:21, 22)

They . . . let them go. The court had no alternative. They simply added empty threats of punishment to save face for the court, which they were restrained from inflicting through fear of the popular support of the apostles' teaching, and then released them. Nor does man ever have an alternative when he is forced to face the verities of divine reality.

[38] Cf. Heb. 7:23.
[39] *Beginnings,* IV, 41.
[40] *Ibid.*

24 And they, when they heard it, lifted up their voice to God with one accord, and said,
O Lord, thou that didst make the heaven and the earth and the sea, and all that in them is:
25 who by the Holy Spirit, *by* the mouth of our father David thy servant, didst say,
Why did the Gentiles rage,
And the peoples imagine vain things?
26 The kings of the earth set themselves in array,
And the rulers were gathered together,
Against the Lord, and against his Anointed:
27 for of a truth in this city against thy holy Servant Jesus, whom thou didst anoint, both
Herod and Pontius Pilate, with the Gentiles and the peoples of Israel, were gathered together,
28 to do whatsoever thy hand and thy counsel foreordained to come to pass.

---

24 The language of this verse seems to indicate praying in concert, a rather infrequent feature in Biblical praying. The extreme circumstances called for spontaneous, earnest praying **with one accord.**

Lord is *despota*. It is the opposite of *doulos*, "slave" (cf. Luke 2:29). Thayer says that *despotēs* "denoted absolute ownership and uncontrolled power." [41] It may be translated here, "Sovereign Lord." [42] The reference to Jesus (vss. 27, 30) shows that the prayer was addressed to God the Father.

25 The Greek of this verse is very difficult to translate. But probably the best sense is given by the Revised versions.[43] The King James Version omits **the Holy Spirit,** which is found in the oldest manuscripts.[44] It was by the inspiration of the Spirit that David wrote these words. The quotation is from Psalm 2:1, 2 (LXX).

26 **His anointed** is "His Christ" (Greek), or "His Messiah" (Hebrew). The Septuagint has *Christou*. This second Psalm was accepted by the Jews as Messianic.[45]

27 **Thy holy Servant Jesus** is probably the best translation.[46] Jesus was both the "Servant of the Lord" of Isaiah and the "Son of David," born in David's city, Bethlehem.[47] **Whom thou didst anoint** is probably a reference to Jesus' baptism, when the Holy Spirit came upon Him and the Father's voice from heaven acclaimed Him "my beloved Son."

Jesus' appearance before **Herod** is described only by Luke (23:6–12). This, of course, is Herod Antipas, ruler of Galilee (4 B.C.—A.D. 39). The part played by **Pontius Pilate** (A.D. 26–36) is related in all four Gospels. It seems natural to take **Herod** as representing "the kings" of verse 26 [48] and **Pilate** "the rulers." Tertullian gives another interpretation of verses 25 and 26. He writes: "In the person of Pilate 'the heathen raged,' and in the person of Israel 'the people imagined vain things,' 'the kings of the earth' in Herod and 'the rulers' in Annas and Caiaphas, were gathered together against the Lord, and against His anointed." [49]

28 The people, both Gentiles and Israelites, raged against Jesus and put Him to death. In this they acted with free wills and so were morally accountable. At the same time they did only what God had **foreordained to come to pass.** This paradox of human freedom and divine sovereignty is one of the great mysteries of life.

IV. THE CHURCH'S PRAYER
(4:23–31)

They . . . lifted up their voice to God with one accord. This prayer embodies three considerations. *First*, there was the release and report of the apostles to the church (vs. 23). How natural that **being let go, they came to their own company.** So does man ever do. They required the understanding and prayer support of the whole Church of which they were but the advance representatives. There they shared their burdens and their victories in Christ. *Second*, the Church took seriously the situation and prayed in

[41] *Op. cit.*, p. 130. [42] So RSV.
[43] Bruce suggests "that which our father David, Thy servant, said by the mouth of the Holy Spirit" (*Acts*, p. 127). Cf. C. C. Torrey, *Composition and Date of Acts* (Cambridge: Harvard University Press, 1916), pp. 17 f.
[44] Aleph A B E. [45] See Edersheim, *op. cit.*, II, 716. [46] Cf. discussion on 3:13.
[47] Cf. Matt. 1:1; 2:1.
[48] While Herod Antipas was actually tetrarch rather than king, he was popularly given the latter designation as a courtesy title (cf. Matt. 14:9; Mark 6:14; etc.).
[49] Tertullian, "On the Resurrection of the Flesh," chap. XX, *The Ante-Nicene Fathers*, eds. A. Roberts and J. Donaldson (Buffalo: Christian Literature Publishing Co., 1887), III, 559.

29 And now, Lord, look upon their threatenings: and grant unto thy servants to speak thy word with all boldness,
30 while thou stretchest forth thy hand to heal; and that signs and wonders may be done through the name of thy holy Servant Jesus.
31 And when they had prayed, the place was shaken wherein they were gathered together; and they were all filled with the Holy Spirit, and they spake the word of God with boldness.
32 And the multitude of them that believed were of one heart and soul: and not one *of them* said that aught of the things which he possessed was his own; but they had all things common.
33 And with great power gave the apostles their witness of the resurrection of the Lord Jesus: and great grace was upon them all.

---

29 These early believers did not pray for protection but for power—to go on preaching the word **with all boldness,** and to take the consequences. This prayer was literally fulfilled (vs. 31, last clause), and it is not surprising to find them back in prison in the next chapter.

30 They asked only that their preaching should be authenticated by manifestations of divine power **through the name of thy holy Servant Jesus.** It is amazing that this prayer is largely a song of praise rather than a sob of petition. It is strikingly similar in spirit to the hymns of the first two chapters of Luke.

31 That God had heard their prayer was proved by the fact that **the place was shaken wherein they were gathered together.** The answer to their prayer was that **they were all filled with the Holy Spirit.** Bruce comments: "While this was a fresh filling of the Spirit, it could not be called a fresh baptism."[50] As a result of this **they spake** (literally, "went on speaking") **the word of God with boldness.**

32 This paragraph (vss. 32–35) is a striking parallel to 2:44–47. Both express not only a close unity of fellowship but also a community of goods.[51] The first clause of this verse underscores the former idea, the second and third clauses the latter.

But the sweeping statement, **they had all things common** (cf. 2:44) must be interpreted in the light of the context. We have noted that in 2:45 the three imperfects clearly indicate that *from time to time* members of the Christian community were selling properties to care for needs that arose within the group. That this did not involve the abolition of private property is shown in the context here by two facts: (1) the case of Barnabas is singled out for special emphasis; (2) Peter told Ananias that he did not have to sell his property and that after he had done so, the money was still his to use as he wished (5:4). It is evident, then, that the general statements about community of goods here and in 2:44 must be modified in terms of the context in both places.

Multitude is *plēthos*. Deissmann points out that in contemporary inscriptions "The word has a technical sense also in the usage of religious associations: it designates the associates in their totality, the *community* or *congregation*."[52] So it does not mean primarily "multitude" or "mass," but *community*.

33 The apostles **gave** their witness, or testimony. The word *apedidoun* (imperfect, "were giving") means "give up or back, restore, return, render what is due." There is perhaps the suggestion here that the apostles felt a sense of obligation to give their testimony; they owed it to Christ to do so.

The **resurrection** was one of the main emphases in early apostolic preaching. It was the proof of Christ's divine sonship and saviourhood.

---

faith unitedly,[g] intelligently, and effectively that God would **grant unto** [his] **servants to speak . . .** [the] **word with all boldness.** *Third,* God heard their prayer and granted their

[50] Bruce, NIC, p. 107.
[51] For a comparison of this with the Qumran community, see Sherman Johnson, "The Dead Sea Manual of Discipline and the Jerusalem Church of Acts," *The Scrolls and the New Testament*, ed. K. Stendahl (New York: Harper and Brothers, 1957), pp. 131 f.
[52] Adolph Deissmann, *Bible Studies*, trans. A. Grieve (Edinburgh: T. & T. Clark, 1901), pp. 232 f.

[g] See Additional Note I, *One Accord*, at end of Chapter I.

34 For neither was there among them any that lacked: for as many as were possessors of lands or houses sold them, and brought the prices of the things that were sold,
35 and laid them at the apostles' feet: and distribution was made unto each, according as any one had need.
36 And Joseph, who by the apostles was surnamed Barnabas (which is, being interpreted, Son of exhortation), a Levite, a man of Cyprus by race,
37 having a field, sold it, and brought the money and laid it at the apostles' feet.

---

34 There are here two imperfects, as well as two present participles: "For as many as were *(hypērchon)* possessors of fields or houses, selling *(polountes)* [them] were bringing *(epheron)* the prices of the things that were being sold *(pipraskomenōn)*." All this suggests, as in chapter 2, an occasional selling of property to meet needs that arose, rather than a single mass sale of all property and putting everything in a common treasury. The latter idea would be expressed by the aorist tense.

35 This verse has three imperfects, as does 2:45. Note the force of this: "And they were placing *(etithoun)* [them] at the feet of the apostles, and distribution was being made *(diedideto)* to each even as any one was having *(eichen)* a need."

36 **Joseph,** a Levite of Cyprus, is singled out for special mention. The apostles called him **Barnabas.** The Greek word *paraklēsis* can mean either "consolation" (KJV) or **exhortation.** Eiher meaning may also be derived from the possible Aramaic original. Macgregor suggests: "Here a good translation is *Son of encouragement*, which includes both ideas."[53]

37 Barnabas **sold** a field and **brought** the money and **laid** it at the feet of the apostles. The three aorist tenses here are in striking contrast to the imperfects of verses 34 and 35.

---

request with a renewed spiritual manifestation, **and they spake the word of God with boldness.** God's answers are sure.

V. THE CHURCH'S PROSPERITY (4:32–37)

The prosperity of the Church consisted in (1) its spiritual unity (vs. 32a), (2) its boundless generosity (vs. 32b, 34–37),[h] (3) its undaunted witness to Christ (vs. 33a), and (4) the measureless grace of God's manifest presence and approval (vs. 33b).

Additional Note I

Christian Communism in the Book of Acts[i]

There are two passages in the Acts of the Apostles which are especially used by some people as proof-texts for the argument that real communism was practiced in the Christian Church after Pentecost. These passages as they appear in the King James Version are as follows: "And all that believed were together, and had all things common; And sold their possessions and goods, and parted them to all men, as every man had need" (Acts 2:44–45).

"Neither was there any among them that lacked: for as many as were possessors of lands or houses sold them, and brought the prices of the things that were sold, And laid them down at the apostles' feet: and distribution was made unto every man according as he had need" (Acts 4:34–35).

These passages supposedly describe a genuine "Christian communism"—a society in which private property was abolished and where the ruling principle could be stated in the words, "From each according to his ability, to each according to his need"—or at least, in which there was a redistribution of wealth, in which all shared equally.

It is evident that this communism, if it was practiced, did not survive for long. Why did it not survive? Two answers fairly well include those which have been offered. The first answer is that the communistic practices were God's will for the Christian community, but that selfishness and other non-Christian

[53] IB, IX, 73.

[h] See Additional Note I, *Christian Communism*, at end of Chapter IV.

[i] J. Harold Greenlee, *The Asbury Seminarian* (Wilmore, Kentucky: Asbury Theological Seminary, Publisher; Fall and Winter, 1950), Vol. V, 92–94. Used by permission.

attitudes made God's ideal impossible and forced a return to "capitalism," where each person had his own personal property. This answer assumes that if we could establish a truly Christian city or country today, it would then be God's will to have such communism again. Indeed, this assumption helped lead to the establishment of the Shaker settlements, the experiment at Zion, Illinois, and other such ill-fated attempts during the past century.

The second answer, which is probably the more common one in our day, is that these early Christians were generous to a fault, becoming starry-eyed idealists who were either so overcome by the joy of their Christian fellowship that they gave their money away unwisely, or else were convinced that Jesus would return to set up His kingdom so soon that money and possessions were worthless. At least one Sunday School lesson commentator, who seems quite sound in many respects, implies that the collections for the Christians in Jerusalem which Paul mentions in his epistles (I Cor. 16:1–4; II Cor: 8–9; etc.) were necessary because this mistaken experiment in communism had so impoverished the Jerusalem Christians that they were thrown on the mercies of other Christians who had not been involved.

Neither of these two answers is satisfactory. In reply to the first, there seems to be abundant evidence that God has ordained the principle of private ownership. The right of private ownership, which is capitalism, and the legitimate rewards of one's own initiative and work, are far more consistent than is communism with the high evaluation which God has placed upon us as individuals, made in His own image. The commandments "Thou shalt not steal" and "Thou shalt not covet" are based upon the right of private property. Sharing with others, based upon love and issuing in love, would be impossible if nothing were our own to share.

The second answer suggested is equally unacceptable. The New Testament nowhere warns us that what these early Christians did in these matters was mistaken. If they were mistaken, then the New Testament is not a completely safe guide for our lives. This conclusion we do not accept.

It seems that the whole assumption of communism in Acts, even a so-called "Christian communism," is due to a misunderstanding of the author of Acts. This misunderstanding is of two kinds. One is a misunderstanding of the author's point of view. He is trying to emphasize very strongly the attitude of generosity which prevailed among the Christians. He was describing an attitude of heart which would be found in any truly Christian home. He meant that the Christian love was so sincere that, if someone was in need, others would share with him as though their possessions were his. A pagan writer about 100 A.D. described the Christians as Acts intends to describe them, with these words: "He who has gives to him who has not without grudging. And if there is a man among them who is poor and needy and they have not an abundance of necessaries, they fast for three days that they may help the needy with the necessary food." Here is not communism, but Christian love. Moreover, the author of Acts shows that he is not describing complete communism by the story of Ananias and Sapphira (Acts 5:2, 4); for he writes that Peter rebuked Ananias with the words, "While it remained, was it not thine own? And after it was sold, was it not in thine own power?" How could Peter have said this if all the Christians were expected to surrender their possessions?

The second misunderstanding of Acts in these passages is a misunderstanding of what the author actually said. The description given in Acts 2:45 and 4:34, 35 is a picture of progressive selling of possessions and distribution of the money. Every verb—five of them—in these descriptions is a Greek imperfect tense, describing not a single act, as implied in the KJV and RSV, but a continuing, repeated, or customary action. We might read them in this way: " . . . they were selling . . . and were distributing . . ."; and " . . . they were bringing the prices . . . and they were placing them . . . and it was being distributed . . ." In other words the disciples were prompted by Christian love to aid those of their company who were in need, *whenever anyone was in need*, even if it meant selling possessions to provide the assistance. This assistance was evidently carried out by the apostles for the church, rather than being a purely individual matter, as Acts 4:35 points out. It may, therefore, have involved some sort of systematic contributions by those who were able. But it is clearly not a case of everyone's selling all his possessions and giving it all to the church.

The misunderstanding is not lessened, moreover, by the translations, ". . . and parted them to all men, as every man had need" (2:45), and ". . . unto every man according as he had need" (4:35). The meaning of each of these passages is more nearly, ". . . and distributed them so often as anyone had need." Indeed, in both passages in the original the words "had need" are preceded by the Greek particle *an* which makes the idea more indefinite—that is, the distribution was made to people *when and if* they were in need.

The translation in 2:44, "*had* all things common," can also easily be misunderstood to mean that the disciples owned everything in common. The verb *echo* usually does mean "to have," in the sense of "to possess."

However, this verb is also used (1) to refer to the people's opinion of John the Baptist—"they *counted* him as a prophet" (Matt. 14:5), "for all *hold* John as a prophet" (Matt. 21:26), "for all men *counted* John, that he was a prophet indeed" (Mark 11:32); (2) to refer to the people's opinion of Jesus —"they *took* him for a prophet" (Matt. 21:46); and (3) in St. Paul's words in Phil. 2:29, "*Hold* such in reputation"—that is, consider such people precious. The meaning of the verb in these passages, in other words, is to have or to hold an opinion about someone or something, or to consider someone or something in a certain light. It is this meaning which should be used in Acts 2:45, which gives the meaning that "they considered all things common"—that is, they had the truly Christian spirit of the motto, "What is mine is yours to share, if you need it."

Perhaps a paraphrase or free translation may summarize what we believe to be the proper meaning of these two passages we have been discussing:

> And all who believed were accustomed to consider their possessions as common property; and they would sell their properties and possessions and distribute them to anyone who was in need (Acts 2:44–45).
>
> For neither was anyone in need among them; for as many as were owners of fields or houses would sell them and bring the price of the things which were sold and would place it at the feet of the apostles, and it would be distributed to anyone who was in need (Acts 4:34–45).

The idea that the Christians were attempting to set up a "communistic utopia" rests upon a view which reads the author's glowing description of vital Christian stewardship and love among what was doubtless a large percentage of poor people, and mistakenly forces into his words a description of a legalistic system which was forced upon the entire Christian community. A fair interpretation of revelant passages does not seem to bear out such a Utopian thesis.

CHAPTER V

But a certain man named Ananias, with Sapphira his wife, sold a possession,
2 and kept back *part* of the price, his wife also being privy to it, and brought a certain part, and laid it at the apostles' feet.

EXEGESIS

1 **Ananias** means "Jehovah is gracious." It is the Greek form of the Hebrew name Hananiah, found frequently in the Old Testament.[1] **Sapphira** (cf. "sapphire") means "beautiful." Klausner calls attention to the fact that in June, 1923, there was unearthed in Jerusalem a beautiful ossuary with this name inscribed on it in Hebrew and Greek, and thinks it probable that this Sapphira is meant.[2] **Possession** here represents land, as indicated by verse 3. The Greek word *ktēma* is so used in Josephus.[3] **Being privy to** is "sharing the knowledge of." The Greek verb *sunoida* is used elsewhere in the New Testament only in I Corinthians 4:4, where it has the connotation of consciousness—"For I know nothing against myself."

2 **Kept back** is translated "embezzled" by Lake and Cadbury.[4] They note that the Greek word always implies "that the theft is secret" and "that part of a larger quantity is purloined"; also that the term is commonly used of misappropriation of public funds by state officials. The same word, *nosphizō*, is used in Joshua 7:1 (LXX) of Achan, who "took of the devoted thing." In the middle voice, as here, it means "set apart for one-

EXPOSITION

Part I

THE CHURCH'S FIRST DIVINE JUDGMENT

I. Divine Judgment and Hypocrisy, Acts 5:1-11.
   A. The Occasion of the Judgment, vss. 1, 2.
   B. The Detection of Hypocrisy, vs. 3.
   C. The Necessity of the Judgment, vs. 4.
   D. The Administration of the Judgment, vss. 5, 6.
   E. The Accomplice in Hypocrisy, vss. 7-10.
   F. The Effects of the Judgment, vs. 11.

II. Divine Judgment and Revival, Acts 5:12-16.
   A. The Church's Prayer Answered, (Acts 4:29-30) 5:12.
   B. The Apostles' Popular Support, vs. 13.
   C. The Revival's Spiritual Fruit, vs. 14.
   D. The Alleviation of Human Suffering, vss. 15, 16.

Part II

THE CHURCH'S SECOND PERSECUTION

I. Imprisonment and Deliverance of the Apostles, Acts 5:17-20.
   A. The Arrest and Imprisonment, vss. 17, 18.
   B. The Divine Deliverance, vs. 19.
   C. The Divine Commission, vs. 20.
   D. The Apostles' Obedience, vs. 21a.

II. Charges and Reply of the Apostles, Acts 5:21b-33.
   A. The Court's Design, vs. 21b.
   B. The Court's Consternation, vss. 22-25.
   C. The Apostles' Rearrest, vss. 26, 27a.
   D. The Court's Charge, vss. 27b, 28.
   E. The Apostles' Reply, vss. 29-32.
   F. The Court's Indignation, vs. 33.

III. Defense and Release of the Apostles, Acts 5:34-42.
   A. The Advice of Gamaliel, vss. 34-39.
   B. The Court's Decision, vs. 40.
   C. The Apostles' Consolation, vs. 41.
   D. The Apostles' Persistence, vs. 42.

[1] There are fourteen different individuals by this name listed in *The Westminster Dictionary of the Bible*.
[2] Joseph Klausner, *From Jesus to Paul*. Translated from the Hebrew by W. F. Stinespring (New York: Macmillan Co., 1943), pp. 289, 290.
[3] *War*, IV, 9, 11. [4] *Beginnings*, IV, 50.

3 But Peter said, Ananias, why hath Satan filled thy heart to lie to the Holy Spirit, and to keep back *part* of the price of the land?

4 While it remained, did it not remain thine own? and after it was sold, was it not in thy power? How is it that thou hast conceived this thing in thy heart? thou hast not lied unto men, but unto God.

---

self." It occurs again in verse 3 and is found elsewhere in the New Testament only in Titus 2:10, where it is translated "purloining" in the King James and American Standard versions and "pilfer" in the Revised Standard Version. It has the same meanings in the papyri.[5]

3 **Satan** was originally a Hebrew common noun meaning "adversary" (cf. I Kings 11:14). In Job (1:6, etc.) and Zechariah (3:1, 2) it is the name of the angel who accuses men before God. In the New Testament it is used as the equivalent of the Greek *diabolos*, "slanderer, false accuser."[6] The Hebrew word was taken over into Aramaic, Greek, and English.

The expression **lie to the Holy Spirit** when compared with verse 4b—**thou hast not lied unto men, but unto God**—clearly affirms both the personality and deity of the Holy Spirit. The latter statement means that Ananias had not lied *only* to men, but, more particularly and seriously, to God.

4 The first two questions in this verse prove conclusively that there was no universal or required community of goods in the Early Church at Jerusalem. Ananias did not have to sell the land nor did he have to donate all the proceeds of the sale. His sin was definitely that of deception, though greed and pride were motivating causes. He wished to receive special commendation

---

Part I

I. DIVINE JUDGMENT AND HYPOCRISY (5:1–11)

This incident of hypocrisy and consequent divine judgment is the first recorded "fly in the precious ointment" (cf. Eccl. 10:1) of the Apostolic Church. The offense is glaring and the punishment severe. Both are intended as a warning to the church, for all time, of God's displeasure with insincerity and its deadening threat to the spiritual life of the church. When insincerity moves into the church, God moves out.

A. The Occasion of the Judgment (5:1, 2)

No one was under compulsion to sell his property and pool the proceeds in the church. Such was purely voluntary (vs. 4). However, the practice appears to have become popular with the Christian community. It gave good standing to the Christians, and herein lay the danger. Who Ananias and Sapphira were, why they sold all their property, or whether they had been sincere believers, we are left to conjecture. We are only told, as Weymouth graphically translates the passage, that "Ananias with his wife, Sapphira, sold some property, but, with her full knowledge and consent, dishonestly kept back part of the price received for it, though he brought the rest and gave it to the apostles."

Plumptre[a] thinks that the account of Ananias' experience here must be understood against the background of the act of Barnabas in selling his property and giving the proceeds to the church (cf. Acts 4:36, 37). Ananias thought he could get the same results of praise and power, acquired by Barnabas at the cost of genuine sacrifice, by a cheaper means. Plumptre sees in Ananias,

> . . . a strange mingling of discordant elements. Zeal and faith of some sort had led him to profess himself a believer. Ambition was strong enough to win a partial victory over avarice; avarice was strong enough to triumph over truth. The impulse to sell came from the Spirit of God; it was counteracted by the spirit of evil, and the resulting sin was therefore worse than that of one who lived altogether in the lower, commoner forms of covetousness. It was an attempt to serve God and mammon; to gain the reputation of a saint, without the reality of holiness.[b]

There are certain respects in which the sin of Ananias resembles that of Achan (Josh.

[5] VGT, p. 430. [6] Compare Mark 1:13 with Matt. 4:1 and Luke 4:2.

[a] E. H. Plumptre, "The Acts of the Apostles," *Commentary on the Whole Bible*, ed. C. J. Ellicott (Grand Rapids: Zondervan Publishing House, n.d.), VII, 26.
[b] *Ibid.*

5 And Ananias hearing these words fell down and gave up the ghost: and great fear came upon all that heard it.

---

from the church, as did Barnabas. But he was too greedy to give everything.

Heart is used in a wider sense in the Scriptures than commonly in English today. Rackham states: "In Hebrew psychology the heart, the centre of life, corresponds most to our will or purpose."[7] That is the meaning here.

5 **Gave up the ghost** is a decidedly old-fashioned expression for "died,"[8] even though retained in the version of 1901. The Greek is literally "expired"—*exepsyxen*, "breathed out" (his life). In the New Testament it is used only here, in verse 10, and in 12:23 of the death of Herod Agrippa I. Hobart writes: "The very rare word *ekpsychein* seems to be almost altogether confined to the medical writers and very seldom used by them."[9]

Did Peter kill Ananias and Sapphira? The

7:1), as also that of Gehazi (II Kings 5: 20–27). However, Ananias' sin was greater than that of either Achan or Gehazi in that he had greater light and consequently his hypocrisy was more glaring. Ananias appears to have been afflicted with the sin of "double-mindedness" against which James warns (James 1:8; 4:8). Possibly it was from this incident that James was impressed with the peril of such a state. It was not the fact that he offered only a part that constituted his sin, but rather because he offered the part as though it were the whole. He was guilty of purloining (cf. Titus 2:10), or "stealthy and dishonest appropriation."

Plumptre understands Peter's rebuke (vs. 3) to imply,

> . . . .the perversion of conscience and will, just at the moment when they seemed to be, and, it may be, actually were, on the point of attaining a higher perfection than before. The question 'Why' implies that resistance to the temptation had been possible (James 4:7).[c]

Insincerity and incomplete obedience are the lessons clearly taught, and the penalty is spiritual death. While on earth, Christ's most severe condemnations were of hypocrisy in the lives of the religionists. The church begins with this same divine disapprobation on insincerity.

B. The Detection of Hypocrisy (5:3)

Why hath Satan filled thy heart to lie to the Holy Spirit?

Ananias' sin was no unpremeditated accident. He had deliberately agreed with his wife to deceive the church by professing to give all the proceeds from the sale, while he was giving only a part. The motive appears to have been twofold: *first*, selfishness in retaining part of the price; and *second*, glory in the recognition for generosity which he hoped to receive from the church. He tarried and toyed with temptation and Satan deceived and ensnared him. Nothing can be clearer than the apostolic belief in the personality of Satan, from this word of Peter. The Holy Spirit of God to whom he lied revealed to Peter Ananias' sin. Sin is ever revealed where the Spirit of God is present.

C. The Necessity of the Judgment (5:4)

Thou hast not lied unto men, but unto God.

All sin is finally against God, and though it may never be detected by man, it is never hidden from God. David realized this fact when he exclaimed: "Against thee, thee only, have I sinned, and done that which is evil in thy sight" (Psa. 51:4a). Weymouth reads: "How is it that you have cherished this design in your heart?" Thus it was an act for which Ananias was fully responsible, and in which he attempted to deceive God so as to realize his unworthy purposes. The judgment that followed was necessary to label hypocrisy in the church as forever condemned of God.

D. The Administration of the Judgment (5:5, 6)

Ananias hearing these words fell down and gave up the ghost (vs. 5a).

Sin will not only be exposed, but it must

---

[7] *Op. cit.*, p. 66.
[8] Cf. Adam Clarke: "'Gave up the ghost' is a very improper translation here" (*op. cit.*, I, 715).
[9] *Op. cit.*, p. 37.
[c] *Ibid.*

6 And the young men arose and wrapped him round, and they carried him out and buried him.

7 And it was about the space of three hours after, when his wife, not knowing what was done, came in.

8 And Peter answered unto her, Tell me whether ye sold the land for so much. And she said, Yea, for so much.

---

account does not so state. It rather indicates that Peter exposed their sin and in the case of Sapphira announced her death. But he pronounced no curse upon the offenders.

Much has been written on the question as to whether their death was a direct judgment of God or a sudden shock (not a supernatural miracle). Most of the older conservative commentators take the former position. Knowling, for instance, writes: "It therefore cannot be regarded as a narrative of a chance occurrence or the effect of a sudden shock caused by the discovery of guilt in St. Peter's words." [10] He further states: "The whole narrative shows that in each case the death was caused by the judgment of God." [11] Adam Clarke says that it was "by an immediate judgment of God." [12] But F. F. Bruce, who is probably the leading conservative New Testament scholar in England today, seems to argue in favor of death by shock.[13] He writes that "the shock produced by the sudden sense of the enormity of such a crime caused their death." [14] However, in his last of three commentaries on Acts, he says: "It was an evident act of judgment." [15]

6 **Young men** is literally "younger men" *(neōteroi)*. Rackham thinks this term refers to "a body of men devoted to such offices as burying." [16] But most recent commentators agree with the judgment of Knowling, who says: "The fact that they are called simply *neaniskoi* [young men] in ver. 10 seems decisive against the view that reference is made to any definite order in the Church."[17] Probably "the younger men" were simply those most fitted for such heavy work.

The exact meaning of *synesteilan*, **wrapped him round,** is rather uncertain. Hobart says that it was used by medical writers in the sense of "bandage a limb" or "compress by bandaging." Here he thinks it means "to shroud." [18] Lake and Cadbury translate it "gathered up." [19] Probably the young men wrapped some kind of cloth around each body,[20] as is the custom in handling dead bodies. There was very likely neither time nor inclination for elaborate preparations for burial. The bearers **carried him out;** that is, outside the walls of the city. Only kings or other notables were buried by the Jews inside the walls.

8 **Answered** *(apekrithē)* in the New Testament often means nothing more than "addressed," although it could mean here that Peter answered Sapphira's unrecorded greeting. The latter, however, seems unlikely.

---

die in the presence of God's revealed holiness. It was not Peter's words, but God's revealed wrath against the sin of hypocrisy, that occasioned the death of Ananias. It was when Isaiah saw God in His exaltation and holiness that he cried out: "Woe is me! for I am undone" (Isa. 6:5a). Sin withers and dies in the presence of God's holiness as surely as snow melts when the sun shines on it. Unless the sinner detaches himself from sin, through repentance and renunciation, he must die with it. God destroys sin, and it remains only for the church to dispose of its remains. **The young men . . . carried him out and buried him** (vs. 6). The immediate effect on the church was most salutary and is graphically portrayed in Weymouth's translation: "all who heard the words were awe-struck."

E. The Accomplice in Hypocrisy (5:7-10)

And it was about the space of three hours after, when his wife, not knowing what was done, came in (vs. 7).

It was either at a subsequent service of the

[10] EGT, II, 142. [11] *Ibid.*, p. 145. [12] *Op. cit.*, I, 716. [13] *Acts*, p. 134.
[14] NBC, p. 905. [15] NIC, p. 114. [16] *Op. cit.*, p. 67. [17] EGT, II, 143.
[18] *Op. cit.*, pp. 37 f. [19] *Beginnings*, IV, 51.
[20] Perhaps their own mantles (EGT, II, 143). For further discussion of the meaning of this word, see Hackett, *op. cit.*, p. 75.

9 But Peter *said* unto her, How is it that ye have agreed together to try the Spirit of the Lord? behold, the feet of them that have buried thy husband are at the door, and they shall carry thee out.

10 And she fell down immediately at his feet, and gave up the ghost: and the young men came in and found her dead, and they carried her out and buried her by her husband.

11 And great fear came upon the whole church, and upon all that heard these things.

---

9 **Try** is perhaps better than "tempt" (KJV). Lake and Cadbury remark: "The concept of 'tempting the Lord' (cf. Exodus xvii. 2) seems to be the primitive one of 'seeing how far you can go.'"[21]

11 The word **church** *(ekklēsia)* is found here for the first time in Acts.[22] The only previous occurrences in the New Testament are in Matthew, where it is found three times.[23] As is commonly known it comes from the verb *ekkaleō*, which means "call out." Hence it means "a convened assembly." Deissmann writes: "This self-bestowed name rested on the certain conviction that God had separated from the world His 'saints' in Christ, and had 'called' or 'convened' them to an assembly, which was 'God's assembly,' 'God's muster,' because God was the convener."[24]

The word was first used for an assembly of the free citizens of a Greek city. This secular usage is found in the New Testament in Acts 19:32, 39, 41, where it is translated "assembly."[25] It was used because the citizens were summoned ("called out") by a herald. "This naturally suggests that in the Bible the reference is to God in Christ calling men out of the world."[26]

The background for the use of this term is to be found in the Greek translation of the Old Testament. "It was the Septuagint which really gave the word *ekklesia* to the N.T., after it has acquired its specific value."[27] Bruce says: "In LXX it is used for the 'congregation' of Israel, the nation in its theocratic aspect, organized as a religious community."[28]

Sir William Ramsay notes that Paul first used *ekklēsia* for a local congregation of believers. Then he used it for "the Unified Church." Both these meanings are found in Acts.[29] Cadbury writes: "Its origins are in Judaism, and it is this Jewish Greek term, with its LXX associations of dignity and of intimate relation with God rather than the usages of secular Greek, or any memory of etymology, that gave the term its appropriateness."[30] Macgregor sums up the signi-

---

church three hours after her husband's death, and probably at a later stated "hour of prayer," or three hours later in the same service in which her husband died, that Sapphira appeared. She had become an accomplice with her husband in his sin, and she intended to carry through with the deception. Peter repeated the question to her, to which she replied as had her husband. She was rebuked by the apostle and the judgment of death swiftly followed. The evident lesson is that as "none . . . liveth to himself" (Rom. 14:7a), so no man sins unto himself, but he must ever draw another into his evil company and partnership. God desired the infant church to learn that sin is contagious and that the one influenced to evil shares the guilt and judgment of the one who influences. Sin is a lonely creature and must soon die in solitude.

F. The Effects of the Judgment (5:11)

And great fear came upon the whole church, and upon all that heard these things, or as Weymouth reads: "all who heard of this incident."

The incident incited three kinds of fear: *first*, a reverential fear of God's holiness and majesty which was revealed; *second*, a disciplinary fear, by reason of the divine judgment against hypocrisy which fell upon and purified the church; and *third*, an arresting

[21] *Beginnings*, IV, 52. [22] It is not genuine in 2:47 (see footnote under 2:47).

[23] Matt. 16:18; 18:17 (twice). It occurs 24 times in Acts, 22 times in I Corinthians, 40 times in Paul's other epistles, twice in Hebrews, four times in the General Epistles and 20 times in Revelation, a total of 115 times in N.T.

[24] Adolph Deissmann, *Light from the Ancient East*. Trans. L. R. M. Strachan (New York: George H. Doran Co., 1927), p. 112. (Hereafter cited as LAE.)

[25] In the other 112 occurrences in N.T. it is regularly translated "church."

[26] Karl Ludwig Schmidt, "The Church," *Bible Key Words*. Trans. J. R. Coates (New York: Harper & Brothers, 1951), p. 24. Schmidt notes that the term occurs about 100 times in the Septuagint (ibid., p. 51.)

[27] *Ibid.*, p. 25. [28] *Acts*, p. 136. [29] William Ramsay, *St. Paul the Traveller*, pp. 124–127. [30] *Beginnings*, V, 387 f.

12 And by the hands of the apostles were many signs and wonders wrought among the people; and they were all with one accord in Solomon's porch.
13 But of the rest durst no man join himself to them: howbeit the people magnified them;
14 and believers were the more added to the Lord, multitudes both of men and women;
15 insomuch that they even carried out the sick into the streets, and laid them on beds and couches, that, as Peter came by, at the least his shadow might overshadow some one of them.

---

ficance of the New Testament usage by saying: "The use of the word by the Christians certainly implies the claim that they, rather than the Jews, were the true 'people of God.'" [31]

12 **Solomon's porch** (better, Portico) was a meeting place of the early Christians in Jerusalem, who would be too numerous by this time to meet in any ordinary hall.

13 The meaning of this verse is not perfectly clear. The first problem is the interpretation of **all** in verse 12. Some refer it to the apostles alone.[32] But probably it denotes the entire Christian community. On the first view, **the rest** would mean the other believers in contrast to the apostles. But this seems unnatural. The second view would indicate that it was non-believing Jews who were afraid to join the Christians. In spite of much disputing about the matter, that seems the most satisfactory conclusion.

14 On the surface there seems here a contradiction of verse 13a, especially as interpreted above. The best explanation is that verse 13 describes a general attitude of awe, fear, and respect on the part of the people (cf. vs. 11), which kept outsiders from joining the Christians insincerely. The miracles performed by the apostles (vs. 12a) added to the reaction produced by the sudden death of Ananias and Sapphira. The final result was that "more than ever believers were added to the Lord" (RSV). The mention of **women** as well as **men** is to be noted, since the Jews did not usually count women in the congregation of Israel. But Luke was probably a Gentile, with more of the Greek point of view. Knowling well remarks: "This constant reference to the share of women in the ministry of the Gospel and the life of the Church is characteristic of St. Luke in both his writings." [33]

15 It is obvious that **insomuch** does not connect with the previous verse but rather with 12a. So the King James translators were probably justified in placing all the intervening matter in parentheses. **Streets** is literally "broadways" *(plateias)*. It may well refer to the "squares" or plazas where the open markets were maintained. It definitely indicates main thoroughfares or places where the people congregated in large numbers.

Luke uses two words here for **beds** and **couches.** The first, *klinarion,* is found only here in the New Testament. The second, *krabattos,* means a "pallet." Luke uses two other words for bed, *klinē* and *klinidion.* The latter is found only in his Gospel. Hobart comments: "The variety of words employed by St. Luke for the beds of the sick is remarkable." [34]

The question naturally arises whether the

---

fear that fell upon the unbelieving who saw or heard of the incident. God is one, but His manifestations and administrations are as varied as the needs of men.

II. DIVINE JUDGMENT AND REVIVAL (5:12–16)

It will be noted that the miraculous events of verses twelve through sixteen are in answer to the prayer of the church following the release of the apostles from prison (see Acts 4:30). Indeed, the tragedy of divine judgment on hypocrisy within the Church had intervened (vss. 1–10), and served to inspire reverence and respect for God and His apostles (vs. 11). God then, as now, worked in mysterious ways His wonders to perform, and indeed "his ways [are] past tracing out!" (Rom. 11:33b). These happenings are the unbroken continuance of the miraculous character of the church from Pentecost onward (Acts 2:43). It was due

[31] IB, IX, 79.
[32] E.g., Hackett, *op. cit.*, p. 77. However, he takes "the rest" as referring to those who were not Christians.
[33] EGT, II, 146.
[34] *Op. cit.*, p. 116.

16 And there also came together the multitude from the cities round about Jerusalem, bringing sick folk, and them that were vexed with unclean spirits: and they were healed every one.

---

last clause of verse 15 reflects faith or superstition on the part of the people. But it is easier to raise the question than it is to put it to rest with a satisfactory answer. The language of the passage, especially when coupled with the context in verses 12a and 16, seems to indicate a connection between Peter's shadow and the healing miracles. However, it should be noted that it is not directly stated here that Peter's shadow actually caused healing to take place. Probably the best solution that could be offered is that of F. F. Bruce, who says: "Peter's shadow was as efficacious a medium of healing power as the hem of his Master's robe had been." [35]

16 A great crowd gathered from the cities, or towns, around Jerusalem,[36] bringing their sick to be healed. They also brought those that were **vexed with unclean spirits.** The verb *ochleō* is found only here in the New Testament. It is from *ochlos*, "crowd," and means in the passive, as here, "be in a tumult." It thus vividly suggests the con-

---

to the prayer of the church, however, that the Pentecostal revival continued.

The unity of the disciples in the Lord (vs. 12b) bespoke their invincibility and afforded the necessary channel for divine manifestation and operation (vs. 12a). Their location was most advantageous. **Solomon's porch** was a spacious court on the east side of the temple, bearing Solomon's name, and was supposed to have been a remnant of the original temple built by him (see II Chron. 4:9; 6:13). The particular location appears to have been advantageous both to Christ and to the Christians (see John 10:23; Acts 3:11; Acts 5:12). So far the Christians had not broken with the temple worship.

The popular support accorded the Christians, and the apostles in particular, is indicated by Luke's words, **howbeit the people magnified them** (vs. 13b), or as Weymouth reads: "the people held them in high honour." God's presence always magnifies human instruments. "Little is much, when God is in it." The resultant revival was more than excitement and mere sensationalism. It was characterized by genuine spiritual fruit. Says Luke: **And believers were the more added to the Lord, multitudes both of men and women** (vs. 14). Two special notes are striking in this passage: *first*, the believers **were added** [joined] **to the Lord**; and *second*, **women** are mentioned as of importance in the church for the first time since Pentecost. Finally, the healings and demon expulsions (vss. 15, 16) represent the beneficent implications of the Gospel extended to suffering humanity. Such was the example that Jesus personally set for the church (Matt. 9:32–35), and such was the commission which He gave His disciples (see Matt. 9:36–38; 10:8 and Mark 3:14, 15). While the so-called modern "social gospel" is scripturally invalid, the social implications of the personal Gospel of Christ are unlimited. Little wonder, or matter, that the pagan thinkers confused magical concepts with the divine miracles of healing (vs. 15b). It is not said, nor is it to be supposed, that the shadow of Peter actually healed anyone. A sharp distinction is made here by Luke between **sick folk** and **them that were vexed with unclean spirits** (vs. 16). The recognition of demon possession and demon expulsion is evident in the Apostolic Church. The modern church may be overlooking an important matter here. It became common practice in the primitive church to appoint a special officer to each church whose ecclesiastical duty consisted in expelling demons from the possessed through the use of Jesus' name.[d]

PART II

THE CHURCH'S SECOND PERSECUTION

I. IMPRISONMENT AND DELIVERANCE OF THE APOSTLES (5:17–20)

The occasion of this second arrest of Peter and John is found in Acts 5:12–16, which incident has been dealt with previously. At

[35] NIC, p. 118. [36] *Eis* ("unto," KJV) is not found in Aleph A B.

[d] See Additional Note I on *Demon Possession and Expulsion*, at end of Chapter V.

17 But the high priest rose up, and all they that were with him (which is the sect of the Sadducees), and they were filled with jealousy,

18 and laid hands on the apostles, and put them in public ward.

---

dition of those who were demon-possessed.

17 **All they that were with him** would seem to refer to the Sanhedrin.[37] But the following clause in parenthesis would, if taken strictly, include only that part of the Sanhedrin that was composed of **Sadducees.** It is clearly indicated here that the high-priestly family was largely Sadducean.

Sect is *hairesis,* from which comes the English word "heresy." The Greek term has had a long and varied history. Coming from *haireō,* "take," it first meant a "capture." But since the middle, *haireomai,* means "choose," the noun was used for "choice." The third step was "that which is chosen," and so one's "chosen opinion." It was only a short transition then to the modern meaning of "heresy." According to Grimm–Thayer the word has this sense only once in the New Testament, in II Peter 2:1.[38] Abbott–Smith would add I Corinthians 11:19 and Galatians 5:20.[39] To these three the King James Version adds Acts 24:14. The other five times the word occurs in the New Testament—all in Acts—it is translated "sect." Probably the best rendering in I Corinthians and Galatians is "dissension" or "faction," and in Acts "party" or "sect." Bartlett goes so far as to say: "*Hairesis* in the common sense of 'heresy' never occurs in N T." [40] He defines it as "a factious division, or the spirit that underlies it." [41] Its use here for "the party of the Sadducees" is paralleled in Josephus, who applies the term to Pharisees, Sadducees, Essenes, and Zealots. He calls them "sects of philosophy," [42] in keeping with the Greek usage of that day.[43] For the phrase **which is the sect** Lake and Cadbury prefer "the local school" [44] and Bruce "the local party." [45]

In Matthew 27:18 and Mark 15:10 it is stated that Pilate knew the chief priests had delivered Jesus to be killed because of their envy of His popularity. Here the same group is **filled with jealousy.** The word *zēlos* is the origin of the English word "zeal." It carries that meaning in seven out of its seventeen occurrences in the New Testament. The other times it means envy or jealousy. The King James translation here, "indignation," completely misses the distinctive connotation of the term.

18 **Public ward** is *tērēsei dēmosia.* The first word—meaning a place where people are kept or guarded—has already been noted in 4:3. It occurs again in the New Testament only in I Corinthians 7:19, in the sense of "a keeping" of the commandments of God. The second word is found only in Acts. In the other three occurrences it is used in the feminine dative form as an adverb meaning "publicly." Since that is also the exact form here Lake and Cadbury would so translate it in this passage—"publicly put them in custody." [46]

---

their first trial they had been strictly warned by the court not to speak nor teach in the name of Jesus (Acts 4:18b). This prohibition they boldly disregarded, and the great revival continued.

A. The Arrest and Imprisonment (5:17, 18)

But the high priest rose up . . . and laid hands on the apostles, and put them in public ward.

Whether by the high priest is meant Annas, the president of the Sanhedrin, or Caiaphas, the actual high priest, it is difficult to know. The former is likely indicated. The high priest, probably Annas the president of the Sanhedrin, was supported by the Sudducean party in his indignation or "angry jealousy" (Weymouth) and intentions against the apostles, at the sight of the influence of the apostles over the multitude. Generally, the arrest was based on the apostles' disregard of the court's command, their continued preaching in Christ's Name, their miracles of healing, and their influence over the people. However, more really and specifically, it was based on the Sadducean opposition to their doctrine of the resurrection and the operations of the Holy Spirit,

[37] So Bruce, *Acts*, p. 140. [38] Thayer, *Lexicon*, p. 16. [39] *Op. cit.*, p. 13.
[40] J. V. Bartlett, "Heresy," HDB, II, 351. [41] *Ibid.* [42] Josephus, *Ant.* XVIII, 1, 1, 6.
[43] HDB, II, 351. [44] *Beginnings*, IV, 56. [45] *Acts*, p. 140. [46] *Beginnings*, IV, 57.

19 But an angel of the Lord by night opened the prison doors, and brought them out,
and said,
20 Go ye, and stand and speak in the temple to the people all the words of this Life.
21 And when they heard *this*, they entered into the temple about daybreak, and taught.
But the high priest came, and they that were with him, and called the council together, and
all the senate of the children of Israel, and sent to the prison-house to have them brought.

---

19 **Angel** comes from the Greek *angelos*, which means "messenger." So some would translate rather than transliterate the word and interpret it as referring to a human messenger who opened the doors. For instance, Macgregor writes: "Here some providential intervention is suggested, perhaps the connivance of a jailer or the help of a friend." [47] Even such a thoroughly conservative commentator as F. F. Bruce says: "The doors were opened by divine agency, whether the agent was a supernatural being or a human 'messenger' of God." [48] But *angelos* in the New Testament—as in the case of *mal'akh* in the Old Testament—is used most commonly for "spiritual attendants of God," as Bruce notes.[49] It seems best, therefore, to take the language in its more usual sense as indicating a miracle performed by direct divine intervention.

Prison here is *phylakē*, from *phylassō*, "guard." Hence it means a guardhouse.

20 **Life** is capitalized in the American Standard and Revised Standard versions, taking the word as having technical significance. In Aramaic the same word can be translated both "life" and "salvation." [50] It apparently has that twofold sense here. The angel would, of course, be speaking in Aramaic to these Jewish disciples.

21 **The council** and **all the senate of the children of Israel** are not two groups but one.

---

both of which the Sadducees denied. It would appear that these court officials so undignified themselves as to have personally laid hands on the apostles and put them in the common prison (vs. 18). As at their first arrest, it was evening, and therefore they could not be legally tried by the Sanhedrin before the next day. Thus they were compelled to spend the night in the common prison among vile criminals. It was not fear of their escape, but desire to stop their work, that accounted for their imprisonment.

B. The Divine Deliverance (5:19)

But an angel of the Lord by night opened the prison doors, and brought them out. God has a master key that will unlock all the prison doors where His servants may be incarcerated by the enemy. "The Lord knoweth how to deliver the godly out of temptation" (II Pet. 2:9). The irony of the situation rests in the fact that the Lord sent an angel to deliver the apostles, while the Sadducees, who dominated the Sanhedrin, did not believe in angels. Man's unbelief does not alter divine reality. The existence and ministry of angels is a clear testimony of the Scriptures (see Additional Note I, Angelology, at end of chapter X). The apostles' deliverance from prison was perfectly right, since it was accomplished by God; and its purpose was to encourage the apostles in their dark hour (**by night** [the angel] **opened the prison doors**), and the church that doubtless prayed for their release, and to confound and convince the rulers who fought against Christ.

C. The Divine Commission (5:20)

Go ye, and stand and speak in the temple to the people all the words of this Life.

The apostles were divinely delivered that they might resume their ministry, not that they might retire into solitude and safety. If it is for personal safety or profit that man seeks deliverance of God he may have little hope of divine intervention. God saves man that he may serve Him (see I Thess. 1:9b).

The commission was to **Go ye, and stand and speak in the temple.** Here was where the people would gather for worship, according to the Law. They were to enter into the very temple itself and boldly stand and proclaim **all the words of this Life,** the whole Gospel of Jesus Christ, to a people condemned to death by the Law. God's true church is ever a "going concern," even in the face of opposition and danger.

[47] IB, IX, 82. [48] NIC, p. 120. [49] *Ibid.*, p. 120, n. 29. [50] *Beginnings*, IV, 57.

22 But the officers that came found them not in the prison; and they returned, and told,

Macgregor says: "*The council and all the senate* are one and the same body, the Jewish Sanhedrin."[51] Schürer writes: "There can be no question as to the identity of the two conceptions *synedrion* and *gerousia*."[52] We cannot agree, however, with Schürer in his conclusion that Luke erroneously supposed them to be two separate bodies. The "and" *(kai)* between the two is epexegetic; that is, the second expression explains further the meaning of the first. It may be translated "even." **Senate** is from the Latin *senatus*, which indicates a council of old men. The Greek word *gerousia*[53] is the source of "geriatrics," the study of old age. The term simply emphasizes the fact that the Sanhedrin was composed of the elders of the people.

Prison-house is still another term for the jail where these disciples were held. The Greek *desmōtērion* comes from *deō*, "bind," and *tēreō*, "keep"; hence, a place where bound prisoners were kept. It occurs also in verse 23, in 16:26, and in Matthew 11:2.

22 **Officers** is *hypēretai*, which occurs again in verse 26. The literal meaning of the word is "under-rowers." The background is the Roman *trireme*, a warship equipped with three banks of oars. The slaves who manned the lowest bank of oars would be far down in the hold of the ship, where they would be the most helpless in case of the sinking or capture of the vessel. Hence they were the lowest order of galley slaves. But the word finally came to be used of any attendant or servant. The translation **officers** for such a humble attendant reflects the modern use of "officer" for an ordinary policeman, for instance. The **officers** were "probably Levites of the Temple watch, under the command of the captain."[54]

D. The Apostles' Obedience (5:21a)

They entered into the temple about daybreak, and taught.

Without hesitation the apostles, encouraged and fortified by their deliverance and the renewed commission, appear to have entered directly into the temple where they resumed their teaching. Weymouth says, "they went into the temple just before daybreak," or as soon as the doors were opened. The divine commission is ever the divine enabling.

II. CHARGES AND REPLY OF THE APOSTLES (5:21b–33)

In this account we have very much of a repetition of the first trial of the apostles as recorded in Acts 4:1–22, with, however, certain important differences which will appear. The rulers' indignation, or "angry jealousy," as Weymouth translates it, was greatly heightened at the apparent defiance of the apostles and their increased influence over the people. They are now wrathfully resolved to stop this whole business forever.

A. The Court's Design (5:21b)

But the high priest . . . called the council together, and all the senate of the children of Israel. The president of the Sanhedrin planned and purposed to make this second trial of the apostles more auspicious and effective than the first. At the first trial the regular court plus certain important persons was present. For this second trial an extraordinary session of the Sanhedrin was evidently called (see exegetical note). This contained, it would appear, the Sanhedrin, with its seventy elders, and two other judicatories, one of which was stationed in the outer-court temple gate, and the other in the inner Gate Beautiful, each of which was comprised of twenty-three judges. The full Sanhedrin thus assembled would have consisted of 116 judges. While the high priest sought to overawe and intimidate the apostles and Christians in general by assembling this extraordinary court and thus finally to stop their activities, God on the other hand turned it into a larger opportunity for the Christian witness.

B. The Court's Consternation (5:22–25)

Behold, the men whom ye put in the prison are in the temple standing and teaching the people (vs. 25). What an embarrassment it

[51] IB, IX, 83. [52] Schürer, *op. cit.*, II, i, 172, n. 464. [53] Found only here in the New Testament.
[54] Bruce, *Acts*, p. 141.

23 saying, The prison-house we found shut in all safety, and the keepers standing at the doors: but when we had opened, we found no man within.

24 Now when the captain of the temple and the chief priests heard these words, they were much perplexed concerning them whereunto this would grow.

25 And there came one and told them, Behold, the men whom ye put in the prison are in the temple standing and teaching the people.

26 Then went the captain with the officers, and brought them, *but* without violence; for they feared the people, lest they should be stoned.

27 And when they had brought them, they set them before the council. And the high priest asked them,

28 saying, We strictly charged you not to teach in this name: and behold, ye have filled Jerusalem with your teaching, and intend to bring this man's blood upon us.

The word for **prison** is *phylakē*, guard-house, as in verse 19. Evidently these different expressions all refer to the same place.

23 **Keepers** is *phylakas*, a word found only here and in 12:6, 19. It is very closely related to the word noted just above. That is feminine, indicating a place. This is masculine, denoting a person. It means "guard" or "sentry."

24 For **captain of the temple,** see on 4:1. For **chief priests** see the exegesis of 4:23. Knowling says: "The word is probably used as including the heads of the twenty-four courses, those who had been high priests and still retained the title, and also those referred to in iv. 6." [55] Schürer defines **chief priests** as consisting "in the first instance, of the high priests properly so called, i.e. the one actually in office and those who had previously been so, and then, of the members of those privileged families from which the high priests were taken." [56]

Them probably refers to **these words,** not the apostles.[57] It must be remembered that **temple** refers to the open courts of the Temple Area and not to a building.

26 The word for **violence** is *bia*, which can also be translated "force." It occurs only in Acts (four times).

27, 28 The first part of verse 28 is treated as a question in the King James Version, but as a declaration in the Revised versions. The word **asked** at the end of verse 27 is the reason for the former. Knowling argues for

---

must have occasioned the president to have summoned this extraordinary court and called it to order, only to find the prisoners docketed for trial, whose arrest and incarceration he had personally conducted the evening before, were missing from the jail. **The officers that came found them not in the prison** (vs. 22a). Man purposes, but God disposes. No prison is sufficiently secure to hold God's true servants. Even Paul was "an ambassador in bonds" (Eph. 6:20), and considered himself not the prisoner of man, but of the Lord Jesus Christ (see Eph. 3:1; 4:1; Philemon 1, 9).

No blame could be placed on the prison guards, for they had done their duty well. Upon learning of the prisoners' escape, the high priest, the temple captain, and the chief priests seem to have recognized that it was by supernatural means that the apostles escaped. Their real concern is expressed by the narrator in his words: **they were much perplexed concerning them whereunto this would grow** (vs. 24b); or in Weymouth's translation, "they were utterly at a loss with regard to it, wondering what would happen next." They had not long to wonder. As if to add to their consternation, a messenger appeared and announced to them: **Behold, the men whom ye put in the prison are in the temple standing and teaching the people.**

C. The Apostles' Rearrest (5:26, 27a)

[They] **brought them, but without violence; for they feared the people, lest they should be stoned** (vs. 26).

The apostles' influence seems to have reached an all-time high, which was doubtless due to a knowledge of their divine deliverance from prison, the many benefits received from God at the hands of the people, and the special manifestations of divine power and favor on their lives and ministry. Fear of stoning by the multitude

[55] EGT, II, 151. [56] Schürer, *op. cit.*, II, i, 206. [57] So Hackett, p. 79, Knowling, EGT, II, 151.

29 But Peter and the apostles answered and said, We must obey God rather than men.
30 The God of our fathers raised up Jesus, whom ye slew, hanging him on a tree.

---

the latter.[58] To adopt this it would probably be better to translate *epērōtēsen* (vs. 27) "questioned," as in the Revised Standard Version. That would simply mean that the declarations of verse 28 were a part of the questioning, or examination.

Strictly charged is literally "with a charge we charged"—a typical Hebraism. In the papyri *parangelia* has the meaning "injunction," [59] which would seem to fit well here. However, Lake and Cadbury think this translation "is probably both too negative and too technical." [60] They render the expression, "We emphatically enjoined," which comes rather close to suggesting an "injunction." The reference is to the command recorded in 4:18.

This name reflects the avoidance by the Jews of the name Jesus, as does **this man's** (cf. 4:17). This same policy is followed consistently in the Talmud.

When the high priest complained that the apostles **intend to bring this man's blood upon us,** he evidently forgot the tragic words recorded in Matthew 27:25. There the people, incited by the priests, had said to Pilate: "His blood be on us, and on our children." But Knowling interprets the last clause of verse 28 as indicating fear of vengeance by the people, rather than divine punishment.[61]

29 With this verse compare 4:19. The statement here is more definite and emphatic, as might be expected. Controversy usually sharpens men's wits and words.

30 **God . . . raised up Jesus** was by many of the older commentators taken as a reference to the resurrection.[62] But probably the majority opinion today would refer to God's sending Jesus to be the Messiah. Hackett defines it as meaning "sent into the world." [63] This was also the view of Calvin,[64] of Gloag,[65] of Brown [66] and others. Bruce comments: "Probably not of the resurrec-

---

only restrained the officers from violently beating and dragging the apostles from the temple. Evidently the apostles accompanied them readily and willingly, possibly having been entreated of the officers, knowing that He who had delivered them from prison would deliver them in court.

D. The Court's Charge (5:27b, 28)

Behold, ye have filled Jerusalem with your teaching (vs. 28).

Having placed the apostles in the midst of this august assembly, arranged as it was in a semicircle, the high priest brought a threefold charge against them. *First*, they had violated the previous command of the court not to teach in Christ's name; *second*, they had filled Jerusalem with the Christian doctrine; and *third*, they had made the rulers of Israel responsible for the death of Christ (vs. 28). Matthew Henry[e] sees in the *second*, disorderly conduct in the disturbance of the public peace through the teaching of an exciting doctrine; and in the *third*, sedition and faction, with a view to setting the people against the rulers. The latter charge doubtless reflects the guilt of their own consciences. It is noteworthy that they were not charged with breaking jail.

E. The Apostles' Reply (5:29–32)

But Peter and the apostles answered (vs. 29a).

Without denial or hesitation, the apostles replied to the charges, indicating in each instance that the rulers were fighting a losing battle against God. *First*, they replied that God's authority was greater than man's, and since they served Him, they said, **We must obey God rather than men** (vs. 29b). They reasoned, *second*, that Jesus was the especially appointed messenger of God whose

[58] EGT, II, 152. [59] VGT, p. 480. [60] *Beginnings*, IV, 58. [61] EGT, II, 153.
[62] E.g., A. C. Hervey, "Acts of the Apostles," *Pulpit Commentary*, ed. H. D. M. Spence and J. S. Exell (Grand Rapids: Wm. B. Eerdmans Publishing Co., 1950), I (of "Acts"), 160. [63] *Op. cit.*, p. 81.
[64] John Calvin, *Commentary on the Acts of the Apostles* (Grand Rapids: Wm. B. Eerdmans Publishing Co., 1949), I, 215.
[65] Paton J. Gloag, *A Critical and Exegetical Commentary on the Acts of the Apostles* (Edinburgh: T. & T. Clark, 1870), I, 189.
[66] David Brown, "Acts," *A Commentary Critical, Experimental, and Practical on the Old and New Testaments*. Edited by R. Jamieson, A. R. Fausset, David Brown (Grand Rapids: Wm. B. Eerdmans Publishing Co., 1948), VI, 31.

[e] Matthew Henry, *op. cit.*, VI, Comment on Acts 5:27b, 28.

31 Him did God exalt with his right hand *to be* a Prince and a Saviour, to give repentance to Israel, and remission of sins.
32 And we are witnesses of these things; and *so is* the Holy Spirit, whom God hath given to them that obey him.
33 But they, when they heard this, were cut to the heart, and were minded to slay them.

---

tion, but the inauguration of His ministry."[67]

The word for **slew** is *diacheirizō*, found only here and in 26:21. It means literally "have in hand" (from *cheir*, "hand"). But in later writers it came to signify "lay hands on, kill," as here. It gives at least a bit of suggestion of the violent way Jesus was treated by the Jewish leaders.

Tree is *xylon*, which literally means "wood." It refers primarily to anything made of wood. It is used of the "staves" (better, "clubs") connected with the arrest of Jesus, and of the "stocks" which held Paul and Silas in Philippi (Acts 16:24). But in ten out of the nineteen times it occurs in the New Testament, it is translated "tree." Here, in 10:39; 13:29; Galatians 3:13; and I Peter 2:24 it refers to the Cross. The Galatian passage quotes the Old Testament statement (Deut. 21:23): "Cursed is every one that hangeth on a tree." This was an integral part of the meaning of Calvary: Christ became accursed for us.

31 But Jesus' shameful treatment by men was matched by His exaltation by God the Father **with his right hand,** or "at his right hand" (ASV margin).[68] The word **exalted** is a reminder of Isaiah 52:13. For **Prince** see the notes on 3:15. The Greek word *archēgos* is used in the Septuagint for Jephthah in Judges 11:6 (B text). **Saviour** *(sōtēr)* is used significantly in Judges 3:9, where it is said that "Jehovah raised up a saviour to the children of Israel, who saved them." So now Christ had been raised up as a Saviour or Deliverer, **to give repentance to Israel,** and **remission of sins.** Hackett says of **repentance**: "i.e., the grace or disposition to exercise it." [69] **Repentance** and **remission** are similarly united in Luke 24:47. It has been suggested that **repentance** is "the condition He imposes as a Prince" and **remission of sins** "the reward He offers as a Saviour." [70]

32 **Witnesses of these things.** This is what Jesus had said they would be (Luke 24:48). The primary meaning of *rhēmatōn* is "words," but the best translation here is probably **things.** [71]

The **Holy Spirit** is also a witness (cf. John 15:26, 27). He witnessed both to and through the apostles. Knowling comments: "Here we have also the twofold witness—the historical witness borne to the facts—and the internal witness of the Holy Ghost in bringing home to men's hearts the meaning of the facts." [72]

Then comes the significant statement that the Holy Spirit is **given to them that obey him.** Faith and obedience can never be divorced in Christian experience. We receive the Holy Spirit and His cleansing by faith (cf. 15:8, 9), but this also comes only by obedience.

33 *Dieprionto*, **they . . . were cut to the**

---

crucifixion at their hands was a direct and vicious affront to God Himself. And *third*, they gave the answer to the second charge of the court, to the effect that the popularity of the Christian doctrine was due to the work of God through His risen Christ, who was now supplanting the Jewish ecclesiastical rulers and teachers (vs. 31). *Finally*, they frankly identified themselves as propagators (witnesses) of the whole and claimed the cooperation and approbation of God. Thus they placed full responsibility upon the court.

F. The Court's Indignation (5:33)

They . . . were cut to the heart, and were minded to slay them. Like maddened beasts, wounded and inescapably cornered, they now saw as their only alternative the destruction of their pursuers. They literally "were sawn asunder"[f] or became violently enraged

[67] *Acts*, p. 143.
[68] Compare the same uncertainty in the parallel passage in 2:33. "At" is used in both places in RSV.
[69] *Op. cit.*, p. 81.
[70] T. E. Page, *Acts of the Apostles* (London: Macmillan and Co., 1886), p. 114.
[71] Cf. Knowling: "the words standing for their contents, i.e., the things, the facts" (EGT, II, 154).
[72] EGT, II, 155.

[f] Dummelow, *op. cit.*, p. 825.

34 But there stood up one in the council, a Pharisee, named Gamaliel, a doctor of the law, had in honor of all the people, and commanded to put the men forth a little while.
35 And he said unto them, Ye men of Israel, take heed to yourselves as touching these men, what ye are about to do.

---

heart, is found only here and in 7:54. Literally it means, "They were sawn asunder." It indicates a state of very sharp vexation, amounting to inward rage. Knowling comments: "Here we have not the pricking of the heart, ii. 37, which led to contrition and repentance, but the painful indignation and envy which found vent in seeking to rid themselves of the disciples as they had done of their Master." [73]

34 The name **Pharisee** appears here for the first time in Acts (cf. 4:1). The term comes from the passive participle of the Aramaic word *perash,* meaning "to separate." Hence the literal sense is "the separated ones." The Pharisees probably originated with the Hasidim (pious ones), who were opposed to the Hellenizing influence of the Seleucids. When Antiochus Epiphanes attempted to force Hellenism on the Jews at the point of the sword, the Hasidim joined the Maccabees in revolt. But when the later Maccabees sought political power, the Hasidim—whose interests were wholly religious—withdrew. Bruce sums up the significance of "separated ones" very well in the following statement: "This name probably indicated both their general tendency to withdraw themselves from contact with those who were careless about ceremonial purity and, in particular, their withdrawal from their alliance with the Hasmoneans after the success of the revolt against the Seleucids in the time of Antiochus IV (175–163 B.C.)." [74]

Apparently the name Pharisee came into use in the time of John Hyrcanus (135–105 B.C.).[75] But it was Queen Alexandra (76–67 B.C.) who first favored this party. "Thenceforth their influence was paramount in the religious life of the Jewish people." [76] Bruce sums up the situation in the period we are studying thus: "Under Herod (37–4 B.C.) their power increased, but in N T times they were in a minority on the Sanhedrin, though their popular support was such that their opponents could not disregard them." [77] The Judaism that survived the fall of Jerusalem and the destruction of the temple in A.D. 70 was Pharisaic Judaism.

Gamaliel, like his grandfather Hillel, was noted for his liberal attitude. He was one of the leading rabbis of his day. Schürer quotes the following statement from the Mishna: "Since Rabban Gamaliel the elder died there has been no more reverence for the law; and purity and abstinence died out at the same time." [78]

---

and **were minded to slay them.** Justice was forgotten and judges' benches were forsaken as personal passion dethroned reason, bared wicked fangs, and viciously panted for blood. "They were disposed to kill the Apostles" (Weymouth).

III. DEFENSE AND RELEASE OF THE APOSTLES

(5:34–42)

Had not the court been restrained by the cool and wise advice of Gamaliel, the rulers probably would have stoned the apostles, as they later did Stephen. However, their work was not done. Three important things are said about Gamaliel; namely, he was **a Pharisee, a doctor of the law,** and he was **had in honor of all the people** (vs. 34). Thus he was best qualified for this defense. Gamaliel was the teacher of Saul who became Paul the apostle (Acts 22:3), and he was the grandson of the great Hillel and the most influential rabbi of his time.[g] His reason for defense of the apostles seems to have sprung from his party affiliation (a Pharisee), and thus his regard for the doctrine of the resurrection, his favorable impression of the lives and ministry of the apostles, his sense

[73] *Ibid.* [74] Bruce, NIC, p. 123, n. 42. [75] WDB, p. 476. [76] *Ibid.*

[77] Bruce, *Acts*, p. 145. Cf. the statement of Josephus (*Ant.* XVIII, 1, 4): "But they [the Sadducees] are able to do almost nothing of themselves; for when they become magistrates . . . they addict themselves to the notions of the Pharisees, because the multitude would not otherwise bear them."

[78] Schürer, *op. cit.*, II, i, 364. Gamaliel died A.D. 57 or 58. He was the first of seven teachers to be given the honorary title "Rabban" (EGT, II, 156).

[g] *Ibid.*

36 For before these days rose up Theudas, giving himself out to be somebody; to whom a number of men, about four hundred, joined themselves: who was slain; and all, as many as obeyed him, were dispersed, and came to nought.

37 After this man rose up Judas of Galilee in the days of the enrolment, and drew away *some of the* people after him: he also perished; and all, as many as obeyed him, were scattered abroad.

38 And now I say unto you, Refrain from these men, and let them alone: for if this counsel or this work be of men, it will be overthrown:

39 but if it is of God, ye will not be able to overthrow them; lest haply ye be found even to be fighting against God.

---

36 The mention of **Theudas** here creates a real problem. The only known insurrectionist named Theudas is thus described by Josephus: "Now it came to pass, while Fadus was procurator of Judea, that a certain magician, whose name was Theudas, persuaded a great part of the people to take their effects with them, and follow him to the river Jordan; for he told them he was a prophet, and that he would, by his own command, divide the river, and afford them an easy passage over it." [79] Fadus made short work of this movement, beheading its leader. [80]

But the difficulty rises from the fact that Fadus became procurator after the death of Agrippa I in A.D. 44, whereas Gamaliel's speech here was much earlier. It cannot be denied that the problem is a serious one, but the best solution is that suggested by Bruce: "It is quite likely that Gamaliel is referring to another Theudas, who flourished before A.D. 6." [81]

37 The mention of this date (A.D. 6) is due to the statement that **after this man** [i.e., Theudas] **rose up Judas of Galilee,** and the latter's rebellion occurred in A.D. 6. Josephus describes it as follows: "A certain Galilean, whose name was Judas, prevailed with his countrymen to revolt, and said they were cowards if they would endure to pay a tax to the Romans." [82]

The time of this rebellion against Rome is dated **in the days of the enrolment.**[83] There is general agreement that this refers to the census taken by Quirinius, legate of Syria, in A.D. 6, when Archelaus was deposed as ruler of Judea.[84]

38, 39 The change from **if this counsel . . . be of men** (*ean* with the subjunctive) to **if it is of God** (*ei* with the indicative) shows that Luke accepted the second condition as true, not the first. But Bruce's warning should be noted: "We cannot argue that Gamaliel regarded the second alternative as the more probable; the interplay of conditional constructions belongs to Luke's Gk., not to Gamaliel's Aram." [85]

---

of justice, and his faith in providence. He cites two examples of Jewish leaders whose work came to naught, and then advised the court to leave these men and their work in God's hands, lest they should fight against God.

Gamaliel's advice was accepted by the court, and though they gave partial vent to their indignation by flogging the apostles for their disobedience to the court's previous command, probably with thirty-nine stripes each, the rulers accordingly released them with a renewal of the futile command, as they must have realized, charging **them not to speak in the name of Jesus** (vs. 40b). The apostles returned forthwith and resumed their ministry to the waiting multitude in the temple and extended their services to private homes as well, where **they ceased not to teach and to preach Jesus as the Christ** (vs. 42b). How futile the efforts of man to stay the work of God!

[79] *Ant.* XX, 5, 1.
[80] *Loc. cit.*
[81] Bruce, *Acts*, p. 147. See further arguments there. Cf. also W. M. Ramsay, *Was Christ Born at Bethelehem* (New York: G. P. Putnam's Sons, 1898), p. 259. Knowling well remarks (EGT, II, 158): "We cannot suppose that St. Luke could have made the gross blunder attributed to him in the face of his usual accuracy."
[82] *War*, II, 8, 1.
[83] "Taxing" (KJV) is incorrect.
[84] This is not the census referred to in Luke 2: 1, which took place in the time of Herod (died 4 B.C.).
[85] Bruce, *Acts*, p. 149.

40 And to him they agreed: and when they had called the apostles unto them, they beat them and charged them not to speak in the name of Jesus, and let them go.
41 They therefore departed from the presence of the council, rejoicing that they were counted worthy to suffer dishonor for the Name.
42 And every day, in the temple and at home, they ceased not to teach and to preach Jesus *as* the Christ.

---

40 It may be surprising, after the speech of Gamaliel, that the Sanhedrin **beat** the apostles. But this was a punishment for their crime of disobeying the previous command of the Sanhedrin to cease teaching **in the name of Jesus** (cf. 4:18).

41 Note the use of **the Name** in an absolute way, corresponding to the expression "the Way" (9:2).

42 **Jesus as the Christ** (i.e., the Messiah) is probably the correct translation of the intended thought here. "In every house" (KJV) is perhaps better rendered **at home** (RV).

Additional Note I

DEMON POSSESSION AND EXPULSION

A significant statement has been made by J. Stafford Wright concerning the problem of demon possession and expulsion. Says this author:

> Demon possession demands serious consideration. It has been accepted as a fact by most nations from early times, and is still recognized today. It was apparently accepted by Jesus Christ, and many of the cures that He and His disciples practised were based on the real existence of demons which had to be cast out. Jesus and His disciples distinguished clearly between normal physical illnesses, that were cured generally by the laying on of hands or anointing with oil, and those cases of possession which were cured by the word of command (e.g., Matt. 10:8; Mark 6:13; Luke 13:32), even though these latter cases often showed the symptoms of ordinary diseases such as dumbness and blindness (Matt. 9:32, 33; 12:22).
>
> The chief characteristic of demon possession appears to have been the control of the body of the possessed in an abnormal way, against what was believed to be the will of the person. Where the possessing spirit was prepared to speak, it spoke of itself as an entity different from the man it was possessing. Thus the spirits in Mark 5 recognized Jesus for what He was, and gave their name as Legion.
>
> Similar characteristics have been noted in recent times from various parts of the world, and they have attracted particular notice in China. The stories may lack the amount of corroboration in detail that we should desire, but their similarity in general outline, as they come from different parts, makes them inherently likely. A person suddenly exhibits another personality, and speaks in a different voice, which Miss Mildred Cable describes as "the weird minor chant of the possessed, the voice, as in every case I have seen, clearly distinguishing it from insanity" (The Fulfilment of a Dream, p. 118). The person often becomes violent, and may exhibit supernatural knowledge. Usually his words are evil, and often blasphemous.
>
> A very full study of cases in China was made by a missionary, Dr. J. L. Nevius, in 1892, in *Demon Possession and Allied Themes* (Fleming H. Revell) . . . Dr. Nevius began his studies with a detailed questionnaire, which he sent to many missionaries and Chinese Christians, so as to discover as much firsthand information as possible. His conclusion in the light of all the evidence is that demon possession is what the name suggests, and it cannot be equated with any ordinary physical or psychological derangement . . . .
>
> Certainly the casting out of demons is no light thing. . . . He [Christ] spoke of the danger of the spirit returning to his former victim, accompanied by other spirits also, unless the victim has in the meantime filled the house of his life with another Owner (Luke 11:24–26).[h]

[h] J. Stafford Wright, *Man in the Process of Time* (London: Paternoster Press, 1955), pp. 131–134. For further discussion of this subject, see Richard Chenevix Trench, *Notes on the Parables of Our Lord* (New York: Revell), pp. 117–138.

CHAPTER VI

Now in these days, when the number of the disciples was multiplying, there arose a murmuring of the Grecian Jews against the Hebrews, because their widows were neglected in the daily ministration.

EXEGESIS

1 The name **disciples** occurs here for the first time in Acts.[1] The Greek *mathētēs* literally means "learner" (from the second aorist stem *math* of *manthanō*, "learn"). It is the most common designation in the Gospels for the followers of Jesus, occurring 74 times in Matthew, 45 in Mark, 38 in Luke, and 81 in John. Outside the Gospels it is found only in Acts, where it appears 28 times, making a total of 266 times in the New Testament. It is always translated "disciples." It is "perhaps the most characteristic name for the Christians in Acts." [2] Other names in Acts are "the saved" (2:47), "saints" (9:13, 32, 41; 26:10), "brethren" (e.g., 1:15), "believers" (10:45), "Nazarenes" (24:5).

Gongusmos, **murmuring**, is an onomatopoetic word; that is, one the sound of which suggests its sense. It reminds one of the buzzing of bees.

Grecian Jews is one word in the Greek, *Hellēnistai*. The best translation is the transliteration, "Hellenists." The commonly accepted connotation of this term (since Chrysostom) is "Greek-speaking Jews." In a lengthy note Cadbury argues for the idea that it means Gentiles.[3] But in collaboration with Lake he comes to this more likely conclusion: "Though 'Greek-speaking' may be the right meaning, it is possible that the reference is to 'Graecizing' Jews who are contrasted with the conservative party of the *Hebraioi*."[4] Bruce thinks that the term means simply "Greek speakers" and that the context must determine the nationality: "here, Greek-speaking Jewish Christians; in ix. 29, probably Greek-speaking Jews in the synagogues;

EXPOSITION

Part I

THE CHURCH'S FIRST ORGANIZATIONAL PROBLEM

I. The New Church Problems, Acts 6:1, 2.
  - A. The Problem of Enlargement, vs. 1a.
  - B. The Problem of Discrimination, vs. 1b.
  - C. The Problem of Responsibilities, vs. 2.

II. The Proposed Solution, Acts 6:3–5a.
  - A. The Necessary Consideration, vs. 3a.
  - B. The Required Qualifications, vss. 3b, 4.
  - C. The Amicable Solution, vs. 5a.

III. The Plan of Procedure, Acts 6:5b, 6.
  - A. The Church's Choice, vs. 5b.
  - B. The Church's Recommendation, vs. 6a.
  - C. The Officer's Dedication, vs. 6b.

IV. The Beneficent Results, Acts 6:7.
  - A. The Word of God Increased, vs. 7a.
  - B. The Church Multiplied, vs. 7.
  - C. The Priests Converted, vs. 7b.

Part II

THE CHURCH'S FIRST MARTYR

I. Stephen's Arrest and Arraignment, Acts 6:8–15.
  - A. The Activities of Stephen, vs. 8.
  - B. The Synagogues' Opposition, vss. 9–12.
  - C. The Accusations against Stephen, vss. 11, 13, 14.
    1. Blasphemed against Moses and God, vs. 11.
    2. Spoke against the Temple, vs. 13b.
    3. Spoke against the Law, vs. 13b.
    4. Threatened the Customs, vss. 14b, 15.

[1] The Textus Receptus has it in 1:15 (see note on that passage).
[2] *Beginnings*, V, 376.
[3] *Beginnings*, V, 59–74. See answer to this in IB, IX, 88.
[4] *Ibid.*, IV, 64.

2 And the twelve called the multitude of the disciples unto them, and said, It is not fit that we should forsake the word of God, and serve tables.

---

in xi. 20, probably Gentiles." [5] That is the best conclusion to which one can come.

Hebrews "apparently means Hebrew or Aramaic-speaking Jews." [6] They were the more conservative Jews who had resisted all Hellenizing influences. The word occurs only here, in II Corinthians 11:22, and in Philippians 3:5.

The **widows** evidently formed a distinct group in the early church.[7] There is considerable evidence for this in the Church Fathers.[8] Knowling says: "It is quite possible that the Hellenistic widows had previously been helped from the Temple Treasury, but that now, on their joining the Christian community, this help had ceased." [9] It is in keeping with Luke's character that *chēra*, widow, occurs nine times in Luke's Gospel and only three times altogether in the other Gospels. It is found three times in Acts.

The word for **neglected,** *paratheōreō*, is found only here in the New Testament. It literally means "look beside," and so "overlook, neglect." *Kathēmerinos*, **daily,** is likewise found only here.

2 The expression **the twelve** is found here alone in Acts, and Paul uses it in I Corinthians 15:5. It occurs six times in Luke's Gospel and ten times in Mark's. Matthias had taken the place of Judas Iscariot in the circle of apostles.

Serve is the verb *diakonein*, "to minister." The related noun, *diakonia*, is translated "ministration" in verse one. It is this, perhaps, which has led to the frequent reference to "the seven deacons." But they are not specifically designated as such. Bruce's comment is wise: "The N T has, generally speaking, no *technical* vocabulary for functions in the churches and for those who discharge them but uses ordinary Gk. words, which had best be rendered by ordinary Eng. words." [10] Perhaps the Pastoral Epistles are an exception (cf. I Tim. 3:1, 8; Titus 1:7).

Part I

The Church's First Organizational Problem

I. THE NEW CHURCH PROBLEMS (6:1, 2)

The apostolic church, like the church of every subsequent generation, had its problems. Those problems were met under divine guidance as they arose. The first was insincerity and was punished by divine judgment (Acts 5:1–11). The second had its origin in the enlargement of the church and consisted in discriminatory accusations, if not practices, and the division of church responsibilities. These problems were settled by divinely aided human wisdom.

A. The Problem of Enlargement (6:1a)

When the number of the disciples was multiplying [Weymouth: was increasing]. The narrator here uses a new arithmetic for the first time in regard to the church's growth. Previously believers have been "added to the church" (see Acts 2:41, 47; 5:14); but now the growth, resultant from the apostolic victories under God's blessings, has become so rapid that it can be referred to as "multiplication." Nor was this rapidly growing church without its growing pains. Growth is normal and healthy, but it always produces its problems of new adaptations, as expansion and maturity continue. An unwillingness to meet and solve those problems will ever stifle the growth and destroy the organism. The apostles accepted it as a challenge.

B. The Problem of Discrimination (6:1b)

There arose a murmuring of the Grecian Jews . . . because their widows were neglected. A muffled undertone of complaint finally broke through and began to evidence itself on the surface. **The Grecians** were Hellenists,

[5] Bruce, *Acts*, p. 151. These are the only three occurrences of the word in the New Testament.
[6] *Ibid.*
[7] Cf. I Tim. 5:9.
[8] See J. B. Mayor, *The Epistle of St. James* (Grand Rapids: Zondervan Publishing House, 1954), p. 77.
[9] EGT, II, 166.
[10] *Acts*, p. 152. Irenaeus, however, speaks of Stephen as "the first deacon" (*Against Heresies*, iii, 12). For further discussion of this point, see IB, IX, 90 f.

3 Look ye out therefore, brethren, from among you seven men of good report, full of the Spirit and of wisdom, whom we may appoint over this business.

Tables has usually been interpreted in relation to eating. But the Greek word *trapeza* is also used of the tables of money-changers (e.g., Matt. 21:12). It has been increasingly felt that perhaps the term should be taken here as indicating "the general financial administration of the community."[11]

3 **Look ye out** is *episkepsasthe*, which elsewhere in the New Testament (ten times) means "visit." But an exact parallel to its use here may be seen in Genesis 41:33 (LXX).

The word **brethren** *(adelphoi)* is here for the first time applied to Christians. This usage is found some thirty-four times in Acts and is frequent in the epistles.

Numerous reasons have been given for the choice of **seven men.** Some have suggested a connection with the sevenfold Spirit (cf. Isa. 11:2; Rev. 1:4). Others have thought that Jerusalem may have been divided into seven districts. Another suggestion is that the Christians met in seven congregations in private homes. But probably the simplest and best interpretation is to relate it to the Hebrew sacred number, seven.[12] It is interesting to note that two centuries later the Roman bishop Cornelius held that there should be exactly seven deacons in each church.[13]

Of good report is all one word in Greek, the participle *marturoumenous.* The original meaning of *martureō* was "bear witness." In later Greek it came to mean "witness favorably, give a good report."[14] So here it would mean "well witnessed to."

The Spirit is used here absolutely. But verse 5 shows that the reference is to the Holy Spirit. **Wisdom** *(sophia)* means "practical wisdom."[15]

The word for **business** is *chreia*, the most common meaning of which is "need." In fact, that is the way the King James Version translates it in 39 of the 49 passages where it occurs in the New Testament. This is the only place where it is rendered "business." It may be translated "office" here.[16]

---

or Jews who had imbibed the Greek culture, including language, of the countries in which they were born in the dispersion. They were considered inferior by the Hebrews, or Palestinian Jews, who were in a majority in the church.[a] The order of widows supported by the church from the common treasury and devoted to prayer and works of mercy (Acts 9:41; I Tim. 5:3, 9–11, 16), was one of the earliest Christian institutions.[b] This neglect of the Grecian widows by the Hebrew–Christian administrators of temporal goods probably was unintentional, but it revealed an essential weakness of early Christian communalism.

C. The Problem of Responsibilities (6:2)

It is not fit [reasonable or proper] **that we should forsake the Word of God, and serve tables.** Originally, in the Christian communal system, the apostles were the administrators of the common treasury (Acts 2:45; 5:2). Increased ministerial responsibilities in the growing church made it inevitable that this could not continue. The apostles' first duty was to minister the Word of God (Matt. 28:18–20; Acts 1:8). They assembled the multitude and declared their first duty to be a direct spiritual ministry. The *apostolate* appeared first in the church, then the *diaconate*, and later the *presbyterate*, as the need of each arose.[c] Whenever the ministry neglects its spiritual service to man for temporal concerns it has failed the divine calling. Janitorial duties or secular employment by the minister may be justifiable in the beginning of a church, but it can seldom be long continued without injury to both the minister and the church.

II. THE PROPOSED SOLUTION (6:3–5a)

The apostolic church here sets forth a workable example for the solution of church

[11] *Beginnings*, IV, 64. [12] See further suggestion in Exposition. [13] Eusebius, *Ecclesiastical History*, VI, 43.
[14] Cf. VGT, p. 389; Deissmann, *Bible Studies*, p. 265. [15] EGT, II, 169. [16] See VGT, p. 691.

[a] Dummelow, *op. cit.*, p. 825.
[b] H. D. M. Spence, ed., *Pulpit Commentary* (Grand Rapids: Wm. B. Eerdmans Publishing Company, rep. 1950), XVIII, p. 192.
[c] *Ibid.*, p. 193.

4 But we will continue stedfastly in prayer, and in the ministry of the word.

5 And the saying pleased the whole multitude: and they chose Stephen, a man full of faith and of the Holy Spirit, and Philip, and Prochorus, and Nicanor, and Timon, and Parmenas, and Nicolaus a proselyte of Antioch;

6 whom they set before the apostles: and when they had prayed, they laid their hands upon them.

---

4 For **continue stedfastly** see note on 1:14. **Prayer**[17] here probably refers to public worship, as in 1:14. **The ministry of the word** means preaching.

5 **Stephen** is the outstanding one of the seven appointees. Probably only martyrdom prevented him from becoming a great leader in the early church. **Philip** is the second most important, holding the center of the scene in chapter 8, after Stephen's prominence in chapters 6 and 7. **Prochorus** is pictured in Byzantine art as the scribe to whom John dictated his Gospel.[18] Nothing further is known of **Nicanor, Timon,** and **Parmenas. Nicolaus** is identified as a **proselyte of Antioch.** Early church tradition said he was the founder of the Nicolaitans mentioned in Revelation 2:6. The mention of Antioch is sometimes taken as suggesting that the author Luke, may have been a native of Antioch.

6 The **apostles . . . laid their hands** on the seven appointees. This was in keeping with the Jewish custom of ordination.[19]

Ramsay characterizes the appointment of the seven as "the first distinct step in the development from the primitive condition of the church."[20] Again he says: "A distinct step towards the Universalized Church was here made; it was already recognized that the Church was wider than the pure Jewish race; and the non-Jewish element was raised to official rank."[21] This statement refers primarily to Nicolaus.

---

problems. The entire church was represented (vs. 2a), and though the apostles suggested the solution, responsibility for the choosing of the officers was left with the church. While these officers are simply designated **seven men** in this early Acts record, it would appear that the office to which they were appointed was that known as the *diaconate* in later times,[d] though this is questioned if not denied by some scholars. The fuller qualifications of deacons are given by Paul (Phil. 1:1; I Tim. 3:8, 12).

A. The Necessary Consideration (6:3a)

Look ye out therefore, brethren, from among you seven men. Here is a perfect model of lay representation in official church matters. Weymouth reads: "Pick out from among yourselves." The church best knew who among its number were efficient, reliable, and impartial. Its careful consideration and choice is reflected in the care of the church under those chosen. No particular significance need be attached to the number seven, unless for the sacredness of the number with the Jews, or that each might supervise the temporal affairs one day a week.

B. The Required Qualifications (6:3b, 4)

Of good report, full of the Spirit and of wisdom. The apostles specify the qualifications of the seven officers to be chosen; namely, (1) *good reputation*, **of good report;** (2) *spirituality*, **full of the Spirit;** and (3) *practicality*, **full . . . of wisdom.** These qualifications are few, but they cover much territory. Such church officers will ever do credit to Christianity, and under them the cause of Christ will prosper; and thus the ministry will be freed from temporal time-consuming interests that it may **continue** [itself] **stedfastly in prayer, and in the ministry of the word.**

C. The Amicable Solution (6:5a)

And the saying pleased the whole multitude. Any solution of such an acute problem that will please the whole church must indeed be of divine origin. How insignificant do personal or group differences become when Christian people are disposed to settle their problems in God's way.

[17] Literally, "the prayer" (*tEi proseuchEi*). [18] *Beginnings*, IV, 65.
[19] Cf. Num. 27:18; Deut. 34:9. For a description of such ordination see Edersheim, *Life and Times*, II, 382.
[20] *St. Paul the Traveller*, p. 372. [21] *Ibid.* p. 375.

[d] Dummelow, *loc. cit.*

7 And the word of God increased; and the number of the disciples multiplied in Jerusalem exceedingly; and a great company of the priests were obedient to the faith.

---

7 Josephus claims that there were 20,000 priests in his day.[22] So the mention of **a great company of the priests** is not preposterous, as some have held. The expression **the faith** for Christianity is similar to that found in the Pastoral Epistles and so eliminates this item as an argument for the late second century date of the latter.

III. THE PLAN OF PROCEDURE (6:5b, 6)

Divine wisdom is clearly reflected in the apostolic plan for the selection, presentation, and dedication of these church officers to their duties. As is revealed by their later ministerial activities, especially in the case of Stephen and Philip, they were more than temporal officials.

A. The Church's Choice (6:5b)

And they chose. While it was the duty of the church to choose the officials, it was the responsibility of the apostles to dedicate (vs. 6b) and appoint them (vs. 3b). All seven of those chosen bore Greek names. However, as it was not uncommon for Jews, especially Hellenist Jews, to have Greek names, this does not argue that all of them were pure Greeks. Three of the seven are of special interest. Stephen turned evangelist and became the first Christian martyr, of whom we learn more later. Philip likewise became an effective evangelist, whose record we have in Acts 8:5; 8:26; and 21:8. Nicolaus is called a proselyte of Antioch, indicating that he was a Gentile converted to the Jewish faith, and from that to Christianity. This mention of his nationality may seem to indicate that the rest were Jews by nationality.

B. The Church's Recommendation (6:6a)

Whom they set before the apostles. Here is a beautiful example of respect for rights within the church. The church has used its best judgment in selecting the officers in accordance with the specifications given, and now they present their choice to the apostles for their approval. It may be seriously questioned whether anyone is divinely called into Christian service who does not have the recognition and recommendation of at least some responsible party or parties within the church.

C. The Officers' Dedication (6:6b)

When they had prayed, they laid their hands upon them. How like the selection and dedication of Barnabas and Paul for their missionary work by the church at Antioch (Acts 13:2, 3). The essential elements in their ordination were prayer and the laying on of hands by the apostles. This custom was very ancient and was borrowed from the Jews by the Christians (see Num. 27:18–23; Deut. 34:9). It simply betokened the Christians' acceptance of God's selection (John 15:16).

IV. THE BENEFICENT RESULTS (6:7)

When the mind and will of God is sought and followed in the solution of problems and the conduct of church business, spiritual prosperity will always follow.

A. The Word of God Increased (6:7a)

With the apostles wholly devoted to prayer, study, and the preaching of the Word of God (vs. 4), and the church's temporal offices wisely and satisfactorily administered by the newly elected officers, there is little wonder that the revival went on. **The word of God increased** in arresting, illuminating, convicting, converting, delivering, and cleansing power. Under the Spirit's quickening power, produced by earnest prayer, God's Word becomes "quick and powerful" (Heb. 4:12, 13). The Spirit-animated Word is ever productive of revivals.

B. The Church Multiplied (6:7)

The number of the disciples multiplied in Jerusalem exceedingly. It is possible that this reference gives a hint of the division of

[22] *Against Apion*, II 8.

8 And Stephen, full of grace and power, wrought great wonders and signs among the people.
9 But there arose certain of them that were of the synagogue called *the synagogue* of the
Libertines, and of the Cyrenians, and of the Alexandrians, and of them of Cilicia and Asia,
disputing with Stephen.

---

8 This verse contains one of the great words of the New Testament, **grace** *(charis)*. It is a favorite word with Luke and Paul. The former uses it eight times in his Gospel and sixteen times in Acts.[23] It occurs over one hundred times in Paul's thirteen epistles. Plummer notes that its earliest meaning was "comeliness, winsomeness";[24] that is, "gracefulness" or "graciousness." He continues: "From this objective attractiveness it easily passes to subjective 'favour, kindness, goodwill,' esp. from a superior to an inferior . . .; and hence, in particular, of finding 'favour' with God."[25] The next stage is dominant in the New Testament. "From the sense of God's favour generally . . . we come to the specially theological sense of 'God's favour to sinners, the free gift of His grace.'"[26] Bruce says: "It is possible that *charis* has here its earlier sense of 'charm', i.e., spiritual charm."[27]

9 The word **synagogue** is found here for the first time in Acts. It occurs nine times in Matthew, eight in Mark, fifteen in Luke, twice in John, twenty times in Acts and only three times elsewhere in the New Testament (James 2:2; Rev. 2:9; 3:9). The English word is simply a transliteration of the Greek

---

the disciples into separate congregations in Jerusalem, for more efficient administrative purposes. Some scholars think that each of the seven officers was appointed to a different congregation. However, there is no evidence of this. It is enough to know that the spiritual movement continued, and that the word **multiplied** best expressed the narrator's concept of the rapid growth.

C. The Priests Converted (6:7b)

A great company of the priests were obedient to the faith. While some scholars doubt the genuineness of this reading, Clarke[e] observes that it represents the greatest of all apostolic miracles, since the priests were the bitterest foes of Christ and Christianity (see John 12:42). Since there were 24 courses in Jerusalem, literally multitudes, there is no problem about the conversion of **a great company of the priests.**

Part II

The Church's First Martyr

I. STEPHEN'S ARREST AND ARRAIGNMENT

(6:8–15)

Stephen was the first of the seven lay church officers chosen to administer the temporal affairs of the disciples (Acts 6:5a). He well met the qualifications of *good reputation*, *spirituality*, and *practicality*, as laid down by the apostles (Acts 6:3). While Peter has been considered the greatest of the apostolic preachers, and Paul the greatest missionary, it is hardly too much to say that Stephen was the greatest first-century Christian. He evidently was a Hellenistic Jew and was possessed with a passion for the conversion of his fellow Hellenists. He evidences a remarkable knowledge of the Jewish Scriptures and history; and he reflects a wider and more liberal view of the Gospel of Jesus Christ as the fulfillment of the Law, and God's provision of salvation for all nations and peoples, than even the apostles themselves. He was willing to seal his testimony to this conviction in martyrdom with his own blood.

A. The Activities of Stephen (6:8)

And Stephen . . . wrought great wonders and signs among the people. Though Stephen had been chosen by the church as an official lay leader, it soon became evident that God had higher designs for his life. He came up through the ranks, as have so many great preachers and church leaders since. As a lay leader he was **a man full of faith and of the**

[23] It is found only four times in the other Gospels (John 1:14, 16 [twice], 17).
[24] Alfred Plummer, *A Critical and Exegetical Commentary on the Gospel According to St. Luke* (ICC) (New York: Charles Scribner's Sons, 1896), p. 124.
[25] *Ibid.*, p. 125. [26] *Ibid.* [27] *Acts*, p. 155.

[e] Clarke, *op. cit.*, V, 725.

synagōgē. This comes from *synagō*, "gather together." So it refers to an assembly of people. As in the case of "church," it came later to denote the building where the people assembled. This is its common meaning in the Gospels.

The synagogue seems to have had its beginning during the captivity in Babylon, when the people could no longer worship in the temple at Jerusalem. The English word occurs only once in the Old Testament (Psalm 74:8). But the Septuagint there has *heortē*. "It is not, therefore, certain that there is any reference to a synagogue in the O.T." [28]

There has been a great deal of discussion as to how many synagogues are indicated in this verse. There are proponents, respectively, of one, two, three, four, and five synagogues. Schürer was "uncertain whether one congregation or five are spoken of." [29] But he finally decided in favor of *five*.[30] By placing **them of Cilicia and Asia** together one could postulate *four* synagogues. Then there are those who hold to *three* synagogues: (1) **of the Libertines**; (2) **of the Cyrenians . . . and Alexandrians**; (3) **of them of Cilicia and Asia.**[31] That there are *two* synagogues mentioned here is the view of Knowling [32] and Plumptre.[33] This is also held by Lake and Cadbury. They write: "The arrangement of the articles *tōn . . . tōn* suggests that there were two groups, (a) Libertini, Cyrenians, and Alexandrians, (b) Cilicians and Asians."[34] They would not, however, coordinate the first three names, but hold that the first synagogue was composed of Libertini from Cyrene and Alexandria.

Calvin held that there was only *one* synagogue, composed of Libertines from the four areas mentioned.[35] Bruce adopts this view. He writes: "I am inclined to think that one synagogue is meant, attended by Jewish freedmen or descendants of freedmen from the various places mentioned." [36] This is perhaps the best conclusion to reach.

Libertines is a transliteration into English of the Greek word *libertinoi*, which in turn is a transliteration of the Latin *libertini*, meaning "freedmen." Deissmann thinks they were "former Imperial slaves." [37] Schürer says: "The *Libertinoi* can only be Roman 'freed men' and their descendants, therefore, descendants of those Jews whom Pompey despatched as prisoners to Rome, and who were soon liberated by their masters." [38]

The **Cyrenians** were from Cyrene, in North Africa. There is evidence that there was a numerous Jewish population there. [39] The **Alexandrians** were from Alexandria, Egypt. It is well known that a considerable part of the population of this city was composed of Jews. Knowling writes: "According to Philo, two of the five districts of the town . . . were called 'the Jewish,' from the number of Jews dwelling in them, one quarter, Delta, being entirely populated by them." [40] Josephus declared that the Jewish quarter of Alexandria was "a large part of that city." [41]

Cilicia would suggest special interest, since that was Paul's home province. Most commentators think that the young Saul may have taken active part in the disputes with Stephen. Lake and Cadbury say: "That Paul was by birth a Roman citizen (see xxii. 28) is not against his belonging to the Libertini

---

Holy Spirit (Acts 6:5a), and now impelled by the quickening power of the Spirit and a passion for the evangelization of his fellows, he is seen doing **great wonders and signs** (vs. 8b). Stephen's temporal office in the church brought him into contact with the poor, the sick, and the suffering, whether from demon possession or otherwise, of the congregation, and thus afforded ample opportunity for the supplying by miraculous means such needs of many of the people as could not be met by the temporal treasury. Filled with faith (some read "grace"), and thus giving unlimited credence to the pro-

[28] *Westminster Dictionary of the Bible*, p. 585. For further discussion of the origin and history of the Jewish synagogue see Paul Levertoff, "Synagogue," ISBE, V, 2877–2879; W. Bacher, "Synagogue," HDB, IV, 636–642; R. W. Moss, "Synagogue," HDCG, II, 689–692; K. Kohler, "Synagogue," HDAC, II, 541–545.

[29] Schürer, *op. cit.*, II, i, 49.

[30] *Ibid.*, II, ii, 57, n. 44. Lechler (Lange's Commentary) *Acts*, p. 109, does the same, as does Hackett, *op. cit.*, p. 87.

[31] Cf. T. E. Page, *Acts of the Apostles* (New York: Macmillan Co., 1886), p. 118.

[32] EGT, II, 174.

[33] E. H. Plumptre, "Acts of the Apostles," *Commentary on the Whole Bible*, ed. Charles J. Ellicott (Grand Rapids: Zondervan Publishing House, n.d.), VII, 35.

[34] *Beginnings*, IV, 66.

[35] *Op. cit.*, I, 241.

[36] Bruce, *Acts*, p. 156.

[37] LAE, p. 441.

[38] Schürer, *op. cit.*, II, ii, 57, n. 44. Pompey took Jerusalem for the Romans in 63 B.C.

[39] Cf. *ibid.*, II, ii, 231, 244.

[40] EGT, II, 1[illegible]

[41] *Ant.* XIV, 7, 2.

10 And they were not able to withstand the wisdom and the Spirit by which he spake.
11 Then they suborned men, who said, We have heard him speak blasphemous words against Moses, and *against* God.

---

but rather in its favour."[42] **Asia,** of course, refers to the Roman province of that name at the west end of Asia Minor (modern Turkey), where many Jews resided at this time.

Disputing is literally "questioning together" *(sunzētountes)*. This word is used in the New Testament "always in the sense of questioning, generally in the sense of disputatious questioning."[43] It carries this same meaning of "discussing, debating, disputing," in the papyri.[44]

10 Strangely, the King James Version spells **Spirit** with a small "s." But most commentators connect this with verse 5 and interpret it as meaning the Holy Spirit.

11 The Hellenistic opponents of Stephen, worsted in debate, now **suborned** men to accuse him falsely. The verb *hypoballō* is found only here in the New Testament. Its literal meaning is "throw under," and so "submit." Then it came to mean "suggest, prompt, instigate." Lake and Cadbury write: "It applies to the secret instigation of persons who are supplied with suggestions of what they are to say, much as in a modern 'frame-up.'"[45] (Cf. RSV—"secretly instigated").

The charge against him was that of speaking **blasphemous words against Moses, and against God.** The accusation was false, but it was similar to the one levelled against Jesus (Mark 14:58, 64). Lake and Cadbury object that legal blasphemy was not involved here, since the name of God was not used. Dalman furnishes a sufficient answer to this objection when he says: "But it is clear that their interpretation of the Mosaic law on blasphemy . . . was less formally developed than the later rabbinic law (Sahn. vii. 5)."[46]

---

mises of God for the people, and of the energizing power of God's Spirit (Acts 1:8), Stephen was enabled to witness mighty miracles of healing, demon expulsion, and spiritual and moral transformations among the peoples he served. The possibilities for Spirit-filled and faithful lay leadership in the Church are quite unlimited. However, this spiritual service was not without its price.

B. The Synagogue's Opposition (6:9–12)

But there arose certain of them that were of the synagogue (vs. 9a). Satan will never see his territory invaded and his subjects lost without a battle. This new activity of a Hellenist Christian especially directed toward the more liberal Hellenistic Jews of the synagogues was particularly dangerous to the cause of the enemy. It is striking that this opposition arose from among the Hellenists. Possibly they were incited by the rulers of the Sanhedrin.

Concerning the synagogue it should be noted that at least 10 adults were required by Law for the organization of a synagogue, and there were at this time about 150 Jewish communities throughout the Roman Empire and beyond, though they may not all have had synagogues.[f] There were 480 synagogues in Jerusalem, according to Josephus (some says 250). They were simpler in form of worship and more liberal than the temple, in that they allowed Gentile proselytes and Godfearing non-proselytes to worship in them. Mould says concerning the Jewish Synagogue of the first century:

> The synagoge controlled by scribes and Pharisees, was the vital center of Jewish religious thought and life. In the time of Jesus it was required that there be a synagogue in every place where ten would agree to be regular attendants. The larger cities had several synagogues. The synagogue building was so constructed and arranged that the worshippers faced toward Jerusalem. At the end of the room which the worshippers faced was the *ark*, a chest or closet in which were kept the rolls of Holy Scripture in linen cases. In front of the ark was a curtain and before that a lamp which was always kept burning. The elders and the Pharisees occupied *chief seats* facing the congregation. There was a reading desk upon a raised platform. Control of the synagogue was vested in the council of elders. Officers of the synagogue consisted of (1) *the ruler of the synagogue*, who had the immediate management of the building and its services, and who sat in the "seat of

[42] *Beginnings*, IV, 68. [43] EGT, II, 175. [44] VGT, p. 607. [45] *Beginnings*, IV, 68, 69.
[46] Dalman, *Words of Jesus* (Edinburgh, T. and T. Clark, 1909), p. 314.

[f] Robinson, *op. cit.*, p. 10.

12 And they stirred up the people, and the elders, and the scribes, and came upon him, and seized him, and brought him into the council,

13 and set up false witnesses, who said, This man ceaseth not to speak words against this holy place, and the law:

---

12 The leaders **stirred up**[47] the people, and Stephen was **seized**[48] and brought before **the council,** or Sanhedrin. There has been some difference of opinion as to where the Sanhedrin met. Josephus states that the "council house" was at the east end of the oldest wall just west of the Temple Area.[49] But the Talmud says that it was a room *in* the temple at the south side of the front court. It was called Gazith, which is usually interpreted as "Hall of Stone." Lake favors Josephus as the earlier witness and one who had firsthand knowledge of the temple before its destruction in A.D. 70. He concludes: "In support of Josephus it should be noted that the trial of Jesus was at night, and it is therefore unlikely to have been in the Temple which was closed at sunset."[50]

13 The **false witnesses** call to mind Mark 14:56, 57. There are a number of parallels between Stephen's trial and that of Jesus.

14 This charge was probably a garbled,

Moses" during service; (2) the *chazzan* or attendant, who had charge of the sacred rolls, kept the building in condition, and administered the scourgings which were meted out to criminals by the local synagogue courts. The chazzan may also have served as village school teacher in the synagogue schools. (3) A third group of synagogue officials was the *almoners* who collected and disbursed the alms.

Synagogue services were held on all Sabbath mornings and feast days. Less formal services occurred on Sabbath afternoons, on Mondays, and on Thursdays. The order of worship included (1) the Shema (Deut. 6:4–9; 11:13–21; Num. 15:37–41), recited in unison with certain benedictions; (2) prayers, with responses by the congregation, standing; (3) a reading of passages selected by the ruler from the Torah and the Prophets, with an accompanying translation from Hebrew into Aramaic; (4) an address by any person selected by the ruler; and (5) a benediction, provided a priest were present to give it; otherwise a prayer was substituted.[g]

Those mentioned here, the members of which attacked Stephen, are **the synagogue of the Libertines,** consisting of freedmen of the Roman descendants of prisoners taken by Pompey (Chrysostom); **Cyrenians,** consisting of members from Cyrene, capital of Upper Libya in Africa, one-fourth part of which city was Jewish; **Alexandrians,** consisting of peoples from Alexandria in Egypt, two-fifths of which city was Jewish, or about 100,000 people, and the place of the translation of the Old Testament into Greek (the Septuagint); **Cilicia,** consisting of people from the province of Cilicia in Asia Minor, which was the home of Paul and the residence of many Jews (see Acts 15:23, 41); and **Asia,** with members from the province of Asia in Asia Minor where many bigoted Jews resided (vs. 9).

Unable to match the wisdom and the Spirit with which Stephen preached and reasoned with these Hellenist Jews in their Jewish synagogue or synagogues, they resorted to the foul means of employing certain lewd fellows to do their dirty work of bringing false witness against him before the Sanhedrin (vs. 12; cf. Acts 17:5); and thus by these means they had him dragged into the court and falsely accused by testimonies designed to inflame the wrath and prejudice the judgments of the rulers (vs. 13).

C. The Accusations against Stephen (6:11, 13, 14)

And set up false witnesses, who said. The accusations brought against Stephen by these hired false witnesses remind one very much of the like proceedings against Christ at His trial. Indeed there is very much in the trial and death of Stephen to remind one of the trial and death of Christ. Nor is this surprising when it is remembered that his attacks on Judaism were but the continuation of the attacks which Christ had made, and that he proclaimed the Gospel of Jesus Christ. Specifically, the accusations brought against Stephen were four. *First,* he was

---

[47] The Greek word (*synkineō*) is found only here in N.T.
[48] *Synarpazō* is used only by Luke. [49] *War*, V, 4, 2.
[50] *Beginnings*, V, 478. Schürer also (*op. cit.*, II, i, 190) supports the position of Josephus.

[g] Mould, *op. cit.*, pp. 479, 480. For further information on the Jewish synagogue, see Edersheim, *Life and Times of Jesus the Messiah* (New York: Longmans, Green and Co., 1899), Vol. I, pp. 430–49.

14 for we have heard him say, that this Jesus of Nazareth shall destroy this place, and shall change the customs which Moses delivered unto us.

15 And all that sat in the council, fastening their eyes on him, saw his face as it had been the face of an angel.

---

distorted version of what Stephen actually was saying (cf. 7:48–50). The accusation brought against Jesus was strikingly similar (Mark 14:58) and was likewise a distortion of His teaching. It is not impossible, however, that Stephen may have made this prediction of what did take place nearly forty years later (cf. Mark 13:2).

15 Under false accusation and facing cruel hatred, Stephen's face shone like **the face of an angel.** No one can miss the similarity to Moses' countenance when he came down from the Mount Sinai, after spending forty days in the presence of God, or to the transfiguration of Jesus on the mount as He was in close fellowship with His Father.

---

accused of blasphemy (a very serious religious crime) against Moses, the Jewish Law-Giver, and against God (vs. 11); *second,* they accused him of blaspheming against, and even predicting, the destruction of the Jewish temple (13b); *third,* he was accused of blasphemy against the Law itself (13b); and *finally,* they accused him of saying that Jesus would destroy the temple and change or destroy the customs handed down from Moses. The accusations are all doubtless a perversion of what Stephen had actually said, but the overall charge is blasphemy. Both the contemptuous scorning of sacred places and the persistent willful transgression of the commands of God and disregard for the word of God (Num. 15:30 f), were regarded as blasphemy of the highest order by the Jews. It was the most frequent charge brought against Jesus by His enemies, the Jews, both on the grounds of His claims to divinity and His interpretation of the Law (Matt. 9:3; 26:65; Mark 2:7; John 10:33, 36). The legal punishment for blasphemy was death (Lev. 24:16), and thus Jesus' death was regarded as just by the Jews (John 8:58, 59; 10:33; 19:7). Likewise Stephen is placed under accusation for the crime of blasphemy, for which, if convicted, he might be executed, though such execution could only be carried out legally by official approval of the Roman procurator of Judea.

The rulers had their last warning from God in His vindication of Stephen before the council, as he stood to make his defense with his face in a halo of divine glory resembling **the face of an angel** (vs. 15).

CHAPTER VII

And the high priest said, Are these things so?
2 And he said, Brethren and fathers, hearken: The God of glory appeared unto our father Abraham, when he was in Mesopotamia, before he dwelt in Haran,
3 and said unto him, Get thee out of thy land, and from thy kindred, and come into the land which I shall show thee.

EXEGESIS

This speech is often referred to as Stephen's defense before the Sanhedrin. But Bruce's comment is well taken: "'Stephen's apology' is not so much a forensic defence as a statement of the teaching which had caused such irritation."[1] The same writer summarizes the two main arguments of the speech as being: "(1) God is not locally restricted and does not inhabit material buildings; . . .(2) the Jewish nation has always been rebellious."[2] The first point is emphasized by calling attention to the obvious fact that the patriarchs had neither temple nor fixed country. Yet they worshipped God, and He blessed them. It was a note of universality that the Jews deeply resented.

2, 3 The opening words, **the God of glory,** "are an implied answer to the charge of blaspheming God."[3] This God **appeared unto our father Abraham, when he was in Mesopotamia.** So God's appearances and blessings were not restricted to the so-called Holy Land. **Mesopotamia** is from two Greek words: *mesos*, "in the middle, between," and *potamos*, "river." Hence it means "the land between the rivers" (that is, the Tigris and Euphrates). Ur of the Chaldees, where Abraham lived (Gen. 11:31), has generally been located in the southern part of the Tigris-Euphrates Valley. Some recent scholars have argued for a location farther north.[4]

The phrase **before he dwelt in Haran** has raised a problem. For in Genesis 12:1 the words quoted here in verse 3 are presented apparently as a call that came to Abraham in Haran. But Genesis 15:7 says: "I am Jehovah that brought thee out of Ur of the Chaldees." The same thing is stated in Nehemiah 9:7. Philo emphasizes the call in Ur.[5] Josephus writes that Abram "left the land of Chaldea when he was seventy-five years old,"[6] which seems a contradiction of Genesis 12:4, where it is specifically stated that "Abram was seventy and five years old when he departed out of Haran."

EXPOSITION

THE CHURCH'S FIRST MARTYR

(cont'd.)

II. Stephen's Defense and Charge, Acts 7:1–53.
   A. The Address to the Council, vss. 1, 2a.
   B. The Answer to the First Charge, vss. 2b–37.
   C. The Answer to the Third Charge, vss. 38–43.
   D. The Answer to the Second Charge, vss. 44–50.
   E. The Indictment of the Council, vss. 51–53.

III. Stephen's Glorious Martyrdom, Acts 7:54–60.
   A. The Council's Indignation, vs. 54.
   B. The Consolation of Stephen, vss. 55, 56.
   C. The Council's Illegal Procedure, vss. 57, 58.
   D. The Prayer of Stephen, vss. 59, 60a.
   E. The Death of Stephen, vs. 60b.

[1] Bruce, *Acts*, p. 160. [2] *Ibid.*, p. 161.
[3] Plumptre, *op. cit.*, p. 27. Blunt explains the phrase as meaning the God "who reveals Himself in the glory (Shekinah) between the cherubim" (*Acts of the Apostles* [Clarendon Bible], p. 162).
[4] Cf. Bruce, *Acts*, p. 161.
[5] *de Abrahamo* 71.
[6] *Ant.* I, 7, 1. He also quotes Nicolaus of Damascus as saying: "Abram reigned at Damascus" (*Ant.* I, 7, 2).

4 Then came he out of the land of the Chaldaeans, and dwelt in Haran: and from thence, when his father was dead, *God* removed him into this land, wherein ye now dwell:
5 and he gave him none inheritance in it, no, not so much as to set his foot on: and he promised that he would give it to him in possession, and to his seed after him, when *as yet* he had no child.
6 And God spake on this wise, that his seed should sojourn in a strange land, and that they should bring them into bondage, and treat them ill, four hundred years.
7 And the nation to which they shall be in bondage will I judge, said God: and after that shall they come forth, and serve me in this place.

The simplest solution of the problem is to hold that the call of God first came to Abraham when he was in Ur of the Chaldees. After his father had migrated with the family to Haran the call was renewed, perhaps with greater intensity and urgency. This solution satisfies all the known facts of the case and is also true to life.

4 Another chronological problem arises in the statement here that **when his father was dead** Abraham migrated from Haran to Canaan. Genesis 11:26 reads: "And Terah lived seventy years and begat Abram, Nahor, and Haran." Verse 32 states that Terah died at the age of 205 in Haran. But, as already noted, Abraham was 75 years old when he left Haran. That would seem to mean that Terah lived for sixty years after Abraham moved to Canaan. But if it could be assumed that Abraham was a younger, rather than the oldest, son of Terah—his name being placed first to honor him—the conflict would be resolved.

It should be clearly recognized, however, that the doctrine of plenary inspiration in no way involves a guarantee of the accuracy of statements attributed to speakers in the Bible (e.g., Job's "comforters"). If it could be proved conclusively that Stephen was guilty of an error in statement of fact, that would in no way affect one's belief in the inspiration of the Scriptures.

5 **Not so much as to set his foot on** is better, "not even a foot's length" (RSV). A literal translation would be "not even a pace of a foot." The word for "pace" is *bēma*, which elsewhere in the New Testament means "judgment-seat." [7]

6 **Should sojourn** is literally "should be a sojourner" *(paroikos)*. The same word is used in verse 29, of Moses. The point Stephen is making is that Abraham was only a sojourner in the land of Canaan. It was not the soil which was sacred but God's presence that accompanied him wherever he went.

7 The statement that the descendants of Abraham would be afflicted for **four hundred years** raises still another historical problem. Exodus 12:40 reads: "Now the time that the children of Israel dwelt in Egypt was four

---

II. STEPHEN'S DEFENSE AND CHARGE (7:1–53)

A semblance of justice appears in the high priest's permission granted Stephen to answer before the Sanhedrin the charges made against him. Bruce correctly observes that Stephen's speech "is obviously not a speech for the defense in the forensic sense of the term." Bruce continues:

> Such a speech as this was by no means calculated to secure an acquittal before the Sanhedrin. It is rather a defense of pure Christianity as God's appointed way of worship; Stephen here shows himself to be the precursor of the later Christian apologists, especially those who defended Christianity against Judaism. [a]

The very crux of Stephen's address reveals that he had grasped the true significance of the universality of Christianity as expressed by Christ to the Samaritan woman at the well of Jacob:

> Woman, believe me, the hour cometh, when neither in this mountain, nor in Jerusalem [the temple], shall ye worship the Father . . . But the hour cometh, and now is, when the true worshippers shall worship the Father in spirit and truth: for such doth the Father seek to be his worshippers. God is a Spirit: and they that worship him must worship him in spirit and truth (John 4: 21b–24).

[7] It is translated thus ten times in KJV, plus once "throne" (Acts 12:21).

[a] F. F. Bruce, *Commentary on the Book of the Acts* (Grand Rapids: Wm. B. Eerdmans Publishing Company, 1954), p. 141.

8 And he gave him the covenant of circumcision: and so *Abraham* begat Isaac, and circumcised him the eighth day; and Isaac *begat* Jacob, and Jacob the twelve patriarchs.

9 And the patriarchs, moved with jealousy against Joseph, sold him into Egypt: and God was with him,

10 and delivered him out of all his afflictions, and gave him favor and wisdom before Pharaoh king of Egypt; and he made him governor over Egypt and all his house.

11 Now there came a famine over all Egypt and Canaan, and great affliction: and our fathers found no sustenance.

12 But when Jacob heard that there was grain in Egypt, he sent forth our fathers the first time.

---

hundred and thirty years." That agrees essentially with Stephen's statement, which he quoted from Genesis 15:13. But Galatians 3:17 presents the 430 years as reaching from Abraham to the Exodus. This, in turn, agrees with the Septuagint and Samaritan Pentateuch, which in Exodus 12:40 read, "in Egypt and Canaan," thus making the four centuries include the sojourn of the patriarchs in Canaan as well as the period of Israelite bondage in Egypt. This chronological scheme is stated with even more exactness in a striking passage in Josephus: "They left Egypt . . . four hundred and thirty years after our forefather Abraham came into Canaan, but two hundred and fifteen years only after Jacob removed into Egypt."[8] This difficult problem cannot be said to have been solved as yet. But the fact that a satisfactory solution has been found for many perplexities of the past should be a warning against undue pessimism at this point.

8 **Covenant** *(diathēkē)* is found in Acts only here and in 3:25. The regular classical word was *synthēkē*. But since this might suggest an agreement made between equals, both the Septuagint and New Testament use *diathēkē* for a divine covenant—one which God, on His own initiative, makes with man.[9]

The significance of *so* is thus expressed by Lake and Cadbury: "Possibly the 'so' is emphatic and means 'thus, while there was still no holy place, all the essential conditions for the religion of Israel were fulfilled.'"[10]

The use of the term **patriarchs** for the twelve sons of Jacob occurs here for perhaps the first time in literature.[11]

9 **Moved with jealousy** is one word in the Greek *zēlōsantes*, derived from *zēlos*. Both the verb and the noun are used in the New Testament with almost equal emphasis on the two connotations of "zealous" and "jealous." Finally the first meaning was adopted for the English derivative. Moulton and Milligan state that the primary idea of *zēlos* as found in the papyri is "fervour."[12]

The word for **sold** is *apedonto*, aorist middle of *apodidōmi*. It is used a number of times in the New Testament for "pay" or "give." But in the middle it means "give up of one's own," and hence "sell." This meaning is found only here, in 5:8, and in Hebrews 12:16. But the Septuagint employs it in the story of Joseph in Genesis 37:28; 45:4. This usage is also found in the papyri.[13]

10 It was God as well as Pharaoh who **made him [Joseph] governor over Egypt** (cf. Gen. 45:8). But Lake and Cadbury probably go too far when they assert categorically: "The subject of *katestēse* is God."[14] The more natural subject is Pharaoh.

11 **Sustenance** is *chortasmata*, found only here in the New Testament. Coming from *chortos*, "grass," its original meaning was "fodder," or food for animals. Later it came to be used also of food for human beings.

12 **Grain** is more correct than "corn" (KJV), at least for American readers. But the word here is not the common term *sitos* ("grain," usually wheat), which occurs some fourteen times in the New Testament. Rather it is *sitia*, which means "bread, food, provisions." The word is found only here in the New Testament.

[8] *Ant.* II, 15, 2. In two other passages (*Ant.* II, 9, 1 and *War*, V, 9, 4), however, he makes the sojourn in Egypt last 400 years.
[9] For further discussion of the meaning of *diathēkē*, see the author's *Gospel According to Mark* ("Evangelical Commentary"), p. 167.
[10] *Beginnings*, IV, 72. [11] *Ibid.* [12] VGT, p. 273. [13] *Ibid.*, p. 61.
[14] *Beginnings*, IV, 72.

13 And at the second time Joseph was made known to his brethren; and Joseph's race became manifest unto Pharaoh.

14 And Joseph sent, and called to him Jacob his father, and all his kindred, three score and fifteen souls.

15 And Jacob went down into Egypt; and he died, himself and our fathers;

16 and they were carried over unto Shechem, and laid in the tomb that Abraham bought for a price in silver of the sons of Hamor in Shechem.

---

13 **At the second time Joseph was made known to his brethren.** There is a parallel in the case of Moses, noted in this chapter. But Lake and Cadbury suggest another when they write: "It is possible that the author is thinking of the first and second 'comings' of Jesus." [15]

14 Stephen states that the total number of Joseph's **kindred was threescore and fifteen souls.** The Hebrew text says 70 persons in Genesis 46:27, Exodus 1:5, and Deuteronomy 10:22. In the passages in Genesis and Exodus the Septuagint says 75, as here, and that number is found in Deuteronomy in the manuscript Alexandrinus. "The LXX does not add Jacob or Joseph, but credits Joseph with nine children instead of two." [16] Josephus states the number as 70.[17] Perhaps that was intended as a round number.

15 **Egypt** is named again. Knowling points out the possible significance thus: "The frequent mention of Egypt may perhaps indicate that Stephen meant to emphasise the fact that there, far away from the land of promise, God's Presence was with the chosen race (who were now all in a strange land), and His worship was observed." [18]

16 **They were . . . laid in the tomb . . . in Shechem** would seem to indicate that all the sons of Jacob were buried there. The Old Testament only states that Joseph was buried at Shechem (Josh. 24:32). But that does not deny the possibility that the bodies of the others were also brought there out of Egypt.[19] Nor is it stated specifically here that Jacob was buried at Shechem, as **they** may refer back only to **our fathers** (vs. 15); that is, the twelve patriarchs. Genesis 50:13 states clearly that Jacob was buried in the cave of Machpelah, at Hebron. There is nothing in the account here that contradicts that.

But the real problem comes in the reference to **the tomb that Abraham bought for a price in silver of the sons of Hamor in Shechem.** The Old Testament record is clear in stating that Abraham purchased the cave of Machpelah at Hebron from Ephron the Hittite (Gen. 23:16, 17), whereas Jacob bought a field at Shechem from the sons of Hamor (Gen. 33:19). How are we to reconcile these statements with Stephen's words here?

Hackett thinks that **Abraham** is due to a corruption of the text, which should be

---

A. The Address to the Council (7:1, 2a)

Addressing the council as **brethren and fathers,** or fellow Jews and official rulers, thus respectfully identifying himself with the nationality and the religion of his accusers, Stephen proceeds to reply to the charges. This same mark of sympathetic identification with the audience addressed is in evidence in each of Peter's and Paul's recorded public addresses. It will characterize the successful gospel minister's message today, or in any day.

B. The Answer to the First Charge (7:2b–37)

The God of glory appeared . . . This is that Moses, who said unto the children of Israel, A prophet shall God raise up unto you from among your brethren, like unto me (vss. 2b, 37).

By a studied and extended recounting of Jewish history, with which his hearers are familiar, Stephen reflects his extreme reverence for, and faith in, both God and His servant Moses and thus refutes their charge that he blasphemed God and Moses.

[15] *Beginnings*, IV, 73.
[16] *Ibid.*
[17] *Ant.* II, 7, 4; VI, 5, 6. Henry J. Cadbury (*The Book of Acts in History* [New York: Harper and Brothers, 1955], p. 108, n. 36) records the claim that "an unpublished Hebrew fragment found about 1953 near the Dead Sea reads at Exodus 1:5, seventy-five like the LXX and Acts."
[18] EGT, II, 184.
[19] Josephus, however, says that the other sons of Jacob were buried in Hebron (*Ant.* II, 8, 2). But Plumptre (*op. cit.* p. 39) argues for the likelihood of their burial at Shechem.

17 But as the time of the promise drew nigh which God vouchsafed unto Abraham, the people grew and multiplied in Egypt,
18 till there arose another king over Egypt, who knew not Joseph.
19 The same dealt craftily with our race, and ill-treated our fathers, that they should cast out their babes to the end they might not live.

---

corrected by substituting Jacob.[20] Lake and Cadbury suggest that the writer of Acts may have "telescoped" together the stories of the two purchases, even as the two calls of Abraham are combined at the beginning of this chapter.[21] Bruce appears to accept this explanation.[22]

Knowling suggests another solution. He calls attention to the fact that Abraham had built an altar at Shechem when he first entered the promised land. Would he not then have been likely to have purchased this sacred spot?[23] Of course, this would assume that Jacob repurchased it at a later date. Plumptre argues at still further length for the plausibility of this explanation, adding the interesting reference in Genesis 48:22.[24] It should be remembered again, as stated above, that one is not required to defend the accuracy of Stephen's statements.

17 For **vouchsafed** *(hōmologēsen)* the King James Version has "sworn" *(ōmosen)*. But the former reading is unquestionably correct, being supported by Aleph A B C. The meaning of the verb here is "agree, promise."

18 **Another king . . . who knew not Joseph** means more than a different individual. It probably signifies another dynasty. It is generally held that Joseph was prime minister of Egypt during the time when the Hyksos kings ruled that country.[25] This period is dated about 1710–1550 B.C.[26] Albright writes, "We have recently discovered that the Hyksos were almost entirely Semitic," and further says that they "spoke the same language as was then spoken by the Hebrews."[27] Albright then adds: "The pharaoh who 'knew not Joseph' must have been one of the kings of the Eighteenth Dynasty."[28]

The significance of the language of this verse then becomes clear. Jacob and his family were warmly welcomed into Egypt by their fellow-Semites who then ruled that country. (This also helps explain how a slave-prisoner, Joseph, could become prime minister.) But when a native Egyptian dynasty expelled the Hyksos, the Hebrews would be hated all the more because of their association with the foreign Hyksos rulers.

19 **Dealt craftily** *(katasophisamenos)* may be rendered "exploited."[29] Lake and Cadbury say: "It implies crafty or deceitful ill-treatment."[30] The word is found only here in the New Testament. But it is used in the Septuagint in Exodus 1:10, where the English reads: "Let us deal wisely with them."

The word **ill-treated** *(ekakōse)*[31] covers a multitude of sins. Josephus says the Egyptians compelled the Israelites to dig canals and build city walls and pyramids "and by all this wore them out."[32]

The facility with which Stephen relates the history of God's chosen people, from the call of Abraham in Ur to the giving of the Law on Sinai, reveals both his thorough knowledge of those historical facts and his grasp of their spiritual significance, culminating in the promise of the Messiah (vs. 37b; cf. Deut. 18:15 and Acts 3:22). Thus Stephen shows, not only that he believes in and reverences God and Moses, but that God through Moses prepared the way for the coming of the Christ whom he preached. Instead of blaspheming God and Moses, as they charged, Stephen shows that faith in God and Moses is established through faith in Christ, who is the Son of the first and the fulfilment of the type of the second.

[20] Hackett, *op. cit.*, p. 95. [21] *Beginnings*, IV, 74.
[22] Bruce, *Acts*, p. 106; NIC, p. 149, n. 39.
[23] EGT, II, 185. [24] Plumptre, *op. cit.*, pp. 39, 40.
[25] G. Ernest Wright and Floyd V. Filson (eds.), *Westminster Historical Atlas to the Bible* (Philadelphia: Westminster Press, 1945), p. 28.
[26] *Ibid.*, (rev. ed., 1956), p. 15.
[27] W. F. Albright, "The Old Testament and Archaeology," *Old Testament Commentary*, ed. H. C. Alleman and E. E. Flack (Philadelphia: Muhlenberg Press, 1948), p. 141.
[28] *Ibid.* [29] *Beginnings*, IV, 74. [30] *Ibid.*
[31] The same word occurs in Exodus 1:11 (LXX), where the English has "afflict." [32] *Ant.* II, 9, 1.

20 At which season Moses was born, and was exceeding fair; and he was nourished three months in his father's house:

21 and when he was cast out, Pharaoh's daughter took him up, and nourished him for her own son.

22 And Moses was instructed in all the wisdom of the Egyptians; and he was mighty in his words and works.

23 But when he was well-nigh forty years old, it came into his heart to visit his brethren the children of Israel.

24 And seeing one *of them* suffer wrong, he defended him, and avenged him that was oppressed, smiting the Egyptian:

That they should cast out their babes has "he" in the margin of the American Standard Version. Knowling comments: "A comparison with Exod. i. 22 (LXX) justifies us in taking these words, as in R.V. margin, as describing the tyranny of Pharaoh, not as declaring that the parents themselves exposed their children." [33] Lechler apparently holds the same view—"he ill-treated them, so that, among other things, he caused their new-born children to be exposed." [34] But the majority of commentators interpret this statement as meaning that Pharaoh's oppression caused the Israelites to expose their own infants.

20 The statement is made that **Moses . . . was exceeding fair.** The Greek says "fair unto God" or "beautiful before God" (RSV). Josephus quotes Pharaoh's daughter as saying to her father: "I have brought up a child who is of a divine form" *(morphē te theion)*.[35]

21 **When he was cast out** would suggest that Moses' parents exposed him to die. But the account in Exodus (2:2–9) seems to indicate that the child was purposely placed where Pharaoh's daughter would discover him.

Pharaoh's daughter can be identified with Queen Hatshepsut (ca. 1490–1468 B.C.) if the fifteenth century date (ca. 1447 B.C.) of the Exodus is accepted.[36] But since that date is still very much disputed, the identification is uncertain.

Took him up *(aneilato)* may be translated "adopted." That is the meaning the word had in common Greek. But the use of this same verb in Exodus 2:5 for taking up the "ark" in which Moses lay would suggest a non-technical sense here.

22 The statement of this verse is not found in the Old Testament; but Jewish legend has greatly elaborated the idea. Schürer says that "the Hellenists" represented Moses as the father of all science and culture. "He was, according to Eupolemus, the inventor of alphabetical writing, which first came from him to the Phoenicians, and from them to the Greeks." [37] One writer, Artabanus, went so far as to say that the Egyptians owed to Moses their whole civilization.[38]

The statement that Moses was **mighty in his words and works** has sometimes been held to conflict with Exodus 4:10. But **words** may refer to his written words.[39] Knowling, moreover, makes another suggestion. He writes: "There is no contradiction with Exod. IV. 10, and no need to explain the expression of Moses' writings, for Stephen has in his thoughts not so much . . . the oratorical form as the powerful contents of Moses' words." [40] Josephus speaks of him as "very able to persuade the people by his speeches." [41]

23 **When he was well-nigh forty years old** (literally, "when the time of forty years was being fulfilled to him"), Moses decided to **visit his brethren.** The Old Testament does not give his exact age at this point but merely says, "when Moses was grown up" (Ex. 2:11). But rabbinical tradition divided Moses' life into three periods of forty years each.

24 **Smiting** equals "killing" here. This meaning of *patassō* is found only in the Septuagint and New Testament.

[33] EGT, II, 186. [34] *Op. cit.*, p. 119. [35] *Ant.* II, 9, 7.
[36] Cf. G. Ernest Wright, *Biblical Archaeology* (Philadelphia: Westminster Press, 1957), p. 60.
[37] Schürer, *op. cit.*, II, i, 323.
[38] *Ibid.*
[39] *Beginnings*, IV, 75.
[40] EGT, II, 187.
[41] *Ant.* III, 1, 4.

25 and he supposed that his brethren understood that God by his hand was giving them deliverance; but they understood not.

26 And the day following he appeared unto them as they strove, and would have set them at one again, saying, Sirs, ye are brethren; why do ye wrong one to another?

27 But he that did his neighbor wrong thrust him away, saying, Who made thee a ruler and a judge over us?

28 Wouldest thou kill me, as thou killedst the Egyptian yesterday?

29 And Moses fled at this saying, and became a sojourner in the land of Midian, where he begat two sons.

30 And when forty years were fulfilled, an angel appeared to him in the wilderness of Mount Sinai, in a flame of fire in a bush.

31 And when Moses saw it, he wondered at the sight: and as he drew near to behold, there came a voice of the Lord,

32 I am the God of thy fathers, the God of Abraham, and of Isaac, and of Jacob. And Moses trembled, and durst not behold.

33 And the Lord said unto him, Loose the shoes from thy feet: for the place whereon thou standest is holy ground.

34 I have surely seen the affliction of my people that is in Egypt, and have heard their groaning, and I am come down to deliver them: and now come, I will send thee into Egypt.

35 This Moses whom they refused, saying, Who made thee a ruler and a judge? him hath God sent *to be* both a ruler and a deliverer with the hand of the angel that appeared to him in the bush.

---

25 This statement is without a parallel in the Old Testament.[42] **Deliverance** is *sotēria*, "salvation."

26 **Would have set them at one** is better, "tried to reconcile." It is the imperfect of *synallassō*, found only here in the New Testament.

27 The one that **thrust him away** was **he that did his neighbor wrong.** Robertson observes: "It is always the man who is doing the wrong who is hard to reconcile."[43]

29 **Moses . . . became a sojourner** *(paroikos)*, though his sojourn lasted forty years. The thought of being a pilgrim is stressed throughout this chapter (cf. vss. 6, 44). **Midian** was "the district round the gulf of Akaba, traditionally inhabited by the children of Abraham by his second wife, Keturah."[44]

30 Verse 23, this one, and 13:18 clearly indicate the three periods of forty years each in Moses' life. That he was 120 years old at death is stated in Deuteronomy 34:7.

Angel here is defined by the Fathers as the Eternal Logos.[45]

Sinai is called Horeb in Exodus 3:1. Page thinks they were "probably peaks of one mountain range."[46] Horeb means "the mountain of dried-up ground," Sinai "the mountain of the thorns."[47]

31 **To behold** is a little weak for the infinitive *katanoēsai*. The verb means "to take note of, perceive, consider carefully." It has the idea of putting one's mind *(nous)* on something.

33 Bruce comments: "The removal of the shoes was a mark of respect to the divine presence, as it was a mark of respect to one's host when visiting him."[48] Moslems today remove their shoes when entering a mosque. The Jews thought the temple in Jerusalem was *the* holy place. But Stephen reminds them that at the bush the voice said **the place whereon thou standest is holy ground.** This, indeed, was completely outside Palestine.

34 **I have surely seen** is literally "having seen I saw." This Semitic expression is quoted from the Septuagint of Exodus 3:7.

35 Just as God had chosen Joseph, when rejected by his brethren, so too He had chosen **this Moses** who was refused by his fellow countrymen. In this way the two men were typical of Jesus Christ, who though rejected by His people was chosen by God

[42] Lumby, *Acts* (CGT), p. 167, says: "The traditions . . . represent the death of the Egyptian as no mere ordinary killing by superior strength, but as brought about by mysterious divine power, which Moses feeling within himself expected his kindred to recognize." But there is nothing in the account in Exodus 2:12 to suggest this.

[43] *Word Pictures*, III, 88. [44] *Beginnings*, IV, 76. [45] EGT, II, 191.

[46] *Op. cit.*, p. 124. See discussion of the location of Mount Sinai in *Time*, LXVIII (Dec. 3, 1956), 71.

[47] *Word Pictures*, III, 89. [48] *Acts*, p. 170.

36 This man led them forth, having wrought wonders and signs in Egypt, and in the Red
sea, and in the wilderness forty years.
37 This is that Moses, who said unto the children of Israel, A prophet shall God raise
up unto you from among your brethren, like unto me.
38 This is he that was in the church in the wilderness with the angel that spake to him
in the mount Sinai, and with our fathers: who received living oracles to give unto us:
39 to whom our fathers would not be obedient, but thrust him from them, and turned
back in their hearts unto Egypt,
40 saying unto Aaron, Make us gods that shall go before us: for as for this Moses, who
led us forth out of the land of Egypt, we know not what is become of him.
41 And they made a calf in those days, and brought a sacrifice unto the idol, and rejoiced
in the works of their hands.
42 But God turned, and gave them up to serve the host of heaven; as it is written in the
book of the prophets,

Did ye offer unto me slain beasts and sacrifices
Forty years in the wilderness, O house of Israel?

---

as both **ruler** and **deliverer.** The words are here applied to Moses, but prefigure Christ. **Deliverer** is literally "redeemer." The Greek word *lytrōtēs* has not been found anywhere in classical Greek. It comes from *lytron*, "ransom," and so means "one who ransoms or redeems." This could be applied to Moses in only a limited way as "deliverer" from Egyptian bondage. But it can carry its full force when used of Christ.

36 Moses was like Jesus also in doing **wonders and signs.** Moses' miracles were performed in Egypt, spectacularly at the Red Sea, and in the wilderness.

37 This prophecy had its first reference to Moses and its second and more complete application to Christ (cf. 3:22). This is what is called the "telescopic" principle of prophecy.

38 Extreme dispensationalists object strenuously to speaking of the "Old Testament church." But it should be noted that *ekklēsia* is here used of the congregation of Israel. Verse 37 is a quotation of Deuteronomy 18:15. Right following that, in Deuteronomy 18:16 *ekklēsia* is used in the Septuagint for the congregation of Israelites assembled at Sinai to receive the Law. So it is properly applied to God's people in Old Testament times. **Angel** here and in verse 35 evidently refers to God's own presence as manifested to Moses. For **living oracles** compare Hebrews 4:12 and I Peter 1:23.

39 Again the idea of rejection is emphasized. This is the main theme running all through Stephen's speech.

40 The quotation is from Exodus 32:1. The Israelites quickly turned away from their God in spite of all He had done for them.

41 **They made a calf** is all one word in the Greek, *emoschopoiēsan*, a compound verb formed from *moschos*, "calf," and *poieō*, "make." The word is not found elsewhere, except in later writers commenting on the Bible.

42 For **gave them up** compare Romans 1:24, 26, 28. **The host of heaven** refers to the sun, moon, and stars. This form of false worship is mentioned a number of times in the Old Testament (cf. Deut. 4:19; 17:3; II Chron. 33:3, 5; Jer. 7:18). **The book of the prophets** evidently means the twelve so-called Minor Prophets, referred to by the Jews as "the Book of the Twelve."

C. The Answer to the Third Charge (7:38–43)

This is he . . . who received living oracles to give unto us (vs. 38). Stephen continues his defense by indicating that Moses was part and parcel of the true **church** [of God] **in the wilderness** (vs. 38a), which culminated in Christ the Messiah, and that it was by the hand of this Moses that God, through an angel, gave Israel the Law, the living oracles. Further, he shows from their own history that their fathers had rejected Moses and the Law which God gave them through him; while he, Stephen, rather than blaspheming the Law, reverenced it for what it was intended of God: **living oracles** designed as a "tutor to bring us unto Christ" (Gal. 3:24b).

43 And ye took up the tabernacle of Moloch,
And the star of the god Rephan,
The figures which ye made to worship them:
And I will carry you away beyond Babylon.

44 Our fathers had the tabernacle of the testimony in the wilderness, even as he appointed who spake unto Moses, that he should make it according to the figure that he had seen.

45 Which also our fathers, in their turn, brought in with Joshua when they entered on the possession of the nations, that God thrust out before the face of our fathers, unto the days of David;

42, 43 The quotation in these two verses is from Amos 5:25–27. The differences between the Septuagint and the Massoretic Text have created a problem for Biblical scholars. The Hebrew of Amos 5:26, 27 reads: "But ye have carried Sikkuth your king and the star-images of Chiun your god, which ye made for yourselves, therefore I will carry you into captivity beyond Damascus."[49] The Septuagint took Sikkuth as meaning **tabernacle** and "your king" as **Moloch.**[50] The difficulty of the translation of this passage may be seen by a comparison of the English versions (KJV, RV, ASV, RSV). **Rephan** was apparently the substitution of the name of an Egyptian god by the Septuagint translators.[51]

Stephen is emphasizing the fact that the idolatry which flowered at Sinai with the worship of the golden calf came to full fruition during the period of the monarchy in the worship of the heavenly bodies. This resulted in the people of Israel being carried captive by Assyria.

The most startling change in this quotation is the change from "beyond Damascus" (found in both the Hebrew and Septuagint of Amos 5:27) to **beyond Babylon.** Bruce gives the best explanation of this: "Amos, foretelling the Assyrian exile of the northern kingdom, described the place of their captivity as 'beyond Damascus'; but the same disloyalty to the God of Israel brought a similar judgment on the southern kingdom more than a century later, in the Babylonian exile, and Stephen accordingly substitutes 'beyond Babylon' for 'beyond Damascus.'"[52]

44 **The tabernacle of the testimony** is what the Septuagint has for "the tent of meeting" (e.g. Ex. 33:7). This tabernacle was **in the wilderness.** God appointed a place of worship which was neither the temple nor in the Holy Land. Thus again Stephen emphasizes the fact that God's presence was not restricted to what the Jews called sacred. **Figure** is contrasted with the "figures" of false gods in verse 43. The Greek word is *typos*, from which comes "type." For the idea of a heavenly pattern for the earthly tabernacle, see Hebrews 9:23, 24.

45 **In their turn** is *diadexamenoi* (only here in N.T.). It means "receive in turn." **Joshua** is correct rather than "Jesus" (KJV). While the Greek does have *Iēsous*, yet the obvious allusion is to the Joshua (Heb.) of the Old Testament. Both words mean "saviour."

D. The Answer to the Second Charge (7:44–50)

Our fathers had the tabernacle of the testimony in the wilderness (vs. 44a). Stephen replies to the charge of blasphemy against the temple by showing that God was worshipped by the Israelites in the wilderness in the tabernacle which was God's pattern for the temple which was later to be constructed by Solomon. However, he clearly implies that the true spiritual worship of God is not confined to material buildings, and that as God was worshipped in the wilderness before there was a temple, so He may now be worshipped without the temple: **Howbeit the Most High**[b] **dwelleth not in houses made with hands . . . The heaven is my throne, And the earth the footstool of my feet** (vss. 48, 49a). To this very fact their own prophet has borne testimony: **as saith the prophet,** (vs. 48b; cf. I Kings 8:27; II Chron. 2:6; 6:18).

[49] *Beginnings*, IV, 79.
[50] *Ibid.*
[51] For a careful discussion of the difficult terms here, see Bruce, NIC, p. 155, n. 63; and Knowling, EGT, II, 195 f.
[52] NIC, p. 156.

[b] See Additional Note I, *The High-God Theory* at end of Chapter VII.

46 who found favor in the sight of God, and asked to find a habitation for the God of Jacob.
47 But Solomon built him a house.
48 Howbeit the Most High dwelleth not in *houses* made with hands; as saith the prophet,
49 The heaven is my throne,
And the earth the footstool of my feet:
What manner of house will ye build me? saith the Lord:
Or what is the place of my rest?
50 Did not my hand make all these things?
51 Ye stiffnecked and uncircumcised in heart and ears, ye do always resist the Holy
Spirit: as your fathers did, so do ye.
52 Which of the prophets did not your fathers persecute? and they killed them that
showed before of the coming of the Righteous One; of whom ye have now become betrayers
and murderers;
53 ye who received the law as it was ordained by angels, and kept it not.

Unto the days of David should be taken with **which also our fathers . . . brought in,** rather than with **they entered on the possession of the nations.** While it is true that the possession of Canaan was not completed until the days of David—with the capture of the Jebusite stronghold of Jerusalem and the defeat of the Philistines on the coast—yet Stephen's point here is that the Israelites worshipped God in the movable tabernacle until the time of David.

46 **God of Jacob** is the reading of A C E P and many of the early versions. But Aleph B D have "house of Jacob." Lake and Cadbury defend the latter as probably original.[53] Bruce says: "Perhaps *theōi* was an early emendation for *oikōi*, itself a still earlier corruption of the original, which Hort, followed by Ropes, suggested might be *kyriōi*." [54]

47 This verse corroborates the interpretation given above for verse 45.

48 The statement of this verse is the heart of Stephen's theme. He is trying to show the unreasonableness of the Jewish attitude toward the temple as the sole place of God's presence among them. Solomon expressed the same idea in his prayer of dedication (II Chron. 6:18).

49, 50 To substantiate his declaration just made (vs. 48), Stephen quotes from Isaiah 66:1, 2a.

51 **Stiffnecked** *(sklērotrachēloi)* is found only here in the New Testament. It is taken from Exodus 33:3 and other passages in the Septuagint. **Uncircumcised in heart** echoes Leviticus 26:41 and Ezekiel 44:7. For **uncircumcised . . . in ears** compare Jeremiah 6:10.

It is sometimes held that perhaps Stephen was interrupted at this point in his speech by furious opposition. [55] But Page thinks "the growing warmth of the speech" led naturally to this outburst. [56]

52 For the charge made here compare Jesus' words in Matthew 5:12, and Luke 13:34; also Matthew 23:29–37. **The Righteous One** means the Messiah (cf. 3:14).

53 **Ordained by angels** is an idea not found in the Old Testament, but occurring in

---

E. The Indictment of the Council (7:51–53)

Ye stiffnecked and uncircumcised in heart and ears, ye do always resist the Holy Spirit; as your fathers did, so do ye (vs. 51). Finally, having incontestably cleared himself of the charge of blasphemy, Stephen turns the whole argument on the rulers of the Jews and directly indicts them with the height of the crime of blasphemy, through their willful and persistent disobedience to, and rejection of, God's Law and its realized fulfillment in Jesus Christ their Messiah (see Num. 15:30, 31). Thus he has established two great facts: *first*, that, as Paul later stated (Gal. 3:23–26), the Law only served to bring man to Christ, and that its instrumental value is now past, since Christ the Messiah has already come; and *second*, that they, his accusers, themselves stand inescapably condemned for the very crime of which they have accused him, blasphemy, which carries the penalty of death.

[53] *Beginnings*, IV, 81.
[54] Bruce, *Acts*, p. 175. See also Knowling, EGT, II, 198 (critical note).
[55] So Bruce, *Acts*, pp. 176, 177.
[56] *Op. cit.*, p. 128.

54 Now when they heard these things, they were cut to the heart, and they gnashed on him with their teeth.
55 But he, being full of the Holy Spirit, looked up stedfastly into heaven, and saw the glory of God, and Jesus standing on the right hand of God,
56 and said, Behold, I see the heavens opened, and the Son of man standing on the right hand of God.
57 But they cried out with a loud voice, and stopped their ears, and rushed upon him with one accord;
58 and they cast him out of the city, and stoned him: and the witnesses laid down their garments at the feet of a young man named Saul.

Galatians 3:19; (cf. also Heb. 2:2). Josephus expresses this mediation of angels.[57]

54 **Cut to the heart** is the same word *(dieprionto)* as in 5:33 (see note there). **Gnashed on him with their teeth** reflects Psalm 35:16.

55 **Full of the Holy Spirit** is a key phrase of Acts. **Looked up stedfastly** *(atenisas)* also occurs frequently. **Jesus standing** has often been interpreted as meaning that Jesus stood to greet this first martyr.[58] But Dalman thinks this is "merely a verbal change in expression" for "sitting" in Mark 14:62.[59]

56 The language of this verse is similar to the words of Jesus before the Sanhedrin recorded in Matthew 26:64; Mark 14:62, and Luke 22:69. **The Son of man** is a phrase found only here outside the Gospels, where it is always used by Jesus of Himself (81 times).[60] The meaning of the title is indicated by Daniel 7:13, 14, where the "son of man" is pictured as a king with a universal and everlasting kingdom. Stephen's vision corroborated Jesus' claim and infuriated the Jewish leaders, who had condemned Jesus to death for that claim.

57 The mob action here is an example of gross unreasonableness. Refusing to listen, **they stopped their ears,** as they **rushed upon him with one accord.** Whether this refers to the members of the Sanhedrin or to the crowd mentioned in 6:12 is not certain. It sounds like a lynching by a mob. But in any case, the Jewish leaders were involved.

58 The mention of **the witnesses** suggests a formal execution, though carried out in an illegal and violent manner. It was enjoined in the Law (Deut. 17:7) that the witnesses who testified at the trial should cast the first stones at the execution.

III. STEPHEN'S GLORIOUS MARTYRDOM (7:54–60)

Stephen became the first Christian Martyr, and he gave his life that the Gospel might be unshackled from Jewish legalism to find its way to the hearts of all men throughout the world.

A. The Council's Indignation (7:54)

They were cut to the heart [sawn asunder], **and they gnashed on him with their teeth.** Weymouth says, "They became infuriated and gnashed their teeth at him." The realization of their humiliating situation, after Stephen's speech, should have brought them to repentance and submission to Christ, as on the day of Pentecost. However, it only inflamed their wrath and dethroned their reason, and thus an orderly and dignified court suddenly became a scene of mob-mad chaotic violence. The volcano had long smouldered, but now it suddenly burst forth in all of its destructive fury, inundating its innocent victim with its scalding wrath.

B. The Consolation of Stephen (7:55, 56)

But he . . . saw the glory of God. Through the hail of death-stones, Stephen caught a vision of God's revealed glory that was laid up in store for him and saw Jesus standing on the right hand of God, in identification with His martyred saint, waiting to receive him into everlasting glory. It is said that this is the only scriptural record of Christ standing, after His ascension. With David he could say: "Yea, though I walk through the valley of the shadow of death, I will fear no evil; for thou art with me" (Ps. 23:4a).

[57] *Ant.* XV, 5, 3.
[58] E.g., Lenski, *op. cit.*, p. 304.
[59] George Dalman, *op. cit.*, p. 311.
[60] See special note in the author's *Mark*, p. 44.

59 And they stoned Stephen, calling upon *the Lord*, and saying, Lord Jesus, receive my spirit.

60 And he kneeled down, and cried with a loud voice, Lord, lay not this sin to their charge. And when he had said this he fell asleep.

This is the first mention of **Saul.** Doubtless this scene was indelibly stamped on his memory.

59 The Greek reads: "And they were stoning Stephen, as he was calling upon and saying, 'Lord Jesus, receive my spirit.'" The comparison with Luke 23:46 is too striking to miss. Stephen had the spirit of his Lord.

60 Again Stephen echoed the words of Jesus, the last cry from the Cross, found in Luke 23:46. Probably this prayer was addressed to Jesus as **Lord,** as is definitely stated of the one in verse 59.

He fell asleep is *ekoimēthē*, from *koimaō*, "put to sleep." The cognate noun *koimētērion* gives the English word "cemetery." It suggests a faith in the resurrection.

C. The Council's Illegal Procedure (7:57, 58)

They cast him out of the city, and stoned him (vs. 58a).

Justice and legality were thrown to the wind as the rulers, **with one accord,** rushed upon the defendant and, without verdict or sentence, dragged him out of the city and violently stoned him to death. Nor had the Jewish Sanhedrin the right of execution without Roman authority, with one exception (see note on Acts 4:5, 6). This was reserved for the Roman government. Thus Stephen's death was a violent, unjust, and illegal murder at the hands of the Jewish rulers, though the people of Acts 6:12 may have been employed as their unwitting instruments.

D. The Prayer of Stephen (7:59, 60a)

Lord Jesus, receive my spirit . . . Lord, lay not this sin to their charge.

Amidst the confusion and fury of violent death, Stephen makes two requests. *First,* he prays for the privilege of continued identification with his Master: **Lord Jesus, receive my spirit.** *Second,* he prays for his enemies: **Lord, lay not this sin to their charge.** St. Augustine is reported to have said, "If Stephen had not prayed, Saul would not have been converted." Saul heard Stephen's prayer. How like the Master's dying prayer was that of Stephen (Luke 23:34a)! Some of Christ's own murderers were present to hear both the dying prayer of the Master and that of His martyred saint, Stephen.

E. The Death of Stephen (7:60b)

Luke had caught the spirit of hope that animated the first Christians when he recorded, concerning Stephen's death, **he fell asleep.** Taylor remarks, "Such a mode of speech suggests a future awakening."[c] Thereafter the Christians appear to have largely substituted the word "sleep" for "death," in the event of the decease of a Christian (cf. John 11:23–26; I Cor. 15; 1 Thess. 4:13–18). The word bespeaks the continuance of the new life which they already enjoyed. It suggests that they had grasped the significance of immortality through Christ.

Vincent significantly observes concerning Stephen's death, as expressed in the words, **He fell asleep,** that this expression marks

> . . . his calm and peaceful death. Though the pagan authors sometimes used *sleep* to signify *death*, it was only as a poetic figure. When Christ, on the other hand, said, 'Our friend Lazarus *sleepeth* . . .,' he used the word, not as a figure, but as the expression of a *fact*. In the mystery of death, in which the pagan saw only nothingness, Jesus saw continued life, rest, waking — the elements which enter into sleep. And thus, in Christian speech and thought, as the doctrine of the resurrection struck its roots deeper, the word *dead*, with its hopeless finality, gave place to the more gracious and hopeful word *sleep*. The pagan burying-place carried in its name no suggestion of hope or comfort. It was a *burying-place*, a *hiding-place*, a *monumentum*, a mere *memorial* of something gone; a *columbarium* or dove-cot, with its little pigeonholes for cinerary urns; but the Christian thought of death as sleep, brought with it into Christian speech the kindred thought of a chamber of rest, and embodied it in the word *cemetery . . . the place to lie down to sleep.*[d]

[c] William M. Taylor, *Paul the Missionary* (New York: Richard R. Smith, Inc., 1930), p. 23.
[d] Marvin R. Vincent, *Word Studies in the New Testament* (New York: Charles Scribner's Sons, 1887, rep. 1906), I, 486.

Additional Note I

THE HIGH-GOD THEORY

Stephen's allusion to **the Most High** (Acts 7:48), here clearly identified with the Jehovah of the Hebrews, is both interesting and provoking. Twice in the Acts the expression occurs (Acts 7:48 and 16:17), and once in Hebrews (Heb. 7:1). Paul's allusion to "The Unknown God" of the Athenians (Acts 17:23) appears to bear the same significance as the other references. At Philippi the demon-possessed damsel referred to the Christian apostles as servants of "the Most High God, who proclaim . . . the way of salvation" (Acts 16:17). Likewise the demon-possessed Gadarene addressed Jesus as the "Son of the Most High God" (Mk. 5:7). In the Epistle to the Hebrews Melchizedek is referred to as the "priest of the God Most High" (Heb. 7:1).

All of the foregoing adds up to a strong suspicion that, even apart from the special divine revelation as given of God to the Hebrew through the law, but later and fuller to the world through Christ, there is in man's moral consciousness the inescapable conviction of a supreme God. In the science of religion this concept has become known as the "High-God Theory."

In general the "High-God Theory" maintains that all people, including the most primitive, have a concept of a Supreme Being, above and beyond their polytheistic concepts. This "High-God" is seldom an object of worship for primitives, though he may be recognized as the supreme God. Zwemer[e] treats the subject at considerable length.

Andrew Lang, nearly half a century ago, was one of the earliest modern scholars to advance and champion this "High-God" theory. Lang spoke of his "anachronistic views regarding the prevalence of the idea of a Sky-god or Highest God among primitive tribes."[f] Though Lang was largely ignored at first, in due time Wilhelm Schmidt, the well-known German anthropologist, revived the theory and brought it to scholarly recognition and wide acceptance. Thus Zwemer writes:

> Through endless transformations, myths, and legends, the Sky-god or High-god is found at the base of all the ethnic religions in the Mediterranean area and in the Far East. We find him also among primitive tribes in most widely scattered areas and the belief in such a Supreme Spirit is characterized by spontaneity, universality, and persistency which can only point to a veritable primitive revelation or an innate perception.[g]

Lang stated:

> Of the existence of a belief in a Supreme Being, among primitive tribes there is as good evidence as we possess for any fact in the ethnographic region . . . certain low savages are as monotheistic as some Christians. They have a Supreme Being and the distinctive attributes of Deity are not by them assigned to other beings.[h]

J. K. Archer,[i] following Wilhelm Schmidt, classifies primitives on the "lower" and "higher" cultural levels. The former include the Negritos, certain Micronesian and Polynesian tribes, Papuans, Aruntas, Andamanese, the Kols and Pariaks, the Pygmies and Bushmen, the Caribs and the Yohgans. The latter include the Samoans, Hawaiians, Kalmuks, Veddas, Todas, Bantus, Eskimos, and the American Indians.

In his Oxford Lectures ("High Gods In North America"—1932), Schmidt asserted:

> It is precisely among the three oldest primitive peoples of North America that we find a clear and firmly established belief in a High-god . . . It is only now that we can produce the final proof that these High-gods, in their oldest form, come before all other elements, be they naturalism, fetishism, Ghost-worship, animism, totemism, or magism, from one or other of which of the earlier evolutionistic theories had derived the origin of religion.[j]

Schmidt[k] further observes that among a large number of these tribes the High-god concept includes the creatorship of the universe *ex nihilo*.

Grace H. Turnbull cites ample evidence from the ritual of the Omaha Indians to the effect that "Wakonda" was their High-god and as such was the creator of all things: "At the beginning all things were in the

e Samuel Marinus Zwemer, *The Origin of Religion, Evolution or Revelation* (New York: Louizeaux Brothers, 1945), pp. 75–99.
f *Ibid.*, p. 75.
g *Ibid.* Cf. "Sky-Gods" by Foucart in *Encyclopedia of Religion and Ethics*, James Hastings, ed. (New York: Charles Scribner's Sons, 1928), pp. 580–585.
h Andrew Lang, *The Making of Religion*, pp. 181, 183.
i J. K. Archer, *Faiths Men Live By* (New York: Nelson, 1934), pp. 18, 19.
j Wilhelm Schmidt, *High Gods in North America* (Oxford University Press, 1933), p. 19.
k *Ibid.*

mind of Wakonda . . . Wakonda [was] the Maker of all things." [l]

Schmidt observes that primitives generally represent the Supreme Being as absolutely good, ascribe to him fatherhood, creative power, and sky residence. African pygmies and bushmen, Philippine Negritos, and Southeast Australians use the name "father" for their High-god. Creator is a common designation for him among the American Indians. The Ainu of Hokkadio have three unusual names for their High-god: Upholder, Cradle (of children), and Protector.[m]

Among the High-god attributes on which there is rather general agreement among primitives, Schmidt [n] observes, are eternity, omniscience, beneficence, omnipotence, and the authority to administer rewards and punishments.

Likewise missionaries and anthropologists have found this High-god concept in the ethnic religions of China (*Shang-ti*=supreme ruler), Japan (*Ama no Mi Naka Nusho no Mikoto*), and India (*Varuna*, perhaps the original *Ouranos*). [o]

Ancient Egypt, Assyria (*Ashur*), and the Arabs (*Orotal*, a corruption of *Alah Taal*) have all had their High-god concepts as expressed in their respective deities. [p]

Zwemer observes that Calvin held that

> . . . in every man there is still a seed of religious truth and an ineradicable consciousness of God. Light is still shining in the darkness and all men still retain a degree of love for truth, for justice, and a social order. This knowledge of God, said Calvin, is innate but quickened by the manifestation of God in nature. It fails in its proper effect because of sin, and could only be restored by special grace in a special objective revelation. [q]

Zwemer concludes that "although Calvin's doctrine of the knowledge of God and of Common Grace was wholly based on the Scriptures, this very doctrine is now largely confirmed by anthropology and the history of religion." [r]

We conclude therefore that the origin of the idea of God is not due to magic, fetishism, manism, animism, or any process of evolution on man's part, but to God himself, the Creator of man and his Redeemer. "For ever since the world was created, his invisible nature, his everlasting power and divine being, have been quite perceptible in what he had made. So they have no excuse. Though they knew God, they have not glorified him as God nor given thanks to him; they have turned to futile speculations till their ignorant minds grew dark . . . Since they have exchanged the truth of God for an untruth, worshipping and serving the creature rather than the Creator who is blessed for ever. Amen. (Rom. 1:20, 21, 25).[s]

Therefore, it appears most probable that the Philippian demoniac's "Most High God" (Acts 16:17), the Athenians' "Unknown God" (Acts 17:23), and Melchizedek's "God Most High" (Heb. 7:1), with their varying concepts, were one and the same with the "Most High God" (Acts 7:48) of Stephen's address and the "Most High God" (Mark 5:7), recognized by the demon-possessed Gadarene. [t]

[l] Grace H. Turnbull, *Tongues of Fire: A Bible of Sacred Scriptures of the Pagan World* (New York: Macmillan Co., 1929), p. 10.

[m] Wilhelm Schmidt, *The Origin and Growth of Religion: Facts and Theories*. Tr. H. J. Rose (New York: Dial, 1935), pp. 263–269.

[n] *Ibid.*, pp. 270–275.

[o] Zwemer, *op. cit.*, pp. 84–88.

[p] *Ibid.*, pp. 89–93.

[q] *Ibid.*, p. 98.

[r] *Ibid.*

[s] *Ibid.*, pp. 98, 99.

[t] For further evidence on the "High-God" theory, the reader is referred to the following works:

P. S. Deshmukh, *Religion in Vedic Literature* (Oxford: 1933).
Alexander LeRoy, *The Religion of the Primitives*. Tr. Newton Thompson (New York, 1922).
R. H. Lowie, *Primitive Religion* (New York: (Liveright Pub., Corp., rep. 1948).
John Murphy, *Primitive Man*: His Essential Quest (Oxford: 1927).
Paul Radin, *The Method and Theory of Ethnology* (London: 1933).
Paul Radin, *Primitive Man As Philosopher* (New York: 1927).
Paul Radin, *The Racial Myth* (New York: 1933).
Benjamin B. Warfield, "Antiquity and Unity of the Human Race," in *Studies In Theology* (New York: 1932), pp. 235–258.
William L. Thomas, *Source Book for Social Origins* (Chicago; 1909).
H. J. D. Ashtey, *Biblical Anthropology* (Oxford U. Press, 1929).
Robert Henry Lowie, *The History of Ethnological Theory* (New York: Rhinebart, 1937).

CHAPTER VIII

And Saul was consenting unto his death. And there arose on that day a great persecution against the church which was in Jerusalem; and they were all scattered abroad throughout the regions of Judaea and Samaria, except the apostles.

EXEGESIS

At the eighth chapter we enter a new division of the book. Hitherto all the events recorded took place in or near Jerusalem. Now the work of the Holy Spirit through the disciples moves out into "all Judaea and Samaria." In chapter eight we read of Philip preaching in Samaria and of Peter and John giving the gospel "to many villages of the Samaritans" (8:25). In the latter part of chapter nine, there is a record of Peter's ministry in Lydda and Joppa, both in Judea. And Judea is the locale of most of the events described in chapters 10–12.

1 **Was consenting** is an imperfect periphrastic. Knowling says: "The formula here indicates the lasting and enduring nature of Saul's 'consent.'"[1] The verb *syneudokeō* is used six times in the New Testament—three times by Luke and three times by Paul—and is translated four different ways in the King James Version. It means literally "think well with," and so "join in approving." **Death** really means "murder" or "slaying." It is not the common Greek word for death, *thanatos*, which occurs well over one hundred times in the New Testament, but *anairesis*, found only here. It definitely suggests a

EXPOSITION

PART I

THE CHURCH'S FIRST DISPERSION

I. The Origin of the Mission, Acts 8:1-4.
   A. The Death of Stephen, vss. 1a, 2.
   B. The Dispersion of the Disciples, vs. 1b.
   C. The Persecutions of Saul, vs. 3.
   D. The Preaching of the Disciples, vs. 4.

II. The Samaritan Mission under Philip, Acts 8:5-13.
   A. The Ministry of Philip, vs. 5.
   B. The Response of the Samaritans, vs. 6.
   C. The Success of the Mission, vss. 7, 8.
   D. The Case of Simon the Sorcerer, vss. 9–13.

III. The Apostles and the Samaritan Mission, Acts 8:14–25.
   A. The Apostles' Commission, vs. 14.
   B. The Apostles' Confirmation, vss. 15–17.
   C. The Apostle's Rebuke of Simon, vss. 18–24.
   D. The Apostles' Evangelization, vs. 25.

PART II

THE CHURCH'S FIRST AFRICAN CONVERT

I. The Messenger of God, Acts 8:26–30, 40.
   A. The Messenger's Commission, vs. 26.
   B. The Messenger's Obedience, vs. 27a.
   C. The Messenger's Opportunity, vss. 27b, 28.
   D. The Messenger's Approach, vss. 29, 30.

II. The Seeker after God, Acts 8:31–34.
   A. The Seeker's Bewilderment, vs. 31a.
   B. The Seeker's Request, vs. 31b.
   C. The Seeker's Interest, vss. 32, 33.
   D. The Seeker's Question, vs. 34.

III. The Ready Instructor, Acts 8:35–37.
   A. The Evangelist's Wisdom, vs. 35a.
   B. The Evangelist's Message, vs. 35b.
   C. The Seeker's Conversion, vss. 36, 37.

IV. The Joyful Convert, Acts 8:38, 39.
   A. The Convert's Baptism, vss. 38, 39a.
   B. The Evangelist's Disappearance, vs. 39a.
   C. The Convert's Joy, vs. 39b.
   D. The Evangelist's Continued Ministry vs. 40.

[1] EGT, II, 207.

2 And devout men buried Stephen, and made great lamentation over him.
3 But Saul laid waste the church, entering into every house, and dragging men and women committed them to prison.

---

violent death (lit., a taking up or away). The word is found frequently in medical writers.[2]

On that day is a literal translation of the Greek and is somewhat stronger and more specific than "at that time" (KJV). It would appear that a persecution broke out immediately. Instead of being ashamed of their disgraceful mob murder of Stephen, the Jewish leaders launched an all-out attack on the young church.

This is the second mention of the Christian "church" (cf. 5:11). From now on *ekklēsia* appears fairly frequently. Found only three times in the Gospels (Matt. 16:18; 18:17, twice), it occurs 24 times in Acts, 62 times in Paul's Epistles, twice in Hebrews, four times in the General Epistles, and 20 times in Revelation—for a total of 115 times in the New Testament.

The Greek word for **scattered abroad** occurs in the New Testament only in connection with this dispersion (cf. vs. 4; 11:19). The related noun, *diaspora*, has been taken over into English as the technical term for dispersion. So this might properly be called the first Christian Diaspora.

The geographical extent of the immediate dispersion is indicated as **Judaea and Samaria.** This statement fitly introduces this section of the book (chaps. 8–12).

Except the apostles seems surprising. But the members of this group, all Jews, probably continued worshiping in the temple. They were in general favor with the populace (cf. 5:13). Apparently it was the Hellenists, who exercised more freedom regarding Jewish customs, that were the special object of opposition. Perhaps, too, the apostles considered it their duty to stay in Jerusalem regardless of the danger.

2 There has been much dispute as to whether **devout men** refers to Jews or Christians. Bruce says: "These were probably Jewish Christians."[3] Knowling's conclusion is perhaps the best: "The word might therefore include both devout Jews and Jewish Christians who joined together in burying Stephen."[4] **Buried,** *synekomisan*, is found only here in the New Testament. It literally means "carried together." The word *kopetos*, **lamentation,** means "a beating of the head and breast." It occurs only here in the New Testament.

3 Saul's persecution was very violent. It is stated that he **laid waste the church.** The

---

Part I

The Church's First Dispersion

I. THE ORIGIN OF THE MISSION (8:1–4)

Prior to the incident of this record, Christian evangelization, since Pentecost, had been confined to Jerusalem, as far as we know. Nor does there appear to be any scriptural evidence that the "apostles" as yet envisioned their responsibility for world-wide evangelization. Indeed Christ had so commissioned them (Matt. 28:18–20; Acts 1:8), but the larger significance of that commission had not as yet dawned upon them. As stated previously, it was Stephen, a Hellenist Jew, who first caught this larger vision of the Gospel for the whole world, and who paid for its declaration with his life.

Devout men buried Stephen, and made great lamentation over him (vs. 2). Jewish law forbade public mourning at the death of a condemned criminal. Thus the **great lamentation** over Stephen testified to his innocence and the illegality of his martyrdom. Nor was the body of a criminal buried by official Judaism (see Christ's burial, Matt. 27:57–60; John 19:28–42).

It was Stephen's heroic and glorious death that shattered the iron bars of Jewish legalism and emancipated the Gospel of Christ for world-wide dissemination. The corn of wheat fell into the ground and died, and it brought forth much fruit (John 12:24). Stephen means "crown," and thus he was the first to wear the "Christian martyr's crown" (see Rev. 2:10). He had "fallen asleep" that a great spiritual awakening might occur. God buries His workmen, but His work goes on.

[2] Hobart, *op. cit.*, p. 209.
[3] *Acts*, p. 171.
[4] EGT, II, 209.

4 They therefore that were scattered abroad went about preaching the word.
5 And Philip went down to the city of Samaria, and proclaimed unto them the Christ.

---

verb, *lymainomai,* is found only here in the New Testament. But it is used several times in the Septuagint of a wild boar ravaging a vineyard (cf. Psa. 80 [79]:13). In classical Greek it was used of scourging or torture and of the devastation caused by an army. Medical writers employed it for the ravages of disease.[5]

It is not clear whether **house** refers primarily to private homes or to the places of worship. In either case the persecution was thorough and severe.

The violence of Paul's methods is further indicated by **dragging**—possibly by the hair of the head. The King James rendering "haling" is old English for "hauling." So to be haled into court is to be hauled (forcibly dragged) before the magistrate.

4 *Hoi men oun,* **they therefore,** is an expression used throughout Acts to signify the beginning of a new narrative.

Went about is more accurate than "went every where" (KJV), which goes beyond the Greek. The verb *dierchomai* means "go through" *(dia),* or "go about." It is a favorite word with Luke. He uses it ten times in his Gospel and twenty-one times in Acts—out of a total of forty-two occurrences in the New Testament. In Acts it is used regularly in connection with missionary journeys.

As those that were **scattered abroad** traveled throughout Judaea and Samaria they were **preaching the word.** The verb *euangelizō* (preach) is a favorite with Luke. He uses it ten times in his Gospel and fifteen times in Acts—about half the total number of times in the New Testament. It occurs only once in the other Gospels (Matt. 11:5). The literal meaning is "announce glad tidings or good news." It is especially appropriate as a missionary word to describe the preaching of those who carried the gospel to new regions.

5 **Philip went down to . . . Samaria.** This was an important step in the transition of Christianity from the Jews to the Gentiles. Macgregor notes: "The Samaritans formed a halfway house between Judaism and the Gentile world."[6]

Many Greek manuscripts have "a city of Samaria" (cf. RSV) rather than **the city of Samaria.** In the Old Testament, "Samaria" regularly refers to the capital of the Northern Kingdom, though it sometimes indicates the nation of Israel. But in the New Testament

---

Stephen's death was followed by the first organized, systematic, concerted persecution of the disciples, which appears to have been directed primarily against the Hellenist Christians who had caught the larger vision of the Gospel from Stephen. Under the impact of persecution, the disciples were **scattered abroad** [thus far they had been concentrated in Jerusalem] **throughout the regions of Judaea and Samaria, except the apostles.** This dissemination was in accord with Christ's command (Matt. 10:23), not for the security of the disciples, but for the spread of the Gospel. It is noteworthy that the apostles are excepted in the scattering: **except the apostles** (vs. 1b), which probably indicates that the persecution fell mainly on the Hellenist disciples, but not on the Jewish Christian apostles.

Saul, who probably was a member of the Cilician synagogue and had been worsted in debate with Stephen (Acts 6:9), who guarded the garments of Stephen's murderers (Acts 7:58b), and who had given his full consent to Stephen's martyrdom (Acts 8:1a), now becomes the ringleader of the Jewish official persecution of the Christians. **Saul laid waste the church.** Disregarding the rights of domestic privacy and sex differences, he hunted down Christians wherever they might be found and **committed them to prison** (vs. 3b). What a dark day for the Church, but what unforeseen blessed results. The concentrated blaze of divine glory in Jerusalem was thereby scattered to become a devouring fire throughout the regions beyond (see Rom. 1:8; Col. 1:6). **They therefore that were scattered abroad** [because of the persecution] **went about** [everywhere] **preaching the word** (vs. 4). "Surely the wrath of man shall praise thee: The residue of wrath shalt thou gird upon thee [restrain]" (Psalm 76:10).

[5] Hobart, *op. cit.,* p. 211. [6] IB, IX, 108.

6 And the multitudes gave heed with one accord unto the things that were spoken by Philip, when they heard, and saw the signs which he did.

---

it always means the district, not the city. Lake and Cadbury suggest that the city of Samaria mentioned here may have been Gitta, which Justin Martyr connects with Simon Magus. But it seems more probable that it was either the capital, Sebaste (modern Sebastiyeh), or the headquarters of the Samaritan religion, Neapolis (ancient Shechem, modern Nablus).

Proclaimed is *ekēryssen* (imperfect of continuous action). The two most common verbs for preaching in the New Testament are *kēryssō* (61 times) and *euangelizō* (55 times). But in Acts the latter is used fifteen times, the former only eight. *Kēryssō* comes from the noun *kēryx*, "herald." So the verb means "to be a herald, to proclaim." Just as the herald stepped out in front of the army, blew his trumpet, and made a proclamation for the general or king, so the preacher of the Gospel is called to proclaim God's good news to man.

The Christ means, of course, "the Messiah." That the Samaritans as well as the Jews were looking for the coming of the Messiah is indicated clearly in John 4:25.

6 **Gave heed** is *proseichon* (imperfect, "were giving heed"). The verb literally means "hold to." The idea is that of holding the mind to something *(to noun* "the mind," is sometimes supplied in classical Greek). So it signifies "give heed" (vs. 10) or "take heed" (5:35; 20:28).

Signs occurred in connection with the preaching of the early disciples, as well as of Jesus. This phenomenon was not confined to the ministry of the apostles, but is mentioned in connection with Stephen (6:8), as well as Philip.

The translation of *sēmeion* in the King James Version is an interesting study. The word occurs 31 times in the Synoptic Gospels and is translated "sign" 30 times. But in the 30 places where it appears in John's Gospel, it is rendered "miracle" 17 times and "sign"

II. THE SAMARITAN MISSION UNDER PHILIP (8:5–13)[a]

The author of Acts seems to single out, from among the many witnessing activities of the disciples scattered abroad under the terrible persecution of Saul, the case of Philip as an example of the tenor of those disciples.

A. The Ministry of Philip (8:5)

And Philip . . . proclaimed unto them the Christ. Philip, like Stephen, was one of the seven lay officers chosen to supervise the temporal affairs of the Church (Acts 6:5). Also, like Stephen, he was doubtless a Hellenist Christian, who with a heart aflame for Christ and a mind illumined by the larger vision of the Gospel for the whole world, derived from the teachings and example of Stephen, found himself among the scattered Hellenist disciples who had gone **about** [everywhere] **preaching the word.** This Philip is not to be confused with the apostle Philip. In evidence of this fact, the apostles did not leave Jerusalem under the persecution of Saul (vs. 1b), nor until they were apprised of the revival in Samaria. A later note of Philip the deacon, who from a lay church officer became an effective evangelist, is found in Acts 21:8, 9. Exactly what city of Samaria Philip went to, whether Sebaste the capital or possibly Sychar, is not certain, nor important. It may have been the latter, where Christ saw the Samaritan woman and many others converted (John 4:3–42). It evidently was a populous center, and it represented the transition of the Gospel from the Jews to the Gentiles. The Samaritans were a racially mixed Jewish-Gentile people, and quite as mongrel in religion. Consequently, they were more despised by the Jews than were the Gentiles. Philip's going **down to the city of Samaria** only indicates the greater importance of Jerusalem, and not geographic elevation. There he preached to these Samaritans Christ as the Messiah, whom they expected, both from the Jewish Scriptures which they possessed and from Christ's earlier ministry among them.

[a] See Additional Note I, *Samaria and the Samaritans*, at end of Chapter VIII.

Literally it reads: "For many of those having unclean spirits, crying out with a great voice, were coming out." The King James and Revised versions give paraphrases which represent the obvious meaning of the passage. Semitic and Greek scholars have labored long to explain the grammatical construction
Literally it reads: "For many of those having unclean spirits, crying out with a great voice, were coming out." The King James and Revised versions give paraphrases which represent the obvious meaning of the passage. Semitic and Greek scholars have labored long to explain the grammatical construction
Literally it reads: "For many of those having unclean spirits, crying out with a great voice, were coming out." The King James and Revised versions give paraphrases which represent the obvious meaning of the passage. Semitic and Greek scholars have labored long to explain the grammatical construction
here. Perhaps the best suggestion is that of Lake and Cadbury, who explain it as a case of mental "telescoping." [7] The readings of a few late manuscripts (ninth century) are

Palsied is the participial form of *paralyō.* Luke uses this twice in his Gospel and twice in Acts. In the parallel passages in the Gospels, Matthew and Mark both have *paralytikos* (paralytic). Luke's usage reflects the fact that as a physician he was familiar with medical language. The only other
Palsied is the participial form of *paralyō.* Luke uses this twice in his Gospel and twice in Acts. In the parallel passages in the Gospels, Matthew and Mark both have *paralytikos* (paralytic). Luke's usage reflects the fact that as a physician he was familiar with medical language. The only other
Palsied is the participial form of *paralyō.* Luke uses this twice in his Gospel and twice in Acts. In the parallel passages in the Gospels, Matthew and Mark both have *paralytikos* (paralytic). Luke's usage reflects the fact that as a physician he was familiar with medical language. The only other
occurrence of *paralyō* is in Hebrews, and there is some patristic tradition that Luke actually composed or translated that epistle.

B. The Response of the Samaritans (8:6)

And the multitudes gave heed with one accord. The height of this expectancy of the coming Messiah quickened these semi-pagan Samaritans to perceive in Philip's preaching of Christ, from the Jewish Scriptures (Acts 8:35), the fulfillment of those Scriptures and of their personal hopes, which faith was confirmed by the accompanying demonstrations of divine power and approval in the miracles wrought among them through Philip (cf. Thess. 1:5). Thus the **multitudes gave heed with one accord,** or with one mind, to Philip's message. That they tended to credulity appears evident from verse ten, but that they had solid ground for their faith in Christ through Philip's ministry is certain from verse twelve. The expression, **gave heed,** is meant to suggest an obedience of faith unto salvation on the part of the people, and not merely a mental assent or mere interest.

C. The Success of the Mission (8:7, 8)

And there was much joy in that city. The validity of demon possession and expulsion among the Samaritans, as opposed to the view that they were merely insane persons whose delusions took the form of a belief that they were possessed, appears evident from two considerations. *First,* Luke clearly states that they were **unclean spirits** and indicates that their personalities are evident from the fact of their **crying with a loud voice** as they came out. Indeed Matthew refers to lunatics who were healed by Christ, but in the same passage he also mentions the demon possessed as a different class (Matt. 4:24, 25). Luke, who was a physician and thus well qualified to judge the nature of maladies of his day, both here and in the case of the Gadarene (see Luke 8:26–36), refers clearly to demon possession. *Second,* the author clearly differentiates, in this passage, between demon possession and the disease of palsy and afflictions of lameness, both of which later are healed, while the former is expelled. Little wonder that there should have been **much joy** in the hearts and homes of emancipated and healed individuals restored to normality. The Gospel wrought social and economic benefits, as well as physical and spiritual.

[7] *Beginnings,* IV, 90.

9 But there was a certain man, Simon by name, who beforetime in the city used sorcery, and amazed the people of Samaria, giving out that himself was some great one:

10 to whom they all gave heed, from the least to the greatest, saying, This man is that power of God which is called Great.

11 And they gave heed to him, because that of long time he had amazed them with his sorceries.

12 But when they believed Philip preaching good tidings concerning the kingdom of God and the name of Jesus Christ, they were baptized, both men and women.

13 And Simon also himself believed: and being baptized, he continued with Philip; and beholding signs and great miracles wrought, he was amazed.

---

9 **Simon**—better known as Simon Magus (the magician, or sorcerer)—is the subject of many legends in the Early Church.[8] The most striking tradition is that he was the founder of Gnosticism. Here it is said that he **used sorcery**, or practised magic. The verb *(mageuō)* is found only here. In modern Greek it means "bewitch." This is the translation in the King James Version of *existanōn*, which is properly rendered **amazed** in the Revised versions. It means "drive one out of his senses," and so "confound, amaze." **People** is the Greek *ethnos*, "nation" (so, correctly, RSV). Just what is indicated by **some great one** is not known.

10 The appraisal of the people is stated somewhat more definitely: **This man is that power of God which is called Great.** This is the reading of the best Greek text. Probably the phrase is equivalent to "God." In other words, the people of Samaria treated Simon as a deity, or at least a revealing angel of the deity.

11 **Amazed** is again "bewitched" in the King James Version. This is an over-translation. **Sorceries** is *magia* (magic), found only here in the New Testament.

12 **Preaching good tidings** is all one word in Greek, *euangelizomenōi.* It takes three English words to bring out the full meaning of this verb. The gospel Philip preached is characterized thus: **concerning the kingdom of God and the name of Jesus Christ.** The first phrase indicates a close connection with the preaching of John the Baptist and Jesus. The second goes beyond that to an emphasis on belief in the Name of Jesus as the only way of salvation. It agrees with what Peter said to the Sanhedrin: "Neither is there any other name under heaven, that is given among men, wherein we must be saved" (4:12). Emphasis on the Name of Jesus was an outstanding characteristic of apostolic preaching.

Those that **believed** were **baptized.** Baptism was especially important as a sign of transference to a new religion, as in mission fields today.

13 **Simon also himself believed: and being baptized, he continued with Philip.** The first two verbs are the same as in verse 12. **Continued** is the same word *(proskartareō)*

D. The Case of Simon the Sorcerer (8:9-13)

But there was a certain man, Simon by name . . . giving out that himself was some great one. It is sufficient to note that this Simon was one of the many opportunist wizards of the land in his day who took advantage of the prevalent expectation of a Messiah popularized by the Jews of the *Diaspora* and played upon the credulity of the people with the practices of conjuring, juggling, and soothsaying. Probably a superpsychic, as well as a trickster and a demon-trafficker, this man had for long amazed the Samaritans and held them bound under his spells of sorcery. These spells were validated, in the minds of the people, by his claim to be **some great one.** Actually he professed deity, and many unsubstantiated legends about him grew up even in the Church. Simon himself was put to consternation by the genuine miracles and wonders wrought through Philip, and then, motivated by selfish evil desires, he professed faith in Christ, was baptized, and for a time followed Philip and studied most diligently **the signs and great miracles wrought** by Philip (vs. 13b). There appears to be little grounds for a belief in his genuine conversion under Philip.

[8] See *Beginnings*, V, 151-163; also EGT, II, 212 f.

14 Now when the apostles that were at Jerusalem heard that Samaria had received the word of God, they sent unto them Peter and John:
15 who, when they were come down, prayed for them, that they might receive the Holy Spirit:

---

that is translated "continue stedfastly" in 1:14; 2:42, 46; 6:4. But was Simon sincere in all of this? This is a much debated question. Roberts thinks his conversion "was sincere as far as it went, but was very superficial."[9] Knowling perhaps gives the best summary of the matter, when he suggests that Simon's faith "rested on the outward miracles and signs," and adds: "He may have believed in the Messianic dignity of Christ, and in His Death and Resurrection, . . . but it was a belief about the facts, and not a belief in Him whom the facts made known, a belief in the *power* of the new faith, but not an acceptance of its *holiness*."[10] In other words, Simon's faith was one of mental assent but not of moral consent. His mind accepted, but his will did not submit.

14 **The apostles . . . at Jerusalem** still constituted the supreme earthly authority in the Church. **Samaria** here means the district or country. **Received the word** is a phrase almost peculiar to Luke (cf. Luke 8:13; Acts 11:1; 17:11). Paul uses it in I Thess. 1:6 (cf. I Thess. 2:13; James 1:21). **Peter and John** are associated here, as in the early part of Acts (cf. 3:1, 3, 4, 11; 4:13, 19), but this is the last time that John appears in this book.

15 It should be noted that the Samaritans were converted under the preaching of Philip and filled with the Spirit under the ministry of Peter and John. In his speech at the Jerusalem Council, Peter identified the receiving of the Holy Spirit and the purifying of the heart by faith as one and the same act (15:8, 9). So it would appear that this was what happened to the Samaritans. Knowling takes issue with those who interpret Holy Spirit as meaning special gifts of the Spirit. He writes: "In a book so marked by the working of the Holy Spirit . . . it is difficult to believe that St. Luke can mean

---

III. THE APOSTLES AND THE SAMARITAN MISSION (8:14–25)

It is noteworthy that the apostles were excepted in the scattering of the disciples under persecution at the martyrdom of Stephen (vs. 1b). This likely indicates that the persecution fell mainly on the Hellenist disciples because of their larger vision of the Gospel for the Gentile world, as Stephen clearly indicated in his defense. Too, it likely indicates that the apostles as yet had thought of the Gospel of Christ for the Jews only.

A. The Apostles' Commission (8:14)

When the apostles . . . heard that Samaria had received the word of God, they sent unto them Peter and John. News of the reception of the Gospel of Christ by the Samaritans was indeed epochal. The word indicates something of a national turning to Christ and not just a revival in a given city. A meeting of the apostolate in Jerusalem was immediately called, and official decision was made to dispatch Peter and John to Samaria with full powers to act in whatever capacity they deemed wise in the interest of the Church. This is the first action of its kind recorded of the Jerusalem apostles.

B. The Apostles' Confirmation (8:15–17)

Who . . . prayed for them . . . then laid they their hands on them, and they received the Holy Spirit. Most authorities seem to agree that the mission of Peter and John to Samaria was to consecrate or ordain, through the imposition of hands and prayer on the human side, and through the special gifts of the Holy Spirit on the divine side, certain of the Samaritans for special Christian service to their own people. While this may be true, it cannot be denied that with the manifestation of the Holy Spirit, in whatever capacity, there is always the sanctifying efficacy of the holiness of His personal presence. Whether the Samaritans were sanctified on this occasion or another, they were sanctified by the Holy Spirit (Acts 15:8, 9). Thus the apostles recognized, approved, and confirmed that God had visited with salvation the Samaritans also.

[9] HDAC, II, 497. [10] EGT, II, 215.

16 for as yet it was fallen upon none of them: only they had been baptized into the name
of the Lord Jesus.
17 Then laid they their hands on them, and they received the Holy Spirit.
18 Now when Simon saw that through the laying on of the apostles' hands the Holy
Spirit was given, he offered them money,
19 saying, Give me also this power, that on whomsoever I lay my hands, he may receive
the Holy Spirit.
20 But Peter said unto him, Thy silver perish with thee, because thou hast thought to
obtain the gift of God with money.
21 Thou hast neither part nor lot in this matter: for thy heart is not right before God.
22 Repent therefore of this thy wickedness, and pray the Lord, if perhaps the thought of
thy heart shall be forgiven thee.

---

to limit the expression *lambanein* **[receive]** here and in the following verse to anything less than a bestowal of that divine indwelling of the spirit which makes the Christian the temple of God."[11]

16 This verse clearly indicates that while the Samaritans had been converted and **baptized,** they had not received the Holy Spirit. **Into the name of the Lord Jesus** is thus explained by Bruce: "The expression *eis to onoma* is common in a commercial context: some property is paid or transferred 'into the name' of someone, i.e., into his account. So the person baptized *eis to onoma tou kyriou Iēsou* bears public testimony that he has become Christ's property."[12]

17 For **laid . . . hands on,** see on 19:6. Compare also 9:17.

18, 19 The effort of **Simon** to purchase the power to bestow the Holy Spirit is the origin of the word "simony," applied to the buying and selling of ecclesiastical authority or position.

20 Peter's wish—expressed by a rare optative—sounds like an imprecation. But Knowling writes: "The words are no curse or imprecation, as is evident from verse 22, but rather a vehement expression of horror on the part of St. Peter, an expression which would warn Simon that he was on the way to destruction."[13] The literal Greek means: "May your silver be with you for perishing." This might be interpreted as a wish that his money, which was helping to drag him down to destruction, might perish. That Peter's ultimate desire and prayer for Simon was the latter's salvation is clearly shown by verse 22.

21 **Matter** is *logos,* the most common meaning of which is "word." So some have interpreted it as meaning the preaching of the Gospel, rather than the bestowal of the Spirit. Hackett, for instance, prefers the translation "word" and explains it thus: "doctrine or gospel, which we preach."[14]

22 **Thought** is *epinoia,* found only here in the New Testament. It is from the verb *epinoeō,* "contrive," and so means "design" or "plot."[15] It was a wicked design that constituted Simon's sin. Yet it was not too late to **repent** and **be forgiven.** The sin was serious, but not unpardonable. But it could not be forgiven until Simon repented. There is no evidence that he did this.

C. The Apostle's Rebuke of Simon (18–24)

Verses 18–24 present the true character of another imposter who, like Ananias, desired Christian connections and divine powers for selfish reasons. He had previously amazed the people with his magic and sorcery before professing Christianity. If he could but obtain these special gifts of the Holy Spirit by the imposition of the apostles' hands, he would be able to supersede his former practices and powers and thus his fame and fortune would grow greatly. He makes his request and Peter, perceiving the wickedness of his heart, delivers to him the withering rebuke contained in verses 20, 21, and 23, and then exhorts him to true repentance and earnest prayer to God for forgiveness. Simon, still thinking magically, asks the prayers of Peter, not for salvation, but that he might escape the consequent judgment of his evil (vs. 24). Luke does not relate the sequel, and we are left to conjecture the outcome.

[11] EGT, II, 216. [12] *Acts,* p. 187. [13] EGT, II, 218. [14] Hackett, *op., cit.,* p. 111. [15] *Beginnings,* IV, 94.

23 For I see that thou art in the gall of bitterness and in the bond of iniquity.
24 And Simon answered and said, Pray ye for me to the Lord, that none of the things which ye have spoken come upon me.
25 They therefore, when they had testified and spoken the word of the Lord, returned to Jerusalem, and preached the gospel to many villages of the Samaritans.
26 But an angel of the Lord spake unto Philip, saying, Arise, and go toward the south unto the way that goeth down from Jerusalem unto Gaza: the same is desert.

---

23 Peter describes Simon as being **in the gall of bitterness and in the bond of iniquity.** But his case was not yet hopeless.

24 Simon's only desire was to escape the consequences of his sin. He does not seem to have had any real Spirit-wrought conviction of the seriousness of sin itself. **Come upon** *(enerchomai)* Luke uses four times in his Gospel and four times in Acts, or a total of eight out of the ten times it occurs in the New Testament.

25 **They therefore** *(hoi men oun)* is taken by some as indicating that Philip returned to Jerusalem with Peter and John. But that does not seem necessary. It is probably best to make verse 25 a transitional paragraph, as in the Revised versions.

26 **An angel of the Lord** seems to be almost equivalent to the Holy Spirit (cf. vss. 29, 39). **Arise** is aorist, **go** imperfect. That is, **Philip** was to get up at once and keep on going. In the Septuagint *mesēmbria*, **south,** almost always has the meaning "noon" (cf. Gen. 18:1). That is the way it is translated in 22:6, its only other occurrence in the New Testament. Some scholars have argued for that rendering here. But most commentators favor "southward."

The way that goeth down from Jerusalem to Gaza was one of two roads leading south from Jerusalem. One went by the way of Hebron, the other, farther to the west. **Gaza** was one of the ancient Philistine cities, the last town in Palestine on the way to Egypt.

There has been a great deal of discussion as to whether **the same is desert** applies to

---

D. The Apostles' Evangelization (8:25)

So enlightened and inspired by God's visitation of the Samaritans with salvation were Peter and John, that as they returned to Jerusalem, they engaged in the evangelization of the villages of the very people upon whom James and John once besought the Master for permission to "bid fire to come down from heaven, and consume them" (Luke 9:54).

Part II

The Church's First African Convert

I. THE MESSENGER OF GOD (8:26–30, 40)

When God has a special mission to perform, He does not appoint someone who is sitting idly by waiting for something to do, but rather chooses one who is actively engaged in the task at hand. Philip was such, and he became God's messenger for the special missionary undertaking in relation to the Ethiopian nobleman. We have already observed Philip engaged in the successful evangelization of the Samaritans. Mighty miracles and powerful conversions were occurring under his ministry among the people, until it could be said that **Samaria had received the word of God** (vs. 14). Likewise, after this mission was completed, **Philip . . . passing through . . . preached the gospel to all the cities, till he came to Caesarea** (vs. 40).

A. The Messenger's Commission (8:26)

An angel . . . spake unto Philip, saying, Arise, and go toward the south . . . the same is desert. It appears most unusual that God should have commissioned Philip, who was being so successfully used in the evangelization of the Samaritans, to leave his labors there among the hungry-hearted multitudes and depart to an uninhabited wilderness in southern Palestine. Since there were several roads leading to Gaza, and God knew well the road over which the nobleman would return to his native land from Jerusalem, he specifies to Philip the exact route to follow, **the way that goeth down from Jerusalem unto Gaza.** It is always safe to follow His directions.

27 And he arose and went: and behold, a man of Ethiopia, a eunuch of great authority under Candace, queen of the Ethiopians, who was over all her treasure, who had come to Jerusalem to worship;

28 and he was returning and sitting in his chariot, and was reading the prophet Isaiah.

---

the road or the city. The former view was held by Edersheim,[16] Schürer,[17] and others. But the reference to Gaza itself is held by George Adam Smith [18] and seems to be supported by Josephus.[19] Lake and Cadbury feel that the best solution of the problem is that there were two cities called Gaza. The old Gaza, which lay two and a half miles from the Mediterranean, had been destroyed by Alexander the Great (332 B.C.) and was still deserted. The new Gaza was a Hellenistic city on the coast and was partially destroyed in A.D. 66. [20] Perhaps the best conclusion is to refer **desert** to the old city destroyed by Alexander.

27 **He arose and went**—both verbs are in the aorist tense, suggesting prompt obedience. If Philip had dallied or stopped to argue, he would have missed his divinely-made appointment.

Ethiopia was a kingdom on the Nile, between modern Aswan and Khartoum. Scholars today usually deny the identification of ancient Ethiopia with modern Abyssinia, though both names are now used for the same territory near the upper Nile.

In the Mosaic Law (cf. Deut. 23:1) a **eunuch** was banned from the congregation of the Lord. But this prohibition seems later to have been lifted (Isa. 56:3–5; cf. also Jer. 38:7). **Of great authority** is all one word in Greek, *dynastēs*, from which comes "dynasty." It is translated "the mighty" in Luke 1:52 (KJV and RSV). Elsewhere in the New Testament it occurs only in I Timothy 6:15, where God is called "Potentate." The word means "prince, ruler, potentate."

Candace was not a personal name, but a title such as Pharaoh. Apparently it was given to the queen mother, the real head of the government, whose son was considered to be "the child of the Sun." [21] Eusebius says that Ethiopia was ruled by queens in his day. [22]

The eunuch had come to Jerusalem **to worship** *(proskynēsōn)*. Since in modern Greek the word *proskynētēs* means "pilgrim," Lake and Cadbury have the rendering "on a pilgrimage." [23] Exactly the same expression as here is used of Paul's last visit to Jerusalem (24:11).

28 The **chariot** may have been an oxwagon.[24] At any rate, it was probably going very slowly so that Philip, walking in the same direction, could catch up with it. A springless wagon would have to move slowly to let an occupant read.

B. The Messenger's Obedience (8:27a)

And he arose and went. Philip was not only living near enough to God to receive His instructions, but his unbounded faith prompted him to immediate obedience to God's will. Had he been a day late, or perhaps even an hour, he would have missed the opportunity of his lifetime to witness the conversion of a great foreign nobleman. Indeed there are times when "the king's business [requires] haste" (I Sam. 21:8b).

C. The Messenger's Opportunity (8:27b, 28)

Behold, a man of Ethiopia. The Ethiopian was most likely a negro from the country south of Egypt in Africa which included the modern Nubia, Cordofan, and northern Abyssinia, of which great kingdom he was treasurer under the queen who bore the dynastic title of Candace. He may not have been a eunuch, in the literal sense of the word, but bore the title as was common with ancient oriental high court officials (see Gen. 37:36 with marginal notes). This important officer was evidently a Jew by religion who had been to Jerusalem to worship at the temple. He most likely was only a *proselyte of the gate*. He was returning and reading en route the prophecy of Isaiah. He clearly expected the Messiah, as all Jews did. This was Philip's opportunity!

[16] *Jewish Social Life*, p. 79. [17] *Op. cit.*, II, i, 71.
[18] *Historical Geography of the Holy Land*, pp. 186–188. [19] *Ant.* XIV, 4, 4.
[20] *Beginnings*, IV, 95. [21] *Beginnings*, IV, 96.
[22] *Ecclesiastical History*, II, 1, 13. [23] *Beginnings*, IV, 96. [24] *Ibid.*

29 And the Spirit said unto Philip, Go near, and join thyself to this chariot.
30 And Philip ran to him, and heard him reading Isaiah the prophet, and said, Understandest thou what thou readest?
31 And he said, How can I, except some one shall guide me? And he besought Philip to come up and sit with him.

The eunuch was **reading** aloud (cf. vs. 30), as was the custom in that day.[25] He was reading from the scroll of **Isaiah.** Handwritten scrolls were in those times expensive, but the Ethiopian was a man of wealth. The rabbis taught that the Law should be read aloud when a man was traveling.

29 **Join thyself** is literally "be glued" *(kollēthēti)*. This verb is found five times in Acts and only five times elsewhere in the New Testament. It is an odd coincidence that the Greek for **chariot** is *harma*, which is from the verb meaning "to join."

30 **Understandest thou what thou readest?** There is a play on words in the Greek: *ginōskeis ha anaginōskeis*. The word for "read," *anaginōskō*, literally means "know again." That is, when one reads he recognizes the written characters, knows them again; or, to look at it another way, he knows again what the writer knew and wrote.

31 **How** is literally "for how" *(pōs gar)*, or "how indeed." It implies: "Why do you ask? for how should I be able, **except someone shall guide me**?" The word **guide** *(hodēgeō)* is used in Jesus' promise that the Holy Spirit would "guide" into all truth (John 16:13). Philip had received the Spirit and so possessed that guidance; the eunuch had not.

D. The Messenger's Approach (8:29, 30)

Understandest thou what thou readest? Philip, whose faith in God had been rewarded in the finding of the hungry-hearted Ethiopian, was quick to respond to the Spirit's prompting to **Go near, and join thyself to this chariot** (vs. 29b). **And Philip ran** [thither] **to him** (vs. 30a). The nobleman may have appeared to be out of the class of the humble, dust-covered, Christian disciple by the way, but God's servants must be ready to reach up for spiritual fruit as well as down. There is a suggestion of sympathetic identification in those words **join thyself,** of urgency in the words **Philip ran to him,** and of wise and understanding tactfulness in Philip's question, **Understandest thou what thou readest?** This is the nobleman's interest which the evangelist wisely seeks.

II. THE SEEKER AFTER GOD (8:31–34)

The nobleman had worshipped at Jerusalem and possibly was present at Pentecost. He had reading knowledge of the Jewish Scriptures, most likely in the Alexandrian Greek version (Septuagint), and was in earnest quest of the Messiah.

A. The Seeker's Bewilderment (8:31a)

How can I [understand] **except some one shall guide me?** In answer to Philip's question, **Understandest thou?** he replied, **How can I?** unless I have a teacher, a guide. His bewilderment immediately opened the way for Philip's exceptional opportunity. Man's sincere quest for God will always be met by God if He can but find a human instrument through whom He can work.

B. The Seeker's Request (8:31b)

And he besought Philip to come up and sit with him. The nobleman's request was both an expression of confidence in the evangelist and a gesture of courtesy and desired companionship. Clearly Philip had won both the confidence and respect of the treasurer. His invitation became the evangelist's enlarged opportunity. It is seriously doubtful if anyone is ever won to Christ until his confidence has been secured by some Christian. Herein lies the weakness of much professional evangelism.

C. The Seeker's Interest (8:32, 33)

The passage of the scripture which he was reading was this. The point of his scriptural interest was most opportune. It spoke to his heart of Christ's shameful trial before Pilate:

[25] Cf. Henry J. Cadbury, *The Book of Acts in History*, p. 18: "I am convinced that such was the universal practice in the ancient world."

32 Now the passage of the scripture which he was reading was this,
He was led as a sheep to the slaughter;
And as a lamb before his shearer is dumb,
So he openeth not his mouth:
33 In his humiliation his judgment was taken away:
His generation, who shall declare?
For his life is taken from the earth.
34 And the eunuch answered Philip, and said, I pray thee, of whom speaketh the prophet this? of himself, or of some other?
35 And Philip opened his mouth, and beginning from this scripture, preached unto him Jesus.
36 And as they went on the way, they came unto a certain water; and the eunuch saith, Behold, *here is* water; what doth hinder me to be baptized?

---

32 **Passage** *(periochē)* is the word used later by ecclesiastical writers for "lection," or a Scripture lesson to be read in public. It is found only here in the New Testament.

32, 33 The quotation in these verses is from Isaiah 53:7, 8. This is a part of one of the "Servant Songs" of Isaiah.

34 **Of whom speaketh the prophet?**—this is the age-old problem of interpretation. It would appear that the oldest Jewish exegesis applied Isaiah 53 to the Messiah. But gradually the interpretation was changed from the Messiah to Israel,[26] until the latter has become the standard Jewish interpretation of the Suffering Servant. Rather obviously, this was due to the Christian application of this passage to Jesus.

35 **Philip . . . preached unto him Jesus.** This is the first specific identification in Acts of Jesus with the Suffering Servant, though it is suggested in the use of *pais* (servant) in 3:13, 26 and 4:27, 30. One of the main tasks of the early Christians was to discover and "expose" Jesus in the Jewish Scriptures.

36 The eunuch's question, **What doth hinder me to be baptized?** perhaps reflects his acquaintance with the fact that Gentile converts to Judaism were baptized. It is also probable that Philip finished his preaching to him in somewhat the same way as did Peter on the day of Pentecost: "Repent ye, and be baptized every one of you in the name of Jesus Christ unto the remission of your sins" (2:38).

He was led as a sheep to the slaughter; of His non-retaliatory sufferings: **so he openeth not his mouth;** of the ignominy and injustice of the treatment accorded Him: **in his humiliation** [sufferings] **his judgment was taken away** [or, He was denied justice]; of the immeasurable wickedness of His opposers and murderers: **His generation who shall declare** [or declare their wickedness]; and of His death: **his life is taken from the earth.** Such a record is sufficient to awaken the moral and spiritual interest of any sincere soul.

D. The Seeker's Question (8:34)

Of whom speaketh the prophet this? The height of interest had become so great in the nobleman's mind that he broke forth with a demand for an explanation. This is always the crucial point in dealing with the sincere seeker after God. It is only the man who knows God himself that can lead another to Christ at this juncture. Philip had patiently and painstakingly awaited this moment. The clock had struck, and now it was Philip's time and turn to speak, and he spoke in season.

III. THE READY INSTRUCTOR (8:35–37)

There are many who can talk about religion, but there are few indeed who can instruct men into a saving relationship with the Lord Jesus Christ, as did Philip in dealing with the Ethiopian.

A. The Evangelist's Wisdom (8:35a)

And Philip opened his mouth. There is a time to listen to the sorrows, griefs, and longings of others, and there is a time to

[26] I. Abrahams, "Jewish Interpretation of the Old Testament" in *The People and the Book*, ed. A. S. Peake (Oxford: Clarendon Press, 1925), p. 409. Cf. also S. Mowinckel, *He That Cometh* (New York: Abingdon Press, n.d.), pp. 255–257.

38 And he commanded the chariot to stand still: and they both went down into the water, both Philip and the eunuch; and he baptized him.

39 And when they came up out of the water, the Spirit of the Lord caught away Philip; and the eunuch saw him no more, for he went on his way rejoicing.

---

37 The entire verse is left out in the Revised Versions for the simple, and adequate, reason that it is not found in the oldest and best Greek manuscripts,[27] as well as many of the ancient versions. It is obviously a later word of explanation added by some scribe, although it may represent very well what took place.

38 **Went down into the water** shows that it was in a pool or running brook that the Ethiopian was baptized. The *Didache* (7:1) directed that baptism should be performed, if possible, in running water.

39 Irenaeus says [28] that the eunuch became a missionary to the Ethiopians, which is probably correct. But the genuine records of the Ethiopian church go back only as far as the fourth century.

---

speak forth in instruction and consolation. Philip had listened until he knew well the thoughts and secret desires of his spiritual patient and then he **opened his mouth** and spoke forth with assurance and certainty. Starting at the point of the seeker's greatest interest and question, concerning the Scripture under consideration, Philip **preached** unto him Jesus. It is always at man's point of extremity that God's greatest opportunity presents itself. Happy and wise is the soul winner who can detect that point. "He that is wise winneth souls" (Prov. 11:30).

B. The Evangelist's Message (8:35b)

Philip . . . preached unto him Jesus. The nobleman earnestly sought, in the Jewish Scriptures, for the Messiah promised by the prophets. Christ the Messiah is the ultimate object of the earnest and sincere religious quest of every man. Many indeed are not following, in their religious quests, the road that leads to God in Christ. This man had found in the Old Testament Scriptures an intimation of the fulfillment of his hopes. Philip began with Isaiah's prophecy of the Christ, the Messiah, and showed the nobleman that this Jesus, of whom he may have heard, was the fulfillment of that Messianic prophecy, and thus the Saviour of all men. Evangelism that does not lead to Christ misses the mark.

C. The Seeker's Conversion (8:36, 37)

Though omitted by the American Standard Version, the King James Version includes verse thirty-seven, which reads in part: "I believe that Jesus Christ is the Son of God." The Ethiopian's request for baptism expressed in his words, **Behold, here is water; what doth hinder me to be baptized?** indicates that Philip's instruction in salvation, even to the outward sign of water baptism, had been thorough, even perhaps well beyond the conversation recorded in Acts. It also indicates the genuineness and sincerity of the man's conversion. But Philip, anxious for a thorough commitment and open confession of Christ, replied: "If thou believest with all thy heart, thou mayest." Philip wanted no halfway conversion of a man who would return to his pagan countrymen with an opportunity for a wide and vital witness to Christ. His open confession, "I believe that Jesus Christ is the Son of God," fully satisfied the evangelist of his thorough conversion to Christ. "For with the heart man believeth unto righteousness; and with the mouth confession is made unto salvation" (Rom. 10:10).

IV. THE JOYFUL CONVERT (8:38, 39)

Philip's personal evangelistic efforts led the Ethiopian to wholehearted faith in Christ, an open confession of Christ, and a joyous experience with Christ.

A. The Convert's Baptism (8:38, 39a)

And he baptized him. The Ethiopian's baptism reveals four things: *first*, that personal salvation precedes water baptism (see

[27] Aleph A B C H L P. [28] *Against Heresies*, III, 12, 8.

40 But Philip was found at Azotus: and passing through he preached the gospel to all the cities, till he came to Caesarea.

---

40 **Azotus** is the old Philistine city of Ashdod, about 20 miles north of Gaza. It formed a sort of "halfway station on the great road between Gaza and Joppa."[29] Philip **preached the gospel to** (evangelized) **all the cities,** which would doubtless include Lydda and Joppa, where believers are mentioned in the next chapter (9:32 ff.). **Caesarea** was on the coast, northward toward Mount Carmel. Originally known as Straton's Tower, it had been rebuilt by Herod the Great at about 13 B.C. He named it Caesarea Sebaste, in honor of the Emperor Augustus. (Augustus is the Latin equivalent of the Greek *Sebastos,* meaning "reverend.") Though actually in the territory of Samaria, it became the capital of the Roman province of Judea, which included Samaria.

---

vs. 37); *second,* that water baptism was a recognized practice of the Apostolic Church (Matt. 28:19); *third,* that performance of the rite of baptism was not restricted to the apostles, since Philip was but a lay evangelist; and *fourth,* that water baptism, whether by immersion or otherwise, was but an outward sign or testimony to the inner-soul work of grace.

B. The Evangelist's Disappearance (8:39a)

The Spirit of the Lord caught away Philip; and the eunuch saw him no more. Without questioning the miraculous disappearance of Philip, let us note the practical effects of that disappearance on the convert. *First,* he was thus early weaned from dependence on the human instrument of his new faith; and *second,* he was left wholly dependent on God and the Scriptures for the sustenance and development of his new Christian life. Little wonder that tradition has assigned to this man the early evangelization of Ethiopia.

C. The Convert's Joy (8:39b)

He went on his way rejoicing. The Ethiopian continued in the course of his former life, but now with a new life in Christ. His joy consisted in the soul rest and satisfaction found in Christ, and in the glorious prospect of carrying his new faith to his native countrymen where his influential position gave him a great advantage for Christ and righteousness.

D. The Evangelist's Continued Ministry (8:40)

He preached the gospel to all the cities. The expression, **But Philip was found at Azotus,** is meant to convey the idea, Wesley thinks, that "Probably none saw him from his leaving the eunuch till he was there."[a] The distance from Gaza, near which place Philip likely met the eunuch, was about twenty miles to Azotus. From here he carried out an evangelizing mission until he reached **Caesarea,** the Roman capital of Judea and an important seaport, where Philip eventually settled and raised his family, including four unmarried daughters who were prophetesses. The cities alluded to, which Philip evangelized, must have included Ashdod, Ekron, Joppa, Jamnia, Ascalon, and Apollonia of the Philistine country, as these all lay in his course between Gaza and Caesarea. The extent of the spiritual fruitage of this evangelism we do not know, but the activities of the evangelist suggest his impelling zeal for Christ and his passion to see men brought under His Lordship. The earlier spiritual fruitage in Samaria and the conversion of the Ethiopian added their impetus to the evangelist's activities. Good fuel always causes the flames to leap higher and the fire to burn brighter. *The evangelistic ministry* of Philip may be summarized as threefold: *first,* mass evangelism at Samaria (Acts 8:5-8); *second,* personal evangelism, as represented in the conversion of the Ethiopian nobleman (Acts 8:26-39a); and *third,* itinerant evangelism, as represented by his preaching to the coastal cities (Acts 8:40).

[29] EGT, 288.

[a] John Wesley, *Explanatory Notes upon the New Testament* (London: Epworth Press, 1954), p. 427, n. 40.

Additional Note I

SAMARIA AND THE SAMARITANS[b]

The district of Samaria lay to the north of Judea and was bounded on the west by the Mediterranean, on the east by the Jordan River, and on the north and northwest by Phoenicia and Galilee. Caesarea, the capital of Judea, of which Samaria was a political part in Paul's day, was located on the seacoast of Samaria. In Solomon's time Samaria was peopled by Israelites (mainly Ephraim and the half-tribe of Manasseh).

Upon the death of Herod the Great (4 B.C.), his will provided for Samaria and northern Idumaea to be given to his son, King Archelaus, who ruled the country until he was deposed by Rome in A.D. 6. Thereafter the country came under the Roman procurators.

When Israel, the Northern Kingdom, fell under the Assyrians in 722 B.C., most of the ruling and artisan classes were taken into captivity. Many of the peasant class were left in the country. Foreigners were introduced to replace the captive Israelites, resulting in a mixed population (Ezra 4:2, 9 ff.). They had neither the Hebrew standards of racial nor religious purity. The resultant condition greatly offended the Judean Jews, in consequence of which an imaginary line was drawn between the two nations which was never to be erased.

After the restoration of the Southern Kingdom, the Jerusalem Jews rejected the proffered assistance of the Samaritans under their governor Sanballat, in rebuilding the temple (Neh. 6). The Samaritans thereafter tried to prevent the rebuilding of Jerusalem (Ezra 4:4–7; Neh. 4:7), and in general opposed the Jewish restoration.[c]

In consequence of their rebuff, the Samaritans built their own temple on Mt. Gerizim and organized themselves into a distinct sect. This was probably accomplished in the fourth century B.C. under permission of Alexander the Great, though it may have been at an earlier date. Thereafter the Jews considered the Samaritans a mongrel people, both racially and religiously, and had no more dealings with them than absolutely necessary. In fact, because of their racial and religious corruption, the orthodox Jews regarded the Samaritans with greater disdain than they did the heathen nations. They denied them the privilege of offerings at the Jerusalem temple, restricted their commerce, and forbade them to intermarry with the Jews. In short the "Jews . . . [had] no dealings with the Samaritans" (John 4:9b).

The Samaritans had much in common with the Jews. They observed the Sabbath, kept the sacred feasts, practiced circumcision, anticipated the Messiah (however He was to be a Samaritan Messiah who would convert all to their religion and nation). On the other hand, they had certain marked differences with the Jews. They held the Pentateuch only to be divinely authoritative, while they rejected the rest of the Old Testament. They believed in a god who was unique and without associate, in Moses, the Torah, the sacredness of Mt. Gerizim, and in future rewards and punishments. Their belief that Mt. Gerizim was the true earthly abode of God was the main theological contention with the Jews who held Jerusalem to be His earthly abode (see John 4:19–25). Thus the Samaritans assigned many Old Testament events to Mt. Gerizim which the Jews attributed to Moriah. Among these were the home of Abraham (Gen. 22), the place of Isaac's intended sacrifice, the vision of Jacob (Gen. 31:13), Joseph's tomb (Josh. 24:32), Jacob's Bethel, and others. They gave many honorific titles to Mt. Gerizim, such as "'the Ancient Mountain,' 'Bethel,' 'the House of Angels,' 'the Gate of Heaven,' 'Luzah,' ('to God in This Place'), 'Sanctuary,' 'Mt. Gerizim,' 'Beth-yhwh, the very name of the Highest,' 'the Beautiful Mountain,' 'the Chosen Place,' 'the Highest in the World,' 'the First of Mountains,' 'God is Seen,' and 'the Mountain of the Inheritance of the Shekinah.'"[d]

The Gerizim temple was destroyed by the Maccabeans under John Hyrcanus and was never rebuilt, though they continued to venerate Mt. Gerizim. The Jewish-Samaritan

[b] The following treatment is largely based upon R. A. S. Macalister, "Samaria and the Samaritans," in *Dictionary of the Bible*, ed. James Hastings (New York: Charles Scribner's Sons, 1909), p. 821; Madelene S. and J. Lane Miller, "Samaria, District of" and "Samaritans," in *Harper's Bible Dictionary* (New York: Harper Brothers, 1955), pp. 638 639; and Elmer W. K. Mould, *op. cit.*, pp. 637–640.

[c] Josephus, *op. cit.*, *Ant.* XII, V, 5.

[d] Madelene S. and J. Lane Miller, *op. cit.*, p. 640.

animosity was finally taken to Rome for settlement.[e]

Throughout the first century the Jewish-Samaritan animosity continued. Samaritans were considered strangers (Luke 17:18), and their mixed Jewish-heathen worship (John 4:22) was an abomination to the Jews. Only a handful of Samaritans remained, sacrificing, and celebrating the Passover and waiting for the Messiah at Mt. Moriah.

While in His earlier ministry, Jesus' disciples appear to have shared the Jewish hostility to the Samaritans (Luke 9:51–56), it is quite evident that Jesus Himself was not infected with this spirit. It is recorded that He cleansed ten Samaritan lepers (Luke 17:11–19) and that an ill-famed Samaritan woman and many of her acquaintances came to believe on Him (John 4:21–42). In conversation with this woman, He set the Kingdom of God in correct perspective as consisting in a spiritual relationship with God and not dependent on earthly sacred places or ritual. Christ paid His highest respects to the Samaritans in His famous parable of "The Good Samaritan" delivered to a Jewish lawyer (Luke 10:25–37).

Persecuted Christians, following Stephen's martyrdom, fled to Samaria among other places, and in Samaria Philip preached and witnessed a great spiritual awakening accompanied by many miracles and conversions (Acts 8:1–25).

[e] Josephus, *op. cit.*, *Wars*, II, XII, 3–7.

CHAPTER IX

But Saul, yet breathing threatening and slaughter against the disciples of the Lord, went unto the high priest,

2 and asked of him letters to Damascus unto the synagogues, that if he found any that were of the Way, whether men or women, he might bring them bound to Jerusalem.

EXEGESIS

1 **Breathing** is "breathing out" in the King James Version. But the Greek has *enpneō*, "breathe on or in" (found only here in the New Testament), not *ekpneō*, "breathe out." The Revised versions wisely say simply "breathing." In Semitic thought the emotion of anger was connected with the breath.[1] **The high priest** was Caiaphas, who held office until A.D. 36.

2 Saul **asked of him letters to Damascus** so that **if he found any** believers there **he might bring them bound to Jerusalem.** In I Maccabees 15:15 ff., it is stated that Numenius brought back from Rome a letter giving the high priest authority to demand the extradition of Jews who broke their law. This was the legal basis for Saul's expedition, which was perhaps mainly to seize the Christians who had fled from Jerusalem.

Damascus had a large colony of Jews. Josephus states that at the time of the Jewish War (ca. A.D. 70) the Damascenes killed 10,500 Jews,[2] or 18,000 including women and children.[3] The Zadokite Fragment describes the "Covenanters of Damascus," as they are commonly known, a very strict Jewish sect. By some they are identified with the Qumran Community of the recently discovered Dead Sea Scrolls.[4] Damascus was the leading city of Syria (the capital today) and lay on the main caravan route from Mesopotamia to Egypt. Located about seventy miles from the Mediterranean (Beirut) just beyond the Lebanon and Anti-Lebanon Mountains, it forms an oasis on the edge of the desert. The Arabs have always referred to it as a paradise.

The use of the primitive expression, **the Way**, seems to point to an early date for

---

EXPOSITION

THE CHURCH'S FIRST PERSECUTOR CONVERTED

I. The Persecutor Arrested, Acts 9:1–9.
   A. The Persecutor's Activities, vss. 1, 2.
   B. The Persecutor's Encounter, vss. 3–7.
   C. The Persecutor's Apprehension, vss. 8, 9.
II. The Persecutor Converted, Acts 9:10–18.
   A. The Human Agent Employed, vs. 10.
   B. The Divine Commission Given, vss. 11, 12.
   C. The Human Objection Offered, vss. 13, 14.
   D. The Divine Purpose Set Forth, vss. 15, 16.
   E. The Divine Transformation Effected, vss. 17, 18.
III. The Persecutor Preaches, Acts 9:19–30.
   A. The Preacher's Associations, vs. 19.
   B. The Preacher's Message, vs. 20.
   C. The People's Amazement, vss. 21, 22.
   D. The Preacher's Escape, vss. 23–25.
   E. The Disciples' Fear, vss. 26, 28.
   F. The Hellenists' Opposition, vss. 29, 30.
IV. The Church Prospers, Acts 9:31–43.
   A. The Church's Rest, vs. 31.
   B. The Healing of Aeneas, vss. 32–35.
   C. The Raising of Dorcas, vss. 36–43.

[1] *Beginnings*, IV, 99. [2] *War*, II, 20, 2. [3] *Ibid.*, VI, 8, 7.
[4] F. F. Bruce, *Second Thoughts on the Dead Sea Scrolls* (Grand Rapids: Wm. B. Eerdmans Publishing Co., 1956), p. 32; W. H. Brownlee, "A Comparison of the Covenanters of the Dead Sea Scrolls with Pre-Christian Jewish Sects," *The Biblical Archaeologist*, XIII, 51. Cf. also Millar Burrows, *The Dead Sea Scrolls* (New York: The Viking Press, 1955), chap. XIII.

3 And as he journeyed, it came to pass that he drew nigh unto Damascus: and suddenly there shone round about him a light out of heaven:
4 and he fell upon the earth, and heard a voice saying unto him, Saul, Saul, why persecutest thou me?

Acts. In China Christianity has been called "the Jesus way" *(tao)*, in contrast to the Confucius and Buddha ways.

3 Since Damascus was located some 200 miles from Jerusalem, the journey—probably by way of Shechem and the Lake of Galilee or by way of Philadelphia (Amman) [5]—would take Saul a full six days between sabbaths, if not longer. That would give him sufficient time for much thinking about this new "heresy."

Suddenly there shone round about him a light out of heaven. The verb *periastraptō* occurs only here and in Paul's report of this incident in 22:6. It means "flash around." In classical Greek the word was used for the flashing of lightning. Whether that is the meaning here or whether it was a supernatural light makes little difference. The conversion of Saul which followed is the important thing.

4 **Fell upon the earth** describes the usual reaction to a heavenly visitation (cf. Ezek. 1:28; Dan. 8:17). **Saul, Saul** is in the Hebrew form here and in the other two accounts of his conversion (22:7; 26:14). Paul reported that the voice spoke to him "in the Hebrew language" (26:14); that is, in Aramaic.

I. THE PERSECUTOR ARRESTED (9:1–9)

Whatever may have been the extent of the persecution that fell upon the Church following the martyrdom of Stephen, it is evident that Saul was the ringleader of these vicious activities.

A. The Persecutor's Activities (9:1, 2)

At the stoning of Stephen he was present and guarded the garments of the murderers (Acts 7:58b), and Luke takes pains to say that Saul gave his full approval of the martyrdom of Stephen (Acts 8:1a). Although the author of Acts has deviated from Saul to relate the conversion of the Samaritans and the Ethiopian nobleman, he resumes the subject in chapter nine. Nor has the persecution abated in the meantime, for we read, "But Saul laid waste [made havoc] the church, entering into every house, and dragging men and women committed them to prison" (Acts 8:3). The intensity of his wrathfully destructive activities is graphically depicted in Luke's words: **But Saul, yet breathing threatening and slaughter against the disciples of the Lord.** Lange observes that "menace and slaughter constituted the vital air which he inhaled (and exhaled)." [a] Time and the growth of the Church under the labors of the apostles, Philip, and the scattered disciples, only served to intensify his wrath and activities against the Christians. As a servant of the Sanhedrin, if indeed not a member, he secured warrants from the high priest for the arrest of any disciples who might be associated with the synagogue at faraway Damascus. This was a civil and religious right permitted the Jews by the Roman government concerning members of their own race. His utter disregard for Christian women is evidenced by the fact that their persecution by Saul is specifically mentioned three times in Acts (Acts 8:3; 9:2; 22:4).

The disciples, not yet called Christians, are here for the first time referred to as the people of **the Way.** The word thus used and capitalized in the ASV occurs six times in the Acts (Acts 9:2; 19:9, 23; 22:4; 24:14, 22).

B. The Persecutor's Encounter (9:3–7)

Who art thou, Lord? . . . I am Jesus whom thou persecutest (vs. 5). Saul's visit to Damascus in quest of Christians indicates something of the wide spread of Christianity by this time, as well as his blind and cruel determination to arrest its progress, or to stamp it out completely. The light of God's

[5] Cadbury, *The Book of Acts in History*, p. 64.

[a] Lange, *op. cit.*, p. 161.

5 And he said, Who art thou, Lord? And he *said*, I am Jesus whom thou persecutest:
6 but rise, and enter into the city, and it shall be told thee what thou must do.
7 And the men that journeyed with him stood speechless, hearing the voice, but beholding
no man.
8 And Saul arose from the earth; and when his eyes were opened, he saw nothing; and
they led him by the hand, and brought him into Damascus.
9 And he was three days without sight, and did neither eat nor drink.

---

5 The first lesson Saul learned was that in persecuting the Christians he was persecuting Christ. When the body (the Church) was stabbed, the Head (Christ) felt the pain.

6 The last clause of verse 5 and the first half of verse 6 are not found in any Greek manuscript, nor in the oldest versions. Knowling concludes: "There seems no Greek authority for the whole insertion; apparently a retranslation by Erasmus from the Latin."[6] Thus it came from the Vulgate by way of the so-called Textus Receptus into the King James Version. "It is hard for thee to kick against the goad" is genuine in 26:14, but not here.

7 The verb *synodeuō*, **journeyed with,** and the adjective *eneos*, **speechless,** are found only here in the New Testament. The fact that it says the men **stood** is no contradiction of Paul's statement in 26:14 that they all fell to the ground. Obviously they would soon stand on their feet again.

A slightly more difficult problem exists in harmonizing the phrase **hearing the voice** with the statement in 22:9 that they did not hear the voice speaking to Paul. There is some ground for holding that the genitive *(phōnēs)* after *akouō*, as here, suggests an audible sound, whereas the accusative (*phōnēn*, 22:9) indicates the intelligible content of what was said.[7] Another solution, preferred by Bruce,[8] is that the reference here is to *Paul's* voice as heard by his companions; they did not hear the voice from heaven. But it seems that the former interpretation is more natural.

8 Paul is sometimes pictured riding on a Roman charger on the road to Damascus. But **led him by the hand** [9] would suggest that he was walking. If he did ride, it was probably on a donkey, since the Pharisees avoided horses as a symbol of Roman power.

9 For **three days** Paul was **without sight, and did neither eat nor drink.** Some interpret this as being the result of his shock.[10] But his fasting was more likely due to a desire to wait penitently before God in prayer.

---

ineffable glory suddenly flashed forth, probably in answer to the prayer of the Christians in Damascus who may have heard of his coming (Acts 9:13, 14), and smote the persecutor down in the road near the city. The voice of God spoke to the arrested and startled enemy of Christ, clearly reflecting that Saul's battle was not against men, but against God and His Son, who is Lord of all. The Lord, in response to Saul's question, **Who art thou, Lord?** immediately identified Himself as the Jesus whom Saul and the Jews rejected. Christ's identification of Himself with His suffering disciples is likewise very clearly intimated. Saul's inevitable capitulation is suggested by Christ's words, as recorded in the King James Version, though omitted from the American Standard Version, "it is hard for thee to kick against the pricks" (vs. 5b; cf. 26:14b). Saul the persecutor, who had made many tremble under his wrath, was suddenly arrested by God and stood trembling and astonished before his conqueror, humbly inquiring for His will.

C. The Persecutor's Apprehension (9:8, 9)

And he was three days without sight (vs. 9a). When man will not heed the overtures of God's mercy, he will have to suffer the judgments of the Lord. He who had dragged innocent men and women away from their homes to prison in chains was now so helpless that he required to be led about by the hand. Startled, shocked, humbled, and

6 EGT, II, 232.
7 Cf. James H. Moulton, *A Grammar of New Testament Greek* (Edinburgh: T. & T. Clark, 1906), I (Prolegomena), 66.
8 *Acts*, p. 199. 9 The verb *cheiragageō* is found only here and in the parallel passage in 22:11.
10 E.g., Bruce, *Acts*, p. 200.

10 Now there was a certain disciple at Damascus, named Ananias; and the Lord said unto him in a vision, Ananias. And he said, Behold, I *am here*, Lord.
11 And the Lord *said* unto him, Arise, and go to the street which is called Straight, and inquire in the house of Judas for one named Saul, a man of Tarsus: for behold, he prayeth;
12 and he hath seen a man named Ananias coming in, and laying his hands on him, that he might receive his sight.

---

10 **Ananias** ("the Lord is gracious") was apparently a Jewish Christian living in Damascus. **The Lord** was Jesus (cf. vs. 17).

11 **The street which is called Straight** probably received that name not because it was perfectly straight but because it was less crooked than most of the streets of that oriental city. Today it is identified as one of the main thoroughfares running across Damascus from east to west. In the bazaar section it is partly covered with a long canopy. The **house of Judas** is supposed to be located near the west end.

Behold, he prayeth. Luke gives special attention to prayer in his Gospel and Acts and several times associates it with visions (cf. Luke 1:10; 3:21; 9:28; Acts 10:9 f.).

---

blinded by the stroke of God, for three days Saul groped helplessly about, eating nothing. He was led, a harmless captive of God, into the very city from which he had purposed to ruthlessly take captive the disciples of God's Son. He had gone to Damascus to imprison Christ's disciples, but he had been arrested by their Master, and for a time was imprisoned in the dismal dungeon of sightlessness that he might become the disciple and love servant of Christ ever after. Paul later reflects this experience in his words, as Weymouth translates them: "I press on, striving to lay hold of that for which I was also laid hold of by Christ Jesus" (Phil. 3:12b; cf. Williams' translation).

II. THE PERSECUTOR CONVERTED (9:10–18)

The conversion of Saul was so momentous that Luke thrice records the event in the Acts (9:1–19; 22:5–21; 26:12–20). Contributing to the conversion of Saul was his likely unsuccessful dispute with Stephen, as a member of the Cilician synagogue (Acts 6:9, 10); the profound impression made on his mind by Stephen's defense, as evidenced by the similarities in all his later recorded messages and arguments to Stephen's address; the practical demonstrations of Christianity which he must have witnessed in the lives of the disciples he so doggedly persecuted; and his growing personal sense of dissatisfaction with the inability of the Law to give peace with God, as he later records (see Rom. 7). The sudden revelation of Christ to him on the Damascus road removed the last objection, and forever convinced him that the Christian way was right. It was this personal appearance of Christ to him upon which he ever after relied to validate his apostleship (Acts 22:7–11, 21; I Cor. 9:1; 15:8; II Cor. 11:5; 12:12; Gal. 2:8). Dummelow significantly remarks:

> Saul's conversion at once gave Christianity a higher social status. He was an educated man, of good family, a rabbi, and (probably) a member of the Sanhedrin. It could no longer be objected to the teachers of the new faith that they were all ignorant and unlettered men. [b]

A. The Human Agent Employed (9:10)

Now there was a certain disciple at Damascus, named Ananias (vs. 10a). Ananias may have been the leader of the Christian disciples at Damascus. Tradition holds that he was one of the Seven, later consecrated a bishop of Damascus by Andrew and Peter, and that he finally became a martyr. He is later described by Luke as "a devout man according to the law, well reported of by all the Jews that dwelt there" (Acts 22:12). That these Damascus disciples were still worshipping in the Jewish synagogue appears evident (vs. 2).

B. The Divine Commission Given (9:11, 12)

Arise, and go to the street which is called Straight (vs. 11a). The task assigned Ananias was indeed a hazardous one, as humanly viewed, but it was definite and specific.

[b] Dummelow, *op. cit.*, p. 830.

13 But Ananias answered, Lord, I have heard from many of this man, how much evil
he did to thy saints at Jerusalem:
14 and here he hath authority from the chief priests to bind all that call upon thy name.
15 But the Lord said unto him, Go thy way: for he is a chosen vessel unto me, to bear
my name before the Gentiles and kings, and the children of Israel:
16 for I will show him how many things he must suffer for my name's sake.
17 And Ananias departed, and entered into the house; and laying his hands on him said,
Brother Saul, the Lord, *even* Jesus, who appeared unto thee in the way which thou camest,
hath sent me, that thou mayest receive thy sight, and be filled with the Holy Spirit.

---

13 **I have heard** suggests that Ananias was not a fugitive from the persecution at Jerusalem (8:1), but that he had lived for some time at Damascus.

Saints occurs here for the first time in Acts as a designation of Christians. It is used again in verses 32 and 41, and in 26:10. Paul employs it frequently (40 times) as his favorite term for followers of Christ. The Greek word is *hagioi*, masculine plural of the adjective *hagios*, holy. So it literally means "holy ones." But it is clear that Paul uses it of all believers as those who have been set apart to God. *Hagios* is thus taken in its minimum sense of "consecrated." In the King James Version *hagios (hagioi)* is translated "holy" some 165 times and "saints" 61 times.

14 Saul had **authority from the chief priests to bind all that call upon thy name.** In the eyes of the Jewish leaders praying to Jesus was a denial of their monotheistic faith.

15 Saul's mission was first to **the Gentiles,** and only secondly to **the children of Israel;** hence the order here. **Kings** would include Herod Agrippa II (chap. 26) and Nero (27:24).

17 This **laying his hands on him** was not "confirmation" or ordination. It was probably connected primarily with Saul's recovery of his sight, although it may have had some connection also with his receiving the Holy Spirit (cf. 8:17).[11] The greeting, **Brother Saul** (same Hebrew form as in vs. 4) must have brought immediate comfort to Saul's heart. One whom he had come to persecute now accepted him as a brother in the Lord. **The Lord, even Jesus** strikingly asserts the deity of Jesus. Saul was not only to **receive** his **sight** again, but to **be filled with the Holy Spirit.** He would need this experience to carry out his commission.

Judas' house was likely the regular lodging place of Saul when in Damascus. Here Luke records perhaps the most hopeful news that the disciples had received since the death of Stephen. **Behold,** said the Lord to Ananias concerning the former persecutor, **he prayeth.** As God prepared Ananias for his mission to Saul by a vision, He at the same time prepared Saul for Ananias' visit.

C. The Human Objection Offered (9:13, 14)

Lord, I have heard from many of this man (vs. 13a). Ananias' objection rested, *first*, on the cruelties of Saul against the disciples at Jerusalem, which were well known at Damascus; and *second*, on the fact that Saul was authorized by the high priest to arrest all who called upon the name of Christ in connection with the synagogue at Damascus. Only a fool would walk into such a dangerous trap, Ananias objected.

D. The Divine Purpose Set Forth (9:15, 16)

Go thy way: for he is a chosen vessel unto me (vs. 15a).

Ananias' objection is met by God's renewal of the commission to fulfill his mission to Saul: **Go thy way: for he is a chosen vessel unto me,** or an instrument of choice, to carry the Gospel to the Gentiles, God informed Ananias.

Saul's birth and upbringing in the Gentile city of Tarsus in Asia Minor, his theological training in the more liberal school of Gamaliel at Jerusalem, his likely graduate training in the Greek university at Tarsus,[c]

---

[11] So Bruce, *Acts*, p. 202. But contra. Knowling, EGT, II, 237.

[c] Jewish boys desiring a liberal education had to study at Alexandria, Tarsus, or Athens. E. W. K. Mould, *op. cit.* p. 473.

18 And straightway there fell from his eyes as it were scales, and he received his sight; and he arose and was baptized;

19 and he took food and was strengthened. And he was certain days with the disciples that were at Damascus.

20 And straightway in the synagogues he proclaimed Jesus, that he is the Son of God.

21 And all that heard him were amazed, and said, Is not this he that in Jerusalem made havoc of them that called on this name? and he had come hither for this intent, that he might bring them bound before the chief priests.

22 But Saul increased the more in strength, and confounded the Jews that dwelt at Damascus, proving that this is the Christ.

---

18 **Scales** *(lepis)* is perhaps better rendered "flakes," [12] or "scaly substance." The word occurs only here in the New Testament. **Fell** *(apopiptō)* also occurs only here. Hobart is probably justified in finding some medical interest in the use of these terms. [13]

19 The new Saul found a new fellowship. Now he spent his time **with the disciples.**

20 **Straightway** Saul started to preach at Damascus. On the surface this seems to conflict with his statement in Galatians 1:17 that after his conversion he went away into Arabia and then returned to Damascus. It is not unreasonable to conclude that he began at once to preach, but then felt the need for more meditation and prayer, and so sought the solitude of Arabia. Many a young person in the zeal of his newly found experience with Christ, coupled with the consciousness of a call, has started to preach, only to find that he needed to take time out first for further preparation.

As was Saul's custom later, his first ministry was **in the synagogues.** There **he proclaimed Jesus, that he is the Son of God.** The latter expression, **the Son of God,** is found only here in Acts. It is evidently here equivalent to "the Messiah," in keeping with Psalm 2:7 (cf. Acts 13:33). That the Jews of Jesus' day thought of the Messiah as God's Son is indicated by the question of the high priest: "Art thou the Christ [Messiah], the Son of the Blessed [God]?" (Mark 14:61).

21 Saul's hearers were **amazed** *(existanto,* stood out of themselves) and asked if this were not the one who in Jerusalem **made havoc** of the followers of Jesus. The same word is used by Paul in Galatians 1:13, 23 to describe his persecution of the believers. The verb, found only in these three places in the New Testament, is *portheō,* "destroy, ravage, sack." [14] **Had come** is the correct translation in the American Standard Version of the pluperfect *elēlythei,* since "as his original purpose in coming no longer existed, the perfect is no longer applicable." [15]

22 **Increased . . . in strength** is *enedynamouto,* found only here and six times in Paul's epistles. This probably means that he was growing stronger (imperfect tense) both in preaching power and in his influence

---

and his membership in the Cilician synagogue, combined to qualify him for this great mission to the Gentiles, a mission which must entail great suffering.

E. The Divine Transformation Effected (9:17, 18)

And straightway there fell from his eyes as t were scales (vs. 18a).

That this experience under the human instrumentality of Ananias culminated in the genuine conversion of Saul, which had begun with his spiritual arrest on the Damascus road, is evident from the following facts: *first,* Ananias' tender prayer and announcement of his divinely appointed mission to Saul (vs. 17b); *second,* the falling away of the scales of blinding pride, prejudice, hatred, and vain imaginations that had darkened his spiritual vision; and *third,* his baptism and experience of the regenerating Holy Spirit and forgiveness of sins through prayer to God in Christ. The last is particularly evident in the account in Acts 22:16, where we read: "arise, and be baptized, and wash away thy sins, calling on his name." This spiritual transformation of Saul marks the turning point in the history of early Christianity.

[12] *Beginnings,* IV, 104. [13] *Op. cit.,* pp. 39 ff.
[14] Cf. *Beginnings,* IV, 105: "The suggestion of *porthein* is the sack of a city." [15] Bruce, *Acts,* p. 204.

23 And when many days were fulfilled, the Jews took counsel together to kill him:
24 but their plot became known to Saul. And they watched the gates also day and night that they might kill him:
25 but his disciples took him by night, and let him down through the wall, lowering him in a basket.

---

on the people. He **confounded** the Jews at Damascus. The verb is *synchynnō*, found only in Acts (2:6; 19:32; 21:31). **Proving** is the verb *synbibazō*, used only in Acts and Paul's epistles. It means literally, "join or knit together, unite," and so to "deduce, prove, demonstrate." Saul joined the Old Testament prophecies with their fulfilment in Christ, and thus proved that Jesus was **the Christ,** the Messiah promised by God to Israel. This was obviously the most important point that had to be made in preaching the gospel to the Jews. They must accept Jesus first as their national Messiah and then, and only thus, as their personal Saviour.

23 The **many days** would be about three years (cf. Gal. 1:18). Instead of persecuting the Christians, Saul was preaching the Christ. It is no wonder that **the Jews took counsel together to kill him.** The verb *symbouleuō* is used similarly in Matthew 26:4 of the Jewish leaders taking counsel together to arrest and kill Jesus.

24 **Plot,** *epiboulē*, is used only in Acts in the New Testament (four times). It has the same meaning in Esther 2:22 (LXX), where it is used of the plot to assassinate the king.

So strong was the Jews' hatred of Saul that **they watched the gates also day and night that they might kill him.** With this and the following verse we need to compare II Corinthians 11:32, 33—"In Damascus the governor [ethnarch] under Aretas the king guarded the city of the Damascenes in order to take me: and through a window was I let down in a basket by the wall, and escaped his hands."

The problem of harmonizing these two accounts has engaged the labors of many. One thing that perplexed earlier scholars was the fact that Damascus was apparently under Roman rule during this period. What then was an ethnarch of Aretas IV—king of the Nabatean Arabs from 9 B.C. to A.D. 40—doing in that city? A striking coincidence is that there have not been found in Damascus any Roman coins for the period A.D. 34–62.[16] (Saul's flight probably was soon after A.D. 34.) It is therefore assumed that the Roman government may have turned over the jurisdiction of that city to the Nabateans for this brief time.[17] A better explanation would probably be that the ethnarch was "an Arab sheik or chieftain who headed the Arabian community in that mixed city." [18]

Kirsopp Lake has still another suggestion. He thinks that Saul's stay in Arabia (the Nabatean kingdom) was not for the purpose of meditation, but of preaching, in fulfilment of his commission to proclaim the Gospel to the Gentiles (cf. vs. 15). This aroused the opposition of the Nabatean authorities. So the ethnarch had posted a guard *outside* the walls to capture Saul if he sought to leave the city again. This explanation can be received without accepting Lake's further contention that the Acts account of the Jews watching *inside* the walls is unhistorical.[19] In any case, this conclusion seems the most satisfactory: the Jews and the Nabatean ethnarch worked together in an effort to prevent Saul's escape.

25 **In the wall** is made more specific in the Corinthian account that Saul was let down "through a window . . . by the wall." [20] The window shown today to tourists is obviously a fabrication of more recent times. But it may represent the approximate situation of Paul's day.

Basket is *sphyridi*,[21] used in connection with the feeding of the 4000 (Matt. 15:37; 16:10; Mark 8:8, 20) and nowhere else in the New Testament. It was probably a large wicker basket. The word used in II Corinthi-

[16] So Knowling (EGT, II, 240). Cadbury (*The Book of Acts in History*, p. 20) says A.D. 37 to 54.
[17] Cf. Cadbury, *The Book of Acts in History*, p. 20. [18] *Ibid.* [19] *Beginnings*, V, 193 f.
[20] Hackett (*op. cit.*, p. 123, n. 2) explains how the exit could be both "through the window" and "through the wall." Just to the left of the east gate of Damascus he noticed two or three windows in the wall, which opened into houses inside the city. The phrase "through the wall" is used by Josephus (*Ant.* V, 1, 2) of the escape of the spies from Jericho.
[21] This is the spelling in Aleph C and adopted by Westcott and Hort. Vaticanus and Alexandrinus have *spyridi* (Nestle and Souter).

26 And when he was come to Jerusalem, he assayed to join himself to the disciples: and they were all afraid of him, not believing that he was a disciple.

27 But Barnabas took him, and brought him to the apostles, and declared unto them how he had seen the Lord in the way, and that he had spoken to him, and how at Damascus he had preached boldly in the name of Jesus.

28 And he was with them going in and going out at Jerusalem,

---

ans 11:33 is *sarganē*—"a large woven or network bag or basket suitable for hay, straw . . . or for bales of wool." [22] Hackett notes that the account here fits well with the customs of the country.[23] The normal way to lower a man into a well or raise him to a second floor is by means of a rope and basket.

26 **When he was come** is one word in the Greek, *paragenomenos*. This verb is characteristically Lukan, being found eight times in his Gospel, twenty-one times in Acts, and only eight times elsewhere in the New Testament. Literally the aorist participle means "having become beside," and so "having arrived."

Assayed represents the earliest sense of *peirazō:* "try, attempt." The more common meaning in the New Testament is "test, prove." In the King James Version it is most frequently translated "tempt" (29 out of 39 times). The new convert, Saul, attempted to **join** the **disciples,** but **they were all afraid of him,** thinking that he was a wolf in sheep's clothing.

27 **But Barnabas,** as always, lived up to his name, "son of consolation" (cf. 4:36, KJV) or "Son of encouragement" (RSV). He "went bond" for the ex-Pharisee, **brought him to the apostles,** and told them about his conversion near Damascus and his preaching in that city. For **seen the Lord** compare I Corinthians 15:8.

Some scholars have claimed a contradiction between this and Paul's own statement in Galatians 1:18, 19 that he saw no apostles on this visit except Peter, together with James the Lord's brother. But this does not necessarily conflict with the statement in Acts that Barnabas brought him **to the apostles.** Paul visited two of the representative leaders.

28 The result of Barnabas' guarantee of

III. THE PERSECUTOR PREACHES (9:19–30)

Immediately following his conversion, Saul identified himself with the Damascus disciples, began to preach Christ as the living Son of God now alive from the dead, amazed the people with his radical change of spirit and purpose from the persecutor of Christ's disciples to the preacher of Christ's Gospel, and began to grow in favor with God and in influence with the people.

Concerning Saul's Damascus road conversion experience, Robinson [d] observes that there was a threefold significance. *First*, in that vision he received the profound personal conviction that Jesus Christ was alive from the dead; *second*, there came to him a clear conception that the fact and saving significance of Christ's resurrection was to be made known to all nations (Acts 9:15; 22:15; 26:17; Rom. 1:5; I Cor. 9:1; 15:8 ff.; Gal. 1:16); and *third*, he was deeply convinced that he was the divinely chosen messenger to bear this gospel message to all nations (Acts 26:16–18; Rom. 1:5; Gal. 1:16).

Soon after his conversion, Saul departed to Arabia, possibly to the ancient Petra, where he prepared himself for his lifework by study, meditation, and prayer. Returning to Damascus, he began to preach Christ in the synagogues openly. The Jews were moved with envy and laid a plot to kill him, from which plot Saul escaped, with the aid of the disciples, over the city wall in a basket. He proceeded to Jerusalem where he met Barnabas who commended him to the apostles. His preaching incited the Hellenist Jews to murderous intent against him, which occasioned his departure to his home country in Cilicia, where he lived and labored for about seven years, until summoned to Antioch to assist Barnabas in the ministry of the church there.

[22] *Beginnings,* IV, 106.
[23] *Op. cit.,* p. 123.

[d] Robinson, *op. cit.,* pp. 54, 55.

29 preaching boldly in the name of the Lord: and he spake and disputed against the
Grecian Jews; but they were seeking to kill him.
30 And when the brethren knew it, they brought him down to Caesarea, and sent him
forth to Tarsus.
31 So the church throughout all Judaea and Galilee and Samaria had peace, being edified;
and, walking in the fear of the Lord and in the comfort of the Holy Spirit, was multiplied.
32 And it came to pass, as Peter went throughout all parts, he came down also to the
saints that dwelt at Lydda.

Saul's sincerity was that the latter was able to associate freely with the disciples at Jerusalem.

29 Saul was never idle. Soon he was **preaching boldly in the name of the Lord.** But when he **spake and disputed against the Grecian** [Hellenistic] **Jews . . . they were seeking to kill him.** He was faced with exactly the same situation as was Stephen some years before (6:9–11).

30 The believers at Jerusalem are here called **brethren.** Knowling comments: "The expression seems expressly used to imply that the disciples at Jerusalem recognized Saul as a brother." [24]

Because Saul's life was in danger, the disciples escorted him to **Caesarea**—the main seaport of Palestine at that time—**and sent him forth to Tarsus,** probably by boat. What he did during the next half dozen years we are not told. Apparently Paul's only reference to it is in Galatians 1:21—"Then I came into the regions of Syria and Cilicia"; that is the province of Syro-Cilicia. But the reference to Syria and Cilicia implies that Paul did not settle down at Tarsus. He probably spent these years evangelizing his native province. Ramsay characterizes them as "ten years of quiet work within the range of the synagogue and its influence." [25]

Tarsus, Paul's birthplace, was the capital of Cilicia. It became a part of the Roman Empire in 64 B.C., and was given the rank of a free city. In the apostle's day it was regarded as one of the three great university cities of the world, surpassed only by Athens and Alexandria. Paul speaks of it as "no mean city" (21:39).

31 **Church** is plural in the King James Version, based on the late manuscripts. That is the easier reading, and is paralleled by "the churches of Judaea" (Gal. 1:22) and "the churches of God which are in Judaea" (I Thess. 2:14). But the oldest manuscripts [26] have *ekklēsia* here, not *ekklēsiai.*[27] Ramsay says that Luke uses *ekklēsia* here "in the sense of the Unified Church." [28]

Judaea and Galilee and Samaria were the three main divisions of Palestine proper, between the Jordan Valley and the Mediterranean Sea. Samaria lay between the other two. Probably the three are named in order of their importance as Jewish territories. **Galilee** appears in Acts only three times. In the other two passages (10:37; 13:31) it refers to Jesus' ministry there. This is the only mention of Christian churches in Galilee.[29]

Edified is literally "built up" (RSV). The verb *oikodomeō* is from *oikos*, house, and *demō*, build. So its first meaning was "build a house." Then it came to be used in the general sense of "build" and metaphorically as "build up." **The comfort of the Holy Spirit** reminds one of the expression "Comforter" applied to the Holy Spirit in John's Gospel (14:16, 26; 15:26; 16:7) and to Christ as "Advocate" in I John 2:1 (the only occurrences of *paraklētos* in the New Testament). **Comfort** is *paraklēsis*, found 29 times in the New Testament.

32 **Peter** appears once more in the narrative and holds the central place, not only for the remainder of this chapter, but also throughout most of the next three chapters (10–12).

Lydda is mentioned only in this passage (vss. 32, 35, 38) in the New Testament. After the destruction of Jerusalem in A.D. 70, it became a renowned center of rabbinical learning. It is of interest now because the main airport in Israel is located there.

[24] EGT, II, 243. [25] Ramsay, *St. Pau the Traveller*, p. 47.
[26] Aleph A B C, and many versions.
[27] Found in Western and Byzantine texts.
[28] *St. Paul the Traveller*, p. 127.
[29] Until Eusebius (cf. Cadbury, *The Book of Acts in History*, p. 122).

33 And there he found a certain man named Aeneas, who had kept his bed eight years; for he was palsied.

34 And Peter said unto him, Aeneas, Jesus Christ healeth thee: arise, and make thy bed. And straightway he arose.

35 And all that dwelt at Lydda and in Sharon saw him, and they turned to the Lord.

36 Now there was at Joppa a certain disciple named Tabitha, which by interpretation is called Dorcas: this woman was full of good works and almsdeeds which she did.

37 And it came to pass in those days, that she fell sick, and died: and when they had washed her, they laid her in an upper chamber.

38 And as Lydda was nigh unto Joppa, the disciples, hearing that Peter was there, sent two men unto him, entreating him, Delay not to come on unto us.

Some of the **saints** at Lydda probably had fled from Jerusalem, which was nearby. Since Lydda was situated between Azotus and Caesarea, it is also probable that Philip had evangelized there (cf. 8:40).

33 **Aeneas** was probably a Christian,[30] although it is not so stated. **Eight years** is literally "out of eight years" *(ex etōn oktō)* and could be translated "since eight years old." For **palsied** Luke uses *paralelymenos*, as in 8:7. Hobart contends that Luke's choice of this rather than *paralytikos* is in line with the medical usage of his day.[31]

34 To the paralytic Peter made a striking declaration: **Aeneas, Jesus Christ healeth thee.** The verb *iaomai* is used in Luke's writings more than in all the rest of the New Testament (17 out of 28 times). Luke uses *therapeuō* (cf. therapeutics, therapy) 19 out of 44 times in the New Testament. **Make thy bed** could be translated "lay the table for yourself." Lake and Cadbury comment: "The command of Peter is not to lift up his *krabattos* [pallet] to show that he is cured . . . but to get himself something to eat (cf. Mark v. 43 = Luke viii. 55)." [32]

35 **Sharon** was, and is, not a town but the coastal plain stretching from Lydda northward to Mount Carmel. It is famous for the "rose of Sharon" and for its fertility. It is still one of the most productive parts of Palestine.

36 **Joppa** is modern Jaffa, now united with the new Jewish city of Tel Aviv to form Tel Aviv-Jaffa, on the coast opposite Jerusalem. Long a Philistine city, it was restored to the Jews in 47 B.C. But its population included many Greeks. It has always been the principal port of southern Palestine, although it has no natural harbor.

The feminine form of **disciple,** *mathētria*, is found only here in the New Testament. **Tabitha** is Aramaic, as **Dorcas** is Greek, for "gazelle," a beautiful, fleet-footed animal.

37 When Dorcas died they **washed her.** This was in keeping with the customs of both Jews and Greeks. Then **they laid her in an upper chamber.** Outside Jerusalem a body could be held for three days before burial, but in Jerusalem it must be buried the day the death occurred.[33]

38 Since **Lydda was nigh unto Joppa**—only ten milee away—the disciples sent for Peter. Perhaps they had heard of the healing of Aeneas.

IV. THE CHURCH PROSPERS

(9:31–43)

Saul's conversion resulted in a cessation of persecution long suffered by the Church at his hands and allowed for the edification and rapid increase of its ministry (vs. 31). Luke follows this account with a notation concerning the disciples at Lydda (vs. 32b), where Peter healed Aeneas of palsy, which healing precipitated a great turning to God (vs. 35). Finally, he relates the restoration to life of Dorcas at Joppa through Peter's prayers (vs. 40) with the resultant spiritual awakening at Joppa (vs. 42).

It is noteworthy that Luke's expression in verse 31, **So the church throughout all Judæa and Galilee and Samaria had peace, being edified,** contains the only reference to Christianity in "Galilee" in the entire Book of Acts.

[30] Contra, *Beginnings*, IV, 108 f.
[31] *Op. cit.*, p. 6.
[32] *Beginnings*, IV, 109.
[33] EGT, II, 247.

39 And Peter arose and went with them. And when he was come, they brought him into the upper chamber: and all the widows stood by him weeping, and showing the coats and garments which Dorcas made, while she was with them.

40 But Peter put them all forth, and kneeled down, and prayed; and turning to the body, he said, Tabitha, arise. And she opened her eyes; and when she saw Peter, she sat up.

41 And he gave her his hand, and raised her up; and calling the saints and widows, he presented her alive.

42 And it became known throughout all Joppa: and many believed on the Lord.

43 And it came to pass, that he abode many days in Joppa with one Simon a tanner.

---

39 The **widows** here are probably not an ecclesiastical order.[34] However, Lake and Cadbury write: "It is possible that the widows came in the capacity, which they certainly had later in the Christian church, of nurses and professional mourners."[35]

40 Before praying, **Peter put them all forth,** as Jesus did at the raising of Jairus' daughter (Mark 5:40). He wanted an atmosphere of faith.

41 **The saints and widows** does not mean, of course, that the widows were not Christians. It means the saints and especially the widows.

42 The results of these two healings are stated in emphatic terms: **many believed on the Lord** (cf. vs. 35). Miracles of healing were a support for evangelism in the early church.

43 In **Joppa** Peter stayed with **one Simon a tanner.** Since tanning was considered an unclean occupation by the Jews, because it involved handling dead bodies, it is surprising that Peter stayed at Simon's house. Evidently as a Christian he had broadened his outlook a little already.

[34] Bruce, *Acts*, p. 212.
[35] *Beginnings*, IV, 111.

CHAPTER X

Now *there was* a certain man in Caesarea, Cornelius by name, a centurion of the band called the Italian *band*,

2 a devout man, and one that feared God with all his house, who gave much alms to the people, and prayed to God always.

EXEGESIS

1 **Cornelius** was a very common name in the Roman Empire. In 82 B.C. Cornelius Sulla had freed 10,000 slaves, who promptly adopted his name in gratitude.

This **Cornelius** was a **centurion.** The word *hekatontarchēs* (often spelled *hekatontarchos*) occurs 21 times in the New Testament. It literally means ruler *(archōn)* of a hundred *(hekaton)*. Mark, writing for the Romans, alone and always (three times), uses the Latin equivalent *kentyriōn*, which has been taken over into English as "centurion." The first Gentile with whom Jesus came into contact, as far as we know, was a centurion (Matt. 8:5).

Band *(speira)* was a cohort (Latin *cohors*). This was the tenth part of a legion. Since a legion normally consisted of 6,000 men, a cohort would naturally have 600 soldiers. But apparently the number differed in some instances.

This cohort was called the **Italian.** Broughton thinks this can be identified as the Cohors II. Italica, which is known to have been in Syria by A.D. 69 and may have been there much earlier.[1]

2 Cornelius was a **devout man.** The adjective *eusebēs* occurs again in verse 7 and elsewhere only once in the New Testament (II Pet. 2:9). It means "pious, godly, devout." This, together with the statement that he **feared God** *(phoboumenos ton theon)*, shows that he worshiped the true God. A similar expression used in Acts is *sebomenos ton theon*, "worshiping God." Bruce notes that these expressions, "though not strictly technical terms . . . , are generally used in

EXPOSITION

THE CHURCH'S FIRST GENTILE EVANGELISM

I. THE HEAVENLY VISIONS, Acts 10:1–16.
   A. The Man Cornelius, vss. 1, 2.
   B. The Vision of Cornelius, vss. 3–8.
   C. The Trance of Peter, vss. 9–16.

II. THE DIVINE MISSION, Acts 10:17–33.
   A. The Mission Summons, vss. 17–23a.
   B. The Mission Accepted, vss. 23b–33.

III. THE APOSTLE'S MESSAGE, Acts 10:34–43.
   A. The Divine Impartiality, vss. 34, 35.
   B. The Universal Divine Lordship, vss. 36–41.
   C. The Way of Salvation, vss. 42, 43.

IV. THE SPIRIT'S EFFUSION, Acts 10:44–48.
   A. The Spirit Outpoured, vss. 44–47.
   B. The Disciples' Baptism, vss. 47, 48.

I. THE HEAVENLY VISIONS (10:1–16)

The first Gentile mission had a most opportune entrance at Caesarea, the Roman colony and Roman capital of Judaea and the most important commercial and political cosmopolitan port of Palestine of the time. Caesarea was built by Herod the Great and named Caesarea Augustus in honor of the emperor, Augustus Caesar. The inhabitants were mostly Greeks and other Gentiles, but the Jews were accorded equal privileges. Besides the governor's royal palace, the city had a theater, amphitheater, and a temple housing the image of the emperor of Rome. The chief characters in the gospel drama were Peter and Cornelius. Peter, the apostle, was at Joppa lodging with Simon the tanner whose house, for ceremonial reasons incident to his tanner's trade, was removed from the city and located near the seaside.

[1] *Beginnings*, V 441f.

3 He saw in a vision openly, as it were about the ninth hour of the day, an angel of God coming in unto him, and saying to him, Cornelius.

4 And he, fastening his eyes upon him, and being affrighted, said, What is it, Lord? And he said unto him, Thy prayers and thine alms are gone up for a memorial before God.

Acts to denote those Gentiles who, though not full proselytes . . . , attached themselves to the Jewish religion, practising its monotheistic and imageless worship, attending the synagogue, observing the Sabbath and food-laws, etc." [2]

It is also said of Cornelius that he **gave much alms to the people** [i.e., the Jewish people] **and prayed to God always.** The description given here indicates that this centurion was a reverent worshiper of God according to the Jewish religion. But there is nothing that would suggest that he was a Christian. Everything said here of Cornelius could probably also be said of Nicodemus, to whom Jesus declared, "Ye must be born again" (John 3:7).

3 *Phanerōs*, **openly,** means "clearly, distinctly." [3] It occurs only here, in Mark 1:45, and in John 7:10. **As it were about** [*hōsei peri*] reflects Luke's habitual caution in using numbers. His keen historical sense made him careful about exact figures. **The ninth hour** (3:00 P.M.) was the time for offering the evening sacrifice in the temple, and devout Jews and God-fearers observed it as an hour of prayer (cf. 3:1).

4 *Atenisas*, **fastening his eyes,** is a strong verb meaning "looking fixedly, stedfastly, earnestly." Luke uses it 12 out of the 14 times it occurs in the New Testament. The other two times are in II Corinthians 3:7, 13.

Lord *(Kyrie)* should perhaps be "sir," since there is no implication of deity here. The vocative form would have the force of "my lord" as used in British circles. **Are gone up** is language reminiscent of the smoke of ancient sacrifices ascending toward heaven.

Mnēmosynon, **memorial,** is used in the Septuagint [4] to translate the Hebrew word which is "a name given to that portion of the vegetable oblation [meat offering, KJV]

A. The Man Cornelius (10:1, 2)

Now there was a certain man in Caesarea, Cornelius by name (vs. 1a). Cornelius was by occupation and position a centurion, or captain, of an Italian century (band) or a cohort. If it were the latter, which appears more likely than the former, then he was in command of 600 soldiers, men recruited in Italy and thus likely Roman citizens. The duties of a Roman centurion were similar to a present-day army captain. Like all the centurions appearing in the New Testament, Cornelius is favorably represented (cf. Matt. 8:5 and Luke 7:1–10). By religion he was an uncircumcised Gentile worshipper of the one true God, "a proselyte of the gate," or a "God-fearer"; a devout, generous, prayerful, and religiously influential man. Luke is specific in designating Cornelius a **devout man,** or a sincere worshipper of the Jewish Jehovah, as opposed to Gentile idolatry. Luke's statement that he was **one that feared God** is to be understood in reference to reverential fear that inspired worship, rather than a servile fear. His sound character and religious influence are evidenced by the fact that his family followed his faith, as Weymouth renders Luke's words, "and so was every member of his household." His Jewish faith is attested by his observance of the stated Jewish hours of prayer (vss. 3, 30), fastings, and almsdeeds (vs. 31).

Although Philip had earlier visited Caesarea and doubtless preached the Christian Gospel there (see Acts 8:40), there appears no evidence that Cornelius had ever heard that message before the appearance of Peter. Thus this "God-fearing" Gentile, one of the first to hear and believe the Gospel of Jesus Christ (see exception Acts 8:27–40), was prophetic of the entrance the Gospel would have into the cities of the empire, where Paul later traveled, through the nucleus of "God-fearers" who formed the gateway to the various communities. Such an individual was Lydia at Philippi (see Acts 16:14).

[2] *Acts*, p. 215. For a full discussion of this subject see Kirsopp Lake, "Proselytes and God-Fearers," *Beginnings*, V, 74–96.

[3] W. F. Arndt and F. W. Gingrich, *A Greek–English Lexicon of the New Testament and Other Early Christian Literature* (Chicago: University of Chicago Press, 1957), p. 860.

[4] Lev. 2:2, 9, 16; 5:12; 6:15; Num. 5:26.

5 And now send men to Joppa, and fetch one Simon, who is surnamed Peter:

---

which was burnt with frankincense upon the altar, the sweet savour of which, ascending to heaven, was supposed to commend the person sacrificing to the remembrance and favour of God." [5]

Prayers and **alms** were closely connected in Jewish thought (cf. Matt. 6:2–15). Alms were considered an especially acceptable offering to the Lord. They constituted a **memorial** with which He was well pleased.

5 **Fetch** is old English for "bring" (RSV). The verb *metapempō* occurs only in Acts (eight times). In the middle (as here) it means "send for, summon."

Simon, who is surnamed Peter is thus identified because Simon was one of the most common names among the Jews. In fact, Peter was staying with **Simon a tanner.** The references to Peter make an interesting study. He is called Peter some 58 times in the first 15 chapters of Acts, and not mentioned thereafter in this book. Outside of the Gospels and Acts the name occurs five times in Galatians,—where Paul is asserting his independence of the Jerusalem apostolate—and once each in I Peter 1:1 and II Peter 1:1. In Mark's Gospel he is called Simon until the list of apostles is given. Thereafter he is called Peter, except in Gethsemane, where he is fittingly addressed in his self-pride and real weakness as "Simon." Matthew and Luke follow the Markan pattern. For some reason that is not clear, John uses "Peter" and "Simon Peter" about equally. Only in connection with this incident do we find the expression **Simon who is surnamed Peter** (10:5, 18, 32; 11:13).

B. The Vision of Cornelius (10:3–8)

He saw in a vision openly (vs. 3a). While praying at about three o'clock in the afternoon, **the ninth hour,** Cornelius was suddenly confronted with a supernatural vision in which an angel appeared to him from God with a special message. Luke is careful to indicate that Cornelius' vision was genuine, since it was at the stated hour of prayer when he would not have been asleep. The word **openly** implies "plainly" or "evidently," thus delivering the worshipper of any suspicion of imposition. Supernatural visions were to be a valid characteristic of the Pentecostal dispensation (Acts 2:17).

In the Old Testament "visions and dreams" are commonly mentioned together, and even Peter's quotation of Joel's prophecy at Pentecost associates the two.

Concerning the earlier Old Testament concept, one has observed:

> The two words are repeatedly used of the same experience, the dream being rather the *form*, the vision the *substance* (e.g. Dan. 1:17; 2:28; 4:5; cf. Jer. 23:28)... The earlier prophets had already attained to the idea of vision as inspired insight. [a]

Among the important visions recorded by Luke in Acts are those of Ananias on the occasion of Saul's conversion (Acts 9:10); Saul in the house of Judas at Damascus (Acts 9:12); Cornelius at Caesarea (Acts 10:3); Peter at Joppa (Acts 10:17, 19; 11:5); Paul at Troas (Acts 16:9, 10); Paul at Corinth (Acts 18:9); and Paul's vision on the occasion of the shipwreck en route to Rome (Acts 27:23, 25).

The special messenger of Cornelius' vision was a divinely commissioned angel. The whole subject of angelology in the Bible, though difficult, is exceedingly interesting. [b]

Cornelius' fear at the sight of the angel in his vision is assuaged by the angel's citation of God's remembrance of his prayers and alms. The devotion and service of a godly man are a standing memorial before God. The angel's directions are specific, including the name of the city, **Joppa.** (Joppa was about thirty miles south of Caesarea and thirty-five miles northwest of Jerusalem, now a flourishing city known as Jafa or Jaffa—one of the most ancient cities of the world, and once the chief seaport of Palestine.)

God's directions were specific: **Simon, whose surname is Peter, . . . Simon a tanner.**

Note the name and occupation of Peter's

EGT, II, 252.

[a] S. W. Green, "Vision," *Dictionary of the Bible*, ed. James Hastings (New York: Charles Scribner's Sons, 1921), p. 959.

[b] See Additional Note I, *Angelology*, at close of chapter X.

6 he lodgeth with one Simon a tanner, whose house is by the sea side.
7 And when the angel that spake unto him was departed, he called two of his household-
servants, and a devout soldier of them that waited on him continually;
8 and having rehearsed all things unto them, he sent them to Joppa.
9 Now on the morrow, as they were on their journey, and drew nigh unto the city, Peter
went up upon the housetop to pray, about the sixth hour:
10 and he became hungry, and desired to eat: but while they made ready, he fell into a
trance;

---

6 Of the location of Simon's house **by the sea side,** Bruce says: "A tanner lived outside the town, since his trade was regarded by the Jews as unclean. He doubtless used sea-water in his work." [6]

7 In Plato, Herodotus, and other Greek writers, the plural of *oiketēs,* **household-servants,** included all the inmates of the house.[7] It differs from other words for servant *(doulos, hypēretēs, diakonos)* in stressing the close relation with the household. It occurs only four times in the New Testament. **Of them that waited on . . . continually** is one word in the Greek, *proskarterounton.* It is found once in Mark, six times in Acts, and three times in Paul's epistles.

8 *Exēgeomai,* **rehearsed,** is used by Luke five times. Elsewhere in the New Testament it occurs only in John 1:18.

9 **On the morrow** after Cornelius' vision, the three messengers sent by him from Caesarea **drew nigh unto the city** of Joppa. **As they were on their journey** is all one word in the Greek, *hodoiporountōn.* The verb is found only here in the New Testament.

There is some difference of opinion as to how long it would take them to make this journey of 30 miles. Lake and Cadbury write: "If they had started at 4 P.M. one day they must have travelled through the night to reach Joppa by noon the next day." [8] That would be on foot. Bruce, on the other hand, says: "If they set off early the next morning on horseback, they would arrive at Joppa . . . about noon." [9] Others have suggested that they started in the late afternoon, after the vision, but stopped overnight on the way.

Dōma, **housetop,** is from *demo,* "build." Originally it signified "house." In the Septuagint and papyri it meant **housetop.** [10] The English word "dome" suggests something very different from the flat roof of a Palestinian home.

The sixth hour (noon) was probably not one of the regular times of public prayer (see note on 3:1). However it may have been observed as a season for private prayer (cf. Psa. 55:17).

10 Of *prospeinos,* **hungry,** Bruce says: "The only other known occurrence of this word is in a passage of Demosthenes, a first-century eye-doctor, quoted by the sixth-century medical writer Aëtius." [11] Dillistone suggests that Luke may have been a student of Demosthenes. [12]

---

host, and the location of Simon's house, **whose house is by the sea side** (cf. Acts 9:10, 11). When we are near enough to hear God's voice, His directions are always clear.

Forthwith Cornelius dispatched two **household-servants,** under the command of **a devout,** or "God-fearing", **soldier** to Joppa to summon Peter, having revealed God's message to them.

C. The Trance of Peter (10:9–16)

Peter went up upon the housetop to pray . . . he fell into a trance (vss. 9, 10). As God prepared Cornelius to receive His message through Peter, so He also prepared Peter to deliver that message to Cornelius. Such was the case with Philip and the Ethiopian treasurer (Acts 8:26–39), with Saul and Ananias (Acts 9:10–19), and with Jacob and Esau (Gen. 32:9–12, 24, 29; 33:4); and such is ever true where God can get the audience and obedience of those through whom He would work.

At about twelve o'clock noon, **the sixth hour,** Peter ascended to the flat roof of his host's house (likely by an outside stairway),

---

[6] *Acts,* p. 216. [7] Abbott-Smith, *op. cit.,* p. 311. [8] *Beginnings,* IV, 114. [9] *Acts,* p. 217.
[10] Arndt and Gingrich, *op. cit.,* p. 209.
[11] *Acts,* p. 217. See also Cadbury, *The Book of Acts in History* (1955), p. 37.
[12] W. F. Dillistone, *Expository Times,* XLVI (1934–35), 380.

11 and he beholdeth the heaven opened, and a certain vessel descending, as it were a great
sheet, let down by four corners upon the earth:
12 wherein were all manner of fourfooted beasts and creeping things of the earth and
birds of the heaven.
13 And there came a voice to him, Rise, Peter; kill and eat.

Becoming hungry Peter **desired to eat.** The verb *geuō* is related to the noun *geume*, which is still used for midday lunch and *progeuma* for breakfast. In Rome it was common to have lunch at noon, and perhaps this custom had extended to the cities of Palestine.

Paraskeuazontōn, **while they made ready**—"while they were preparing it" (RSV)—reflects the fact that Orientals often spend much time in the preparation of a meal. The verb is found only three other places in the New Testament (I Cor. 14:8; II Cor. 9:2, 3).

While waiting, Peter fell into a **trance.** The Greek word is *ekstasis*, which has been taken over into English as "ecstasy." It literally means a putting out of place, and so a driving one out of his senses. The word occurs seven times in the New Testament. In three of these (Acts 10:10; 11:5; 22:17), it indicates a trance. In the other four (Mark 5:42; 16:8; Luke 5:26; Acts 3:10), it simply means "amazement" and does not involve any cessation of self-control such as is suggested in "trance," a state in which one stands *(stasis)* outside *(ek)* himself.

11 In the trance Peter **beholdeth** *(theōrei)*. This is one of Luke's rare historic presents. Another, "findeth," occurs in verse 27. From the opened heavens Peter saw a **vessel** descending. This word *(skeuos)* is translated in the King James Version "vessel," "goods," "stuff," and "sail" (Acts 27:17).

The vessel, or utensil, looked like a **sheet** (*othonēn*, found only here and in 11:5). Originally signifying "fine linen," it came later to mean "a sheet or sail." The combination of this word with *archai* (**corners,** literally "beginnings") is very common in medical writers and perhaps reflects this special interest on the part of Luke.[13] Zahn remarks: "If Galen expressly comments on the customary use of *archai*, by himself as previously by Hippocrates, to denote the ends *(perata)* of a bandage *(hoi epidesmoi*, and often *othonia* and *othonē)*, it is clear that Acts x.ii, xi.5 were written by a physician." [14]

12 The same threefold division of the animal kingdom as here occurs in Genesis 6:20, though not in the same order. Fish are not mentioned—perhaps because there is no suggestion that the vessel contained any water—even though they also were divided into clean and unclean.

13 **Kill** is *thyson*, which originally meant "offer, sacrifice." But in the New Testament it appears in a number of passages to mean "slay," without any suggestion of sacrifice (cf. Matt. 22:4; Luke 15:23).

---

for prayer and meditation while he awaited the preparation of the midday meal. These housetops of oriental houses commonly served as places of prayer, meditation, recreation, and even for sleeping purposes (cf. I Sam. 9:25, 26; II Sam. 11:2; II Kings 23:12; Neh. 8:5, 6). Overcome with hunger and drowsiness, he fell into a trance. Nor is Peter's trance to be identified with the vision as such. The trance, of far less importance than the vision in Bible experiences, was a sort of waking vision. Webster defines the trance as: "1. A state of partly suspended animation or of inability to function; a daze; a stupor. 2. A state of profound abstraction of mind or spirit, as in religious contemplation; ecstasy. 3. A sleeplike state such as that of deep hypnosis."

And Willett defines the trance as:

> A condition in which the mental powers are partly or wholly unresponsive to external impressions while dominated by subjective excitement, or left free to contemplate mysteries incapable of apprehension by the usual rational processes.[c]

In the entire Bible there are but two occurrences of the trance recorded: namely, that of Peter at Joppa, and of Paul's early Christian experience at Jerusalem when he was warned of impending danger (Acts

[13] Cf. Hobart, *op. cit.*, p. 218; EGT, II, 253 f.
[14] *Op. cit.*, III, 162.

[c] H. L. Willett, "Trance," *Dictionary of the Bible* ed. James Hastings, p. 946

14 But Peter said, Not so, Lord; for I have never eaten anything that is common and unclean.
15 And a voice *came* unto him again the second time, What God hath cleansed, make not thou common.
16 And this was done thrice: and straightway the vessel was received up into heaven.

---

14 *Oudepote ... pan* (**never ... anything**) is a typical Semitic expression, found often in the Septuagint. But "it can also be paralleled from the vernacular of the papyri."[15] They are words of strong negation, characteristic of the vehement Peter. The laws concerning **common and unclean** foods are given in the eleventh chapter of Leviticus. The only animals that were clean were those which both chewed the cud and had cloven hoofs.

15 **Make not thou common** is *su mē koinou.* The present imperative means that Peter is to stop doing what he has been doing. The verb *koinoō* in the classics meant "make common" (from *koinos,* common). In the Septuagint it signifies "make ceremonially unclean, profane." It carries this meaning also in the New Testament, except in connection with this incident. Here (10:15; 11:9) it means "count unclean."[16] For this message to Peter compare the parenthetical statement in Mark 7:19, which is perhaps based on this saying.

16 Instead of "again" (KJV) the oldest Greek manuscripts have **straightway,** Mark's favorite word *euthus.*

22:17). Other implied trances may be found in Isa. 6; Dan. 7:1, 2; 9:21; II Cor. 12:2; and Rev. 1:10.

During this trance experience, God gave Peter an object lesson in the form of a **great sheet** filled with all manner of animals, both clean and unclean. The **great sheet-like vessel** which was **let down by the four corners upon the earth** may be best understood as a "sail canvas," perhaps suggested in part by Peter's fishing trade and in part by the appearance of sail ships at sea near Simon's house (see Acts 10:6). Likewise Peter's hunger may account for the revelation having centered about food.

Weymouth's translation of the passage is illuminating:

> He had got very hungry and wished for some food; but, while they were preparing it, he fell into a trance. The sky had opened to his view, and what seemed to be an enormous sheet was descending, being let down to the earth by ropes at the four corners. In it were all kinds of quadrupeds, reptiles, and birds, and a voice came to him which said, "Rise, Peter, kill and eat."

Clarke significantly observes concerning Peter's revelation, that it was

> Perhaps intended to be an emblem of the *universe,* and its *various nations,* to the four corners of which the Gospel was to extend, and to offer its blessings to all the inhabitants, without distinction of nation (cf. Matt. 28:18–20; Acts 1:8; 2:21, 39).[d]

It appears that God's command to Peter to **kill and eat** carried the idea of sacrificial slaughter, rather than simply slaughter for food, suggesting Peter's appointed mission to offer up Jews and Gentiles alike as a spiritual sacrifice to God through a universal gospel ministry (cf. Rom. 12:1, 2).

The expression, **What God hath cleansed, make not thou common** (vs. 15b), is intended to shatter Jewish conservatism and prejudice. Indeed God had earlier, under the Levitical system, distinguished between the clean and the unclean beasts and had forbidden the Jews to eat or sacrifice the latter, as He had also distinguished between Jew and Gentile, all for a purpose in that preparatory period. But now that Christ has come "and brake down the middle wall of partition" (Eph. 2:14b) by His sacrificial death, these distinctions have been forever abolished (see Eph. 2:11–22). Happy are the people who are discerning of divine progress and are adaptable to the onmoving program of God in human history. Prejudice and undue conservatism lock the gates of the Kingdom of God against the world for whose salvation Christ died (cf. Matt. 23:13).

Three times this array descended before the gaze of Peter, thus fulfilling the requirements of the Mosaic law, "that at the mouth of two witnesses or three every word may be established" (Matt. 18:16b; cf. Deut. 19:15).

[15] Bruce, *Acts,* p. 218. [16] Abbott-Smith, *op. cit.,* p. 251.

[d] Clarke, *op. cit.,* V, 761.

17 Now while Peter was much perplexed in himself what the vision which he had seen might mean, behold, the men that were sent by Cornelius, having made inquiry for Simon's house, stood before the gate,
18 and called and asked whether Simon, who was surnamed Peter, were lodging there.
19 And while Peter thought on the vision, the Spirit said unto him, Behold, three men seek thee.
20 But arise, and get thee down, and go with them, nothing doubting: for I have sent them.
21 And Peter went down to the men, and said, Behold, I am he whom ye seek: what is the cause wherefore ye are come?

---

17 Peter was **perplexed** *(diēporei)*. Luke is especially fond of compounds with *dia*. **Having made inquiry** *(dierōtēsantes)* is another example. Occurring only here in the New Testament, it is used in classical Greek for asking constantly or continually. It may imply that the messengers had asked several times in the town for the house of Simon. **What... might mean** *(ei an eiē)* is the optative with indirect question, a construction used only by Luke in the New Testament. [17]

Gate is not the usual word *pylē*, but *pylōn* (cf. English "pylon"). It is used five times in the New Testament for the "porch" or "vestibule" of a house or palace and seven times for the gateway of a walled town (cf. Rev. 21:12, 13, 15, 21, 25; 22:14). Here it is the passage which led from the street to the inner court. Actually **before the gate** would be the same as before the outer court; the messengers stood in front of the outer gate opening into the passage *(pylōn)*.

18 The messengers **called and asked** if Peter was **lodging there** as a guest *(xenizō*, from *xenos*, "stranger"). Orientals still stand outside the door and call for the one they want.

19 **Thought** is a strong compound, *dienthymeomai*, found only here in the New Testament. It means "ponder" [18] (cf. RSV).

Peter, on the housetop, was alerted by **the Spirit** that **three men** were seeking him. Codex Vaticanus has "two men," which would mean the two messengers, with the soldier acting only as guard.

20 **Arise** and **get thee down** are both aorist, suggesting instantaneous action. **Go** is present imperative meaning "be going." **Nothing doubting** is another compound with *dia*,

---

Clearly the admixture of clean and unclean animals, which Peter was commanded of God to kill and eat, an act repugnant to Peter's Jewish training and taste (cf. Lev. 11), was designed to convey to the apostle that the Gospel of Christ was for Gentiles, who were considered by the Jews unclean, as well as for the Jews. Finally convinced that the revelation was from God, Peter's Jewish prejudices against the admission of the Gentiles into the Church were shattered, and he was thus prepared for the reception of the Gentile messengers from Cornelius (vs. 28).

However, the distinction between clean and unclean meats had to be abolished before the barriers to social intercourse between the Jews and Gentiles in the Church could be removed, and thus Christian equality be established. Jesus clearly taught this in principle (Mark 7:19).

God's supernatural acts toward men are always validated by their moral worth.

II. THE DIVINE MISSION (10:17–33)

As Peter meditated on the significance of the housetop sheet or canvas sail object lesson, Cornelius' servants arrived at Simon's house and inquired for him.

A. The Mission Summons (10:17–23a)

Arise, and get thee down, and go with them, nothing doubting: for I have sent them (vs. 20). While the messengers were inquiring for Peter at the gate of the house, the Spirit was prompting Peter to descend to meet them. In ready obedience Peter descended and inquired of their quest. Accordingly, the messengers related their mission and Peter, recognizing the hand of God in it all,

[17] Robertson, *Grammar*, p. 1030.
[18] Arndt and Gingrich, *op. cit.*, p. 193. They note that it is used only by Christian writers.

22 And they said, Cornelius a centurion, a righteous man and one that feareth God, and well reported of by all the nation of the Jews, was warned *of God* by a holy angel to send for thee into his house, and to hear words from thee.
23 So he called them in and lodged them. And on the morrow he arose and went forth with them, and certain of the brethren from Joppa accompanied him.
24 And on the morrow they entered into Caesarea. And Cornelius was waiting for them, having called together his kinsmen and his near friends.
25 And when it came to pass that Peter entered, Cornelius met him, and fell down at his feet, and worshipped him.
26 But Peter raised him up, saying, Stand up; I myself also am a man.
27 And as he talked with him, he went in, and findeth many come together:

---

diakrinō; literally "judge through or thoroughly." In the middle and passive *(diakrinomenos)*, it was used in Hellenistic Greek with the sense "be divided in one's mind, hesitate, doubt." "Without hesitation" (RSV) expresses well the meaning here.

22 **Warned** is the verb *chrēmatizō*. Josephus, the Septuagint, and the New Testament use it of divine communications, with the meaning "instruct, admonish, warn." Bruce translates it "was instructed (divinely)," and adds: "The sense 'to give a divine warning' is paralleled in papyri . . . and in inscriptions." [19] Here "instructed" or "directed" (RSV) seems to fit the passage best.

23 **Called** is the verb *eiskaleō*, found only here in the New Testament. **Lodged** is the same word *(xenizō)* as in verse 18. It means "to be his guests" (RSV). This would seem to imply that they arrived too late in the afternoon to start out on the return trip.

24 *Prosdokōn*, **waiting for,** is another favorite Lukan word. Used twice in Matthew and three times in II Peter, *prosdokaō* occurs six times in Luke's Gospel and five times in Acts. It means "await, expect." *Anagkaios*, **near,** is literally "necessary." In this passage alone it means "intimate, familiar."

25 **When . . . Peter entered** the house, **Cornelius . . . worshipped him.** Rackham comments: "Such prostrations before royal and superior personages were common in the east, as to this day." [20] But ". . . the idea of prostration was alien to the western mind, and the custom was not introduced into the imperial court till the reign of Diocletian." [21] So Rackham thinks that Cornelius must have regarded Peter as "a heaven-sent messenger or inspired prophet."

26 Peter's reaction was immediate. He **raised him up, saying, Stand up; I myself also am a man.** A similar situation is described in Acts 14:13–15 and Revelation 19:10; 22:9. On the contrary, Christ received the worship of His followers. Hackett has well expressed the implication, when he writes: "This different procedure on the part of Christ we can ascribe only to his consciousness of a claim to be acknowledged as divine." [22]

27 **As he talked with** is *synomilōn*, found only here in the New Testament. It means "converse with." [23] **Went in** (cf. vs. 25) probably means into the room where the group was assembled.

---

received and entertained the messengers until the following day.

B. The Mission Accepted (10:23b–33)

And on the morrow he arose and went forth with them (vs. 23b). Accompanied by six Jewish brethren (Acts 11:12), as witnesses to what was about to occur, Peter set out with Cornelius' messengers the following day. Upon arrival at Caesarea, evidently a day later, Cornelius awaited them, together with his **kinsmen and his near friends.** These latter probably included his domestic servants, as well as such "devout soldiers" from the barracks as the one sent in charge of the party that summoned Peter (vs. 7). That the company assembled was sizable is evident from verse 27.

Cornelius' conduct toward Peter upon his arrival at Caesarea, as he **fell down at his feet, and worshipped him** (vs. 25), seems to indicate that he mistook Peter for an angel

[19] *Acts*, p. 220. [20] *Op. cit.*, p. 154. [21] *Ibid.* [22] *Op. cit.*, p. 132.
[23] Arndt and Gingrich, *op. cit.*, p. 799.

28 and he said unto them, Ye yourselves know how it is an unlawful thing for a man that
is a Jew to join himself or come unto one of another nation; and *yet* unto me hath God
showed that I should not call any man common or unclean:
29 wherefore also I came without gainsaying, when I was sent for. I ask therefore with
what intent ye sent for me.
30 And Cornelius said, Four days ago, until this hour, I was keeping the ninth hour of
prayer in my house; and behold, a man stood before me in bright apparel,
31 and saith, Cornelius, thy prayer is heard, and thine alms are had in remembrance in
the sight of God.
32 Send therefore to Joppa, and call unto thee Simon, who is surnamed Peter; he lodgeth
in the house of Simon a tanner, by the sea side.

---

28 The first thing Peter did was to remind his hearers that he was ostensibly breaking the Jewish law by associating with Gentiles. *Athemitos*, **unlawful,** is found in the New Testament only here and in I Peter 4:3. *Allophylos*, **another nation** (from *allos*, "other" and *phylon*, "tribe"), is found only here in the New Testament. Peter's use of this instead of *ethnoi* ("Gentiles," "heathen") showed a fine courtesy.

The last part of this verse gives Peter's interpretation of his trance-vision. He was not to consider Gentiles **common or unclean.**

29 *Anantirētōs*, **without gainsaying,** is found only here in the New Testament. It means "without contradiction," or "without demur"; literally "not spoken against." **With what intent** *(tini logōi)* might be rendered "with what reason."

30 Cornelius stated that it was **four days ago** that he had his vision. Apparently the messengers had left Caesarea that same afternoon—or possibly the next morning—and reached Joppa the next afternoon. After having stayed overnight they left, with Peter and his companions, on the morning of the third day. With ten in the party they evidently traveled more slowly and so did not arrive in Caesarea until about 3:00 P.M. on the fourth day. **Fasting** is not found in the oldest and best Greek manuscripts,[24] and so is rightly omitted in the Revised Versions.

---

who had come to fulfill the implied promise of the angel in his vision (vs. 3). However, it is evident that that former announcement concerned a man **Simon, who is surnamed Peter.** In any event Cornelius' act is one of reverential obeisance commonly accorded superiors in the Orient (see Gen. 33:3), and not an act of worship directed to God (cf. Gen. 18:3; 19:3). Peter's humility and sense of divine mission is reflected in his courteous refusal of superior recognition, even when offered by a Gentile: **But Peter raised him up, saying, Stand up; I myself also am a man** (vs. 26), or as he seems to imply, I am but your equal, and not your superior. The true Christian spirit is ever the world's greatest social equalizer.

Possibly for the sake of the Gentile proselytes and God-fearers, as well as Jews present in Caesarea who had knowledge of his mission, Peter reiterates his "housetop trance experience," recounting the manner in which God had shattered his anti-Gentile prejudice. Indeed Peter goes beyond the verbal message of God regarding the animals and reveals that he had grasped the significance of the revelation as it concerned the relation of Jews and Gentiles in the plan of Christian redemption: **unto me hath God showed that I should not call any man common or unclean** (vs. 28b).

As a preparatory factor to the message he was about to deliver, Peter requested a fuller statement of Cornelius' purpose in sending for him (vs. 29). Cornelius proceeded to relate a full account of his vision before the entire company, which account corroborates Peter's trance experience and confirms the faith of all, in preparation for Peter's message. This is most remarkable in the light of the strict Jewish prohibitions against Jewish social intercourse with Gentiles (see John 4:9; 18:28; Acts 11:3; Gal. 2:12, 14).

[24] Aleph A B C.

33 Forthwith therefore I sent to thee; and thou hast well done that thou art come. Now therefore we are all here present in the sight of God, to hear all things that have been commanded thee of the Lord.
34 And Peter opened his mouth, and said, Of a truth I perceive that God is no respecter of persons:
35 but in every nation he that feareth him, and worketh righteousness, is acceptable to him.

---

33 **Thou hast well done that thou art come** is rendered "you were so kind as to come" by Lake and Cadbury. They comment: "There can be little doubt that the affirmative phrase here conveys the polite gratitude of Cornelius."[25] This meaning is found in the papyri. The receptive attitude of Cornelius and his friends is emphasized in his closing words: **we are all here . . . to hear all things that have been commanded thee of the Lord.**

34 **God is no respecter of persons** is literally "God is not a receiver of face." It is a typical Hebraistic expression. To receive one's face was to show favor, and in a bad sense to show favoritism. The word *prosōpolēmptēs* occurs only here in the New Testament, and apparently this is its first appearance in Greek literature. It is used later only by ecclesiastical writers.

35 The language of this verse has been taken as indicating that Peter assumed Cornelius to be a proselyte, and that he would thus enter Christianity by way of Judaism. But this is not a necessary deduction. What Peter meant was that all nations are equal before God. **Righteousness** was especially applied by the Jews to almsgiving, mentioned in connection with Cornelius (vss. 2, 4). *Dektos*, **acceptable**, is from *dechomai*, "receive, accept."

III. THE APOSTLE'S MESSAGE (10:34–43)

The message of Peter to the household of Cornelius consists of three essential considerations; namely, the impartiality of God, the universal lordship of Jesus Christ, and the way of salvation for all men.

A. The Divine Impartiality (10:34, 35)

Of a truth I perceive that God is no respecter of persons (vs. 34b). Peter **opened his mouth** and began his message to the Gentile household of Cornelius, probably including many Italian soldiers from the barracks, by frankly acknowledging his shattered Jewish prejudices and his new understanding of the impartiality of God in His great plan of human redemption. While with us today the universality of divine redemption is taken for granted, to both Jew and Gentile in Peter's day the whole matter was an entirely new concept. Indeed, it was implicit in the teachings of the prophets and in Christ's works and words, but it required a special divine revelation for it to become explicit in the ministry of the Christian apostles. Thus, in a single sentence, Peter's utterance is effective, as Bruce[e] phrases it, in "sweeping away the racial prejudices of centuries." Peter had "perceived" the divine impartiality, and he was prompt to declare it.

Race prejudice has been one of the persistent problems of society from early ages. Nor has man as yet been successful in his attempts to eradicate this loathsome disease from the social organism. Notwithstanding the high ideals and clear teachings of the equality of man and the unity of the body of Christ, the Church has not infrequently stood self-condemned as a result of her racial attitudes that have closed the doors of the Kingdom of God to the souls of men. An early indication of this racial problem is reflected by one of the Pharaohs, as recorded by Groves:

> Egypt varied with political and military fortunes, but may be taken as passing just below the First Cataract, and including the island of Philae, the most famous centre in all Egypt in Roman times for the worship of Isis, and one of the last pagan strongholds to yield to Christianity. The First Cataract was the ethnological as well as the geographical boundary. As early as 2000 B.C. the Pharaoh set this as the frontier no Negro should pass save in special circumstances. There is good evidence however, of active commercial intercourse, and of Egyptian

[25] *Beginnings*, IV, 119.

[e] F. F. Bruce, *op. cit.*, p. 224.

36 The word which he sent unto the children of Israel, preaching good tidings of peace by Jesus Christ (he is Lord of all)—
37 that saying ye yourselves know, which was published throughout all Judaea, beginning from Galilee, after the baptism which John preached;
38 *even* Jesus of Nazareth, how God anointed him with the Holy Spirit and with power: who went about doing good, and healing all that were oppressed of the devil; for God was with him.

---

36 The main body of Peter's speech (vss. 36–43) is strikingly parallel to the outline of Mark's Gospel. It is a significant sample of early apostolic preaching.

36–38 The Greek of this sentence is admittedly awkward. Some of the construction seems due to an Aramaic original. Bruce suggests: "Peter no doubt addressed his audience in Greek, or spoke through an interpreter, but the narrative was possibly preserved in an Aramaic document." [26] Then he adds: "The Greek is certainly not Luke's free composition; if it were, it would be much clearer." [27]

37 **Saying** is *rhēma* (contra. *logos*, **word,** vs. 36). It is used similarly in 5:32, where it is translated "things." **Published** is an exceedingly free translation of *genomenon*, "became." *Rhēma* sometimes equals "fact" or "history" (cf. Luke 2:15, where the same words as here, with perfect tense instead of aorist, are translated "this thing that is come to pass"). So the phrase could be rendered "the event which happened." [28]

Judaea is used in the broader sense of all Palestine, including **Galilee.** The parallels to Mark are striking: Jesus' ministry begins in Galilee and is first patterned **after the baptism which John preached**; that is, repentance.

38 Jesus was **anointed . . .** with the **Holy Spirit and with power** at His baptism (cf. Luke 4:1, 14). Mark's Gospel especially presents Him as one **who went about doing good, and healing all that were oppressed of the devil.** "Oppress" is a strong compound, *katadynasteuō*, "exercise power over," found only here and in James 2:6. **Devil** is *diabolos*, "slanderer," which is the Greek equivalent of the Hebrew Satan.

With regard to Jesus' anointing at His baptism, Bruce makes this remark: "The Christology of this sermon, like that of the earlier speeches in Acts, is the primitive Christology of Mark, rather than the more developed Christology of Paul; this is significant in view of the traditional dependence of Mark on Peter." [29]

---

influence on Nubian culture. The people were of mixed Hamitic and Negro descent. [f]

The foregoing citation clearly indicates that while the racial barrier stood opposed to both social and religious intercourse between the Nubian Negro and the Egyptian, it did not prevent an "active commercial intercourse," nor the influence of Egyptian culture on the Negro Nubian.

Indeed, Stephen and Philip, both Jewish Hellenist Christian laymen, had earlier grasped the broader significance of the Gospel for the Gentiles as well as the Jews, but Peter was the first Jewish Christian "apostle" to enter into that universal concept.

Nothing new or great is ever undertaken or accomplished until someone has "perceived," or seen through, and grasped the pattern and possibilities of things yet unrealized. Divine revelations, when properly understood, ever have a transforming moral and spiritual effect on man and human history. "Where there is no vision, the people perish" (Prov. 29:18a, KJV). Let it be noted that Peter refers to **nations,** a political designation, and not "races," a physical designation. The latter term is not found in the Bible in reference to divisions of mankind.

B. The Universal Divine Lordship (10:36–41)

He is Lord of all (vs. 36). Peter's first gospel message to this eager Gentile congregation is a succinct, but dynamic, summation of the entire person and work of

[26] *Acts*, p. 225. [27] *Ibid.* [28] *Beginnings*, IV, 120. [29] *Acts*, p. 226.

[f] C. P. Groves, *The Planting of Christianity in Africa* (London and Redhill: Lutterworth Press 1948), I, 47; see also Serigman, *Races of Africa*, p. 111.

39 And we are witnesses of all things which he did both in the country of the Jews, and in Jerusalem; whom also they slew, hanging him on a tree.
40 Him God raised up the third day, and gave him to be made manifest,
41 not to all the people, but unto witnesses that were chosen before of God, *even* to us, who ate and drank with him after he rose from the dead.
42 And he charged us to preach unto the people, and to testify that this is he who is ordained of God *to be* the Judge of the living and the dead.
43 To him bear all the prophets witness, that through his name every one that believeth on him shall receive remission of sins.

---

39 **Country of the Jews** is equivalent to "Judaea" (vs. 37); that is, all Palestine. For **hanging him on a tree**, see on 5:30.[30]

40 Only here in Acts is **the third day** mentioned, but Luke has it six times in his Gospel. **Gave him to be made manifest** is a literal translation of the Greek.

41 The fact that Jesus did not appear to the general public—**not to all the people**—but only to chosen **witnesses** is in agreement with the picture of His post-resurrection appearances as given in the Gospels. *Prokecheirotonēmenois,* **chosen before,** is found only here in the New Testament. The fact that Jesus **ate** with His disciples after His resurrection is recorded in Luke 24:41–43.

42 **Judge of the living and the dead** was a popular emphasis in the first century (cf. I Peter 4:5; II Timothy 4:1).

43 **Every one that believeth on him**—both Jews and Gentiles—comes last in the Greek sentence, for emphasis. Here is the heart of the gospel message: **remission of sins** through faith in Jesus Christ.

Jesus Christ in relation to the redemptive scheme. In rapid succession he presents Jesus Christ in the clear aspects of His peace, His universal lordship, His requirement of repentance, His humanity, His deity, His sacrificial death, His victorious resurrection, His post-resurrection appearances, His universal judgeship, and remission of sins through faith in His Name.

Analytically outlined, Peter's message to Cornelius' household would look something like the following:

1. *The Gospel of Peace by Jesus Christ:* **preaching good tidings of peace by Jesus Christ** (vs. 36).
2. *The Universal Lordship of Jesus Christ:* **he is Lord of all** (vs. 36b).
3. *The Repentance of Sins through Jesus Christ:* **the baptism which John preached** (vs. 37b).
4. *The Humanity of Jesus Christ:* **Jesus of Nazareth** (vs. 38a).
5. *The Deity of Jesus Christ:* **God anointed him with the Holy Spirit and with power** (vs. 38).
6. *The Crucifixion of Jesus Christ:* **whom also they slew, hanging him on a tree** (vs. 39b).
7. *The Resurrection of Jesus Christ:* **Him God raised up the third day** (vs. 40a).
8. *The Appearances of Jesus Christ:* **and gave him to be made manifest** (vs. 40b).
9. *The Universal Judgeship of Jesus Christ:* **this is he who is ordained of God to be the Judge of the living and the dead** (vs. 42b).
10. *The Impartial Remission of Sins through Jesus Christ:* **through his name every one that believeth on him shall have remission of sins** (vs. 43b).

C. The Way of Salvation (10:42, 43)

It is significant that Peter concludes his message with the clear implication that the way of salvation for these Gentiles, as also for the Jews, is open through faith in the name, and submission to the lordship of Jesus Christ.

Thus Peter sets an example of expository evangelistic preaching in the first Christian century, which was both eagerly received by his Gentile hearers and signally approved and blessed of God. Nor has this type of preaching ever lost its usefulness throughout the subsequent centuries.

[30] "Slew" in 5:30 is a different verb.

44 While Peter yet spake these words, the Holy Spirit fell on all them that heard the word.
45 And they of the circumcision that believed were amazed, as many as came with Peter,
because that on the Gentiles also was poured out the gift of the Holy Spirit.
46 For they heard them speak with tongues, and magnify God. Then answered Peter,
47 Can any man forbid the water, that these should not be baptized, who have received
the Holy Spirit as well as we?
48 And he commanded them to be baptized in the name of Jesus Christ. Then prayed they
him to tarry certain days.

---

45 **They of the circumcision that believed** would be Jewish Christians. These were **amazed** that the Gentiles should be given **the Holy Spirit,** for this was contrary to all Jewish teaching.

46 The main feature mentioned in connection with speaking with tongues was that those involved did **magnify God.** Whatever magnifies, or glorifies, God, is of the Spirit.

48 Baptism was **in the name of Jesus Christ.** This does not preclude a trinitarian baptismal formula, but simply indicates that the main distinctive emphasis was on the Name of Jesus.

IV. THE SPIRIT'S EFFUSION (10:44–48)

That Peter's hearers believed on Christ unto the salvation of their souls is evidenced by two facts: *first*, that God poured forth upon them the gift of the Holy Spirit; and *second*, that they were judged by Peter as worthy candidates for water baptism.

A. The Spirit Outpoured (10:44–47)

While Peter yet spake these words, the Holy Spirit fell on all them that heard the word (vs. 44).

Usually the outpouring of the Holy Spirit followed water baptism and the laying on of hands by the apostles (cf. Acts 2:38; 8:17; 19:6); but in this instance the order was reversed. While God may honor and use human symbols, He is never confined to them for His spiritual operations. The reversal of the order here is probably the miraculous evidence that the Gentiles were to be included in the gift of the Holy Spirit, and thus were to be baptized.

That the spiritual significance of the outpouring of the Holy Spirit on these Gentiles is identical with that of the Pentecostal effusion of Acts 2 is attested by Peter's declaration, on the occasion of his defense of the Gentile cause at the Jerusalem Council. In this rehearsal he states:

> And God, who knoweth the heart, bare them witness, giving them the Holy Spirit, even as he did unto us; and he made no distinction between us and them, cleansing their hearts by faith (Acts 15:8, 9).

Thus as the baptism of the Holy Spirit wrought purity of heart in the disciples on the day of Pentecost, so the hearts of these Gentile believers were cleansed by His gracious personal manifestations at the close of Peter's message to them. One is reminded of Christ's words to His disciples: "Already ye are clean because of the word which I have spoken unto you" (John 15:3). **While Peter yet spake these words, the Holy Spirit fell on all them that heard the word** (vs. 44), "cleansing their hearts by faith" (Acts 15: 9b). A purported Pentecost that does not purify the Christian's inner nature of the carnal principle and pollution is spurious indeed, notwithstanding the external manifestations or significations of such a purported experience. The manifestation of the personality of the Holy God, to the inner nature of the unholy heart, inevitably consumes the sin nature of that heart and recreates it in His likeness (cf. Ps. 51:10).

This spiritual effusion on the Gentiles amazed Peter's Jewish–Christian companions, for they **heard them speak with tongues, and magnify God** (vs. 46). This miraculous phenomenon of **tongues,** or "languages," recurred at Caesarea as an aid to the evangelization of the polyglot Gentile inhabitants of this great seaport city.[g] But as Clarke observes:

> They had got *new hearts* as well as *new tongues;* and, having believed with the heart unto

[g] See Additional Note II, *The Bible Gift of Tongues at Caesarea,* at the close of Chapter X.

righteousness, their tongues made confession unto salvation; and God was magnified for the mercy which he had imparted.[h]

Through faith they had believed unto righteousness of heart, and by the miraculous divine gift of languages these Spirit-baptized Gentile believers began to proclaim that righteousness to their polyglot neighbors, and thus they "magnified God."

The amazement of the Jewish-Christian believers present with Peter at this Gentile Pentecost is due to the fact that the Jews held that the Divine Spirit could not be communicated to any Gentile, or be bestowed upon anyone who dwelt beyond the promised land.[i]

B. The Disciples' Baptism (10:47, 48)

Can any man forbid the water, that these should not be baptized, who have received the Holy Spirit as well as we? (vs. 47). The incontestable right of these uncircumcised Gentile Christians to be baptized, as a token of their acceptance into the body of Christ, is made evident by the miraculous divine approval, and the apostle's declaratory question of verse 47. Peter then commands their baptism and thus shows a vital, saving relationship through faith in Jesus Christ, the Son of God and the Savior of men. God had witnessed to His acceptance of the Gentiles by giving them the Holy Spirit, and Peter witnesses to their acceptance into the Church by baptizing them in the Name of Jesus without the requirement of circumcision. On the question of the baptismal formula employed by Peter on this occasion, Wesley remarks:

> *In the name of the Lord*—Which implies the Father who anointed Him, and the Spirit with which He was anointed, to His office. But as these Gentiles had before believed in God the Father, and could not but now believe in the Holy Ghost, under whose powerful influence they were at this very time, there was the less need of taking notice that they were baptized into the belief and profession of the sacred Three; though doubtless the apostle administered the ordinance in that very form which Christ Himself had prescribed.[j]

Certainly, in the light of Wesley's explanation, no ground remains for a Unitarian interpretation of this passage.

Additional Note I

ANGELOLOGY

The following discussion of angelology is based in part upon Oesterley's[k] treatment of the subject. In general angels are recognized in the Bible as divinely created beings (Col. 1:16), who possess superhuman powers (II Kings 6:17; Zech. 12:8). They assume human forms and converse (I Kings 19:5); eat (Gen. 18:8) and fight in defense of men on earth (Gen. 32:1, 2; II Sam. 5:24; Joel 3:11). Though they are regarded as wise (II Sam. 14:17, 20), they do not possess divine perfection (Job 4:18). If angels and seraphim are identical, they move by flight (Isa. 6:2, 6).

The mission of angels in relation to men appears to be that of guidance (Gen. 24:7, 40; Exod. 23:20 ff.; Job 33:23); instructors of the Old Testament prophets (I Kings 13:18; 19:5 ff.; II Kings 1:3, 15; Zech. 1:9); the destroyers of the evil and destructive (II Sam. 24:16, 17; II Kings 19:25; Job 33:23; Ps. 35:6; 78:49; Acts 12:23); the guardians of men (Gen. 19:15 ff.; Ps. 34:7; 91:11); carriers of the answers to men's prayers on earth (Dan. 10:10–21); and messengers for God to men (Matt. 1:20; 2:13; 28:5; Luke 1:28; 24:23).

In their relation to God the function of angels consists principally in reporting the affairs of men on earth (Job 1:6; 2:1; cf. Zech. 1:8–10; Ps. 18:11; Isa. 19:1), and of participating in praise to God (Gen. 28:12; Ps. 103:20; Isa. 6:2).

Christ indicates in the gospels that heaven is the dwelling place of angels (Matt. 18:10; Luke 12:8, 9; John 1:51); that they are above men (Luke 20:36); that they escort the souls of the righteous dead to their heavenly abode (Luke 16:22); that they are without sex (Matt. 22:30); and that they are very great in number (Matt. 26:53). They are represented as accompanying Christ at his second coming (Matt. 13:39; 16:27; 24:31; 25:31; Mark 8:38; Luke 9:26; John 1:51). The Bible indicates that there are evil as well as good angels (Matt. 25:41); but that they are limited in knowledge (Matt. 24:36). Children have their guardian angels

h Clarke, *op. cit.*, V 767.
i *Ibid.*
j Wesley, *op. cit.*, pp. 436, 437, n. 48.
k W. O. E. Oesterley, "Angels," *Hastings Dictionary of the Bible*, pp. 31–33.

(Matt. 18:10). Angels are represented as rejoicing at the repentance of sinners and their return to the heavenly Father (Luke 15:10).

The ministry of angels seems to play a larger part in the Acts account than in the gospel stories. Luke gives us the account of the release of Peter and John from their imprisonment at the hands of an angel (Acts 5:19). An angel carried the Law to Moses on Mount Sinai (Acts 7:30, 35, 38). It was an angel that spoke to Philip during his work in Samaria (Acts 8:26). An angel appeared to Cornelius in his home at Caesarea (Acts 10:3, 7, 22; 11:13). Peter was released from his prison by an angel (Acts 12:7–11, 15). The judgment of death was inflicted upon Herod by an angel (Acts 12:23). Just before his shipwreck experience at Malta, an angel visited Paul with a message of assurance (Acts 27:23).

That angels and spirits are not one and the same is fairly attested (Acts 23:8, 9). Paul's treatment of angels accords in general with the Acts account (see Rom. 8:38; I Cor. 4:9; 11:10; I Tim. 5:21), except that he seems to give greater place to the direct communication of God to man (Gal. 1:12; cf. Acts 9:5). Paul forbids the worship of angels (Col. 2:18), and goes so far as to equate this practice with the worship of demons (I Cor. 10:20).

If the traditional view be true that one third of the angels fell with Lucifer, and if Lucifer is to be identified with Satan, then it would be a logical conclusion that two thirds of the angels remain righteous and unfallen. Thus it is a logical conclusion that to every evil angel attacking righteous man upon earth, there may be assigned two unfallen protecting angels to preserve him against their attacks. Thus indeed "They that be for us are more than they that be against us."

Additional Note II

The Bible Gift of Tongues at Caesarea

The first clear record of the miracle of "tongues," following the Jerusalem Pentecost, is found in Acts 10, when the household of Cornelius received the Holy Spirit and spake with tongues, under the ministry of Peter. The record is specific and very significant. It reads in part as follows:

> While Peter yet spake these words, the Holy Spirit fell on all them that heard the word. And they of the circumcision that believed were amazed, as many as came with Peter, because that on the Gentiles also was poured out the gift of the Holy Spirit. For they heard them speak with tongues, and magnify God (Acts 10:44–46).

In his defense of the Gospel for the Gentiles at Jerusalem, following his return from Caesarea, Peter identifies this divine phenomenon that occurred at Caesarea with that of the Pentecost at Jerusalem. Says Peter:

> And as I began to speak, the Holy Spirit fell on them, even as on us at the beginning [or on the day of Pentecost]... If then God gave unto them the like gift as he did also unto us, when we believed on the Lord Jesus Christ, who was I, that I could withstand God? (Acts 11:15, 17).

Now, there are two circumstances that validate the evangelistic significance of the gift of tongues at Caesarea. The first lies in the location of Caesarea and the second in the person and the position of Cornelius. As to the first, it must be noted that Caesarea was the most important seacoast and port city of Palestine at that time. It was a Roman colony and the Roman capital of Palestine. Caesarea was a large and important commercial and political cosmopolitan city, to which came, and through which passed, peoples of all parts of the Roman empire, representing the many linguistic divisions of that empire. Caesarea was the main port for the East-West overland route through southern Palestine, and it was the principal Palestinian port of call for the marine intercourse of the Mediterranean world with Egypt. Here, where Christianity first invaded the polyglot Gentile world, it was fitting that the gift of tongues should have occurred as an instrument for Gentile evangelization.

As to Cornelius and his position, it remains to be noted that he was a Gentile "proselyte of the gate"[1] or "devout man," in relation to the Jewish religion, and a Roman cen-

[1] 'Proselytes of the gate,' Gentiles "who dwelt in the land of Israel, or even out of that country, and who, without obliging themselves to circumcision, or to any other ceremony of the law, feared and worshipped the true God, observing the [seven] rules that were imposed upon the children of Noah." Alexander Cruden, *A Complete Concordance* (New York: Fleming H. Revell Company).

turion of the Italian cohort,[m] in relation to the Roman government. As such he had in his garrison of a hundred or more men (some hold a cohort of 600 men rather than a century of a 100),[n] a considerable linguistic representation of soldiers recruited from the various parts of the Roman Empire. It is easily possible that "the household of Cornelius" included the soldiers' barracks, as well as his servants and the members of his family. When these factors are considered, then the gift of tongues, both in getting the message to the soldiers of the barracks and perhaps his servants as well, and in turn aiding these Gentile Christian soldiers to witness for Christ to others who were of a different language, begins to take on meaning at Caesarea. Nor is it necessary to assume that there was no time element between their reception of the Holy Spirit and their speaking with tongues, any more than is such an assumption warranted concerning the day of Pentecost, or in subsequent occurrences of this miraculous phenomenon. It is entirely likely that between the records of verses 45 and 46 in Acts 10, these Spirit-baptized Christians scattered throughout the city witnessing for Christ to the peoples of various languages. Such was likewise most probable in Jerusalem, on the day of Pentecost, and elsewhere when the disciples of Christ received this gift of tongues.

m Italian cohort: one of the 10 divisions consisting of 600 soldiers, of a Roman military legion.
n Lange, *op. cit.*, p. 191.

CHAPTER XI

Now the apostles and the brethren that were in Judaea heard that the Gentiles also had received the word of God.

2 And when Peter was come up to Jerusalem, they that were of the circumcision contended with him,

3 saying, Thou wentest in to men uncircumcised, and didst eat with them.

4 But Peter began, and expounded *the matter* unto them in order, saying,

---

EXEGESIS

1 **The apostles** are still thought of as being the divinely appointed leaders of the Church. **In Judaea** is rather "throughout Judaea" (*kata tēn Ioudaian*).

2 The Western text of this verse has **Peter** preaching the Word and teaching on his way **up to Jerusalem.** This is not unlikely (cf. 8:25). **They that were of the circumcision** would be the Judaistic party, which insisted that all Christians must keep the Mosaic law.

3 The Judaizers did not find fault with Peter for preaching to the Gentiles, but for eating with them. *Akrobystia*, **uncircumcised,** is found only here in Acts.

4 Verses 4–17 are a repetition of the material in the previous chapter. Also Cornelius repeated (10:30–33) the story of his vision (10:3–8). Bruce comments: "It is therefore clear that Luke regards the Cornelius incident as epoch-making in his history." [1] (Compare the three accounts of

---

EXPOSITION

PART I

THE CHURCH'S FIRST GENTILE EVANGELISM (cont'd)

V. THE DEFENSE OF PETER (Continued from Chapter 10), Acts 11:1–18.
   A. The Occasion of the Defense, vss. 1–4.
   B. The Explanation of Peter, vss. 5–10.
   C. The Obedience of Peter, vss. 11–14.
   D. The Reward of Peter, vss. 15–18.

PART II

THE CHURCH'S FIRST GENTILE MISSIONARY CENTER

I. THE CHURCH AT ANTIOCH, Acts. 11:19–21.
   A. The Jewish Evangelization, vs. 19.
   B. The Grecian Evangelization, vs. 20.
   C. The Extent of the Evangelization, vs. 21.

II. THE MINISTRY OF BARNABAS, Acts 11:22–24.
   A. The Commission of Barnabas, vs. 22.
   B. The Consolations of Barnabas, vs. 23.
   C. The Character of Barnabas, vs. 24.

III. THE ENGAGEMENT OF SAUL, Acts 11:25–26.
   A. The Summons of Saul, vss. 25, 26a.
   B. The Service of Saul, vs. 26.
   C. The Disciples' New Name, vs. 26b.

IV. THE JERUSALEM FAMINE RELIEF, Acts 11:27–30.
   A. The Prophets from Jerusalem, vs. 27.
   B. The Prophecy of Famine, vs. 28.
   C. The Provisions of the Christians, vss. 29, 30.

Part I

V. THE DEFENSE OF PETER (11:1–18)

The news of the success of Peter's mission to the Gentiles at Caesarea spread rapidly throughout Judea as the apostles and disciples heard of the mighty workings of God in the household of Cornelius and passed that good news along to their fellows. In addition to their moral and spiritual transforming power in the lives, homes, and communities of people, spiritual awakenings always have a restraining influence against wickedness among non-Christian people.

[1] *Acts*, p. 231.

5 I was in the city of Joppa praying: and in a trance I saw a vision, a certain vessel descending, as it were a great sheet let down from heaven by four corners; and it came even unto me:
6 upon which when I had fastened mine eyes, I considered, and saw the fourfooted beasts of the earth and wild beasts and creeping things and birds of the heaven.
7 And I heard also a voice saying unto me, Rise, Peter; kill and eat.
8 But I said, Not so, Lord: for nothing common or unclean hath ever entered into my mouth.
9 But a voice answered the second time out of heaven, What God hath cleansed, make not thou common.
10 And this was done thrice: and all were drawn up again into heaven.

Saul's conversion in chapters 9, 22, 26.)

Ektithēmi (**expounded**) occurs only in Acts (four times). In 7:21 it means "set out, expose" (of Moses by his parents). In the other three passages it is used metaphorically with the sense, "set forth, expose."

5 The narrative is somewhat more vivid than in 10:11, 12.

6 **Wild beasts** *(thēria)* is an added item, not mentioned in 10:12 (except KJV).

8 Note the slight change of wording with no difference in meaning. This is a common phenomenon in parallel passages of Scripture.

10 **Drawn up** *(anespasthē)* is found only here and in Luke 14:5. It is used in the papyri of pulling up barley.[2] The word is more striking than the parallel expression *anelēmphthē* ("received up") in 10:16. The latter is found thirteen times in the New Testament.

However, they are no less likely to arouse opposition from unsympathetic sources. Such was the case with the Gentile awakening at Caesarea.

A. The Occasion of the Defense (11:1–4)

Upon his return to Jerusalem, Peter was met by a delegation of the anti-Gentile Jewish Christians. This was likely the Judaising party (Acts 15:1–5), which soon charged him with illegal association with Gentiles (vs. 3). These Jewish-Christian legalists did not attack the baptism of the Gentiles, perhaps because of the Lord's command and God's evident visitation of these Gentiles, but they made an acute issue of Peter's breach of Jewish ceremonial law and custom: **Thou wentest in to men uncircumcised, and didst eat with them** (vs. 3). Legalism always places externalities above spirituality and seeks to stifle the latter by enforcement of the former. Paul declared, "the letter killeth, but the spirit giveth life" (II Cor. 3:6). The legalists wished at best to regard the Gentiles as an inferior class and require of them subscription to the Jewish ceremonial law (Gal. 2:12–21). Legalism invariably tends toward "classism" in the Church, the "holier-than-thou" attitude.

B. The Explanation of Peter (11:5–10)

What God hath cleansed, make not thou common (vs. 9b). Peter by-passed the general principles embodied in their accusation and built his defense on the grounds of the special divine revelation that commanded, and thus authorized, his act in the special case in question. He proceeded to expound in order unto his opponents the details of the Caesarean incident (vs. 4). It originated in answer to prayer to God at Joppa, was revealed to the apostle in a vision from God, in which God clearly (by a thrice repeated revelation) showed him that the Gentiles were not to be considered ceremonially unclean by the Jews. The genuineness of the sheet-vision is accentuated, Peter indicates, by the fact that it was not only thrice lowered but finally retracted into heaven from whence it had been let down. Peter intimates that he had been quite as reluctant to break ceremonial rules and eat meat considered unclean by the Jews, as the Jewish Christians were to see that the ceremonial law had been fulfilled and abrogated by Christ, and thus that the Gentiles were to be admitted to fellowship in the body of Christ without imposition of the Jewish law. In short, it was God's doing, and who were the Jewish Christians to object?

[2] VGT, p. 37.

11 And behold, forthwith three men stood before the house in which we were, having been sent from Caesarea unto me.
12 And the Spirit bade me go with them, making no distinction. And these six brethren also accompanied me; and we entered into the man's house:
13 and he told us how he had seen the angel standing in his house, and saying, Send to Joppa, and fetch Simon, whose surname is Peter;
14 who shall speak unto thee words, whereby thou shalt be saved, thou and all thy house.
15 And as I began to speak, the Holy Spirit fell on them, even as on us at the beginning.
16 And I remembered the word of the Lord, how he said, John indeed baptized with water; but ye shall be baptized in the Holy Spirit.

---

12 **Making no distinction** *(mēden diakrinanta)* is similar to "nothing doubting" *(mēden diakrinomenos)* in 10:20. The difference in translation is due to the fact that it is active in 11:12, middle or passive in 10:20. The fact that there were **six brethren** who accompanied Peter is not stated in chapter ten.

14, 15 These verses are important as indicating that Cornelius was to receive from Peter information on how to **be saved.** Apparently Peter also understood that to be his mission, for in his sermon at Cornelius' house (10:34–43) he said nothing about Pentecost. In fact, the last words recorded as uttered by him were: "... through his name every one that believeth on him shall receive remission of sins" (10:43). He was telling them how to be **saved.** To hold that Cornelius was a Christian before he met Peter is very precarious exegesis. The better explanation seems to be that as Peter told the ones gathered in Cornelius' house about salvation through Jesus Christ, his hearers believed the truth and accepted Jesus as Saviour. Then since they were walking in the light, with their hearts open to receive all of God's will, they also were filled with the Holy Spirit.

16 The quotation here is from Acts 1:5. In the Gospels this statement is attributed to John the Baptist, not Jesus. Both John and Jesus asserted this truth.

C. The Obedience of Peter (11:11–14)

And the Spirit bade me go with them, making no distinction (vs. 12a). As Peter continued his defense of the Gospel for the Gentiles before the Jewish-Christian opposition, he clearly implied the divine origin and authorization of the mission, and then adduced a number of evidences in support of his obedience in ministering to, and associating with, the Gentiles. *First,* no sooner had the trance of divine origin been withdrawn than three men appeared from Caesarea inquiring for him in behalf of Cornelius, who had been instructed of God in a vision to send for him (vs. 11). *Second,* the Holy Spirit spoke directly to him, prompting him to accompany the messengers to Caesarea, and that without misgivings (vs. 12). *Third,* six Jewish Christian men accompanied Peter to Caesarea to testify to the divine leadings and approval in all the events (vs. 12). *Fourth,* by comparing notes with Cornelius, after arriving at Caesarea, Peter found that all the circumstances of the divine directions, both on his part and with Cornelius, perfectly corresponded. And *fifth,* he stated the object of the mission as being the salvation of Cornelius and his household (vs. 14), a most worthy mission indeed.

D. The Reward of Peter (11:15–18)

And as I began to speak, the Holy Spirit fell on them, even as on us at the beginning (vs. 15). Peter clearly saw that the divine approval and reward of his obedience (in transcending the ceremonial bounds of Judaism to take the Gospel to the Gentiles) was the outpouring of the Holy Spirit upon them, even as on the day of Pentecost (vs. 15). We have previously observed that the significance of the divine spiritual effusion at Pentecost was fourfold (see Acts 2:1–4). So likewise, Peter relates, the Holy Spirit was outpoured on the Gentiles in His *personal power, sanctifying purity, spiritual enduement and possession,* and in a *miraculous proclamation* through the gift of **tongues** (or languages) for the purpose of evangelization. This spiritual effusion Peter then recognized to be the fulfillment of Christ's promise (vs. 16).

Verses 17 and 18 clearly reveal that

17 If then God gave unto them the like gift as *he did* also unto us, when we believed on the Lord Jesus Christ, who was I, that I could withstand God?

18 And when they heard these things, they held their peace, and glorified God, saying, Then to the Gentiles also hath God granted repentance unto life.

19 They therefore that were scattered abroad upon the tribulation that arose about Stephen travelled as far as Phoenicia, and Cyprus, and Antioch, speaking the word to none save only to Jews.

---

17 **Who was I, that I could withstand God?** is in reality two questions: "Who was I? Was I able to withstand God?" [8]

18 An important victory was won, for the time being. That it was not permanently settled is shown by the crisis that arose in chapter fifteen. In any case the matter of the relation of Jewish and Gentile Christians was not faced here. The only conclusion at this point was: **Then to the Gentiles also hath God granted repentance unto life.**

19 This verse begins with exactly the same words as 8:4—*hoi men oun diasparentes,* **they therefore that were scattered abroad.**

Peter's vivid and convincing presentation of the events at Caesarea won, for the time being, the complete approval of the Jewish Christians at Jerusalem upon the mission to the Gentiles.

Part II

THE CHURCH'S FIRST GENTILE MISSIONARY CENTER

I. THE CHURCH AT ANTIOCH (11:19–21)

We have previously noted the approval of the Gentile evangelization at Caesarea, by the Jewish Christians at the close of Peter's defense (Acts 11:17, 18). It becomes clear, however, from verse 19 that the evangelization of Antioch was carried out by the disciples scattered abroad under the persecution that followed Stephen's death (Acts 8:1), rather than by Gentile disciples from Caesarea, as some have supposed. The dispersed disciples followed the great trade routes by land and sea northward to Phoenicia, Cyprus, and Antioch. Antioch in northern Syria ranked the third greatest city (about 800,000 inhabitants, including suburbs[a]) of the Roman Empire and was called "The Queen of the East," "Antioch, the Beautiful," and "Antioch the Great." It was beautifully situated on the Orontes river about 15 or 20 miles from its seaport city of Seleucia. It was the capital of Syria and seat of the Roman governor. The population was mainly Syrian, but Greek in language and culture, with a considerable Jewish representation who had equal rights with the Greeks. Here Christianity first contacted and came to grips with Roman and Greek civilization. The moral corruption of Antioch is reflected in Juvenal's statement, when he wished to say the worst about Rome: "The Orontes has flowed into the Tiber."[b] Antioch soon superseded Jerusalem as the center of Christianity and remained so for long, producing such honorable Christian names as Ignatius and John Chrysostom, and a famous school of theology.

A. The Jewish Evangelization (11:19)

They therefore that were scattered abroad [preached] **. . . the word to none save only to Jews.** The dispersion that took place after the martyrdom of Stephen seems at first to have extended only into Judea and Samaria. However, Jewish Christians, many of whom may have been present for Pentecost and were converted there, soon moved on northward, visiting and witnessing in the Jewish synagogues throughout the coastland of Phoenicia (Phenice), on the western Mediterranean island of Cyprus (home of Barnabas) and in Antioch of Syria. That they preached **the word to none save only to Jews** seems evidence that these evangelists were themselves Jewish Christians, and not proselytes. While accpeting Christ as the Messiah, they thought of Christianity only as a new spiritual life movement within the Jewish religion. They knew nothing of Peter's vision and did not understand that God had opened the door of faith to the Gentiles also.

[8] EGT, II, 266.

[a] Madeline S. and J. Lane Miller, *op. cit.*, p. 21.

[b] James Hastings, *Dictionary of the Bible*, p. 37.

The reader is taken back to the dispersion of the disciples from Jerusalem following the death of Stephen. The further extent of that diaspora, into definitely Gentile territory, is now given.

What is called "persecution" (*diogmos*) in 8:1 is here called **tribulation** (*thlipsis*). It **arose about Stephen** (RSV, "over Stephen"). The preposition *epi* is literally "upon," but has many meanings. It can be translated "against." But probably "about" or "over" fits best here. **Phoenicia** is modern Lebanon, on the coast of southern Syria. In Bible times its main cities were Tyre and Sidon, which still exist as towns. **Cyprus** is the easternmost of the larger islands of the Mediterranean.

Antioch was founded in 300 B.C. At the time of its evangelization it was said to have been composed of four cities, each with its own surrounding wall. Reaching around the whole was a long wall which enclosed more area than the city of Rome. The four cities were separated by the two main streets of Antioch.[4] Situated five miles from the city was Daphne, a main center for the worship of Apollo and Artemis. This contributed a great deal to the notorious immorality of Antioch. Yet it had a large Jewish colony, with many proselytes,[5] which provided a starting point for the evangelization of the city. Josephus states that it was the third city in the Roman Empire, surpassed only by Rome and Alexandria.[6]

B. The Grecian Evangelization (11:20)

But there were some of them, . . . [who] **spake unto the Greeks also, preaching the Lord Jesus.** These particular Christian disciples were Hellenists (Greek-speaking Jews), or perhaps some were even converted proselytes, and consequently were more liberal in their views than were the Jewish Christians. Representatives of Cyrenean Africa and Cyprus are named. The mention of Cyreneans at Antioch, who naturally would have returned to their homes in Africa, may indicate a purposeful evangelization mission to the Greeks of Antioch, on their part. In any event, to Hellenist Africans and Cyprian Christians belongs credit for the first-known Grecian evangelization after Pentecost. Groves remarks:

> That there were Christians quite early in Cyrenaica seems clear. The existence of a Jewish community in contact with Jerusalem is attested in Acts (2:10; 6:9); these more enlightened Jews of the Dispersion, when converted, were not unnaturally among the first missionaries to the Gentiles (11:20; 13:1). That their own home settlements received the Gospel early is to be safely presumed. We know nothing, however, about Christian beginnings in Cyrenaica (alternatively known as Pentapolis). Catacombs are said to have been discovered in Cyrene belonging to the period before Constantine.[c]

Further, the foregoing authority[d] observes that Simon of Cyrene, who bore Christ's cross, came from northern Africa (Luke 23:26). He is regarded as a Jewish settler in a Greek settlement of Barca, a district of modern Tripoli (cf. Acts 2:10; 6:9; 11:20; 13:1). Apollos (Acts 18:24–19:1) is declared to have been an Alexandrian Christian (cf. Acts 6:9). Luke's account of the conversion of the Ethiopian nobleman (Acts 8:26–40) further testifies to the early impact of Christianity upon Africa.

Tradition in the apostolic age gives no account of any of the original apostles evangelizing in Africa. Indeed, tradition depicts Thomas as the apostle to India, whose route likely took him via the Nile and across the Red Sea, and possibly through Alexandria. J. N. Farquhar regarded this tradition very favorably and actually considered Thomas as one of the evangelists who proclaimed Christ in Egypt, Cyrene, and westward in Africa. Eusebius is the authority for a tradition that John Mark was a missionary to Egypt, but especially the establisher of churches in Alexandria. Demetrius, Pantanus, Clement, and Origen were all associated with the famous Catechetical School of Alexandria, which became a center of Christian learning which stood unrivaled in the Christian world of its day.

Returning to the dispersed disciples, we note that some of them preached **only to Jews** (vs. 19b), while others **spake unto the Greeks also, preaching the Lord Jesus.** As previously noted, the population of Antioch was mainly Gentiles of Greek culture and with many pure Greek residents, and the

[4] *Beginnings*, IV, 128. [5] Josephus, *War*, VII, 3, 3. [6] *Ibid.*, III, 2, 4.

[c] Groves, *op. cit.*, p. 46. [d] *Ibid.*, p. 34.

20 But there were some of them, men of Cyprus and Cyrene, who, when they were come to Antioch, spake unto the Greeks also, preaching the Lord Jesus.
21 And the hand of the Lord was with them: and a great number that believed turned unto the Lord.
22 And the report concerning them came to the ears of the church which was in Jerusalem: and they sent forth Barnabas as far as Antioch:

---

20 Some disciples from **Cyprus and Cyrene** (see on 2:10) adopted the new policy of preaching to Gentiles (cf. vs. 19). The choice between **Greeks** (ASV and RSV) and "Grecians" (KJV) is difficult to make. *Hellēnas* is found in the uncials A and D, and the versions have "Greeks." *Hellēnistas* is the reading of B E 33. Aleph originally read *euangelistas*. This obvious mistake may suggest that the text back of Aleph had *Hellēnistas*. Bruce thinks that perhaps this reading should be accepted, as being the more difficult, but interpreted in a non-technical way; that is, "Greek speakers." He says: "In vi, 1 and ix, 29, the context implies that the Greek speakers were Jews; here the contrast with *Ioudaioi* in ver. 19 (which probably refers to Greek-speaking Jews) plainly implies that the Greek speakers of ver. 20 are Gentiles." [7] So, whichever reading is correct, the reference is evidently to Gentiles.

Preaching the Lord Jesus means telling the good news *(euangelizomenoi)* that Jesus is Lord. This was the approach to the Gentiles. To the Jews and proselytes, Jesus was presented as the Messiah (cf. 2:36; 5:42).

21 **The hand of the Lord** is a typical Semitic expression for the power of the Lord.[8] It is perhaps a metaphor for the Spirit of God. The result of this powerful, Spirit-inspired ministry was that **a great number that believed turned unto the Lord.** The first step in turning to the Lord is acceptance of the gospel message.

22 **The report concerning them came to the ears of the church** is literally: "The word was heard in the ears of the church . . . concerning them." So the Jerusalem church **sent forth Barnabas.** The verb is *exapostellō*. The leaders at Jerusalem made Barnabas their apostle to Antioch.[9] Since Barnabas was a Cyprian Jew (4:36), with broader outlook than most Jerusalem Christians, he could appreciate this new Gentile work.

---

church that subsequently developed in Antioch was largely Gentile in membership.

C. The Extent of the Evangelization (11:21)

And a great number that believed turned unto the Lord. These disciples had preached **the Lord Jesus** (vs. 20b), or Jesus as the Messiah and Lord, to the Greeks, and a great number of them were saved, or **believed,** and were converted, **turned,** to the Lordship of Christ in their lives. How many were converted we are not told, but that the demands of the church soon required Saul to assist Barnabas in the pastoral care of the flock indicates an extensive movement. Further, Antioch was very soon to become the missionary center from which the Gospel would be sent to the Gentile world afar.

Something of the extent of this early evangelization movement among the Grecian Antiocheans is indicated by the fact that by the time of the Nicean Council in A.D. 325, there are reported to have been more than 200,000 Christians in Antioch alone. Between A.D. 253 and 380, Antioch was the seat of no less than ten church councils,[e] and its patriarchs took precedence over those at Rome, Constantinople, Jerusalem, and Alexandria.[f]

II. THE MINISTRY OF BARNABAS (11:22-24)

The fame of the Antiochen mission among the Greeks soon reached the Jerusalem church. The Jewish Christians there, restrained by God's acknowledged visitation of the Caesarean Gentiles, wisely did not condemn the movement at Antioch, but rather selected and authorized a most

[7] *Acts*, pp. 235 f. [8] JFB, VI, 76.
[9] Page (*op. cit.*, p. 153) calls him "a commissioner to examine and report."
[e] For an account of Christianity at Antioch, see Additional Note I, *Christianity at Antioch*, at end of Chapter XI.
[f] Hastings, *op. cit.*, p. 37.

23 who, when he was come, and had seen the grace of God, was glad; and he exhorted them all, that with purpose of heart they would cleave unto the Lord:
24 for he was a good man, and full of the Holy Spirit and of faith: and much people was added unto the Lord.

---

23 When Barnabas saw the **grace** [*charin*] **of God, he was glad** *(echarē)*. There is a play on words, which may or may not have been intentional. **He exhorted** *(parekalei)* reminds us that Barnabas was a "son of exhortation" *(paraklēsis)*. Both "son of consolation" (KJV) and "son of exhortation" (ASV) well describe his character and ministry. **Purpose of heart** means "determination."

---

honorable and trustworthy man of their number, Barnabas (vs. 24), to proceed to that city.

A. The Commission of Barnabas (11:22)

They sent forth Barnabas as far as Antioch. Barnabas' commission was evidently principally to investigate the situation and report to the Jerusalem church. The extent of his commission may be inferred from the duration of his service there and his acquisition of Saul to assist him in the ministry of the church. His more liberal Cypriote background well qualified him for work among the Gentiles. If Barnabas may not have had the honor of founding the church at Antioch, he at least holds the credit for being the first known pastor. That he was not one of the original (Acts 14:14) apostles, but a Jewish Levite who owned land in Cyprus, which land he sold and gave the proceeds to the church, we learn from Acts 4:36. This passage likewise informs us of his special gifts for Christian service, as the very name Barnabas signifies, "the son of consolation" (ASV).

B. The Consolations of Barnabas (11:23)

He exhorted them all, that with purpose of heart they would cleave unto the Lord. Upon his arrival in Antioch, Barnabas evidently wisely played the part of an unbiased auditor and observer of the Gentile revival. The evidences of transforming divine grace at work in the lives of these Gentile people were soon sufficient to convince him that it was indeed a genuine and great work of God. Concerning Barnabas, Luke says: **Who, when he was come, and had seen the grace of God, was glad.** Though he was neither the originator nor director of this work, he was sufficiently magnanimous to appreciate and rejoice in it. Barnabas at once adjusted himself to the new situation, stepped into the movement, and lent the full weight of his support by exhortations (encouragements: Weymouth) to them all; that is, Jews as well as Gentiles. The import of his exhortations was unity in the body of Christ and fixedness of purpose and steadfastness in the Lord Jesus Christ. His very name, Barnabas, means "Son of Prophecy" (see Acts 13:1), and this name may have been gained from an especially comforting or consoling prophecy which he delivered to the disciples at Jerusalem after his conversion.[g] Thus he consoled or encouraged the Antioch church.

C. The Character of Barnabas (11:24)

For he was a good man, and full of the Holy Spirit and of faith. Something of the esteem in which Barnabas was held by the author of the Book of Acts is indicated by the fact that he is mentioned in Acts no less than twenty-five different times, beside five references to him by Paul outside Acts. Luke here characterizes Barnabas as a man of sterling "character": **a good man**; a man of "spirituality": **full of the Holy Spirit**; and a man of "faith": **full of . . . faith.** His character stems from two sources: *first*, his strict Levitical training in the moral law; and *second*, his sound Christian conversion (Acts 4:36, 37). His spirituality was attributable to the sanctifying work and abiding presence of the Holy Spirit in his life. His faith was the natural fruit of the first two, plus an unwavering devotion to Christ and an unquestioned obedience to His will. His fulness of faith may imply: *first*, that "natural or intellectual faith" that is the property of every normal man, without

[g] Dummelow, *op. cit.* p. 824.

25 And he went forth to Tarsus to seek for Saul;
26 and when he had found him, he brought him unto Antioch. And it came to pass, that even for a whole year they were gathered together with the church, and taught much people; and that the disciples were called Christians first in Antioch.

25, 26 **Seek** and **found** suggest that it took Barnabas some time to locate Saul. Moulton and Milligan state that in the papyri *anazēteō* (seek) "is specially used of searching for human beings, with an implication of difficulty, as in the NT passages." [10] This lends strong support to the idea that Saul was not waiting idly at Tarsus but evangelizing his home province. Only those who are busy with tasks at hand are called to larger spheres of service.

On the name **Christians** Lake and Cadbury say: "The termination—*ianos* is a Latinism, and is used to express partisans . . . it implies that *christos* was already taken by the Gentile population as a proper name." [11]

---

which life would be impossible; *second*, "evangelical faith" by which he experienced a saving and sanctifying relationship with Christ; *third*, "fiduciary faith" by which he maintained the constancy of his relationship with Christ; and *fourth*, "achieving faith" by which he saw the mighty works of God performed.

Little wonder that Luke states, after this characterization of Barnabas: **and much people was added unto the Lord** (vs. 24b). The fruit of increased spiritual conversions was consequent upon the divine commission, consolation, and unimpeachable character of Barnabas as a prophet of God to Antioch. Nor did Barnabas win men to himself, only for them to be lost to the cause of Christ after his departure, but rather to the Lord Christ, for they were **added** [joined] **unto the Lord.** This building up of the Antioch church under the ministry of Barnabas probably extended over a considerable period of time.

III. THE ENGAGEMENT OF SAUL (11:25, 26)

Following the attack made on Saul's life by the Hellenist Jews at Jerusalem he had gone to Tarsus, his home city in Cilicia, where he had most likely engaged in evangelistic labors until called to Antioch to assist Barnabas. It is possible, and some scholars think likely, that Barnabas and Saul had attended the Greek university together at Tarsus, and that Barnabas had known for long the character and worth of Saul. In any event, his thorough acquaintance with, and confidence in, Saul are evident (see Acts 9:27).

A. The Summons of Saul (11:25, 26a)

And he [Barnabas] **went forth to Tarsus to seek for Saul** (vs. 25). When the Antioch church had grown beyond Barnabas' ability to shepherd it alone, it was Saul that he desired to aid him. Saul's more liberal education, long residence among Gentiles,[h] thorough spiritual transformation, and his subsequent evangelistic activities at Damascus, possibly in Arabia for some time, at Jerusalem, and then in Cilicia for approximately seven years, combined to recommend him to Barnabas as a man fitted to assist him in the work at Antioch. Thus Barnabas departed to Tarsus, not far distant from Antioch, where he sought Saul. The fact that he probably did not have definite knowledge of Saul's exact whereabouts may suggest that Saul was already travelling somewhere in Asia Minor evangelizing. When found, Saul readily accompanied Barnabas to Antioch.

B. The Service of Saul (11:26)

A whole year they were gathered together with the church, and taught much people. Saul's service at Antioch was primarily a teaching ministry. In consideration of his thorough Jewish theological training, his radical conversion to Christianity, and his sympathetic understanding of the Gentiles (see Acts 15), Saul was in a strategic position to indoctrinate and edify in the Christian faith these Gentiles recently converted to that faith, many of them at least from gross paganism, and to effect a workable plan of church membership and fellowship between them and the Jewish-Christian element of the Church.

[10] VGT, p. 32. [11] *Beginnings*, IV, 130 (cf. also V, 383–386).

[h] Mould, *op. cit.*, pp. 570 ff.

27 Now in these days there came down prophets from Jerusalem unto Antioch.
28 And there stood up one of them named Agabus, and signified by the Spirit that there
should be a great famine over all the world: which came to pass in the days of Claudius.
29 And the disciples, every man according to his ability, determined to send relief unto
the brethren that dwelt in Judaea:
30 which also they did, sending it to the elders by the hand of Barnabas and Saul.

---

27 **Prophets** ranked next to apostles in the Early Church (cf. I Cor. 12:28; Eph. 4:11). They were evidently primarily preachers, but sometimes predicted, as here.

28 **Agabus** is mentioned again in 21:10, 11, and there also he predicts evil. The **great famine** occurred **in the days of Claudius.** Lake and Cadbury say: "The evidence of Suetonius (*Claudius* xix.) and Tacitus (*Ann.* xii, 43) shows that widespread famine was a feature of the reign of Claudius."[12] Josephus mentions a famine in Judea at this time (A.D. 44–48).[13] Some would make **all the world** a Semitic expression for "all the land"; that is, Judea. **Claudius** reigned from A.D. 41 to 54.

29 **According to his ability** is literally "even as he had plenty" (*euporeito*, found only here in the New Testament). **Determined to send relief** is literally "arranged to send for a ministry" *(diakonia)*. "Arranged" *(hōrisan)* perhaps means "fixed a definite amount."

30 **Barnabas and Saul** became the official delegates of the Antioch church to Jerusalem. There is much dispute as to whether or not this "Famine Visit" is to be equated with Paul's visit to Jerusalem described in Galatians 2:1–10. Bruce thinks so.[14] He would place it at about A.D. 46, which would agree well with Josephus' dating (between 44 and 48) for the famine in Judea.

C. The Disciples' New Name (11:26b)

And . . . the disciples were called Christians first in Antioch. Until now the followers of Christ were known by such designations as **disciples, believers, brethren, saints,** the people of **the Way** (or **this Way), the church of God, Galileans,** or **Nazarenes** (Acts 24:5). This last name was likely given in derision, as nothing good was supposed to come out of Nazareth (John 1:46). The term **Christian** occurs only three times in the New Testament (Acts 11:26; 26:28; I Peter 4:16), and only in the last instance is it used by a Christian of Christians. It is quite clear that they did not assume the name themselves, as they were so **called,** and the Jews could not have given them this name without admitting the Messiahship of Christ. Therefore, it probably was given to them by the Antiochenes, not in derision as some suppose, but in recognition of their avowed devotion to Christ as their Lord and leader. It was here at Antioch that the disciples of Christ more nearly earned the right to the name Christian than at any previous place or time, and they were rewarded with it. Harnack gives an interesting and illuminating treatment of the various names accorded the early Christians.[i]

IV. THE JERUSALEM FAMINE RELIEF (11:27–30)

This incident reflects the important part played by prophets, as distinguished from apostles or deacons in the Apostolic Church, and the spirit of genuine charity that characterized the Antioch Christians in their relief of the needy at Jerusalem. It further indicates the good will of these young Gentile Christians toward the mother Judeo-Christian church at Jerusalem (see note on Acts 2:41–47).

Additional Note I

CHRISTIANITY AT ANTIOCH

Harnack furnishes the following most enlightening information on the status of Christianity in Antioch:

> In accordance with its tendency towards universal dominion, Christianity streamed from Jerusalem as far as Antioch (Acts xi), the greatest city of the East and the third city in the Roman empire, ere a few years had passed over its head. It was in Antioch that it got its name, which in all probability was originally a nickname; for Antioch was a city of nicknames and of low-class literature. Here the first Gentile Christian community grew up; for it was adherents of Jesus drawn from paganism who were called

[12] *Ibid.*, IV, 131. [13] *Ant.* III, 15, 3. [14] *Acts*, p. 241.

[i] See Additional Note II, *Early Names of Christ's Followers*, at close of Chapter XI.

"Christians" (cf. vol. i, pp. 411 f.). Here Barnabas labored. Here the great apostle Paul found his sphere of action for some years, and ere long the Christian community became so important, endowed with such a vigorous self-consciousness and such independent activity, that its repute rivalled that of the Jerusalem church itself. Between the churches of Jerusalem and Antioch the cardinal question of the Gentile Christians was debated; it was the church of Antioch—mentioned along with Syria and Cilicia in Acts xv, 23, and the only city noted in this connection—which took the most decided step forward in the history of the gospel; and as early as the second century it gave further expression to its church-consciousness by designating the apostle Peter as its first bishop—although, to judge from Gal. ii, 11 f., it was no glorious role that he had played in Antioch. One of its churches was traced back to the apostolic age.

. . . .

Its fame is established by Ignatius, after Paul. Several features (though they are not many) in the contemporary situation of the church at Antioch can be made out from the epistles of Ignatius, who proudly terms it "the church of Syria." In Smyrn., xi, 2, he says that after the persecution it had regained its proper size. The claim which he advances, under cover of an exaggerated modesty, to instruct foreign churches probably sprang, not simply from his personal attainments as a confessor, but also from the ecclesiastical and commanding position of the city of which he was bishop. The central position of the church is indicated by the fact that all the Asiatic churches sent envoys to congratulate the church of Antioch upon its recovery. It now occupied the place once held by Jerusalem.

. . . .

Once more, it was in this church that the dynamic Christology received its most powerful statement; here Arianism arose; and here the ablest school of exegesis flourished. Thanks to the biblical scholarship of Lucian, the teacher of Arius, Antioch acquired a widespread importance for the development of exegesis and theology in the East (Arianism, the Antiochene school of exegesis, Nestorianism).

The central position of the church is reflected in the great synods held at Antioch from the middle of the third century onwards.

. . . .

It is impossible to draw up any statistical calculations with regard to the church about 320 A.D., but at any rate there were several churches in the city (Theod., H.E., i, 2), and if the local Christians really were in the majority in Julian's reign, their number must have been very large as early as the year 320. Diodorus and Chrysostom [347–407] preached in what was substantially a Christian city, as the latter explicitly attests in several passages. He gives the number of the inhabitants (excluding slaves and children) at 200,000 (Hom. in Ignat. 4), the total of members belonging to the chief church being 100,000 (Hom. 85, 86, c. 4). Antioch in early days was always the stronghold of Eastern Christianity, and the local church was perfectly conscious of its vocation as the church of the metropolis. The horizon and effective power of the Antiochene bishop extended as far as Mesopotamia and Persia, Armenia and Georgia He felt himself in duty bound to superintend the missions and the consolidation of the church throughout these countries. The execution of this task led to the steady growth of certain rights, which were never formally defined, but which were exercised by the Antiochene bishop throughout the East. Similarly, he recognized his duties with regard to the defence of the church against heretics, who were fond of resorting to the East. It was from Antioch that the missionary impulse of Chrysostom proceeded, as well as the vigorous campaign against the heretics waged by the great exegetes, by Diodorus and Theodoret, and by Chrysostom and Nestorius.[j]

Additional Note II

EARLY NAMES OF CHRIST'S FOLLOWERS[k]

The term "disciples" fell into disuse, because it no longer expressed the relationship in which Christians now found themselves placed. It meant at once too little and too much. Consequently other terms arose, although these did not in every instance become technical.

The Jews, in the first instance, gave their renegade compatriots special names of their own, in particular "Nazarenes," "Galileans," and perhaps also "Poor" (though it is probably quite correct to take this as a self-designation of Jewish Christians, since "Ebionim" in the Old Testament is a term of respect). But these titles really did not prevail, except in small circles. "Nazarene" alone enjoyed, and for long retained, a somewhat extensive circulation.

. . . .

The Christians called themselves "God's people," "Israel in spirit" . . . "the seed of Abraham," "the chosen people," "the twelve tribes," "the servants of God," "believers," "saints," "brethren," and "the church of God."

. . . .

The three characteristic titles, however, are those of "saints," "brethren," and "the church of God," all of which hang together.

. . . .

Closely bound up with the name of "saints" was that of "brethren" (and "sisters"), the former denoting the Christians' relationship to God and to the future life . . . the Kingdom of God, the latter the new relationship in which they felt themselves placed towards their fellow-men, and, above all, towards their fellow believers (cf. also the not infrequent title of "brethren in the Lord"). After Paul, this title became so

[j] Adolf Harnack, *The Mission and Expansion of Christianity*, II, 125, 127, 128, 133.
[k] Harnack, *op. cit.*, I, 401–406, 410, 414.

common that the pagans soon grew familiar with it, ridiculing and besmirching it, but unable, for all that, to evade the impression which it made. For the term did correspond to the conduct of Christians.

. . . .

Yet even the name of "the brethren," though it outlived that of "the saints," lapsed after the close of the third century; or rather, it was only ecclesiastics who really continued to call each other "brethren."

. . . .

We now come to the name "Christians," which became the cardinal title of the faith. The Roman authorities certainly employed it from the days of Trajan downwards (cf. Pliny and the rescripts, the "cognitiones de Christians"), and probably even 40 or 50 years earlier (I Pet. iv, 16; Tacitus), whilst it was by this name that the adherents of the new religion were known among the common people (Tacitus; cf. also the well-known passage in Suetonius).

. . . .

One name still falls to be considered, a name which of course never became really technical, but was (so to speak) semi-technical; I mean that of . . . (miles Christi, a soldier of Christ). With Paul this metaphor had already become so common that it was employed in the most diverse ways.

It is indeed strange that Harnack appears to overlook one name by which the early Christians were well known and often called, that is the designation "Friends."

CHAPTER XII

Now about that time Herod the king put forth his hands to afflict certain of the church.
2 And he killed James the brother of John with the sword.

EXEGESIS

1 **About that time** (more literally, "at that time") evidently connects this chapter chronologically with the closing verses of chapter eleven. **Herod the king** (Herod Agrippa I) is mentioned in the New Testament only in this chapter. The Greek expression for **put forth his hands** is used in the sense of seized or arrested in the Septuagint, the papyri, and the New Testament (cf. 4:3; 5:18; 21:27). **To afflict** is literally "to ill-treat" *(kakōsai)*. The verb is found five times in Acts and only once elsewhere in the New Testament (I Pet. 3:13).

2 The tradition that John the son of Zebedee was martyred with his brother James (cf. Mark 10:39) is both too late and too weak to deserve the attention sometimes given to it.[1] Clement of Alexandria, as quoted by Eusebius,[2] says that the officer who led James to the judgment-seat was so impressed by the apostle's witness that he himself accepted Christ and was beheaded with James.

EXPOSITION

THE CHURCH'S FIRST SECULAR PERSECUTION

I. THE DESIGNS OF HEROD, Acts 12:1–4.
   A. The Persecutions of Herod, vs. 1.
   B. The Execution of James, vs. 2.
   C. The Imprisonment of Peter, vss. 3, 4.
II. THE DELIVERANCE OF PETER, Acts 12:5–11.
   A. The Prayer of the Church, vs. 5.
   B. The Plight of Peter, vs. 6.
   C. The Intervention of God, vss. 7–10.
   D. The Considerations of Peter, vss. 11, 12a.
III. THE DILIGENCE OF THE CHURCH, Acts 12:12b–17.
   A. The Church's Concern, vs. 12b.
   B. The Church's Surprise, vss. 13–15.
   C. The Church's Reward, vss. 16, 17.
IV. THE DEFEAT OF HEROD, Acts 12:18–25.
   A. The Disappearance of Peter, vss. 18, 19a.
   B. The Execution of the Guards, vs. 19.
   C. The Death of Herod, vss. 19b–23.
   D. The Progress of the Church, vss. 24, 25.

I. THE DESIGNS OF HEROD (12:1–4)

From the prosperity of the Gentile work at Antioch (Acts 11:19–30), Luke returns in chapter twelve to the Jerusalem church, where for the third time the cruel hand of organized persecution had fallen upon the disciples. The *first* persecution was by the Sadducees and the chief priests (Acts 4:1; 5:17); the *second* was incited by the Hellenists (Acts 6:9–15), though executed by the Jewish council (Acts 7:1–60), and followed up by the Pharisees and Hellenists with Saul as their chief representative, until his conversion (Acts 8:1; 9:1, 2, 29). This *third* persecution came by the hand of **Herod the king,** though doubtless it was incited by the anti-Christian Jews. The next great Christian persecution was to come from the official Roman government. That this persecution occurred at about the time of the Jerusalem famine relief (Acts 11:29, 30; 12:1) is evident from the known date of Herod's death, 44 A.D.

This **Herod the king** was Herod Agrippa I,[a] grandson of Herod the Great and nephew to Herod Antipas, who beheaded John the

[1] Those who wish to examine the evidence will find it set forth at length in R. H. Charles, *Revelation* (ICC), I, xlv ff., and refuted in J. H. Bernard, *The Gospel According to St. John* (ICC), I, xxxvii ff. and W. F. Howard, *The Fourth Gospel in Recent Criticism and Interpretation*, p. 234.
[2] *Ecclesiastical History* II, 9.

[a] Mould, *op. cit.*, pp. 550, 551.

3 And when he saw that it pleased the Jews, he proceeded to seize Peter also. And *those* were the days of unleavened bread.

---

3 **Pleased the Jews** expresses well the policy of Herod Agrippa I. **Proceeded** is literally "added" (*prosetheto*, "put to"). That is the way the verb is translated in the King James Version in 11 out of its 18 occurrences. There would be immense crowds in Jerusalem during **the days of unleavened bread,** so that Agrippa's zeal for the law and for the suppression of "heresy" would receive wide attention.

Baptist. It may be noted that upon the death of Herod the Great, king of the Jews, in about 4 B.C., his kingdom was divided between his three sons as follows: Philip was made tetrarch of Iturea, the country north and east of the Sea of Galilee, where he reigned until A.D. 34; Herod Antipas became tetrarch of Galilee and Perea until his recall by Rome for maladministration and a suspected plot against the emperor's life in A.D. 39. Archelaus was made ethnarch of Judea, which also included Samaria to the north and Idumaea in the south, with his capital at Caesarea, until his deposition and banishment to Gaul by Rome in A.D. 6, also for maladministration. Though some of the Jews, especially the political party of the Herodians, wished another descendant of Herod the Great to succeed Archelaus, many of the Judean Jews preferred a direct Roman rule. Thus Rome added Judea to the province of Syria and established in Judea the procuratorship which lasted from A.D. 6 until A.D. 41. There were seven of these procurators, between Archelaus and Herod Agrippa I, of which Pilate was the fifth in order. Caponius ruled from A.D. 7–9; M. Ambibulus A.D. 9–12; Annius Rufus A.D. 12–15; Valerius Gratus A.D. 15–26; Pontus Pilatus A.D. 26–36; Marcellus A.D. 36; and Marullus A.D. 37–41.

These procurators were chiefly fiscal agents for Rome. Judea was divided into eleven toparchies, or major towns with their adjacent country and villages, with Jerusalem as the Jewish capital. Each toparchy had a synagogue with a minor Sanhedrin responsible to the Temple and Sanhedrin at Jerusalem.

While the Sanhedrin was permitted to administer Jewish law relating to civil, criminal, moral, and religious questions involving Jews within Judea, except where such Jews possessed Roman citizenship, the execution of all capital punishment and the charge of all Gentiles, fell under Roman authority. There was the one exception that the Jews had the right to kill on the spot any Gentile who ventured beyond the court of the Gentiles at the Jerusalem Temple. The procurator was the final court of appeal, except that Roman citizens had the right of direct appeal to Caesar. The procurator had the power to appoint and remove the Jewish high priest of the Sanhedrin. In fact, the robes of the Jewish high priest were kept in the tower of Antonia. Otherwise the Jews were allowed complete religious freedom. Taxes were collected by the procurators mainly through the local Sanhedrins of the eleven toparchies.[b]

For a brief period of three years (A.D. 41–44) the whole of Palestine was ruled by Herod Agrippa I. This Herod Agrippa I had a checkered career. He grew up in Rome where from luxury and extravagance he descended to poverty and want. To evade his debts he fled to southern Judea where he contemplated suicide in despondency over his bankruptcy, but from which he was saved by his wife Kypros, who gained favor for her husband with Herod Antipas through his wife Herodias, who was the sister of Agrippa I. Agrippa I was given a minor appointment in Tiberias, but he soon fell out with Antipas and resigned. He then found brief favor with Flaccus the legate of Syria at Damascus until his own brother Aristobulus charged him with bribery. He eluded his Palestinean creditors and fled back to Rome via Alexandria, where he borrowed a vast sum of money from Alexander, the brother of the Jewish philosopher Philo.

Back in Rome he developed a friendship with Caius Caligula, who succeeded his foster father to the throne upon the death of the latter in A.D. 37. Caligula released Agrippa I from prison where Tiberius had

[b] *Ibid.*, pp. 391, 467, 468.

4 And when he had taken him, he put him in prison, and delivered him to four quaternions of soldiers to guard him; intending after the Passover to bring him forth to the people.

---

4 **Prison** *(phylakēn)* and **guard** *(phylassein)* are from the same root, *phylax*, "guard, sentry." Peter was guarded by **four quaternions of soldiers.** Each quaternion of four soldiers would be on duty for a three-hour watch at night and also in the daytime. **Passover** here quite obviously refers to the entire festival of eight days. Strictly speaking, the Passover lasted one day and was followed immediately by the feast of unleavened bread (cf. vs. 3). Here both expressions are used for the whole period. The rendering "Easter" in the King James Version is an obvious anachronism. The reference here is to the Jewish Passover. *Anagagein*, **to bring . . . forth,** is literally "to lead or bring up." Probably Agrippa intended to make a public spectacle of Peter's trial and execution, in order to receive greater gratitude from the Jews. Moulton and Milligan cite a parallel use of this word from a first century inscription.[3]

---

incarcerated him for wishing his death, and appointed him king over the former tetrarchy of Philip. Two years later (A.D. 39), Caligula extended Agrippa's domain to include the tetrarchy of Herod Antipas, who was banished through the instigation of Agrippa.

When Caligula was murdered and succeeded by Claudius in A.D. 41, Claudius, out of a sense of obligation to Agrippa, added Judea and Samaria to his kingdom. Thus Agrippa became the king of all the territory which had belonged to his grandfather Herod the Great.

With the Jews Agrippa I was successful as a ruler. He deferred to their scruples, observed their regulations, and was careful to avoid offense in every respect. It was this disposition toward, and deference to, his Jewish subjects at Jerusalem that elicited his persecution of the Christians, his beheading of the apostle James, and his intention to execute Peter during the Jewish feast of the Passover at Jerusalem. These acts were all designed to curry favor with the Jews: **And when he saw that it pleased the Jews, he proceeded to seize Peter also** (vs. 3a).

In A.D. 44, at the conclusion of an oration at Caesarea to the peoples of Tyre who had sued for his favor, Herod Agrippa I suddenly died by a stroke of God for receiving the ascriptions of divinity from his favor-seeking subjects (Acts 12:21–24).

Following Herod's death Rome returned the government of Judea to a succession of seven procurators, until the destruction of Jerusalem and the end of Jewish national life in A.D. 70. These later procurators were Fadus, A.D. 44–48; Alexander, A.D. 48; Cumanus, A.D. 48–52; Felix, A.D. 52–60; Festus, A.D. 60–62; Albinus, A.D. 62–64; and Florus, A.D. 64–66. After declining to appoint him king of Judea in A.D. 44, Claudius did, in A.D. 48, give Herod's twenty-one-year-old son, Agrippa, the small kingdom of Chalcis in Lebanon. In A.D. 50 he exchanged this for Philip's former kingdom, and later Nero gave him parts of Galilee and Julias in Perea. His capital was Caesarea Philippi and, though he maintained a residence in Jerusalem, he had no authority in Judea. It was this Agrippa II that heard Paul's defense at Caesarea (Acts 25:13—26:32). He reigned from A.D. 48 until about A.D. 100.[c]

Whatever the immediate incitement of this persecution of the Christians, with the resultant martyrdom of James and the intended martyrdom of Peter may have been, it is evident that it arose with the Jews. Herod, out of respect for his Jewish subjects, had proceeded to Jerusalem to be present for the great annual Jewish feast of the Passover. Here he observed the cumulative opposition of the non-Christian Jews to the progress of the new Christian movement, and considering it good policy to please these troublesome Jewish subjects (vs. 3a), "laid hands on certain members of the church, to do them violence" (Weymouth). James the Great, son of Zebedee and brother of John (see Matt. 20:20)—not James the less, son of Alpheus—was the first victim to fall. The Jews, Clarke[d] observes, had four methods of execution: namely, *stoning*, *burning*,

[3] VGT, p. 32.

[c] *Ibid.*, pp. 466–470; 550–554.

[d] Clarke, *op. cit.* V, 774.

5 Peter therefore was kept in the prison: but prayer was made earnestly of the church unto God for him.

---

5 While Peter **was kept in prison** *(phylakē)*, **prayer was made earnestly** *(ektenōs)*.[4] The adverb is used by Luke also in his Gospel (Luke 22:44) and elsewhere in the New Testament only in I Peter 1:22 ("fervently," KJV). The adjective *ektenēs*, found here in the Textus Receptus, occurs only in I Peter 4:8. These words come from *ekteinō*, which literally means "stretch out or forth." **The church** was stretching out its hands **unto God** in prayer for Peter. The Christians did not take a fatalistic attitude, but believed that God could change bad circumstances.

---

beheading with the sword, and *strangling*. Crucifixion was later adopted, probably from the Romans. Beheading with the sword was the punishment (according to the Talmud) for one who drew the people away to a strange worship. This probably accounts for the verdict against James and thus indicates something of his influence. He had the honor of being the *first apostle* to be martyred for Christ. No more is known of the incident. Herod evidently sought to stamp out the new movement by eliminating James and Peter, whom he thought to be the ringleaders. Therefore, after beheading James and observing that it improved his position with the Jews, as a foreign ruler, he proceeded to arrest and securely imprison Peter by placing him under a special guard of sixteen soldiers, intending to publicly execute him after the Jewish passover.

II. THE DELIVERANCE OF PETER (12:5–11)

Why God allowed James to be executed while He miraculously delivered Peter from the same fate is not known for certain. That an apostle's heroic martyrdom should have strengthened the faith of the Church, as well as convinced the unbelieving of the worthfulness of the Christian Way, seems most likely. Possibly James was Christ's best example of devotion, even unto death. The Hebrew children did not claim immunity from the fiery furnace, but they did declare their undivided devotion to God, even unto death, if necessary (Dan. 3:16–18). David likewise did not claim immunity from "the valley of the shadow of death," but he did claim Jehovah's comforting presence in that valley (Ps. 23:4). Perhaps James, like certain other ancient worthies, was "tortured, not accepting their deliverance; that they might obtain a better resurrection" (Heb. 11:35). In any event, for reasons best known to God, He allowed James to be martyred and spared Peter for further service.

A. The Prayer of the Church (12:5)

Prayer was made earnestly of the church unto God for him. Is it possible that the martyrdom of James may have been due to the Jerusalem disciples having slacked their prayer vigil when rest from persecution came to the Church with the conversion of the persecutor Saul (Acts 9:31)? Possibly it required this advantage of the enemy to drive them back to earnest and incessant prayer for Peter's deliverance from prison and impending execution. That these disciples knew the power of prayer is evident from Peter's earlier deliverances from the murderous designs of the Sanhedrin (Acts 4). Weymouth's translation of the passage is instructive: "but long and fervent prayer was offered to God by the church on his behalf." With Peter locked in prison and secured by a sixteen-man guard, the only hope of his deliverance lay in a miracle. Man's extremity again becomes God's opportunity, and the Church learned the power of prayer in a crisis. Never was it truer than then that prayer alters apparently impossible situations.

B. The Plight of Peter (12:6)

Herod was about to bring him forth. Just how a condemned man may feel the night before his scheduled execution probably only that individual can know. Peter had likely watched the recent trial and bloody execution of his brother-apostle James. The memory of that gory spectacle was fresh in his mind. How would he stand up to the ordeal on the morrow? Many a man has lost

[4] So Aleph A B.

6 And when Herod was about to bring him forth, the same night Peter was sleeping between two soldiers, bound with two chains: and guards before the door kept the prison.

7 And behold, an angel of the Lord stood by him, and a light shined in the cell: and he smote Peter on the side, and awoke him, saying, Rise up quickly. And his chains fell off from his hands.

8 And the angel said unto him, Gird thyself, and bind on thy sandals. And he did so. And he saith unto him, Cast thy garment about thee, and follow me.

---

6 **The same night**—just before the scheduled trial and execution—**Peter was sleeping between two soldiers, bound with two chains.** Interestingly, Josephus tells how Herod Agrippa I had been bound to a soldier during his imprisonment by Tiberius at Rome.[5] Perhaps the added caution taken in Peter's case was due to the apostle's previous escape from prison (5:19).

7 **An angel of the Lord stood by**—exactly the same expression *(angelos kyriou epestē)* occurs in Luke 2:9. Because *angelos* means "messenger" some have argued that a human agent secured Peter's release—perhaps an "inside job." But Bruce puts the case well, when he writes: "The expression used, and the name *angelos kyriou* (see on v. 19, viii, 26) seem to exclude the idea that a human messenger is meant."[6]

A light shined continues the comparison with Luke 2:9, where it is stated: "An angel of the Lord stood by them, and the glory of the Lord shone round about them." **Cell** is *oikēma*, related to *oikos*, "house." Found only here in the New Testament, the word means "a dwelling." But it was used euphemistically by Demosthenes and Thucydides for a "prison"[7] (cf. KJV).

The angel **smote** Peter to waken him. This suggests how soundly the apostle was sleeping, in spite of what apparently awaited him the next day. Miraculously, **his chains fell off from his hands.** He was now free within his cell.

8 While it took a miracle to loosen Peter's chains, the apostle was instructed to dress himself. It is characteristic of Biblical miracles that God does not do for men what they can do for themselves.

---

his reason under similar circumstances. But we read concerning Peter: **the same night Peter was sleeping.** Indeed he slept between two soldiers to whom he was bound with two chains, **and guards before the door kept the prison,** or "were keeping" the prison. The language of the text seems to be intended to emphasize the security and apparent inescapableness of the prison, and at the same time the "rest of faith" that characterized the apostle. Peter had learned the secret that "he giveth unto his beloved sleep" (Ps. 127:2b). Perhaps it was from this experience that Peter later wrote: "The Lord knoweth how to deliver [rescue: Weymouth] the godly out of temptation" (II Pet. 2:9a).

C. The Intervention of God (12:7–10)

And behold, an angel of the Lord stood by him. As the hour for execution drew near and the victory looked certain for the Jews who had instigated Peter's arrest and intended execution, and the disciples saw no hope of Peter's escape outside of God, it was then that the angel of the Lord appeared and things began to happen. The glory of God's presence illumined the inky black cell in which Peter was incarcerated. The angel gently smote Peter, awakening him without so much as disturbing the guards, took him by the hand and raised him to his feet, as the chains that had bound him to the soldiers fell as noiselessly to the floor as a feather to a cushion (vs. 7). The angel then bade Peter, in a soundless language, to gird himself and follow him (vs. 8). The whole procedure seemed to Peter to be too good to be real, and he thought it to be only an illusion or dream (vs. 9). They passed the first and second guards without even arousing their suspicions that a major jail-break was in progress and then came to the great outer iron gate of the prison which, like an electric-eye door, automatically opened as they approached it. From here they passed into the open street where the angel left Peter a free man. What a miraculous and glorious deliverance! Who but God could have executed it? How utterly futile are man's efforts to outwit God.

[5] *Ant.* XVIII, 6, 7. [6] *Acts*, p. 245. [7] Arndt and Gingrich, *op. cit.*, p. 559.

9 And he went out, and followed; and he knew not that it was true which was done by the angel, but thought he saw a vision.

10 And when they were past the first and the second guard, they came unto the iron gate that leadeth into the city; which opened to them of its own accord: and they went out, and passed on through one street; and straightway the angel departed from him.

11 And when Peter was come to himself, he said, Now I know of a truth, that the Lord hath sent forth his angel and delivered me out of the hand of Herod, and from all the expectation of the people of the Jews.

---

9 Peter **thought he saw a vision.** The word *horama* (from *horaō*, "see"), means "that which is seen." The whole expression thus becomes equivalent to: "thought he was seeing things." Outside of Acts (ten times), *horama* occurs in the New Testament only in Matthew 17:9.

10 **The first and the second guard** would probably be the two sentries who, with the two soldiers chained to Peter, made up the quaternion on duty at that particular watch. Ramsay argues that *prōtos*, **first** should be taken absolutely and concludes: "There were obviously three gates and three wards to pass (Peter was allowed to pass the first and the second, being taken presumably as a servant; but no servant would be expected to pass beyond the outermost ward at night, and a different course was needed there)." [8]

Iron is *sidēran*, found only here and four times in Revelation. The **iron gate** is described as one **that leadeth into the city,** suggesting that the prison was inside the walls of Jerusalem. This lends support to the idea that it may have been the Tower of Antonia, located at the northwest corner of the Temple Area. The heavy iron gate opened **of its own accord.** This entire phrase is one word in Greek, *automatē;* that is, automatically. The term is found in the New Testament only here and in Mark 4:28.

When Peter was safely out of prison, **straightway the angel departed from him.** Again it is to be noted that miraculous power is not wasted in doing what human strength and wisdom can do. Peter no longer needed direct divine intervention.

11 **When Peter was come to himself** is literally "Peter having become in himself" *(en heautōi genomenos)*. He had been out of himself, in a sort of trance. But when the angel disappeared, he discovered that he was actually out of prison. **Expectation** is *prosdokia*, found only here and in Luke 21:26. The danger from **Herod** was actually due to the opposition from **the Jews.**

D. The Considerations of Peter (12:11, 12a)

And when Peter was come to himself . . . [he] considered the thing. The events of his deliverance had been so rapid that it took Peter a while to get his bearings as he stood there alone in the dark street a free man.

The circumstances of Peter's deliverance from prison may be summed up as follows: he was conscious that he had his freedom; he stood alone in the street; he realized that he must go somewhere; and he thought of the prospect of the friendly shelter of Mary's home where the comforts of life and kindly friends would welcome him. Perhaps he took in much more than the foregoing as he **considered the thing.** How much more we often see after some great deliverance than we were able to see before the deliverance came. God's emergency movements are too rapid for men either to follow or fully comprehend by reflection.

III. THE DILIGENCE OF THE CHURCH (12b–17)

Mention of the house of Mary greatly humanizes the church at Jerusalem. This Mary, mother of John Mark and thus an aunt to Barnabas, was evidently a Christian widow of considerable wealth and influence, as her home would indicate. She evidently played an important part in the lay life of the Early Church at Jerusalem. It should be observed that her house was approached by an imposing gate at which the portress Rhoda (Rose) attended (vs. 3). Her spacious home provided for the assemblage of the church for worship (vs. 12b), though this occasion could not have been an official meeting of the church since James and the

[8] *St. Paul the Traveller*, p. 28.

12 And when he had considered *the thing*, he came to the house of Mary the mother of John whose surname was Mark; where many were gathered together and were praying.
13 And when he knocked at the door of the gate, a maid came to answer, named Rhoda.
14 And when she knew Peter's voice, she opened not the gate for joy, but ran in, and told that Peter stood before the gate.
15 And they said unto her, Thou art mad. But she confidently affirmed that it was even so. And they said, It is his angel.

---

12 **When he had considered the thing** is one word in Greek, *synidōn.* The verb is found in the New Testament only here and in 14:6. It means "*to see in one view,* hence, of mental vision, *to comprehend, understand.*" [9]

John was the Jewish name, **Mark** (Marcus) the Roman name, of the individual who appears here for the first of four times in Acts. In the rest of the New Testament he is mentioned four times (Col. 4:10; II Tim. 4:11; Philemon 24; I Pet. 5:13). It seems very probable that Luke derived his information about this incident from Mark.

13 **The door of the gate** was the street door opening into the outer court or passageway (*pylōn;* see on 10:17). **Rhoda** is the Greek name from *rhodē,* "Rose," [10] a common name in that day. In view of Lake and Cadbury's treatment of verses 7–10 as "one of the most obviously legendary in Acts" [11] it is interesting to read their following comment on this verse: "It is impossible to deny the convincing nature of the behaviour of Rhoda and of the family." [12]

14 That Rhoda **knew Peter's voice** suggests that he often visited this home. If so, his contact with Mark was early. The fact that he calls him "Mark my son" (I Pet. 5:13) probably indicates that John Mark was converted under his ministry.

15 **Thou art mad** is *mainē.* The verb occurs again in 26:24, 25, where Festus accuses Paul of being "mad" and Paul denies it. Elsewhere in the New Testament it is used only in John 10:20 (by the Jews of Jesus) and I Corinthians 14:23. **Confidently affirmed** is *diischyrizeto,* found only here and in Luke 22:59. The second **said** is *elegon* (imperfect), which suggests repetition. Edersheim describes the Jewish belief that a guardian **angel** might assume the form and voice of the one it protected.[13]

---

other apostles were absent (vs. 17b). It has been previously suggested (see note on Acts 1:12, 13) that her house was the scene of the Last Supper and the location of the Pentecostal effusion.

A. The Church's Concern (12:12b)

Many were gathered together and were praying. This was no ordinary perfunctory midweek prayer meeting. The life of the leading apostle, Peter, and perhaps the very existence of the Church was at stake, and at this special, though unofficial, prayer meeting **many were gathered together and were praying.** Perhaps from this experience James learned that: "The effectual fervent prayer of a righteous man availeth much" (James 5:16–KJV).

B. The Church's Surprise (12:13–15)

And they said, It is his angel. Common Jewish opinion held that guardian angels were generally provided for God's servants. However, only twice in the New Testament are special personal guardian angels mentioned: namely, in this instance and in Matthew 4:11. Popular belief allowed that on occasion one's guardian angel might assume his physical appearance and represent him. Such seems to have been the first thought of the disciples on the appearance of Peter at the home of Mary. Indeed, the damsel was convinced that Peter was present, but the disciples first judged her mad and then concluded that what she saw was Peter's angel. How human were these early disciples to fear to believe that God had answered their prayers.

C. The Church's Reward (12:16, 17)

When they had opened [the door], **they saw him, and were amazed** (vs. 16b). In amazement they beheld Peter. Here was the answer to their prayers knocking for recognition while

[9] Abbott-Smith, *op. cit.*, p. 427. [10] Thayer, *op. cit.*, p. 563. [11] *Beginnings*, IV, 135. [12] *Ibid.*, IV, 138.
[13] *Life and Times*, II, 752.

16 But Peter continued knocking: and when they had opened, they saw him, and were amazed.

17 But he, beckoning unto them with the hand to hold their peace, declared unto them how the Lord had brought him forth out of the prison. And he said, Tell these things unto James, and to the brethren. And he departed, and went to another place.

18 Now as soon as it was day, there was no small stir among the soldiers, what was become of Peter.

19 And when Herod had sought for him, and found him not, he examined the guards, and commanded that they should be put to death. And he went down from Judaea to Caesarea, and tarried there.

20 Now he was highly displeased with them of Tyre and Sidon: and they came with one accord to him, and, having made Blastus the king's chamberlain their friend, they asked for peace, because their country was fed from the king's country.

---

17 **Beckoning unto them with the hand** is one of the many touches that indicate the report of an eye-witness. Young Mark would not soon forget that night.

James here is not the son of Zebedee (vs. 2) but the brother of Jesus. This is the first indication in Acts that James was the leader of the church at Jerusalem (cf. 15:13; 21:18; Gal. 2:9).

18 In the morning **there was no small stir.** *Tarachos* is found only here and in 19:23. It means "trouble, disturbance." *Ouk oligos*, **no small,** is used only in Acts (8 times). *Ara*, "then, therefore" is an inferential particle not translated into English. It suggests: since he was not in prison, what had happened to him?

19 Herod ordered the guards to be **put to death.** Lake and Cadbury comment: "According to the Code of Justinian, which doubtless represents Roman custom, a guard who allowed a prisoner to escape was liable to the penalty which the prisoner would have paid." [14]

Herod then **went down from Judaea to Caesarea;** that is, he left Jerusalem and returned to Caesarea on the coast. Though Caesarea was the capital of the Roman province of Judaea, it was a Gentile city, built along Roman lines.

20 **Highly displeased** is *thymomachōn*. The verb, found only here, means "to fight desperately, have a hot quarrel." [15] It may be rendered "furious." The reason for this anger is unknown. The only hint we have is that it was at Tyre that Agrippa and his cousin Antipas quarreled.[16] **Blastus** is unknown, aside from the statement here that he was the **king's chamberlain.** The Greek word suggests that he was over the king's bedchamber. The people of Tyre and Sidon **asked for peace, because their country was fed from the king's country.** Phoenicia was dependent on Galilee for much of its food.

---

they prayed on for what they already had. Nowhere is the reality of answered prayer more clearly taught than in this instance. For their edification Peter rehearsed the details of the deliverance, authorized them to relay the report to James and the brethren, and then departed for regions unknown.

IV. THE DEFEAT OF HEROD (12:18–25)

Once again God outwitted Satan and removed the carefully designed plot to defeat and destroy the Church. Peter made good his escape. Only once again is he mentioned in Acts, that in chapter fifteen, where some six years later he was present at the general church council held in Jerusalem in A.D. 49 or 50.

The guards were unable to give a satisfactory account of the escape of the special prisoner, and consequently suffered execution. Herod suffered a horrible death, as divine judgment, at Caesarea consequent upon his assumption of a divine prerogative.

Consequent upon these events **the word of God grew and multiplied** (vs. 24). The prosperity and progress of the Church are assured when she finds her victories through faith in her glorified head, Christ (For the meaning of verse 25, see exegetical note).

[14] *Beginnings*, IV, 139.
[15] Abbott-Smith, *op. cit.*, p. 210.
[16] Josephus, *Ant.* XVIII, 6, 2.

21 And upon a set day Herod arrayed himself in royal apparel, and sat on the throne, and made an oration unto them.
22 And the people shouted, *saying*, The voice of a god, and not of a man.
23 And immediately an angel of the Lord smote him, because he gave not God the glory: and he was eaten of worms, and gave up the ghost.
24 But the word of God grew and multiplied.
25 And Barnabas and Saul returned from Jerusalem, when they had fulfilled their ministration, taking with them John whose surname was Mark.

---

21 **A set** [*taktēi*, found only here in the New Testament] **day** is identified by Josephus as a festival celebrated to make vows for the safety of the Emperor, at which Herod "exhibited shows in honour of Caesar." [17] At this festival **Herod arrayed himself in royal apparel.** The description of Josephus adds color to this statement. He says of the king: "He put on a garment made wholly of silver, and of a contexture truly wonderful, and came into the theatre early in the morning; at which time the silver of his garment being illuminated by the fresh reflection of the sun's rays upon it, shone out after a surprising manner, and was so resplendent as to spread a horror over those that looked intently upon him." [18] (*Edēmēgorei*, **made an oration,** is found only here in the New Testament.)

22 Josephus continues: "And presently his flatterers cried out . . . that he was a god; and they added, 'Be thou merciful to us; for although we have hitherto reverenced thee only as a man, yet shall we henceforth own thee as superior to mortal nature.'" Josephus also says that the king "did neither rebuke them, nor reject this impious flattery." [19]

23 This account of Herod Agrippa's death is in striking agreement with that of Josephus. Luke says that the king was smitten **immediately.** Josephus says: "A severe pain also arose in his belly, and began in a most violent manner." [20] The fact that Josephus says Herod continued in pain for five days before he finally died is obviously not in conflict with Luke's account.

Eaten of worms is an adjective, *skōlēkobrōtos*, found only here in the New Testament. It was used of diseased grain by Theophrastus.[21] Josephus does not mention the precise disease that afflicted Herod. But Hobart well observes: "St. Luke, however, had ample opportunity of learning on the spot the exact nature of the malady inflicted on him, as he spent two years at Caesarea with St. Paul, where the occurrence took place." [22]

Gave up the ghost is an old-fashioned way of saying "expired" (*exepsyken*, literally "breathed out," found only here and in 5:5, 10, of Ananias and Sapphira).

24 This is the third such statement of progress in the church (cf. 6:7; 9:31).

25 This verse presents an undeniably serious textual problem. The English versions read, **Barnabas and Saul returned from Jerusalem.** But the two oldest manuscripts, Vaticanus and Sinaiticus, have *eis Ierousalēm*, "to Jerusalem." This does not seem to make sense, since Barnabas and Saul were last mentioned as going up to Jerusalem (11:30), and it would be assumed that here they are returning to Antioch. The mention of **John whose surname was Mark** as accompanying them also fits a return from Jerusalem (where Mark lived) to Antioch, not the reverse. Bruce indicates that the Greek could be translated "Barnabas and Saul returned [to Antioch], having fulfilled their ministry at Jerusalem" but that this "supposes an unnatural order of the Greek words." [23]

Various solutions have been proposed for this difficult problem. Hort would invert the order of the Greek words and thus give the translation offered above by Bruce.[24] But this lacks manuscript support.

The only alternative appears to be that of regarding *eis Ierousalēm* as a scribal gloss. This is the position of Bartlet in his commentary on Acts in the Century Bible series.[25] Ramsay writes: "This seems to be an alteration made deliberately by an editor, who, because these passages referred to the same visit, tampered with the text of XII 25

[17] *Ibid.*, XIX, 8, 2. [18] *Ibid.* [19] *Ibid.* [20] *Ibid.*
[21] VGT, p. 580. [22] *Op. cit.*, p. 42. [23] *Acts*, p. 251.
[24] Westcott and Hort, *Greek New Testament*, II, Appendix, 94.
[25] J. V. Bartlet, "The Century Bible" *The Acts*, (Edinburgh: T. C. + E. C. Jack, n.d.), p. 252.

to bring it into verbal conformity with XXII 17."[26] Bruce, whose conservative position is unquestioned, adopts this alternative. He says: "In view of the variety of readings, this solution has claims to be regarded as the most satisfactory one, even though it cuts the knot instead of untying it."[27]

[26] *St. Paul the Traveller*, p. 64.
[27] *Acts*, p. 252.

CHAPTER XIII

Now there were at Antioch, in the church that was *there*, prophets and teachers, Barnabas, and Symeon that was called Niger, and Lucius of Cyrene, and Manaen the foster-brother of Herod the tetrarch, and Saul.

EXEGESIS

1 **Antioch** in Syria, third largest city of the Roman Empire—after Rome and Alexandria (see on 11:19, 20)—now becomes the home base of the great foreign missionary enterprise. This was indeed providential. The church at Jerusalem was still so prejudiced against the Gentiles that it could never have sponsored an untrammeled campaign for the evangelization of the Roman Empire. Christianity could not have become a world-wide religion if it had not moved its base of operations to a great Gentile center. In Jerusalem it was still considered to be a sect of Judaism. In this chapter, it burst its nationalistic boundaries and ceased to be in any sense a racial religion.

In the church that was there *(kata tēn ousan ekklēsian)* is translated "in the local church" by Lake and Cadbury. Reference has already been made to the church at Antioch (11:26). This shows that the believers in that city had now become a settled congregation. Hitherto in Acts "church" has been used mainly for the congregation at Jerusalem (5:11; 8:1, 3; 11:22).[1] The two exceptions are "the church in the wilderness" (7:38) and the very singular expression, "the church throughout all Judaea and Galilee and Samaria" (9:31). The regular use of "church" in Acts is for a local congregation.

Five **prophets and teachers** are named. The repetition of *te* with Manaen has suggested the division of the list into three **prophets** (Barnabas, Symeon, Lucius) and two **teachers** (Manaen, Saul).[2] Lake and Cadbury object to this—"It may be doubted whether an enclitic can quite bear the strain of this interpretation" —but probably Ramsay is justified in his comment: "In Acts VI:5, the list of seven deacons is given without any such variation; and it seems a fair inference that the variation here is intentional." [4] Lake and Cadbury's citation of the repetition of *te* . . . *kai* in 2:9–11 is no valid argument for their position, since geographical groupings are

EXPOSITION

THE CHURCH'S FIRST GENTILE MISSIONARY CAMPAIGN

Date: A.D. 45 or 46–48 or 49; Geographic Scope: Cyprus to Asia Minor.

I. The Mission Initiated, Acts 13:1–3.
   A. The Source of the Mission, vss. 1, 2a.
   B. The Personnel of the Mission, vs. 2b.
   C. The Consecration of the Mission, vs. 3.

II. The Mission Inaugurated, Acts 13: 4–12.
   A. A Divinely Approved Campaign, vs. 4a.
   B. A Thoroughly Executed Campaign, vss. 4b–6a.
   C. A Strongly Opposed Campaign, vss. 6b–11.
   D. A Definitely Victorious Campaign, vs. 12.

III. The Mission Extended, Acts 13:13–43.
   A. The Geographical Extension, vss. 13, 14a.
   B. The Evangelical Extension, vss. 14b–43.

IV. The Mission Interrupted, Acts 13: 44–52.
   A. The Cause of the Interruption, vss. 44, 45.
   B. The Nature of the Interruption, vss. 46–51.
   C. The Results of the Interruption, vs. 52.

[1] *Ekklēsia* is not genuine in 2:47.
[2] So Ramsay, *St. Paul the Traveller*, p. 65.
[3] *Beginnings*, IV, 141.
[4] *St. Paul the Traveller*, p. 65.

2 And as they ministered to the Lord, and fasted, the Holy Spirit said, Separate me Barnabas and Saul for the work whereunto I have called them.

---

evidently intentionally indicated thereby. While Paul was both a prophet and a teacher (I Cor. 14:6), he was primarily the latter.

There is no proof for the identification of **Symeon that was called Niger** with Simon of Cyrene (Mark 15:21). Nor is Lucius of Cyrene to be identified with Luke, the author of Acts. The word *syntrophos*,[5] **foster-brother** ("brought up with," KJV), is perhaps best translated "a member of the court" (RSV). Moulton and Milligan note the literal meaning "foster-brother" in a second-century papyrus. They add, however: "From its widespread use as a court title, it is better understood as = 'courtier' or 'intimate friend.'"[6] This appears to be its most common use in the inscriptions of that period. Deissmann cites several such examples.[7] In modern Greek the term means "companion."[8]

2 **Ministered** is *leitourgounton.* This verb was first used at Athens with the meaning "to supply public offices at one's own cost, render public service to the State." Then it came to have the more general sense, "to serve the State, do a service, serve."[9] It is used in the Septuagint for the official service

---

I. THE MISSION INITIATED (13:1–3)

The missions of Philip to Samaria (Acts 8:5–13) and to the Ethiopian nobleman (Acts 8:26–40), of Peter to Caesarea (Acts 10:23–48), and the general preaching of the scattered disciples after the martyrdom of Stephen (Acts 8:1, 4), were all expressions of the infant Church's missionary spirit and outlook. However, the record of Acts 13 gives us the first account of an organized missionary campaign to the great Gentile world outside of Judaism. Further, with the launching of the first missionary campaign, we observe the transfer of the base of missionary operation from the Jewish church at Jerusalem where she experienced her Pentecostal enduement, to the prodominantly Gentile Christian church at Antioch, from which all three of the great missionary campaigns of Paul were launched.

A. The Source of the Mission (13:1, 2a)

Now there were at Antioch, in the church that was there, prophets and teachers (vs. 1a). The first great Gentile missionary campaign found its origin among a spiritually vital and active corps of preachers (**prophets**), and **teachers,** who were carrying forth the work of the church at Antioch. Nor were their services merely perfunctory, but rather vital, as is evidenced by the fact that **they ministered to the Lord, and fasted** (vs. 2a). A praying, supplicating, fasting, and praiseful church will ever be an active and fruitful church. One of the first laws of life in the spiritual organism, as in nature, is vital insurgency, or a disposition for life to break out of bounds and express itself. A second law of life is self-reproduction. The noted soul winner and church builder, Dr. John Timothy Stone, once presented the following telling illustration, bearing on the question of soul-winning. Hypothetically he produced two objects, the one a beautiful, ornate, symmetrical, and attractive agate, which any boy would desire. Beside it was placed an object that was rough and coarse in exterior appearance, unsymmetrical and unattractive, just a worthless acorn admired and desired by no one. "Should these two objects," stated Dr. Stone, "be buried together in fertile soil where the rain would moisten and the sun warm the earth, producing conditions favorable to germination, the acorn would soon sprout, grow, and eventually develop into a great spreading oak of beauty and value. The agate, on the other hand, would remain forever unresponsive to the atmospheric challenges. The difference in these two objects is the fact that the acorn is possessed of the germ of life, and life is insurgent and must ever reproduce itself, while the agate is inanimate and can never reproduce itself; it can never be other than what it is—just a beautiful, glossy, cold agate. It may detoriate, but it will never

[5] Found only here in the New Testament. [6] VGT, p. 615.
[7] *Bible Studies*, pp. 310 ff. [8] *Beginnings*, IV, 141. [9] Abbott-Smith, *op. cit.*, p. 266.

3 Then, when they had fasted and prayed and laid their hands on them, they sent them away.

---

of priests and Levites (cf. Heb. 10:11). In Romans 15:27, it is employed by Paul for the contribution the Gentile churches were making to the Jewish Christians at Jerusalem. These are the only three occurrences of the word in the New Testament. The cognate noun *leitourgia* (six times in N.T.) is the basis of the English word "liturgy." But it is very doubtful that any reference should be found here to the observance of the Lord's Supper. Probably Knowling is correct in interpreting it as meaning "the ministry of public worship." [10] **Fasted** emphasizes a state of uninterrupted concentration which made it possible to ascertain the will of the Lord. That is the main purpose and value of fasting.

Just how **the Holy Spirit said** is not divulged. Knowling says: "We may reasonably infer by one of the prophets; it may have been at a solemn meeting of the whole Ecclesia held expressly with reference to a project for carrying the Gospel to the heathen." [11]

Separate me. Paul uses the same word *(aphorizō)* of himself (Rom. 1:1; Gal. 1:15). The Spirit selected **Barnabas and Saul** for the most important task ever undertaken by the Church. These two were doubtless the outstanding leaders in Antioch.

3 There has been some discussion as to the identity of the **they** who **fasted and prayed.** It would seem that "they" in verse 2 means the prophets and teachers. But Ramsay thinks that here "It cannot be the five officials just mentioned, because they

---

reproduce itself. Likewise the church, regardless of culture, beauty of form, perfection of ritual, architectural impressiveness or material prosperity, that does not have in it the germ of spiritual life will die with the generation that produced it. The church possessed of the Spirit of God, though lacking any or all of these other admiral graces and characteristics, will reproduce itself spiritually, and there will be another generation of Christians."

When the ministers and teachers of a church sustain the vital relationship of the branch to the vine (John 15:5), there will be spiritual fruition.

There were no apostles in the Antioch church at this time. Prophets were of secondary rank to apostles. Both apostles and prophets characterized first-century Christianity and distinguished it from subsequent ages. Upon the foundation of the divine revelation given through these two offices, the Church of Christ is built (Eph. 2:20). While the predictive element was not absent, New Testament prophets were for the most part "forth tellers" or preachers of the Gospel. Paul defines their function as "edification," "exhortation," and "consolation" (I Cor. 14:3). The gift of prophecy was widely diffused (I Cor. 14:1), and even women not uncommonly exercised it (Acts 2:17). Philip is said to have had "four virgin daughters who prophesied" (Acts 21:9). Five prophets, or prophets and teachers, are here named in the Antioch church. Judas and Silas are later referred to as prophets at Antioch (Acts 15:32). Paul lists the divine order of the officers as "apostles, prophets, teachers, miracle workers, gifts of healing, helps, governments, and gifts of languages" (I Cor. 12:28). Those named at Antioch are Barnabas (see Acts 11:22–24), later the missionary companion of Paul; Symeon, otherwise known as Niger or Black, the latter a Roman surname, possibly a freedman from Africa; Lucius of Cyrene, an ancient African city state (see Acts 11:20); Manaen, here designated the foster brother of Herod the tetrarch, but designated by the RSV, "a member of the court of Herod the tetrarch." Herod Antipas became ruler of Galilee and Perea after his father (Herod the Great) died, but was exiled to Gaul where he died in A.D. 39. Finally, Saul, who was to become the Great Apostle, is named.

The vital relationship of these Christians with Christ made them sensitive to the will of God and the directions of His Spirit (see Acts 8:29, 39; 10:19; 11:12; 13:4; 16:6). The Spirit, possibly through one of the several prophets, instructed the church to separate Barnabas and Saul for special

[10] EGT, II, 282 f.
[11] *Ibid.*, p. 283.

cannot be said to lay their hands on two of themselves."[12] This interpretation involves an awkward change in subject—a feature, however, that is very common in the Hebrew Old Testament and not uncommon in the Greek New Testament. Ramsay holds that **they** means the whole church. He writes: "*Codex Bezae* makes all clear by inserting the nominative 'all' *(pantes)*; and on our view this well-chosen addition gives the interpretation that was placed in the second century on a harsh and obscure passage."[13]

Either the whole church or just the leaders —we cannot be positive which—**laid their hands on them.** This seems rather clearly to have been some kind of ordination. It is rather commonly assumed that the two men were here ordained as apostles. Again Ramsay disagrees. He says: "The Apostle was always appointed by God and not by the church."[14] Knowling maintains that Barnabas and Saul are called Apostles by Luke in connection with this first missionary journey, and that "under no other circumstance does he apply the term to either, xiv, 4, 14, and it is possible that the title may have been given here in a limited sense with reference to their special mission."[15] Bruce feels the laying on of hands was a recognition of the divine call.[16]

Sent them away is *apelysan*. This is the only place in Acts where the verb is translated thus in the King James Version. Thirteen times it is rendered "let go." Since God had called these men, the church "released" them from further service in Antioch to follow God's leading to the foreign field.

---

missionary service. Thus the first great missionary campaign of the Church was initiated by the Holy Spirit in and through a vitally spiritual ministering, fasting, and praying church at Antioch. Such situations always give birth to missionary endeavor. It was in a "haystack prayer meeting" that the modern American foreign missionary movement had its inception.

B. The Personnel of the Mission (13:2b)

The Holy Spirit said, Separate me Barnabas and Saul for the work whereunto I have called them.

The voice of God by the Holy Spirit (**the Holy Spirit said**) here indicates both His personality and office work in directing the affairs of the Church.

Selection unto divine service is always conditioned upon spiritual relationship to God, moral worth, special gifts and graces, and holy zeal for Christ. A call to special divine service is characterized by: *first*, a period of unconscious preparation; *second*, a secret inner consciousness of God's will; *third*, the church's recognition and confirmation of the call; *fourth*, a period of specific preparation for the special service; *fifth*, human dedication to the field of service; *sixth*, an open door of service; and *seventh*, a fruitful ministry (see John 15:16). Careful examination will reveal how well Barnabas and Saul met these qualifications.

While it is Luke's primary purpose to narrate the history of Paul, rather than Barnabas or another, throughout the remaining chapters of Acts, the evidence is conclusive that the divine wisdom was fully justified in selecting these men to become the first, great, Christian missionaries.

C. The Consecration of the Mission (13:3).

Then, when they had fasted and prayed and laid their hands on them, they sent them away.

The church's separation of Barnabas and Saul, at the Spirit's command, may well be regarded as their ordination unto apostleship by the church, as well as a sacred consecration to missionary service. Hereafter, from Acts 14:4, 14, they are both designated "apostles" by Luke. Whether Barnabas had met the requirements laid down by Peter for apostleship is a matter of doubt. That Paul had not, his enemies persistently contended (see Acts 1:21, 22). However, Paul's right of claim to the apostleship is well established: *first*, by his training (Acts 22:3); *second*, by his Christian experience on the Damascus road when the Lord appeared to him in a vision (I Cor. 15:8); *third*, by Christ's direct revelation of His Gospel unto him (Gal. 1:11, 12 and Eph. 3:1-4); *fourth*, by the

[12] *St. Paul the Traveller*, pp. 65 f.
[13] *Ibid.*, p. 66. Bruce agrees with this interpretation (*Acts*, p. 254).
[14] *Ibid.*, p. 67. [15] EGT, II 284. [16] *Acts*, p., 254.

4 So they, being sent forth by the Holy Spirit, went down to Seleucia; and from thence they sailed to Cyprus.

5 And when they were at Salamis, they proclaimed the word of God in the synagogues of the Jews: and they had also John as their attendant.

---

4 **Being sent forth** is *ekpemphthentes*, found only here and in 17:10. These two verses (3, 4) give the ideal combination. The missionaries were sent forth both by the Holy Spirit and by the church. This is the norm for all Christian service. The verb *ekpempō* is used in II Samuel 19:31 (LXX) where it says that Barzillai "went over Jordan with the king, to *conduct* him over Jordan" (KJV), italics mine). So it has been suggested that the full meaning here is that the Holy Spirit personally conducted the two missionaries on their way.

Went down is *katēlthon*. Bruce writes: "Compounds in *kata* are regularly used of movement towards the coast, either from inland (as here) or from the high seas." [17]

Seleucia was the port of Antioch. Luke was a widely traveled man, and it is his custom in Acts to mention the harbors into which or from which people sailed (cf. 14:25; 16:11; 18:18). Seleucia, founded about 300 B.C. by Seleucus Nicator, was sixteen miles west of Antioch and five miles north of the mouth of the Orontes.

Leaving Seleucia, they **sailed.** The verb *apopleō* occurs only in Acts (here and in 14:26; 20:15; 27:1). It was about 100 miles from Antioch to **Cyprus,** a large island (150 × 40 miles) noted for its production of copper, to which it gave its name.

5 **Salamis,** a Greek city, was the chief town of the island. **Attendant** does not have the modern meaning of "minister" (KJV). **John** Mark did not do the preaching. Rather he acted as an assistant to the two apostles. The Greek word *hypēretēs* literally means "underrower" (see on 5:22).

Jerusalem apostles' recognition of him (Gal. 2:6–10; *fifth,* by the Antioch church's ordination and consecration of him to missionary service (Acts 13:2, 3); *sixth,* by the fruit of his service (Acts 13:49; 14:1, 21); *seventh,* by the divine miracles that accompanied his ministry (Acts 13:11; 14:3, 10); and *eighth,* by his success in founding Christian churches in Asia Minor during his first missionary journey (Acts 14:23), and subsequently throughout much of the Roman world.

The moral and spiritual security afforded these heroic Christian apostles by the imposition of hands, backed up by fastings and earnest prayers on the part of the church at Antioch, doubtless accounted in large measure for the success of their enterprise. There is no substitute for the prayers of the home church in the missionary enterprise.

II. THE MISSION INAUGURATED (13:4–12)

The missionary campaign which was initiated by God through the Antioch church was now launched by the apostles under the evident direction of the Holy Spirit.

A. A Divinely Approved Campaign (13:4a)

They [the church] **sent them away,** but the higher commission and personal direction of the campaign is expressed in Luke's statement, **So they, being sent forth by the Holy Spirit, went.** Thus the divine commission and the human consecration collaborated in the inauguration of the first missionary enterprise of the Church. On these words, **being sent forth by the Holy Spirit,** Clarke significantly observes: "By his *influence*, *authority,* and his *continual direction.* Without the *first,* they were not *qualified* to go; without the *second,* they had no *authority* to go; and without the *third,* they would not know *where to go.*"[a]

B. A Thoroughly Executed Campaign (13:4b–6a)

So they . . . went down to Seleucia; and from thence they sailed to Cyprus . . . And when they had gone through the whole island [they came] **unto Paphos** (vss. 4, 6a). That Barnabas and Paul had a very definite strategy in their missionary campaign be-

[17] *Loc. cit.*

[a] Clarke, *op. cit.*, V, 780.

6 And when they had gone through the whole island unto Paphos, they found a certain sorcerer, a false prophet, a Jew, whose name was Bar-Jesus;

6 **When they had gone through** is *dielthontes* which Ramsay labels "the technical term for making a missionary progress through a district."[18] A comparison with its use in 15:41 suggests that they evangelized their way across **the whole island.** Ramsay further comments: "The word 'whole' is probably intended to bring out clearly that they made a complete tour of the Jewish communities in the island, preaching in each synagogue."[19]

Paphos was New Paphos, the official capital of the island. **Sorcerer** is *magos*, used again in verse 8. Elsewhere in the New Testament, it is found only in Matthew 2:1, 7, 16 (twice), where it is translated "wise men" and probably refers to astrologers. It was used originally for a priestly caste in Media. Regarding its meaning here Bruce observes: "As this man was a Jew, *magos* is not used here in its original or technical sense . . . , but in the sense of 'magician.'"[20] **False prophet** Bruce defines as "one who claims falsely to be a medium of divine revelations."[21] **Bar-Jesus** means "son of Jesus" (or Joshua). The term is Aramaic.

comes increasingly evident, both from the first and subsequent campaigns. Robinson[b] sees four elements in Paul's plan of advance. *First*, there was the selection of the strategic points of the empire as bases of operation; *second*, the establishment of self-sustained churches in each of these centers; *third*, the charging of these churches with the responsibility of evangelizing the surrounding area; *fourth*, the projection of Paul's personal evangelistic efforts through Asia Minor, Greece, Italy, and possibly Spain, thus planting Christianity clear across the Roman Empire.

Seleucia, from where the apostles set sail, was the seaport city of Antioch located near the mouth of the Orontes River, and about sixteen miles from Antioch. From thence they sailed in a southwesterly direction across the eastern Mediterranean Sea to the island of Cyprus. Cyprus, an island in the eastern Mediterranean Sea, sixty miles west of Syria, the chief cities of which were Salamis in the east and Paphos located at the west end, was the first target of the missionary campaign. The island had many Jewish communities.

At Salamis two important factors came to light. The first was Paul's lifelong strategy of evangelizing the Gentile world via the Jewish synagogue. Robinson[c] reckons that there were some 150 Jewish communities (and most, if not all, likely had synagogues in them) throughout the empire by the time of Paul. He further observes that they were relatively simple in structure and form of worship; that they maintained a close tie with the Jerusalem temple; and that they exercised a liberalizing influence upon Judaism by reason of their adaptation of the Jewish religion to their environment. Robinson also notes their reduction of the ceremonial law and greater emphasis upon the ethical and spiritual elements of religion, plus wide use of the Greek Septuagint in the services, and their intensive proselyting activities among the Gentiles, with special concessions to these converts. Paul, brought up in the synagogue of Tarsus, could best use the synagogue as a springboard for his evangelizing activities. The second factor was the appearance of John Mark at Salamis. Luke notes (Acts 12:25) that Barnabas and Saul took Mark with them from Jerusalem. Whether he accompanied them via Antioch or met them at Salamis is not known definitely. That Barnabas was from Cyprus (Acts 4:36) and that Mark was his cousin, may account for the expedition having been directed first to Cyprus where they had friends and acquaintances, and where already the Gospel had been introduced (11:19, 20); and that John Mark was a sort of apprentice missionary appears likely; **they had also John [Mark] as their attendant** (vs. 5b).

For a distance of 140 miles they traversed the island, visiting the towns and proclaiming the Gospel until they came to Paphos. The

[18] *St. Paul the Traveller*, p. 384. [19] *Ibid.*, p. 73. [20] *Acts*, p. 256.
[21] *Ibid.* The word is found only here in the New Testament.

[b] Robinson, *op. cit.*, pp. 74, 75. [c] *Ibid.*, pp. 9–12.

7 who was with the proconsul, Sergius Paulus, a man of understanding. The same called unto him Barnabas and Saul, and sought to hear the word of God.

8 But Elymas the sorcerer (for so is his name by interpretation) withstood them, seeking to turn aside the proconsul from the faith.

---

7 This Jewish magician was **with the proconsul, Sergius Paulus.** Archaeology has confirmed Luke's accuracy here—as at many other points in Acts.[22] It is now known that the island of Cyprus was incorporated with the Roman province of Cilicia in 55 B.C. In 27 B.C. it became an imperial province, governed by a propraetor. But in 22 B.C. it became a senatorial province, under a proconsul. **Of understanding** is *synetos* (four times in N.T.), which describes one who is able to "put things together."

8 Bar-Jesus is called **Elymas.** The origin of this name is not certain. Knowling says: "In *Elymas* we have the Greek form either of Aramaic *Alima*, strong, or more probably of an Arab word *alim*, wise." [23] Bruce favors the latter.[24] The explanation in parenthesis, **for so is his name by interpretation,** is difficult to explain, since scholars agree that *Elymas* is not a translation of **Bar-Jesus.** The difficulty has not yet been resolved.

---

incidents and fruits of their ministry en route from Salamis to Paphos are passed over by Luke, since his primary concern is with certain important events at Paphos.

Paphos ranked second in importance to Salamis, but while Salamis was the capital of eastern Cyprus, Paphos, in the west, was the seat of the Roman government. Cyprus was a Roman senatorial province over which a proconsul (Sergius Paulus) presided, rather than a Caesarean or imperial province presided over by propraetors. The island was annexed by Rome in 57 B.C. and had formerly enjoyed the latter status but was given to the people by Augustus. Paphos was, further, the seat of the island's chief deity, Aphrodite or Venus, a form of worship that rendered Paphos one of the most immoral and dissolute centers of the world. The superb temple of Venus here with all its elaborate, but immoral, rites won for her the title "Queen of Paphos." To this stronghold of Satan, the Holy Spirit with purpose led the Christian apostles.

C. A Strongly Opposed Campaign (13:6b–11)

But Elymas [Bar-Jesus] **the sorcerer (for so is his name by interpretation) withstood them, seeking to turn aside the proconsul from the faith** (vs. 8). Several things concerning Elymas or Bar-Jesus are noteworthy. *First*, he was an apostate Jewish prophet (vs. 6), a man who had known the light of the divine revelation and had turned from that light to darkness (cf. Matt. 6:23; Luke 11:35; John 3:19–21). *Second*, he was **a false prophet** who subtly used his knowledge of the secret mysteries of the divine revelation, into which he had been initiated as a Jewish prophet, to pervert the truth of God (vs. 10b). *Third*, he was a **sorcerer**, or one who trafficked in "black magic," the wickedest and most demonical of all known practices (vs. 6). *Fourth*, he was a learned, wise, shrewd, cunning man, as his name Elymas (wise, skilled, learned) signifies. Since Bar-Jesus was his Jewish name, ironically signifing his purposes, in its Anglicized form, Elymas was probably the title given him by the inhabitants of Paphos in recognition of his skillful, though wicked, practices. Thus he was known at Paphos as Elymas, Bar-Jesus, or a doctor. *Fifth*, he seems to have been totally devoid of any remnants of such moral principles as sincerity, honesty, or good intentions, and so far depraved as to be capable of the most vicious or heinous crimes, as suggested by Paul's rebuke: **O full of all guile and villany.** *Sixth*, he appears to have so yielded himself to Satanic influence as to become partaker of the demoniacal nature to the extent that Paul could address him as **thou son of the devil.** *Seventh*, though strategically situated in a position of tremendous influence as the proconsul's moral and religious adviser or court chaplain (vs. 7a), his evil influence was cast against

[22] Cf. A. T. Robertson, *Luke the Historian in the Light of Research* (New York: Charles Scribner's Sons, 1920), pp. 179–182.
[23] EGT, II, 287.
[24] *Acts*, p. 256.

9 But Saul, who is also *called* Paul, filled with the Holy Spirit, fastened his eyes on him,
10 and said, O full of all guile and all villany, thou son of the devil, thou enemy of all righteousness, wilt thou not cease to pervert the right ways of the Lord?
11 And now, behold, the hand of the Lord is upon thee, and thou shalt be blind, not seeing the sun for a season. And immediately there fell on him a mist and a darkness; and he went about seeking some to lead him by the hand.

---

9 **Saul, who is also called Paul** introduces us for the first time to the apostle's Roman name. But after this late beginning it occurs 132 times in Acts (plus 30 times in the epistles, all Pauline, except II Pet. 3:15). It was very natural, and wise, for Paul to identify himself to a Roman governor by his Roman name, probably informing his host that he was a Roman citizen, born in the famous city of Tarsus.[25]

There was an accompanying change. Hitherto it has always been "Barnabas and Saul." From now on, it is Paul and Barnabas, with only two exceptions. At the Jerusalem Council, as would be expected, Barnabas is recognized as having priority over Paul (15:12, 25). This would very naturally be the attitude of the Jewish Christians in Jerusalem, who were never overly enthusiastic about Paul. The other exception is in connection with Lystra, where Barnabas is called Zeus (Jupiter), the chief god, and Paul Hermes (Mercurius), because he was the speaker. Hence we have "Barnabas and Paul" (14:14).

10 **Villany** is *rhadiourgia*, found only here in the New Testament. Literally it means "ease in doing," and so, "laziness." But it came to be used for "recklessness, wickedness," such as lewdness (Xenophon) and fraud (Plutarch).[26] In the papyri it is used for "theft."[27] **Son of the devil** was perhaps intended as a contrast to "son of Jesus" (vs. 6).

11 *Achlys*, **mist,** is found only here in the New Testament. Hobart cites its frequent use as a medical term by Galen (on the Diseases in the Eyes) and other Greek physicians.[28] Abbott-Smith notes that it is used especially for "a dimness of the eyes."[29] **Darkness** seems to describe the final stage of complete blindness. **Seeking** is literally "he was seeking" (*ezētei*, imperfect), suggesting that he was unable to find anyone who cared or dared to help him. **Some to lead him by the hand** is all one word, *cheiragogous*, found only here in the New Testament.

---

every moral, religious, social, economic, and political good of humanity and the community. This appears evident from Paul's charge: **thou enemy of all righteousness.** What a formidable foe these "first term" missionaries confronted! Men of lesser conviction, courage, and faith might well have forsaken the field at this first serious engagement as they attempted to invade these fortified realms of Satan's dark domain.

Paul's assumption of the initiative in handling the case of Elymas may indicate a recognition of his superior wisdom and training to that of Barnabas, required to match the skill and cunning of this servant of Satan. That God wisely selects His servants with a view to their fitness for the occasion or situation is evidenced by successful experience and history alike. Nor are we to overlook the influence of the **Holy Spirit,** with whom Paul was **filled,** for this encounter with Satan. The wisest are helplessly weak in the presence of satanic forces without the wisdom and power of God's Spirit, and the unlearned and weak often become spiritual giants under the Spirit's influence (see I Cor. 1:26–29). Further, at this juncture Luke introduces the apostle's Gentile name "Paul," by which he is consistently designated throughout the remainder of Acts and the New Testament, except in the reiteration of his conversion experience (see Acts 14:14; 15:12, 25; 22:13; 26:14). While "Saul" was his Jewish name, now that his ministry has carried him into contact with the official Roman world, in which empire he has legal citizenship, it is both to his personal advantage and that of the Kingdom of Christ which he represents to be officially known as "Paul." Again, hereafter the order of names presented by Luke is usually Paul and Barnabas, instead of Barnabas and Saul as

[25] See Ramsay. *St. Paul the Traveller*, pp. 81–87. Josephus gives several examples of this interesting custom of Jews having two names (e.g., *Ant.* XII, 9, 7; XIII, 12, 1).
[26] Abbott-Smith, *op. cit.*, p. 396. [27] VGT, p. 562. [28] *Op. cit.*, p. 44. [29] *Op. cit.*, p. 73.

12 Then the proconsul, when he saw what was done, believed, being astonished at the teaching of the Lord.

---

12 Someone has remarked: "The blindness of Elymas opened the eyes of the proconsul."[30] The proconsul **believed,** which most naturally means that he became a Christian.

---

before, thus indicating the prominence of leadership into which Paul had entered.

Sergius Paulus gave every evidence of intelligent sincerity as he **called unto him Barnabas and Saul, and sought to hear the word of God** (vs. 7b). The very presence of Elymas at his court may indicate a spiritual concern on the ruler's part. The Christian message is as obligated to reach up to those in high positions as to reach down to the social outcaste. According to Finegan, "An inscription of the year A.D. 55 has been found at Paphos with the words 'in the time of the proconsul Paulus.'"[d] This evidence adds validity to Luke's account.

Paul's withering rebuke administered to Elymas produced results vividly reminiscent of the apostle's own Damascus road encounter with Christ (see Acts 9:3–9, 18). Origen and Chrysostom mention a tradition to the effect that Elymas became a Christian, and indeed the words of Paul, **thou shalt be blind . . . for a season,** seem to offer a ray of hope.

D. A Definitely Victorious Campaign (13:12)

Then the proconsul, when he saw what was done, believed. A practical-minded Roman officer could not be other than profoundly impressed by such demonstration of divine power. The miracle of judgment inspired his faith in Christ's power to save and conditioned his mind for the reception and understanding of the teaching of the Lord. Thus Paul's first recorded convert is both a Gentile and a distinguished government official; "a member of the ancient patrician gens of the Sergii."[e]

The larger success of this mission of planting Christianity in Cyprus is indicated by Harnack's[f] citation of three bishops, Gelasues of Salamis, Cyrl of Paphos, and Spryidon of Trimithus, who attended the council of Nicaea in A.D. 325. Again, Harnack relates that the register of the synod of Sardica (A.D. 343) reveals the signatures of twelve bishops from Cyprus; both of which evidences are a testimony to the rapid growth of Christianity in Cyprus.

III. THE MISSION EXTENDED (13:13–43)

Having rapidly covered the homeland of Barnabas on Cyprus, the missionary party set sail across 170 miles of the Mediterranean toward the native country of Paul, for whose salvation his impassioned soul yearned.

A. The Geographical Extension (13:13, 14a)

Now Paul and his company set sail from Paphos, and . . . passing through from Perga, came to Antioch of Pisidia (vss. 13a, 14a).

Perga was the capital of the province of Pamphylia. Here Mark, for reasons unknown forsook the party and evidently returned to Jerusalem. Whether he resented the ascension of Paul to leadership of the party over his cousin Barnabas, or became homesick, or was unable to stand the rigors of pioneer missionary travel, or was fearful of the wild mountain country before them, or whether Paul's more liberal views irked his Jewish prejudices, is left to conjecture. That Paul was displeased with Mark's conduct and made an issue of this incident at the outset of the second missionary journey, Luke frankly records (see Acts 15:36–39). However, Paul later testifies to the worth of Mark and thus indirectly credits the judgment of Barnabas as superior in having given Mark another chance (see II Tim. 4:11).

Though some hold that a possible case of malaria or other illness contracted by Paul in the lowlands of Pamphylia accounted for his having moved on to the higher country northward (see Gal. 4:13–15), it would seem that the more likely explanation lies in Paul's

[30] Quoted in EGT, II, 288.

[d] Jack Finegan, *Light from the Ancient Past* (Princeton: Princeton University Press, 1946), p. 260.
[e] Dummelow, *op. cit.*, p. 835. [f] Harnack, *op. cit.*, II, 141.

13 Now Paul and his company set sail from Paphos, and came to Perga in Pamphylia: and John departed from them and returned to Jerusalem.

13 **Paul and his company,** literally "those around Paul" *(hoi peri Paulon)*, is a very significant expression. From now on Paul is the acknowledged leader of the party. Big-hearted Barnabas graciously takes second place. **Set sail** is literally "having put out to sea" *(anachthentes)*. *Anagō* is a typically Lukan term, used by him 21 times (17 in Acts), and elsewhere only three times in the New Testament (Matt. 4:1; Rom. 10:7; Heb. 13:20). Luke alone employs it in its nautical sense, reflecting his knowledge of the sea.[31] From Paphos to Perga was about 170 miles.

Perga was about eight miles up the Cestrus and about five miles in from the river. Probably the party landed at Attalia (cf. 14:25), a large harbor about twelve miles away.

Pamphylia was "a small poor region"[32] of Asia Minor between the Taurus mountains and the Mediterranean, bordered on the west by Lycia—with which it was joined at this time as a Roman province—and on the east by Cilicia (Paul's home territory).

Why **John departed from them** is not known. In addition to the reasons listed in the Exposition, mention might be made of the following suggestion by Lake and Cadbury: "It is quite possible that the original plan did not contemplate anything more than Cyprus and that Mark did not feel it his duty to continue with the new enterprise."[33]

passion to evangelize the regions beyond throughout Galatia. The Galatian letter's reference to Paul's infirmity appears more likely to indicate an eye affliction (see Gal. 4:15). The cities falling within the scope of his immediate objective were Pisidian Antioch, Iconium, Lystra, and Derbe, all of which were located in the southern section of the Roman province of Galatia.

Certain scholars of note, including Bishop Lightfoot, support the "Northern Galatian Theory," to the effect that the churches to which Paul wrote the Galatian letter were located in north Galatia proper, and included Tavium, Ancyra, and Pessimus. However, this position seems to lack sufficient support, especially in the light of the fact that there is no specifically recorded missionary journey nor account of the establishment of churches in those parts. On the other hand, Luke records the missionary journey to the cities of southern Galatia and gives an account of the establishment of the several churches there. This latter view holds that the Galatian epistle was written to churches of Pisidia, Antioch, Iconium, Lystra, and Derbe, established on Paul's first missionary journey.

In support of the southern view are the following evidences: *first*, we have a clear record of the apostle's visit to, and establishment of churches in, the cities of the Roman province of southern Galatia, whereas we have no definite record of either a visit to, or establishment of, churches in northern Galatia proper; nor is there any reference to the existence of any churches in northern Galatia until about a century and a half later. *Second*, the Roman province of Galatia included the southern states mentioned in Acts 13 and 14, as well as northern ethnic Galatia (see I Pet. 1:1). *Third*, Paul repeatedly alludes to Barnabas in the Galatian letter as though he were well known to the Galatians, and we know that he accompanied Paul on this first journey to southern Galatia, whereas he was not with Paul on his second or any subsequent journey as far as is known. *Fourth*, Paul refers to his readers as Galatians (Gal. 3:1), the customary Roman designation and the only term by which he could correctly address both Lycaonians and Phrygians. The principal exponents of this southern Galatian theory are Ramsay and Findlay. If this more likely position is adopted, then Paul's letter to the Galatians will serve as an illuminating commentary on the Acts account of this missionary journey to Asia Minor. It is noteworthy that, outside of the Galatian letter, there are but five New Testament references to Galatia (Acts 16:6; 18:23; I Cor. 16:1; II Tim. 4:10; I Pet. 1:1).

Antioch of Pisidia, the next objective of the apostles, was the Roman capital of Antioch of Pisidia or "Pisidian Antioch,"

[31] He also uses *katagō* nine out of its ten times in the New Testament and *eisagō* eight out of ten times.
[32] *Beginnings*, IV, 147.
[33] *Ibid.* See also *St. Paul the Traveller*, p. 90.

14 But they, passing through from Perga, came to Antioch of Pisidia; and they went into the synagogue on the sabbath day, and sat down.

---

14 **Passing through from Perga** would take them over the Taurus mountains into the province of Galatia, a journey beset with many perils of robbers and rivers. The reason for leaving Pamphylia is not stated. Ramsay held that it was a recurrence of Paul's chronic malaria.[34] Lake and Cadbury write: "The generally malarious nature of the coast and the far more healthy climate of Antioch (3600 feet above the sea) render very probable Ramsay's guess that Paul had fever in Perga." [35]

Antioch of Pisidia is the reading of generally inferior manuscripts, such as D E H L P. The earliest and best manuscripts (Aleph, A B C Papyrus 45) all have *tēn Pisidian*, "Pisidian Antioch." Most scholars today are agreed that this is the correct reading. Ramsay says that "Pisidian Antioch" is the right form [36] and that it means "a Phrygian city towards Pisidia." [37] He further contends that it was "the centre of the *Region* called Phrygia in inscriptions enumerating the parts of the province." [38] Lake and Cadbury assert: "Antioch was not in but near to Pisidia." [39] Bruce agrees [40] and quotes Strabo (XII, 6, 4) as employing the expression "Antioch near Pisidia." This would seem to be fairly conclusive evidence. Probably the inferior variant reading *tēs Pisidias*, "of Pisidia," was due to the fact that in A.D. 295 Antioch became the leading city of the enlarged province of Pisidia. Josephus says the Jews had special privileges "in the metropolis itself, Antioch." [41]

---

and is so called because of its unusual location. It was situated at an altitude of approximately 3,600 feet and was traversed by the great overland highway passing from Syria and the East to Ephesus, and thence by sea route to the West. It had been made a free city about 189 B.C., and a Roman colony with citizenship rights by Augustus Caesar sometime before 11 B.C. Its extensive ruins indicate its prominence in Paul's day. It was located near the modern Turkish city of Yalovath. It was a thoroughly Hellenized and Romanized city, though the Phrygians and Pisidians were a less highly civilized people. It was the seat of Roman civil and military administration for southern Galatia. Being a Roman citizen (Acts 22:29) as well as a citizen of the kingdom of heaven, Paul's wisdom and the Holy Spirit's leadings are clearly evidenced in the selection of this advantageous location for the apostles' ambassadorial entry into Galatia. Main overland routes, governmental capitals, centers of population, and Jewish synagogues were a part of Paul's strategy for the spread of the Gospel.

B. The Evangelical Extension (13:14b–43)

And they went into the synagogue on the sabbath day, . . . And Paul stood up, and beckoning with the hand said (vss. 14b, 16a). No inconsiderable number of Jews dwelt in the cities of Asia Minor, and it was natural that they should have possessed a synagogue at this important location. As was his strategy, Paul with Barnabas resorted to the synagogue at Antioch on their first sabbath in the city, both for worship and with a view to an opportunity to present the Gospel of Christ. Here they sat down until after the customary reading of the Law and the Prophets. Dummelow's Commentary outlines the order of the synagogue services as follows:

> (1) the recitation of the Shema (i.e., of Deut. 6:4-9; 11:13-21; Num. 15 : 37-41); (2) fixed prayers and benedictions; (3) a lesson from the Law; (4) a lesson from the Prophets, intended to illustrate the law; (5) a sermon or instruction. The ruler of the synagogue (at Antioch there appears to have been more than one) decided who was to read or preach.[g]

Recognized by the rulers of the synagogue

[34] *St. Paul the Traveller*, pp. 91–97.
[35] *Beginnings*, IV, 148.
[36] *St. Paul the Traveller*, p. 91.
[37] *Ibid.*, p. 104.
[38] *Ibid.*
[39] *Beginnings*, IV, 148.
[40] *Acts*, p. 260.
[41] *Ant.* XII, 3, 1.

[g] Dummelow, *op. cit.*, p. 835.

15 And after the reading of the law and the prophets the rulers of the synagogue sent unto them, saying, Brethren, if ye have any word of exhortation for the people, say on.
16 And Paul stood up, and beckoning with the hand said, Men of Israel, and ye that fear God, hearken:

---

15 **The law,** of course, is the Pentateuch, the first five books of our Old Testament. **The prophets** in the Hebrew canon include Joshua, Judges, I and II Samuel, I and II Kings, Isaiah, Jeremiah, Ezekiel, and the Book of the Twelve (Minor Prophets). In the synagogues of Palestine the reading would be in Hebrew, with an Aramaic Targum (paraphrase) recited along with it. But with regard to Antioch Ramsay says: "The Scriptures were probably read in Greek in this synagogue of Grecized Jews." [42]

Rulers of the synagogue is one word, *archisynagōgoi.* This is found four times in the fifth chapter of Mark (vss. 22, 35, 36, 38). Elsewhere it is used only by Luke (twice in his Gospel, three times in Acts). The use of the plural here (as in Mark 5:22) implies that sometimes there was more than one ruler in a synagogue. The duties of a synagogue ruler are listed as follows by Bruce: "take charge of the building, see that nothing unseemly happened in it, make arrangements for public worship, appoint members of the congregation to read the prayers and lessons, and invite fit persons to speak." [43] A contemporary inscription shows that this office was sometimes held for life.[44] Bruce suggests that **word of exhortation** was "probably a synagogue expression for the sermon which followed the Scripture lessons." [45]

16 **Stood up** is in marked contrast with the habitual practice of Jesus, who followed the custom of the Jewish rabbis in sitting to teach (cf. Matt. 26:55; Luke 4:20). Paul here adopted the method of the Greek orators, who stood to speak. Their manner was further copied in his **beckoning with the hand,** to gain the attention of the audience. The verb *kataseiō* is found only in Acts (12:17; here; 19:33; 21:40).

Josephus indicates that there were many among the Gentiles **that fear God.** He writes: "The multitude of mankind itself have had a great inclination of a long time to follow our religious observances; for there is not any city of the Grecians nor any of the barbarians, nor any nation whatsoever, whither our custom of resting on the seventh day hath not come . . . , and many of our prohibitions as to our food, are not observed." [46]

---

as Jewish brethren, though strangers, Paul and Barnabas were bidden to bring the congregation an exhortation, or better a "consolation," or encouragement to their hopes. Scattered throughout the ancient world with no independent national life, these people, like Simeon at the birth of Christ, were "looking for the consolation of Israel," their coming Messiah (Luke 2:25). Any message by a credentialed Jew that could direct their hopes to the soon-coming of their long-awaited Messiah would be welcome indeed; and so especially welcome were the messengers from Jerusalem, as was the case with Paul and Barnabas. Such an invitation afforded a coveted opportunity for Paul to deliver to his brethren in Israel at Antioch the glorious Gospel that this Messiah of their fond hopes was at hand. The sermon that follows is Paul's first recorded address and here, as in all of his subsequent recorded sermons, is clearly revealed the influence of the underlying principles of Stephen's valedictorian address of Acts seven. Indeed the influence of Peter's Pentecostal Sermon on Paul may not be entirely lacking, but even this may more likely have come to the apostle indirectly through Stephen's address to which Paul, as Saul the youthful persecutor, listened and from the influence of which he was never quite able to free himself (cf. Acts 7:58; 8:1; 26:10b; and 26:14).

An analysis of Paul's sermon which follows in verses 16 through 47 might appear as follows:

1. *An address of recognition and courtesy* (vs. 16).
2. *A Jewish historical frame of reference,* with the facts of which his audience was familiar (vss. 17–25).

[42] *St. Paul the Traveller*, p. 100. See also Rackham, *Acts*, pp. 207 f.
[43] *Acts*, p. 261. [44] VGT, p. 82. [45] *Acts*, p. 261. [46] *Against Apion* II, 40.

17 The God of this people Israel chose our fathers, and exalted the people when they sojourned in the land of Egypt, and with a high arm led he them forth out of it.

---

17 The fact that God **chose** Israel as His covenant people is one of the outstanding emphases of the Old Testament (cf. Ex. 6:1, 4, 6; 13:14, 16; Deut. 7:6–8). God **exalted** the nation; that is, "made them numerous and powerful." [47] Thirdly, **with a high arm**—symbol of great power and authority—**he led them forth.** In harmony with the teaching of the entire Scriptures, Paul presented God as the Initiator of redemption.

---

3. *Certain scriptural, historical, and logical deductions from the foregoing*, concerning Christ as the Messiah of the Jews and the Savior of all mankind (vss. 26–37).
4. *A practical application of these truths to his audience* (vss. 38, 39).
5. *A solemn warning and impassioned appeal to his hearers*, lest they suffer the fate of their ancient forefathers in the wilderness (vss. 40, 41).

First, concerning the address, it need be noted that when **Paul stood up, and** [beckoned] **with the hand,** he was employing a familiar gesture designed to arrest attention and establish rapport with his audience. Further, the address, **Men of Israel, and ye that fear God,** clearly indicates that Paul recognized two general classes of hearers before him: *first*, the "Jews of the dispersion;" and, *second*, "God-fearers," or those Gentiles who were privileged to worship the true God, Jehovah, in the non-liturgical services of the synagogue, but who did not subscribe to the Jewish ceremonials of circumcision or strict observance of the Law. They were "God-fearers," but not full proselytes. That there were many such Gentiles out in the empire and beyond who benefited from the spiritual worship of Jehovah through the synagogue is clearly evident. When a minister fails to properly recognize his audience and its components, he will usually fail to gain its attention and interest for his message. When a minister duly recognizes and respects his audience, he will usually gain the respect of the audience for himself and his message.

Whether Paul meant to include the **devout proselytes** of verse 43 in the class of **Men of Israel,** or **ye that fear God,** in verse 16, is not quite clear. However, from the foregoing facts it would seem that they were among the former, and that the special mention made of these **devout proselytes** in verse 43 is intended to indicate that they, like the Jews, had a more profound understanding of the relationship of the Law of Moses to the promised Messiah and consequently grasped more easily and clearly the implications of Paul's message. Further, to have recognized them as **Men of Israel** in his address would have been a distinct compliment to them and no offense to the Jews. if indeed not a compliment to the Jews also,

Second, Paul launches abruptly into his message by (1) sympathetically relating his congregation to the God of Israelitish history, then by identifying himself with all three: **The God of this people Israel chose our fathers** (vs. 17); (2) he makes a patriotic allusion to the Israelitish nation's deliverance from Egyptian bondage under the direct intervention of God; **exalted the people** [delivered and vindicated them] **when they sojourned in the land of Egypt, and with a high arm** [a demonstration of divine power over their enemies] **led them forth out of it** (vs. 17b); (3) in a sweeping statement he covers forty years of wilderness wanderings followed with a reminder of God's patience with, and care over, them: **as a nursing-father bare he them in the wilderness** (vs. 18b); (4) next he summarily reviews God's power and the fulfillment of His promise in destroying the Caananites, after which He fulfilled His promise and **gave them their land for an inheritance for about four hundred and fifty years** (vs. 19); (5) the period of the Judges is briefly cited with the notation of its termination with their illustrious prophet Samuel (vs. 20); (6) God's compliance with their request for a king follows with the coronation of Saul of the tribe of Benjamin whose reign lasted forty years (vs. 21); (7) a delicate reference to Saul's removal follows (vs. 22a), after which Paul arrives at the crux of his message in the introduction of King David of whom God testified: **a man after my heart, who shall do all my will**

[47] Hackett, *op. cit.*, p. 155.

18 And for about the time of forty years as a nursing-father bare he them in the wilderness.
19 And when he had destroyed seven nations in the land of Canaan, he gave *them* their land for an inheritance, for about four hundred and fifty years:
20 and after these things he gave *them* judges until Samuel the prophet.

---

18 **As a nursing-father bare he them** is in place of "suffered he their manners" (KJV). The difference is due to variant readings. The manuscript evidence is not decisive enough to permit certainty as to which is correct. Aleph B D H L P have *etropophorēsen*, "suffered he their manners." A C E have *etrophophorēsen*. This verb means "nourish, bear like a nurse." Neither verb is found elsewhere in the New Testament. The matter is complicated by the fact that both readings are found in the Septuagint of Deuteronomy 1:31, from which Paul quoted. So the textual corruption came very early in the New Testament manuscripts and is probably due to the confusion in the Septuagint. The original Hebrew may mean either "carry" or "endure" and so could be translated by either Greek word.[48] Westcott and Hort, as might be expected, adopt the reading of Aleph B. The Revised Standard Version follows this—"he bore with them"—and thus agrees in thought with the King James Version. Lake and Cadbury think that "nourished" gives the better meaning, and that while *etropophorēsen* "is undoubtedly the right spelling, it is much less certain that 'endured' is the right rendering." [49] And yet that is the rendering they adopted in their translation! The best we can say is that "both here and in Deuteronomy either reading gives excellent sense." [50] That is the judgment of Westcott and Hort in their "Appendix."

19, 20 The **seven nations** are listed in Deuteronomy 7:1—Hittites, Girgashites, Amorites, Canaanites, Perizzites, Hivites, and Jebusites.

The overwhelming evidence of the best manuscripts (Aleph A B C, 33, 81) supports the reading adopted by the Revisers, which places **about four hundred and fifty years** in verse 19 instead of verse 20 (as in KJV). The latter would make the period of the Judges (after Samuel) last about 450 years. But this conflicts seriously with the statement in I Kings 6:1 that the fourth year of Solomon was 480 years after the Exodus. The **four hundred and fifty years** probably cover the 400 years' sojourn, the 40 years in the wilderness, and about ten years spent in the actual conquest of Canaan (see on 7:7). Perhaps they begin with the promise to Abraham that his seed should have the **land for an inheritance.**[51]

20 **Samuel** was commonly regarded as the last of the **judges** and the first **prophet** in the new succession that continued through the rest of the Old Testament period.

(vs. 22b); (8) through the posterity of David, Paul declares that God has fulfilled His age-old promise to Israel, of a Messiah (**a Saviour**) in the person of **Jesus** (vs. 23); (9) this conclusion is then collaborated by John the Baptist's prediction of Christ's coming, his mission of repentance to Israel, and the personal testimony of John to Christ as the Messiah (vss. 23, 24), all facts with which his hearers were familiar. Thus the historical foundation of this sermon is complete.

Third, the apostle proceeds to make his deductions, from these known and acknowledged facts, concerning Christ as the Jews' Messiah and the Saviour of all men.

Paul (1) tightens his psychological grasp upon his audience by a renewed direct address: **Brethren, children of the stock of Abraham, and those among you that fear God** (vs. 26a); (2) he then boldly asserts that Israel has already given birth to the child of her age-old expectations, and that his mission is to announce to them that glorious consummation: **to us is the word of this salvation sent forth** (vs. 26); (3) then anticipating their likely objections to his identification of Jesus Christ with the Messiah, because of the Jews' rejection of Christ at Jerusalem, of which fact they would have had knowledge, Paul proceeds to disqualify the adverse judgment of the Sanhedrin on the grounds (a) that they really did not know Jesus Christ, (b) that they did not understand the real significance of the prophetic

[48] Bruce, *Acts*, p. 263. Lake and Cadbury, however, say: "The Hebrew means to 'carry' rather than to 'endure'" (*Beginnings*, IV, 149).
[49] *Beginnings*, IV, 149.
[50] EGT, II, 292.
[51] So Rackham, *op. cit.*, p. 211.

21 And afterward they asked for a king: and God gave unto them Saul the son of Kish, a man of the tribe of Benjamin, for the space of forty years.
22 And when he had removed him, he raised up David to be their king; to whom also he bare witness and said, I have found David the son of Jesse, a man after my heart, who shall do all my will.
23 Of this man's seed hath God according to promise brought unto Israel a Saviour, Jesus;
24 when John had first preached before his coming the baptism of repentance to all the people of Israel.
25 And as John was fulfilling his course, he said, What suppose ye that I am? I am not *he*. But behold, there cometh one after me the shoes of whose feet I am not worthy to unloose.
26 Brethren, children of the stock of Abraham, and those among you that fear God, to us is the word of this salvation sent forth.

---

21 But instead of a prophet to rule them, the people **asked for a king.** Paul's mention of **Saul . . . of the tribe of Benjamin** doubtless reflects the apostle's pride in his name and ancestry (cf. Phil. 3:5).

For the space of forty years is an item of information not found in the Old Testament. Josephus agrees with this when he writes: "Now Saul, when he had reigned eighteen years while Samuel was alive, and after his death two and twenty, ended his life in this manner."[52] However, in another place he says that Saul retained the government twenty years.[53]

22 Paul emphasized the fact that God **gave** (vs. 21) Saul as king and then **removed** him. The point he is making is that God's choices are conditioned on man's obedience. He had chosen Israel. But if she sinned against Him, He would "remove" her from being His people.

After God had removed Saul, He **raised up** David to the position of king. The **witness** borne to him is a bit unusual. This brief quotation (vs. 22b) is composed of three parts. The first is from Psalm 89:20 (LXX, 88:21); the second, from I Samuel 13:14; the third, from Isaiah 44:28. The first two are combined in I Clement 18:1. Furthermore Acts and I Clement both have *andra* instead of the Septuagint reading, *anthrōpon*. This suggests strongly that Clement knew and used Acts.[54] I Clement is usually dated about A.D. 96.

23 After this brief historical introduction Paul comes to the heart of his message: **A Saviour, Jesus.** Here He is presented as of the **seed** of David, a Saviour-King.

24 Verses 24–31 are strikingly similar in content to 10:36–43. This was the early Kerygma of the apostles.

This verse reads literally: "When John had proclaimed [*prokēryxanto*, found only here in the New Testament] before the face of His entrance a baptism of repentance to all the people of Israel." **Coming** *(eisodou)* refers to Jesus' "entrance" upon His public ministry.

---

writing which they regularly read, (c) that they actually fulfilled those prophecies concerning Christ by their official condemnation of him, (d) that they had dishonestly and unjustly rendered their judgment in demanding the death sentence for Christ when **they found no cause of death in him** (vss. 28, 28).

Next (4) Paul proceeds to declare the culminating fact of Christianity that **God raised him from the dead** (vs. 30a), and he (5) supports this claim by the fact of His post-resurrection appearances to His disciples who, including the speaker, **are now his witnesses unto the people** (vs. 31b). How well Paul has grasped the significance of Christ's words in Acts 1:8! Paul (6) personally applies the benefits of Christ's resurrection from the dead to his hearers (vs. 33) and then supports the resurrection of Christ by reference to the Psalms of David wherein His eternal victory over death is clearly predicted (vss. 34–37).

Fourth, Paul offers the practical benefits of Christ's atoning death and resurrection to his hearers as (1) remission of sins (vs. 38b); (2) justification by faith (vs. 39a); and (3) superiority of Christian grace to the Mosaic Law in doing for man what the Law could never do (vs. 39b).

Fifth, while Paul's sermon differs from

[52] *Ant.* VI, 14, 9. [53] *Ant.* X, 8, 4. [54] Cf. *Beginnings*, IV, 152.

27 For they that dwell in Jerusalem, and their rulers, because they knew him not, nor the
voices of the prophets which are read every sabbath, fulfilled *them* by condemning *him*.
28 And though they found no cause of death *in him*, yet asked they of Pilate that he should
be slain.
29 And when they had fulfilled all things that were written of him, they took him down
from the tree, and laid him in a tomb.
30 But God raised him from the dead:
31 and he was seen for many days of them that came up with him from Galilee to Jerusalem,
who are now his witnesses unto the people.
32 And we bring you good tidings of the promise made unto the fathers,
33 that God hath fulfilled the same unto our children, in that he raised up Jesus; as also
it is written in the second psalm, Thou art my Son, this day have I begotten thee.

27–29 The exact text of these verses is somewhat uncertain. Rackham remarks: "This brings the apostle to the most difficult part of his message, and the difficulty is reflected in the broken and uncertain character of the text." [55] But the English versions give the sense satisfactorily.

30 The resurrection of Jesus appears here again as a paramount emphasis in early apostolic preaching.

31 The post-resurrection appearances were all made to disciples of Jesus, who **came up with him from Galilee to Jerusalem.**

33 **Unto our children** *(tois teknois hēmōn)* has the overwhelming support of the earliest manuscripts (Aleph A B C D), but does not make good sense. The King James rendering, "unto us their children," is based on the later manuscripts, but much easier to understand. Scholars have labored long over the difficulty. Westcott and Hort would retain *hēmin*, "to us," alone.[56] On the other hand, Rackham writes: "Perhaps the original reading was simply *to the children* [of promise] which the copyists did not understand and tried to correct." [57] Lake and Cadbury conclude: "The evidence for this reading [*tois teknois hēmōn*] is overwhelming . . . , yet all the editors rightly agree that it is impossible and that it is a primitive corruption of a text, which, however it is read, meant 'to us, their children.'" [58] Thus the textual critics have returned to the thought, though not necessarily the textual basis, of the King James rendering (cf. "to us their children," RSV).

Does raised up refer to Jesus' resurrection or to His incarnation? Hackett agrees with Luther, Meyer, and others in favoring the former.[59] Calvin, Bengel, Olshausen, and others [60] lean to the latter. Rackham makes the reference apply to both.[61] Bruce writes: "The promise of ver. 23, the fulfilment of which is here described, has to do with the sending of Messiah, not His resurrection (for which cf. ver. 34)." [62] Lake and Cadbury refer it to "the whole career of Jesus." [63]

The quotation in the last part of this verse is from Psalm 2:7. This Psalm was interpreted Messianically by the early rabbis.

Peter's and Stephen's in his appeal to David as against their appeal to Moses for support, it does nevertheless correspond with their addresses in his conclusion. This conclusion consists of (1) a solemn warning against his hearers suffering the fate of their forefathers who rejected the voice of God in the wilderness (vss. 40, 41a); (2) a reference to the exhibition of divine power designed to produce their salvation (vs. 41b).

In this, Paul's first recorded sermon, is distinctly advanced his great doctrine of "justification by faith," as opposed to justification by the works of the Law (vs. 39), a doctrine the discovery of which spiritually awakened the slumbering soul of a German monk nearly fifteen centuries later and produced the history-changing Protestant Reformation of A.D. 1517. Further this sermon reveals that the people, to whom he later wrote the Galatian epistle on this subject of justification, had already been enlightened (see Gal. 2:16; 3:1–15). Some doctrines that emerge from this sermon are divine providence, divine omnipotence, divine judgment, repentance, divine revela-

[55] *Op. cit.*, p. 24. [56] "Appendix," p. 95. [57] *Op. cit.*, p. 215, n. 9.
[58] *Beginnings*, IV, 154. [59] Hackett, *op. cit.*, p. 158. [60] E.g., Knowling, EGT, II, 295 f.
[61] *Op. cit.*, pp. 215 f. [62] *Acts*, p. 269. [63] *Beginnings*, IV, 154 f.

34 And as concerning that he raised him up from the dead, now no more to return to corruption, he hath spoken on this wise, I will give you the holy and sure *blessings* of David.
35 Because he saith also in another *psalm*, Thou wilt not give thy Holy One to see corruption.
36 For David, after he had in his own generation served the counsel of God, fell asleep, and was laid unto his fathers, and saw corruption:
37 but he whom God raised up saw no corruption.
38 Be it known unto you therefore, brethren, that through this man is proclaimed unto you remission of sins:
39 and by him every one that believeth is justified from all things, from which ye could not be justified by the law of Moses.
40 Beware therefore, lest that come upon *you* which is spoken in the prophets:
41 Behold, ye despisers, and wonder, and perish;
For I work a work in your days,
A work which ye shall in no wise believe, if one declare it unto you.
42 And as they went out, they besought that these words might be spoken to them the next sabbath.
43 Now when the synagogue broke up, many of the Jews and of the devout proselytes followed Paul and Barnabas; who, speaking to them, urged them to continue in the grace of God.

---

34 The quotation in this verse is from Isaiah 55:3. The Hebrew reads, "I will give you the sure mercies of David," and the King James Version reproduces that here. But the Greek text quotes the Septuagint: "[I will give] to you . . . the holy things of David, the sure things." Lake and Cadbury observe: "It is important to notice that the whole argument is based on the LXX, and disappears if the speech be not in Greek." [64]

35 The quotation is from Psalm 16:10.

36 The argument is similar to that in Peter's Pentecost address (2:29–32). David died and remained dead; Jesus was raised from the dead.

37 Jesus alone is the fulfilment of the prophecy quoted in verse 35.

38 This is the reiterated theme of apostolic preaching: **remission of sins** only **through this man,** Jesus.

39 Here Paul asserts boldly his doctrine of justification by faith alone, apart from the works of the Law. It is what he later wrote in his epistle to these same Galatians.

41 The message closes appropriately with a word of warning, contained in a quotation from **the prophets** (The Book of the Twelve Prophets), specifically from Habakkuk 1:5.

On the general character of this first recorded sermon by Paul, Bruce says: "It forms a bridge between the primitive preaching of the early chapters of Acts and the mature doctrine of the Epistles." [65]

42 **Next** is *metaxy*, the regular meaning of which is "between." Here alone in the New Testament it means "next," but this usage is common in Josephus and is also found in the Epistle of Barnabas and I Clement. [66]

43 The phrase **devout proselytes** *(sebomenōn prosēlyton)* is found only here. It evidently differs from "God-fearers," in that the ones mentioned here were full proselytes.

---

tion, the death of Christ, the resurrection of Christ, the appearances of Christ, the divine sonship of Christ, and forgiveness of sins. Interestingly, the doctrine of baptism is totally absent, even though there were converts (vss. 48, 52).

The spiritual interest and desire awakened in the minds of Jew and Gentile alike by Paul's sermon is evident; **and as they went out, they** [both Jews and Gentile proselytes] **besought that these words might be spoken to them the next sabbath** (vs. 42). The apostles, taking advantage of their awakened souls, further instructed and encouraged these new believers **to continue in the grace of God** (vs. 43).

[64] *Ibid.*, p. 156.
[65] *Acts*, p. 272.
[66] *Beginnings*, IV, 158.

44 And the next sabbath almost the whole city was gathered together to hear the word of God.

45 But when the Jews saw the multitudes, they were filled with jealousy, and contradicted the things which were spoken by Paul, and blasphemed.

46 And Paul and Barnabas spake out boldly, and said, It was necessary that the word of God should first be spoken to you. Seeing ye thrust it from you, and judge yourselves unworthy of eternal life, lo, we turn to the Gentiles.

---

44 **Next** is here a different word from that in verse 42. Aleph B C D have *erchomenōi*, "coming," while A E have *echomenōi*, "next." This is an interesting example of a slight variation in reading which does not affect the sense of the passage. *Schedon*, **almost**, is found only here, in 19:26, and in Hebrews 9:22.

45 **Blasphemed** is from the Greek *blasphēmeō*, which means "to speak lightly or profanely of sacred things, to speak impiously of God." When the object is human beings, as frequently in the New Testament, it means, "to revile, rail at, slander." The usage in 26:11 would perhaps indicate that these Jews were blaspheming God rather than slandering Paul.

46 **Spake out boldly**, *parrēsiasamenoi*, is used seven times in Acts and twice by Paul. **It was necessary** [in the divine will] **that the word of God should first be spoken to you.** This is in line with Paul's later declaration in Romans 1:16.

IV. THE MISSION INTERRUPTED (13:44–52)

As at Paphos, so at Antioch, the enemy would not allow his domain to be invaded and his subjects taken captive by the Gospel of Christ without violent opposition. At Antioch, as usual in the ministry of Paul, the Jews were the greatest opponents of the Gospel of Christ.

A. The Cause of the Interruption (13:44, 45)

But when the Jews saw the multitudes, they were filled with jealousy (vs. 45a). The broadcasting of Paul's sermon throughout the week by those who had heard him, especially the God-fearers, and those who were spiritually awakened, resulted in an assemblage of **almost the whole city** on the following sabbath **to hear the word of God** (vs. 44).

The resultant jealousy and opposition of the Jews likely arose from two causes: *first*, out of their envy at seeing the God-fearing Gentiles, whom they had hoped to convert to Judaism, drawn away to Christianity; and *second*, from their fear that the teachings of the apostles would undermine and destroy the whole structure of Judaism, and thus the new faith would supersede that system, as indeed Paul had already intimated in his first sermon (vss. 27–31). The form of their opposition is said to be "contradiction" and "blasphemy." The former probably consisted of historical and theological arguments, and the latter of insinuations and charges against the person and character of Christ, based on reports they had acquired from Jerusalem.

B. The Nature of the Interruption (13:46–51)

Seeing ye thrust it from you [the word of God], **and judge yourselves unworthy of eternal life, lo, we turn to the Gentiles** (vs. 46b). In verse 46 Paul clearly indicates that it is a part of his missionary strategy to preach the Gospel first to the Jews, using the synagogue as a door of entrance to the Gentile world (see Rom. 1:14–16). Herein Paul reveals what so many Bible scholars until today have failed to see: namely, that the Jews were not a people chosen especially of God unto salvation, to the exclusion of the Gentiles, but rather they were chosen and prepared to become a missionary nation to proclaim the Gospel of God to all people of the earth. This is the thesis of Paul in his Roman letter where in chapter nine he presents God's election of Israel as a missionary people, in chapter ten His rejection of Israel from this office and function because of their rejection of Christ and His Gospel (thus leaving them without a message), and in chapter eleven, His partial restoration of Israel because of their acceptance of Christ. Nowhere in His word has God revealed an election of the Jews, as a nation, to salvation,

47 For so hath the Lord commanded us, *saying*,
I have set thee for a light of the Gentiles,
That thou shouldest be for salvation unto the uttermost part of the earth.
48 And as the Gentiles heard this, they were glad, and glorified the word of God: and as
many as were ordained to eternal life believed.
49 And the word of the Lord was spread abroad throughout all the region.
50 But the Jews urged on the devout women of honorable estate, and the chief men of the
city, and stirred up a persecution against Paul and Barnabas, and cast them out of their
borders.

---

47 In Isaiah 49:6 these words are addressed to Israel as the servant of the Lord. In Luke 2:32 they are applied to Jesus. Here Paul claims them for himself as **a light for the Gentiles.** A striking parallel is found in Jesus' two statements, "I am the light of the world" (John 8:12) and "Ye are the light of the world" (Matt. 5:14).

48 **As many as were ordained to eternal life believed.** The verb *tasso* is used in the papyri in the sense of "put in its place, appoint, enrol." [67] But it also has the meaning "arrange." [68] Adam Clarke points out the fact that there is no suggestion here of *fore*ordination nor of *pre*destination. He says that the verb may be taken "as implying the *disposition* or *readiness of mind*" of those who believed; "they therefore in this good *state* and *order* of mind, believed." [69]

50 *Parōtrynan*, **urged on,** is found only here in the New Testament. In regard to the **devout women** Ramsay says: "The influence attributed to the women at Antioch, *v*. 50, is in perfect accord with the manners of the country. In Athens or in an Ionian city, it would have been impossible." [70] *Euschēmon*, **of honorable estate,** may mean "of position" or "rich." [71] **Chief men** is literally "the first ones" *(tous prōtous)*; that is, the magistrates. Throughout Acts, Luke portrays the Roman officials as protecting rather than persecuting the Christians. The only exceptions were when they were incited to action, usually by the Jews, as here. *Epēgeiran*, **stirred up,** is found in the New Testament only here and in 14:2. It means "to rouse up, excite." **Borders** is "coasts" in the King James Version. But the latter is now used for the margin of a sea. The Greek *horion* means "boundary." Ramsay thinks the missionaries' stay at Antioch lasted at least two to six months.[72]

---

to the exclusion of the Gentiles, nor their rejection, as a nation, from salvation. Salvation is always and everywhere a matter of the "personal" acceptance of God's offered mercy in Christ.

Paul's declaration, **lo, we turn to the Gentiles** (vs. 46b), does not close the door of hope to the Jews, nor does it indicate that he will not hereafter preach to the Jews. It is to be understood that since the Jews at Antioch have rejected the Gospel and thus "judged themselves" (not "are judged") **unworthy of eternal life,** the apostles will henceforth address themselves to the Gentiles at Antioch. This decision the apostles justify by reference to their own prophet who foresaw the universal implications of the great plan of redemption (cf. Isa. 49:6 and Acts 2:39; see also Acts 18:6 and 28:28).

The Gentiles having grasped the universal implications of Paul's words greatly rejoiced and **glorified the word of God** (vs. 48a).

Luke's statement, **and as many as were ordained to eternal life believed,** receives a most illuminating treatment by Dummelow:

> This expresses the Pauline and Apostolic doctrine of predestination, according to which God desires the salvation of all men (I Tim. 2:4; 4:10, etc.), but insomuch as He foresees that some (in the exercise of their free will) will actually repent and believe, while others will refuse to do so, He ordains the former to eternal life, and the latter to eternal death (Rom. 8: 28–30, etc.)[h]

What is clear from this passage and its setting, and is consistent with the whole plan of divine redemption, is that while God ordains unto eternal life all that will believe, and to eternal death all that do not believe,

[67] VGT, p. 626. [68] *Ibid.* [69] *Op. cit.*, I, 790.
[70] *St. Paul the Traveller*, p. 102. [71] *Beginnings*, IV, 160. [72] *St. Paul the Traveller*, p. 105.

[h] *Ibid.*, p. 836.

51 But they shook off the dust of their feet against them, and came unto Iconium.
52 And the disciples were filled with joy and with the Holy Spirit.

---

51 **Iconium** is "the modern Konia, always important because it is at the junction of several roads." [73] In 25 B.C. it became a part of the newly formed Roman province of Galatia.

52 Those are **filled with joy** who are also **filled with the Holy Spirit.** The deepest joy comes only in the consciousness of His abiding presence. He it is who enables one to rejoice even in times of trouble.

---

it must be observed that God neither ordains the "act of believing" nor the "act of unbelief." These are acts of man's intelligent moral volition, for the exercise of which he bears full moral responsibility (see John 3:16-21 and 3:36).

When it is understood that the words of verse 44, **almost the whole city was gathered together,** would imply not just the town residents but the country as well, or the regions of Pisidia (Clarke), then Luke's statement of verse 49 takes on meaning: **And the word of the Lord was spread abroad throughout all the region.** Thus the apostles' wisdom is justified in their selection of Antioch as their first strategic Galatian center from which to evangelize.

The **devout women of honorable estate** affected by the Jewish propaganda against the apostles were likely the wives of prominent Gentile citizens, if not government officers, who had become proselytes to the Jewish faith. These women were now used by these Jews to influence their husbands, the chief men of the city, to take action against Paul and Barnabas by arresting, roughly treating, and expelling them from Antioch and Pisidia. How like the tactice of the Sanhedrin in handling the case of Jesus, and later those against Paul at Jerusalem upon his arrest.

The action of Paul and Barnabas, upon leaving Antioch, when **they shook off the dust of their feet against them** (vs. 51), was well understood by the Jews who regarded it as a curse pronounced upon their enemies. When traveling in heathen lands outside of Canaan, the Jews paused at the borders and shook the contaminated dust from their feet and garments before re-entering their sacred land, lest they defile it. Thus, this act of the apostles signified that the Jews of Antioch had taken a curse upon themselves in rejecting the Gospel and its messengers (see Matt. 10:14; Mark 6:11; Luke 9:5; and Acts 18:6).

C. The Results of the Interruption (13:52)

And the disciples were filled with joy and with the Holy Spirit. Again the irony of the situation turns out to the glory of God and the benefit of His disciples. These disciples, like those at Thessalonica, "received the word in much affliction," but "with joy of the Holy Spirit" (I Thess. 1:6b). Such discipleship bids fair for the success of the Church in any situation.

The ultimate success of this initial invasion of Antioch with the Gospel is in evidence at a later date. Says Finegan:

> Also there was a Christian basilica at Antioch which was more than 200 feet long, and which dates, according to an inscription, in the time of Optimus, who was bishop of Antioch in the last quarter of the fourth century.[i]

[73] *Beginnings*, IV, 160.

[i] Finegan, *op. cit.*, p. 262.

CHAPTER XIV

And it came to pass in Iconium that they entered together into the synagogue of the Jews, and so spake that a great multitude both of Jews and of Greeks believed.

2 But the Jews that were disobedient stirred up the souls of the Gentiles, and made them evil affected against the brethren.

EXEGESIS

1 **Together** is better rendered "after the same manner," or "in the same way" *(kata to auto);* that is, as at Pisidian Antioch. Ramsay translates it: "after the same fashion." [1]

2 **The Jews that were disobedient** can be translated "the unbelieving Jews" (KJV, RSV). *Apeitheō* is properly "to disobey, be disobedient." It is the negative of *peithō*, "persuade." In the King James Version it is taken about an equal number of times as "disbelieve" (nine times) and "disobey" (seven times). The contrast with **believe** (vs. 1) would favor "unbelieving" here. Bruce appropriately observes: "Unbelief and disobedience are both involved in the rejection of the Gospel." [2] **Made them evil affected** is *ekakōsan*, found five times in Acts and in I Peter 3:13. It means "to ill-treat, afflict, distress." Abbott-Smith would here translate it "embitter." [3] Lake and Cadbury render it "irritated." [4] It has this meaning in Josephus and the papyri.[5]

EXPOSITION

THE CHURCH'S FIRST GENTILE MISSIONARY CAMPAIGN (cont'd)

- V. The Mission Resumed, Acts 14:1-7.
  - A. The Methods Employed, vss. 1-3a.
  - B. The Results Achieved, vss. 3b-7.
- VI. The Apostles Idolized, Acts 14:8-20.
  - A. The Occasion of Idolization, vss. 8-10.
  - B. The Attempt at Idolization, vss. 11-13.
  - C. The Renunciation of Idolization, vss. 14-20.
- VII. The Christians Revisited, Acts 14:21-25.
- VIII. The Results Reported, Acts 14:26-28.

V. THE MISSION RESUMED (14:1-7)

Feeling that their work in Antioch was completed and nothing daunted by their persecution, Paul and Barnabas followed the injunctions of the Lord (Matt. 10:23) and moved on to the next important city of Iconium. This distance of 60 miles southeastward they traversed by the Roman highway that followed the ancient Alexandrian route eastward to a verdant and fruitful plateau watered by Pisidian mountain streams. Here Iconium, a flourishing city of strategic importance located at a crossroads in Pisidia and honored with the title Caludiconium but later named a Roman colony by Hadrian, met the vision and challenged the spirits of these Christian ambassadors. A modern Turkish city of 47,000 people, bearing the name of Konia, is located at the site of ancient Iconium.

A. The Methods Employed (14:1-3a)

Luke employs three phrases that subtly suggest the successful methods of the apostles at Iconium: namely, **entered together into the synagogue ... so spake ... Long time therefore they tarried there speaking boldly in the Lord** (vss. 1, 3a). Here, as always, the missionaries singled out the little synagogue for the initiation of the Gospel among the Iconians. Experience gained and success attained at Antioch afforded them definite advantages here.

[1] *St. Paul the Traveller*, p. 107. [2] *Acts*, p. 277. [3] *Op. cit.*, p. 227.
[4] *Beginnings*, IV, 161. [5] *Ibid.*

3 Long time therefore they tarried *there* speaking boldly in the Lord, who bare witness unto the word of his grace, granting signs and wonders to done by their hands.

4 But the multitude of the city was divided; and part held with the Jews, and part with the apostles.

5 And when there was made an onset both of the Gentiles and of the Jews with their rulers, to treat them shamefully and to stone them,

---

3 Some scholars have claimed to find a contradiction between this and the preceding verse. If opposition arose, how can it be true that **long time therefore they tarried there**? But there is certainly no difficulty in assuming that the Jewish opposition was not sufficient to compel the missionaries to leave town until the Gentiles joined in (vs. 5).

4 It is noticeable that Barnabas is here included as one of **the apostles.** He probably met the requirement of having seen Jesus after His resurrection (cf. 1:22).

5 *Hormē*, **onset,** is found elsewhere in the New Testament only in James 3:4, where it means "a violent movement, impulse." [6] But here it probably means "a hostile movement, assault." [7] The position of **their rulers,** in close proximity to **the Jews** suggests that it was the leaders either of the Jews or **of the Gentiles and of the Jews** together. The latter is more probable. **To treat . . . shamefully** is *hybrisai*, which means "to outrage, insult, treat insolently." [8]

The words **so spake** characterize the ministry of Paul and Barnabas as probably tactful in approach, understanding of the constituency and mental attitudes of their audiences, but with such faith and holy boldness as enabled the Spirit of God to be demonstrated in mighty power (cf. I Thess. 1–5). Their recent success at Antioch revealed its influence on the beginning of their ministry at Iconium. Experience may serve to either strengthen or weaken the ministry of God's servants, depending on the manner in which it is used.

Luke's expression, **Long time therefore they tarried there speaking boldly in the Lord** (vs. 3a), can only be properly understood in the light of the persecution directed against Paul and Barnabas at Iconium. The first persecution likely consisted in a legal attempt of the Jews to have the apostles officially expelled. This would appear to be the sense of the words, **But the Jews . . . stirred up the souls of the Gentiles** [likely the Roman officials, as they are not called Greeks], **and made them evil affected against the brethren** (vs. 2). Whether considered as disturbers of the peace, or slanderously charged, the attempt apparently failed. However, it evidently required time among this strange people for the apostles to "live down" the false accusations and prejudices and prove to the people the truth of the Gospel. As when God sought to deliver Israel from Egypt by the hand of Moses, He demonstrated His power as superior to that of the Egyptian magicians and deities, so God here manifested Himself through Paul and Barnabas in **signs and wonders . . . done by their hands** (vs. 3b). Thus their ministry of the Word, their perseverance, and God's manifest power combined to accomplish success in Iconium.

B. The Results Achieved (14:3b–7)

Luke's statement in verse one, **that a great multitude both of Jews and of Greeks believed** (Jews and Greek God-fearers or proselytes to the Jewish faith), indicates the initial success of the gospel ministry in Iconium.

However, the great success of their ministry had the further effect of precipitating a second persecution in which **the city was divided; and part held with the Jews, and part with the apostles** (vs. 4). Doubtless it was the sword of truth that sharply divided the believing from the unbelieving (Matt. 10:34–36), but it was the Jews who instigated the actual attack against the apostles, of which Luke says: **there was made an onset both of the Gentiles and of the Jews with their rulers, to treat them shamefully and to stone them** (vs. 5). Legal procedure having evidently failed in the first attempt (vs. 2), the Jews finally resorted to mob violence, as at Thessalonica (see Acts 17:5), to rid themselves of these emissaries of the Gospel of

[6] Abbott-Smith, *op. cit.*, p. 323. [7] *Ibid.* [8] *Ibid.*, p. 453.

6 they became aware of it, and fled unto the cities of Lycaonia, Lystra and Derbe, and the region round about:
7 and there they preached the gospel.
8 And at Lystra there sat a certain man, impotent in his feet, a cripple from his mother's womb, who never had walked.

---

6 **Fled** is the compound *katapheugō*, found only here and in Hebrews 6:18. It means "flee for refuge."

The language of this verse, identifying **Lystra and Derbe** as **cities of Lycaonia,** implies definitely that Iconium belonged to Phrygia, not Lycaonia, at this time. Regarding the description here, Ramsay writes: "It was accurate at the period when Paul visited Lycaonia; . . . it was accurate at no other time except between 37 and 72 A.D." [9] Before and after that Iconium was Lycaonian. This is one of the many evidences of Luke's exact accuracy as a reliable historian.

The site of **Lystra** was identified by Sterrett in 1885, when he found an inscription which indicated that it had been made a Roman colony by Augustus (A.D. 6). Coins found there since then have confirmed the inscription. The site of **Derbe** is "not yet completely identified," [10] though its general location is fairly certain.

7 **They preached the gospel** is the strong periphrastic construction, "they were preaching the gospel" *(euangelizomenoi ēsan)*. This implies continued evangelization over a period of time. Ramsay renders it: "They were engaged in preaching the gospel." [11]

8 **Impotent** is *adynatos*. Here alone it means physically "powerless." [12] In Romans 15:1 it means "weak." In the other eight places it occurs in the New Testament, it is used of things and means "impossible."

That the healing was a supernatural miracle is underscored by three items here: **impotent in his feet, a cripple from his mother's womb, who never had walked.** The middle phrase occurs in 3:2. The parallels between the two healings have led some scholars to claim that they are two accounts of the same miracle. But the differences equal the similarities. The man at the Beautiful Gate was a beggar, asking for alms. Here nothing is said of that. In the earlier miracle there is no mention of the man's faith, while here it is explicitly stated. Peter is described as taking the man by the hand and raising him to his feet, but Paul simply spoke to this man. The main things in common in the two accounts are the phrase noted above, the word **atenisas,** and the fact that both men leaped and walked.

Christ. Seeing that every principle of justice was cast to the wind by their enemies, so that they could accomplish nothing further under the circumstances and that the new believers would be safer for their absence, the apostles decided, as in like circumstances at Thessalonica (Acts 17:9, 10), to evade further trouble by departing to **the cities of Lycaonia, Lystra and Derbe, and the region round about:** [where] **they preached the gospel** (vss. 6b, 7).

Three items of interest accompany the introduction of the Gospel at Iconium. In the *first* place, it is here that Paul and Barnabas are first called "apostles" by Luke, though they were evidently ordained or consecrated to that office at Antioch of Syria (Acts 13:1–3). The *second* item concerns a legend recorded by Dummelow:

> The curious second-century romance, 'The Acts of Paul and Thecla,' gives many additional particulars of St. Paul's proceedings at Iconium, some of which, perhaps are authentic. Thecla, who belonged to one of the chief families of Iconium, overheard from a window the preaching of the apostle. She was at that time engaged to a young man named Thamyris, but on hearing St. Paul's words, she became so enamoured of virginity that she broke off her engagement. For this interference with family life, and for impiety, St. Paul was scourged and expelled from the city, and Thecla was condemned to be burnt alive. A fall of rain extinguished the fire, and she escaped and followed Paul to Antioch. Here again she was persecuted, but was rescued by Tryphaena, a lady of great influence. The presbyter who composed this romance (though it was probably founded on a fact) was deposed from his office.[a]

The *third* item of interest associated with Iconium is a famous description of Paul, as contained in the apocryphal *Acts of Paul*

[9] *St. Paul the Traveller*, pp. 110 f. [10] *Beginnings*, IV, 163. [11] *St. Paul the Traveller*, p. 110.
[12] Hobart gives numerous examples of its medical use in this sense (*op. cit.*, p. 46).

[a] Dummelow, *op. cit.*, p. 836.

9 The same heard Paul speaking: who, fastening his eyes upon him, and seeing that he had faith to be made whole,

10 said with a loud voice, Stand upright on thy feet. And he leaped up and walked.

9 The impotent man **heard Paul speaking.** "Listened to Paul speaking" (RSV) perhaps brings out better the force of the imperfect, *ēkouen*.[13] As a good listener he had developed faith. **Fastening his eyes** *(atenisas)* on the man, Paul perceived that he had **faith to be made whole** *(pistin ton sōthēnai)*. *Sōzō* occurs some 111 times in the New Testament. Ninety-four of those times it is translated "save." That is its usual meaning in the epistles. So Ramsay translates the phrase here "the faith that belongs to salvation." [14] While recognizing value in Ramsay's point of view, Bruce says: "Primarily, *sōthēnai* here means 'to be healed' in the bodily sense." [15]

10 **Upright** is *orthos*, "straight," found only here and in Hebrews 12:13 (in a quotation from the Septuagint). **Leaped up** is the verb *hallomai*. It is used elsewhere in the New Testament only in John 4:14 (of water "springing up" unto eternal life). The aorist of this verb and the imperfect "walked" *(periepatei)* suggest that he "jumped up" immediately and "began to walk" or "went on walking."

and recorded by Finegan. The account reads as follows:

> A man of little stature, thin-haired upon the head, crooked in the legs, of good state of body, with eyebrows joining, and nose somewhat hooked, full of grace; for some times he appeared like a man, and sometimes he had the face of an angel.[b]

VI. THE APOSTLES IDOLIZED (14:8–20)

To understand the attempted worship of the apostles at Lystra it is necessary to understand, at least in a measure, these Lycaonian peoples of **Lystra and Derbe, and the region round about** (vs. 6b).

The distance from Iconium to Lystra was eighteen miles in a south-southwestward direction, and the elevation of this city was approximately 3,800 feet. The modern city of this site is likely Zolders. Both Lystra and Derbe were in the Lycaonian region, and at the time of the apostles' visit, the peoples spoke the Lycaonian vernacular (Acts 14:11), though Latin was the official language. Lystra, like Antioch, was a Roman colony. Derbe was located some twenty miles southeast of Lystra and is supposed to be represented by the modern village of Zosta or Losta.

No mention is made of a synagogue here, and it is apparent that the inhabitants were largely without Judaistic influence. They were a grossly superstitious heathen people who had descended from the Gauls, who in turn had settled there in the third century B.C. They were characterized (if we are to judge from Paul's letter to the Galatians) by mental alertness, generosity, impressibility, impulsiveness, inconstancy, vehemence, treacherousness, quarrelsomeness, discouragement, extreme and gross superstition (see Gal. 1:6; 4:8; 5:15; Acts 14:11, 12). It is noteworthy that of the fifteen works of the flesh listed in Galatians 5:20, 21, five are sins of strife. Such were the people to whom the apostles preached the Gospel at Lystra and Derbe (cf. Acts 5:42; 13:32: 14:15).

A. The Occasion of the Idolization (14:8–10)

And at Lystra there sat a certain man, impotent in his feet, a cripple from his mother's womb, who never had walked . . . And he leaped up and walked (vss. 8, 10b).

How similar is this incident to the healing of the cripple at the Gate Beautiful in Acts 3:1–10! Here sat, or probably better sprawled a pitiable wretch of humanity who had likely been born with clubfeet that were totally useless for locomotion, a familiar daily spectacle to the citizens of the city, an object of charity to whom they tossed an occasional alms. As is common among such primitive pagans, his deformity was likely regarded as a curse of the gods or fate, for some sin

[13] Found in B C P. The aorist, *ēkousen*, is the reading of Aleph A D E H L. Most of the editors—Tischendorff is an exception—prefer the former.
[14] *St. Paul the Traveller*, p. 114.
[15] *Acts*, p. 280.
[b] Finegan, *op. cit.*, p. 263.

11 And when the multitudes saw what Paul had done, they lifted up their voice, saying in the speech of Lycaonia, The gods are come down to us in the likeness of men.
12 And they called Barnabas, Jupiter; and Paul, Mercury, because he was the chief speaker.

---

11 Probably these people of Lystra could speak Greek. But when they became excited it was only natural that they should revert to their mother tongue. Of the **speech of Lycaonia** nothing further is known. It is eivdently mentioned here, as Chrysostom noted long ago, to explain why the apostles did not sooner recognize what was taking place.

12 Ramsay says the reason the people **called Barnabas, Jupiter; and Paul, Mercury** was that "the Oriental mind considers the leader to be the person who sits still and does nothing, while his subordinates speak and work for him." [16] Hence in Oriental religions "the chief god sits apart from the world, communicating with it through his messenger and subordinate. The more statuesque figure of Barnabas was therefore taken by the Orientals as the chief god, and the active orator, Paul, as his messenger." [17] In the neighborhood of Lystra two Greek inscriptions have been found, one of which mentions priests of Zeus, and the other of which is on a statue of Hermes with a sundial dedicated to Zeus.[18]

---

committed by his ancestry, a fatalistic view (Karma) imbibed also by some of the Jews (see John 9:1–3) and refuted by the experiences and faith of Job. How utterly helpless is paganism to alleviate the sufferings and elevate the status of unfortunate humanity! But what an opportunity and challenge was afforded the Christian apostles to demonstrate to this pagan community the power of the God of Christianity!

What this cripple **heard Paul speaking** we are not told. Possibly he related an incident of healing from the ministry of Christ, or possibly the very incident of the healing of the cripple at the Gate Beautiful. In any event what he heard awakened faith within him (see Rom. 10:14–17), a fact Paul was quick to detect: **seeing that he had faith to be made whole** (vs. 9b). A twofold human assistance was afforded his faith. The first was the electrifying eye contact through which the apostle radiated the faith of his own living soul to the dormant soul of the cripple, thereby awakening and inspiring him to life and hope. The second consisted in the apostle's authoritative command, most probably given in the name of the Lord Jesus, when he **said with a loud voice, Stand upright on thy feet** (vs. 10a). In the first, "faith begets faith," while in the second, "authority begets action." God's living messengers are always animating, and his authoritative commands are always action-producing. The full evidence of his miraculous healing is seen in the fact that **he leaped up and walked** (vs. 10b). His was not a psychological superimposed benefit by a super-psychic healer giving him temporary relief, only to slump back into a deeper despair after the excitement subsided and the human inspiration had been removed; but now, restored, he proceeded on a normal course of life, as suggested by the word **walked.** The word **leaped** may suggest a natural and joyful emotional reaction to the sudden realization of his having been made whole, as well as prompt obedience to Paul's command, but the word **walked** suggests the permanence of his cure. Thus God selected for the demonstration of His power before these pagans a hopeless, organically disordered victim which no power or trick of magic or super-psychic influence could change, but which His power could make every whit whole.

B. The Attempt At Idolization (14:11–13)

And the priest of Jupiter whose temple was before the city, brought oxen and garlands unto the gates, and would have done sacrifice with the multitudes (vs. 13).

So profoundly overcome by the evident miracle of divine healing were these impressionable peoples that with one voice they gave expression in their Lycaonian vernacular to their natural, pagan, religious concepts: **The gods are come down to us in the likeness of men** (vs. 11b). Nor was this anthropomorphic idea of the pagan divinities

[16] *St. Paul the Traveller*, p. 84. [17] *Ibid.*, pp. 84 f. [18] *Beginnings*, IV, 164.

13 And the priest of Jupiter whose *temple* was before the city, brought oxen and garlands unto the gates, and would have done sacrifice with the multitudes.

14 But when the apostles, Barnabas and Paul, heard of it, they rent their garments, and sprang forth among the multitude, crying out

---

13 Though the word **temple** is not in the original, most scholars agree that it should be supplied. That **oxen,** or bulls *(taurous)*, were sacrified to Zeus and Mercury is stated in the contemporary literature, as also that **garlands,**[19] or woolen wreaths, were put on the sacrificial victims.[20] It is not indicated whether **the gates** *(polōnas)* were those of the city, of the temple, or of the house where the apostles were staying.

14 Some think that **sprang forth** *(exepēdēsan,*[21] found only here in the New Testament) suggests that the sacrifices were brought to the gateway of the home where **Barnabas and Paul** were lodging. On the other hand, Knowling says: "But the verb may mean that they ran hastily out of the city to the temple, and there mingled with the crowd." [22] Lake and Cadbury think they "rushed from the gate into the crowd, which was between the gate and the temple." [23]

---

new to the Lycaonians. It was commonly believed that the gods visited men in human form. In part, the idea may have been a corrupt borrowing by the pagans from Jewish history and theology, taken from such accounts as the visit of the angels to Abraham. In the main, it probably reflected the disposition of the pagan mind to conceive of the gods as being human, with a view to attaining a sense of kinship with them. One legend has it that Jupiter and Mercury visited Baucis and Philemon, virtuous peasants in the neighboring province of Phrygia.

It appears from Luke's account that the Roman Jupiter or Greek Zeus, their chief deity, was best represented by Barnabas who was likely older, larger, heavily bearded, and more impressive in physical appearance, than was Paul. On the other hand, the smaller stature, more youthful appearance, quick movements, and eloquent speech of Paul best represented their concept of the Roman Mercury or Greek Hermes. Luke phrases it thus: **because he was the chief speaker** (vs. 12b).

It appears that Jupiter was the patron deity of Lystra, and it is likely that there was an image of Jupiter in the temple dedicated to him and situated before the city gates, where also the priest of Jupiter officiated.

Believing the apostles to be the gods, it was quite natural that the officiating priest should have sought to honor these deities with a special sacrifice. Thus oxen for sacrifice and garlands for festive decoration were brought, and the animals were about to be slain in their honor before the apostles realized what this priest and the populace were about. Likely their use of the Lycaonian language, a tongue unknown to the apostles, accounted for their ignorance of the procedures.

C. The Renunciation of Idolization (14:14–20)

They rent their garments, and sprang forth among the multitude, crying out and saying, Sirs, why do ye these things? We also are men of like passions with you . . . And with these sayings scarce restrained they the multitude from doing sacrifice unto them (vss. 14b, 15a, 18).

The apostles rent their garments in a familiar token of horror at the thought of so blasphemous a consideration as their deification (see Matt. 26:65).

The apostles appear to have run in among the peoples, possibly waving their arms in violent protest, in an attempt to prevent the sacrificial slaughter of the oxen. While the language barrier would have prevented the apostles from understanding the Lycaonian speech, the Lycaonians evidently understood and spoke the Greek used by the apostles.

The speech that follows, likely an address by Paul, differs radically from Paul's syna-

---

[19] The word *stemma* is found only here in the New Testament.

[20] Cf. EGT, II, 307.

[21] Found in Aleph A B C D E. The late, medieval manuscripts have *eisepēdēsan* ("ran in," KJV).

[22] EGT, II, 307.

[23] *Beginnings*, IV, 165. See also Rackham (p. 232, n. 5), who calls attention to the fact that a different Greek word is used for city gates and also that the narrow streets would probably preclude sacrifice in front of a house. He favors the "pylons" of the temple.

15 and saying, Sirs, why do ye these things? We also are men of like passions with you, and bring you good tidings, that ye should turn from these vain things unto a living God, who made the heaven and the earth and the sea, and all that in them is:

15 **Sirs** is "men" *(andres)*. *Homoiopatheis*, **of like passions,** is found only here and in James 5:17 (of Elijah). It would perhaps be better to translate it "of like feelings or affections," [24] or "of like nature" (RSV). The latter is Ramsay's rendering. [25] **Bring... good tidings** is *euangelizomenoi*. This is the first case recorded in Acts of preaching the Gospel [26] to a purely pagan audience, which apparently had had no connection with the Jewish faith. The main emphasis with this class of hearers was on the **living God,** in contrast to **these vain things.** *Mataios*, **vain,** means "useless." Here alone in the New Testament is it used of heathen gods and their worship. The exact phrase **the heaven and the earth and the sea, and all that in them is** occurs in 4:24.

gogue sermons, in that it is an address on "natural religion" such as these pagan Lycaonians could understand, rather than on "revealed religion" designed for the Jewish mind. There are close similarities between this address and Paul's Mars' Hill sermon, likewise delivered to pagan hearers (cf. Acts 17:22–31).

Even under the extremity of the circumstances, the apostles retained their equilibrium and maintained a courteous manner toward the people, as witnessed their address: **Sirs, why do ye these things?** (vs. 15a); not a condemnation of their conduct, but an arresting question. Nor did the apostles make a tirade of attacks upon their pagan deities, but rather positively and sympathetically identified themselves with the humanity of the Lycaonians and thus denied any suspicion of their personal divinity: **we also are men of like passions with you** (vs. 15). Here it should be remarked that the words, **of like passions,** are to be understood as identifying their human nature, and not an allusion to the base or perverted nature of sinful man, as some have mistakenly supposed.

In the apostles' words, [we] **bring you good tidings** (vs. 15), the Christian evangel appears as natural and as fresh as the water that flows from the nearby mountain source to irrigate the arid plateau on which Lystra stood. This is the evangel of the **living God** who vitalizes all that He touches. How different from the **vain things,** valueless and meaningless objects of their pagan worship, from which they are exhorted to turn in true repentance.

The brief address on "natural religion," contained in verses 15 through 17, likely delivered by Paul, while not primarily a Christian sermon is nevertheless foundational to Christianity for the thought of the Lycaonians. This address may be analyzed as follows:

1. *The Vitality of God;* **a living God** (vs. 15).
2. *The Creatorship of God*: **who made the heaven and the earth and the sea, and all that in them is** (vs. 15b).
3. *The Mercy of God*: **who in the generations gone by suffered all the nations** [Gentiles] **to walk in their own ways** (vs. 16).
4. *The Revelation of God*: **and yet he left not himself without witness** (vs. 17a).
5. *The Providence of God*: **he did good and gave you from heaven** (vs. 17).

First, Paul's letter to the Thessalonians affords an illuminating commentary on the striking contrast between pagan idolatry and Christian theism: "and how ye turned unto God from idols to serve a living and true God" (I Thess. 1:9). Their conversion was: (1) "voluntary," in that it represented an intelligent moral choice on their part—"ye turned." Thus Paul exhorts the Lycaonians to turn from vanity to reality. Their conversion was (2) "vital," in that they established relationship with "a living God," as opposed to the non-living character of their former idols, called **vain things** among the Lycaonians. And (3), their conversion was "victorious," as it involved deliverance from slavish servitude to vain idolatry, and liberty "to serve a living and true God" (cf. Acts 26:18). How many of the Lycaonians entered into this gracious experience we do

[24] Abbott-Smith, *op. cit.*, p. 317. [25] *St. Paul the Traveller*, p. 117.
[26] In KJV, *euangelizo* is translated "preach" 23 times and "preach the gospel" 22 times (out of a total of 55 times in N.T.).

16 who in the generations gone by suffered all the nations to walk in their own ways.

---

16 This statement is very similar to that in 17:30. **Gone by** is the verb *paroichomai*, found only here in the New Testament. **Suffer** is the verb *eaō*, which means "let, permit." Luke uses it nine out of its eleven occurrences in the New Testament.

---

not know, but that some did we know from the subsequent life of Timothy (see Acts 16:1–3).

Second, faith in the existence and creatorship of God is absolutely essential to evangelical or saving faith (see Heb. 11:1–6). Naturalistic evolution strikes at the very foundation of man's hope of salvation, "the creatorship of God." This humanistic scheme seeks to rob God of His rightful ownership of all things and thus render impossible their redemption by, and to, God.

Third, the thought of God's mercy in allowing the unenlightened pagan Gentiles **to walk in their own ways** (vs. 16b) [religiously] until light should be afforded them, when He might have destroyed them in their ignorance and vanity, should influence them to comprehend His goodness and repent and turn to Him for saving grace (cf. Acts 17:29, 30).

Fourth, God's revelation of Himself to the Lycaonians through nature makes them responsible for faith in His unitary nature, divine creatorship, and providential goodness. In the Roman letter Paul argues the fourfold revelation of God to man, in chapters one and two, and then makes him morally responsible to each of these revelations. In the *first* place, he presents the revelation of God in the very moral constitution of man who is created in the personal spiritual image of God (Rom. 1:19 and 2:14, 15); *second*, he represents God as revealed in nature, His handiwork (Rom. 1:20); *third*, God is revealed in the Mosaic Law (Rom. 2:12); and *finally*, God is revealed in Christ and His Gospel (Rom. 2:16). To these first two revelations of God the Lycaonians had been responsible. To what extent they had been enlightened by the law of Moses through the Jewish religion we cannot say, but that they now had a far greater responsibility because the Gospel of Christ had been delivered to them by the apostles is evident.

Fifth, God's revelation of Himself through His providential goodness in so directing the seasons and elements as to afford the earth's fruit for the supply of their temporal necessities is presented in verse 17. This last citation is especially designed to impress upon the hearers the goodness and love of God with a view to producing repentance and acceptance of His spiritual goodness through Jesus Christ.

How much more was contained in the apostle's message Luke does not tell us, but how little they were impressed with what was said is suggested by the author's words: **And with these sayings scarce restrained they the multitudes from doing sacrifice unto them** (vs. 18).

Like persistent bloodhounds on the trail of a criminal, the Antioch and Iconian Jewish enemies of the Gospel of Christ trailed Paul and Barnabas to Lystra where they took advantage of the half-civilized, fickle Lycaonians (see Gal. 1:6; 3:1; 4:15), whose minds they poisoned and perverted and whose emotions they inflamed to violent action against the apostles of the Lord. Thus under their influence these very people who had but so recently sought to worship the apostles as gods, now sought to destroy them as devils: **they stoned Paul, and dragged him out of the city, supposing that he was dead** (vs. 19b).

How changeable is popular acclaim. One day the crowds acclaimed Christ king (Matt. 21:9, 15), but another day not far distant they cried for His blood (Luke 23:21). First Paul is Mercury from heaven; now he is an impostor worthy of death by stoning.

The violence enacted against Paul, but from which Barnabas and the new disciples were evidently exempt, is probably due to the fact that Paul was regarded by the Jews as the most damaging to their cause, by reason of his courage, wisdom, logic, and convincing eloquence in preaching the Gospel of Christ. It was these qualities in Stephen that so enraged his enemies and precipitated his martyrdom by stoning at the hands of the Sanhedrin (see Acts 6:10).

Whether the Jews took part in the actual

17 And yet he left not himself without witness, in that he did good and gave you from heaven rains and fruitful seasons, filling your hearts with food and gladness.

18 And with these sayings scarce restrained they the multitudes from doing sacrifice unto them.

19 But there came Jews thither from Antioch and Iconium: and having persuaded the multitudes, they stoned Paul, and dragged him out of the city, supposing that he was dead.

---

17 *Amartyron*, **without witness,** *agathourgon*, **did good,** and *karpophorous*, **fruitful,** occur only here in the New Testament. *Ouranothen*, **from heaven,** is found also in 26:13, and *euphrosynēs*, **gladness,** in 2:28.

In reference to **rains** Knowling makes this comment: "The rain was regarded in the East as a special sign of divine favour, and here, as in the O.T., God's goodness and power in this gift are asserted as against the impotence of the gods of the heathen" [27] (cf. Jer. 14:22).

18 *Molis*, **scarce,** means, "with difficulty, hardly." Luke uses it five of the seven times it occurs in the New Testament. *Katepausan*, **restrained** (lit., "caused to cease") is found only here and three times in the Epistle to the Hebrews.

19 The hatred and zeal of the **Jews** is shown in their coming all the way from **Antioch,** over 100 miles away.[28] In II Corinthians 11:25 Paul refers to this one time when he was **stoned.** Adding insult to injury, they **dragged him out of the city.** The verb *syro* is used three times in Acts (cf. 8:3; 17:6) and only twice elsewhere in the New Testament.

---

stoning, or whether Paul was actually dead, Luke does not say. Since stoning was the Jewish method of punishment, while flogging, decapitating, and crucifixion were the Roman methods, this is decidedly a Jewish-incited mob, and they likely participated in the violence. The fact that he was dragged outside the city may indicate their utter disdain for him and their purpose that his blood should not pollute their town. How like the rejection and execution of the Christ whom Paul preached! (Heb. 13:12). How reminiscent of the occasion on which Paul had cast his lot with the persecutors of Stephen! (Acts 7:58 and 8:1). One may wonder if Paul, like Stephen, had any vision of heaven during his ordeal (see Acts 7:55, 50).

Whether Paul was actually dead, or whether the life was still in his body and his persecutors just "supposed that he was dead," it was their full intent to have killed him, and in either case his recovery is miraculous (cf. Acts 20:9–12 and Rom. 8:11). Luke's notation that **the disciples stood round about him** (vs. 20a) is likely intended to mean that their sympathies were deeply stirred and their hearts were lifted in passionate and faithful prayer for his recovery. What part those prayers played in his restoration to life and service only heaven will reveal. Paul's return to the city after his restoration probably was due to the fact that his enemies thought him dead and supposed that his friends had disposed of his body. On the other hand, what an encouragement to the faith of these young Christians to see Paul so miraculously restored by the power of the **living God** he preached, and what an example of Christian courage that he should return to the very city from which he had been dragged to his supposed death. Likely the home of Timothy, a new Christian disciple (II Timothy 1:3–6), was the abode of Paul and Barnabas while in Lystra.

The extent of Paul's early recovery from this ordeal is suggested by Luke's words: **And on the morrow he went forth with Barnabas to Derbe** (vs. 20b), though the mention of his having accompanied Barnabas may indicate the temporary safeguard of the protection afforded him by this fellow apostle.

The success of their ministry at Derbe is indicated by Luke's statement that they **made many disciples** (vs. 21). Among those **many disciples** made at Derbe was one Gaius, who later became one of Paul's trusted assistants in the gospel ministry (Acts 20:4).

The importance of Derbe, a small Lycaonian city on the extreme borders of Galatia, is indicated by the Roman title accorded it, Claudio-Derbe. Zoska is the modern city on the site of ancient Derbe.

[27] EGT, II, 309. [28] Knowling says 130 miles (EGT, II, 310 f.).

20 But as the disciples stood round about him, he rose up, and entered into the city: and on the morrow he went forth with Barnabas to Derbe.
21 And when they had preached the gospel to that city, and had made many disciples, they returned to Lystra, and to Iconium, and to Antioch,
22 confirming the souls of the disciples, exhorting them to continue in the faith, and that through many tribulations we must enter into the kingdom of God.

---

20 *Epaurion* (an adverb), **on the morrow** occurs ten times in Acts, five times in John's Gospel, and once each in Matthew and Mark. It would be a day's walk to **Derbe,** some twenty or thirty [29] miles away.

21 **Preached the gospel** is the same verb *(euangelizō)* as "bring good tidings" in verse 15. **Made . . . disciples** is the verb *mathēteuō*, found elsewhere in the New Testament only in Matthew (13:52; 27:57; 28:19). It comes from *mathētēs*, "disciple." This translation is obviously preferable to "taught" (KJV). It declares the success of the apostolic mission in Derbe.

The lack of opposition in this city is a bit surprising, in view of the missionaries' fortunes in the other three cities of Galatia. There is a striking coincidence in II Timothy 3:11, where Paul mentions his persecutions "at Antioch, at Iconium, at Lystra," but omits Derbe. The fact that the apostles **returned** to the cities where their lives had so recently been in danger shows both courage and consecration. They put the needs of the Church ahead of their own safety or selfish interests.[30]

22 *Epistērizontes*, **confirming,** is found only here and in 15:32, 41. **That** *(hoti)* should be rendered "saying" (RSV), as introducing a direct quotation in the first person, **we.** The Greek, when properly translated, is not as awkward as the older English versions suggest. *Hoti* is frequently equivalent to quotation marks.

VII. THE CHRISTIANS REVISITED (14:21–25)

Luke's record states that the apostles **returned to Lystra, and to Iconium, and to Antioch** (vs. 21b), in the face of their former opposition and persecution, and in full consideration of the fact that they could easily have crossed the Taurus Mountains through the Cilician Gates and returned via Tarsus, Paul's home. This indicates the extent of their devotion to the Christian cause. The work of the apostles on the return trip may be summed up as consisting in *confirmation*, *exhortation*, *organization*, and *commendation* of the new Asia Minor disciples.

First, as they revisited these cities where the Gospel had been introduced, they did so for the purpose of **confirming the souls of the disciples** (vs. 22a). A disciple is a follower of a master, a learner, or a scholar. These new believers are so designated, and as such Luke's choice of words here is apt. The apostles confirmed their souls by instruction in the Christian doctrines and principles which Luke designates as **the faith** (vs. 22). To convert but not to confirm the souls of men is to leave them a likely prey to vicious error. Probably in small classes by day and by flickering lights at night, in homes, in the markets, or by the wayside, these apostles confirmed the young disciples in the Christian truth.

Second, they set themselves to the task of **exhorting them to continue in the faith, and that through many tribulations we must enter into the kingdom of God** (vs. 22). While confirmation was primarily instructional and its principal appeal was to the intelligence, exhortation, on the other hand, was primarily hortatory, and its appeal was mainly to the emotions and will. Citation of the Lord's teaching concerning the Christian heritage of suffering (Mark 10:29, 30), examples from Old Testament history, and the recent vivid personal experiences of the apostles themselves, doubtless served as data for these exhortations delivered with a view to encouraging and fortifying these new believers in the midst of immoral pagan environment and violent Jewish opposition. To have left them unwarned would have been to leave them unarmed against powerful godless foes (see Acts 20:31).

Third, for the conservation of their evangelistic work, the apostles effected a simple

[29] Rackham, *op. cit.*, p. 235.
[30] Tarsus was only 160 miles away.

23 And when they had appointed for them elders in every church, and had prayed with fasting, they commended them to the Lord, on whom they had believed.
24 And they passed through Pisidia, and came to Pamphylia.
25 And when they had spoken the word in Perga, they went down to Attalia;

---

23 **Appointed** is *cheirotonēsantes*, found elsewhere in the New Testament only in II Corinthians 8:19. The verb was used in connection with the free assembly *(ekklēsia)* at Athens with the meaning "to vote by stretching out *(teinō)* the hand *(cheir)*." It later came to be used in the more general sense of "appoint." Abbott-Smith says that in the Corinthian passage it means to appoint "by vote" but here "without vote."[31] Probably the basis for that distinction is the implication here that **they** means Paul and Barnabas. Josephus uses this verb in reference to Saul's having been "ordained king by God," [32] and also in quoting Alexander as writing to Jonathan: "We therefore do ordain thee this day the high priest of the Jews." [33] However, Ramsay writes: "It must, I think, be allowed that the votes and voices of each congregation were considered." [34]

24 **They passed through** is *dielthontes*, "having made a missionary journey through" (see on 13:6). **Pisidia** was the southernmost part of Galatia, just north of **Pamphylia.**

25 The apostles had visited **Perga** before (13:13, 14), but it is not recorded that they preached there. This time, however, they did not leave until **they had spoken the word** in that city. Then they **went down** to the coast **to Attalia,** the main harbor of Pamphylia. It is represented now by Andaliya, at the mouth of the Cataractes River (the name sufficiently reveals the nature of that stream).

---

form of organization for each church by appointing **for them elders in every church** (vs. 23a). The question of church officers has been dealt with elsewhere (see Acts 6, Pt. I). These men were selected for their faith, character, wisdom, conduct, and perseverance. This selection was delayed until the apostles' return journey in order to give opportunity for those with leadership qualities and moral worth time and opportunity to be revealed to their fellow Christians, as well as the apostles (see Acts 16:1–3a). In this Paul was practicing what he later enjoined upon Timothy (I Tim. 5:18–22). It would appear to be a valid inference from this incident that wherever Paul established churches he provided a ministry for them. The method of selecting and electing these under-shepherds (**elders**) for their office is aptly treated by Clarke thus:

> I believe the simple truth to be this, that in ancient times the people chose by the *cheirotonia* (lifting up of hands) their spiritual pastor; and the *rulers* of the Church, whether *apostles* or *others*, appointed that person to his office by the *cheirothesia*, or *imposition of hands;* and perhaps each of these was thought to be equally necessary: the *Church agreeing* in the *election* of the person; and the *rulers* of the church appointing, by *imposition of hands*, the person thus elected.[c]

The accompanying fasting and prayer were customary to ascertain God's will and insure God's approval and blessings upon the church's ministry (Acts 13:2, 3). Here is a first century apostolic precedent and model of democratic congregational church government.

The *final act* of the apostles in relation to these young churches was performed when **they commended them to the Lord, on whom they had believed** (vs. 23b). Here, as always, there is no safer refuge for the young Christian believers than in the hands of the Lord.

VIII. THE RESULTS REPORTED (14:26–28)

In rapid succession Luke carries the apostles homeward through Pisidia and Pamphylia to Perga, where they are said to have **spoken the word** (vs. 25), from whence they went to Attalia, the seaport of Perga, and sailed to Antioch of Syria.

Luke is careful to note that upon their return the apostles could report that the work to which they had been committed by the Church **they had fulfilled** (vs. 26b). Their conference report was completed.

[31] *Op. cit.*, p. 481. [32] *Ant.* VI, 13, 9. [33] *Ant.* XIII, 2, 2.
[34] *St. Paul the Traveller*, p. 122.

[c] Clarke, *op. cit.*, V, 797.

26 and thence they sailed to Antioch, from whence they had been committed to the grace of God for the work which they had fulfilled.

27 And when they were come, and had gathered the church together, they rehearsed all things that God had done with them, and that he had opened a door of faith unto the Gentiles.

28 And they tarried no little time with the disciples.

---

26 From here they **sailed to Antioch,** evidently by-passing Cyprus on the return trip.

27 Apparently a special meeting was called to hear the report of the missionaries who had been sent out by **the church.** **Rehearsed** is the verb *anangellō*, which means "to bring back word, report." [35] That sense fits very well here.

28 It is not stated how long the "furlough" lasted. **No little time** suggests a period of months, if not a year or two.

The last two verses of this chapter record the first church missionary service ever conducted by returned missionaries sent forth by the church body. Several items of interest appear in conjunction with this event. *First,* **they . . . gathered the church together** (vs. 27a). Thus they assembled the whole church which had been responsible for sending them on the mission, that they might benefit from the report. The missionary task and concern is one belonging to the entire church, and not a small group of "special interest" enthusiasts. *Second,* they made a complete positive report of their tour in which they **rehearsed all things that God had done with them** (vs. 27). Whatever apparent adversities had befallen them, they seem to have regarded as in the permissive will of God, and thus were counted to His glory. They gave these "investors" in the cause of world evangelism what they expected, a report of the returns on their investment in the cause. One might like to know if they related the departure of Mark from the work at Lystra, but Luke does not say. Even that may have been regarded as one of the **all things that God had done with them** (vs. 27). *Third,* they threw out a new and greater challenge to the churches in their report, that God **had opened a door of faith unto the Gentiles** (vs. 27b).

It was the last item of their report that challenged the Antioch church to launch a second and third missionary enterprise with Paul as the principal organizer and leader. Successful endeavor for God always inspires and challenges to further and more heroic undertakings.

It is striking that no mention of baptism is made by Luke, either throughout the First Missionary Journey or in the apostles' report to the church at Antioch (see I Cor. 1: 14–17).

The entire journey covered about 1,400 miles, and the total time may have occupied about 18 months or more.

The furlough time spent at Antioch, between one and two years, was for rest, recuperation, replenishment, recruitment, and reorganization for a second mission.

[35] Abbott-Smith, *op. cit.*, p. 28.

CHAPTER XV

And certain men came down from Judaea and taught the brethren, saying, Except ye be circumcised after the custom of Moses, ye cannot be saved.

2 And when Paul and Barnabas had no small dissension and questioning with them, *the brethren* appointed that Paul and Barnabas, and certain other of them, should go up to Jerusalem unto the apostles and elders about this question.

EXEGESIS

1 **Taught** is better rendered "were teaching" (RSV), since *edidaskon* is imperfect. **Custom** is preferable to "manner" (KJV). The latter may be a temporary usage, whereas the former refers to habitual practice. *Ethos* (from *ethō*, be accustomed) is translated "custom" in the King James Version in seven out of its twelve occurrences in the New Testament. **Saved** was evidently thought of more in terms of Messianic salvation than of personal deliverance from sin.

2 **Dissension** is *stasis,* which literally means "a standing" (from *histēmi*), and so "place" or "status." In the New Testament it has this meaning only in Hebrews 9:8. Occurring nine times, it is translated in the King James Version as "sedition" (3),

---

EXPOSITION

Part I

THE CHURCH'S FIRST GENERAL COUNCIL

I. The Occasion of the Council, Acts 15:1-5.
   A. The Activities of the Judaizers, vs. 1.
   B. The Appointment of the Antioch Delegation, vss. 2, 3.
   C. The Report of the Delegation, vs. 4.
   D. The Opposition of the Pharisees, vs. 5.

II. The Defense of the Gentiles, Acts 15:6-12.
   A. The Defense of Peter, vss. 6-11.
   B. The Declaration of Barnabas and Paul, vs. 12.

III. The Decision of the Chairman, Acts 15:13-21.
   A. The Position of the Chairman, vs. 13.
   B. The Summary of the Chairman, vss. 14-18.
   C. The Sentence of the Chairman, vss. 19-21.

IV. The Decrees of the Council, Acts 15:22-29.
   A. The Support of the Decrees, vs. 22.
   B. The Script of the Decrees, vss. 23-29.

V. The Delivery of the Decrees, Acts 15:30-35.

Part II

THE CHURCH'S FIRST EUROPEAN MISSION

I. The Apostles' Plans for the Mission, Acts 15:36-41.
   A. The Proposal of Paul, vs. 36.
   B. The Problem of John Mark, vss. 37, 38.
   C. The Parting of the Apostles, vss. 39-41.

I. THE OCCASION OF THE COUNCIL (15:1-5)

In this chapter Luke records the greatest crisis with which the young Church had yet been confronted, if indeed not the greatest crisis the Church has yet faced in her history. It was the first serious internal conflict of the body ecclesiastic, and it threatened to precipitate a cleavage in the body that might never have been healed. The apostles' handling of the situation has set a model for all time.

Two different views of the circumcision controversy in relation to the Jerusalem Council have characterized the thinking of scholars. Both are summarily presented here.

The position which is probably the most widely accepted places the Jerusalem Council "dissension" (3), "insurrection" (1), "uproar" (1), and "standing" (1). It has the same spread of meaning in the papyri.[1] **Questioning** may be rendered "debate" (RSV).

The subject of **appointed** *(etaxan)* is not stated and so is left indefinite in the King James and Revised Standard versions. Most commentators agree with the insertion, **the brethren,** in the American Standard Version. The Western text presents an interesting variation (probably a later interpretation): "Those who had come from Jerusalem ordered *(parēngeilan)* Paul and Barnabas themselves and some others to go up to the apostles and elders at Jerusalem to be judged before them about this question." After reading the Epistle to the Galatians, it is difficult to believe that Paul would have taken any such orders from the Judaizers.

Question is *zētēma,* found only in Acts (five times). In modern Greek it means "controversy."[2]

---

between the First and Second Missionary Journeys. *First,* word of the conversion of the Gentiles on Paul's First Missionary Journey, and that he had not required their circumcision, had reached Jerusalem and there greatly disturbed the strict Judeo-Christian legalist party. *Second,* this party sent representatives to Antioch, who falsely professed to have authority from the Jerusalem apostles, to teach that all Gentile converts had to be circumcised before they could be saved (Acts 15:1). *Third,* Paul challenged the validity of their doctrines and ecclesiastical authority and questioned the sincerity of their motives (Gal. 2:4). *Fourth,* Paul, possibly challenged by the Judaizers, decided to go to Jerusalem and present the question to the Jerusalem church for solution. This he finally decided to do only after he had received a special divine revelation that it was God's will and that the results would accord with God's former revelation to him (Gal. 2:4). *Fifth,* the Antioch church accorded with this plan and endorsed a delegation to the Jerusalem Council, consisting of Paul, Barnabas, and Titus (Gal. 2:1–5), and possibly unnamed others. Galatians 2:1–10 is an account of this third visit of Paul to Jerusalem after his conversion. *Sixth,* Paul and his party met with the apostles and elders of the Jerusalem church in a private pre-council session in which they presented the cause of Gentile freedom and apparently secured their concurrence. *Seventh,* the legalist party made a test case of Titus in which they demanded his circumcision, since he was a Gentile, to which Paul steadfastly refused to give consent. The apostles evidently favored the legalists' contention at first, since Titus was to be Paul's companion; but, judging from James' decision, as expressed in the decrees of the Council (Acts 15:19, 20), and Paul's argument in the Galatian letter (Gal. 2:6–10), they eventually concurred with Paul. *Eighth,* the Council unanimously rendered its decision in favor of the exemption of the Gentile Christians from circumcision (see Acts 15:19–21) and approved the ministry of Paul and Barnabas to the Gentiles (cf. Acts 15:25–27 and Gal. 2:9). *Ninth,* Paul and Barnabas, in company with Judas and Silas, returned to Antioch where they delivered the decrees, to the great joy and edification of the church (Acts 15:30, 31). *Tenth,* subsequently Peter, under pressure from the disgruntled Judaizers, whose cause had been lost at the Council, went to Antioch where his divisive conduct in the church was openly condemned by Paul (Gal. 2:11–14). *Eleventh*' the Galatian letter was written after the Jerusalem Council and before the Second Missionary Journey. *Twelfth,* the Second Missionary Journey was launched from Antioch, with its attendant incidents (Acts 15:36–41).

Certain other scholars take quite a different view of the incidents outlined in the foregoing view. In brief they contend: *first,* the Jerusalem visit of Galatians 2:1–10 is not the same as that of Acts 15, but rather of that described in Acts 11:29, 30; *second,* that the Galatian letter was written sometime before the Jerusalem Council during the heat of the circumcision controversy; and *third,* that Peter's visit to Antioch, related in Gal. 2:11–21, occurred before the Jerusalem Council.

Ramsay is possibly the ablest supporter of the latter view in general. However, the first view is the most generally accepted, and all factors considered it appears to fit most

[1] VGT, p. 586. [2] *Ibid.,* p. 274.

satisfactorily the recorded events. This view is held by Clarke, Wesley, Lightfoot, and many other eminent scholars. It will afford the frame of reference for the exposition of this chapter, except for the time of Peter's visit to Antioch and the possible date of the Galatian letter, both of which are in dispute among scholars.

A. THE ACTIVITIES OF THE JUDAIZERS (15:1)

And certain men came down from Judaea and taught the brethren, saying, Except ye be circumcised after the custom of Moses, ye cannot be saved.

That these **certain men** of verse one were the representatives of the "believing" **sect of the Pharisees** in the Jerusalem Christian church, mentioned in verse five, appears evident. Further, that they were sent by this Judeo-Christian legalist party to Antioch to propagate their doctrines, though they falsely claimed to have been sent by the Jerusalem apostles (see Gal. 2:4), is equally evident. Again, that they were the same as those mentioned in Galatians 2:12 is likely. This sect of Pharisees consisted of Jews whom Christ frequently rebuked (see Matt. 23:4, 15, 23 and Luke 11:42, 46), and from which party there had been converts to Christianity (vs. 5).

To properly understand these Judaizers, as they are called, it is necessary to know something of the strict Jewish Pharisaic party, from which they were converted to Christianity. It appears from history that the sect of the Pharisees came into existence for the preservation and propagation of the essence of Judaism following the exile and during the Inter-Testament period, when they developed a "Theocracy" in lieu of their former "Monarchy." Thus they became the rulers of a religious state in which Mosaic monotheism was preserved, the Mosaic Law was strictly imposed, and the Messianic hope was widely diffused.

This was all to their credit, and to them both Judaism and the Christian world are deeply indebted. However, by the dawn of the Christian era, their religious beliefs and practices had crystallized into a fanatical advocacy of binding and blinding legalism that stifled the last breath of life from religion. They had become blind leaders of the blind (Matt. 15:14), and bound burdens upon their followers which none could bear (Matt. 23:4; Luke 11:46; Acts 15:10b). They had made the fatal mistake of confusing means with ends and had mistaken the former for the latter. Whereas the Mosaic law was designed as a tutor to lead men to Christ and liberty, they thought it to be the saviour in itself (see Gal. 3:24, 25). They failed to recognize in Christ the fulfillment of the law, never attained to the spiritual idea of "the church," and placed their interpretations of the law above the law itself (see Matt. 23:2). Rabbi Eleazer is reported to have said: "He who expounds the Scriptures in contradiction to tradition has no inheritance in the world to come." They degraded Judaism into a narrow nationalistic religion with an elaborate ritual and extreme Sabbatarianism, from which all but the strictest were excluded. Of this persuasion they became fanatical advocates (Matt. 23:15), and from this sect Paul had sprung (Acts 26:5).

The Jewish-Christian legalists consisted of those from this Judeo-Pharisaic party who had embraced Christianity but had attempted to incarcerate it behind the iron bars of Jewish legalism, both for themselves and for the Gentiles. The Epistles to the Galatians, to the Romans, and to the Hebrews at a later period, were all written to refute this error, and the segment of the church at Jerusalem that held it never outlived the first Christian generation. In fact, its influence seems to have extended widely over the Jerusalem church in time, and to have robbed that church of her vital spirituality and mission to the world. There is evidence that there developed in the Jerusalem church an increasing disposition to restrict the privileges of membership to those who had conformed strictly to the Jewish law. That the "Pillar Apostles" did not fully share this position is equally evident from the decisions of the Jerusalem Conference (Acts 15:19–21). Harnack observes that this Jewish-Christian church fled to Pella, a small pagan town to the north and across the river in Decapolis, in A.D. 68 upon the first Roman attack on Jerusalem, where it remained for the most part, and evidently never enjoyed prosperity nor wielded any noticeable influence on its hosts.

3 They therefore, being brought on their way by the church, passed through both Phoenicia and Samaria, declaring the conversion of the Gentiles: and they caused great joy unto all the brethren.

3 **Being brought on their way** is one word, *propemphthentes*. This verb sometimes means "accompany" (cf. 20:38), but that is probably not the meaning here (see Exposition). Literally it is "send before," and is used thus in the papyri; but Moulton and Milligan feel that "set forward" fits all the (nine) New Testament occurrences.[3] **Passed through** is literally "were passing through"—*diērchonto*, Luke's favorite missionary word for evangelizing a territory (see on 8:4 and 13:6).

Declaring is the verb *ekdiēgeomai*, found (in N.T.) only here and in the quotation in 13:41. It means "tell in detail, relate." **Conversion** is *epistrophē*, which occurs only here in the New Testament. It means literally "a turning about." **Caused** is *epoioun*, imperfect. The missionaries were creating **great joy** in all the cities along the coast from Antioch down perhaps to Caesarea, a distance of over 200 miles.

Of the disappearance of this legalistic Jewish-Christian church, Lietzmann remarks:

> The original church disappeared with the migration to Pella and the destruction of Jerusalem. At the same time it sank below the horizon of Gentile Christianity which was in process of conquering the world and which had thereby become dominant in Christendom after the judgment of God over the Holy City had made plain to all eyes His punishment for the crucifixion of the Lord, i.e., by the destruction of the temple and its worship and the abolition of the Law. Jewish Christianity had lacked not only a racial, but also a religious basis for its former claims and thus was forgotten in the church Catholic. It sank to oblivion in the lonely deserts of East Jordan.[a]

Had these legalists won their contention at the Jerusalem Conference, either the Church would have been divided into Judeo-Christian and Gentile-Christian sections, or the whole body would have likely suffered the fate described above.

This legalistic teaching was extremely disturbing to the faith of the young Gentile disciples at Antioch, since they already believed on Christ for salvation, and were now told that **Except ye be circumcised after the custom of Moses, ye cannot be saved** (vs. 1b). It further threatened to effect a cleavage between the Jewish and Gentile Christians of the Antioch church (see Gal. 2:11–13).

B. The Appointment of the Antioch Delegation (15:2, 3)

The brethren appointed that Paul and Barnabas, and certain other of them, should go up to Jerusalem unto the apostles and elders about this question (vs. 2b).

When it is remembered that no Gentile, in the first generation, could become a true proselyte to the Jewish religion without circumcision, if indeed at all, it is understandable that these representatives of Judeo-Christian legalism should have contended for the circumcision of the Gentile disciples at Antioch before they could regard themselves as being truly saved and worthy of membership in the Christian Church. Since the principle of salvation with them was "law," while it was "grace" with the apostles, there naturally arose strong differences of opinions and points of view, as well as pointed and sharp questionings. Contentiousness is no stranger to legalism, and *dissensions* are her favored devices. She looks on externals and judges spiritual values by appearances, while God looks on the heart and judges spiritual values by true moral worth and purity of motives (cf. I Sam. 16:7).

Because of the dangers involved to the Antioch church, as well as the issues involved for the whole Christian movement, the Antioch church decided to send a delegation to the apostles at Jerusalem for a decision on the matter. This decision may have been due in part to the fact that these Judaizers claimed to have been sent on their mission by the Jerusalem apostles, a claim likely suspected by Paul and Barnabas (Acts 15:24).

While Paul and Barnabas were the elected delegates of the church at Antioch, Paul claims the support of direct divine revelation

[3] *Ibid.*, p. 544. Knowling prefers "escorted on their way" (EGT, II, 316), as does Rackham (p. 245).

[a] Hans Lietzmann, *The Beginnings of the Christian Church* (New York: Charles Scribner's Sons, 1937), pp. 78–80.

4 And when they were come to Jerusalem, they were received of the church and the apostles and the elders, and they rehearsed all things that God had done with them.

---

4 **Jerusalem** was another 60 miles from Caesarea. **When they were come** is *paragenomenoi*, a favorite Lukan term (see on 9:26). **Received** *(paradechthēsan)* could be translated "welcomed," as in the papyri.[4] It is a strong compound, meaning literally "receive by the side of." **Rehearsed** is the verb *anangellō*, which in the classics means "bring back word, report" (cf. 14:27). But in Hellenistic Greek it is often equivalent to *parangellō*,[5] which means "announce, declare." Probably this meaning fits best here.

---

in the venture (see Gal. 2:2). Among the **certain other of them** sent to Jerusalem was Titus, who became a test case in this matter of Gentile circumcision (see Gal. 2:3–5), and who later became one of Paul's most trusted companions and emissaries for delicate and difficult tasks (see II Cor. 7:6; 8:6, 16–18), but who strangely is not mentioned in the Acts account. Paul's justification in not allowing the circumcision of Titus at the Jerusalem Council, while requiring it in the case of Timothy at a later date (see Acts 16:3), is found: first, in the fact that Titus was evidently a pure Gentile, while Timothy was of mixed parentage, his mother a Jewess and his father a Greek; second, since "they all knew that his father was a Greek" (Acts 16:3b) and he was to be Paul's traveling companion, the apostle realized that, uncircumcised, Timothy would be a barrier to the Gospel with the prejudiced Jews wherever they traveled throughout the empire. This reason is given by Luke: "because of the Jews that were in those parts; for they all knew that his father was a Greek" (Acts 16:3b). However, since his mother was a Jewess and Timothy had followed her religion (II Tim. 1:5), it seemed logical that he should bear the outward signs of his nationality. Thus, for expediency's sake, Paul had him circumcised (cf. I Cor. 8:9–13; Acts 18:18; 20:16; 21:23). Again, Titus was a test case at Jerusalem involving the question of the observance of the Jewish law as necessary to salvation, which for Paul to have yielded would have been against his cause of freedom for the Gentiles, in that he would have sacrificed a religious principle, while such was not true in the case of Timothy.

Since the question concerning circumcision is purported to have arisen with the apostles at the mother church in Jerusalem, it is only logical that it should be referred to them.

The expression, **They therefore, being brought on their way by the church** (vs. 3a), is probably meant to suggest that the church which delegated them to attend the conference provided the necessary means, financial and otherwise, to meet their travel expenses, rather than that members of the church accompanied them for a distance, as some suppose (cf. Rom. 15:24).

This was to be Paul's third visit to Jerusalem since his conversion. The first occurred about A.D. 37 or 38 and followed his escape from Damascus (Acts 9:26); the second took place about A.D. 45 on the occasion of the famine offering taken to Jerusalem by Paul and Barnabas (Acts 11:29, 30).

The apostle's reports, concerning Gentile conversions, to the disciples in Phoenicia and Samaria as they were en route to Jerusalem, were received with joyful gratitude on their part. Though there were evidently Jewish Christians in Phoenicia (Acts 11:19), they seem not to have been prejudiced against the apostle's ministry to the Gentiles.

C. Report of the Delegation (15:4)

They rehearsed all things that God had done with them (vs. 4b).

Upon arrival in Jerusalem, the delegation was cordially and warmly received by the church body, its elders, and the apostles. Whether the latter included all the apostles, or just the "pillar apostles," James, Cephas, and John, who are named in this connection (Gal. 2:9), we are not informed. From Luke's statement that **they were received of the church** (vs. 4a), we may safely infer that the Judaizers were greatly in the minority.

Here, as at Antioch, Paul and Barnabas gave a full and detailed report of their missionary activities and experiences. This initial report appears to have been made to

[4] VGT, p. 482. [5] *Ibid.*, p. 30.

5 But there rose up certain of the sect of the Pharisees who believed, saying, It is needful to circumcise them, and to charge them to keep the law of Moses.
6 And the apostles and the elders were gathered together to consider of this matter.

5 **Rose up** is a double compound, *exanestēsan;* literally, "stood up out of." It is found elsewhere in the New Testament only in quotation (Mark 12:19; Luke 20:28). For **sect** see note on 5:17. Lake and Cadbury assert: "*Hairesis* means a 'party'; not a heresy, and not even a 'sect.'"[6] They also declare: "The use of the word in the sense of heresy is probably not to be found before the middle of the second century."[7] The Western text identifies these Judaizers with those who caused trouble in Antioch. This is not impossible, but neither is it necessarily the case. The margin of the King James Version follows Beza and some older commentators in making this verse a quotation from what Paul and Barnabas said. But this view has not gained wide acceptance.

6 Just how this verse is related to Galatians is not certain. Some would make this the private session (Gal. 2:2), and have the public conference begin with verse seven.[8] But the text does not seem to indicate any change of locale between verses six and seven.

To consider of (antiquated construction) is literally "to see concerning" *(idein peri)*. The English equivalent is "to see about." **Matter** is *logos* (cf. 8:21).

a private session of the apostles (Gal. 2:2) before the opening of the full church conference on the matter. This report included a detailed statement of the doctrinal content of Paul's Gentile message: "I laid before them the gospel which I preach among the Gentiles" (Gal. 2:2). Paul's strategy in this pre-conference session with the apostles is evident from his words, "but privately before them who were of repute, lest by any means I should be running, or had run, in vain" (Gal. 2:2b), a strategy which appears to have been effective, judging from the support given him by the apostles in the subsequent church conference.

D. The Opposition of the Pharisees (15:5)

But there rose up certain of the sect of the Pharisees who believed.

This is the sole mention by name of believing Pharisees, though it is likely that the Judaizers in general were of this sect. It is possible that the words of verse five are a part of the report of Paul and Barnabas to the apostles concerning the activities of these Pharisees at Antioch. However, it seems more likely that they are a record of the concerted opposition of this party at Jerusalem, possibly in the pre-conference session. Concerning these Pharisees, see the note on verse one. The Pharisaic requirements of the Gentile disciples for church membership, **It is needful to circumcise them, and to charge them to keep the law of Moses** (vs. 5b), are even more demanding here than as stated at Antioch, according to verse one. As the crisis approaches, the emotional temperature of these legalists rises. They foresee the issues involved, in which Christianity may become an extra-Jewish movement embracing the Gentile world and resulting in the disintegration of the whole Mosaic economy.

II. THE DEFENSE OF THE GENTILES (15:6–12)

This is the occasion of the first general Christian council ever held, and certainly the greatest of the first century. It dealt with some of the weightiest problems ever considered by the Church.

A. The Defense of Peter (15:6–11)

And when there had been much questioning, Peter rose up, and said unto them (vs. 7).

The speech of Peter here delivered in defense of the Gentiles clearly reveals the principles involved. They are: *first*, the direct will of God for the salvation of the Gentiles by faith, as attested by Peter's experience at Caesarea (vs. 7b); *second*, the divine impartation of the Holy Spirit in the regeneration of the souls of the believing Gentiles (vs. 8); *third*, the divine impartiality in sanctifying the souls of the Gentile believers in response to their faith (vs. 9); *fourth*, the insulting affront to God in substituting an

[6] *Beginnings*, IV, 171. [7] *Ibid.* [8] See *Beginnings*, IV, 172.

7 And when there had been much questioning, Peter rose up, and said unto them, Brethren, ye know that a good while ago God made choice among you, that by my mouth the Gentiles should hear the word of the gospel, and believe.
8 And God, who knoweth the heart, bare them witness, giving them the Holy Spirit, even as he did unto us;
9 and he made no distinction between us and them, cleansing their hearts by faith.

---

7 **A good while ago** is more accurately rendered "in the early days" (RSV). The Greek is *aph' hēmerōn archaiōn*, "from beginning days." The reference may be to Jesus' statement at Caesarea Philippi (Matt. 16:19), or to the beginning of the Christian Church,[9] but most definitely to Peter's preaching in the house of Cornelius (chap. 10), which in a sense began the evangelization of **the Gentiles.**

The noun *euangelion*, **gospel,** is used by Luke only here and in 20:24. He uses the verb *euangelizō* ten times in his Gospel and fifteen times in Acts. This is the last mention of **Peter** in Acts, the only occurrence of the name outside the first twelve chapters (57 times).

8, 9 These two verses make a very significant identification. It is sometimes said that while Acts has much to say about being filled with the Holy Spirit, it makes no mention of sanctification. But here Peter declares that when the hearers in Cornelius' house received **the Holy Spirit,** they also experienced the **cleansing** [of] **their hearts.** These are two aspects of one and the same Christian experience. **Even as he did unto us** refers to the day of Pentecost (2:4). Peter indicates that the disciples at that time received the same twofold experience (vs. 9).

For **who knoweth the heart** see 1:24, the only other occurrence in the New Testament of *kardiognōstēs*, "heart-knower." **Made no distinction** is *diekrinen*. This verb is found elsewhere in Acts only three times (10:20; 11:2, 12), all in connection with the Cornelius incident. The same is true with the other two occurrences (10:15; 11:9) of *katharizō*. Of **cleansing** [*katharisas*] **their hearts** Knowling says: "Here it stands in contrast to the outward purification of circumcision upon which the Judaizers insisted." [10]

Lake and Cadbury call attention to the great difficulty of translating aorist participles into English, as illustrated here by **giving** *(dous)* and **cleansing** *(katharisas)*.[11] These participles indicate simultaneous but not continuous action. It is impossible to express this exactly in English.

An interesting parallel to this passage is found in the text of Luke 11:2 (part of the Lord's Prayer) in at least two minuscules (162 and 700), which in place of "Let thy kingdom come" have "Let thy Holy Spirit come upon us and cleanse us." [12]

---

unbearable and ineffective human device for the grace of God (vs. 10; cf. Gal. 5:1); *fifth*, the grace of God received through faith is the only means of salvation for Jews as well as Gentiles (vs. 11; cf. Rom. 3:24; Gal. 2:16; 3:6).

Clarke succinctly summarizes Peter's address as follows:

> 1. Circumcision is a sign of the purification of heart. 2. That purification can only be effected by the Holy Ghost. 3. This Holy Spirit was hitherto supposed to be the portion of those only who had received circumcision. 4. But the Gentiles, who were never circumcised, nor kept any part of the law of Moses, have had their hearts purified by faith in Christ Jesus. 5. As God, therefore, has given them the thing signified, He evidently does not intend that the sign should be administered. 6. Should we impose this burdensome rite, we should most evidently be provoking God, who plainly shows us that He intends no more to save in this way. 7. Therefore it is evident that both Jews and Gentiles are to be saved through the grace of the Lord Jesus Christ.[b]

Peter's entire speech is in full accord doctrinally with the theology of the apostle Paul, though Paul claims independence of all the apostles in the origin of his theology (Gal. 2:6). That James and the other apostles were in accord with Peter's defense of the Gentiles is clear from James' address recorded in verses 13–21.

There is an apparent divergence in point

[9] So Bruce (*Acts*, p. 292), Knowling (EGT, II, 319), Rackham (p. 252). [10] EGT, II, 319.
[11] *Beginnings*, IV, 173. [12] B. H. Streeter, *The Four Gospels*, p. 277.

[b] Clarke, *op. cit.*, V, 801.

10 Now therefore why make ye trial of God, that ye should put a yoke upon the neck of the disciples which neither our fathers nor we were able to bear?

11 But we believe that we shall be saved through the grace of the Lord Jesus, in like manner as they.

12 And all the multitude kept silence; and they hearkened unto Barnabas and Paul rehearsing what signs and wonders God had wrought among the Gentiles through them.

---

10 Lake and Cadbury call attention to the fact that the phrase **make trial of God** is borrowed from such Old Testament passages as Exodus 17:2 and Deuteronomy 6:16, and add: "It seems to mean acting against the declared will of God, and so tempting Him to inflict punishment." [13]

The **yoke** was a very familiar figure to the Jews. Rabbinical writers speak of "the yoke of Torah" (the Law); [14] that is, the obligation to keep the commandments. But Peter emphasizes here the idea of a heavy burden. Some scholars have objected to Peter's description of the Law as an unbearable yoke. But probably Schürer is justified when he writes: "Life was a continual torment to the earnest man, who felt at every moment that he was in danger of transgressing the law; and where so much depended on the external form, he was often left in uncertainty whether he had really fulfilled its requirements." [15] Bruce has pointed out that the Rabbinical writings "rarely reflect the conditions . . . of the first century A.D." and adds: "The relevant parts of the NT are among the best evidence we have for the attitude to the law in Palestine in the first 70 years of the Christian era." [16]

11 This is a clear statement of the Pauline principle that all are saved **through the grace of the Lord Jesus,** not by works of the Law. **In like manner as they** probably means that Jews are saved in the same way as Gentiles; that is, by faith in Jesus Christ.

12 **All the multitude** would seem to indicate a public meeting of the church, which would mean a different session from that described in verse six. But Lake and Cadbury say of the expression here: "It is not impossible that it implies no larger company than the apostles and elders." [17] The same term *(to plēthos)* is used of the Jewish Sanhedrin in 23:7. However, it is probably best to assume that here the whole church was called together by the apostles and elders to decide the matter (cf. 6:2). This is definitely implied in verse 22. Rackham says: "Though the initiative rested with the apostles, the consent of the whole church was required." [18] **Was silent** could mean "the meeting came to order." [19] **Hearkened** is *ēkouon,* "were hearing." It suggests continued, respectful attention.

Barnabas and Paul are named in this order for the second time since 13:7. In 14:14 (at Lystra) it was because Barnabas was

---

of view between Paul and Peter in their concept of God's choice of an apostle to the Gentiles. In the Acts account (15:7), Peter appears to claim the priority on the divine election to Gentile apostleship, whereas in Paul's account (Gal. 2:7, 8), he claims for himself the divine right to Gentile apostleship and ascribes to Peter the divine right of apostleship to the Jews. However, this apparent difference may find its reconciliation in the chronological fact that Peter was divinely called to preach to the Gentile household of Cornelius at Caesarea before Paul had begun his larger Gentile ministry, but that Peter's larger ministry was to the Jews.

B. The Declaration of Barnabas and Paul (15:12)

And all the multitude kept silence: and they hearkened unto Barnabas and Paul.

The arguments presented by Peter based upon experience, Scripture, and logic evidently left his opponents totally defeated and disarmed for the time being, and the assembled multitude awesomely convinced.

Paul and Barnabas corroborated the conclusions of Peter by a vivid recital of instances of divine manifestations and the gracious salvation of the Gentiles through their ministry on the First Missionary Journey. Doubtless the blinding of Elymas,

[13] *Beginnings,* IV, 173. [14] EGT, II, 320. [15] *Op. cit.,* II, ii, 124.
[16] *Acts,* p. 294, n. 1. [17] *Beginnings,* IV, 172.
[18] *Op. cit.,* p. 249. This view would involve two public meetings (vss. 4, 12) and a private session between (vs. 6).
[19] *Beginnings,* IV, 175.

13 And after they had held their peace, James answered, saying, Brethren, hearken unto me:
14 Symeon hath rehearsed how first God visited the Gentiles, to take out of them a people for his name.

---

taken as the chief god. Here and in verse 25 (the only other instance), it is obviously because Barnabas was held in higher esteem than Paul by the Jerusalem Christians.

Rehearsing is the verb *exēgeomai.* It means "to lead, show the way," and so metaphorically, "to unfold, narrate, declare." [20] It occurs again in verse 14 (see on 10:8). **Signs and wonders** (see note on 2:22) occur here together for the last of nine times in Acts (cf. 2:19, 22, 43; 4:30; 5:12; 6:8; 7:36; 14:3). The phrase is also used three times by Paul (Rom. 15:19; II Cor. 12:12; II Thess. 2:9) and in Hebrews 2:4. It is a common expression for miracles in the Septuagint.

13 **Held their peace** means "finished speaking" (RSV). It is the same verb, *sigaō*, which is translated "kept silence" in the previous verse. Luke uses it six times and Paul four times. **Answered** is often a pleonastic Semitism in the New Testament.[21] But here it may be similar to the Latin *responsa* for legal decisions.

Hearken unto me is *akousate mou*, found elsewhere in the New Testament only in James 2:5. J. B. Mayor has pointed out a number of striking agreements between this speech of James and the Epistle of James, which tend to corroborate the authenticity of the account here.[22]

14 **Symeon** is applied to Peter only here and in II Peter 1:1. It is the Septuagint form for Simeon in the Old Testament and is nearer the original Hebrew than the more common *Simon.* It was "probably therefore

---

the conversion of Sergius Paulus, the effect of the Gospel on the Gentiles at Antioch of Pisidia, the healing of the lame man, the conversion of Timothy, and Paul's deliverance from death at Lystra were among the **signs and wonders God had wrought among the Gentiles through them** (vs. 12b). And all of this was accomplished by, and approved of, God, quite independent of the Jewish ceremonial law. What a fitting conclusion to, and what a convincing demonstration of, the truth of Peter's apologia for Gentile salvation by grace and freedom from the burden of ceremonial law.

III. THE DECISION OF THE CHAIRMAN (15:13–21)

Naturally Peter would be expected to have taken charge of the assembly and rendered the decision concerning the status of the Gentiles in the Christian Church, as well as the requirements to be met by them for membership. Certainly, if the contention of the Roman church, that Peter was the pope, were correct, he should have presided at this first general church council. However, the office is assumed by another while Peter quite gracefully gives place.

A. The Position of the Chairman (15:13)

And after they had held their peace, James answered, saying, Brethren, hearken unto me.

James, the Lord's brother, who was pastor of the Jewish-Christian church at Jerusalem, evidently assumed the role of president or moderator of the Council, by calling the assembly to attention. A note of recognized authority seems to characterize his manner and ring in his introductory words, **Brethren, hearken unto me** (vs. 13b). While humbly and sympathetically identifying himself with the Council, he had a decision to render, and he demanded a hearing. Since the Judaizers centered in the mother church of which he was pastor, and since it was from this church that their activities had been launched, it was quite logical that James should have assumed command, as chairman of the assembly, as also in a certain sense, the judge who rendered the final decision.

B. The Summary of the Chairman (15:14–18)

Symeon hath rehearsed how first God visited the Gentiles, to take out of them a people for his name (vs. 14).

Though a Jewish Christian himself and

[20] Abbott-Smith, *op. cit.*, p. 160.
[21] See Arndt and Gingrich, *op. cit.*, p. 93; Gustaf Dalman, *The Words of Jesus*, pp. 24 f.
[22] *Op. cit.*, pp. iii f.

15 And to this agree the words of the prophets; as it is written.
16 After these things I will return,
And I will build again the tabernacle of David, which is fallen;
And I will build again the ruins thereof,
And I will set it up:
17 That the residue of men may seek after the Lord,
And all the Gentiles, upon whom my name is called,

---

the form current in Jerusalem."[23] Further support is given in the fact that this Hebraic form is found in the list of early Jerusalem bishops in Eusebius.[24] Lake and Cadbury comment: "It was fitting that Peter should be addressed by a Palestinian Jew by his Jewish name and even in its most Jewish spelling."[25]

Visited is the verb *episkeptomai*, which is related to *episkopos*, "overseer," "bishop" (cf. episcopal). Its original meaning was "inspect, examine." Then it came to mean "visit," and even "visit with help." In modern Greek it is used especially for visiting the sick and afflicted. In 6:3 it has the rarer sense of "look out." All three of these meanings are illustrated in the papyri.[26]

The combination of *ethnē*, **Gentiles,** and *laos*, **people,** is indeed striking. In the Old Testament they are always contrasted. The Jews, and they alone, were the people of God. Now God had selected from the Gentiles **a people for his name.** This may mean a people who should bear His Name (the people of God), or simply a people for Himself (name being used for person).

15 **The prophets** probably refers to the roll of the Twelve Prophets.[27]

16–18 The quotation is from Amos 9:11, 12. There is a definite problem involved, in that James bases his argument on the Septuagint—quoted here somewhat freely—which differs strikingly from the Massoretic Hebrew text.

16 For **after these things** Amos has "in that day," in the Hebrew and Septuagint. Probably both signify the time of the Messiah.[28] Meyer writes: "The meaning is the same: after the pre-Messianic penal judgments, in the day of the Messianic restoration."[29]

17 While verse 16 has some variations

---

primarily concerned with the affairs of the Jewish-Christian church, James nevertheless had caught the significance of Christ's commission and the universal implications of His Gospel. He threw the full weight of his authority behind the address of Peter delivered in favor of the Gentiles' salvation by grace and freedom from the ceremonial law. He fully approved Peter's conduct in preaching the Gospel to Cornelius' household, and he credited their conversion as a genuine work of God. Further, James quoted to this Jewish-Christian assembly a Jewish prophecy from Amos 9:11, 12, which he declared to be in full agreement with the contention of Peter. Thus the Jewish prophets knew better than the Judaizers, God's place for the Gentiles in His spiritual kingdom.

Amos prophesied before the exile and foretold the partial historical restoration of Israel, but thereby implied the spiritual inclusion of this Jewish remnant who should **seek after the Lord** (vs. 17) together with **all the Gentiles, upon whom my name is called** [better, who call upon my name]—(see Acts 2:21), in His great spiritual kingdom, the Church of Jesus Christ. This divine purpose was made known by God **from of old** or "from the beginning" (vs. 18b), and was revealed to Amos and the other Messianic prophets, but only now is it discovered that the prophecy is being fulfilled. God is giving the Gentiles a spiritual visitation for the purpose of completing His spiritual kingdom, the *ecclesia*, the body of Christ of which He is the rightful head (cf. 1:22, 23; 2:11–22; 3:6).

It is interesting that James here called Peter by his common Hebrew name **Symeon,** and not Peter, a fact that would not honor him with any special significance on this important occasion.

[23] EGT II, 321. [24] *Ecclesiastical History*, IV, 5. [25] *Beginnings*, IV, 175.
[26] VGT, p. 243 f. [27] *Beginnings*, IV, 176. [28] Cf. Edersheim, *Life and Times*, II, 734.
[29] H. A. W. Meyer, *Critical and Exegetical Handbook to the Acts of the Apostles*. Translated from the 4th Ger. ed. by Paton J. Gloag (New York: Funk & Wagnalls, 1883), p. 287.

18 Saith the Lord, who maketh these things known from of old.
19 Wherefore my judgment is, that we trouble not them that from among the Gentiles turn to God;

---

from both the Hebrew and Septuagint, it is in this verse that the real problem arises. The Massoretic text reads: "That they may possess the remnant of Edom and all the nations which are called by my name." It is a prophecy of the restoration of the Davidic kingdom to its ancient power and proportions. But the Septuagint altered the meaning—apparently adopting *yidreshu* (will seek) in place of *yireshu* (will possess) and *adam* (man) in place of *Edom.* Moreover, the Hebrew clearly indicates that **residue** (remnant) is the object, not the subject as in the Septuagint. In the present state of textual studies, it appears impossible to give a satisfactory solution for this problem.

Upon whom my name is called is closely paralleled in James 2:7 and nowhere else in the New Testament.

18 **Known from of old** is not in the Old Testament, either Hebrew or Greek. The words were apparently added by James. The phrase *ap' aiōnos* occurs in the New Testament only in Luke's writings. In Psalms of Solomon (8:7) it seems to mean "from creation."

While we cannot solve the textual problem the significance of this prophecy is apparent. It is a prediction of the Messianic kingdom, fulfilled in the Son of David. Bruce summarizes well the meaning of verses 16 and 17 when he writes: "As the presence of believing Jews in the Church fulfilled the prediction of the rebuilding of the tabernacle of David, so the presence of believing Gentiles fulfilled the next part of the prophecy." [30]

19 **My judgment is** *(egō krinō*—"I for my part judge") may mean "I decree," or perhaps only, "I recommend." *Parenochlein,* **trouble,** is found only here in the New Testament. The present tense indicates clearly that the meaning is "*stop* annoying." **Turn** is "are turning" (present participle).

C. The Sentence of the Chairman (15:19–21)

Wherefore my judgment is, that we trouble not them that from among the Gentiles turn to God (vs. 19).

James speaks with the authority vested in him as chairman of the Council. This is evident in the decision which he renders, and it is recognized by the Council in its adoption of his recommendations.

It is noteworthy that James recommends that the decisions he is about to make be sent to the churches by letter from the Council. This is probably intended not only to make the decision official but also to prevent its denial or distortion by the Judaizers.

Negatively considered, James cast his decision in favor of the position of Peter, Barnabas, and Paul; **that we trouble not . . . the Gentiles** (vs. 19b) with the burden of the Mosaic ceremonial law. Positively, James advanced four prohibitions to be observed by Gentile Christians, designed, in part at least, to facilitate Jewish-Gentile social and religious relationships, but all of which pertained to approved Christian deportment and were not requisites to salvation. When analyzed, these prohibitions appear to fall into four categories as follows:

1. *A Religious Prohibition*: **that they abstain from the pollutions of idols** (vs. 20).
2. *A Moral Prohibition*: **that they abstain from . . . fornication** (vs. 20b).
3. *A Hygienic Prohibition*: **that they abstain from . . . what is strangled** (vs. 20b).
4. *A Civil Prohibition*: **that they abstain from . . . blood** (vs. 20b).

The *first*, or religious prohibition, did not pertain primarily to the worship of idols, a practice renounced by Gentiles at their conversion (see I Thess. 1:9b), but rather to meat which had been sacrificed to the heathen idols, as indicated in verse 29. This prohibition would be observed by refusing to buy such meat in the markets as was known to have been sacrified to idols; by declining to receive or to eat, in heathen homes, meat known to have been offered to idols; by avoiding heathen religious feasts which were both an incentive to idolatry and moral impurities.

Second, the moral prohibition was directed, not only against **fornication** as such, but as

[30] *Acts,* p. 298.

20 but that we write unto them, that they abstain from the pollutions of idols, and from fornication, and from what is strangled, and from blood.

21 For Moses from generations of old hath in every city them that preach him, being read in the synagogues every sabbath.

---

20 **Write** is the verb *epistellō*, "send a message by letter" (epistle). It is used for a written injunction, and so may be translated either "write" or "enjoin."

Pollutions of idols is the word *alisgēma*, which has not been found elsewhere in Greek literature. It is from *alisgeō*, "pollute," and so means simply "pollution." But its significance here is indicated by verse 29 and 21:25, both of which have *eidōlothyta*, "things sacrificed to idols." Bruce favors the interpretation of **fornication** as referring to breaches of the Jewish marriage laws (Lev. 18).[31] **What is strangled** is *pniktou*, found (in N.T.) only in connection with these decrees (15:20, 29; 21:25).

The Western text (D, g, Latin of Irenaeus) omits *pniktou*—thus leaving only three prohibitions—and adds "and not to do to others what they do not wish done to themselves." This makes the decree purely ethical. Bruce comments: "Idolatry, fornication, and murder were the three cardinal sins in Jewish eyes."[32] The Western text is consistent in omitting **strangled** in verse 29 and in 21:25. Harnack thinks this was the original form of the decree.[33]

21 The significance of **for** *(gar)* has been a matter of dispute among commentators. Knowling suggests the following explanation: "The Gentile proselytes could long ago in the synagogues have been acquainted week by week with the spirit and enactments of the Mosaic law, and they would thus be the more easily inclined to take upon themselves the few elementary precepts laid down in the decree of the Jerusalem Church."[34] Bruce writes: "Possibly James means that since Jews are to be found everywhere, their scruples are to be respected."[35] Hackett gives much the same view.[36] Rackham reasons thus: Moses would continue to be read in the synagogues every sabbath, so that Jewish Christians could still hear the Law. The liberty given Gentile converts would not rob the synagogues of their worshipers.[37]

---

the word seems to allow, against adultery (I Thess. 4:3-7), prostitution, homosexuality (Rom. 1:26, 27), incest, and bestiality (cf. Lev. 15 and I Cor. 5:1). These vices, frequently practiced in connection with heathen worship, were an especial danger to the young Gentile converts environed by evil influences as they were. Wesley remarks: "Which even the philosophers among the heathens did not account any fault. It was particularly frequent in the worship of their idols; on which account they [**pollutions of idols** and **fornication**] are here named, together."[c] Lightfoot holds that this prohibition was especially directed against the Gentile practice of marriage within the forbidden degrees, especially such as is described in Leviticus chapter 18, against which the Jews had a strong antipathy but which was common among the Gentiles (I Cor. 5:1).

Third, the hygienic prohibition pertained to the heathen practice of strangling, rather than butchering an animal killed for meat. Such meat was considered a delicacy by some of the pagans, but the practice was forbidden by God (see Lev. 17:10-14 and Deut. 12:16, 23, 25), and it was highly obnoxious to the Jews, a fact which would have caused the Gentile Christians no limit of difficulty in their religious and social intercourse with the Jewish Christians.

On the *fourth* prohibition scholars have differed, some holding that *blood* here refers to the use of animal blood as food, a position apparently rendering the fourth prohibition quite unnecessary because of its close similarity, if not identity, with the third prohibition. Another and more likely view is that it is a prohibition against cruelty, murder, manslaughter, or other acts of violence (Clarke). God's prohibitions contained in Genesis 9:4-6 appear to have a bearing on this question. Weymouth remarks on this problem:

[31] *Acts*, p. 300. [32] *Ibid.*, p. 299. [33] Adolph Harnack, *The Acts of the Apostles*, pp. 255-263.
[34] EGT, II, 325. [35] *Acts*, p. 300. [36] *Op. cit.*, p. 176. [37] *Op. cit.*, p. 254.

[c] Wesley, *op. cit.*, p. 454, n. 20.

22 Then it seemed good to the apostles and the elders, with the whole church, to choose men out of their company, and send them to Antioch with Paul and Barnabas; *namely*, Judas called Barsabbas, and Silas, chief men among the brethren:

23 and they wrote *thus* by them, The apostles and the elders, brethren, unto the brethren who are of the Gentiles in Antioch and Syria and Cilicia, greeting:

---

22 **It seemed good** is *edoxe.* Knowling says: "The word is often found in public resolutions and official decrees." [38] Lake and Cadbury go a step further and state: "*Edoxe* is the technical term in Greek of all periods for 'voting' or 'passing' a measure in the assembly." So they translate it here, "It was voted." [39]

23 **And they wrote thus by them** is literally, "having written through their hand" *(grapsantes dia cheiros autōn).* But clearly these men were the messengers who carried the letters, not the secretaries who wrote them. The Revised Standard Version gives an excellent paraphrase: "with the following letter." **The apostles and the elders, brethren** could be rendered "the apostles and the elder brethren," as in the English Revised Version. Lake and Cadbury argue for the American Revised rendering.[40] The King James reading must be rejected, since "and" before "brethren" is not in Aleph A B C D. **Syria and Cilicia** formed a double province, with Antioch as the chief city.

It is a very striking fact that *chairein,* **greeting,** is found here in the council's letter (perhaps dictated by James) and in James 1:1, but nowhere else in the New Testament at the beginning of an Epistle. Paul uses *charis,* "grace," instead.

There is some evidence, both in verses 20 and 29, for the omission of 'things strangled,' as well as for the addition of a negative form of the Golden Rule, 'Do not to others what you would not have done to yourselves.' Some interpreters, accepting the shortened text, regard the Decree as a threefold *moral* prohibition, of idolatry, bloodshed (murder), and fornication.[d]

One view of verse 21 is that James considered these prohibitions unnecessary for the Jewish Christian, since they were all contained in the Scriptures which they regularly heard read in the synagogues and with which they would be familiar (Clarke). Another view holds that these prohibitions are rendered necessary for the amicable relations of the Gentile Christians with the Jews, who were so widely diffused over the empire. Yet another view holds that James is simply recommending that the Jewish Christians are still to attend the synagogues and observe the ceremonial law (Dummelow).

IV. THE DECREES OF THE COUNCIL (15:22–29)

With no dissenting voice, and an apparent satisfaction on the part of all with the conclusions reached, the Council proceeded to formulate the decrees.

A. The Support of the Decrees (15:22)

Then it seemed good to the apostles and the elders, with the whole church . . . and they wrote thus (vss. 22a, 23a).

Concurring in the decision to formulate and publish the decrees stated by James were the body of original apostles at Jerusalem, who were responsible for the general oversight and direction of the Church, the ruling elders of the local churches as represented at the Council, and the entire lay membership of the Jerusalem church and the Council. No voice of dissent is heard from the Judaizers, and had they been content to leave the matter as settled by the Council, how much trouble the young Church would have been saved (see Gal. 1:6–10)!

Had the decrees been left with Paul and Barnabas to deliver, they might have been suspected by the Judaizers, since they were involved in the controversy. Therefore, in accordance with the Mosaic legal requirement for the establishment of evidence, and recommended by Christ (Matt. 18:16), they, the whole Council in democratic concurrence, chose two honored and representative man from the Council to accompany Paul and Barnabas and deliver the decrees, primarily

[38] EGT, II, 325.
[39] *Beginnings,* IV, 178.
[40] *Ibid.,* p. 180.

[d] Richard Francis Weymouth, *The New Testament in Modern Speech* (Rev. Ed., New York: Harper and Brothers, Publishers), p. 312, n. 20.

24 Forasmuch as we have heard that certain who went out from us have troubled you with words, subverting your souls; to whom we gave no commandment;
25 it seemed good unto us, having come to one accord, to choose cut men and send them unto you with our beloved Barnabas and Paul,
26 men that have hazarded their lives for the name of our Lord Jesus Christ.

---

24 **With words** "may mean with words only, words without true doctrine."[41] **Subverting,** *anaskeuazontes,* is found only here in the New Testament. It means "properly *to pack up baggage,* hence, *to dismantle, ravage, destroy;* metaphorically, *to unsettle, subvert.*"[42] In a military sense it was used for plundering or dismantling a town.[43] This is what the Judaizers were doing to the Christian church at Antioch. Lake and Cadbury put it thus: "It means reversing what has been done, tearing down what has been built, or cancelling what has been agreed upon."[44] The insertion of "such" in the last clause of this verse in the King James Version weakens, and so distorts, the statement. The church at Jerusalem declared that it had not authorized the Judaizers in their mission to Antioch.

25 **Having come to one accord** expresses very accurately the Greek, *genomenois homothymadon;* literally, "having become of the same mind." The rendering of the Revised Standard Version, "in assembly," is evidently due to the contention of Lake and Cadbury that in Hellenistic Greek *homothymadon* "probably had come to mean simply 'together.'"[45] The King James rendering, "being assembled with one accord," is a combination. The next words read literally, "having chosen men, to send" *(eklexamenois andras pempsai).*

Agapētos, **beloved,** occurs only here in Acts. Paul uses it some 28 times in his epistles. James has it three times, Peter about eight times, and John nine times. It was the latter three who, probably at this time, gave to Paul and Barnabas the right hand of fellowship (Gal. 2:9). The word **our** here is significant as showing the attitude of the Jerusalem leaders toward the two apostles to the Gentiles.

26 **Hazarded** is the verb *paradidōmi,* the basic meaning of which is "give" or "hand over." Occurring about 120 times in the New Testament, it is translated "hazard" only here. Lake and Cadbury assert: "The English rendering 'hazarded' for *paradedōkosi* is indefensible; it means 'given up,' not 'risked.'"[46] Yet "risked" is the translation in the Revised Standard Version. Knowling claims it has this meaning in classical Greek and the Septuagint.[47] Perhaps the best rendering is "devoted,"[48] with the overtones of "risking."

---

to the church at Antioch where the controversy had arisen. **Judas,** called Barsabbas, a Hebrew Christian, and possibly the brother of Joseph Barsabbas who was a candidate for apostleship to replace Judas (Acts 1:23), was the first elected, likely to represent the Christian-Jewish point of view. **Silas,** or Silvanus, whose Latin name identifies him as a Hellenist, is next chosen to represent the Gentile interest and point of view. How providential that Silas, one of the **chief men among the brethren** (vs. 22b) at the Council, should have been chosen for this mission. The appointment opened the door to him for a larger ministry as the companion of Paul on his Second Missionary Journey (see Acts 15:40; 16:19; 17:4, 10, 14; 18:5 and II Cor. 1:19). His Roman citizenship, like that of Paul, was a valuable credential for travel and missionary service out in the empire (see Acts 16:37–39). At a later date he appears to have been associated with Peter (I Peter 5:12).

B. The Script of the Decrees (15:23–29)

And they wrote thus by them (vs. 23a).

In writing the decrees to the churches, they supplied a threefold witness to the decisions of the Council; *first,* that of Paul and Barnabas; *second,* that of Judas Barsabbas and Silas; and *third,* that of the written statement (Matt. 18:16). Further, a written

[41] EGT, II, 327. [42] Abbott-Smith, *op. cit.*, p. 33. [43] VGT, p. 37. [44] *Beginnings*, IV, 180.
[45] *Ibid.*, p. 54. Interestingly, Bruce supports this idea (see *Acts*, p. 302—"having met together").
[46] *Beginnings*, IV, 180. [47] EGT, II, 327.
[48] So Bruce (*Acts*, p. 302), following Lake and Cadbury.

27 We have sent therefore Judas and Silas, who themselves also shall tell you the same things by word of mouth.
28 For it seemed good to the Holy Spirit, and to us, to lay upon you no greater burden than these necessary things:
29 that ye abstain from things sacrificed to idols, and from blood, and from things strangled, and from fornication; from which if ye keep yourselves, it shall be well with you. Fare ye well.

---

27 *Apestalkamen*, **we have sent**, is a good example of the epistolary perfect (cf. epistolary aorist). Though the messengers had not yet been sent when these words were penned, the letter is written from the point of view of its readers—perhaps a fine touch of ancient courtesy. For **Judas and Silas** compare verse 22.

28 **Necessary**—not for salvation, but for good fellowship between Jewish and Gentile Christians.

29 **It shall be well with you** *(eu praxete)* is common in the papyri in the sense of "you will prosper." [49] But in Ignatius and Justin Martyr, it definitely means "you will be doing right," and Lake and Cadbury prefer that rendering here as suiting the context better.[50] Since the epistolary usage in the papyri favors the former, probably both senses should be allowed.

Errōsthe, **fare ye well**, is the perfect imperative of *rhōnnymi*, "strengthen." It is used most frequently in the perfect tense, with the meaning, "be strong." In the New Testament it occurs only here and in the Received Text of 23:30 (see note there) at the close of the letter from Lysias to Felix.

---

record of the decrees would prevent distortion of the Council's decision, support the oral report of the apostles, and preserve a record of the historic Council's agreement on the issue.

The address of the epistle reflects, not only the unanimity of the participating personnel (**The apostles and the elders, brethren** (vs. 23a), but also a tender and endearing fraternalism and Christian affection, as suggested by the words of specific greeting which may be read: from the brethren of the Jerusalem Council **unto the brethren who are of the Gentiles, in Antioch and Syria and Cilicia, greeting** (vs. 23b). Further, here is designated both the places and persons for which the epistle was intended. It had been designed for the Gentile disciples in whose interest the decrees had been made. It was directed to those disciples in Antioch where the controversy had arisen, and throughout Syria and Cilicia where Gentile Christians were located among the Jews and would require the decrees both for their protection and instruction. There was no need to address the Jewish Christians, as the epistle concerned only the Gentile Christians.

The epistle takes passing note of the Judaizing adversaries who had given rise to the necessity of this epistle. The Council assumes a proportionate share of responsibility for the activities of these disturbing legalists, who, they write, **went out from us** [and] **have troubled you with words, subverting your souls** (vs. 24). So must the Church ever assume responsibility for her whole constituency, the defective or injurious as well as the saintly and benevolent (cf. Isa. 6:5 and Gal. 6:1-3). Indeed the Church owns them, **they went out from us;** but the Church does not approve their subversive activities nor take responsibility for their unauthorized teachings: **to whom we gave no commandment** (vs. 24b).

Briefly the epistle reviews the account of the Council proceedings, by relating the unanimity of spirit (see Additional Note I, *One Accord*, at end of chapter I) and judgment in the decisions reached and the plans formulated. A special word of confidence is accorded the apostles; **our beloved Barnabas and Paul, men that have hazarded their lives for the name of our Lord Jesus Christ** (vss. 25b, 26). This is especially significant in view of the fact that they have been, and will again be, under attack by the Judaizers.

Special divine inspiration is claimed for the decrees about to be written: **For it seemed good to the Holy Spirit** (vs. 28a). Paul claimed divine revelation in attending the Council

[49] VGT, p. 534.
[50] *Beginnings*, IV, 181.

30 So they, when they were dismissed, came down to Antioch; and having gathered the multitude together, they delivered the epistle.
31 And when they had read it, they rejoiced for the consolation.
32 And Judas and Silas, being themselves also prophets, exhorted the brethren with many words, and confirmed them.
33 And after they had spent some time *there*, they were dismissed in peace from the brethren unto those that had sent them forth.

---

30 **Came down to Antioch** reflects the point of view that still accepted Jerusalem as the main headquarters. **The multitude** is the literal meaning of *to plēthos*. Here it clearly means the church (cf. RSV—"the congregation"). *Epedōkan*, **delivered** was a technical term in later Greek for handing over a letter.[51] In the papyri it was "the ordinary formula for sending in a report to a magistrate or official body."[52]

31 *Paraklēsis*, consolation, also means "encouragement" and "exhortation." In the King James Version it is translated "consolation" fourteen times, "exhortation" eight times, "comfort" six times, and "intreaty" once. The context would seem to favor **consolation** here rather than "exhortation." Ramsay adopts "encouragement."[53]

32 **Exhorted** is the verb *parakaleō*, from which is derived the noun *paraklēsis*, translated "consolation" in the previous verse. Lake and Cadbury maintain that the same meaning must be given to both, although they admit that "... 'comfort' is less usual with the verb than with the substantive."[54] They use "comfort" in both places, the Revised Standard Version "exhortation" (exhort). But it seems that the double rendering in the King James and American Standard versions is preferable. **Confirmed** is a compound, *epistērizo*, "make stronger." It is found only here, in verse 41, and in 14:22. They made the church "firm and compact after its recent shaking and divisions."[55]

33 **After they had spent some time there** is literally "having done time" *(poiēsantes chronon)*. There is no indication of the length of this stay. **In peace** reflects the most common greeting of the East, "Peace to you" (John 20:19), and farewell, "Go in peace."

(Gal. 2:2), Peter claimed divine direction in his ministry to the Gentiles as reported at the Council (Acts 15:7), and there was every evidence of divine approval in the decisions reached by the Council. Therefore it is in order that these decrees be sent forth as the voice of God.

Reference to **these necessary things** (vs. 28b) indicates the disposition of the Church to keep external regulations of the Church over its members at a minimum (cf. Matt. 11:28–30).

Finally, the admonitions contained in the decrees set forth in the letter are reiterated with some change in their order from James' original statement (see comment on verse 20). The observance of these regulations will be in the interest of their spiritual welfare and prosperity, the letter informs them, and then closes with an expression of Christian good will (vs. 29b).

V. THE DELIVERY OF THE DECREES (15:30–35)

And having gathered the multitude together, they delivered the epistle (vs. 30b).

Officially released from, and authorized by, the Council, the delegation proceeded to Antioch where before the assembled church they read the epistle, with the result that the disciples **rejoiced for the consolation** (vs. 31b), which its message afforded them. They were now officially free from the threatened yoke of legalism and could devote themselves to spiritual edification and vital evangelism. Judas and Silas, both of whom were prophets (preachers), took advantage of the Antiocheans' jubilant spirits and delivered a series of exhortations, probably on brotherly love, spiritual unity, loyalty, steadfastness in the Christian faith, and devotion to the continued evangelization of their non-

[51] *Beginnings*, IV, 182.
[52] VGT, p. 238.
[53] *St. Paul the Traveller*, p. 174.
[54] *Beginnings*, IV, 182.
[55] Rackham, *op. cit.*, p. 257.

35 But Paul and Barnabas tarried in Antioch, teaching and preaching the word of the Lord, with many others also.

---

34 This verse is omitted in the Revised Versions because absent in Aleph A B E H L P. In the King James Version it reads: "Notwithstanding it pleased Silas to abide there still." The Western text adds: "and only Judas went." The addition is obviously intended to explain why Silas was in Antioch to accompany Paul on his second missionary journey (vs. 40).

Ramsay defends the genuineness of this verse. He writes: "At some period *v.* 34 was deliberately omitted from the text, from the mistaken idea that *v.* 33 declared the actual departure of Judas and Silas: but the officials of the Church in Antioch (the Elders?) simply informed Judas and Silas that their duties were concluded and they were free to return home, and Silas did not avail himself of the permission." [56] But this interpretation seems strained and the textual criticism precarious. It is probably best to take the natural implication of verse 33 that Judas and Silas returned to Jerusalem and that the latter came back to Antioch again before verse 40.

Christian fellows. They concluded by confirming them in the truths they had previously been taught. How long they remained we are not told, but that they were farewelled under the blessings of God is suggested by Luke's words, **they were dismissed in peace from the brethren unto those that had sent them forth** (vs. 33b).

How long Paul and Barnabas remained at Antioch, **teaching and preaching the word of the Lord** (vs. 35), we are not told, but the entire time elapsing between the First and Second Missionary Journeys certainly did not exceed two years.

The problem of fitting the conduct of Peter, as recorded in Galatians 2:11–21, into the pattern of events at Antioch has plagued the minds of many scholars. Certainly the view that Peter went to Antioch soon after the Jerusalem Council and became guilty of the divisive conduct attributed to him in the Galatian account hardly seems logical, if possible. On the other hand, to relate the second chapter of Galatians to the eleventh chapter of Acts is highly unsatisfactory. Where then does the conduct of Peter, described in Galatians 2, best fit?

First, let it be observed that in the Galatian letter Paul is arguing the case for Gentile freedom, and not recording history, as is the case with Luke in Acts. Indeed, Paul is drawing on historical events to enforce his argument, but that without necessary regard to the sequence of events.

Second, therefore, we shall assume that Peter's conduct as recorded in Galatians 2:11–21 actually occurred at some time before the Jerusalem Council events recorded in Galatians 2:1–10. Thus Peter's conduct and Paul's rebuke of that conduct may have taken the form of an afterthought with the apostle. This he relates to the Galatians to show what issues were finally settled at the Council and that even Peter and Barnabas, who had been influenced by Peter at Antioch, were both so far convinced as to champion the cause of Gentile freedom at the Council.

Third, granted the foregoing conclusions, then the conduct of Peter in Galatians 2:11–21 would appear to best fit into an earlier visit of this apostle to Antioch, possibly in a supervisory capacity during the ministry of Paul and Barnabas, prior to the First Missionary Journey. It might best fit into the period described in Acts 11:25, 26.

The foregoing conclusion has the following support: (1) there were both Jew and Gentile Christians in the Antioch church (Acts 11:19–21); (2) that Barnabas faced difficulty in reconciling the Jew and Gentile elements at Antioch likely accounted for his seeking Saul, who possessed special qualification by nature and training for such a delicate task (Acts 11:25–26); (3) Paul who labored at this task with Barnabas for a year (Acts 11:26) would naturally have been greatly disturbed at such a time by the official conduct of Peter on a social occasion among the Christians at Antioch, which even influenced Barnabas, just when the reconciliation of the Jews and Gentiles seemed imminent; (4) the conduct of Peter did not involve the question of circumcision, which was dealt with at the Jerusalem Council, but rather

[56] *St. Paul the Traveller*, pp. 174 f.

36 And after some days Paul said unto Barnabas, Let us return now and visit the brethren in every city wherein we proclaimed the word of the Lord, *and see* how they fare.
37 And Barnabas was minded to take with them John also, who was called Mark.
38 But Paul thought not good to take with them him who withdrew from them from Pamphylia, and went not with them to the work.

---

36 **After some days,** while indefinite, probably suggests a short period.[57]

37 **Was minded** is perhaps better than "determined" (KJV). The oldest manuscripts [58] have *ebouleto*. *Boulomai* means "will, wish, desire, purpose, be minded." [59] The Textus Receptus has *ebouleusato*, which means "resolved" or "determined with himself" (in the middle, as here).

38 **Thought . . . good** is a strong verb, *axioō*, meaning "think fit" or "deem worthy." **To take** is present infinitive here, *synparalambanein*, "to keep on taking along with them." In verse 37 it is the aorist infinitive, *sunparalabein*. Paul thought it fit not to keep on taking one who had proved unreliable. Barnabas wanted to give him one more chance.

---

the matter of the social relations of the two nationalities. Peter had been severely censured by the Pharisaic party at Jerusalem for this same breach of Jewish religious and social etiquette while at Caesarea (Acts 11:1–3), and their presence at Antioch could easily account for his deflection there; (5) both Peter and Barnabas seemed to have fully recovered themselves, without resentment, after Paul's rebuke, and thus after a lapse of between two to three years, it is not surprising that they defended the Gentiles' liberty so vigorously at the Council.

Part II

The Church's First European Mission

I. THE APOSTLES' PLANS FOR THE MISSION

(15:36–41)

Certainly the Second Missionary Journey was more opportune at this juncture than had it occurred before the Jerusalem Council, as now the Christian Gentiles' relation to the Church has been officially determined. That the apostles had long contemplated this second evangelistic enterprise is likely.

A. The Proposal of Paul (15:36)

Paul said unto Barnabas, Let us return now and visit the brethren in every city wherein we proclaimed the word of the Lord.

Three things become evident in the plans for the second missionary campaign. *First,* it is Paul who takes the initiative and suggests the plans and purposes of this campaign. *Second,* it seems clear that in his original plans, Paul purposed to follow the course of the First Missionary Journey, judging from his reference to **every city wherein we proclaimed the word of the Lord** (vs. 36). *Third,* the objective of the campaign is specifically stated to be a review of the progress of the Christian faith where they planted it during the first campaign, as the words, **and see how they fare** (vs. 36b), would imply.

That Paul did not have a European mission in mind at this time seems further evident from the fact that his plans to evangelize in the province of Asia (Acts 16:6) were thwarted by the Holy Spirit, as were his subsequent plans to evangelize in Bithynia (Acts 16:7).

Thus it would appear that the whole procedure of the divine scheme for the Second Missionary Journey was revealed step by step as the apostles followed the divine leadings. While Paul proposed a worthy missionary plan, God purposed a much more extensive and fruitful campaign that was to penetrate to the very heart of first-century European-Hellenist civilization. Paul's plans were always subject to revision by the divine wisdom. Only a careful review of the fruits of this second journey will reveal the spiritual losses, had Paul missed God's plan for the campaign. How much more is seen by Him who looks down from above the circle of heavens (Isa. 40:22), than by man who looks up from the valley hemmed in by mountain walls.

[57] Hackett, p. 179. [58] Aleph A B C E. [59] Abbott-Smith, *op. cit.*, p. 84.

39 And there arose a sharp contention, so that they parted asunder one from the other, and Barnabas took Mark with him, and sailed away unto Cyprus:

---

39 **Sharp contention** is *paroxysmos*, which (without the ending) has been taken over bodily into English. It means "stimulation, provocation; irritation." [60] Elsewhere in the New Testament it occurs only in Hebrews 10:24—"Let us consider one another *to provoke* unto love and good works." It may be doubted whether the common English rendering **sharp contention** is fully justified. Yet it must be admitted that there was a strong enough provocation to separate these companions of years. Bruce is right in his observation: "It is a tribute to Luke's honesty that he should describe a quarrel between two apostles by so strong a term." [61]

Parted assunder is *apochoristhēnai*, found elsewhere in the New Testament only in Revelation 6:14. It emphasizes essentially the idea of separation.

Barnabas . . . sailed away unto Cyprus.

B. The Problem of John Mark (15:37, 38)

And Barnabas was minded to take with them John also . . . but Paul thought not good to take . . . him (vss. 37a, 38a).

The first serious recorded Apostolic Church leadership problem arose over the question of John Mark's accompanying Paul and Barnabas on the Second Missionary Journey. The departure of Mark from the missionary party at Perga, on the first journey, was treated in relation to Acts 13:13. At the outset of the Second Missionary Journey, John Mark is at Antioch with plans to accompany the apostles. Barnabas, his cousin, has a deep interest in him and his welfare, as well as a devotion to the missionary cause. Paul, a nonrelative of Mark and possessed of a supreme devotion to the cause of Christ, is unable to see in Mark the values discernible by Barnabas. Paul remembers the departure of Mark from the work at Perga and thinks of the words of Christ (Luke 9:62). Robinson[c] thinks, further, that there may have been other problems involved in the contention, including too ambitious a program for Barnabas; Barnabas' act of siding with Peter (Gal. 2:11); difference of opinion as to the route to be followed; and Paul's desire to visit his own Cilician country first.

C. The Parting of the Apostles (15:39–41)

Leaving the foregoing speculations, we are on certain ground when we center the problem in John Mark and observe that the sharp contention over the problem resulted in their parting asunder, Barnabas taking Mark and Paul taking Silas. Barnabas followed the former route to Cyprus where we lose sight of him. Paul takes a northwesterly route through Syria and into Cilicia confirming the churches en route. Paul and Silas are said to have been **commended by the brethren to the grace of the Lord** (vs. 40b). Nothing is said of the church's approval of the program of Barnabas and Mark. However, this may be due to Luke's purpose to record the history of Paul henceforth and thus may have no bearing on Barnabas.

Notwithstanding the nearly, if not quite, facetious remark of D. A. Hayes, that he is quite sure one of the two brethren lost his perfect love over the contention, Clarke argues with learning and force that there is nothing in the expression, **sharp contention** (vs. 39a), to justify the conclusion that ill will characterized either of them. That they were both perfectly sincere in their positions may well be granted. That they were both right from their respective points of view is possible. Let us sum up the resultant facts: *first*, there appears to have been no breach of fellowship between Paul and Barnabas (I Cor. 9:6); *second*, Barnabas was evidently right in giving Mark another chance, as his history reveals and as Paul later recognizes (see Col. 4:10; Philemon 24; II Tim. 4:11); *third*, two missionary parties went forth, each of which had special qualifications for its respective fields of service; *fourth*, the division appears to have had no ill effects on the church at Antioch, nor to have created any problems on the fields visited;

[60] *Ibid.*, p. 347. [61] *Acts*, p. 306.

[c] Robinson, *op. cit.*, pp. 111, 112.

40 but Paul chose Silas, and went forth, being commended by the brethren to the grace of the Lord.
41 And he went through Syria and Cilicia, confirming the churches.

For him this was going home—perhaps for the last time. There is a pathetic sadness about this parting.

40 **Silas** would be an especially appropriate companion for Paul, since he was mentioned by name in the letter they were to take with them (cf. 16:4).

41 For **confirming** see note on verse 32.

---

fifth and finally, the incident apparently opened the door of opportunity for Silas to accompany Paul on his Second Missionary Journey, and thus to gain experience that developed him into one of Paul's closest companions and most useful co-workers in the gospel ministry.

Thus we are taught the lesson from first-century Christianity that even great men may forcefully disagree on what they regard as principles and still maintain Christian grace and charity while proceeding on their respective courses, and that out of such vigorous disagreements of energetic men may come greater good than from apathetic acquiescence (Rom. 8:28).

CHAPTER XVI

And he came also to Derbe and to Lystra: and behold, a certain disciple was there, named Timothy, the son of a Jewess that believed; but his father was a Greek.

EXEGESIS

1 **He came** is singular *(katēntēsen)*, showing that Paul was definitely the leader. The verb *katantaō* occurs here for the first of nine times in Acts. Elsewhere in the New Testament it is used four times by Paul, always in the figurative sense of "attain to." It has that metaphorical meaning once in Acts (26:7). Here it may be translated "arrived at."

It is not stated positively in which city **Timothy** lived. Origen placed him in Derbe.[1] But the best manuscripts[2] have *eis* (to) before Lystra as well as Derbe,[3] which would normally indicate that **was there** refers only to Lystra.[4] This conclusion is strengthened by the combination of **to Derbe and to Lystra** in this verse with "Lystra and Iconium" in the next. The natural inference is that Paul found Timothy at Lystra.

The young disciple was **the son of a Jewess . . .; but his father was a Greek.** The statement that Timothy's mother **believed** and the lack of such description of his father implies that the latter was a heathen, neither a proselyte to Judaism nor a Christian.

EXPOSITION

THE CHURCH'S FIRST EUROPEAN MISSION (cont'd.)

- II. The New Missionary Personnel, Acts 16:1–5.
  - A. The Heritage of Timothy, vss. 1, 2.
  - B. The Circumcision of Timothy, vs. 3.
  - C. The Help of the Decrees, vss. 4, 5.
- III. The Enlarged Prospect, Acts. 16: 6–10.
  - A. The Divine Prohibition, vss. 6–8.
  - B. The Macedonian Invitation, vss. 9–10.
- IV. The Ministry at Philippi, Acts 16: 11–15.
  - A. The Mission's Advance, vss. 11, 12.
  - B. The Mission's Success, vss. 13–15.
- V. The Expulsion of a Demon, Acts 16: 16–18.
  - A. The Occasion of the Demon Expulsion, vss. 16–18a.
  - B. The Accomplishment of Demon Expulsion, vs. 18b.
- VI. The Victory over Persecution, Acts 16:19–34.
  - A. The Cause of the Persecution, vss. 19–21.
  - B. The Nature of the Persecution, vss. 22–24.
  - C. The Consequence of the Persecution, vss. 25–30.
  - D. The Fruits of the Persecution, vss. 31–34.
- VII. The Departure in Peace, Acts 16: 35–40.
  - A. The Missionaries' Acquittal, vss. 35, 36.
  - B. The Missionaries' Reprisal, vss. 37–39.
  - C. The Missionaries' Departure, vs. 40.

II. THE NEW MISSIONARY PERSONNEL (16:1–5)

Reference to Acts 15:41, which logically belongs to the sixteenth chapter, indicates that Paul's course at the commencement of the Second Missionary Journey led overland through northern Syria, likely touching at Issus and Alexandria, and then passed through the Syrian Gates (now the Belian or Beilan Pass) in Mount Amanus and thence into the Cilician province of Asia Minor. In Cilicia he most probably visited

[1] Latin *Commentary* on Romans 16:21. [2] Aleph A B. [3] The omission in KJV is due to the Textus Receptus.
[4] So Ramsay, *St. Paul the Traveller*, p. 179. He also notes that Derbe and Lystra formed a *region* in the Roman classification.

2 The same was well reported of by the brethren that were at Lystra and Iconium.
3 Him would Paul have to go forth with him; and he took and circumcised him because of the Jews that were in those parts: for they all knew that his father was a Greek.

---

2 **Well reported of** is literally "witnessed of" *(emartyreito)*. But in Hellenistic Greek the word came to mean "witness favourably, give a good report, approve" [5] (see note on 6:3). While Derbe and Lystra are grouped together as a Roman *region* (vs. 1), **Lystra and Iconium** were linked together more closely geographically, commercially, and socially.[6]

3 Paul took along Timothy in the place of Mark, as he had already chosen Silas in place of Barnabas. But it would appear that in Paul's affections Timothy became a true "son of consolation."

Timothy was probably **circumcised** at Lystra,[7] not Iconium as held by some.[8] **Those parts** would be the cities of the southern section of the province of Galatia. **Was** *(hypērchen)* implies that Timothy's father was dead; otherwise we should expect *hyparchei*.[9]

Tarsus, the metropolis of Cilicia and Paul's home, from whence he ascended toward Mount Taurus and on to the Lycaonian plateau via the Cilician Gates and thence to Derbe and Lystra. Luke's statement, "confirming the churches" (Acts 15:41b), expresses the primary purpose and nature of Paul's visit to the churches of Syria and Asia Minor. Whether or not the reading of some versions of Acts 15:41 is valid (namely, "They delivered unto them the decrees of the apostles and elders to keep"), certainly Acts 16:4 expresses an essential part of their ministry to all the churches revisited on this journey. That their faith had been disturbed by Judaizing activities appears evident from Paul's Galatian letter (cf. Gal. 1:6–9 and 3:1), if we regard this letter as having been written after the Jerusalem Council and before the Second Missionary Journey, even to the extent of undermining confidence in the validity of his apostleship. Their reception of the Jerusalem Council decrees (Acts 15:23–29) afforded an official statement of their Christian freedom from the Mosaic Law (Gal. 5:1–13), and that their faith should rest in divine grace producing hope and brotherly love (Gal. 5:5–14), and not in the ceremonial law that could but lead to bondage and the forfeiture of their relationship with Christ (Gal. 5:2–4), with inevitable resultant confusion, strife, and destruction (Gal. 5:15).

A. The Heritage of Timothy (16:1, 2)

Timothy's home was at Lystra. An element of surprise and amazement are suggested by the manner in which Luke introduces him into the narrative, **And behold a certain disciple was there, named Timothy** (vs. 1). At Lystra a cripple had been healed, the apostles had been beaten, and then Paul was stoned by the Jewish-incited mob and left for dead (see Acts 14:8–20). Could any good possibly have emerged from these misfortunes? In just one phrase of verse 20, Luke gives us the key to the almost hidden success of the apostle's first mission to Lystra: "But as the disciples stood round about him." Among those new converts who were present and witnessed the miraculous restoration of Paul was a lad in his late teens whose name was Timothy, and likely his newly converted Jewish mother, Eunice, and grandmother, Lois, in whose home the apostles may have resided. Possibly the souls of the great apostle and this bright, lovable young lad had been "knit together" in love and mutual admiration, like Jonathan and David of old, as they lived and associated together in the home of his mother. Or is it too fanciful to suppose that, since as some hold, Timothy's mother was a widow, Paul came to fill the place of an absent father's love in the boy's life? Such seems to have been the subsequent relationship of the two (cf. I Tim. 1:2, 18; II Tim. 1:2; 2:1). There was indeed great cause for amazement as this young man, physically mature and spiritually developed, stands before the apostle upon his re-entry into Lystra. His name Timothy, or Timotheus, simply means "dear to God," likely suggesting his pious Jewish mother's hopes at his birth. Or did

[5] Abbott-Smith, *op. cit.*, p. 279. [6] *St. Paul the Traveller*, p. 179. [7] *Ibid.*, p. 180. [8] E.g., *Beginnings*, IV, 184.
[9] The Greek normally uses the present tense in a subordinate clause where the English would have the same tense as the main verb.

4 And as they went on their way through the cities, they delivered them the decrees to keep which had been ordained of the apostles and elders that were at Jerusalem.

---

4 **The cities** were those where Paul had founded churches on his first journey (chaps. 13, 14). **Decrees** is the Greek word *dogma*. Originally meaning "an opinion," it was later used for public decrees and ordinances. In the New Testament it is used elsewhere only for the decrees of Roman rulers (Luke 2:1; Acts 17:7) and the ordinances of the Jewish law (Eph. 2:15; Col. 2:14). It is used similarly in III Maccabees 1:3 for the requirements of the Mosaic law. All this seems to give the **decrees** the force of authoritative commands. Moulton and Milligan state that the general idea conveyed by *dogma* was that of "a positive ordinance, emanating from a distant and unquestionable authority."[10] It should be noted, however, that *dogma* is derived from *dokeō* ("be of opinion"), the verb used in 15:22, 25, 28.

To keep is *phylassein*, which means "guard, watch, protect," and so metaphorically "keep, preserve, observe."[11] One guards the law by observing it. **Ordained** is *kekrimena*. This is the same verb *(krinō)* as in 15:19—"my judgment is." Of 114 occurrences in the New Testament, this is the only place where it is translated **ordained** in the King James Version. The most frequent rendering, of course, is "judge" (88 times). The Revised Standard Version perhaps best reflects the actual situation with its translation, "the decisions which had been reached."

Paul rechristen him "Timothy" at his conversion?

No mention is made of Timothy's father, except that he was a Greek; thus he was the son of one of those forbidden, but not uncommonly practiced, mixed marriages of that day. That he had the advantages of upbringing by a pious Jewish mother and grandmother, both of whom became Christians, we know (cf. II Tim. 1:5; 3:14, 15; and Acts 16:1). Further, such had been the exemplary faith and conduct of this young man that Luke can observe that he was held in high esteem by the Christians at Lystra and Iconium, 18 miles away. A vital faith always manifests itself in an energetic service for Christ (cf. I Thess. 1:8).

B. The Circumcision of Timothy (16:3)

Him would Paul have to go forth with him; and he took and circumcised him because of the Jews that were in those parts. Paul's judicious decision to take Timothy with him on this journey finds its justification both in Timothy's reputation in the church (vs. 2) and his subsequent usefulness to the apostle in the cause of Christ. (For a record of their later relationship, compare the following Scriptures: Acts 17:14; I Thess. 3:2; Acts 18:5; I Thess. 1:1; II Thess. 1:1; Acts 19:22; I Cor. 4:17; 16:10; II Cor. 1:1; Rom. 16:21; Acts 20:4; Col. 1:1; Phil. 1:1; Philemon 1.)

The circumcision of Timothy finds its justification in the fact that while his father was a Greek, his mother was a Jewess, and Timothy had been brought up in her faith. Thus he would be regarded as a Jew in religion, and consequently, uncircumcised, he would have been regarded by the Jews as unclean. Therefore, both Paul's association with him and any attempt on his part to minister in the synagogue, would have been resented and resisted by the Jews everywhere they traveled. His circumcision was voluntary and for the sake of expediency, and not necessary for his salvation. For a reconciliation of this incident with Paul's refusal to circumcise Titus at Jerusalem, see the comment on Acts 15:2, 3. While Paul's policy was never to compromise where principle was involved, he was always ready to compromise, even sacrifice, when expediency not involving principle, required it for the sake of the cause of Christ (cf. Gal. 2:3–5 and I Cor. 8:8–13; 9:22, 23).

C. The Help of the Decrees (16:4, 5)

So the churches were strengthened in the faith, and increased in number daily (vs. 5). The subsequent cities visited in Asia Minor are not specified by Luke, but they most certainly included Iconium and Antioch of Pisidia, where churches were planted on the First Missionary Journey, if not others, that these disciples might have the benefit of the

[10] VGT, p. 166. [11] Abbott-Smith, *op. cit.*, p. 475.

5 So the churches were strengthened in the faith, and increased in number daily.
6 And they went through the region of Phrygia and Galatia, having been forbidden of the Holy Spirit to speak the word in Asia;

---

5 **Strengthened** is the verb *stereoō*, which occurs only in Acts (3 times). In 3:7, 16 it is used physically, here figuratively. The word means "make firm or solid, make strong." It has much the same sense as "confirm" (15:32, 41).

This is the fourth brief report of progress in Acts (cf. 6:7; 9:31; 12:24). It indicates both an inward, intensive growth (**strengthened in the faith**) and an outward, extensive growth (**increased in numbers**). The mention of daily additions is very striking.

6 **Went through** *(diēlthon)* suggests a missionary journey (see on 8:4; 13:6). **The region of Phrygia and Galatia** is preferable to "Phrygia and the region of Galatia" KJV), since the article *(tēn)* occurs only before Phrygia and thus brackets together the two place names as modifying **region** (*chōran*, country). Ramsay translates it: "the Phrygian region of *the province* Galatia."[12] But Bruce prefers to take Galatia in the popular rather than political sense here—not in the Epistle to the Galatians—and so to refer this to the boundary between the ethnic regions of Phyrgia and Galatia,[13] indicating a route farther north than Ramsay's.

Having been forbidden *(kolythentes)*[14] suggests that they received this prohibition before they left the cities (vs. 4) of southern Galatia. Since they were not to preach in **Asia**—the Roman province, founded in 133 B.C.—they headed northward.

---

decisions of the Jerusalem Council and the confirmation of Paul's ministry, since such was Paul's original purpose for this Second Journey (see Acts 15:36). Concerning the decrees of verse four, see the comment on the introduction to chapter sixteen.

Two benefits accrued from Paul's second ministry to these churches. The first was "edification," they **were strengthened in the faith,** and the second was "evangelization." The first was a passive benefit received by them from the missionaries, the second an active benefit communicated by them to the world. This is an abiding divine principle exemplified by Christ in the training and commission of His disciples, and everywhere found in His teachings (cf. John 7:37–39; Gal. 5:6). Here is a recurrence of the normal spiritual life of the Church of Pentecost (see Acts 2:42, 47b). When disturbing and divisive factors are eliminated from the body of Christ, confidence and faith will be restored, and the Church will return to her supreme mission of world evangelization. Such is the spiritual norm of the body ecclesiastic. The "spiritually animate" will always seek to reproduce itself as normally as does the "naturally animate" world.

The early and widespread growth of the Church in these regions, as suggested by Luke's words, **the churches . . . increased in number daily** (cf. Acts 13:44, 48, 49; 14:1, 21) is amply attested by extra-Biblical sources. Harnack indicates two factors that especially prepared the soil of Asia Minor for Christianity. *First,* he declares,

> Here there were no powerful and unifying national religions to offer . . . fanatical resistance to Christianity . . . although there were strong local sanctuaries and several attractive cults throughout the country.

Second, he continues,

> The older national memories had almost died out everywhere. There was a total lack of any independent political life. Here, the imperial cultus established itself, therefore, with success. But while the imperial cultus was an anticipation of universalism in religion, it was a totally unworthy expression of that universalism, nor could it permanently satisfy the religious natures of the age . . . Here Hellenism had assumed a form which rendered it peculiarly susceptible to Christianity.[a]

III. THE ENLARGED PROSPECT (16:6–10)

That Paul had plans for the further evangelization of Asia Minor which were not immediately in accord with the divine will is clearly evident from Luke's account.

[12] *St. Paul the Traveller*, p. 194 (see also note 1, p. 210).
[13] *Acts*, pp. 309 f. Cf. *Beginnings*, V, 228—"two localities conceived as a single district."
[14] A favorite word with Luke, used by him 12 out of its 23 occurrences in the New Testament.
[a] Harnack, *The Mission and Expansion of Christianity in the First Three Centuries*, II, 181–184.

7 and when they were come over against Mysia, they assayed to go into Bithynia; and the Spirit of Jesus suffered them not;
8 and passing by Mysia, they came down to Troas.

---

7 Arriving **over against** [opposite the eastern border of] **Mysia**—the northwest part of the province of Asia—they **assayed** (*epeirazon*, were trying or attempting) **to go into Bithynia.** This Roman province, formed in 74 B.C., lay northeast of the province of Asia. Since they were forbidden to preach in the latter, this seemed the only course to take. But again they were turned aside, this time by **the Spirit of Jesus.** The additional phrase **of Jesus** (cf. KJV) is found in Aleph A B D E, as well as many ancient versions. This striking expression does not occur elsewhere in the New Testament. The verb *eaō* **(suffered)** is used by Luke ten out of its thirteen times in the New Testament. Though translated "suffer" nine times in the King James Version, its proper meaning today is "permit" or "allow" (RSV).

8 **Passing by** *(parelthontes)* is rendered "neglecting" by Ramsay,[15] for the only way that Paul could reach Troas was by going west through Mysia. Perhaps this word was purposely chosen instead of *dielthontes,* which is used in Acts for a missionary journey (cf. vs. 6). Mysia was a part of Asia. However, they were not forbidden to go through that province; the prohibition was against preaching there.[16]

Katebēsan, **went down,** is the regular term for going down to the coast. **Troas**—its full name was Alexandria Troas, in honor of Alexander the Great—was an important port for commerce between Macedonia and northwestern Asia Minor.[17]

A. The Divine Prohibition (16:6–8)

Having been forbidden of the Holy Spirit to speak the word in Asia . . . and the Spirit of Jesus suffered them not (vss. 6b, 7b). While at Lystra, Paul and his party received a divine intimation that they should not attempt the evangelization of Proconsular Asia in western Asia Minor, for reasons left to conjecture. Possibly a further seasoning of the Galatian Christians with a view to a gradual penetrating impact of their new faith on the western peoples, through travel and commercial intercourse, was needed to prepare the soil of Asia for Christianity. Possibly an encircling of Asia by Christian influences, through the planting of churches in Macedonia and Achaia, was necessary as a preparatory factor. Possibly the "occupational missionary service" of Priscilla and Aquila, whom Paul was to meet and engage at Corinth, was a requisite to the establishment of Christianity in Ephesus, from which location Asia was eventually evangelized. Possibly the ripeness of Europe for the gospel message accounted for the divine prohibition to preach in Asia; or a combination of two or more of these factors, if not others, may have occasioned the divine directive. The Holy Spirit's directives are always right, when properly understood and obeyed. Man can always afford to lay his plans aside in deference to the divine will. It is wise that he should plan, but his plans must always be subject to alteration by the will of God.

Phrygia and Galatia, through which Paul passed, doubtless visiting Iconium and Antioch, may be best understood, Goodwin thinks, by considering Phrygia and Galatia as adjectives rather than nouns, and thus reading, "the country which is Phrygian and Galatic."[b]

Arriving at the borders of Mysia, Paul's party made plans to enter **Bithynia,** evidently with the purpose of the evangelization of that territory, since the Spirit had forbade them to preach in Asia; **the Spirit of Jesus**

[15] *St. Paul the Traveller*, p. 194.
[16] Bruce suggests (*Acts*, p. 310) that since Mysia seems to be distinguished from Asia, the latter may be used here in its earlier popular application to a smaller territory in the western part of what finally became the province. See also Ramsay, *The Church in the Roman Empire*, p. 150: "But during the first century before Christ the province was greatly increased in size, and it is difficult to determine after this time whether the name Asia is used in the popular sense of the Aegean coast lands or denotes the entire Roman province." For a full discussion of this point, as indeed of the whole problem involved in verses 6–8, see Kirsopp Lake, "Paul's Route in Asia Minor," *Beginnings*, V, 224–240 (especially pp. 228–237).
[17] W. A. McDonald, "Archaeology and St. Paul's Journeys in Greek Lands," *Biblical Archaeologist*, III, (1940), 18 f.

[b] Frank J. Goodwin, *A Harmony and Commentary on the Life of St. Paul* (Grand Rapids: Baker Book House, 1951), p. 65.

9 And a vision appeared to Paul in the night: There was a man of Macedonia standing, beseeching him, and saying, Come over into Macedonia, and help us.
10 And when he had seen the vision, straightway we sought to go forth into Macedonia, concluding that God had called us to preach the gospel unto them.

---

9 *Horama*, **vision** (from *horaō*, see), occurs ten times in Acts and only once elsewhere in the New Testament (Matt. 17:9). **Macedonia,** made famous by Philip and his greater son, Alexander, was formed into a Roman province in 146 B.C.

10 **Concluding** is the verb *synbibazō*, the literal meaning of which is "join or knit together" (cf. Eph. 4:16; Col. 2:2). In the Septuagint it regularly signifies "instruct" (cf. I Cor. 2:16; Acts 19:33). In Acts 9:22 it means "prove." Only here does it mean "conclude." [18]

We occurs here for the first time in the narrative of Acts. This "we-section" continues through verse 17, indicating that the author joined the missionary party at Troas and accompanied it to Philippi.

This fact has led Ramsay to identify "the man of Macedonia" (vs. 9) as Luke.[19] He feels that the epochal importance attached to the new move made at this time can best be explained on the basis that the author himself met Paul here and accompanied him into Macedonia. Ramsay considers Luke a Macedonian, who "though evidently acquainted with Philippi and looking to it as his city, had no home there." [20] He thinks that Paul and Luke "met accidentally as strangers," [21] and that the occasion of their meeting may have been Paul's need for the services of a physician.[22]

In stressing the importance of the new step taken by Paul at this time, it should be recognized that the move from one continent to another probably did not assume the same significance then as now, for "Macedonia and Asia were merely two provinces of the Roman Empire, closely united by common language and character." [23]

---

suffered them not (vs. 7b). Of these words, **Spirit of Jesus,** Dummelow remarks:

> This remarkable expression, which makes the Holy Spirit the Spirit not only of the Father, but also of the Son, is an evidence that the true divinity of Jesus was firmly held when St. Luke wrote.[c]

That these divine prohibitions had a purpose, as they always have in man's life becomes evident in the next verse.

The divine method of forbidding Paul to preach in Asia (vs. 6b), or enter Bithynia (vs. 7b), needs to be considered circumstantial, as God often manifests His will directly to His servants, as also sometimes circumstantially. Says Wesley: "Sometimes a strong impression, for which we are not able to give any account, is not altogether to be despised." [d]

B. The Macedonian Invitation (16:9, 10)

There was a man of Macedonia standing, beseeching him, and saying, Come over into Macedonia, and help us (vs. 9).

The missionary party arrived at Troas, the chief port of Mysia on the Aegean Sea, which was located near the site of the legendary Troy, the scene of Homer's Illiad. Troas had been made a Roman colony by Augustus, and was afforded special privileges by the Romans because of their traditional origin in this region.

While at Troas Paul most certainly preached and founded a church, as he met disciples there on a subsequent visit (Acts 20:7). Here the apostle experienced one of the several significant visions of his life (cf. Acts 9:3–6, 12; 18:9; 27:23–25; II Cor. 12:1–7). While Paul stands alone in the significance of his visions, there are many historic parallels of the fact of his vision, including Socrates, Mohammed, St. Bernard, Saint Francis, Ansgar, George Fox, Jacob Boehme, David Joris, and Swedenborg. That this or any other vision of Paul was indicative of epilepsy, as some hold, is too fanciful for serious consideration. If epileptic seizures produced such results as to influence human history as did the visions of Paul, then it

[18] The verb occurs only these six times in the New Testament.
[19] *St. Paul the Traveller*, pp. 198–205 (especially p. 203).
[20] *Ibid.*, p. 204. [21] *Ibid.*, p. 203. [22] *Ibid.*, p. 205. [23] *Ibid.*, p. 199.

[c] Dummelow, *op. cit.*, p. 840. [d] Wesley, *op. cit.*, p. 458, n. 7.

11 Setting sail therefore from Troas, we made a straight course to Samothrace, and the day following to Neapolis;

11 **Setting sail** is the verb *anagō*, used by Luke 21 out of its 24 occurrences in the New Testament. Luke alone uses it (14 times) in the nautical sense, "put to sea," which is found in Homer, Herodotus, and Thucydides. The implication is that Luke was both well read and widely traveled. **We made a straight course** is another nautical term, *euthydromēsamen*, found in the New Testament only here and in 21:1. It means "sailed before the wind." [24] Ramsay says of Luke, "He has the true Greek feeling for the sea." [25] **Samothrace** was a mountainous island, with an elevation of 5000 feet, and so a prominent landmark. The total distance from **Troas** to **Neapolis** was about 140 miles.[26] That this voyage was accomplished in two days shows very favorable winds. Coming against these winds on an opposite voyage took the party five days (20:6). **Neapolis** ("New City") is the modern Cavalla, "the only real port on the south coast of Macedonia, except Salonica."[27]

---

would be to the interest of God and humanity that world religious and political leaders have "epileptic fits."

Says Wesley:

> *A vision appeared to Paul by night*—It was not a dream, though it was by night. No other dream is mentioned in the New Testament, than that of Joseph and of Pilate's wife. *A man of Macedonia*—Probably an angel clothed in the Macedonian habit, or using the language of the country, and representing the inhabitants of it. *Help us*—Against Satan, ignorance, and sin.[e]

It is entirely possible that Paul became ill at Troas and was attended by a young Gentile Christian physician from Philippi whose name was Luke, who was on business or conducting a clinic at Troas and who may have told the apostle of the great needs and opportunities for the Gospel in his home city. Some have even surmised that Luke was the man of Macedonia who appeared in Paul's vision. Others have thought the man to have been the guardian angel of Macedonia (Dan. 10:10–14). His Macedonian speech or dress may have identified him (Dummelow). Be this as it may, we have scriptural evidence that it was at Troas that Luke joined the party, for here the author of Acts identifies himself for the first time with the missionaries by the use of the pronoun "we" in verse ten. Paul's vision produced the European mission, and this is sufficient to validate its divine origin. Such was to characterize the Spirit-baptized Church (see Acts 2:17). In any enterprise, sacred or secular, the vision is essential to afford the form, ideal, or pattern, as a guide for actualization.

How fitting that Christianity should have been introduced into Europe by a special divine revelation to Paul. God forever stands at the threshold and opens the doors for His servants into great new spiritual enterprises.

IV. THE MINISTRY AT PHILIPPI (16:11–15)

Though not revealed to Paul in the divine prognostication at Troas, nevertheless God foresaw the open door for the Gospel at Philippi and unerringly directed the missionary party to the **place of prayer,** which was not only to afford access to God but also to the great country of Macedonia, by way of the heart of a prominent merchant woman.

A. The Mission's Advance (16:11, 12)

Setting sail therefore from Troas, we made a straight course . . . to Philippi, which is a city of Macedonia, the first of the district, a Roman colony (vss. 11a, 12a).

Luke makes clear that there was now a sense of certainty and urgency characterizing the missionaries. **And when he had seen the vision, straightway we sought to go forth into Macedonia, concluding that God had called us to preach the gospel unto them** (vs. 10). Zeal, good intentions, and earnest or feverish efforts for God will all end in failure and

---

[24] W. J. Conybeare and J. S. Howson, *The Life and Epistles of Saint Paul* (Hartford, Conn.: S. S. Scranton Co., 1902), p. 246. Conybeare and Howson give an excellent description of this voyage (pp. 246—248).

[25] *St. Paul the Traveller*, p. 205.

[26] So E. J. Bicknell, "The Acts of the Apostles," *A New Commentary on Holy Scripture*, edited by C. Core, H. L. Goudge, A. Guillaume (New York: Macmillan Co., 1928), Part III, p. 361. Rackham (*op. cit.*, p. 278) says 125.

[27] *Beginnings*, IV, 187.

[e] *Ibid.*, n. 9.

12 and from thence to Philippi, which is a city of Macedonia, the first of the district, a *Roman* colony: and we were in this city tarrying certain days.

---

12 The statement that **Philippi** was **the first of the district** has created considerable discussion, since it is agreed by all that at that time Amphipolis, not Philippi, was the chief city of this one of the four administrative districts of **Macedonia.** Several explanations have been offered. One is that Philippi was the **first** Macedonian city to be reached by Paul,[28] omitting Neapolis because it was only the seaport [29] or because it was regarded as Thracian, not Macedonian.[30] Another view places *prōtē* with *polis*, translating it as "a chief city" [31]—there is no article in the Greek. Codex D changes *prōtē* to *kephalē*, and omits *meridos*, thus making Philippi "the capital of Macedonia." But this is clearly wrong, for Thessalonica was the capital of the province of Macedonia.[32] Meyer calls attention to the fact that "the formal epithet *prōtē* is given to Greek cities which were not capitals." [33]

Ramsay suggests that the language used here reflects Luke's pride in his own city. He adds: "Perhaps he even exaggerates a little the dignity of Philippi, which was still only in process of growth, to become at a later date the great city of its division." [34] Macgregor concludes: "The more general meaning given to the words in RSV [the leading city of the district of Macedonia] is therefore probably here correct." [35] Hervey thinks that because of its gold mines, Philippi may have already become the leading city by Paul's day.[36]

It is known that Philippi was in the first division of Macedonia.[37] But the suggested emendation of *prōtē* to *prōtēs* (giving "a city of the first part of Macedonia") must be rejected because it has no support in the Greek manuscripts.[38]

Kolōnia, **colony,** is a transliteration of the Latin *colonia.* It is found only here in the New Testament. Originally Roman colonies were "settlements of Roman citizens in captured territory as garrisons." [39] They were often populated with veteran soldiers. These colonies were given the following rights: autonomous government, freedom from taxation, and the same legal privileges as if they were living in Italy.[40] Although several other cities mentioned in Acts were Roman colonies—Pisidian Antioch, Lystra, Troas, Ptolemais, Corinth, Syracuse, Puteoli—only in this case does the author mention the fact. This would seem to indicate his special interest in Philippi. Ramsay holds that the ancient tradition that Luke was a native of Antioch (Syria) is due to a confusion of Lucas with Lucius.[41]

---

frustration until the divine will is ascertained (see vss. 6 and 7). When God's will is clearly understood by His obedient servants, there comes to their hearts a rest of conviction and purposefulness that clears the moral and spiritual atmosphere and gives drive and direction to life and service. There is no stabilizing and securing force in the life of man equal to a clear knowledge of God's will, when the mind of man accords with that divine will.

Since Philippi was the party's goal, Luke hurried on with only a passing notice of **Samothrace,** an island midway of the northern Aegean Sea, to their port of disembarkation on the following day at **Neapolis,** the seaport of **Philippi.** Luke's special notes on **Philippi** indicate its importance as the **first** city of the district, and a **Roman colony.** Whether **first** in importance, or in the course of travel from the sea, is in doubt; probably the former is meant.

Finegan gives an interesting account of this once proud city. Philippi was founded in the middle of the fourth century B.C. by Philip of Macedonia, father of Alexander the Great; but a small settlement named Crenides had preceded it, according to Strabo. It was made a Roman colony to celebrate the victory of Antony and Octavian over Brutus and Cassius in the battle of Philippi 42 B.C. and given the name Colonia Julia Philippenis, in honor of Julius Caesar, with the first citizenship rights accorded the veterans of

[28] Conybeare and Howson, *op. cit.*, p. 250, n. 9.
[29] H. Olshausen, *Biblical Commentary on the New Testament* (New York: Sheldon, Blakeman & Co., 1857), III, 345.
[30] J. B. Lightfoot, *St. Paul's Epistle to the Philippians* (London: Macmillan Co., 1894), p. 50, n. 1.
[31] Hackett, *op. cit.*, p. 184. [32] EGT, II, 356. [33] *Op. cit.*, p. 309. [34] *St. Paul the Traveller*, p. 206.
[35] IB, IX, 218. [36] *Pulpit Commentary, Acts*, II, 28. [37] Livy, *Annals*, XLV, 29. [38] Bruce, *Acts*, p. 313.
[39] *Beginnings*, IV, 190. [40] *Ibid.* [41] *St. Paul the Traveller*, p. 209.

13 And on the sabbath day we went forth without the gate by a river side, where we supposed there was a place of prayer; and we sat down, and spake unto the women that were come together.

---

13 **Gate** is substituted for "city" (KJV) on the basis of the oldest manuscripts.[42] **By a river side** refers to the Gangites or Angites, not the Strymon some miles away.[43] Ramsay thinks the omission of the article is "one of the touches of familiarity which show the hand of one who knew Philippi well." [44] Robertson explains it as an idiomatic anarthrous prepositional form,[45] which allows "the" to be supplied in English.

Where we supposed there was a place of prayer (also RSV) is the reading of Vaticanus and Alexandrinus. Sinaiticus originally had "he supposed," but it was later "corrected" to "we supposed." The rendering "where prayer was wont to be made" (KJV) is based on the later manuscripts (E H L P). But it is preferred by Ramsay.[46]

Whether *proseuchē* should be translated **place of prayer** or "prayer" is a debated point. In the King James Version it is rendered "prayer" in all but one (James 5:7—"pray earnestly") of the 37 times it occurs in the New Testament. But Moulton and Milligan cite numerous examples of its clear use for a Jewish place of prayer in both the papyri and the inscriptions.[47] It was even used for heathen places of worship.[48] Josephus says of one *proseuchē:* "It was a large edifice, and capable of receiving a great number of people." [49] He also quotes the decree at Halicarnassus as giving the Jews the right to make their prayers *(proseuchai)* "at the seaside, according to the customs of their forefathers." [50] Conybeare and Howson say of *proseuchē:* "Probably it was the usual name of the meeting-place of Jewish congregations in Greek cities." [51] Meyer thinks the description here favors an open space, not a building.[52] Because only **women** are mentioned, Bruce thinks *proseuchē* should be rendered "prayer," and the King James reading preferred.[53]

That **women** were given greater freedom in Macedonia than elsewhere is suggested by the specific mention of them at the three Macedonian towns—Philippi, Thessalonica, and Beroea. The inscriptions of that period indicate that women had more liberty there than at Athens.[54]

---

this battle. Neapolis, located nine miles from Philippi, was included in the Philippian territory. The famous overland route from Asia to Rome (the Via Egnatia) passed from Neapolis over Mount Symbolum into Philippi, traversing the full length of the city's forum, a structure 300 by 150 feet. The fame of this once proud city is further indicated by the acropolis, Roman baths, the theater, and the "colonial archway," the latter located at the west entrance of the city, which forbade foreign deities to enter the city. About a mile west of Philippi, the Via Egnatia crossed the river Ganga or Gangites. Thus the gate of Acts 16:13 is likely the "colonial archway" through which the apostles passed to the riverside where Paul ministered to the women assembled for prayer, in the absence of a Jewish synagogue.[f]

B. The Mission's Success (16:13–15)

And a certain woman named Lydia, . . . one that worshipped God, heard us: whose heart the Lord opened to give heed unto the things which were spoken by Paul (vs. 14).

Luke's words in verse thirteen suggest five things. *First*, that there were either insufficient Jews in Philippi to afford a synagogue, or that their religion was forbidden by the Romans to be practiced within the city. The latter may be intimated by the author's words, **And on the sabbath day we went forth without the gate** (vs. 13a). *Second*, they indicate that the Jews maintained a place of prayer (Gr. *proseuche*), "a *place* used for *worship*, where there was no synagogue. It was a large building uncovered, with seats, as in an amphitheatre. Buildings of this sort the Jews had by the seaside, and by the sides

[42] Aleph A B C D.
[43] Conybeare and Howson, *op. cit.*, p. 254, n. 3.
[44] *St. Paul the Traveller*, p. 213.
[45] A. T. Robertson, *Grammar*, p. 792.
[46] *St. Paul the Traveller*, p. 213.
[47] VGT, p. 547.
[48] Schürer, *op. cit.*, II, ii, 69.
[49] *Life*, 54.
[50] *Ant.* XIV, 10, 23.
[51] *Op. cit.*, p. 254, n. 1.
[52] *Op. cit.*, p. 310.
[53] *Acts*, p. 314.
[54] Lightfoot, *Philippians*, pp. 55 f.

[f] Finegan, *op. cit.*, pp. 269–271.

14 And a certain woman named Lydia, a seller of purple, of the city of Thyatira, one that worshipped God, heard us: whose heart the Lord opened to give heed unto the things which were spoken by Paul.

---

14 **Lydia was a seller of purple.** *Porphyropōlis* [55] is from *porphyra*—which first meant "the purple fish," then "purple dye," and finally (in the N.T.) "a purple garment"—and *pōleō*, "sell." So it means "a seller of purple fabrics" [56] (cf. RSV—"a seller of purple goods"). **Thyatira,** says Ramsay, "was famous for its dyeing; and its guild of dyers is known from the inscriptions." [57] It also had a Jewish colony, so that Lydia learned about the true God.[58] It belonged to the province of Asia.

---

of rivers." [g] *Third*, this passage suggests that such Jews or proselytes as may have resided at Philippi were women, since no men are mentioned. Clarke's suggestion that this may have been a pre-service assembly of women to whom Paul spoke appears quite unlikely. *Fourth*, the riverside location of the *proseuche* was likely due to the convenience of water for ceremonies or purification purposes. And, *fifth*, it is clear that Paul's manner of approach was one of informal religious conversation with these women, rather than a direct formal proclamation of the Gospel, as indicated by the record: **we sat down, and spake unto the women that were come together** (vs. 13b). Paul usually stood to preach. How like Christ's informal approach to the Samaritan woman at Jacob's well (John 4:6–26), or that of Philip with the Ethiopian nobleman (Acts 8:29–39). The most effective preaching has not always been done from the high pulpits, nor to great audiences. The Christian message is a witness, and to be effective it must ever be on the personal level.

Lydia was likely an influential leader of these women of Jewish faith, possibly even the director of this simple act of worship. That she was a Gentile proselyte to the Jewish faith, as were the other women, is most likely. That she was a native of Thyatira, the city of Thyatira in Lydia of Asia Minor (the country that probably gave her her name), and a merchandiser of a very beautiful and expensive cloth of purple dye, Luke suggests. Her circumstances indicate that she was a woman of considerable means (vs. 15). It was such a person as this that God sought out to become the human door of entrance for the Gospel in Macedonia.

Luke's statement that she was **one that worshipped God** implies a sincerity and devotion out of the usual course. Wesley suggests that she was "Probably acquainted with the prophetic writings";[h] in which case she would have been one of those Grecian-Jews who earnestly expected the Messiah and gladly heard the message of the apostle. She was near to the Kingdom of God, and Paul's message of truth was used of God to turn the key that unlocked her heart to the entrance of Christ. The same Spirit that directed and inspired the apostle's message conditioned her spiritual understanding to receive that message. Wesley remarks concerning Luke's expression, **whose heart the Lord opened** (vs. 14), "The Greek word properly refers to the opening of the eyes. And the heart has its eyes (Eph. 1:18). These are closed by nature; and to open them is the peculiar work of God."[i] This very thing Paul declares to be the purpose and function of the Gospel: "to open their eyes, that they may turn from darkness to light and from the power of Satan unto God, that they may receive remission of sins and an inheritance among them that are sanctified by faith in me" (Acts 26:18). On the contrary, he asserts that Satan, "the god of this world hath blinded the minds of the unbelieving, that the light of the gospel of the glory of Christ, who is the image of God, should not dawn upon them" (II Cor. 4:4).

Satan darkens, God illumines; Satan closes the spiritual eyes, Christ opens the eyes of the spiritually blind. No amount of oratory, elocution, logical argumentation, exposition, or persuasion can effect this spiritual illumination. It is a work that belongs exclusively to God. Until the Lord opens the hearts of the unsaved, they will remain entombed in

55 Found only here in the New Testament.
56 Abbott-Smith, *op. cit.*, p. 374.
57 *St. Paul the Traveller*, p. 214.
58 *Ibid.*

g Clarke, *op. cit.*, V, 815.
h Wesley, *op. cit.*, p. 459, n. 14.
i *Ibid.*

15 And when she was baptized, and her household, she besought us, saying, If ye have judged me to be faithful to the Lord, come into my house, and abide *there*. And she constrained us.

16 And it came to pass, as we were going to the place of prayer, that a certain maid having a spirit of divination met us, who brought her masters much gain by soothsaying.

---

15 It is not stated, and is perhaps unlikely, that she was baptized the first sabbath. **Constrained** is the verb *parabiazomai*, found only here and in Luke 24:29. The literal meaning is "to force against nature or law." In the classics it meant "to compel by force." But in the New Testament it means "to constrain by entreaty." [59] It probably indicates "the vehement urgency of the feeling of gratitude." [60]

16 **Maid** is more properly "slave girl" (RSV). Moulton and Milligan state that *paidiskē* "from meaning originally 'a young woman' came in later Greek to denote 'a female slave.'" [61]

A spirit of divination is literally "a spirit, a Python" *(pneuma pythōna)*. The latter word, found only here in the New Testament, was used for the serpent (cf. python) at Delphi slain by Apollo, who was therefore called the Pythian god. In Plutarch it is used for ventriloquist soothsayers.[62] It seems evident that this slave girl was a demon-possessed ventriloquist.

Gain is *ergasian*, "work, business," [63] used by Luke five out of its six occurrences in the New Testament.[64] **Soothsaying** is a participle of *manteuomai*, found only here in the New Testament. It is from *mantis*, "diviner," and so means "practise divination."

---

the dark dungeon of this world of spiritual death.

Awakened and illumined Lydia gave **heed unto the things which were spoken by Paul** (vs. 14b). In his Ephesian letter Paul implies that the soul may be truly awakened without responding and realizing the benefits of salvation: "Awake thou that sleepest, and arise from the dead, and Christ shall shine upon thee" (Eph. 5:14). Thus the apostle suggests that initial salvation consists of a threefold process: (1) spiritual awakening, (2) spiritual resurrection, and (3) spiritual illumination. Such appears to have been the experience of this first European convert.

And when she was baptized (vs. 15a). Like the Ethiopian nobleman converted and baptized under the personal ministry of Philip (Acts 8:36–39), this European noblewoman, converted under Paul's ministry, sealed her faith and offered her testimony to the pagan citizens of Philippi by that outward material symbol of a gracious inner work of grace already wrought by God in her inner spiritual nature. So genuinely converted and so influential was her life that her entire household followed her in baptism. Her household would have included her domestic servants and slaves, as well as her children and relatives, if any resided with her (cf. 16:33; 18:8; I Cor. 1:16; Matt. 19:13–15). Since no mention is made of her husband, it is as logical to believe that she was a widow, if indeed she was married and had children, as it is to so conclude concerning Eunice, the mother of Timothy (Acts 16:1). Renan is reported to have entertained the unsupported notion that Lydia became Paul's wife.

Lydia's conversion served the further practical benefit of providing lodging and entertainment for Paul's missionary party while they remained in Philippi and this by constraint of Lydia and not of choice by the missionaries. God's doings are always practical, when properly understood. Though she was God's chosen instrument in the gospel's European initiation, she appears either to have left Philippi or died, as Paul does not mention her name in the Philippian letter.

V. THE EXPULSION OF A DEMON (16:16–18)

Though the Gospel had a peaceful European entrance through the conversion of Lydia, this state of affairs was not to last for long.

[59] Abbott-Smith, *op. cit.*, p. 337.
[60] Meyer, *op. cit.*, p. 312.
[61] VGT, p. 474.
[62] Abbott-Smith, *op. cit.*, p. 393.
[63] *Ibid.*, p. 178.
[64] The sixth is Ephesians 4:19.

17 The same following after Paul and us cried out, saying, These men are servants of the Most High God, who proclaim unto you the way of salvation.

17 **Following after** is the verb *katakoloutheō*, used only by Luke (cf. Luke 23:55). **Us** marks the end of the first we-section, which began at verse ten. The next one begins at 20:6, when Paul returns to Philippi. The implication is that Luke remained at Philippi during the intervening years.

Cried out is literally "was crying out" (*ekrazen*, imperfect). She kept on doing it day after day (vs. 18). **The Most High God** was an expression used in both heathen and Jewish connections. After noting the Hebrew equivalent Lake and Cadbury say: "Not only is there evidence of the actual use of the corresponding Semitic word in pagan religion, but a considerable body of inscriptional evidence from many lands attests the use of *hypsistos theos*."[65] But they warn us that "In many cases it is either purely Jewish or due to Jewish influence."[66] **Unto you** is substituted for "unto us" (KJV) because found in the earliest manuscripts.[67] **The way of salvation** is probably the correct translation, even though the definite article is missing in the Greek. On this subject Lake and Cadbury make this sane observation: "When the article is used, the English definite article is a safe translation, but it does not follow that when the article is not used in Greek, we should use the English indefinite article."[68]

A. The Occasion of Demon Expulsion (16:16–18a)

As we were going to the place of prayer, . . . a certain maid having a spirit of divination met us (vs. 16).

The evangelistic activities of the missionaries by the riverside were disturbing to Satan's interests. Interference began through the annoying conduct of a "clairvoyant" slave girl whose "mediumship" had been exceedingly gainful to her masters. That she was both possessed of a demon and mentally unsound is a reasonable inference from Luke's account. Her supposed, if not real, ability to divine, or clairvoyantly explore and discern the transomatic world, and then to display this occult knowledge in soothsaying or fortune-telling, was unquestionably due to the intelligence of the unclean demon by whom she was possessed. Such individuals and practices were not uncommon in the ancient Orient, nor are they uncommon in the dark regions of paganism today. Though in a more refined fashion and with greater cultural pretenses, occultism is experiencing a shocking recrudescence in the modern western world through practices of clairvoyance, telepathy, spiritualistic mediumship and materialization, palmistry, and crystal gazing. Especially has this become increasingly true in the wake of three great wars when so many devoid of a knowledge of Bible truth or faith in God have attempted to make contact with their deceased loved ones. There are always those who are ready to sell their souls and service to forbidden occultism.

Jan Karl Van Baalen has analyzed this occult practice as consisting in either trickery, such as sleight of hand performance, superpsychic powers of occult personalities, demon possession, or possibly a combination of any two or all three of these factors. Again the same authority has outlined the results of occultism under the heading of three "Black I's," namely, "infidelity," "immorality," and "insanity."[j]

That ventriloquism has been associated with divination and soothsaying is not strange when it is remembered that not infrequently these practitioners are characterized by dual personalities, one of whom may be a possessing demon. Many soberminded thinkers are becoming increasingly aware of the reality of demon possession as accounting for much personality abnormality even in modern civilized society, as witnesses the appearance of a recent significant publication by J. Stafford Wright, Principal of Tyndale Hall, Bristol, England.[k] A chapter in this book entitled, "Man and His Unseen Neighbours" treats and gives full credence to "Demons," "Fallen Angels," "Demon Possession," and "The Method and Manner

[65] *Beginnings*, IV, 193. [66] *Ibid.* [67] Aleph B D E. [68] *Beginnings*, IV, 193.

[j] J. K. Van Baalen, *The Chaos of Cults* (Grand Rapids: Wm. B. Eerdmans Publishing Co., 1949), pp. 33–38.
[k] Wright, *op. cit.*.

18 And this she did for many days. But Paul, being sore troubled, turned and said to the spirit, I charge thee in the name of Jesus Christ to come out of her. And it came out that very hour.

19 But when her masters saw that the hope of their gain was gone, they laid hold on Paul and Silas, and dragged them into the marketplace before the rulers,

---

18 For *diaponētheis,* **being sore troubled,** see on 4:2, the only other place where the word occurs in the New Testament. This is the first instance in Acts of exorcism **in the name of Jesus Christ.** The cure was instantaneous—that very hour.

19 **Gone** is the same verb *(exerchomai)* as "come out" in verse 18. **The hope of their gain** was the spirit that possessed the girl. **Paul and Silas,** as leaders, were seized. The **marketplace** (better two words, as in RSV) was the *Agora.* The word is used in all three Synoptics, but in Acts only here and in 17:17 (at Athens). In the earliest writers (Homer and Xenophon), it meant "an assembly." Later it indicated "a place of assembly," "a forum."[69] Lake and Cadbury comment: "The word is better transliterated than translated."[70] **Rulers** is *archontes,* "the general Greek name for the magistrates of a city."[71] Meyer calls them "city-judges."[72]

---

of Possession." A widely read work of C. S. Lewis of Oxford University likewise reflects faith in demon personality.[l]

That Luke, a physician capable of distinguishing between symptoms of a natural physical or mental disorder and those superimposed by a demon personality, should diagnose this and other cases as demon possession cannot be without significance.

This unfortunate girl's discernment reflected in her often repeated exclamation, **These men are servants of the Most High God** (vs. 17), is not surprising in the light of Christ's experiences when the demons recognized Him (cf. Matt. 8:28, 29 and Acts 19:15). Possessed of a knowledge of Christ's person, the demon would also know His redemptive work and thus the exclamation, **who proclaim unto you the way of salvation** (vs. 17b). Paul neither required nor desired this demoniacal counterfeit publicity, as it threatened to weaken the missionaries' position with the people by reason of the demon's profession of a knowledge of God and His salvation and a proclamation of this through the possessed girl. Paul, like Jesus (Mark 1:25), while recognizing that what the demon said was true, rejected the testimony, because of its source. The demon-possessed girl's reference to the **Most High God** antedates the "High-god" discoveries of modern anthropologists by nearly two thousand years (See Additional Note I, **The High-God Theory,** at close of Chapter VII).

B. The Accomplishment of Demon Expulsion (16:18b)

Paul . . . said to the spirit, I charge thee in the name of Jesus Christ to come out of her. And it came out that very hour (vs. 18).

The girl recognized in Paul a servant and minister of the **Most High God,** or the supreme God, and therefore supreme over the demon that possessed her. Consequently, Paul's authoritative command in the Name of Jesus Christ, that the spirit leave the girl, automatically expelled the demon, who by reason of his inferiority to Christ was compelled to obey. Note that it was Paul's command **in the name of Jesus Christ** that expelled the demon (cf. Mark 5:8).

VI. THE VICTORY OVER PERSECUTION (16:19–34)

Though the Gospel had a peaceful entrance into Philippi, the enemy was soon to raise a storm of violent opposition against the invasion of his territory.

A. The Cause of the Persecution (16:19–21)

But when her masters saw that the hope of their gain was gone, they laid hold on Paul and Silas (vs. 19a).

This slave girl was the chattel of unprincipled mercenary pagan men who had no respect for her personal worth nor con-

[69] Abbott-Smith, *op. cit.,* p. 7. [70] *Beginnings,* IV, 194. [71] *Ibid.* [72] Meyer, *op. cit.,* p. 314.

[l] C. S. Lewis, *The Screwtape Letters* (New York: Macmillan Co., 1948).

20 and when they had brought them unto the magistrates, they said, These men, being Jews, do exceedingly trouble our city,
21 and set forth customs which it is not lawful for us to receive or to observe, being Romans.

---

20 *Stratēgoi* (**magistrates**) was the Greek equivalent of the Latin *praetores*. Ramsay calls it a "courtesy title." [73] Bruce says: "They were two in number, whence their official title *duouiri*, 'duumvirs.'" [74] Meyer [75] distinguishes between the *archontēs* and *stratēgoi*, but probably they are two names for the same person.[76] *Ektarassō* (**do exceedingly trouble**) is a strong verb, found only here in the New Testament. It means "to throw into great trouble, agitate." [77] Meyer translates it, "bring into utter disorder." [78]

21 On the expression **not lawful** Lake and Cadbury comment: "Though Judaism was tolerated and protected in the Empire, its adherents were not allowed to make proselytes of Romans." [79] **Being Romans** is in proud contrast to the contemptuous **being Jews** of the previous verse.

---

cern about the teachings of the missionaries, until their monetary gain was affected. She was to them but an instrument, and when her instrumental worth to them was destroyed, they were enraged. Paul's expulsion of the evil spirit from the girl had left her quite incapable of divining for stolen goods or telling fortunes to their material profit. Clarke sees no evidence that the girl was converted, and therefore the protests of her masters were from mercenary and not religious or patriotic motives, as they represent their cause before the magistrates. How helpless are the evil devices of unprincipled men apart from the support of Satanic intelligence! How much evil would be eliminated from society were the profit motive absent! (see I Tim. 5:10). Truth always suffers opposition when it touches the purse of the greedy.

Doubtless the missionaries were ruthlessly dragged to the market place with a view to exciting and inflaming the passions of the rabble gathered there and thus gaining support for their accusers.

Note that when Paul and Silas were arraigned before the magistrates (or Praetors),[m] whose offices were likely near the central market, they do not present their real reasons for attacking them, the loss of gain (vs. 19a), but from pretense of patriotism they make a threefold charge against them. *First*, they prejudice the minds of the magistrates at the outset by representing Paul and Silas as Jews, **These men, being Jews** (vs. 20b), (only a half-truth as Silas was likely a Gentile proselyte), a people despised by the Romans as troublemakers throughout the empire. Roman hostility to the Jews may account for the absence of many Jews, or even a synagogue at Philippi. *Second*, they charge them with disturbance of the peace, **these men, being Jews, do exceedingly trouble our city** (vs. 20b), a charge totally devoid of factual evidence. On the contrary, Paul had silenced a disturbance of the peace by casting the demon out of the noisy damsel. *Third*, they were charged with introducing religious customs forbidden to Romans, though not to non-Roman citizens. Nor is there any validity to this charge since there is no evidence that the missionaries had preached to other than Jews. As a slave the soothsaying damsel would not have been a citizen nor is there evidence that she was converted. Thus there is not a valid charge against them.

B. The Nature of the Persecution (16:22–24)

And the multitude rose up together against them: and the magistrates rent their garments off them . . . they . . . laid many stripes upon them . . . cast them into the inner prison, and made their feet fast in the stocks (vss. 22, 23a, 24b).

The likely protest of Paul and Silas that they were Roman citizens and should be treated as such was probably drowned by the clamor of the excited and inflamed mob. Six steps are clearly discernible in the persecution proceedings against Paul and Silas.

[73] *St. Paul the Traveller*, p. 218. [74] *Acts*, p. 317. [75] *Op. cit.*, p. 314. [76] *Beginnings*, IV, 195.
[77] Abbott-Smith, *op. cit.*, p. 142. [78] *Op. cit.*, p. 314. [79] *Beginnings*, IV, 195.

[m] Weymouth observes, "Their proper title was 'duumviri,' but they often assumed the higher rank of praetors, to which they had no right, although Luke concedes it to them five times in this chapter."

22 And the multitude rose up together against them: and the magistrates rent their garments off them, and commanded to beat them with rods.
23 And when they had laid many stripes upon them, they cast them into prison, charging the jailor to keep them safely:
24 who, having received such a charge, cast them into the inner prison, and made their feet fast in the stocks.

---

22 The false accusations of the slave-owners set off a popular anti-Semitic uprising—**the multitude rose up together against them.** The strong double compound *synephistēmi* is found only here in the New Testament. **Rent** is the verb *perirēgnymi,* also found only here in the New Testament. It means "to break or tear off all around." [80] Ramsay says that the praetors "rent their clothes in loyal horror." [81] Hackett more wisely comments: "Not their own, but those of Paul and Silas." [82]

23 *Desmophylax* **(jailor)**, one who guards those who are bound, is found in the New Testament only in this chapter (vss. 23, 27, 36).

24 *Esōteran,* **inner,** is a comparative with probably superlative force, as commonly in the New Testament. The meaning then would be "the inmost prison." *Asphalizō* **(made . . . fast),** "make firm, secure," occurs only here and in Matthew 27:64, 65, 66. **Stocks** is **xylon** (see on 5:30). In its other three occurrences in Acts (5:30; 10:39; 13:29) it is translated "tree" and refers to the Cross. Only here in the New Testament does it mean **stocks.** To add to the torture, the legs were often spread apart for days at a time.[83] Origen is said to have been "stretched to the distance of four holes on the rack." [84]

First, every semblance of rationality or justice was removed from their makeshift trial by the influence of the mob spirit that motivated the proceedings (vs. 22a). *Second,* official shame and regard for justice and legal procedure were cast aside as the magistrates stripped the missionaries of their clothing and commanded them to be beaten (vs. 22b). *Third,* they were mercilessly beaten with rods by the police (lictors). Though the Jews had borrowed this form of punishment from the Romans, they limited it to thirty-nine stripes, whereas the Romans applied it without limit. Paul possibly alludes to this very incident at Philippi in his later words, "stripes above measure" (II Cor. 11:23). *Fourth,* they were thrown or cast, like vicious criminals, into the dark, damp, unsanitary, prison dungeon and secured there (vs. 23b). *Fifth,* for self-protection the jailer cast them into the solitary confinement of the inner prison cells. *Sixth,* their feet were securely and painfully locked in the heavy wooden stocks of the prison. This cruel form of punishment the writer has often witnessed among the West Africans. A heavy hardwood log, twelve to eighteen inches in diameter and ten to fifteen feet long, is hewn square and then sawed in half lengthwise. Round holes the size of a man's ankles are then cut at the division of the log at intervals of about two feet. The halves are hinged together at one end and then tapered off to a flat point at the opposite end and provided with a hasp and staple for locking. The prisoner secured in such a set of stocks is required to place his feet in the grooves of the lower half of the log while attendants raise the upper half from the unhinged end. When the feet are in place, the upper section is lowered over the victim's feet and securely padlocked. Here prisoners are sometimes left for days in a dark, unventilated room without food, water, or sanitation. This device is aptly named an "alligator" (u-quie) in the Temne language of Sierra Leone. In a similar device Paul and Silas were secured in the inner prison. The likelihood of Luke's residence in Philippi and Timothy's youthfulness, if not his Greek father's resemblance, may have exempted these men from the punishment accorded their companions.

---

80 Abbott-Smith, *op. cit.*, p. 357.
81 *St. Paul the Traveller*, p. 219.
82 *Op. cit.*, p. 189. So also Meyer (*op. cit.*, p. 315), Knowling (EGT, II, 349), Lake and Cadbury (*Beginnings*, IV, 195).
83 Olshausen, *op. cit.*, p. 350.
84 Eusebius, *Ecclesiastical History*, VI, 39.

25 But about midnight Paul and Silas were praying and singing hymns unto God, and the prisoners were listening to them;
26 and suddenly there was a great earthquake, so that the foundations of the prisonhouse were shaken: and immediately all the doors were opened: and every one's bands were loosed.
27 And the jailor, being roused out of sleep and seeing the prison doors open, drew his sword and was about to kill himself, supposing that the prisoners had escaped.
28 But Paul cried with a loud voice, saying, Do thyself no harm: for we are all here.

---

25 **Were listening** correctly brings out the force of the imperfect, *epēkroōnto*. The verb *epakroaomai* occurs only here in the New Testament.

26 **Prison-house** reflects the fact that the Greek word is a compound, *desmōtērion;* literally, a place where bound persons are kept (see on 5:21). *Anethē*, **were loosed,** is used in this literal sense only here and in 27:40.

27 *Exypnos*, **roused out of sleep,** occurs only here in the New Testament. *Spaō* **(drew)** is found only here and in Mark 14:47—in both cases of drawing a sword. Conybeare and Howson note: "Philippi is famous in the annals of suicide." [85]

28 The question has sometimes been raised as to why the prisoners did not flee Ramsay's answer is: "An earthquake strikes panic into the semi-oriental mob in the Aegean lands." [86] The prisoners were too awed to escape.

C. The Consequences of the Persecution (16:25–30)

But about midnight Paul and Silas were praying and singing hymns unto God, and the prisoners were listening to them; and suddenly there was a great earthquake . . . and every-one's bands were loosed (vss. 25, 26).

The sequence, as well as significance, of transpiring events recorded by Luke is striking.

Wearied, beaten, maltreated and bloody, these two missionaries uncomfortably sat in their inner dungeon cell with feet secured in the torturesome stocks. Then *first*, in these circumstances and at the darkest hour of the night, **about midnight** (vs. 25a), Paul and Silas were praying and singing hymns **unto God** (vs. 25a). What Paul and Silas prayed about we are not told; we may suppose that they prayed for their persecutors, for the salvation of their fellow prisoners and for grace to sustain them in this situation. Nor do we know the hymns that they sang, except that they were **unto God.** All self-pity was absent. What better occupation could they have engaged in at such a time and place. They had learned with afflicted Job that God "giveth songs in the night" (Job 35:10). Their physical sufferings had been spiritually sublimated, and they were transported into "heavenly places, in Christ Jesus" (Eph. 2:6). Nor have they been the last to experience mental and spiritual transcendence in the hour of most intense affliction. *Second*, though cut off from the normal channels of missionary activity, they were not without an audience, and such an audience as without their presence could not have heard the Gospel. Their prayers and songs of praise ascended to the ears of God and extended to the ears of the prisoners: **the prisoners were listening to them** (vs. 25b). Who can say that some of these very prisoners were not among Paul's beloved disciples to whom he later wrote the endearing epistle to the Philippians? Possibly it was from this experience that Paul learned the great philosophy which he phrased in Romans 8:28. *Third*, the earth began to rise and fall, like a panting monster, under a seismic shudder that vibrated the stones out of their positions and sent iron doors clattering to the prison floor. Freed from their cells, the prisoners quickly assisted one another in gaining freedom from their bonds. Clarke regards this incident as symbolical of the shattering dynamic of the Gospel with its consequent liberation of the spiritually bound, and consternation of the impenitent and wicked (see Luke 4:18). There need be no question about the miraculous character of an incident so productive of moral and spiritual benefit as was this earthquake. *Fourth*, the same jailer, who had so heartlessly and ruthlessly

[85] *Op. cit.*, p. 265.
[86] *St. Paul the Traveller*, p. 221. Ramsay's description of a Turkish prison (*ibid.*) seems beside the point, since this was a well-constructed Roman prison.

29 And he called for lights and sprang in, and, trembling for fear, fell down before Paul and Silas,
30 and brought them out and said, Sirs, what must I do to be saved?
31 And they said, Believe on the Lord Jesus, and thou shalt be saved, thou and thy house.

---

29 **Lights** is plural in the Greek *(phōta) Eisepēdēsen*, **sprang in,** is found only here in the New Testament. It may be translated "rushed in" (RSV), as it carries this meaning in the papyri.[87]

30 The jailer **brought them out.** The Western text has this interesting addition: "having fastened up the others." The explanatory and supplementary Western interpolations are usually true to life and perhaps often represent correctly what actually took place.

The jailer's question may well reflect his acquaintance with the words of the soothsayer (vs. 17).

31 "Christ" (KJV) is found in C D and the later manuscripts (H L P S and minuscules) but is omitted in the earliest authorities.

---

thrust them into the prison, now frightfully awakened, first thought to commit suicide and then sought and found peace with God. Roman law demanded that in the event prisoners escaped, the prison keeper or guard should suffer the same punishment intended for the escaped prisoner (cf. Acts 12:19). Pagan philosophy of the day, especially Stoicism, commended suicide to escape execution, and the jailer thinking death inevitable, supposing that the prisoners were escaped, in desperation intended suicide. Little did he realize that though so near the gates of death and hell, the doors of mercy and eternal life were about to open to him. The alertness of Paul became the means of his salvation. From fear and despair his mind turned to hope and inquiry: **Sirs, what must I do to be saved?** (vs. 30b). If man could but see that the calamities of life are often God's methods of leading him to hope and salvation how different would be the issues of life.

D. The Fruits of the Persecution (16:31–34)

And they said, Believe on the Lord Jesus, and thou shalt be saved, thou and thy house . . . and [he] **rejoiced greatly, with all his house, having believed in God** (vss. 31, 34b).

How different the attitude and address of the jailer toward Paul and Silas now than yesterday. Then he ruthlessly cast them into prison as malefactors; now he falls down before them in reverence and addresses them as **Sirs.** The arrester has been arrested by God.

Certainly, as Clarke observes, it is absurd to think that the jailer was concerned about his personal safety when he asked this question, **What must I do to be saved?** (vs. 30b). It was now certain that none of the prisoners had escaped. Rather let us soberly and realistically conclude with Wesley that his question, **What must I do to be saved?** (vs. 30b), implied: "From the guilt I feel, and the vengeance I fear. Undoubtedly God then set his sins in array before him, and convinced him in the clearest and strongest manner that the wrath of God abode upon him."[n]

Their answer was confident and unequivocal: **Believe on the Lord Jesus** [or believe that Jesus is Lord supreme even to your need] **and thou shalt be saved** (vs. 31). To supply the needed further instruction for the salvation of the jailer and his family, Paul and Silas spoke the word of the Lord unto him, with all that were in his house, and this may have included the prisoners by now. This was no vague or shallow personal instruction which Paul and Silas gave these spiritually awakened souls. The genuineness of the jailer's repentance and faith in God is further evidenced by his restitutional service to Paul and Silas in the washing of their wounds and the likely application of soothing and healing ointment. A profession of religion that does not right the wrongs of the past, where possible and practical, is of little value to either the professor or society.

Like the Ethiopian nobleman, this jailer seals the inner work of divine grace wrought in his heart by the outward symbol of water baptism. By what mode he was baptized we

[87] VGT, p. 188.

[n] Wesley, *op. cit.*, p. 461, n. 30.

32 And they spake the word of the Lord unto him, with all that were in his house.
33 And he took them the same hour of the night, and washed their stripes; and was baptized, he and all his, immediately.
34 And he brought them up into his house, and set food before them, and rejoiced greatly, with all his house, having believed in God.
35 But when it was day, the magistrates sent the serjeants, saying, Let those men go.

---

32 **House** is *oikos* in verse 31, *oikia* here. Knowling comments: "The first word is most frequently used in Attic Greek, and in the N.T. for household, *cf.* ver. 15, but both words are used in Attic, and in the N.T., for *familia.*" [88]

33 The jailer **washed** the wounds of Paul and Silas and **was baptized.** Probably these activities took place at a well or cistern in the courtyard of the prison. The expression *elousen apo tōn plēgōn* (literally, "bathed from the stripes") is a bit odd. But Deissmann cites instances of this very construction in inscriptions of that period.[89] Lake and Cadbury suggest: "He bathed them so that they were relieved from their stripes." [90]

34 The word **up** has been taken by some as implying that the inner prison was underground. Conybeare and Howson say of the earlier part of the narrative: "The whole phraseology seems to imply that the dungeon was subterraneous." [91] But it is more likely that the jailer brought Paul and Silas from the inner prison through the outer prison into the courtyard, where they were bathed and he baptized, and then **up** into his quarters above the prison.[92]

Set food is literally "set a table" *(parethēken trapezan)*—an idiomatic expression found in Homer and Herodotus. In Homer mention is made of a separate table for each guest.[93] **Rejoiced,** *hēgalliasato,* is the same word used in 2:26, its only other occurrence in Acts. **With all his house** is one word, *panoikei,* found only here in the New Testament.

35 The Western text of this verse [94] is indeed interesting: "And when it was day the praetors assembled together in the Agora, and when they remembered the earthquake which had taken place they were afraid, and sent the lictors to say, 'Let those men go whom you received yesterday.'"

Magistrates is *stratēgoi* (see on vs. 20). **Serjeants** is *rhaddouchoi.* The word, which occurs only here and in verse 38, is from *rhaddos,* a staff or rod. Hence it means "rod-bearers"; that is, those who carried their staff of office. These lictors (Lat.) bore the *fasces* before the praetors *(stratēgoi).*

---

are not told, nor is that of primary importance; but Clarke's argument against the employment of immersion under the circumstances will hardly stand in the light of the modern archeological discovery of elaborate baths in ancient Philippi.

Though the profound influence of the jailer's conversion on his household in bringing them to repentance and salvation is not to be discredited, it should also be observed that it was not unusual for whole households to be proselytized to Judaism, and it not infrequently occurred in the Christian Church. That they were individually saved on the grounds of their own faith appears evident from verse 34. His newfound faith in Christ was productive of generosity and joy, as the saving grace of Christ must ever be (vs. 34b).

VII. THEIR DEPARTURE IN PEACE (16:35–40)

The magistrates have sent to let you go: now therefore come forth, and go in peace . . . And they went out of the prison, and entered into the house of Lydia; and when they had seen the brethren, they comforted them, and departed (vss. 36b, 40).

It is quite possible that when the fervor of the frenzied mob had subsided, the magistrates had learned the truth concerning the supposed offense of the men who had been beaten and imprisoned, and sought to wash their hands of this miscarriage of justice. Wesley thinks, and that not without reason, the earthquake may have influenced their decision to release the missionaries. In any event they ordered the prisoners' release the following day (vs. 35).

[88] EGT, II, 352. [89] *Bible Studies*, p. 227. [90] *Beginnings*, IV, 199.
[91] *Op. cit.*, p. 226, n. 4. [92] Cf. Meyer, *op. cit.*, p. 317.
[93] *Odyssey*; XII, 74; XVII, 333. [94] Found in **D** and the margin of the Harklean Syriac.

36 And the jailor reported the words to Paul, *saying*, The magistrates have sent to let you go: now therefore come forth, and go in peace.

37 But Paul said unto them, They have beaten us publicly, uncondemned, men that are Romans, and have cast us into prison; and do they now cast us out privily? nay verily; but let them come themselves and bring us out.

38 And the serjeants reported these words unto the magistrates: and they feared when they heard that they were Romans;

39 and they came and besought them; and when they had brought them out, they asked them to go away from the city.

40 And they went out of the prison, and entered into *the house of* Lydia: and when they had seen the brethren, they comforted them, and departed.

---

36 **In peace** seems almost to reflect the jailer's new Christian experience.

37 By decrees made in 509 B.C. and 248 B.C. "exemption from the disgrace of being scourged by rods and whips was secured to every Roman citizen."[95] *Akatakritos*, **uncondemned,** has not yet been found anywhere, except here and in 22:25.[96] It is a compound of the classical term *akritos*. Ramsay renders it "without investigation" *(re incognita)*.[97] **Men that are Romans** implies definitely that Silas, as well as Paul, was a Roman citizen.

Let them come themselves was not an assertion of pride or self-will. Paul wanted public vindication for the sake of the reputation of the newly founded Christian church at Philippi.

38 The question has often been raised as to how one could prove his Roman citizenship. Lake and Cadbury comment: "It is curious that we seem to have no knowledge of the 'papers' or other means by which a claim to citizenship could be substantiated."[98] But to make a false claim of citizenship was punishable by death.[99]

39 The magistrates asked Paul and Silas **to go away from the city,** probably because they were afraid of further riots. Evidently the missionaries felt that it was best for the new church that they depart, though apparently they left Luke in charge of the work.

40 *Parekalesan*, **comforted,** is probably best translated here "exhorted" (RSV). This is what the new converts would especially need.

Paul asserted their Roman citizenship rights and demanded a respectable release by the very magistrates who had unjustly treated them. The reply by the sergeants brought to light the citizenship of Paul and Silas, which fact struck terror to the hearts of the magistrates. Such official conduct might, if known at Rome, cost them their positions or even severe punishment. In compliance with Paul's request, the magistrates came personally and besought them, probably apologized for the treatment accorded them, and then asked them to leave the city.

For how long we are not told, but they returned to the home of Lydia where they ministered to the disciples, and then feeling that their work in Philippi was done, they went on their way.

No New Testament church became dearer to the heart of the apostle Paul than that at Philippi. His epistle addressed to the Philippians exceeds all the others in its spirit of personal affection, abounding gratitude, and exuberant joy, notwithstanding the fact that it was written from Paul's Roman jail cell. The care of these Christians for the apostle of their salvation finds its fullest expression in his words: "And ye yourselves also know, ye Philippians, that in the beginning of the gospel, when I departed from Macedonia, no church had fellowship with me in the matter of giving and receiving but ye only; for even in Thessalonica ye sent once and again unto my need" (Phil. 4:15, 16). This epistle is so joyful and grateful in its spirit and tone that one has said that it may be summed up in a single sentence, "I rejoice, do you rejoice?"

[95] Meyer, *op. cit.*, p. 318.
[96] *Beginnings*, IV, 200.
[97] *St. Paul the Traveller*, p. 223.
[98] *Beginnings*, IV, 201.
[99] *Ibid.*

CHAPTER XVII

Now when they had passed through Amphipolis and Apollonia, they came to Thessalonica, where was a synagogue of the Jews:

EXEGESIS

1 *Diodeusantes*, **when they had passed through,** is literally "having taken the road through." Luke, a much traveled man, was especially fond of compounds of *hodos*, "way, road," which occurs 20 times in his Gospel and 20 times in Acts (100 times in N.T.). He alone uses the simple verb *hodeuō* (Luke 10:33), and its two compounds *synodeuō*, "travel with" (Acts 9:7), and *diodeuō*, travel through" (here and Luke 8:1). Perhaps he purposely chose this verb to emphasize the fact that Paul took the main *road*, the Via Egnatia, which stretched over 500 miles from the Hellespont to Dyrrhachium and was one of the great highways of the Empire.[1]

Amphipolis is from *amphi*, "on both sides," and *polis*, "city." It probably received its name because of its location on a bend of the Strymon, so that the river flowed almost around it. It may, however, have been due to its prominent position three miles from the Aegean, so that it could be seen from both land and sea. The latter view is supported somewhat by the city's earlier name, "Nine Ways." [2]

Apollonia was apparently one of three cities in Macedonia with that name. The exact location is unknown today. But we know the distances, from ancient Roman itineraries. The total distance from Philippi to Thessalonica was one hundred miles. Lake and Cadbury make the interesting observation that if the two cities mentioned were the only stopping places for the nights enroute, then "Paul must have used horses." [3]

Thessalonica was the largest city in Macedonia. It shared with Ephesus and Corinth the commerce of the Aegean. The mention of **a synagogue of the Jews** there implies, though it does not prove, that there was no synagogue in Amphipolis and Apollonia.

EXPOSITION

THE CHURCH'S FIRST EUROPEAN MISSION (cont'd)

VIII. The Evangelization of the Thessalonians, Acts 17:1–9.
- A. The Proclamation of the Gospel, vss. 1–3.
- B. The Acquisition of Converts, vs. 4.
- C. The Jews' Attack on the Missionaries, vss. 5–9.

IX. The Spiritual Quest of the Beroeans, Acts 17:10–15.
- A. The Beroeans' Pursuit of Eternal Life, vss. 10–12.
- B. The Jews' Pursuit of the Missionaries at Beroea, vss. 13–15.

X. The Ministry at Athens, Acts 17: 16–31.
- A. The Ministry in the Synagogue, vss. 16, 17.
- B. The Message on Mars' Hill, vss. 18–31.
- C. The Product of the Ministry, vss. 32–34.

VIII. THE EVANGELIZATION OF THE THESSALONIANS (17:1–9)

And some of them were persuaded (vs. 4a). Perhaps nowhere is the immediate record of Paul's evangelistic success more pronounced than at Thessalonica. The fuller account of this initial ministry at Thessalonica is revealed in Paul's first and second letters written to the Thessalonian Christians from Corinth on his second missionary journey.

[1] For a photograph of a section of the Via Egnatia near Philippi, see L. H. Grollenberg, *Atlas of the Bible*. Trans. and ed. J. M. H. Reid and H. H. Rowley (New York: Nelson, 1956), p. 134, no. 395.
[2] Conybeare and Howson, *op. cit.*, p. 276.
[3] *Beginnings*, IV, 202.

2 and Paul, as his custom was, went in unto them, and for three sabbath days reasoned with them from the scriptures,

3 opening and alleging that it behooved the Christ to suffer, and to rise again from the dead; and that this Jesus, whom, *said he*, I proclaim unto you, is the Christ.

---

2 **As his custom was** is found only here and in Luke 4:16. **Three sabbath days** is changed to "three weeks" in the Revised Standard Version. Lake and Cadbury argue at length that there is no evidence in the Septuagint or New Testament for the latter usage. The Synoptic Gospels have *sabbaton* 22 times in the singular, 16 in the plural. In John's Gospel it is always singular (12 times). Acts has it six times in the singular and four times in the plural. Usually there is no difference in meaning between the singular and plural of this word. With regard to its use here Lake and Cadbury say: "The present phrase *tria sabbata* is apparently the only example in the N.T. of a true plural (= three Sabbaths) as distinct from a plural with a singular meaning." [4] Aside from the four Gospels and Acts *sabbaton* occurs in the New Testament only in I Corinthians 16:2 (sing.) and Colossians 2:16 (pl.). The former of these has the phrase *mia sabbaton*, "first day of the week." Lake and Cadbury maintain that only in the genitive does *sabbaton* mean "week."

Reasoned is *dielexato*. The verb occurs ten times in Acts, and only three times elsewhere in the New Testament.[5] It means "discourse, discuss, argue." Perhaps **from the scriptures** should be construed with the participles that follow in verse three.[6]

3 *Dianoigōn*, **opening,** is a favorite word with Luke (six out of eight times in the N.T.). It means "open up completely." Paul was opening to the Jews their own Scriptures, so that they could see Christ there. Jesus did the same for His disciples (Luke 24:32, 45). **Alleging** is the verb *paratithēmi*, one meaning of which is "bring forward, quote as evidence." Ramsay renders the participle, "quoting to prove"; [7] Bruce, "bringing forward as evidence." [8] Paul was quoting from the Scriptures (O.T.) to prove that they taught a suffering, resurrected Messiah. These two points, **to suffer, and to rise again,** were the foundation for presenting **Jesus** as **the Christ.** Until the Jews recognized these teachings in their Scriptures, they could not accept Jesus as their Messiah.

A. The Proclamation of the Gospel (17:1–3)

Since Luke drops the "we" of personal identification with the missionary party from his historical record as they leave Philippi, it is generally assumed that he remained there, which likely signifies that either Philippi was his home or that he remained as pastor of the new church, or possibly both. Nor is Luke identified with Paul again until Paul arrives at Philippi the second time on his third missionary journey (see Acts 20:5, 6), after which Luke is with him to the close of the Acts record. Leaving Philippi, the party followed a southwesterly course for thirty-three miles over the *Via Egnatia* to **Amphipolis,** originally the Roman capital of one of the four districts of Macedonia, but now having taken second place to Philippi and being devoid of a synagogue or Jewish population and generally decadent, Paul passes it by as a field of missionary activity. Thirty miles farther southwest they passed through the important city of **Apollonia,** without stopping to evangelize, and from thence on westward upward of forty miles to **Thessalonica.** This was the important capital of the entire province of Macedonia, and it had a large Jewish population and a synagogue. Thessalonica was founded by Cassander about 315 B.C. and named after his wife, Thessalonica, who was the sister of Alexander the Great. It was made a free city in reward for "its support of Antony and Octavian in the Battle of Philippi." [a] Thessalonica was the modern Salonika, an important Allied military base during the First World War, having a present population of about one-quarter million. It is located on the favored Thurmic Bay.

[4] *Ibid.*, p. 203. [5] Mark 9:34; Heb. 12:5; Jude 9. [6] So Meyer, *op. cit.*, p. 325.
[7] *St. Paul the Traveller*, p. 226. [8] *Acts*, p. 324.

[a] Finegan *op. cit.*, p. 271.

4 And some of them were persuaded, and consorted with Paul and Silas; and the devout Greeks a great multitude, and of the chief women not a few.

4 **Them** apparently refers to Jews.[9] *Prosekl̄erōthēsan*, **consorted**, is found only here in the New Testament. In the active it means "to allot to, assign to by lot." [10] Hence Meyer takes it as meaning "they were assigned by God *to them*." [11] But perhaps "joined" (RSV) is the best translation.

Ramsay prefers the Western text, which inserts *kai* (and) between *sebomenōn* **(devout)** and *Hellēnōn* **(Greeks).** This would give four classes. He writes: "Between the two opposite groups, the Jews and the Hellenes, there is interposed the intermediate class of God-fearing proselytes; and there is added as a climax a group of noble ladies of the city." [12] Doubtless Ramsay is correct in emphasizing the fact that Paul labored in Thessalonica much longer than the three weeks mentioned here. This is evidenced by the Gentile majority in the Thessalonian church (see Exposition), as well as by Paul's statement to the Philippians: "For even in Thessalonica ye sent once and again unto my need" (Phil. 4:16).

Here Paul, in keeping with his strategy to evangelize the capitals and commercial centers on the main trade routes that the Gospel might spread from these centers throughout the empire, addressed himself to the Jewish synagogue as was his custom, where the way had been prepared for the Gospel by the Old Testament revelation and the Gentile proselytes, mediums which Paul always sought to use for the evangelization of the Gentile world. Clarke thinks that the use of the definite article in reference to the Thessalonian synagogue indicates that this was the only synagogue in Macedonia, all other places of Jewish worship being only *proseuchas*, as at Philippi (see comment on Acts 16:13).

Paul's method of ministry in the synagogue is made evident in verses two and three. *First*, he, like Philip with the Ethiopian nobleman (Acts 8:30–35), began at the point of Jewish interest in their own Scriptures concerning the promised Messiah, from which he reasoned with them (vs. 2b). *Second*, he expounded the prophecies to the effect that this Messiah was to redeem humanity, not by the route of a materialistic earthly kingdom as they supposed, but through His suffering and atoning death and His glorious universal Lordship through the conquest of death in His resurrection, and this he did positively and with strong conviction as Luke suggests in his use of the word **alleging**, which means to declare as under oath (vs. 3a). How great was the apostle's passion for their salvation! *Third*, he identified the Jesus of his message with the Messiah of the Jewish Scriptures. Thus did Paul tactfully, logically, and passionately lead his hearers from the Scriptures to the Christ that he knew as Saviour and Lord. He proceeded from promise in the Scriptures to fulfillment in his Christ.

That Paul remained at Thessalonica much longer, evangelizing the Gentiles with greater success, appears to be suggested by Luke's references to his three weeks' initial ministry in the synagogue.

B. The Acquisition of Converts (17:4)

And some of them were persuaded, and consorted with Paul and Silas (vs. 4a).

That those who were persuaded went beyond mental assent to the logically inescapable conclusions of Paul is evidenced by the fact they **consorted with Paul and Silas.** Wesley renders these words, "And some of them believed and were joined to Paul and Silas"; while Weymouth's version states: "Some of the people were won over, and attached themselves to Paul and Silas." Thus they joined the company of the Christians. That these conversions were deep and genuine, effecting a saving relationship with Christ, there can remain no reasonable doubt. The great multitude of **devout Greeks** (vs. 4b) who became Christians indicates, *first*, the extensive influence of the Jewish synagogue in winning Gentiles to the Jewish faith at Thessalonica; *second*, that these were not full proselytes, but "God-fearers" or those Greeks who worshipped Jehovah in

[9] Hackett, *op. cit.*, p. 195.
[10] Abbott-Smith, *op. cit.*, p. 385.
[11] *Op. cit.*, p. 325.
[12] *St. Paul the Traveller*, p. 227.

5 But the Jews, being moved with jealousy, took unto them certain vile fellows of the rabble, and gathering a crowd, set the city on an uproar; and assaulting the house of Jason, they sought to bring them forth to the people.

---

5 *Apeithountes*, "unbelieving" (cf. KJV), is omitted in the earliest manuscripts.[13] **Vile** is perhaps a bit strong for *ponēros*, as is "lewd" (only this one time in KJV). Of its 76 occurrences *ponēros* is translated "evil" 51 times in the King James Version and "wicked" (cf. RSV) 16 times. "Worthless" would be a good rendering. **Rabble** is the plural of the adjective *agoraios*, from *agora*, "market place." Hence it means "frequenting the agora, a lounger in the agora." But in late writers it took the meaning "proper to the agora."[14] That is its sense in its only other occurrence in the New Testament (Acts 19:38). Lake and Cadbury say: "It is doubtful whether *agoraios* retained any suggestion of loafing in the agora."[15] Their translation is: "bad men of the lower class."

The compound *ochlopoiēsantes*, **gathering a crowd** (literally, making a crowd), has not been found elsewhere.[16] **Set . . . on an uproar** is *ethoryboun*, used again in 20:10.[17] It means "throw into confusion." **Assaulting** is the verb *ephistēmi*, used by Luke 18 out of its 21 occurrences in the New Testament. Only here is it translated thus in the King James Version. Interestingly this uncommon use of the verb for hostile action is paralleled in I Thessalonians 5:3.

It is not known whether or not **Jason** was a Jew. Bruce thinks so, although it was a common name among the Greeks because of the leader of the Argonauts in quest of the Golden Fleece.[18] *Dēmos*, **people**, is rendered "public meeting" by Ramsay.[19] Bruce seems to agree, when he uses "citizen-body,"[20] as does Hackett.[21] But Lake and Cadbury think the attackers (cf. RSV) wanted to subject the missionaries "to the violence of the crowd."[22] Knowling allows both ideas.[23]

---

the synagogue but did not subscribe to the Jewish ceremonials; and *third*, that the Greeks at Thessalonica much more readily became Christians than did the Jews. In fact, there is evidence from the Thessalonian letter that the church here was largely comprised of Gentile believers, as indeed it could not have been said of Jews, "ye turned unto God from idols, to serve a living and true God" (I Thess. 1:9b), since Jews were not idol worshipers at this time, and they already professed to be servants of the "living and true God," in contrast with the inanimate false idols. **The chief women not a few** (vs. 4a) likewise were most probably the wives of prominent Gentile citizens and governmental officials, as was the case at Antioch of Pisidia (see note on Acts 13:50). Here, as in so many other places, women figured largely in the Church of the first century.[b]

C. THE JEWS' ATTACK ON THE MISSIONARIES (17:5-9)

But the Jews, being moved with jealousy, took unto them certain vile fellows of the rabble, and gathering a crowd, set the city on an uproar (vs. 5a).

At Thessalonica, as at Antioch (Acts 13:45, 50), the deflection of so many Gentiles from the synagogue to Christianity, whom the Jews had hoped to win as proselytes to Judaism, aroused within them a jealous hatred that expressed itself in a most incredible manner. Unleashed jealousy knows no principles. Nor are religious people immune to its impassioned, blinding, perverting, cruel venom, if they are not cleansed and sustained by the Holy Spirit of God. Motivated by the cruel monster, the subjects throw to the wind every principle of right and justice and pant for the blood of their innocent victims. Jealousy was one of the viperous brood of the "sins of the spirit" characterizing the elder son in Christ's parable (Luke 15:25-32). That this elder son represented the Pharisees and scribes in their jealous resentment of Christ's receiving and eating with the Gentiles (publicans and sinners) is made clear in Luke 15:1. And though the lost sheep, coin, and son were all

[13] Aleph A B E. [14] Abbott-Smith, *op. cit.*, p. 7. [15] *Beginnings*, IV, 204.
[16] Abbott-Smith, *op. cit.*, p. 331. [17] Elsewhere in N.T. only in Matt. 9:23; Mark 5:39.
[18] *Acts*, p. 326. [19] *St. Paul the Traveller*, p. 228. [20] *Acts*, p. 326.
[21] *Op. cit.*, p. 195. [22] *Beginnings*, IV, 205. [23] EGT, II, 360.

[b] See Additional Note I, "The Place of Women in the Primitive Church," at end of Chapter XVII.

6 And when they found them not, they dragged Jason and certain brethren before the rulers of the city, crying, These that have turned the world upside down are come hither also;
7 whom Jason hath received: and these all act contrary to the decrees of Caesar, saying that there is another king, *one* Jesus.

---

6 For **dragged** see on 8:3 (cf. 14:19). Knowling comments: "The word indicates the violence of the mob." [24]

Rulers of the city is the compound *politarchas*, found only here and in verse eight. It was once fashionable to question Luke's accuracy at this point. But in 1898 E.D. Burton published an article in the *American Journal of Theology* (pp. 598–632) in which he called attention to seventeen inscriptions containing this word, and "of these thirteen [fourteen now] are referred to Macedonia, and of these again five to Thessalonica, extending from the beginning of the first to the middle of the second century, A.D." These inscriptions also show that there were five politarchs in Thessalonica in the time of Augustus and six in the time of Antoninus and Marcus Aurelius.[25] More recently the word has been found in a papyrus letter from Egypt.[26]

World is *oikoumenē*, "inhabited earth." In classical writers it signified "the countries occupied by Greeks, as distinguished from barbarian lands." [27] In later times it meant the Roman world. That is evidently its meaning here. **Turned . . . upside down** is *anastatōsantes*. The verb means "to stir up, excite, unsettle." [28] In the New Testament it occurs only here, in 21:38, and in Galatians 5:12. Deissmann gives as its meaning: "incite to tumult, stir up to sedition, upset." [29] He gives in full a fascinating papyrus letter written by a spoiled Egyptian boy in which he quotes his mother as saying: "he driveth me mad [*anastatoi*]: away with him." [30] Moulton and Milligan render it: "He quite upsets me—off with him." [31] The letter comes from the second or third century.

7 **Received** is the compound *hypodechomai*, used three times by Luke (cf. Luke 10:38; 19:6) and in James 2:25. It means "to receive under one's roof, receive as a guest, entertain hospitably." [32] Lake and Cadbury give the very fitting translation "harboured." [33] They also think that **king** *(basilea)* may well be rendered "emperor," since the Romans recognized many kings but only one emperor.[34] **These all** may mean "all these people"; that is, Christians everywhere.[35] *Apenanti*, **contrary to,** has this meaning only this once in the New Testament. Elsewhere it means "over against" (Matt. 27:61) or "in the presence of" (Acts 3:16; Rom. 3:18). But the meaning here is found in Ecclesiasticus (36:14; 37:4). The agitators were smart enough to bring against the missionaries the serious political charge of treason.

---

recovered and restored, the curtain falls on the elder son, leaving him out of the Kingdom of God. When jealousy motivates the pursuer, the victim's only hope is in the "divine city of refuge," as witnesses the relation of Saul and David.

There are two views concerning the **vile fellows of the rabble** (vs. 5a) whom these Jews used as instruments against the missionaries. One holds that they were idle, unprincipled, underworldling scavengers of the city who loafed about the central market and eked out a living by stealing, cheating, or begging, spending as much of their time in jail as outside, fellows everywhere alert to engage in any disorder that would afford them either excitement or personal gain. The other view holds that these **vile fellows of the rabble** were, rather, cheap, incompetent, unprincipled, and largely unemployed shyster lawyers with a degree of judicial authority, comparable perhaps to the so-called American "justice of the peace," of whom there were many in the country in Paul's day. Clarke calls them "wicked men of the forensic tribe." They were likely the descendants of the Greek Sophists and were ever ready to be employed for a pittance. Strange bedfellows for these proud Jewish religionists in their attack upon the missionaries.

Whichever view is taken, these **vile fellows** were employed by the Jews to the great discredit of the religion of Jehovah in

[24] *Ibid.* [25] *Ibid.* [26] VGT, p. 525. [27] Abbott–Smith, *op. cit.*, p. 313. [28] *Ibid.*, p. 34. [29] *Light from the Ancient East*, p. 80. [30] *Ibid.*, p. 188. [31] VGT, p. 38. [32] Abbott-Smith, *op. cit.*, p. 460. [33] *Beginnings*, IV, 205. [34] *Ibid.*, p. 206. [35] Henry Alford, *New Testament for English Readers*, I, 767.

8 And they troubled the multitude and the rulers of the city, when they heard these things.
9 And when they had taken security from Jason and the rest, they let them go.

---

9 **When they had taken security** is *labontes to hikanon,* which is "a literal rendering of the Roman legal term . . . and means to take security or a bond which can be forfeited if the offence be repeated."[36] Ramsay thinks the bond was a guarantee that peace would be kept, which involved assurance that Paul would not return to Thessalonica. He links this with Paul's statement that he was hindered by Satan (action of Roman authorities) from revisiting the Thessalonian Christians (I Thess. 2:18).[37]

Thessalonica. They were employed, either to shout slogans or taunts and thus inflame the passions of the ignorant masses and set them like packs of dogs on Paul and Silas, or, if lawyers, then their approach probably was to charge them with religious heresy and, or, political sedition. In either event, they gathered **a crowd,** [and] **set the city on an uproar** (vs. 5).

Learning that the missionaries were housed in the home of Jason, these Jews attempted, either directly or through their representatives, to secure custody of them, not legally to try them for any supposed misdemeanor, but to turn them over to the mob violence of the waiting, frenzied, populace. How like the incident in Sodom when the sin-intoxicated Sodomites attacked the house of Lot, demanding custody of the heaven-sent investigating angels (cf. Gen. 19:1–11).

Jason was evidently a Jew who had believed on Christ and, like Lydia at Philippi, had become the host of the missionaries. He may be the same Jason from whom Paul sends greetings to the Romans from Corinth (Rom. 16:21), having gone to that city from Thessalonica to be with Paul on the occasion of the apostle's second visit there. Unable to find the missionaries, for reasons untold—possibly Jason hid them—they apprehended Jason and certain of the new believers and hauled them into the court before the magistrates with one of the most complimentary charges, ironically made against the missionaries in absentia, that they ever received, **These that have turned the world** [the inhabited earth] **upside down are come hither also** (vs. 6b). These accusers appear to have had an inverted perspective of the world. Actually, it was already upside down, and the missionaries were simply turning it right side up. Men may become so accustomed to inverted circumstances and ways of life that wrong appears right, and right appears to be wrong. Widespread knowledge of the power and effectiveness of the Gospel at this early stage of Christian progress is suggested in these words of accusation.

Their accusation of sedition (vs. 7) was totally without foundation. Indeed, the missionaries declared Jesus to be Lord of the universe by His resurrection from the dead, but always and everywhere they made clear that His was a spiritual kingdom and never after Pentecost did they confuse it with the material. Nor is there any evidence that the missionaries' conduct contravened Roman law, as is implied in their words, **these all act contrary to the decrees of Caesar** (vs. 7). By these devices the accusers poisoned the minds of the populace and strongly prejudiced them against the Christians.

The **security** (vs. 9), which the rulers took from Jason and the other Christians arraigned before the rulers for harboring and consorting with the missionaries, appears to have been a guarantee that the missionaries would leave the city (see I Thess. 2:17, 18). Paul was never cowardly when the Gospel or its interests were at stake, but always considerate of the interests and welfare of others; having completed his service at Thessalonica, he peacefully went on his way, but not until a powerful church had been planted there.

Paul's first and second letters to the Thessalonians, written from Corinth, are illuminating commentaries on his first visit to this city. At the very outset of the first letter, he remarks that he has only thanks to God for them, and that always (1:2); after which he commends them for the three greatest and abiding Christian virtues (1:3) with which Paul closes his dissertation on the *Summum Bonum* in First Corinthians, the thirteenth chapter. Note, however, that

[36] *Beginnings,* IV, 206. [37] *St. Paul the Traveller,* pp. 230 f.

10 And the brethren immediately sent away Paul and Silas by night unto Beroea: who when they were come thither went into the synagogue of the Jews.

11 Now these were more noble than those in Thessalonica, in that they received the word with all readiness of mind, examining the scriptures daily, whether these things were so.

---

10 The immediate departure of **Paul and Silas** was demanded either in fulfilment of the assurances given by Jason, or the imminent danger of another riot, or both.

Beroea lay south of the Via Egnatia, which Paul had followed from Philippi. Though off the road to Rome, it was on the way to Athens. The modern Verria is a Franco-Turkish transliteration of the ancient name.

Went into is the verb *apeimi*, found only here in the New Testament.[38] It literally means "to depart." [39] Lake and Cadbury suggest the translation "went their way to the synagogue." [40]

11 **More noble** is the comparative form of *eugenēs*, which literally means "well born." It is used in that sense in its only other occurrences in the New Testament (Luke 19:12; I Cor. 1:26). Here it has the metaphorical meaning "noble-minded." The Latin equivalent *generosus* (generous) means "liberal, free from prejudice." Knowling says: "Its meaning here is that the Beroeans were far from the strife and envy of the Thessalonian Jews." [41]

Readiness is *prothymia,* found only here and four times in II Corinthians (8:11, 12, 19; 9:2). It means "eagerness" (RSV), "willingness." **Examining** is the verb *anakrinō*, which was used commonly for a judicial investigation (cf. Luke 23:14). This meaning is found in the papyri.[42] The verb is used in the New Testament only by Luke (six times) and Paul (ten times in I Cor.). **Daily** suggests a somewhat prolonged stay in Beroea.

---

the Thessalonian Christians possessed *a working faith, a laboring love*, and *a patient hope*. In verse five he reviews the effectiveness with which he preached the Gospel at Thessalonica—"in power, and in the Holy Spirit, and in much assurance." Further, he relates of them that they "became imitators of us, and of the Lord, having received the word in much affliction, with joy of the Holy Spirit" (I Thess. 1:6). The apostle continued to the effect that they lived exemplary lives before all (1:7), and that from these Christians "sounded forth the word of the Lord" (1:8a) to the extent that they had largely, if not completely, covered Macedonia and Achaia with their witness. Salvation, suffering, and the Second Coming of Jesus Christ are the three golden strands that run throughout the whole of First Thessalonians and form the essential structure of the epistle.

A word need be said concerning the **rulers** at Thessalonica, since they are unique in the New Testament record. Finegan observes concerning these rulers, who are called *politarchai*, that an inscription found on an arch (the Vardar Gate), spanning the *Via Egnatia* at the western entrance to the city but now in the British Museum, begins with these words: "In the time of the Politarchs . . ." He further states that this inscription should probably be dated between 30 B.C. and A.D. 143. Other Thessalonian inscriptions, he states, one mentioning *Politarchs*, are definitely dated in Augustus' reign. Then says Finegan, "The term is otherwise unknown [outside of Acts 17:6] in extant Greek literature, but Luke's accuracy in the matter is entirely vindicated by the inscriptions." [c]

IX. THE SPIRITUAL QUEST OF THE BEROEANS (17:10–15)

Now these were more noble . . . examining the scriptures daily, whether these things were so (vs. 11).

Under the protective cover of darkness, the Christian disciples at Thessalonica sent Paul and Silas away. While Timothy is not mentioned by name, he certainly accompanied Paul and Silas in the escape, since he is later mentioned with Silas at Beroea in verse fourteen.

[38] Not to be confused with the other *apeimi*, used seven times by Paul. [39] Abbott-Smith, *op. cit.*, p. 46.
[40] *Beginnings*, IV, 206. [41] EGT, II, 362. [42] VGT, p. 35.

[c] Finegan, *op. cit.*, p. 271. See also Ernest De Witt Burton, *The American Journal of Theology*. II (1898), pp. 598–632.

12 Many of them therefore believed; also of the Greek women of honorable estate, and of men, not a few.

13 But when the Jews of Thessalonica had knowledge that the word of God was proclaimed of Paul at Beroea also, they came thither likewise, stirring up and troubling the multitudes.

---

12 The natural result of such a careful investigation was that **many . . . believed** on Jesus as the Messiah. **Of honorable estate** is *euschēmonōn*, which literally means "of good figure or fashion" *(eu-schēma)*. First meaning "graceful" or "comely" (cf. I Cor. 12:24), in later Greek it often meant "wealthy." Here it probably means "of good position," or "of high standing" (RSV).

13 **Of Thessalonica** is literally "from [*apo*] Thessalonica." While the exact sense of the preposition may have weakened in later Greek, the Beroeans would think of these Jews as *from* Thessalonica.[43]

Paul and his company proceeded overland southwest from Thessalonica for a distance of about fifty miles to the small city of Beroea, now known as Verria or Veroia and presently having a population of about 6,000. The city lay on the eastern side of Mount Olympus near Pella, the birthplace of Alexander the Great. It had a community of Jews and a synagogue. It is thought that Paul resorted to Beroea for rest and comparative seclusion for a time, but if so, he had not long to enjoy it. Cicero designates the city as "an out of the way place."

A. The Beroeans' Pursuit of Eternal Life (17:10–12)

Many of them therefore believed (12a). As usual Paul resorted to the Jewish synagogue at Beroea. Here he found not only sincere, earnest-hearted Jews but many prominent Greek women and men. The nobility of these Beroean Jews is evidenced *first*, by their likely higher culture and learning than those of Thessalonica; *second*, by their sincerity and eager-mindedness, **they received the word with all readiness of mind** (vs. 11); *third*, by their unbiased, earnest quest for truth, **examining the scriptures daily, whether these things were so** (vs. 11b). That is, they heard the word of the Gospel readily, and then they earnestly examined the Old Testament prophecies with which they were conversant to ascertain whether the allegations of Paul concerning Christ and His redeeming work were in truth the fulfillment of these prophecies concerning the Messiah. They were following the injunction of Christ to the Jews of His day to "search the scriptures" which testified of Him (John 5:39).

There appear to have been three classes among the many who came to believe on Christ unto salvation at Beroea. *First*, there were many believers from the class of noble Scripture-searching Jews; *second*, there were prominent Greek women, probably wives of governmental officials and merchantmen; *third*, there were not a few Greek men who also came into the faith. Luke has taken special pains to note this latter class who have not been prominent, when present elsewhere.

Thus if Paul thought to rest at Beroea, the results of these evangelistic activities appear to indicate otherwise.

B. The Jews' Pursuit of the Missionaries at Beroea (17:13–15)

How long Paul remained at Beroea we do not know, but as soon as word reached Thessalonica concerning Paul's preaching at Beroea, the Jewish enemies there hotly pursued him to Beroea, thirsting for his blood and employing the same tactics of inciting the multitudes to violence against the apostle.

Since it was evident that Paul was the object of their jealous wrath and they could not rest until they were done with him, the disciples held council and decided that in the interest of the work and Paul's safety, it would be best for him to depart. However, Silas and Timothy were left at Beroea to confirm the faith of the disciples.

An apparent camouflage move was made by Paul's Beroean escorts who pretended to take him to the sea as though to take shipping out of the country. However, it appears likely that they escorted him overland to

[43] Cf. *Beginnings*, IV, 207.

14 And then immediately the brethren sent forth Paul to go as far as to the sea: and Silas and Timothy abode there still.

15 But they that conducted Paul brought him as far as Athens: and receiving a commandment unto Silas and Timothy that they should come to him with all speed, they departed.

---

14 **As far as** *(heōs)* is preferable to "as it were" *(hōs,* KJV) because found in the older manuscripts.[44] Hence there is no suggestion here of a feigned movement toward the sea.[45] But the lack of mention of a harbor by Luke is in favor of the view that Paul went by land to Athens.[46]

15 *Kathistanontes,* **conducted,** is used only here in the New Testament in this sense. But the meaning is supported in both classical and later Greek.[47] It occurs in the papyri with this signification.[48] The superlative form *tachista* is found only here in the New Testament. *Hōs tachista,* **with all speed,** is better rendered "as quickly as possible" (cf. RSV—"as soon as possible"). *Exēisan,* **departed,** is found only in Acts (cf. 13:42; 20:7).

Athens. Others hold that they actually took shipping at Driem and sailed to Athens. However that may be, he gave his escorts a command to deliver to Silas and Timothy that they should come to him at Athens immediately.

There appears to be evidence in First Thessalonians (3:1–3) that Silas and Timothy joined Paul at Athens in accordance with his instructions, but that Paul's anxiety over the welfare of the Christians at Philippi and Thessalonica was such that he soon dispatched Silas to Philippi and Timothy to Thessalonica to ascertain their welfare, confirm them in the faith, and report to him, which they did. They then returned with their favorable reports to find Paul at Corinth (Acts 18:1, 5).

X. THE MINISTRY AT ATHENS (17:16–31)

Arriving at Athens, Paul found himself in one of the most famous centers of philosophy, religion, art, and architecture the ancient world had ever known. It was in "the city of the violet-crown" that the greatest pinnacle of ancient world culture was attained. Its golden age was realized during the administration of Pericles about 443–429 B.C. While not the political capital of Achaia or Greece, a position held by Corinth, it was the cultural capital of the whole ancient world. It was located five miles northeast of the Saronic Gulf between two streams, Caphessus and Ilissus. Long walls connected the city with its two seaports, and the Piraeus and Phaleric Gulfs. It was surrounded by mountains and within its walls were four famous hills; (1) A precipitous rocky eminence of 512 feet altitude, known as the Acropolis, was surmounted by the crown of Greek architecture, the Parthenon, (2) The Areopagus, or Hill of Ares, lay northwest of the Acropolis and was perhaps the location of Paul's famous Mars' Hill sermon. This Areopagus was provided with rock benches constituting three sides of a square, the meeting place of the Areopagus court, which exercised both religious and political authority, but with special interest in religion and education. However, some hold that the Areopagus sometimes met in the Stoa Basileios or Royal Stoa and that Paul's sermon may have been delivered there. (3) The Pynx was farther west. (4) The Museum was located to the south. Says Finegan:

> Of the Parthenon-crowned Acropolis J. P. Mahaffy wrote, 'There is no ruin all the world over which combines so much striking beauty, so distinct a type, so vast a volume of history, so great a pageant of immortal memories . . . All the Old World's culture culminated in Greece —all Greece in Athens—all Athens in its Acropolis—all the Acropolis in the Parthenon.'[d]

The next most important structure was the Agora or marketplace, which constituted the center of the commercial and civic life of the city. The Agora covered a large area to the north of the west end of the Acropolis.

[44] Aleph A B E. [46] Cf. EGT, II, 363.

[45] Cf. *Beginnings*, IV, 207 f. Knox thinks that Paul went westward to the Adriatic, visiting (cf. Rom. 15:19) Illyricum. (Ronald Knox, *A New Testament Commentary* [New York: Sheed & Ward, 1954], II, 40).

[47] EGT, II, 363. [48] VGT, p. 313.

[d] *Ibid.*, p. 273.

16 Now while Paul waited for them at Athens, his spirit was provoked within him as he beheld the city full of idols.

17 So he reasoned in the synagogue with the Jews and the devout persons, and in the marketplace every day with them that met him.

---

16 **Waited** is the verb *ekdechomai*, occurring in Acts only here. This is a late meaning for it, rare in the classics.[49] But it is supported in the papyri.[50] *Athēnais*, **Athens,** is plural because it consisted of several parts.[51] The name occurs only here (vss. 15, 16), in 18:1, and I Thessalonians 3:1.

Lake and Cadbury note that the description of Paul's visit to Athens "commends itself at once as a genuinely historical narrative. The Agora, the Stoics and Epicureans, and the Areopagus are all correct local details." [52]

Provoked is the verb *paroxynō*, used only here and in I Corinthians 13:5 (of love—"not provoked"). It means "rouse to anger." Meyer translates it here "was irritated." [53] The meaning "provoke" is supported by the papyri, as well as by Josephus and Xenophon.[54] **Full of idols** is a better rendering of *kateidōlon* than "wholly given to idolatry" (KJV). The word has not been found elsewhere. But the truth of this description is verified by many writers of that day, such as Livy, Pausanias, Strabo, and Sophocles.[55]

17 For **reasoned** see on verse two. Paul had a twofold ministry: **in the synagogue** and **in the marketplace.** This is the first mention in Acts of Paul conducting a mission specifically to the heathen.[56] At Athens, Corinth, and Ephesus, Paul started in the synagogue and then moved out to the Gentiles.

Eastward from the Agora stood the Stoa of Attalos, a colonnaded portico, and nearby the Stoa of the Giants. On the south were two large parallel stoas, and on the west several other important buildings including the Stoa of Zeus Eleutherios, the Temple of Apollo Patroos, the Sanctuary of the Mother of the Gods, the Bouleuterion, the assembling place of the famous Athenian Council of Five Hundred, and the Tholos where the executive divisions of the Council were held. Other buildings were the Temple of Ares, the Odeum or Music Hall, and the Library which was dedicated to Trajan, south of the Stoa of Attalos.

The Temple of Hephaistos, the god of fire and metallurgy, overlooked the Agora from the hill of Kolonos Agoraios westward. A variety of shops and arcades and the Horologium or Tower of the Winds were located to the east of the Roman Agora.

Achaia was a Roman senatorial province governed by a proconsul such as Cyprus (see comment on Acts 13:4–6), though the city of Athens was governed by the aristocratic court of the Areopagus (vs. 19).

The modern city has a population of approximately one-half million.

It was to this awe-inspiring city of ancient culture, filled with altars and temples to the uncounted gods, that Paul made his way alone from Beroea to await the arrival of Silas and Timothy.

A. The Ministry in the Synagogue (17:16, 17)

So he reasoned in the synagogue with the Jews and the devout persons, and in the marketplace every day with them that met him (vs. 17).

To the sensitive Jewish soul of Paul, cultured in opposition to all forms of idolatry, the ornate imagery and idols of Athens were naturally exceedingly repugnant. Little wonder that Luke records, **his spriit was provoked within him as he beheld the city full of idols** (16b). Paul must have felt as Quartilla is made to say of Athens in Petronius' Satyr (Cap. XVIII): "Our region is so *full of deities* that you may more frequently meet with a *god* than a *man*." [e]

Little wonder that Paul resorted to the Jewish synagogue where from the Old Testament Scriptures he could reason with the **Jews** and **devout persons,** or God-fearing Gentiles, concerning Christ as the fulfillment

[49] Abbott-Smith, *op. cit.*, p. 136. [50] VGT, p. 192. [51] Abbott-Smith, *op. cit.*, p. 11.
[52] *Beginnings*, IV, 208. For extended descriptions of Athens see Conybeare and Howson, *op. cit.*, chap. X; and H. V. Morton, *In the Steps of St. Paul* (New York: Dodd, Mead & Co., 1936), pp. 298–330.
[53] *Op. cit.*, p. 328. [54] VGT, p. 496. [55] *Beginnings*, IV, 209.
[56] The case at Lystra (14:15-18) was an emergency not planned.
[e] Clarke, *op. cit.*, p. 824.

18 And certain also of the Epicurean and Stoic philosophers encountered him. And some said, What would this babbler say? others, He seemeth to be a setter forth of strange gods: because he preached Jesus and the resurrection.

The Agora was the very place where Socrates had "taught" with his inimical method. Of Paul's ministry there Ramsay says: "Luke places before us the man who became 'all things to all men,' and who therefore in Athens made himself like an Athenian and adopted the regular Socratic style of general free discussion in the Agora."[57] He notes that "the mere Jew" could not have functioned thus, and continues: "He was in Athens the student of a great university [Tarsus], visiting an older but yet a kindred university, . . . mixing in its society as an equal conversing with men of like education."[58] Of all the ancient beauty of the Agora at Athens only one building remains, the Stoa of Attalos.

Every day suggests a somewhat protracted stay in Athens. *Paratygchanontas*, **that met him,** occurs only here in the New Testament. It means "happened to be present" (cf. RSV—"chanced to be there"). Ramsay translates it "chance comers."[59]

18 The **Epicurean** school was founded by Epicurus (341–270 B.C.). The **Stoic** philosophers claimed Zeno (340–265 B.C.) as their founder. Their name was derived from the Stoa Poikile (Painted Porch), where he taught. **Encountered** is *syneballon*[60] (imperfect), which literally signifies "throw together." It may mean "discuss, confer," and that is the way Abbott-Smith would render it here.[61] Ramsay has: "engaged in discussions with."[62] It also means "meet with, fall in with," and sometimes with a hostile sense (cf. Luke 14:31). So Lake and Cadbury translate it, "took issue with."[63] **What would** *(ti an theloi)* is correct, rather than "what will" (KJV).

Babbler is *spermologos*, "seed-picker." It was used first of birds, then "in Attic slang, of an idler who lives on scraps picked up in the agora."[64] It therefore suggests "a parasite," "a hanger-on." Eustathius in his comments on Homer's Odyssey uses it in the sense of "ignorant plagiarist,"[65] and that is the way Ramsay renders it.[66] Weymouth has "beggarly babbler"; Moffatt, "fellow with scraps of learning"; Goodspeed, "rag-picker." Cadbury suggests "gossip" or "cock-sparrow."[67] The word occurs only here in the New Testament.

---

of their Messianic prophecies. It would appear that his daily meetings in the marketplace were at first with the peoples of these classes. The synagogue itself at Athens appears to have been near the marketplace.

B. The Message on Mars' Hill (17:18–31)

And Paul stood in the midst of the Areopagus, and said, Ye men of Athens, in all things I perceive that ye are very religious (vs. 22).

Erelong Paul was encountered by the Epicurean and Stoic philosophers who misjudged him to be another of the wandering teachers who gathered bits of information here and there and dispensed it at will.

Athens was the famed city and center of philosophy. The four famous historic schools had been founded and had flourished here. They were the Academy of Plato, the Lyceum of Aristotle, the Porch of Zeno, and the Garden of Epicurus. However, only the Stoics and the Epicureans remained in Athens until Paul's day. The former were the predominant philosophers of the religious and sober-minded thinkers, while the latter characterized the irreligious and loose-living element. One may doubt whether the Epicureans, who regarded pleasure in one way or another as the *Summum Bonum*, had many points of contact with Pharisaic Judaism, or much in common with Christianity. Josephus sees the similarities of the Stoics and Pharisees as consisting in (1) their common narrowness and austerity; (2) their willingness to suffer for piety and virtue's sake rather than compromise; (3) their devotion

[57] *St. Paul the Traveller*, p. 237. [58] *Ibid.*, p. 238. [59] *Ibid.*, p. 237.
[60] Used only by Luke (three times in his Gospel, four times in Acts).
[61] Abbott-Smith, *op. cit.*, p. 426. [62] *St. Paul the Traveller*, p. 241.
[63] *Beginnings*, IV, 211. Cf. Meyer: "fell into conflict with" (p. 328). [64] Abbott-Smith, *op. cit.*, p. 413.
[65] EGT, II, 367. [66] *St. Paul the Traveller*, p. 241. [67] *Book of Acts in History*, p. 45.

19 And they took hold of him, and brought him unto the Areopagus, saying, May we know what this new teaching is, which is spoken by thee?

A setter forth is *katangeleus*, found only here in the New Testament. It means a "proclaimer," or "herald." The word has been discovered on a marble stele which records a decree of the Mytilenians in honor of Augustus and which comes from 27 to 11 B.C.[68]

Strange gods *(xenōn daimoniōn)* means "foreign deities." Lake and Cadbury write: "*Daimonia* is here used in the true Greek sense, without the connotation of evil."[69] This is the only time the word occurs in Acts. In the rest of the New Testament it is found some 60 times (52 times in the Gospels), always in a bad sense. But in classical Greek (Herodotus, Plato, etc.) it signified "the Divine power, Deity."[70] It was used in magical papyri for demons.[71] In the Septuagint it signifies heathen deities, or false gods. In the New Testament it regularly indicates "evil spirits." The correct translation here is "foreign divinities" (RSV). The parallel with Socrates, who was tried for the same offence 450 years earlier, is too striking to be missed.

Older commentators often suggested that *anastasis*, **resurrection,** was taken by the Greeks as the name of a new goddess (see Exposition). But Meyer objects to this,[72] as do also Hackett,[73] and Lake and Cadbury.[74] Rackham favors the older view,[75] while Knowling[76] and Bruce[77] leave the question open.

19 For **Areopagus** see on verse 22, the only other place where this word occurs in the New Testament.

---

to law, the Pharisees to the law of Moses and its commentaries and the Stoics to the law of nature; (4) the Stoics were naturalistic fatalists and the Pharisees, predestinarian fatalists; (5) the Pharisees held to a theistic providence; the Stoics, to a pantheistic providence; (6) the Pharisees were monotheists; the Stoics, though pantheists, approximated this position in their concept of the *Nous* or Divine Reason or *Logos*, that pervaded and ordered all things; (7) they both held a view of a future life, though the Stoics' pantheistic concept necessarily precluded personal immortality; (8) and both were severe ethicists, though neither was highly consistent in this respect.

The Epicureans, on the other hand, were irreligious materialists whose atheistic outlook ascribed all good to pleasures of the senses and of necessity limited them to the present life. Theirs was a world of chance without God or meaning.

Cushman presents an interesting table of comparisons and contrasts between these two schools of philosophy. In agreement: both subordinated theory to practice, and both had the same practical purpose in their philosophy; namely, to gain peace of mind for the individual and to gain independence of the world for the individual. In disagreement: with the Stoics universal law was supreme, with the Epicureans the individual was supreme; to the Stoics man was a rational being, to the Epicureans he was a feeling being; with the Stoics independence was attained by idealizing the feelings through serenity; the Stoics were religious, the Epicureans anti-religious, though both subscribed to the popular gods; to the Stoics the world was a moral order, to the Epicureans it was a mechanical order; with the Stoics the universal determined the individual, with the Epicureans the universal was the result of the individual; to the Stoics the world was the expression of an imminent reason, but with the Epicureans it was but a combination of atoms.[f]

Thus it is not difficult to understand that, while finding many points of sympathy and agreement with the Stoics, Paul would have had little, if any, kinship with the Epicureans.

That neither the Stoics nor Epicureans initially understood the nature of Paul's message appears evident from their remarks.

[68] Deissmann, *Light from the Ancient East*, p. 97.
[69] *Beginnings*, IV, 211 f.
[70] Abbott-Smith, *op. cit.*, p. 97.
[71] VGT, p. 135.
[72] *Op. cit.*, p. 329.
[73] *Op. cit.*, p. 200.
[74] *Beginnings*, IV, 212—"though ingenious is improbable."
[75] *Op. cit.*, p. 310, n. 1.
[76] EGT, II, 367 f.
[77] *Acts*, p. 333.

[f] Hubert Ernest Cushman, *A Beginner's History of Philosophy* (New York: Houghton Mifflin Company, 1946), I, 225, 226.

20 For thou bringest certain strange things to our ears: we would know therefore what these things mean.

21 (Now all the Athenians and the strangers sojourning there spent their time in nothing else, but either to tell or to hear some new thing.)

---

21 **Athenians** is found in the New Testament only here and in verse 22. **New** is literally "newer" (*kainoteron*). Bruce says: "The comparative in classical Greek can often be rendered by the positive degree in English." [78] The characterization of the Athenians given here is abundantly confirmed by writers of that period.[79] For **some new thing** Lake and Cadbury have "the last new idea." [80]

What would this babbler say? . . . He seemeth to be a setter forth of strange gods (vs. 18). The first remark is highly uncomplimentary in that it accuses Paul of being one who picked up knowledge indiscriminately. There were many itinerate philosophers of such a nature in the country in Paul's day, heirs of the Sophist rhetoricians of an earlier day in Athens. In the second remark they fell far short of comprehending Paul, in that they appear to have understood him to refer to a new female deity, possibly the wife of Jesus, when he spoke of **the resurrection,** a conclusion likely drawn from the feminine gender of the noun. The Stoics conceived only of an impersonal continuance of life after death, while the Epicurean materialism terminated all with death; and thus to both schools of thought, the doctrine of the resurrection was entirely new and strange indeed. Clarke contends, as noted in the comment on Acts 16:21, that both among the Athenians and Romans it was unlawful to teach or worship legally unauthorized gods. If this contention is valid, then Paul was in grave danger of arrest at Athens, as at Philippi. This would seem to be the reason he was taken to the Areopagus, or court, that they might assure themselves of the true nature of his teachings (vss. 19, 20). If Paul was actually arrested at this time and made to appear before the Areopagus, as Luke's words, **and they took hold of him, and brought him unto the Areopagus** (vs. 19a), would seem to warrant, their treatment of the apostle is eloquent testimony to Athenian justice in allowing Paul to defend himself and prohibiting such mob violence as had occurred at Philippi and Thessalonica. And indeed the Areopagus was famous for its justice, where the court of twelve superior judges so impartially and fairly conducted the trials of the accused that it became proverbial that "both the plaintiff and defendant departed satisfied with the decision" (Clarke). This was indeed a high standard of justice and approximated the ideal set forth by the founder of the Academy, Plato, who said, "Justice is having and doing what is one's own." However, Luke remarks that it was the custom of the Athenians to pass their time in idle speaking and hearing new speculations. Such was the degeneracy of philosophy at Athens by this time. The profounder meaning of the old schools had been lost, and this generation dabbled in the foamy surf of a departed tide of learning.

As Paul stood in the midst of the Areopagus, he delivered a sermon to the proud Athenians on natural religion, which sermon bears many similarities to his address to the Lycaonians at Lystra (see notes on Acts 14:15–18).

Paul had clearly discerned the Athenian mind and presented a divinely inspired message suited to meet their greatest needs, something "newer" to them indeed than they had ever heard. Certainly if our thesis is correct that Paul's address before the Areopagus was his defense against charges of advocating a new, unauthorized, and in Athens illegal, religion, then his choice of the inscription from the altar, **TO AN UNKNOWN GOD** (vs. 23), was indeed a master stroke. Their **UNKNOWN GOD** whose worship was fully authorized and thus made legal in Athens, Paul declared to be the subject of his preaching in Athens. Thus the Athenian charge, **He seemeth to be a setter forth of strange** [*foreign divinities*] **gods** [*demons*] (vs. 18), was abrogated by Paul's declaration concerning their authorized

[78] *Ibid.*, p. 334. Cf. *Beginnings*, IV, 214—"not to be confused with the Hellenistic use of the comparative for the superlative."
[79] See quotations in *Beginnings*, IV, 214.
[80] *Ibid.*

22 And Paul stood in the midst of the Areopagus, and said, Ye men of Athens, in all things, I perceive that ye are very religious.

---

22 **Areopagus** is two words in Greek: *Areios* (Ares or Mars) and *Pagos* (hill). It is indeed strange that the King James Version transliterates the Greek term in verse 19 but translates it here. Obviously it should be treated the same way in both cases.

Whether Paul appeared before the Court of the Areopagus in the Agora or was led to the top of Mars' Hill is a topic of perennial dispute. Ramsay argues at length that Paul spoke in the Agora. He says, for instance: "The top of the little hill is a most unsuitable place from its small size and its exposed position." [81] Knowling follows Ramsay in holding that Paul did not go to Mars' Hill,[82] as do also Rackham,[83] Lake and Cadbury,[84] and apparently Bruce.[85] The phrase **in the midst of** would lend support to this view, especially when taken with "went out from among them" (vs. 33). In the first century, the Court of the Areopagus met in a portico northwest of the Agora, which was "called alternately the Stoa Basileios and the Stoa of Zeus Eleutherios." [86] Perhaps the best conclusion to which we can come is that expressed recently by Cadbury, who favors a meeting in the Agora rather than on Mars' Hill. Yet he warns us: "The possibilities must be left open that the council sometimes met on the hill Areopagus and not in the Agora even in later times, or that Paul spoke on the hill but not to an official group." [87] Stonehouse gives his own judgment in much the same terms, though likewise concluding that the hill is not the place.[88]

Ye men of Athens is literally "men, Athenians" *(andres Athēnaioi)*. **Very religious** is perhaps better than "too superstitious" (KJV), which would seem to be a rather tactless approach by Paul. The word *deisidaimones*, found only here in the New Testament, is from *deidō* (I fear) and *daimōn* (deity). So its basic meaning is "fearers of the gods." Deissmann would translate the comparative form here "extremely religious." [89] The word is used by Xenophon and other early writers in the sense of "god-fearing," but "in Polybius and Plutarch [2nd. cent. B.C. and 2nd. cent. A.D.] it is usually a term of reproach rather than compliment." [90] So Lake and Cadbury translate it "very superstitious." [91] But it has the meaning "reverent" in a third century (A.D.) epitaph.[92] Two arguments for "superstitious" are the declaration that Paul was "provoked" (vs. 16) at the sight of their idolatry, and the statement of Lucian (De Gymnast. 19) that complimentary words to gain the goodwill of the Areopagus were forbidden.[93] But Knowling says: "It is incredible that St. Paul should have commenced his remarks with a phrase calculated to offend his hearers." [94] Rackham agrees that such an approach would be "quite contrary to the custom of orators and the tact of S. Paul." [95] Hackett translates: "As *(hōs)* more religious (than others) I see you." [96] Meyer suggests a good compromise: "Paul therefore, without violating the truth, prudently leaves the religious *tendency* of his hearers undetermined, and names only its source—*the fear of God.*" [97]

UNKNOWN GOD, What therefore ye worship in ignorance, this I set forth unto you (vs. 23b). If Paul could but prove that his preaching concerning **Jesus and the resurrection** (vs. 18b) was an exposition of their **UNKNOWN GOD,** then his indictment by the Areopagus of preaching an illegal religion in Athens could not stand. How well Paul succeeded in establishing this claim his address and its effect on the court revealed. Of course, this defense afforded Paul a coveted opportunity to proclaim the Gospel of Jesus Christ to a people who had never learned of the Messiah.

Paul presents his address in three clearly discernible steps. The choice of the apostle's words of address, **Ye men of Athens** (vs. 22), is apt. If it was the Areopagus that he was

[81] *St. Paul the Traveller*, p. 244. On the contrary, the present writer has been impressed with the spaciousness of the top of this solid ledge of rock adjacent to the Acropolis.
[82] EGT, II, 368 f. [83] *Op. cit.*, p. 311. [84] *Beginnings*, IV, 212 f.
[85] *Acts*, p. 335. [86] *The Book of Acts in History*, p. 57, n. 43. [87] *Ibid.*
[88] N. B. Stonehouse, *Paul Before the Areopagus* (Grand Rapids: Wm. B. Eerdmans Publishing Co., 1957), p. 8 f.
[89] *Light from the Ancient East*, p. 285. [90] *Beginnings*, IV, 214. [91] *Ibid.* [92] VGT, p. 139.
[93] Bruce, *Acts*, p. 335. [94] EGT, II, 370. [95] *Op. cit.*, p. 314. [96] *Op. cit.*, p. 203. [97] *Op. cit.*, p. 331.

23 For as I passed along, and observed the objects of your worship, I found also an altar with this inscription, TO AN UNKNOWN GOD. What therefore ye worship in ignorance, this I set forth unto you.

Stonehouse perhaps offers as satisfactory a solution as can be found. He first states: "Although the translation of the A.V. 'too superstitious' is unacceptable from a linguistic and contextual viewpoint, the same cannot be as dogmatically asserted of the E.R.V. 'somewhat superstitious.'" [98] He continues: "It has become clear that the word is sufficiently ambiguous and comprehensive to bear both connotations," and concludes: "It does appear definitely more satisfactory in the present connection to conclude that Paul is underscoring their religiosity rather than their superstition." [99]

23 **As I passed along** is *dierchomenos;* literally, "while I was going through" (the streets). **Observed** is the verb *anatheōreō*, found in the New Testament only here and in Hebrews 13:7. It means "observe carefully, consider well." **Objects of . . . worship** is *sebasmata*, which occurs elsewhere in the New Testament only in II Thessalonians 2:4. It is used in Wisdom 14:20; 15:17, clearly in the sense of images. That is its meaning here. "Devotions" (KJV) is misleading to the modern reader. **Also** means "in addition to those with definite dedications." [100] *Bōmon*, **altar,** is found only here in the New Testament, though frequent in the Septuagint. **With this inscription** is literally "on which had been inscribed" *(en hōi epegegrapto)*.

The inscription, **TO AN UNKNOWN GOD,** has occasioned the flow of much printer's ink. Kirsopp Lake expresses the attitude of many scholars when he says: "It is doubtful whether there ever was an inscription which read exactly *agnōstōi theōi*."[101] Cadbury is more cautious when he writes: "We can probably never say positively that no altar in Athens bore the exact phrase in the singular, though nearly all the evidence we have suggests the plural." [102] Meyer thinks that the passages in Pausanias (see Exposition) and Philostratus *(Life of Apollonius of Tyana*. VI, 3, 5) give evidence "that at Athens there were *several* altars, each of which bore the inscription: *agnōstōi theōi*."[103] Kirsopp Lake does go so far as to admit that the story of Diogenes Laertius—about how Epimenides of Crete purified Athens by the offering of black and white sheep in the time of a severe pestilence—"suggests that the singular may have been used in the formula *tōi prosēkonti theōi*, meaning 'to the unknown god who is concerned in the matter.'" [104] Foakes-Jackson goes a step further when he writes: "Paul implies that on careful inspection he found a single altar thus dedicated, which may well have escaped the notice of those who had written about Athens." [105] There is no justification whatever for the dogmatic assertion of Schweitzer: "There can never have been such an inscription." [106] As Stonehouse well notes, such a declaration is based on "nothing more than an argument from silence." [107]

As to the significance of the inscription, Knowling writes: "In such an inscription Paul wisely recognized that there was in the heart of Athens a witness to the deep unsatisfied yearning of humanity for a clearer and

---

addressing, then they were honored as the "first men of Athens"; if otherwise, he still was speaking respectfully. He recognized their all pervasive religious interest and implied that for this reason he was especially happy to address them, since his chief interest also was religion.

The genuineness of the text of Paul's address, purportedly taken from an altar **TO AN UNKNOWN GOD** (vs. 23), has been called into question by some scholars. However, Finegan points out that near the time of Paul, Apollonius of Tyana, a noted Neo-Pythagorean philosopher, visited Athens

[98] *Op. cit.*, p. 16.
[99] *Op. cit.*, p. 17. Compare Cadbury (*The Book of Acts in History*, p. 50): "ultra religious."
[100] EGT, II, 371.
[101] *Beginnings*, V, 245.
[102] *The Book of Acts in History*, p. 51.
[103] *Op. cit.*, 331.
[104] *Beginnings*, V, 242.
[105] F. Foakes-Jackson, *The Acts of the Apostles* ("Moffatt N.T. Commentary") (New York: Harper and Brothers [1931]), p. 165.
[106] Albert Schweitzer, *The Mysticism of Paul the Apostle*. Trans. W. Montgomery (New York: Henry Holt and Co., 1931), p. 6.
[107] *Op. cit.*, p. 11.

24 The God that made the world and all things therein, he, being Lord of heaven and earth, dwelleth not in temples made with hands;

---

closer knowledge of the unseen power which men worshipped dimly and imperfectly." [108]

Eusebeite, **ye worship,** is found in the New Testament only here and in I Timothy 5:4. It means "reverence, show piety toward." This incidentally favors "religious" rather than "superstitious" in verse 22.

In ignorance is the participle *agnoountes*, "not knowing." Paul probably was intentionally pointing back to the *agnōstōi* ("unknown") of the inscription. This is lost in most English versions. But the Revised Standard Version happily preserves it thus: "What therefore you worship as unknown." This rendering also guards against the insulting insinuation that the Athenians were "ignorant"!

Set forth *(katangellō*, proclaim) is Paul's answer to the charge in verse 18 ("setter forth"—*katangeleus)*.

24 **World** is *kosmos* (cosmos), found only here in Acts, though frequent throughout the rest of the New Testament (some 187 times). John uses it over 100 times, almost always in a bad sense. But here it has the Greek meaning of "orderly universe," and so probably includes **heaven and earth.** For *cheiropoiētois*, **made with hands,** see on 7:48, its only other occurrence in Acts. **Temples** is *naois*, "sanctuaries."

---

and is reported by his biographer to have remarked that it is proof of wisdom "to speak well of all the gods, especially at Athens, where altars are set up in honour even of unknown gods." [g] Further, Finegan cites the geographer Pausanias, who visited Athens sometime between A.D. 143 and 159 and produced extensive and accurate topographical accounts of the city, who says that "on the road from the Phaleron Bay harbor to the city he had noticed 'altars of the gods named Unknown, and of heroes,' and also mentions 'an altar of Unknown Gods' at Olympia," [h]

Other instances are cited by Finegan, such as the inscription on the altar found at Pergamum in 1909 in the temple of Demeter which is thought to read, "To unknown gods, Capito, torch-bearer." Thus the absence at present of such an altar in Athens is no disproof of its existence in Paul's day. Whether the Athenians identified this "unknown God" with the Supreme Being, or the "High-God" of the modern science of religion, is an unanswered question. That Paul made this application of the "altar text," there can be no reasonable doubt.[i]

Paul recognizes the philosophical cast of mind of his audience and presents his message understandingly to them in answer to the three great questions of philosophy: "Whence," "What," "Whither"; or otherwise stated, "the origin," "the nature," and "the end of all things." Analyzed, his message would appear something as follows:

1. *The Origin of All Things*, vss. 24–26.
2. *The Nature of All Things*, vss. 27–30.
3. *The End of All Things*, vs. 31.

Neither the Epicureans nor Stoics believed in, or understood, the doctrine of creation by a divine fiat. The materialistic Epicureans regarded matter as eternal and thus uncreated, while the Stoics, being pantheistic, did not distinguish the Divine Reason from Matter. Neither naturalistic materialism nor pantheistic naturalism can ever answer the question of origins, since neither recognizes an originator. Paul's presentation of a personal, supreme, and transcendent God (vs. 24b), who created all things by a divine fiat (vs. 24a) was an answer to the question of origin, for which pagan philosophers had long sought in vain. God then is not only, as the Stoics suppose, the directive, spiritual principle living and working within nature, but a personal, divine Providence. Further, Paul declared that this "unknown God" is the providential dispenser of life and breath to all things and therefore is quite independent of man, thus abrogating the necessity of sacrificial worship (vs. 25). Paul then proceeded to show that man himself is the creature of this "unknown God" and thus dependent upon

[108] EGT, II, 372.

[g] Finegan, *op. cit.*, p. 276. [h] *Ibid.*
[i] See Additional Note I, "The High-God Theory," at close of Chapter VII.

25 neither is he served by men's hands, as though he needed anything, seeing he himself giveth to all life, and breath, and all things;

26 and he made of one every nation of men to dwell on all the face of the earth, having determined *their* appointed seasons, and the bounds of their habitation;

27 that they should seek God, if haply they might feel after him and find him, though he is not far from each one of us:

---

25 **Served** is the verb *therapeuō*, which elsewhere in the New Testament (43 times) refers to physical healing (cf. therapy). The unique usage here reflects the original meaning of the verb, "do service." Then it came to be used in a medical sense as "treat," and so finally "heal." The cognate noun *therapōn* (only in Heb. 3:5 in N.T.) means "attendant, servant." The verb is used in the Septuagint and classical Greek of service to the gods.[109] **As though he needed** is *prosdeomenos*, found only here in the New Testament. It means "to want further, need in addition." [110] **Himself** is missing in the King James Version, though emphatic in the Greek. Of **life, and breath** Meyer says: "The former denotes *life in itself*, the latter the *continuance of life*." [111]

26 **Of one** is literally "out of one" *(ex henos)*. "Blood" (KJV) is not in the oldest manuscripts.[112] *Horisas*, **having determined** (having marked off by boundaries), is closely related to *horothesias*, **bounds.** The former is used by Luke six out of the eight times it occurs in the New Testament. The latter, found only here, in the singular means a placing of boundaries. Paul's speech is marked by several plays on words. *Katoikias*, **habitation,** is found only here in the New Testament.

27 *Theon*, **God,** is the reading of the earliest manuscripts,[113] instead of *Kyrion*, "Lord" (KJV). *Ei ara ge*, **if haply,** is literally "if therefore indeed" (cf. "in the hope that"—RSV). **Feel after** is the verb *psēlaphaō*, which means "to feel or grope about." [114] It is used in the Septuagint for groping in the dark.[115] **Though he is** is *hyparchonta*. Bruce makes the observation: "The prevalence of *hyparchō* in this speech (cf. vv. 24, 29) is in keeping with its elevated style." [116]

Him. Nor are men to be categorized, as do the proud Greeks, into Greek and barbarian, with a decided discount on the latter; a proposition with which the Stoics, who believed in the spiritual equality of man through pantheism, would have readily agreed.

Though Paul declared the providential supervision and location of the various nationalities, as to the places and times of their respective locations in the various parts of the earth, for which in the divine wisdom they were best fitted (vs. 26b), at the same time he declared the essential unity of the human race. And indeed the apostle is supported in his view of "homo sapiens" (vs. 26a) by the testimony of modern science. The science of religion testifies that men are homogenous in their disposition to worship a supernatural being, and indeed anthropology points to a universal concept of a High or Supreme God, though he is not the direct object of worship by all. Psychology testifies to the psychological unity of the human race. Biology witnesses to the fact that mankind is one specie. Physiology predicates a common anatomical structure and blood content, as witnesses the modern blood bank. Sociology finds all people with common social characteristics. Indeed three and a half centuries before Paul in Athens, Socrates had discovered a common universal ethical principle in mankind which neither the ancient Sophists' relativism nor its modern social relativistic counterpart has been able to successfully deny. The apostle used the term **nation** and not "race" to distinguish the varied peoples, for he recognized that there is but one race. The word "race" is not used in the Bible, except in regard to contest of speed. **Nation** is a political designation, whereas "race" is a physical designation. God recognizes no essential physical or psychological difference of peoples, nor does modern science. Again Paul refuted the hoary doctrine of evolution

[109] EGT, II, 373. [110] Abbott-Smith, *op. cit.*, p. 384. [111] *Op. cit.*, p. 334. [112] Aleph A B.
[113] Aleph A B H L. [114] Abbott-Smith, *op. cit.*, p. 488. [115] EGT, II, 375. [116] *Acts*, p. 337.

28 for in him we live, and move, and have our being; as certain even of your own poets have said,

For we are also his offspring.

29 Being then the offspring of God, we ought not to think that the Godhead is like unto gold, or silver, or stone, graven by art and device of man.

---

28 **In him we live, and move, and have our being** is treated as a quotation in the Revised Standard Version: "In him we live and move and are" *(esmen)*. Bruce says: "The language here is quoted from an address to Zeus by his son Minos." [117] This theory is based on a Syriac commentary on Acts by the ninth-century Nestorian Isho'dad, published in 1913, which attributes to Minos the following four lines: [118]

They carve a tomb for thee,
O holy and high one,
The Cretans always liars, evil beasts,
slow bellies;
For thou art not dead for ever but
alive and risen,
For in thee we live and move and
have our being.

The second line, it will be recognized, is quoted in Titus 1:12. It is attributed by Clement of Alexandria to Epimenides of Crete.[119] Cadbury calls attention to the coincidence of the relation of the inscription, "To the Unknown God," with Epimenides the Cretan. Could Paul have had this connection in mind? He also points out the play on words between Zeus and the verb *zaō*, "live." The argument is: "He is called Zeus, 'living.' A tomb for him is a lie. He is alive himself and we live in him." [120]

Kirsopp Lake thinks this line came from Epimenides.[121] He says of Paul's poetical references: "The really significant thing is that Greek quotations seem here to play the same part as the Old Testament in speeches to Jews or in a synagogue." [122] Dibelius at first supported the reference to Epimenides and then renounced it.[123]

The plural, **certain . . . of your own poets,** has been explained three ways. The most obvious explanation would be that the quotation following is found in both Aratus and an earlier poem of Cleanthes (see Exposition). The second is that the expression looks backward and forward referring to both lines noted as quotations in the Revised Standard Version.[124] The third explanation is offered by Cadbury. He says: "The indefinite plural 'some' [certain] used in citing the poets is characteristic of the ancient method of quoting a single and known passage." [125] He is not sure that the earlier line is a quotation.

About the last clause of verse 28 there is little question. The line is quoted from Aratus (*Phainomena* 5). **His** refers to Zeus.

29 **Godhead** is the neuter of the adjective *theios*, divine. So it means "the divine," or "deity." Elsewhere in the New Testament the word occurs only in II Peter 1:3, 4. But Moulton and Milligan give a long list of examples from the papyri.[126] *Charagmati*, **graven,** occurs in this sense only here in the New Testament. Elsewhere it is found only in Revelation (eight times), where it is always translated "mark" (KJV). **Art** is *technēs* (cf. technique), found only here and in 18:3. **Device** is *enthymēseōs*, which means "pondering."

---

which was born in the unenlightened minds of the ancient Greeks and has reappeared in a but slightly altered garb in modern pagan thought. Creation, and not evolution or emanation, is the answer to origins, Paul told his Greek auditors.

Next Paul proceeded to the nature and meaning of all things. First, he declared that since man is the creation of the supreme personal God, he should search after God, even though it may be the groping of a blind man in unfamiliar and uncertain circumstances, not through the pride of intellect, for "the [Greeks] through . . . wisdom knew

[117] *Acts*, p. 338.
[118] Cadbury, *The Book of Acts in History*, pp. 46 f.
[119] *Ibid.*, p. 47.
[120] *Ibid.*
[121] *Beginnings*, V, 250.
[122] *Ibid.*, p. 251.
[123] Martin Dibelius, *Studies in the Acts of the Apostles*. Ed. H. Greenen (New York: Charles Scribner's Sons, 1956), p. 50, n. 74.
[124] *Beginnings*, V, 246.
[125] *The Book of Acts in History*, p. 49.
[126] VGT, pp. 285 f.

30 The times of ignorance therefore God overlooked; but now he commandeth men that they should all everywhere repent:
31 inasmuch as he hath appointed a day in which he will judge the world in righteousness by the man whom he hath ordained; whereof he hath given assurance unto all men, in that he hath raised him from the dead.

30 **Overlooked** is the verb *hypereidon,* found only here in the New Testament. "Winked at" (KJV) sounds almost irreverent, if not flippant.

31 *Kathoti,* **inasmuch as,** used only by Luke (six times), in the classics meant "according as" (cf. Acts 2:45; 4:35). But in Hellenistic Greek it came to be used as the equivalent of *dioti,* "because," which is the reading here in the Textus Receptus. **The man** (no article in the Greek) is Jesus Christ. **Given assurance** is *pistin paraschōn,* second aorist participle of *parechō,* "have beside," and so "furnish, provide." This is the only place *pistis* is translated "assurance" in the King James Version (of 244 times). The phrase means "having provided proof."[127] For the same thought as here see 10:40–42.

not God" (I Cor. 1:21a). But even in the absence of the Jewish divine revelation, man has the revelation of God in nature about him and in his ethical values, which could aid him in finding peace with God, for **he is not far from each one of us** (vs. 27b. See also Rom. 1:18–20 and 2:11–16). Paul quoted, in support of the eminence of God, from the Greek poet Aratus, who was from Paul's home country of Cilicia, though some 300 years earlier, and also a Stoic (cf. I Cor. 15:33 and Titus 1:12). Since the same lines are found in Cleanthus' Hymn to Jupiter, Paul may have referred to both poets. Nor does this mean that Paul was going beyond certain bounds in his agreement with the Stoics. Indeed Christian Theism has many more points of agreement with Stoicism than with Epicureanism, but neither are Christian philosophies, and both have serious divergences from, and irreconcilable conflicts with, Christianity. Concerning this dependence of man on God, Clarke quotes from Synopsis Sohar, p. 104: "The holy blessed God never does evil to any man. He only withdraws his gracious presence from him, and then he necessarily perisheth"; and then Clarke adds, "This is philosophical and correct."[j]

Paul drove to an inescapable conclusion in verse 29, concerning the nature of God and man. Since man is the creature, **offspring,** of God and thus bears the nature of God in His creation, then God must be superior to man; else He could not be his Creator Father. But these gold, silver, and stone, graven images of Athens are inferior to man, as his proud Greek Areopagus auditors would readily agree. Therefore, how can they be likenesses of God who is superior to man? Thus Paul had shown the nature of God to be a personal, transcendent, and yet eminently spiritual being; and man, whose nature is by creation God-like, is therefore an essentially personal, spiritual being. From the answer to the second great philosophical question concerning the nature of things, Paul proceeded to the third and last great question concerning the ends or purposes of all things.

In verse 30 Paul argues that, though God has in His providential goodness overlooked this insulting idolatry, **now he commandeth men that they should all everywhere repent;** or, like the Thessalonians, turn to "God from idols, to serve a living and true God" (I Thess. 1:9b). In the light of this new truth, they cannot continue in the wickedness of idolatry without condemnation now and judgment to come. Such a day of universal righteous judgment for the inhabited world of unrepentant mankind is assured by reason of the resurrection of Jesus Christ, who is to be the judge, since the salvation He provided by His death will have been spurned. The end of man is fellowship with God through repentance and saving faith in the resurrection of Christ. To reject God is certain self-destruction. What a profound impression such an argument must have made upon the august Areopagus that prided itself in pure justice!

127 Bruce, *Acts,* p. 340.

j Clarke, *op. cit.,* p. 827.

32 Now when they heard of the resurrection of the dead, some mocked; but others said, We will hear thee concerning this yet again.
33 Thus Paul went out from among them.
34 But certain men clave unto him, and believed: among whom also was Dionysius the Areopagite, and a woman named Damaris, and others with them.

---

32 The Greeks believed in immortality, but not in a bodily **resurrection.**

34 **Dionysius the Areopagite** was said to have been the first bishop of Athens.[128] It was a real honor to be a member of the Areopagus, which perhaps consisted of about 30 persons.[129]

It is often maintained that Paul's ministry in Athens was a failure. Ramsay has given the classic statement of that view: "It would appear that Paul was disappointed and perhaps disillusioned by his experience in Athens." [130] In view of the prevalence of this attitude it is interesting to note the conclusion of Lake and Cadbury: "It is rash to say that the author of Acts regarded Paul's sermon at Athens as comparatively fruitless, or that I Cor. ii, 7 ff. shows that Paul himself regarded his encounter with philosophy as a failure." [131] The title **Areopagite** was proof of a considerable victory.

Dibelius says that Paul's speech before the Areopagus "in its form of expression and its line of thought, is foreign to the New Testament." [132] Stonehouse has given an extended refutation of this, which satisfactorily answers the charge.[133]

C. The Product of the Ministry (17:32-34)

But certain men clave unto him, and believed: among whom also was Dionysius the Areopagite, and a woman named Damaris, and others with them (vs. 34).

Whether Paul had finished his sermon when the assembly broke up, on the occasion of his mention of the resurrection, is not clear. It was likely the Epicurean element that mockingly laughed and scorned at Paul's doctrine of the resurrection of Jesus Christ and not the Stoics who expressed a desire to hear him further. Wesley says concerning Luke's word, **some mocked,** "They took offence at that which is the principal motive of faith, from the pride of reason. And having once stumbled at this, they rejected all the rest."[k] In any event, the court found no cause for punishment in his teachings and thus Paul, seeing no possibility of further discourse, left the Areopagus.

How many were won over to faith in Christ by Paul's message we are not told; but among the believers was Dionysius the Areopagite, who was a member of the august court of Areopagus and had of necessity passed through the office of Archon or chief governor of the city. This meant that he was a man of the highest intelligence, of good reputation in the city, and of high social position. Thus in Athens, as at Paphos on Cyprus, the Christian message first bore fruit in a governmental person of high rank. **Damaris, and others**—how many we are not told—with Dionysius constituted the first fruits of the Gospel in Athens. Paul's reference to the household of Stephanas as being the first fruits of the Gospel in Achaia may be due to his having considered Athens as a free and independent city. Dummelow[l] observes that tradition made Dionysius a bishop of Athens and a martyr of the Christian faith.

Whether a church immediately developed out of Paul's ministry in Athens is a matter of difference of opinion among scholars. That the high court of Athens and many of the populace had the opportunity of hearing the glorious message of redeeming grace from the lips of Paul is evident.

Additional Note I

THE PLACE OF WOMEN IN THE PRIMITIVE CHURCH

It is most interesting and instructive to note Harnack's observation on the recognition given to, and the prominence of, women in the Church of the first century.

> No one who reads the New Testament attentively, as well as those writings which immediately succeeded it, can fail to notice that in the

[128] Eusebius, *Ecclesiastical History* III, 4, 11; IV, 23, 3.
[129] *Beginnings*, IV, 220.
[130] *St. Paul the Traveller*, p. 252.
[131] *Beginnings*, IV, 219.
[132] *Op. cit.*, p. 57.
[133] *Op. cit.*, chap. I.

k Wesley, *op. cit.*, p. 467, n. 32.
l Dummelow, *op. cit.*, p. 843.

apostolic and sub-apostolic age women played an important role in the propaganda of Christianity and throughout the Christian communities. The equalizing of man and woman before God (Gal. iii, 28) produced a religious independence among women, which aided the Christian mission. Jesus himself had a circle of women among his adherents, in addition to the disciples . . .

Concerning the Roman and Philippian letters, as also Priscilla in Acts, Harnack states:

Thus no fewer than fifteen women are saluted, alongside of eighteen men, and all these must have rendered important services to the church or to the apostle, or to both, in the shape of the work with which they are credited . . .

In Philippians, which contains a few personal items, we read (iv, 2): "I exhort Euodia and I exhort Syntyche to be of the same mind in the Lord. Yea, I pray thee also, true yokefellow, to help these women, for they have wrought with me in the service of the gospel, together with Clement and the rest of my fellow-workers, whose names are in the book of life." These two women, then, had helped to found the church at Philippi, and consequently occupied a position of high honour still (perhaps as presidents of two churches in their houses, like Nymphe at Colosse) . . .

Yet in Acts also (xviii, 18, 26) the woman is first, and it was the woman who—as Chrysostom rightly infers from xviii, 26—converted Apollos, the disciple of John the Baptist. As the latter was a cultured Greek, the woman who was capable of instructing him, must have been herself a person of some culture. She was not merely the mother of a church in her house. As we find from Paul as well, she was a missionary and a teacher. The epistle to the Hebrews probably came from her or from her husband." [m]

[m] Harnack, *op. cit.*, II, 64, 67, 68.

CHAPTER XVIII

After these things he departed from Athens, and came to Corinth.

2 And he found a certain Jew named Aquila, a man of Pontus by race, lately come from Italy, with his wife Priscilla, because Claudius had commanded all the Jews to depart from Rome: and he came unto them;

EXEGESIS

1 **After these things** is one of Luke's phrases for continuing the narrative (cf. Luke 10:1). **Departed from**[1] is *chōristheis ek*. Usually this verb is followed by *apo*, "from." The use here of *ek*, "out of," may emphasize Paul's sudden exit from Athens, "because it was a violation of the intended plan under the compulsion of events."[2] Perhaps Paul suffered more keenly under the mockery of the Areopagites (17:32) than with the mobbing in other cities. Ramsay thinks that the apostle's stay in Athens "can hardly have been longer than six weeks, and was probably less than four."[3] But that is largely conjecture.

2 **Aquila** is Latin for "eagle." **Priscilla** is evidently the Prisca of the epistles (Rom. 16:3; I Cor. 16:19; II Tim. 4:19). Her name usually precedes his, which may indicate that she was of higher rank.[4] She was perhaps not a Jewess.[5] **Lately** is the adverb *prosphatōs*, found only here in the New Testament. Literally it means "freshly slaughtered." But in later Greek it meant "recently."

The decree of **Claudius** is very likely the one mentioned by Suetonius in his *Life of Claudius*, 25, 4 (see Exposition).[6] Dio Cassius (LX, 6, 6) states, however, that because of the large number of Jews, it was found impossible to expel them. A fifth-century writer, Orosius, claims the support of Josephus for

EXPOSITION

PART I

THE CHURCH'S FIRST EUROPEAN MISSION (cont'd)

XI. THE CORINTHIAN MISSION, Acts 18:1–4.
XII. THE CORINTHIAN PEOPLE, Acts 18:5–11.
XIII. THE CORINTHIAN PROCONSUL, Acts 18:12–17.
XIV. THE EPHESIAN PROSPECT, Acts 18:18–21.

PART II

THE APOSTLE'S THIRD MISSIONARY JOURNEY

I. THE RETURN OF THE APOSTLE, Acts 18:22, 23.
II. THE EMERGENCE OF APOLLOS, Acts 18:24–28.

Following his Mars' Hill address at Athens, Paul traversed the forty miles westward to Corinth, the political capital of Achaia, which was situated on the isthmus between Hellas and Peloponnesus. Corinth was in Paul's day both the political and commercial metropolis of Greece and was the residence of the Roman Proconsul.[a]

The wickedness of Corinth made it a byword for corruption and licentiousness throughout the Roman world. Allusions to its sensuality and moral corruption are found in Paul's Corinthian letters and were such, in fact, as to outrage even pagan sentiment. Without question Paul got his inspiration and much of his information for his description of the revolting degeneracy and immorality of the Gentiles, as recorded in the first chapter of Romans (see Rom. 1:21–32), from observation of the Corinthian situation,

[1] "Paul" (KJV) is omitted in Aleph B and the Latin.
[2] Ramsay, *St. Paul the Traveller*, p. 241. He thinks Paul had planned to wait at Athens for the return of Silas and Timothy.
[3] *Ibid.*, p. 239. [4] *St. Paul the Traveller*, p. 268. [5] EGT, II, 384 (cf. Josephus, Ant. XVIII, 3, 5).
[6] Meyer (p. 347) holds that "Chrestus" was "the name of a Jewish agitator at Rome." But most scholars refer it to Christ.

[a] See Additional Note I, "Corinth," at end of chapter XVIII.

3 and because he was of the same trade, he abode with them, and they wrought; for by their trade they were tentmakers.

---

his statement that the decree was in the ninth year of Claudius (A.D. 49).

Unfortunately no such reference can be found in the extant writings of that Jewish historian.[7] Probably the facts are that Claudius ordered all Jews expelled from Rome in A.D. 49, but was unable to carry out the decree. Because of this failure, the matter is not mentioned by Josephus. However, some Jews left, including Aquila. This fits in well with Paul's arrival in Corinth in A.D. 50. Though Aquila was a Jew, it seems likely that he and his wife were Christians before they left Rome.[8]

3 *Homotechnos*, **of the same trade,** occurs only here in the New Testament. Hobart notes that physicians were called *homotechnoi.*[9]

Skēnopoioi (found only here in N.T.) is literally **tentmakers** (from *skēnē*, "tent," and *poieō*, "make"). But a number of the Church Fathers, including Origen, say that Paul was a "leather-worker." Lake and Cadbury write: "The early and widespread nature of this evidence seems to prove that though *skēnopoios* etymologically means 'tentmaker,' it does actually mean 'leather-worker.'" [10] However, this conclusion has not been widely accepted by modern scholars. The Revised Standard Version—Acts was translated by Cadbury—has "tentmakers." Olshausen says of Cilicia: "The hair of a species of very shaggy goat was there wrought into a thick stuff like felt, which was very much employed in covering tents." [11] Bruce writes: "Paul's calling was closely connected with the chief manufacture of his native province, *cilicium*, a cloth of goat's hair." [12] Probably Paul made tents rather than wove material for them.[13]

It would be easy for Paul to find those who worked in his trade for they all clustered together. Even now in the bazaar at Damascus one can visit the sections of leather-workers, metal-workers, weavers, and other tradesmen. Furthermore "in Alexandria the different trades sat in the synagogue arranged into guilds; and St. Paul could have no difficulty in meeting in the bazaar of his trade with the like-minded Aquila and Priscilla." [14]

---

especially as he wrote Romans from Corinth while there on his third missionary journey.

The worship of Aphrodite, the goddess of love and beauty, identified by the Romans with Venus, the worship of whom was cleverly designed to excite lust, was the distinctive cult of Corinth from ages past. The temple of Aphrodite was situated on the summit of Acro Corinth, a mountain 1,500 feet in elevation above the city and 1,886 feet above the sea. North of the market place on a low hill stood the temple of Apollo.

Finegan's description of the topography of Corinth is helpful. He locates the large agora or market place in the center of the city, surrounded by colonnades and monuments. Northwest of the market was the theater of Corinth. In 1898 a heavy stone was found which had formed the lintel over a doorway and which bore the Greek inscription, "Synagogue of the Hebrews." The inscription has been dated between 100 B.C. and A.D. 200. Since it was found near the market place, it appears likely that the synagogue was located near the agora. The lettering is poorly carved which, Finegan thinks, suggests that the Jews of Corinth were poor, and thus it accords with Paul's characterization of the Corinthian Christians (see I Cor. 1:26–31). If the synagogue was on the east side of the street opposite the shops and colonnades of the west side, then, as Finegan supposes, it was located in the residential section as indicated by the remaining house walls, and thus Titus Justus' house could have **joined hard to the synagogue** (Acts 18:7).

The **judgment-seat** where Paul appeared before Gallio is thought to have been the Latin *rostrum*, or elevated platform, located in the agora and constituting one of its most prominent features (see Acts 18:12–17).

[7] *Beginnings*, V, 459 f. [8] Olshausen, *op. cit.*, III, 359. [9] *Op. cit.*, p. 239.
[10] *Beginnings*, IV, 223. [11] *Op. cit.*, p. 360.
[12] *Acts*, p. 343. However, Bruce agrees with Lake and Cadbury on the meaning "leather-worker."
[13] So Meyer, *op. cit.*, p. 349; Knowling (EGT, II, 385).
[14] Edersheim, *Jewish Social Life*, p. 89.

4 And he reasoned in the synagogue every sabbath, and persuaded Jews and Greeks.

---

4 **Reasoned** is in the imperfect *(dielegeto)*, as is **persuaded** *(epeithen)*. This suggests a continuing ministry week after week. After **reasoned** the Western text adds: "and introduced the name of the Lord Jesus."

XI. THE CORINTHIAN MISSION (18:1–4)

And he reasoned in the synagogue every sabbath, and persuaded Jews and Greeks (vs. 4).

At Corinth Paul associated himself with two Jews who were evidently Christian believers, since it is not recorded that they were converted under Paul, and who were to assist him greatly in his evangelization of Corinth and elsewhere later. The home of this man Aquila and his wife Priscilla was in Pontus, one of the two easternmost provinces of Asia Minor. Whether for commercial or other reasons, they had settled in Rome. But due to a disturbance there among the Jews which appears to have centered around a contention over Christ, the Emperor Claudius, not able to distinguish between Jews and Christians, nor understanding the nature of the controversy, expelled the Jews from Rome, including Christian believers, in about A.D. 49. These disturbances likely arose as a result of the Christian witness and preaching by converted Jews who returned to Rome after Pentecost (see Acts 2:10), or possibly they were some of Paul's converts from Asia Minor who had traveled to Rome. The real source of the trouble was always the Christ-rejecting Jews of Paul's day. Suetonius wrote, "He [Claudius] expelled the Jews from Rome, because they were in a state of continual tumult at the instigation of one Chrestus."[b] By Chrestus is likely meant "Christus" or Christ.

At Corinth Aquila and Priscilla became the hosts of Paul, even as Eunice and Lois at Lystra, Lydia at Philippi, and Jason at Thessalonica. Apart from their common faith in Christ, Paul had an occupational affinity with this couple, since they were all tent makers. In fact, it was required of every Jewish boy, regardless of the wealth, education, or social standing of the parents, that he learn a manual trade by which he would be capable of supporting himself in case of necessity. It appears from Luke's words, **they wrought** (vs. 3), that they may have earned a livelihood while preaching the Gospel in Corinth. We hear more of this Jewish-Christian couple, who accompanied Paul to Ephesus (vs. 18), and later returned to Rome where they likely prepared for the coming of Paul and also established a Christian church in their house, as at Ephesus (cf. I Cor. 16:19 and Rom. 16:3–5). They are last seen in the Biblical record at Ephesus where they returned following Paul's trial at Rome (II Tim. 4:19). Only eternity will reveal the credit due such faithful, sacrificing, occupational missionaries who have contributed so much to the spread of the Gospel and the establishment of Christianity, both in Paul's day and throughout subsequent centuries. Often have evangelistic reapers been credited with the fruit of their labors. The self-support of Paul and his companions in the Gospel at Corinth, as well as with Paul at Thessalonica and elsewhere, enabled them to introduce the Gospel among a new people without laying themselves liable to the charge that they were preaching for material gain, as was the custom with the wandering philosopher-teachers of that day and formerly.

On the one hand, Paul did thus labor and support himself when he first arrived at Corinth (vs. 3), in Thessalonica (II Thess. 3:8–12), and later at Ephesus (Acts 20: 33–35; I Cor. 4:9–13). However, on the other hand, he saw the advantage to his disciples of their giving of their material means for the support of the Gospel and its ministers, and he both commended them for so doing and recommended their continuance in giving. This is especially evident in the Philippian letter (Phil. 4:10–20), but it also appears in the Corinthian letter (II Cor. 9), and possibly Paul alludes to a gift from the Thessalonians in his first Thessalonian letter (I Thess. 3:6–10).

If, as evidence would seem to indicate, the

[b] Dummelow, *op. cit.*, p. 843.

5 But when Silas and Timothy came down from Macedonia, Paul was constrained by the word, testifying to the Jews that Jesus was the Christ.

---

5 **Silas and Timothy** were last mentioned in 17:15, when Paul sent instructions from Athens for them to join him quickly. From I Thessalonians 3:1, 2 it appears that they fulfilled his request and then were sent out again from Athens—Timothy to Thessalonica, and Silas probably to Philippi.[15] Now, perhaps two months later, they **came down from Macedonia.** *Syneicheto,*[16] **was constrained,** is literally "was held together." **By the word** is the reading of the oldest manuscripts,[17] instead of "in spirit" (KJV). Ramsay takes the passage as meaning, "wholly possessed by and engrossed in the word," and translates it, "wholly absorbed in preaching." [18] *Diamartyromenos,* **testifying,** is a strong compound, meaning "solemnly protesting." Moulton and Milligan say it suggests "solemn and emphatic utterance." [19] **Jesus was the Christ** is "the Messiah was Jesus."

---

synagogue was near the market place, it is understandable that Paul would likely have had an interested hearing, as **he reasoned in the synagogue every sabbath** (vs. 4a), from the Gentiles who heard him in the market preaching and teaching daily throughout the week. Thus Luke informs us that in these sabbath synagogue services Paul persuaded Jews and Greeks alike. While the initial fruit of his sabbath-to-sabbath synagogue labors is not evident in Luke's record, such fruit is suggested by Luke's statement that he **persuaded Jews and Greeks** (vs. 4b). From Paul's epistles we glean information concerning the identity of these "first-fruit converts" in Corinth. Indeed, Epenetus is given in some versions as the first fruit of the Gospel in Achaia, but in other versions he is recorded as the first fruit of proconsular Asia. Wesley takes the latter view while Clarke as confidently takes the former view. We are on surer ground however when we note the family of Stephanas (I Cor. 1:16), and Crispus and Gaius (cf. I Cor. 1:14 and Acts 18:8). That there were many more we learn from verse eight.

XII. THE CORINTHIAN PEOPLE

(18:5–11)

I have much people in this city (vs. 10b). In Acts 17:15 it was noted that Paul had instructed his Beroean escorts to dispatch Silas and Timothy to him at Athens immediately (see exegetical note on this problem). Upon their final arrival at Corinth, they evidently delivered to him an offering from the Philippian church (cf. II Cor. 11:8, 9 and Phil. 4:15, 16). Doubtless Luke means to imply in the words, **Paul was constrained by the word** [the Gospel-Acts 4:4; 16:6, 32; 17:11], **testifying to the Jews that Jesus was the Christ** (vs. 5b), that Paul had found great encouragement in their reports of the progress of the work in Macedonia, as well as the relief of his stringencies by the offering which they brought and the support of their presence. And thus his faith was rewarded, and he took courage to renew and intensify his evangelistic efforts toward the Jews. He was now released from the necessity of manual employment and could, together with Silas and Timothy, give himself wholly to the preaching of the Gospel. Vincent gives the meaning to the effect that "Paul was engrossed by the word." This appears to be the true meaning of this rather difficult passage. It should be noted at this juncture that this is the last Biblical mention of Silas. Clarke thinks he may have died in Macedonia. Since Luke's primary concern is with Paul, Silas is henceforth dropped from the record.

The Jews' reaction to Paul's intensified evangelistic efforts at Corinth was an *organized* or *concerted* resistance against Paul and his preaching. It is noteworthy that in railing and blaspheming against the Gospel of Christ these Corinthian Jews actually **opposed themselves** (vs. 6a). And so does man always work against his own best interest when he opposes truth. Paul's act of shaking his garments was typical and signified the transfer of responsibility for truth preached and witness given to these blasphemous Jews.

[15] So Ramsay, *St. Paul the Traveller,* p. 240; also Kirsopp Lake, *The Earlier Epistles of St. Paul* (London: Rivingtons, 1911), p. 74.
[16] Luke uses the word nine out of its twelve occurrences in the New Testament.
[17] Aleph A B D E.
[18] *St. Paul the Traveller,* pp. 252 f.
[19] VGT, p. 152.

6 And when they opposed themselves and blasphemed, he shook out his raiment and said unto them, Your blood *be* upon your own heads; I am clean: from henceforth I will go unto the Gentiles.

7 And he departed thence, and went into the house of a certain man named Titus Justus, one that worshipped God, whose house joined hard to the synagogue.

8 And Crispus, the ruler of the synagogue believed in the Lord with all his house; and many of the Corinthians hearing believed, and were baptized.

---

6 *Antitassomenōn*, **opposed themselves,** was originally used of armies drawn up in battle array against each other.[20] Then, in the middle (as here), it meant "resist." *Blasphēmountōn*, **blasphemed,** may also be translated "reviled" (RSV)—see on 13:45. But Rackham may be right in thinking that the Jews cried out, "Anathema Jesus." [21] *Ektinaxamenos*, **shook out,** occurs in 13:51 and Matthew 10:14 = Mark 6:11. In these other three passages it is used of shaking off dust. Here it is shaking out **raiment** (*himatia*, garments). Rackham interprets it thus: "S. Paul as it were excommunicated them: he *shook out his lap*, as if he were shaking out their lot from the kingdom of God." [22] **Your blood be upon your own heads** indicates solemn responsibility (cf. 20:26; Matt. 27:25; also Ezek. 33:6).

7 *Metabas*, **departed,** suggests the idea of exchange or transference from one place to another.[23] **Justus** (KJV) is preceded by **Titus** (ASV) or "Titius" (RSV). The latter is the reading in Vaticanus, the former in Sinaiticus, Laudianus (6th cent.), and several versions. Alexandrinus (5th cent.), Bezae (6th), and the late minuscules have only Justus.[24] **Worshipped God** shows that Justus was connected with the synagogue, as well as living next to it. The verb *synomoreō* (**joined hard to**) is found only here in the New Testament.

The home of Justus may have been chosen as a place of easy access for those Jews and proselytes who wished to follow Paul.[25] At the same time, Justus' citizenship "would afford Paul an opening to the more educated class of the Corinthian population." [26] These factors perhaps justified Paul in taking the very undiplomatic step of locating adjacent to the synagogue. It may be that this was the only Christian home in Corinth suitable for services.

8 **Corinthians** probably means Greeks (cf. vs. 6b). Paul's move proved beneficial for the work.

It may further indicate that they were soon to be delivered to their enemies by God.[c] Paul's testimony had been so given that he bore no further responsibility to these Jews. **I am clean** (vs. 6b), or as Weymouth renders it, "I am not responsible" any longer for you. The apostle's expressed purpose to turn to the Gentiles was here limited to his ministry at Corinth. He subsequently goes first to the Jews at Ephesus and elsewhere.

Paul's entry into the house of Titus Justus, likely a Roman colonist who was a "God-fearer" or "proselyte of the gate" and whose house was next door to the synagogue, was for the purpose of finding a new preaching place after leaving the synagogue. He doubtless continued to lodge with Aquila and Priscilla.

The conversion of the chief ruler of the synagogue, Crispus, was a signal victory for Christianity at Corinth. By his office he presided at all meetings in the synagogue, interpreted and rendered technical decisions in law, solemnized marriages, granted divorces, declared excommunications, and performed other important functions.

It appears likely that Sosthenes was chosen to fill the office of Crispus after the latter's conversion to Christianity. The conversion of this prominent Jewish leader, even after the apostle had been closed out of the synagogue, was the signal for many to follow him in the faith; first those of his own household, as with the Philippian jailer, and then **many of the Corinthians hearing believed, and were baptized** (vs. 8b), most likely

20 *Ibid.*, p. 49. 21 *Op. cit.*, p. 325. 22 *Ibid.*
23 Cf. Ramsay, *St. Paul the Traveller*, p. 255—"he changed his place."
24 Cf. Barsabbas Justus (1:23) and Jesus Justus (Col. 4:11).
25 EGT, II, 387. 26 Ramsay, *St. Paul the Traveller*, p. 257.

c Wesley, *op. cit.*, p. 468, n. 6.

9 And the Lord said unto Paul in the night by a vision, Be not afraid, but speak and hold not thy peace:

10 for I am with thee, and no man shall set on thee to harm thee: for I have much people in this city.

11 And he dwelt *there* a year and six months, teaching the word of God among them.

---

9 In the words of the Lord to Paul, the first two verbs *(phobou, lalei)* are present imperative, while the third *(siōpēsēis)* is aorist. The literal meaning is: "Stop being afraid; go on speaking; do not become silent." It would appear that Paul sensed growing opposition, which caused him to fear.

10 This verse suggests that the apostle's life was in danger. They might **set on** [27] him—as indeed they did (vs. 12)—but not so as **to harm** him. *Kakoō* is found only in Acts (five times) and I Peter 3:13.

11 **Dwelt** is not the usual verb for remaining *(menō)* but *ekathise*, "sat." It is used nowhere else in the New Testament in this sense. Knowling writes: "The word may be purposely used here instead of the ordinary *menein* to indicate the quiet and settled work to which the Apostle was directed by the vision which had calmed his troubled spirit." [28]

Gentiles. How effective for Christ's Kingdom is such a key individual when brought to the Lord. In I Corinthians 1:14 Paul indicates that Crispus was one of the few of his converts who was baptized by his own hands.

It would appear from verse nine that Paul may have been near discouragement or even departure from Corinth. The odds were against him, humanly speaking (cf. I Cor. 2:3). However, "the Lord knoweth how to deliver the godly out of temptation" (II Pet. 2:9a). God had further work for Paul in Corinth, and thus he appeared to him in a vision of the night with instructions to continue his ministry (cf. Acts 27:23–26), and assurance that he will not be prevented in his work nor personally harmed: **For I am with thee, and no man shall set on thee to harm thee** (vs. 10a; cf. Matt. 28:18–20). However, Paul's greater encouragement comes with the Lord's prophetic declaration concerning the spiritual fruit of the apostle's ministry: **for I have much people in this city** (vs. 10b). How often are souls who are not yet saved cut off from a future saving faith in Christ because of the fear or failure of God's messengers to stand by and declare the offered mercies of God in Christ!

Reassured of God, Paul remained at Corinth for about eighteen months during which time he established the Corinthian church and wrote the first and second letters to the Thessalonians. Some scholars hold that he wrote the Galatian letter at this time, though this is not the conviction of the present writer.

XIII. THE CORINTHIAN PROCONSUL

(18:12–17)

But when Gallio was proconsul of Achaia... [he] cared for none of these things (vss. 12a, 17b).

Gallio, brother of the Roman philosopher Seneca (tutor of the emperor Nero) and uncle of the poet Lucan, was a well-educated, accomplished, and amiable Roman who had been advanced from the office of consul to the proconsularship of Achaia, with its capital at Corinth, in about A.D. 52. He was noted for his sense of justice and administrative ability.

Exasperated with his success in winning believers to the Lord, **the Jews with one accord** [d] **rose up against Paul and brought him before the judgment seat** (vs. 12). Though divided among themselves on many issues, **the Jews** were of **one accord** in their purpose to destroy Paul and stop the preaching of the Gospel of Christ. They had no legal right under Roman law to punish Paul, as they had not to crucify Christ, so they charged him before Gallic in hopes of his execution by the Romans. Roman law permitted the Jewish religion, as well as the authorized Gentile religions to be present, in the

[27] Only here in the New Testament does *epitithēmi* have the meaning "attack."
[28] EGT, II, 389.

[d] See Additional Note I, *Homothumadon–One Accord*, at close of Chapter I.

12 But when Gallio was proconsul of Achaia, the Jews with one accord rose up against Paul and brought him before the judgment-seat,
13 saying, This man persuadeth men to worship God contrary to the law.

---

12 Gallio became proconsul of Achaia in the summer of A.D. 51 or 52. The evidence for this provides one of the most certain points in the entire chronology of Paul's life. An inscription at Delphi reads in part as follows:

> Tiberius Claudius Caesar Augustus Germanicus, Pontifex Maximus, in the 12th year of his tribunical power, . . . sends greetings to the city of Delphi . . . A report has been made by Lucius Junius Gallio, my friend, and proconsul of Achaia.[29]

Apparently the twelfth year of the reign of Claudius was the twenty-fifth of January, 52, to the twenty-fourth of January, 53.[30] The narrative in Acts suggests that Paul's trial before Gallio occurred soon after the latter became proconsul.[31]

It is definitely stated that Paul spent a year and a half at Corinth. Correlating the account in Acts with the inscription at Delphi, Kirsopp Lake reaches the following conclusions: "Assuming (*a*) that Gallio was proconsul for only one year, and (*b*) that he came to Achaia in the summer of 51 or 52 and stayed until 52 or 53, Paul's trial before Gallio must have been somewhere in the twenty-four months (or a little more) between the summers of 51 and 53, and his arrival in Corinth must have been eighteen months earlier, that is, probably in the spring of 49 or 50."[32] It seems best to conclude that Paul's stay in Corinth was from the spring of 50 to the fall of 51. Bruce says: "Probably from the late summer of 50 to the early spring of 52."[33]

Luke's accuracy has again been vindicated by archaeology. It is also incidentally confirmed by the fact that "Achaia was governed by a proconsul from B.C. 27 to A.D. 15 and from A.D. 44 onwards."[34] In between these periods it was an imperial province, governed by a propraetor.

Rose up is the verb *katephistēmi*, found only here in the New Testament. *Bēma*, **judgment-seat,** is from *bainō*, "go," and so originally meant a "step, stride,"[35] (see on 7:5). Then it came to be used for "a raised platform" reached by steps. Nine times in the New Testament it is used for the tribunal of a Roman ruler. The ruins of the *bema* at Corinth, where Gallio held court, can still be seen.

13 *Anapeithei*, **persuadeth,** is a strong compound, found only here in the New Testament. It carries the sense of evil persuasion in the papyri.[36] Liddell and Scott indicate that in Herodotus it means "seduce, mislead."[37] **Law** was probably intended by the Jews to mean Roman law (cf. 16:21; 17:7).

---

colonies. However, the introduction of any new and unauthorized religion was forbidden and even punishable by death. Thus in the Jews' charge, **This man persuadeth men to worship God contrary to the law** (vs. 13), is implied a criminal act on Paul's part in introducing and propagating a new religion that was neither of an authorized Gentile brand nor Jewish, and consequently he was guilty of a grave civil offense and liable to execution.

Before Paul could open his mouth in explanation or self-defense, the astute Gallio discerned the wicked devices of the Jews and completely abrogated their designs. Indeed, Gallio asserted, "were Paul allegedly a villainous person, possibly suspect of sedition, then it would be a matter for my court and it would be for me to hear your charges against him." However, coolly and disdainfully Gallio continues, **O ye Jews,** since your complaints concern doctrines, practices, and names (as perhaps whether Jesus was their Messiah) within your own religion, then that is something for you to settle without violence, but it is not a matter for the civil court. With this he dismissed the case and expelled the Jews from the court.

The Jews'[e] violent treatment of Sosthenes, the ruler of the synagogue who had suc-

[29] *Beginnings* V, 461. [30] *Ibid.*, p. 463. [31] *Ibid.*, p. 464. [32] *Ibid.* [33] *Acts*, p. 346.
[34] *St. Paul the Traveller*, p. 258. [35] Arndt and Gingrich, *op. cit.*, p. 139. [36] VGT, p. 37.
[37] Henry D. Liddell and Robert Scott, *A Greek-English Lexicon*. Ed. Henry S. Jones (2 vols.; Oxford: Clarendon Press, 1925), I, 115.

e While Bruce (p. 375) regards Sostenes' assaulters as bystanding Greeks, Wesley (p. 469), with apparent better reasons, regards them as the Jews who were disappointed with Sosthenes' efforts to obtain a conviction against Paul.

14 But when Paul was about to open his mouth, Gallio said unto the Jews, If indeed it were a matter of wrong or of wicked villany, O ye Jews, reason would that I should bear with you:

15 but if they are questions about words and names and your own law, look to it yourselves; I am not minded to be a judge of these matters.

16 And he drove them from the judgment-seat.

17 And they all laid hold on Sosthenes, the ruler of the synagogue, and beat him before the judgment-seat. And Gallio cared for none of these things.

---

14 *Adikēma*, **wrong** (found only here, 24:20, Rev. 18:5), means "injury done to others." [38] *Rhadiourgēma*, **wicked villany** (found only here in the N.T.; cf. *rhadiourgia*, found only in 13:10), may refer to "such vicious practices as were a public scandal or caused danger to the state by their violation of the elementary laws of morality." [39] The two terms might thus signify *civil* and *criminal* cases. **Reason would** is *kata logon*, "according to reason." **I should bear with** is the verb *anechō*, which probably here means "listen to" [40] (cf. II Cor. 11:1).

15 **Questions** is plural (contra. KJV) in the oldest manuscripts.[41] **About words** is *peri logou* (singular) which Hackett translates "concerning a doctrine." [42] Meyer has "concerning doctrine." [43] Lake and Cadbury render it "about talk." [44] Ramsay paraphrases the passage as follows: "If they are questions of word, not deed, and of names, not things, and of your law, not Roman law." [45] **Your own law** is literally "law according to you folks" *(nomon tou kath'hymas)*.

17 **They** is the reading of the earliest manuscripts,[46] not "the Greeks" (KJV). This has led some to suggest that the Jews themselves beat Sosthenes (see Exposition). Ramsay says that "such action is inconceivable in the Roman governor." [47] Knowling agrees with this.[48] In answer to the question, "Who beat Sosthenes?," Bruce says: "Probably the Greeks." [49] Lake and Cadbury suggest: "Possibly Sosthenes was beaten by both parties." [50]

The identification of *Sosthenes* with the one mentioned in I Corinthians 1:1 is likely, but not certain. Knowling goes so far as to say: "There is no occasion to suppose that the Sosthenes here is the same as in I Cor. i, 1." [51] Meyer definitely opposes the identification.[52] Both of these scholars say the name was common. But Lake and Cadbury declare it "rare" and think that "perhaps" the two may be identified.[53] Bruce is noncommittal.[54]

The epithet "the careless Gallio," based on the last statement of this verse, is an unfair slander on the name of this honorable ruler. Gallio fulfilled his duties as a Roman judge when he threw out of court a case which had nothing to do with Roman law.

---

ceeded Crispus on the occasion of the latter's conversion to Christianity, was likely due to the fact that he had already embraced Christianity and defended Paul, or that he was known to have been influenced by Paul and was inclining toward Christianity. That he eventually became a Christian and one of Paul's closest companions we infer from I Corinthians 1:1. Possibly his treatment at the hands of the Jews sealed his decision to become a Christian. How many other converts Paul made in Corinth we do not know. Of the following we have record: Stephanas and his household (I Cor. 16:15), Fortunatus (I Cor. 16:17), Achaicus (I Cor. 16:17), Erastus (Rom. 16:23), Gaius (I Cor. 1:14), Tertius (Rom. 16:22), Quartus (Rom. 16:23), Chloe (I Cor. 1:11), and Phoebe of Cenchrea (Rom. 16:1).

Gallio's attitude as expressed in the words, [he] **cared for none of these things** (vs. 17b), is not to be taken as an indifference toward religion, but rather toward the internal disputations and religious wranglings of the Jews. He was doubtless well informed of their disorderly conduct that eventuated in their expulsion from Rome under the rule of Claudius in ca. A.D. 49. How faithfully is God's promise to Paul, as recorded in verses nine and ten, fulfilled in these threatening circumstances. His promises are always worthy of man's implicit faith.

[38] Rackham, *op. cit.*, p. 331. [39] *Ibid.* [40] Abbott–Smith, *op. cit.*, p. 36. [41] Aleph A B E.
[42] *Op. cit.*, p. 214. [43] *Op. cit.*, p. 351. [44] *Beginnings*, IV, 228. [45] *St. Paul the Traveller*, p. 257.
[46] Aleph A B. [47] *St. Paul the Traveller*, p. 259. [48] EGT, II, 391 f. [49] *Acts*, p. 348.
[50] *Beginnings*, IV, 228. [51] EGT, II, 391. [52] *Op. cit.*, p. 352. [53] *Beginnings*, IV, 228. [54] *Acts*, p. 348.

18 And Paul, having tarried after this yet many days, took his leave of the brethren, and sailed thence for Syria, and with him Priscilla and Aquila: having shorn his head in Cenchreae; for he had a vow.

19 And they came to Ephesus, and he left them there: but he himself entered into the synagogue, and reasoned with the Jews.

---

18 **Took his leave** is the verb *apotassō*. In the active it means "set apart." But in the New Testament it appears only in the middle, with the meaning "take leave of." Though not classical, this sense is supported by the papyri.[55] **Syria** is used in the larger sense, including Palestine.

The question as to whose head was shaved cannot be settled conclusively. Meyer says Aquila's.[56] Ramsay writes: "Though the grammatical construction . . . would suggest that Aquila made the vow, and one old Latin version makes this sense explicit, yet the natural emphasis marks Paul as the subject here." [57] That is also the opinion of Lake and Cadbury.[58] **Cenchreae** was the eastern harbor of Corinth. The **vow** was probably "a temporary Nazirite vow." [59]

19 The voyage to Ephesus would usually take two or three days.[60] **He left them** [Aquila and Priscilla] **there** seems awkward at this point. We should naturally assume that they accompanied Paul to **the synagogue,** although **himself** seems to suggest otherwise. Meyer holds that Paul alone entered the synagogue and then hastened on his way.[61] **Reasoned** is *dielexato* (cf. vs. 4). It means "conversed," "discoursed."

XIV. THE EPHESIAN PROSPECT (18:18–21)

And they came to Ephesus, . . . he himself entered into the synagogue, and reasoned with the Jews (vs. 19).

Paul's continued stay, expressed as **yet many days** (vs. 18), was at the close of his eighteen months' ministry at Corinth and after his arraignment before Gallio; and it was doubtless employed in the edification of the Christian converts.

While Paul left Corinth with a view to returning to Antioch of Syria, he nevertheless had in his plans a brief visit to Ephesus where he intended leaving Priscilla and Aquila to prepare the way for the founding of a church in this great center of western Asia Minor.

It is of interest that the names of this couple here appear in the order of Priscilla and Aquila, thus placing the woman first. They occur likewise in Romans 16:3 and II Timothy 4:19. This is probably due to the greater ability, prominence, and personality of Priscilla over her husband Aquila.

Luke's statement, **having shorn his head at Cenchreae: for he had a vow** (vs. 18b), most likely is spoken in reference to Paul, though Weymouth remarks: "[He] Probably Paul, possibly Aquila." In any event, this was a Jewish custom in the keeping of vows (cf. Acts 21:24; Num. 6:18). What this particular vow was we are not told. It was likely a private vow voluntarily assumed in appreciation of some great mercy or deliverance wrought by God. Vincent thinks that this was not the Nazarite vow, though similar in its obligations, since that vow could only be concluded by the cutting of the hair in Jerusalem, whereas this one was marked by the shearing of the head at the small seaport village of Cenchrea, en route to Ephesus. However, this may have been a modification of the Nazarite vow which began and ended with the shaving of the head. For the duration of the vow, intercourse with the Gentiles was forbidden. Thus Paul may have postponed the initiation of the vow until he had left Corinth and then concluded it at Jerusalem where the hair, grown during this period, was offered on the altar at the temple together with certain specified sacrifices. This was not a conciliatory vow for the benefit of the Jews or Jewish Christians, but just the usual Jewish way of rendering thanks to God for blessings received. Nor is there any reason to suppose that Paul violated his Christian principles in deferring to a Jewish custom, any more than in the circumcision of Timothy at Lystra. An imposing array of scholars are found on either side of the

[55] VGT, p. 70. [56] *Op. cit.*, pp. 352 f. [57] *St. Paul the Traveller*, p. 263. [58] *Beginnings*, IV, 229.
[59] Bruce, *Acts*, p. 349. [60] EGT, II, 393. [61] *Op. cit.*, p. 355. Contra Knowling (EGT, II, 393 f.).

20 And when they asked him to abide a longer time, he consented not;
21 but taking his leave of them, and saying, I will return again unto you if God will, he set sail from Ephesus.
22 And when he had landed at Caesarea, he went up and saluted the church, and went down to Antioch.

---

20 **Consented** is the verb *epineuō*, found only here in the New Testament. Literally it means "nod," and so "nod approval," "consent."

21 "I must by all means keep this feast that cometh in Jerusalem" (KJV) is not in the earliest manuscripts,[62] but it may well represent the true picture. If Paul left Corinth in the fall, the feast would be Pentecost; if in the spring, the Passover.

22 **Landed** is literally "come down"; that is, from the high seas to the coast (cf. 27:5). **Caesarea** was the main seaport of Jerusalem. Whether **the church** here was at Caesarea or Jerusalem is the subject of perennial debate. Lake and Cadbury write: "The 'church' mentioned would naturally be the church in Caesarea; 'going up' means going up from the port to the city." [63] To explain why Paul should go to Caesarea on his way to Antioch they suggest that the prevailing winds favored this route. But the majority of commentators favor Jerusalem.[64] Ramsay gives two strong arguments for this view: (1) **Went down** would not be used of going from Caesarea to Antioch (this is well-nigh unanswerable); (2) the terms "going up" and "going down" are used so frequently of journeys to and from Jerusalem that this usage cannot be ignored.[65]

---

question, some assigning the vow to Aquila and others with equal force to Paul. The weight of evidence seems to point to Paul. This appears the more likely when it is noted that Paul evidently was planning to keep the feast of Pentecost (or possibly the Passover) at Jerusalem, though reference to this feast is omitted from the RV.

Upon arrival at Ephesus (see comments on Ephesus-Acts 19:1), Paul apparently left Priscilla and Aquila there to do occupational missionary work in preparation for his return and his three-year evangelistic ministry on his third missionary journey. Paul himself seems to have spent but a single Sabbath in Ephesus (Clarke) reasoning with the Jews concerning Christ as the Messiah. This initial contact appears favorable, as the record states that **they asked him to abide a longer time** (vs. 20), which invitation he declined, taking his leave with the promise of a future return if such were God's will.

It is interesting to note that the former divine prohibition to preach in Asia (see Acts 16:6) has now been lifted, and Paul apparently plans the Ephesian campaign under the direction of God. As one has said, "God's clock keeps perfect time." He closes doors that no man can open and opens doors that no man can close (Rev. 3:7). The omniscient mind knows best when to prohibit and when to permit. To run before God is as hazardous as to refuse to follow. Here, indeed, "a great door and effectual is opened" (I Cor. 16:9a) for the gospel ministry.

Paul may have sailed on a ship especially chartered by Jews bound for the Jerusalem Passover.

Part II

The Apostle's Third Missionary Journey

Time: A.D. 53–57?

Personnel: Paul, Timothy, Titus, Priscilla and Aquila, Tychicus, Trophimus, Luke, Sopater, Aristarchus, Secundus, Gaius, Erastus, Silas?

Area: Asia Minor, Macedonia, Achaia.

I. THE RETURN OF THE APOSTLE (18:22, 23)

And when he had landed at Caesarea, he went up and saluted the church, and went down to Antioch. And having spent some time there, he departed (vss. 22, 23a).

Having disembarked at Caesarea in Palestine, Paul **went up** to Jerusalem where he greeted the mother church. The prominence of Jerusalem in Jewish and Christian thought was sufficient to justify the omission of the

[62] Aleph AB E. [63] *Beginnings*, IV, 230.
[64] See lists in Meyer, *op. cit.*, p. 356; EGT, II, 395.
[65] *St. Paul the Traveller*, p. 264.

23 And having spent some time *there*, he departed, and went through the region of Galatia, and Phrygia, in order, establishing all the disciples.

24 Now a certain Jew named Apollos, an Alexandrian by race, an eloquent man, came to Ephesus; and he was mighty in the scriptures.

---

23 It is generally held that the second journey ended with Paul's return to Antioch and the third begins here.[66] **Some time** (see on 15:33) depends for its length on whether Paul arrived in Antioch in the fall or spring. If the first, he would stay all winter; if the second, he would start out soon again.

24 **Eloquent** is *logios*. Lake and Cadbury say: "Originally it meant 'learned,' as it does in modern Greek."[67] But in the first century it began to mean "eloquent." While concluding that no decisive choice can be made between these two renderings, they adopt "eloquent." [68] Moulton and Milligan prefer "some such general phrase as 'a man of culture.'" [69]

---

name of Jerusalem—thus the expression **went up** (cf. John 7:8, 10; John 12:20; Acts 24:11).

Luke's statement that Paul **saluted the church,** indicates the prominence of the Jerusalem church in the First Century. Of this expression Wesley says, "Eminently so called, being the mother church of Christian believers."[f] And on this expression Clarke remarks:

> That is, the Church at Jerusalem, called emphatically **The Church,** because it was the **first** church—the **Mother,** or **Apostolic** *Church;* and from it all other Christian Churches proceeded: those in *Galatia, Philippi, Thessalonica, Corinth, Ephesus, Rome,* &c. Therefore, even this last [Rome] was only a *daughter* Church, when in its *purest* state. [g]

Paul evidently kept the feast of the Passover at Jerusalem before he proceeded down to Antioch of Syria where he most likely gave a full account of the activities of his second missionary journey (cf. Acts 14: 26-28) to the church which had commissioned him to both the first and second journeys (see Acts 13:2, 3 and 15:40).

It does not appear that Paul remained long at Antioch, as the language employed seems to indicate that he moved anxiously back toward Ephesus where a great challenge awaited him. En route he **went through the region of Galatia, and Phrygia, in order, establishing all the disciples** (vs. 23). Weymouth remarks: "In the South Galatian view the phrase may mean the shorter hill route from Antioch to Ephesus, a little north of the main road down the Lycus Valley." [h] Wesley thinks that Paul spent about four years in Asia Minor, including the time spent in Ephesus on this third journey. Though not recorded in detail, to judge from the words, **in order,** Paul likely revisited the churches at Derbe, Lystra, Iconium, and Antioch in Pisidia, where he confirmed and established these converts of his first missionary journey.

II. THE EMERGENCE OF APOLLOS (18:24–28)

Now a certain Jew named Apollos, an Alexandrian by race, an eloquent man, came to Ephesus; and he was mighty in the scriptures (vs. 24).

During the time intervening Paul's first and second visits to Ephesus, Apollos made his appearance at that city.

It is strange indeed that this man, designated a Jew, should bear the Roman name of a heathen deity "Apollo," in view of the Jewish aversion to idolatry. Possibly, as Clarke suggests, his parents were Gentiles who were converted to Judaism as proselytes after his birth and christening, and thus Apollos was a Jew by religion but not by nationality. Dummelow's Commentary regards his name as a contraction of Apollonius. Other references to Apollos are found in I Corinthians 1:12; 3:4, 5; 4:6; 16:12 and Titus 3:13.

In any event, he was by religion a Jew who was designated **an Alexandrian by race** (vs. 24). For more than three centuries before Christ, Alexandria of Egypt had been one of the most cosmopolitan centers of the

[66] For objection to the terms "second" and "third" journey, see *Beginnings*, IV, 185.
[67] *Beginnings*, IV, 233. [68] *Ibid.* [69] VGT, p. 378.

[f] Wesley, *op. cit.*, p. 470, n. 22. [g] Clarke, *op. cit.*, I, 838. [h] Weymouth, *op. cit.*, p. 321, n. 24.

25 This man had been instructed in the way of the Lord; and being fervent in the spirit, he spake and taught accurately the things concerning Jesus, knowing only the baptism of John:

25 **Instructed** is the verb *katēcheō*, which means "to teach by word of mouth" [70] (cf. catechize). **Fervent** is a participle of *zeō*, found only here and in Romans 12:11. Lake and Cadbury write: "It does not, however, mean that his own spirit was 'fervent,' but that he was 'boiling over' with the Holy Spirit that had come into him." [71] But why not both?

The things concerning Jesus would most naturally be the story of Jesus' life and labors, of which Mark's Gospel is a good example, and the Messianic implications. Ignorance of the Holy Spirit was probably his greatest lack.[72] **The baptism of John** would involve primarily an emphasis on repentance and righteousness.

ancient world. Here Egyptians, Hindus, Greeks, Latins, Jews, and other nationalities met and pooled their wisdom to produce the greatest university of the day. Of this school Philo Judaeus (20 B.C.–A.D. 54), the Jewish Hellenistic philosopher, is probably the greatest representative. His purpose was to reconcile Greek philosophy with Jewish theology. Out of Jewish scholarship influenced by this Alexandrian school of thought, the famous Septuagint version of the Old Testament was produced.

While there is no other reference to Alexandrian or Egyptian Christianity in the New Testament, extra-Biblical records reveal that by the opening of the Second Century A.D. there were approximately a million Christians in Egypt. It has been previously noted that in the Third Century B.C. a great migration of Jews to the region of Alexandria occurred. Exactly when, how, and by whom Christianity was first carried to Egypt we do not know. Luke's mention of Christ's African cross-bearer, Simon a Cyrenian (Luke 23:26), the presence of those from "Egypt, and the parts of Libya about Cyrene" at Pentecost (Acts 2:10), those of the synagogues of the Cyrenians, and of the Alexandrians" who were "disputing with Stephen" (Acts 6:9) just before his martyrdom, "men . . . of Cyrene" (Acts 11:20) who preached to the Greeks at Antioch, "and Symeon that was called Niger, and Lucius of Cyrene" (Acts 13:1), who were included among the prophets and teachers at Antioch, are all tantalizingly interesting, but what, if any, part they played in carrying the Gospel to Egypt we do not know for certain. Whether Apollos became a disciple of John the Baptist and learned of the promised Messiah on the occasion of a visit to Judea during an annual feast, or whether he was converted to John's gospel by another in Egypt, we are not certain. In coming to Ephesus he likely had in mind the enlightenment and instruction of the Jews in the Christian way, so far as he understood it. How far his knowledge of Christ went seems not too clear. He certainly regarded Christ Jesus as the Messiah (Mark 1:1–11), and he likely knew Him as the divine "Son of God" and "the world's sin bearer" (John 1:29–34). It appears that his knowledge was factually accurate so far as it extended. That he was genuinely sincere is without question, even to the point of **being fervent in spirit** (vs. 25). Of this expression Vincent remarks: "Fervent . . . *to boil* or *ferment*, is an exact translation of this word, which means to *seethe* or *bubble*, and is therefore used figuratively of mental states and emotions." [i] (Cf. Matt. 13:33.) Nor was this a religious zeal without knowledge, for Luke remarks concerning him that he was both **an eloquent man** and **mighty in the scriptures** (vs. 24).

Of Apollos' eloquence (*Logios*) Vincent observes that this is the only New Testament usage of the term. The term *Logios* has several usages in Greek literature, however. Thus Vincent remarks, "As *logos* means either *reason* or *speech*, so this derivation [logios] may signify either one who has thought much and has much to say, or one who can say it well." [j] Vincent continues to observe that Herodotus uses it in the sense of "one *skilled in history*"; or as "an *eloquent* person," especially the "epithet of Hermes or Mercury, as the god of speech and eloquence," or "a *learned* person generally." [k]

From the foregoing it may be deduced

[70] Abbott-Smith, *op. cit.*, p. 241. [71] *Beginnings*, IV, 233. [72] Rackham *op. cit.*, p. 343.

[i] Vincent, *op. cit.*, I, 549. [j] *Ibid.* [k] *Ibid.*

26 and he began to speak boldly in the synagogue. But when Priscilla and Aquila heard him, they took him unto them, and expounded unto him the way of God more accurately.
27 And when he was minded to pass over into Achaia, the brethren encouraged him, and wrote to the disciples to receive him: and when he was come, he helped them much that had believed through grace;

---

26 **Expounded** is the verb *ektithēmi*, found only in Acts (cf. 7:21; 11:4; 28:23). It means "set out, expose"; and so, "expound." **More accurately** is *akribesteron* (cf. *akribōs*, vs. 25). The comparative is found only here and in 23:15, 20; 24:22.

27 The Western text begins the verse thus: "And some Corinthians staying in Ephesus who had heard him, asked him to cross with them to their own country." Though the text is probably not original, this may well be what took place. **Encouraged** is the verb *protrepō*, found only here in the New Testament. It means "to urge forwards, exhort, persuade." [73] **Helped** is *synebalon*, which here alone in the New Testament has the meaning "contribute," [74] "help." It is not clear whether **through grace** goes with **helped** or with **believed.** The former arrangement is preferred by Knowling,[75] Meyer,[76] Page,[77] and Rackham.[78]

---

that the intellectual acumen, thorough training in the general history and philosophy of the ancients, a reasoned knowledge of Jewish history and religion, plus an acquaintance with the teachings of John the Baptist to the effect that Jesus was the Messiah, wrought a burning conviction of these truths in the soul of Apollos that expressed itself in a zealous, logical flow of brilliant eloquence which his opponents found it difficult to match and under which his hearers found themselves swept into his persuasions.

Whether Apollos had experienced true Christian conversion before coming to Ephesus is not quite certain. However, Luke's characterization of him would seem to indicate that he had. In any event, he knew John's baptism of repentance and believed Jesus to be the promised Messiah. If he was not "in" he certainly was "near" the Kingdom of God. He seems to have received Christian baptism at the hands of Priscilla and Aquila. Even that he entered into a deeper sanctifying relationship with Christ under the ministry of this Christian couple appears likely from Luke's account (see Acts 18:26b). What a great ministry, though indirectly rendered, some of God's humble lay-servants have performed. The earnest prayers of two saintly, fervent ladies that D. L. Moody might receive the baptism of the Holy Spirit resulted in the mighty ministry of that man. Natural or acquired abilities without God are utterly meaningless to the Kingdom, but when filled, possessed, and employed of God, they become mighty to the destruction of Satan's kingdom and the construction of Christ's Kingdom.

The vision and zeal of Apollos impelled him to move on to Achaia where at Corinth he was to render a great service to the young church. In the enterprise he was encouraged by the brethren at Ephesus, likely including Priscilla and Aquila, even to the extent of their writing a letter of introduction to the Corinthian church in which letter he was earnestly commended to their confidence (cf. II Cor. 3:1).

The success of the ministry of Apollos at Corinth is attested by the fact that he soon became so popular that his admirers formed a faction or party of Apollos within the Corinthian church (see I Cor. 1:12–3:6).

Luke informs us that the ministry of Apollos at Corinth was twofold: first, **he helped them much that had believed through grace** (vs. 27b), and second, **he powerfully confuted the Jews** (vs. 28a). Thus, in the first instance, his newly acquired grace at Ephesus became the means of edifying the Corinthian converts, and that grace plus his learning and eloquence became an effective instrument for confuting the Jews publicly, both to the encouragement of the Christians and the discouragement of Jewish opposition to Christianity.

Of the word **confuted,** used here by Luke,

[73] Abbott-Smith, *op. cit.*, p. 390. [74] *Ibid.*, p. 426. [75] EGT, II, 398.
[76] *Op. cit.*, p. 358. [77] *Op. cit.*, p. 203. [78] *Op. cit.*, p. 344.

28 for he powerfully confuted the Jews, *and that* publicly, showing by the scriptures that Jesus was the Christ.

---

28 *Eutonōs*, **powerfully**, is found only here and in Luke 23:10. It means "vigorously," "vehemently." Hobart says that it is "one of the words most frequently employed in the medical writers." [79] **Confuted** is the double compound, *diakatalegchomai*, "to confute completely." [80] It has not been found anywhere else. *Epideiknys*, **showing**, means "proving" onlv here and in Hebrews 6:17.

Vincent observes that it is not elsewhere used in the New Testament and that it implies that "he confuted them *thoroughlv* (diá), *against* (Katá) all their arguments." [l]

On the work of Apollos at Corinth Wesley remarks:

> **Who greatly helped through grace**—It is through grace only that any gift of any one is profitable to another. **Them that had believed**—Apollos did not plant, but water [I Cor. 3:6]. This was the peculiar gift which he had received. And he was better able to convince the Jews than to convert the heathens.[m]

The burden of Apollos' ministry at Corinth was **that Jesus was the Christ** (vs. 28b). Any ministry that falls short of this objective is short of Christianity, and the ministry that attains this objective is the true Christian ministry.

Additional Note I

CORINTH

Finegan aptly describes the Corinth of Paul's day as follows:

> In going from Athens to Corinth (Acts 18:1), Paul was moving from the intellectual center of Greece to its most splendid commercial city . . . Corinth was just across the isthmus which connected central Greece with the Peloponnesus. This isthmus was a natural meeting place for trade from East and West. Ships from Asia Minor, Syria, and Egypt put in to the port of Cenchreae, (cf. Romans 16:1) on the east side of the isthmus, those of Italy, Sicily, and Spain docked at Lechaeum, the harbor on the west side. The distance between these two ports was less than ten miles . . . Situated but one and one-half miles south of this isthmus and commanding the ports on either side of it, the city of Corinth obviously was destined for commercial greatness. Pindar called the Isthmus of Corinth 'the bridge of the sea' and Strabo summed up the situation accurately when he said, "Corinth is called 'wealthy' because of its commerce, since it is situated on the Isthmus and is master of two harbors, of which the one leads straight to Asia, and the other to Italy; and it makes easy the exchange of merchandise from both countries that are so far distant from each other.
>
> . . . She dominated extensive trade routes, and Corinthian bronze and pottery were exported widely over the Mediterranean. About 146 B.C., Corinth warred with Rome and upon defeat was completely destroyed, probably because of commercial jealousy. The inhabitants were sold into slavery and for one hundred years the site of the city lay desolate. Then in 46 B.C. Julius Caesar refounded the city as the colonial Laus Julia Corinthiensis, and peopled it with Italian freedmen and dispossessed Greeks. Its commercial prosperity was recovered rapidly, and Augustus made Corinth the capital of Achaia and seat of its proconsul (Acts. 18:12).[n]

[79] *Op. cit.*, p. 241.
[80] Abbott-Smith, *op. cit.*, p. 107.

[l] *Ibid.*, p. 550.
[m] Wesley, *op. cit.*, pp. 470, 471, n. 27.
[n] Finegan, *op. cit.*, pp. 278–279.

CHAPTER XIX

And it came to pass, that, while Apollos was at Corinth, Paul having passed through the upper country came to Ephesus, and found certain disciples:

EXEGESIS

1 *Anōterika,* **upper,** is found only here in the New Testament. Hobart says: "It is a very rare word, and in medical language was applied to the upper part of the body—medicines which acted there—emetics."[1] Cadbury claims to have exploded Hobart's theory of distinctive medical terms in Luke's writings.[2] But here he and Lake admit that "there is no evidence for *anōterikos* except in medical books."[3]

Upper country is literally "upper parts" *(merē)*. The King James rendering "coasts" (15 times in N.T.) is an outmoded use of that term. Lake and Cadbury suggest that the expression means "hinterland" from the Ephesian point of view.[4] Knowling makes it synonymous with "the region of Galatia, and Phrygia" (18:23).[5] But it is probably better to assume that 19:1 continues on from 18:23, after the intervening parenthesis about Apollos. Knowling is more helpful when he writes: "The main road to Ephesus which passed through Colossae and Laodicea was not apparently taken by Paul, but a shorter though less frequented route running through the Cayster valley."[6]

Who were these **certain disciples**? It has been common in the past to label them disciples of John the Baptist. For instance, Meyer's American editor, Ormiston, writes: "The disciples of John, who were numerous and scattered, may be divided into three classes: those, including a large majority,

---

EXPOSITION

THE APOSTLE'S THIRD MISSIONARY JOURNEY (cont'd)

III. The Apostle's Mission to Ephesus, Acts 19:1–22.
   A. Paul Returns to Ephesus, vs. 1a.
   B. Paul Finds Certain Disciples at Ephesus, vss. 1b–7.
   C. Paul Ministers in the Jewish Synagogue, vss. 8, 9a.
   D. Paul Ministers in the School of Tyrannus, vss. 9b–20.
   E. Paul Purposes to Visit Jerusalem, vs. 21a.
   F. Paul Plans to Visit Rome, vss. 21b, 22.
IV. The Apostle's Maltreatment at Ephesus, Acts 19:23–41.
   A. The Cause of the Opposition, vss. 23–27.
   B. The Nature of the Attack, vss. 28–34.
   C. The Arrest of the Attack, vss. 35–41.

III. THE APOSTLE'S MISSION TO EPHESUS

(19:1–22)

On his first missionary journey Paul did not go farther west than Antioch of Pisidia in Asia Minor. On his second missionary journey he by-passed Ephesus on the north, because he was "forbidden of the Holy Spirit to speak the word in Asia" (Acts 16:6b). However, when returning from Corinth to Jerusalem at the close of his second missionary journey, he briefly visited Ephesus where he "entered into the synagogue, and reasoned with the Jews," after which he departed leaving them Priscilla and Aquila and his personal promise to return again in God's will (Acts 18:19, 21). Thus it would appear that Ephesus must have been an objective of the Apostle from the beginning of his missionary career. But until now the time for its invasion by the Gospel had not been propitious. An earlier attempt might

[1] *Op. cit.*, p. 148.
[2] See Henry J. Cadbury, *The Making of Luke-Acts* (New York: Macmillan Co., 1927), pp. 118, 219, 273, 358.
[3] *Beginnings*, IV, 237.
[4] *Ibid.*, p. 236. Cf. Meyer (p. 364): "*lying more inland* from Ephesus."
[5] EGT, II, 402.
[6] *Ibid.*, p. 401. Cf. also Bruce, *Acts*, p. 353.

who became disciples of Christ; those, who formed a small sect of their own, holding that John was the Messiah; and those who, being removed from Palestine, held just what John taught." He adds: "To this class Apollos and the twelve disciples at Ephesus belonged."[7] Meyer himself says that **disciples** *(mathētas)* means Christians. He explains their ignorance thus: "It is most probable that they were strangers, who had just come to Ephesus and had attached themselves to the Christians of that place."[8] They had not even been under Apollos' ministry. Hackett agrees that they were "strangers who had just arrived at Ephesus," but thinks that when Paul met them they "had not yet come in contact with any of the Christians there."[9] Olshausen suggests that "the apostles treated them only as immature disciples, who were in a state of transition from the Old Covenant to the New, . . . without having felt the power of the blood of sprinkling."[10] In view of the older prevailing view, from Chrysostom onward, that these men were merely disciples of John the Baptist, it is interesting to note the conclusion of Lake and Cadbury: "This must mean Christians, both from the use of *mathētas* in Acts and from the context."[11] Bruce agrees.[12]

---

easily have proved abortive. The discernment of God's will for God's work in God's time is indeed a work of divine wisdom.

A. Paul Returns to Ephesus (19:1a)

Paul having passed through the upper country came to Ephesus.

Luke's description of Paul's return to Ephesus is probably designed to indicate that he revisited and confirmed the churches of Asia Minor established on his first missionary journey, en route to Ephesus. This would have constituted his third pastoral visit to these churches since their establishment. Thus Antioch of Pisidia would have been the last and westernmost church from which Paul departed for Ephesus. From this point he evidently proceeded, not by the usual level trade route that passed through the Lycus and Maeander valleys and the cities of Colossae and Laodicea, but rather by the more direct mountainous northern route that passed down through the Cayster valley. Paul's words to the Colossians (Col. 2:1) seem clearly to indicate that he had never been to that city.

In certain respects (especially religiously) Ephesus was the most important city which Paul had so far visited in his missionary travels. Indeed there is a noticeable ascending order in the successive cities attacked by the Apostle in his missionary strategy. His next and probably last great objective was to be the city of Rome itself.

Ephesus was a city of Lydia located on the west coast of Asia Minor, at the mouth and on the left bank of the Cayster River, about midway between Miletus on the south and Smyrna on the north and just opposite the island of Samos, about three miles from the open sea. The city was situated at a transportation junction of the main sea and land trade routes between Rome and the Orient (Acts 19:21; 20:1, 17; I Tim. 1:3; II Tim. 4:12). It possessed an elaborately constructed harbor.

Ephesus came under Rome's control about A.D. 133. While it evidently became the capital of the province of Asia in western Asia Minor, it is uncertain whether it was such in Paul's day. It ranked along with Antioch in Syria and Alexandria in Egypt as one of the three great cities of the eastern Mediterranean."[a] Eventually the mouth of the river silted up, the harbor became a marsh, and the city disappeared, except for its extensive ruins. Only the small village of Ayasoluk, or Seljuk (Turkish), constructed mainly of stone from the ruins of Ephesus, located a mile or so to the northeast, remains to memorialize the once illustrious city.

At the harbor's head stood the famed temple of Diana (Roman) or Artemis (Greek), which goddess was represented in statue as a multi-breasted mother goddess.

Croesus and Cyrus (Sixth Century B.C.) and Alexander the Great (Fourth Century B.C.) had all left their mark on the Asiatic people in general and the Ionian Greeks, who originally populated the province of

[7] Meyer, *op. cit.*, p. 362. [8] *Ibid.*, pp. 364 f. So also Gloag, *op. cit.*, p. 196. [9] *Op. cit.*, p. 219.
[10] *Op. cit.*, III, 368. Knowling (EGT, II, 402) calls them disciples in the "immature stage of knowledge."
[11] *Beginnings*, IV, 237. [12] *Acts*, p. 353. Contra. Lumby (CGT), p. 331.

[a] Finegan, *op. cit.*, p. 265.

2 and he said unto them, Did ye receive the Holy Spirit when ye believed? And they *said* unto him, Nay, we did not so much as hear whether the Holy Spirit was *given.*

---

2 The question, **Did ye receive the Holy Spirit when ye believed?**, involves a problem of translation. The Greek says: "Did you receive, having believed?" *(elabete pisteusantes)*. Meyer translates the latter word "after ye became believers." [13] (Cf. KJV). But most commentators agree with the Revised rendering. The recent grammarians support them. Moulton writes: "The coincident aorist participle is doctrinally important: cf. R.V." [14] Robertson notes that usually the aorist participle indicates action antecedent to that of the main verb but says that here it signifies action contemporaneous with it.[15] But why here? Actually, however, either translation makes good sense, since the Holy Spirit is received only through believing.

It should be obvious that this question cannot be used as a proof text for the view, either that the receiving of the Holy Spirit is subsequent to conversion or that it is simultaneous with it. That matter must be decided on other grounds

What is meant by **when ye believed?** Most commentators take the phrase as meaning "when you became Christians." [16] Knowling [17] and Rackham [18] refei it specifically to baptism.

The literal Greek of the reply to Paul's question is: "No, we did not even hear that there is a Holy Spirit." So the King James rendering is correct (cf. RSV). But is the interpretation **whether the Holy Spirit was given** justifiable? Bengel thinks so. He says: "They could not have followed either Moses or John the Baptist, without hearing of the Holy Spirit " [19] Gloag agrees.[20] So does Knowling.[21] Lake and Cadbury think that the Western text—"We have not even heard if any do receive the Holy Spirit"—"presumably gives the correct sense." [22] Meyer would take "is" as meaning "already present on earth." [23] Rackham says: "The meaning of the Greek *is*, is fixed by S. John's phrase" (John 7:39).[24]

But there are a few dissenting voices. Hackett declares: "It is unnecessary and

---

Asia, in particular. From Croesus' time (ca. 560 B.C.) a fertility goddess of Lydia, who resembled Ashtoreth of the Phoenicians, had been the chief deity of the city. Her worship was characterized by a magnificent temple, commercialized subsidiaries, and legalized prostitution. Ephesus was "a worshiper" (AV), "a temple-keeper" (ASV), and "a warden" (Moffatt) of the goddess (Acts 19:35). Magic was commercialized and widely practiced at Ephesus. Charlatans exacted fees for consultation (Acts 19:13–16, 19), and the general prevalence of superstition was evidenced by inscriptions on buildings and walls throughout the city. The Millers aptly remark: "Under liberal Roman rule, . . . Ephesus became a racial melting pot, a cosmopolitan commercial center of the Empire, and a battlefield of religion."[b]

The temple of Diana was discovered by the English architect and anthropologist, J. T. Wood, on May 2, 1869. It was 120 years in building and the original temple, according to tradition, burned in 356 B.C. However, it was replaced by the "Hellenistic temple" which was completed in the latter part of the Fourth Century B.C. The temple rested on a platform about 240 feet wide and over 400 feet long. The temple proper was over 160 feet wide and 340 feet long with 100 columns over 55 feet high. Gold and silver images, weighing from three to seven pounds each, were made of the goddess by the smiths (Acts 19:23–26). Little wonder that this temple was regarded as "one of the seven wonders" of the ancient world.

The great Ephesian theater, which was the scene of the tumult raised against Paul (Acts 19:29), was a semicircular auditorium 495 feet in diameter, excavated in the hollow of a hill that commanded a clear view of the city and accommodated an audience of nearly 25,000 people.

[13] *Op. cit.*, p. 365. [14] *Op. cit.*, I, 131, n. [15] *Grammar*, p. 860 f.
[16] *Beginnings*, IV, 237. Cf. Meyer (p. 365). [17] EGT, II, 403. [18] *Op. cit.*, p. 346.
[19] *Op. cit.*, I, 876. [20] Paton J. Gloag, *op. cit.*, II, 195 f. [21] EGT, II, 403.
[22] *Beginnings*, IV, 237. [23] *Op. cit.*, p. 365. [24] *Op. cit.*, p. 346.

[b] Madeleine S. Miller and J. Lane Miller, *Harper' Bible Dictionary* (New York: Harper & Brothers, 1955), p. 167.

incorrect to supply *given.*" [25] Olshausen says: "The meaning of the words undoubtedly is, that those men knew nothing even of the existence of the Holy Ghost." [26] Page interprets the reply thus: "At our baptism . . . we did not even hear of the existence of a Holy Spirit." [27] He calls this "the only possible rendering of the Greek." [28]

It should be remembered that while frequent references are made in the Old Testament to the Spirit of the Lord, the actual expression "Holy Spirit" occurs there only three times (Ps. 51:11; Isa. 63:10, 11) and even then with a modifying "his" or "thy." Bruce is correct in suggesting that these men may not have been familiar with the term, but adds: "Possibly *pneuma hagion* is to be understood here in a special sense, of the Holy Spirit as sent at Pentecost with outward manifestation." [29] That is the best conclusion.

The further magnificence of this city is suggested by Finegan's description:

> Another important feature of ancient Ephesus was the agora or marketplace. This was a great rectangular, colonnaded area entered by magnificent gateways and surrounded by halls and chambers. Nearby was the library, built with fine columns and with its walls recessed with niches for bookcases [cf. Acts 19:9b]. Other buildings which have been excavated include gymnasia, baths, and burial monuments. One of the city's finest streets ran directly from the theater to the river harbor, being nearly one-half mile long and about 35 feet wide, and lined with halls on either side. Also at the harbor there were monumental gateways.[c]

At this famous, ancient city Paul evangelized for upward of three years between the autumn of A.D. 52 and the spring of A.D. 55, and out from Ephesus the whole of western Asia Minor was evangelized. Here a great Christian church was founded by Paul, over which Timothy was later made pastor. And if tradition is reliable, at Ephesus both the apostle John and Mary the mother of Christ spent their last days. The churches' third general council, which defined the doctrine of Christ's person as "two natures, but one person," was held at Ephesus in 430 A.D. To this church Paul later wrote the Ephesian Epistle, though likely intended for other churches as well, and to this church Christ directed the message recorded in Revelation 2:1–7.

There appear to be indications that Paul may have regarded Ephesus as the third great missionary base from which the Gospel was to radiate forth to the central eastern section of the Roman Empire, Jerusalem and Antioch of Syria having been the first two and the city of Rome designed to become the fourth.

B. Paul Finds Certain Disciples at Ephesus (19:1b–7)

[He] **found certain disciples** (vs. 1b).

Paul's discovery of these disciples at Ephesus is one of the most momentous and, in certain respects at least, vexing accounts of the Book of Acts. If they were at Ephesus when he briefly visited that city near the close of his second missionary journey (Acts 18:19–21), he evidently did not meet them then. Dummelow holds that they had arrived at Ephesus between the departure of Apollos for Corinth (vs. 1a) and the return of Paul to Ephesus, else Apollos would have instructed them in the Christian doctrine after "Priscilla and Aquila . . . took him unto them and expounded unto him the way of God more accurately" (Acts 18:26). However, this need not be supposed, as Apollos appears to have left Ephesus for Corinth almost immediately after having met Priscilla and Aquila (Acts 18:26, 27).

Clarke thinks that these men were Asiatic Jews who, a quarter-century earlier, had heard John preach at Jerusalem (perhaps at an annual feast) and were there baptized by him, in anticipation of Christ's coming. Bruce allows that

> They may have received their knowledge of Christianity from a source similar to that from which Apollos received his, or they may have received it from Apollos and been baptized by him during his earlier days in Ephesus, when he knew only the baptism of John.[d]

Of greater importance, however, is the state of grace that characterized these disciples. There seems to be no warrant for the common assumption that these **certain disciples** were the disciples of John the Baptist. Indeed they had received **John's baptism**

[25] *Op. cit.*, p. 219. [26] *Op. cit.*, p. 370. [27] *Op. cit.*, p. 203. [28] *Ibid.* [29] *Acts*, p. 354.

[c] Finegan, *op. cit.*, pp. 268, 269.
[d] Bruce, *op. cit.*, p. 385. Davidson likewise allows this latter likelihood (see note on Acts 18:24–28).

3 And he said, Into what then were ye baptized? And they said, Into John's baptism.
4 And Paul said, John baptized with the baptism of repentance, saying unto the people that they should believe on him that should come after him, that is, on Jesus.
5 And when they heard this, they were baptized into the name of the Lord Jesus.

---

3 Perhaps **into** (twice) may be translated "with."[30] Gloag interprets the second one thus: "into a belief of the truths which John's baptism declared."[31]

4 John's identification of **him that should come after him** with **Jesus** is not stated in the Synoptics, but is in John's Gospel (1:29-34).[32]

5 This verse would seem to indicate that these men had never before been **baptized** into the Christian community.

(vs. 3b), which Paul defines as **the baptism of repentance** (vs. 4b), a factor common to all baptisms that were administered to proselytes by the Jews, but faith in Him that was to come was peculiar to John's baptism (Clarke: vs. 4b). Thus they were the disciples of Christ, though imperfectly instructed, and not John's disciples, as many mistakenly suppose. Bruce is specific and significant in his statement:

> But that these men were Christians is certainly to be inferred from the way in which Luke describes them as "disciples"; this is a term which he commonly uses for Christians, and had he meant to indicate that they were disciples, not of Christ but of John the Baptist (as has sometimes been deduced from v, 3), he would have said so explicitly.[e]

Paul's question, **Did ye receive the Holy Spirit when ye believed?** (vs. 2a), was answered by these disciples in the negative: **Nay, we did not so much as hear whether the Holy Spirit was given** (vs. 2b). This reply probably does not warrant the inference that these disciples had no knowledge of the person, dispensation, or office work of the Holy Spirit in the life of the believer. No more can be deduced from their reply than that they were uninformed concerning the fulfillment of His dispensation and effusion which occurred at the Jerusalem Pentecost. Dummelow remarks:

> Of course they had heard of the Holy Ghost, but St. Paul means, had they experienced that new power of holiness, that peace and love and joy which the ascended Messiah had first given at Pentecost, and was still ready to bestow on all believers.[f]

On this problem Bruce remarks:

> Paul's question . . . suggests strongly that he regarded them as true believers in Christ . . . the addition of the word "given," as in A.R.V., may give the real intention of their words. Even if they had only been baptized with John's baptism, they conceivably knew that John had spoken of a coming baptism with the Holy Spirit [see Matt. 3:11]; they did not know, however, that this expected baptism was now an accomplished fact.[g]

Thus it may be safely concluded that these disciples had been instructed in the teaching of John concerning the saving efficacy of the coming Christ, had believed on Him (cf. Eph. 1:13), had received water baptism as a token of their repentance, "A baptism of expectation rather than one of fulfillment as Christian baptism now was."[h] They had become recipients of a measure of Christian grace through the ministry of the Holy Spirit (Rom. 8:5) and had lived in anticipation of a spiritual Pentecost, the historical occurrence of which they had not been informed.

The re-baptism of these Ephesian disciples is the only New Testament account of such an occurrence. Whoever of the apostles had been baptized with John's baptism, it appears that "their Pentecostal enduement with the Spirit transformed the preparatory significance of the baptism which they had already received into the consummative significance of Christian baptism."[i]

However, these Ephesian Christian disciples had neither experienced nor learned of the Pentecostal baptism. Therefore, it was evidently their desire and Paul's judgment that they should be re-**baptized into the name of the Lord Jesus** (vs. 5b). It appears most likely that if these disciples had already received Christian baptism they would have heard of the Holy Spirit, and it further appears probable that the Trinitarian formula (Matt. 28:19) was used at this time.

More important, however, is the fact that

---

[30] So *Beginnings*, IV, 237; Bruce, *Acts*, p. 354.
[31] *Op. cit.*, p. 196.
[32] For the odd position of *hina*, see *Beginnings*, IV, 237; Bruce, *Acts*, p. 354.

[e] *Ibid.* [f] Dummelow, *op. cit.*, p. 845. [g] Bruce, *op. cit.*, pp. 385, 386. [h] *Ibid.*, p. 386. [i] *Ibid.*

6 And when Paul had laid his hands upon them, the Holy Spirit came on them; and they spake with tongues, and prophesied.
7 And they were in all about twelve men.

---

6 The situation here parallels that in 8:15–17, except that it is not stated that they **spake with tongues** at Samaria. This is the third and last time that speaking in tongues is mentioned in Acts (cf. 2:4; 10:46).

7 **Men** is *andres*—men as distinct from women. Nothing is said of their wives, and it may be that these men were ascetic celibates.

In summarizing this incident, Lake and Cadbury make this striking comment: "The 'baptism of John' does not for our author necessarily imply direct or indirect influence from the Baptist, it is his name for Christian water baptism without the Spirit." [33]

---

this second baptism was not likely administered by Paul personally but by some other, such as Priscilla or Aquila, if we are to take Paul's own words to the Corinthians seriously (see I Cor. 1:14–16). Thus whatever measure of Christian grace accompanied their second water baptism, by whatever mode they were baptized, that experience of grace is not to be confused with what they experienced **when Paul had laid his hands upon them,** [and] **the Holy Spirit came upon them; and they spake with tongues, and prophesied** (vs. 6). Under John's teaching they had experienced the baptism of repentance and faith in the coming Messiah. Under their second baptism at Ephesus their Christian experience had been confirmed, animated and enriched by the accompanying power and grace of the Holy Spirit (cf. John 20:22, 23). But under the imposition of hands by Paul, they received the baptism of the Holy Spirit and fire in the purification of their natures, as promised by John (Matt. 3:11; Luke 3:16) and provided by the very nature of God (Heb. 12:29). Thus the complete possession and empowerment of their lives, as experienced by the Christian disciples on the day of Pentecost (cf. Acts 1:8; 2:1–4; and 15:8, 9), as well as by the Samaritans under the ministry of Peter and John (Acts 8:14–17) and the Gentile household of Cornelius at Caesarea under Peter's ministry (Acts 10:44–48; 11:15–17; 15:8, 9), became a reality with these believers.

Luke's remark, that **they spake with tongues, and prophesied** (vs. 6b), seems clearly to indicate that these twelve disciples were divinely earmarked for special witnessing to the Gentiles of Ephesus and western Asia Minor. There is no reason for believing that their prophesyings were other than "forth-telling" or witnessing for Christ to their fellow countrymen, from their personal experiences and possibly also from the Jewish Scriptures with which they may have had an acquaintance. As previously noted, it is not known for certain whether they were Jews, Gentiles, proselytes, or God-fearers. But if they were not Jews, they were most likely either Gentile proselytes to Judaism or God-fearers. In any event, there is every evidence of the fact that when **they spake with tongues** (vs. 6) they had received a divine gift of languages designed to enable them to minister the Gospel of Christ to the exceedingly polyglot cosmopolitan city of Ephesus, as well as the entire western section of Asia Minor. Who can say that from among these very disciples there may not have come some of Paul's most efficient and effective helpers in the evangelization of western Asia Minor from his Ephesian base during the nearly three years that followed? It is entirely possible that some of his helpers named in his epistles were from this original company of disciples who **spake with tongues, and prophesied.** In support of this interpretation, Bruce says:

> Ephesus was to be a new centre of the Gentile mission—the next in importance after the Syrian Antioch—and these twelve disciples were to be the nucleus of the Ephesian church. By this exceptional procedure, then, they were associated in the apostolic and missionary task of the Christian Church.[j]

Clarke adds the further weight of his testimony to this position thus:

> They [the Ephesian twelve] received the miraculous gift of different languages; and in those languages they *taught* to the people the great doctrines of the Christian religion; for this appears to be the meaning of the word *Proefateuon*, prophesied, as it is used above.[k]

[33] *Beginnings*, IV, 238.

[j] *Ibid.*, p. 387. [k] Clarke, *op. cit.*, V, 842.

8 And he entered into the synagogue, and spake boldly for the space of three months, reasoning and persuading *as to* the things concerning the kingdom of God.

9 But when some were hardened and disobedient, speaking evil of the Way before the multitude, he departed from them, and separated the disciples, reasoning daily in the school of Tyrannus.

---

8 *Eparrēsiazeto,* **spake boldly** (literally "was speaking freely or boldly"), is a verb found seven times in Acts and only twice elsewhere in the New Testament (Eph. 6:20; I Thess. 2:2). In view of Paul's bold speech, it is surprising that his ministry in the **synagogue** lasted **three months,** longer than any place else. Josephus indicates that there were at Ephesus many Jews, some of whom were Roman citizens and were given the special privilege of exemption from military service.[34]

9 For **the Way,** see 9:2. He **departed,** just as in Corinth (18:7). For **separated** see 13:2, the only other place in Acts where *aphorizō* occurs. *Scholē,* **school** (only here in N.T.) at first meant "leisure." Beginning with Plato it signified: "(*a*) that for which leisure is employed, *a disputation, lecture;* (*b*) the place where lectures are delivered, *a school.*" [35] Lake and Cadbury say that *scholē* means "a hall used for lectures or other meetings" [36] (cf. RSV). Meyer held that *Tyrannus* was "a Jewish teacher who had a private synagogue." [37] But the vast majority of commentators consider it to have been a Greek lecture hall.

The Western text adds, after Tyrannus: "from the fifth to the tenth hour"; that is, from 11:00 A.M. to 4:00 P.M. Though probably not original, this reading may well preserve an authentic tradition. Ramsay says: "Public life in the Ionian cities ended regularly at the fifth hour." [38] He adds: "Thus Paul himself would be free, and the lecture-room would be disengaged, after the fifth hour; and the time, which was devoted generally to home-life and rest, was applied by him to mission-work." [39] Lake and Cadbury remark: "At 1 P.M. there were probably more people sound asleep than at 1 A.M." [40]

And Matthew Henry significantly remarks,

> This was indeed to introduce the gospel at Ephesus, and to awaken in the minds of men an expectation of some great things from it; and some think that it was further designed to qualify these twelve men for the work of the ministry, and that these twelve men were the elders of Ephesus, to whom Paul committed the care and government of the church. They had the spirit of prophecy, that they might understand the mysteries of the kingdom of God themselves, and the gift of tongues, that they might preach them to every nation and language.[i]

Certainly, while there is found no basis in this incident for the interpretation of an "unknown tongue," there is strong evidence for a valid conclusion that what occurred was a miraculous divine gift of *bona fide* languages designed for the enablement of these Spirit-baptized Christian disciples to preach (*prophesy*) Christ to the polyglot peoples of one of the greatest centers of the ancient world.

Luke records two specific localities of Paul's ministry at Ephesus: namely, the Jewish synagogue and the school of Tyrannus. However, it is not to be supposed that Paul confined his ministry to these places while he remained in Ephesus. Paul's associates here were Timothy, Titus, Erastus, and Sosthenes (Acts 19:22; I Cor. 1:1; II Cor. 1:1; and 12:17 f.).

C. Paul Ministers in the Jewish Synagogue (19:8, 9a)

And he entered into the synagogue, and spake boldly for the space of three months (vs. 8a).

Paul followed his usual custom, as at Antioch of Pisidia (Acts 13:14), at Thessalonica (Acts 17:2), at Beroea (Acts 17:10), at Athens (Acts 17:17), and at Corinth (Acts 18:4), by beginning at Ephesus in the Jewish synagogue. On his earlier visit to Ephesus (Acts 18:19–21), Paul had established contact with the Jews here by ministering in their synagogue. It appears from Luke's words, "they asked him to abide a

[34] *Ant.* XIV, 10, 13. [35] Abbott-Smith, *op. cit.*' p. 436. [36] *Beginnings*, IV, 239.
[37] *Op. cit.*, p. 368. [38] *St. Paul the Traveller*, p. 271. [39] *Ibid.* [40] *Beginnings*, IV, 239.

[i] Matthew Henry, *op. cit.*, VI. Comment on Acts 19:6, 7.

10 And this continued for the space of two years; so that all they that dwelt in Asia heard the word of the Lord, both Jews and Greeks.

11 And God wrought special miracles by the hands of Paul:

12 insomuch that unto the sick were carried away from his body handkerchiefs or aprons, and the diseases departed from them, and the evil spirits went out.

---

10 Because of the strategic importance of Ephesus and the attraction of great crowds to its famous temple, **all . . . Asia** (province) heard the Gospel.

11 *Ou tychousas* (participle), **special,** means "not common or ordinary," [41] and so "extraordinary" (RSV). The idiom is found elsewhere in the New Testament only in 28:2. **Miracles** is *dynameis,* powerful works.

12 *Chrotos,* **body,** found only here in the New Testament, means "the surface of the body, skin." [42] Hobart writes: "The use of *chros,* to mean the body, not the skin, continued in medical language from Hippocrates to Galen." [43] Both *soudaria,* **handkerchiefs,** and *simkinthia,* **aprons,** are from the Latin. The latter, meaning workman's aprons, is found only here. Lake and Cadbury, however, claim that "kerchiefs and handkerchiefs" is the best rendering.[44]

Apallassesthai, **departed,** occurs elsewhere in the New Testament only in Luke 12:58 and Hebrews 2:15. In the active it means "remove, release." *Ponēra,* **evil,** is used for evil spirits only by Luke (three times in his Gospel and four times here), except in Matthew 12:45.

---

longer time" (Acts 18:20), that their impression of his person and ministry had been favorable. This is further borne out by the fact that he continued to minister in **the synagogue . . . for the space of three months** (vs. 8), an unusually long time before opposition forced him out. However, here as always, when the light of Christ's Messiahship had sufficiently illumined their darkness, **some were hardened and** [became] **disobedient** (vs. 9a), with the consequence that they spoke **evil of the Way before the multitude** (vs. 9), thus poisoning their minds against the Christian missionaries and the Christian Gospel. Consequently Paul was forced to leave the synagogue, as he had had to do in so many other instances.

Thus having offered the Gospel first to the Jews at Ephesus, who had been providentially placed there as God's emissaries to the Gentiles, Paul then turns to the Gentiles, seeing that certain Jews were determined to reject and oppose the light of God's truth (cf. Acts 18:6).

Luke's expression, **reasoning and persuading** (vs. 8), or conversing with them, with a view to persuading them of the truth of the Christian doctrine, may suggest that there were those of the synagogue who believed unto eternal life. However, apparently a majority closed their minds, hardened their hearts, and set themselves in active opposition against Christianity. Thus prejudiced they became active propagandists against the Christian mission. Here at Ephesus, as always, the Word of God was "to the one a savor from death unto death; to the other a savor from life unto life" (II Cor. 2:16). The twelve initial subjects of Paul's Ephesian ministry (vss. 1b–7) affectionately received his message and became partakers of the Holy Spirit, but these latter propagandists were hardened by their unbelief and rejection of the same truth. Thus they not only brought condemnation upon themselves but became the active agents of Satan among the multitude, perhaps both those within and outside the synagogue, prejudicing their minds against the Christian **Way** (cf. Acts 17:5).

D. Paul Ministers in the School of Tyrannus (19:9b–20)

He departed from them, and separated the disciples, reasoning daily in the school of Tyrannus (vs. 9b).

In the face of Jewish opposition in the synagogue, there was nothing left for Paul to do, in fairness to the believers, but to separate them from the unbelieving Jews and launch his Christian mission quite independent of the synagogue. When existing sources of spiritual truth and life are deliberately and determinately clogged, new fountains of

[41] Abbott-Smith, *op. cit.,* p. 452. [42] *Ibid.,* p. 486. [43] *Op. cit.,* p. 242. [44] *Beginnings,* IV, 239.

spiritual life will break forth elsewhere. Paul said, "But the word of God is not bound" (II Tim. 2:9b). The many branches of Christianity have largely arisen as a result of the failure of the existing nominal church to express, or allow expression of, spiritual life. Jan Karel Van Baalen, in his book, *The Chaos of Cults*, goes so far as to suggest that the recrudescence of "Sects and cults [has represented] 'the unpaid bills of the [Christian] church.'"[m]

The school of Tyrannus to which Paul resorted for the continuance of his gospel ministry in Ephesus, was either rented or borrowed for his purposes at such hours as this philosopher did not require it for his lectures. It was a secular lecture hall with no other consecration than that given it by Paul's ministry there. Who Tyrannus was, what school of philosophy he represented, or how Paul happened to acquire the building we are not told. That this new and likely central location for Paul's ministry was a decided advantage over the synagogue appears evident from the fact that he no longer was identified with the Jews. Consequently, the Gentiles would experience a freedom to listen to his discussions, which they could not have had in the Jewish synagogue. This appears evident from Luke's words, **reasoning daily in the school of Tyrannus** (vs. 9b), and again, **this continued for the space of two years; so that all they that dwelt in Asia heard the word of the Lord, both Jews and Greeks** (vs. 10). Thus Paul's long entertained desire, hitherto prevented (Acts 16:6), to evangelize the peoples of Proconsular Asia in western Asia Minor, was now fulfilled.

Concerning Paul's hours of discussion in Tyrannus' lecture hall, it may be observed that believers and others favorably impressed by his previous ministry in the synagogue accompanied him, as well as new people attracted to the truth. His messages and discussions were conducted in the hall at such time as Tyrannus did not require the building for his lectures. Indeed, the Western Text indicates that Paul used the building from 11 A.M. to 4 P.M. Tyrannus likely held his classes in the early morning. General public activities in the Ionian cities terminated at 11 A.M. Thus Paul probably spent the early morning hours in tent-making (cf. Acts 20:34), and then devoted the succeeding hours to his evangelistic ministry in the hall of Tyrannus.

Bruce[n] thinks Paul's unusual display of energy and personal sacrifice in preaching while the populace customarily slept may have so impressed the Ephesians as to have induced them to sacrifice their siesta to hear him preach.

Paul's **two years'** ministry in **the school of Tyrannus** is likely meant as an approximate period and may have been longer, which taken together with the **three months** (vs. 8) spent in the synagogue, made up the approximate three-year period spent at Ephesus (Acts 20:31). Luke's statement, **all they that dwelt in Asia heard the word of the Lord, both Jews and Greeks** (vs. 10), indicate the extent of Paul's evangelizing ministry during this period and accounts for the establishment of the several churches of Asia: namely. Ephesus, Smyrna, Pergamum, Thyatira, Sardis, Philadelphia, Laodicea, Colossae, Hierapolis, and Troas, the first seven of which are mentioned in Revelation 1:11. Nor is it to be supposed that Paul visited and evangelized all these locations personally, but rather that he directed the campaign from his Ephesian headquarters, which campaign was carried out in large part by his faithful helpers. Possibly these included the twelve earlier recipients of the Holy Spirit (vss. 5–7), who were likely the elders of the Ephesian church to whom Paul later gave his final charge at Miletus (Acts 20: 17 ff.).

The special miracles attributed to Paul in verses eleven and twelve are reminiscent of the people's faith in Peter's shadow at an earlier period (Acts 5:15), and they bear a definite resemblance to the healings attributed to the touching of Jesus' garments (Mark 5:25–34; 6:53–56).

It should be noted that there is a distinction between the **special miracles** which God wrought **by the hands of Paul** (vs. 11) and the statement **that unto the sick were carried away from his body handkerchiefs or aprons, and the diseases departed from them, and the evil spirits went out** (vs. 12).

In the first instance it would seem that the miracles were wrought by the power of God

[m] Van Baalen, *op. cit.*, p. 17. [n] Bruce, *op. cit.*, pp. 388, 389.

13 But certain also of the strolling Jews, exorcists, took upon them to name over them that had the evil spirits the name of the Lord Jesus, saying, I adjure you by Jesus whom Paul preacheth.

14 And there were seven sons of one Sceva, a Jew, a chief priest, who did this.

---

13 **Strolling** is *perierchomenon*, "going around," and so "itinerant" (RSV). **Exorcists is** a transliteration of the Greek *exorkistes*, literally "one who administers an oath." The word is found only here in the New Testament. Exorcism was usually performed by pronouncing a name. Josephus tells of a Jewish exorcist who cast out demons in the presence of Vespasian, using the name of Solomon.[45] Cadbury says: "The modern discoveries on papyrus of the actual books of ancient Greek magic show the influence, not only of intelligently used Old Testament passages but the mixing in, as of mystifying hocus pocus, of many untranslated Semitic words."[46] **I adjure you by Jesus**—Deissmann gives excerpts of the great Paris magical papyrus 574 (at the Bibliotheque Nationale). Lines 3019-3020 have this striking parallel: "I adjure you by the God of the Hebrews, Jesus."[47]

14 **Sceva** apparently advertised himself[48] as a **chief priest.** Because the high priest alone could enter the Holy of Holies and pronounce the Name, he would be considered as having unusual magical powers.

---

working directly in Paul through the imposition of his hands on the sick, afflicted, and demon-possessed. Such was the usual divine method in the Early Church. However, in the second instance, the faith of his Ephesian followers seems not unmixed with the magical concepts rife in Ephesus (vss. 18, 19). They conceived of the divine power transmitted from his person to his personal effects, especially his handkerchiefs and aprons, or "sweatrags being used for tying round his head and the aprons for tying round his waist,"[0] as he applied himself to his arduous task of tent-making. Magic has always associated personal or supernatural powers with the personal effects of those regarded as possessed of such powers, especially soiled or perspiration-soaked clothing. That even some of Paul's Ephesian disciples were not completely free from these magical concepts appears evident from verse eighteen. To recognize these magical concepts on the part of some of Paul's Ephesian followers at this early stage of their faith is neither to attribute such concepts to Paul or the Christian religion which he preached, nor is it to say that the healings or demon expulsions were occasioned by any power resident in the handkerchiefs or aprons. However, that these objects, coming as they did from the person of so spiritually animated and popularly acclaimed a person as Paul, should have served as an aid to the faith of both those who bore them and those to whom they were borne appears entirely likely. Nor does Luke state that Paul either ordered or approved the practice. That God may have wrought miracles of healing and demon expulsion in response to the faith of these believers, though not because of, nor through, the **handkerchiefs or aprons** borne by them, is indeed credible, and such Luke doubtless means.

The incident of the attempted exorcism of the demons from the possessed man by the sons of Sceva, in verses thirteen through seventeen, is the most remarkable of its kind in the Bible. **And there were seven sons of one Sceva, a Jew, a chief priest, who did this** (vs. 14). It appears from verse thirteen that the practice of demon exorcism by a certain class of vagabond Jews who may have capitalized on this art for monetary gain was not uncommon nor limited to the sons of Sceva. Such an individual was Bar-Jesus or Elymas (Acts 13:6, 8) whom Paul earlier rebuked; and, while his nationality is not given, such may Simon the sorcerer (Acts 8:9–13) have been. Such conditions are indeed an illuminating though sad commentary on the degenerate state of Judaism in the first Christian century. Magic was the means employed in this art of demon exorcism. Correct formulae employing the

[45] *Ant.* VII, 2, 5.
[46] *The Book of Acts in History*, p. 95.
[47] *Light from the Ancient East*, p. 252.
[48] Cf. *Beginnings*, IV, 241; Bruce, *Acts*, p. 358.

[0] *Ibid.*, p. 389.

15 And the evil spirit answered and said unto them, Jesus I know, and Paul I know; but who are ye?

16 And the man in whom the evil spirit was leaped on them, and mastered both of them, and prevailed against them, so that they fled out of that house naked and wounded.

---

15 The first **know** is *ginōskō*, the second, *epistamai*. Page comments: "It is easy, but unsafe, to say that *ginōskō* = 'acknowledge,' i.e. as recognizing His power, whereas *epistamai* = 'know' merely expresses acquaintance with a fact." [49] The variation seems strange, and the reason for it is not clear. Gloag translates it: "Jesus I know, and with Paul I am acquainted." [50] In the closing question **ye** *(hymeis)* is put first for contemptuous emphasis: "But *you*, who are you?"

16 **Leaped on** is the verb *ephallomai*, found only here in the New Testament. It is easy to understand why the Western text omits *amphoterōn*, **both** (cf. KJV), since it appears to conflict with "seven" (vs. 14). But in late Byzantine Greek this word is equivalent to "all." Moulton and Milligan cite a London papyrus dated A D. 167 in which five men are named and then referred to as *amphoteroi*, and a fourth-century papyrus where the same is done with four men.[51] So it is no longer necessary to seek a further solution for this problem.

---

sacred name of Jehovah were recited over the possessed, in the effort to deliver him of his demon.

Whether a **chief priest** (vs. 14), as Luke suggests, or an impostor as may be allowed, this man had seven sons who were all vagabond magicians who practiced, or pretended to practice, demon exorcism. Beholding the miracles wrought by God through Paul (vss. 11, 12) in the use of Christ's name, these lewd fellows conceived the prospect of material gain through the use of this divine name and so attempted its employment on a demoniac (vs. 15).

Immediately the accosted demon recognized and acknowledged the name of Christ (Mark 1:23, 24), as demons must ever do, and admitted acquaintance with Paul, whose activities were well known in Ephesus, but disclaimed the authority of Sceva's sons over him: **Jesus I know, and Paul I know; but who are ye**? (vs. 15b). Whatever other magical formulae they may have known and successfully used, they certainly fouled on this one; for they were overcome by the enraged demon, stripped of their garments, and severely beaten.

Luke suggests in verse seventeen that this incident served to reveal the superior power of Paul's use of the Name of Christ to that of the Jewish exorcists, and thus Christ's name was magnified in the minds of the populace. Again God made the wrath of man to praise Him. Wesley remarks:

> Several of the Jews about this time pretended to a power of casting out devils, particularly by certain arts or charms, supposed to be derived from Solomon. *Undertook to name*—Vain undertaking! Satan laughs at all those who attempt to expel him either out of the bodies or the souls of men but by divine faith. All the light of reason is nothing to the craft and strength of that subtle spirit. His craft cannot be known but by the Spirit of God; nor can his strength be conquered but by the power of faith.[p]

Evidence seems to indicate that this class of vagabond Jewish exorcists commonly employed or professed to employ the Ineffable Name of the Jehovah of the Jews in magical practices, and this the more effectively with the Gentiles because of the Jews' supposed secret knowledge of this name.

That it was the man possessed by this evil spirit, enraged and animated by the demon, and not the disembodied demon himself, **who leaped upon them and mastered both of them, and prevailed against them, so that they fled out of the house naked and wounded** (vs. 16), is made clear by Luke. Further, it is in question whether Sceva's seven sons who were engaged in this nefarious business all participated in this incident, or whether only two of them were involved (see Exegesis).

The resultant effects of the foregoing incident upon the Ephesians is suggested by Luke's statement: **Many also of them that had believed came, confessing, and declaring their deeds** (vs. 18) . . . **So mightily grew the word of the Lord and prevailed** (vs. 20).

[49] *Op. cit.*, p. 206. [50] *Op. cit.*, p. 204. [51] VGT, p. 28.

[p] Wesley, *op. cit.*, p. 472, n. 13.

17 And this became known to all, both Jews and Greeks, that dwelt at Ephesus; and fear fell upon them all, and the name of the Lord Jesus was magnified.
18 Many also of them that had believed came, confessing, and declaring their deeds.
19 And not a few of them that practised magical arts brought their books together and burned them in the sight of all; and they counted the price of them, and found it fifty thousand pieces of silver.

---

18 Of *praxeis*, **deeds**, Lake and Cadbury say: "The noun also has the technical meaning of 'magic spell,' so that the probable meaning here is that the former exorcists now disclosed the secret formulae they had used." [52]

19 *Perierga*, **magical arts,** is used elsewhere in the New Testament only in I Timothy 5:13 ("busybodies"). But it is also "a technical term for magic." [53] **Books** is *biblous*, the Greek word for papyrus.[54] These would be parchment or papyrus scrolls with magical charms written on them. Deissmann gives numerous examples of these.[55] Moulton and Milligan assert that *biblos* always has "the connotation of sacredness and veneration."[56] Gloag notes that the term "Ephesian Letters" was commonly used for magical charms or amulets worn by the Ephesians and widely prescribed by the magicians of that day.[57] So this scene is especially appropriate to Ephesus.

Counted is the verb *sympsēphizō*, found only here in the New Testament. It means "reckon together, count up." *Pieces of* **silver** is *argyriou*. These are generally assumed to be *drachmai*, worth about twenty cents apiece. So the total "value" (RSV) was about $10,000. It is apparent that these magical papyri brought fantastic prices for that day.

The evident contrast, between the effectiveness of Paul's use of the name of Jesus in benevolent miraculous deeds and the utter failure and humiliating defeat of these Jewish extortionists in their attempt to practice demon exorcism by the same divine name, was so rapidly and widely heralded throughout the city that **this became known to all, both Jews and Greeks, that dwelt at Ephesus** (vs. 17a). The result was a reverential fear of God and a heightened respect for His servant Paul, in the minds of the populace. Thus it appears from Luke's words, **and the name of the Lord Jesus was magnified** (vs. 17b), that this whole incident became "the talk of the town" and consequently focused general interest on Paul and his preaching in the hall of Tyrannus, with the result that a powerful spiritual awakening occurred in Ephesus. Wesley remarks: "*And the name of the Lord Jesus was magnified*—So that even the malice of the devil wrought for the furtherance of the gospel." [q]

Luke's statement, **Many also of them that believed came, confessing, and declaring their deeds** (vs. 18), seems clearly to indicate that, to this juncture, many in Ephesus had come under the influence of the Gospel and had partially yielded to its claims, who had not fully grasped the spiritual significance of the Christian Gospel nor purified themselves from their pagan practices. Dummelow supports this conclusion as follows:

> The incident led to a reformation within the church. Many converts had continued their magical practices after their baptism. They now came forward and publicly renounced them, proving their sincerity by burning their books of spells.[r]

Wesley's remarks on this passage are pertinent:

> *Many came, confessing*—Of their own accord. *And openly declaring their deeds*—The efficacy of God's word, penetrating the inmost recesses of their soul, wrought that free and open confession to which perhaps even torments would not have compelled them.[s]

So will the genuinely revealed presence of God ever produce conviction for sin and wrongdoing and elicit frank and open confession, with the resultant forsaking of that which is unlike and opposed to God (cf. John 16:7-11; Acts 26:18; I Thess. 1:9, 10; Ps. 51:1-3). Spiritual manifestation always awakens, illumines, and inspires moral ideals. Without divine illumination, man will always grope in moral darkness and error.

[52] *Beginnings*, IV, 242. [53] Deissmann, *Bible Studies*, p. 323, n. 5. [54] VGT, p. 111.
[55] *Light from the Ancient East*, pp. 250-260, 304-309. [56] VGT, p. 111. [57] *Op. cit.*, II, 206.

[q] Wesley, *op. cit.*, p. 472, n. 17. [r] Dummelow, *op. cit.*, p. 845. [s] Wesley, *op. cit.*, p. 472, n. 18.

Their **confessing, and declaring their deeds** (vs. 18), or divulging the secrets and forces of their magical spells, had the effect of rendering them valueless, both to the users and to the people, as all confidence in them would now be destroyed. So must the works of Satan ever be treated if genuine righteousness is to be established. Whenever the secrets of Satan are known, his power is broken.

Luke takes pains to specify the nature of the pagan practices at Ephesus. Topping the list was the practice of magical arts (vs. 19). It appears that the cult of magic throve in the city of Ephesus among the Jews as well as Gentiles (Acts 19:19 f.). The books of magic which were sold about the country were formulas in the form of amulets or inscriptions for doorposts, garden gates, and such like. Many of the magical papyri still survive. Mould states that "The emperor cult was there,"[t] and there is Scriptural reference to the Ephesian high priests of this cult, which priests are known as Asiarchs (Acts 19:31). However, Artemis or Diana was the most important cult at Ephesus.

How like the half-Mohammedan, half-pagan practices of so many peoples influenced by Mohammedanism in Africa today. Sebbies (portions of Koranic writings encased in leather), worn as charms about the neck, around the forehead and forearms or the ankles, or suspended by cords under the clothing about the waist, are common in these lands.

Luke's account indicates that these magical practices were of such great reputation as to enhance the value of the "books." Wesley[u] sees in the bringing together of these books an evidence of common consent on the part of those who became Christians. Certainly when they **brought their books together and burned them in the sight of all** (vs. 19), they were thoroughly convinced of the truth of Christianity and of the unlawfulness of their former practices. By thus publicly (**in the sight of all**) burning these things, they witnessed to their valuelessness, cleared themselves of any possible temptation to return to their former use, and declared to the Ephesian populace their change of religious loyalties from Satan to Christ. He who does not burn his bridges behind him when he crosses the great gulf between "the kingdom of Satan" and "the Kingdom of God" may find future occasion to return over those bridges to his former loyalties.

The value of these works, stated by Luke to be **fifty thousand pieces of silver** (vs. 19b), is somewhat in dispute among scholars (see the exegetical note on this passage).

Here again, Luke's observation indicates the beneficent effects of a great spiritual victory: **So mightily grew the word of the Lord and prevailed** (vs. 20). This statement appears to suggest both the geographic expansion of Christianity in western Asia Minor and the intensification of its power and efficacy, both in Ephesus and wherever it spread.

Paul's ministry at Ephesus was now nearly completed. Though accompanied by many personal hazards and even possible sufferings, the fruits of his enterprise for Christ at Ephesus were rewarding. Whether Paul was actually imprisoned at Ephesus is uncertain. Luke is silent concerning the matter. In the second Corinthian letter, probably written from Philippi shortly after Paul left Ephesus, he alludes to imprisonments and sufferings, some of which may have occurred at Ephesus (II Cor. 11:23–27). Bruce[v] notes that Deissmann supports this position, as also do H. Lisco, W. Michaelis, G. S. Duncan, and M. Dibelius, while it is opposed by T. W. Manson.

During his three (approximately 2½) years at Ephesus, Paul had thoroughly evangelized that city and western Asia Minor. Having securely planted an indigenous church in those parts, he now felt confident in leaving these young converts to carry on their Christian witness under the superintendency of the Holy Spirit. The Apostle's soul was restless with a passion for the evangelization of regions yet unreached. Says Wesley:

> "Paul sought not to rest, but pressed on as if he had yet done nothing. He is already possessed of Ephesus and Asia. He purposes for Macedonia and Achaia. He has his eye upon Jerusalem; then upon Rome; afterward on Spain (Rom. XV, 24). No Caesar, no Alexander the Great, no other hero, comes up to the magnanimity of this little Benjamite. Faith, and love to God and man, had enlarged his heart, even as the sand of the sea."[w]

[t] Mould, *op. cit.*, p. 575.
[u] Wesley, *op. cit.*, p. 473, n. 19.
[v] Bruce, *op. cit.*, p. 393, n. 29.
[w] Wesley, *op. cit.*, p. 473, n. 21.

20 So mightily grew the word of the Lord and prevailed.
21 Now after these things were ended, Paul purposed in the spirit, when he had passed through Macedonia and Achaia, to go to Jerusalem, saying, After I have been there, I must also see Rome.

---

20 This is the fifth brief report of progress (cf. 6:7; 9:31; 12:24; 16:5; 28:31). *Kata kratos*, **mightily,** was "a frequent military term." [58]

21 This verse summarizes the remainder of Acts, alluding to the visit to Jerusalem and the journey to Rome. It is the first record of Paul's mentioning **Rome** (cf. Rom. 1:13; 15:22–29).

Does **in the spirit** mean "in the Spirit" (RSV)? Lake and Cadbury think so and adopt the translation "was inspired to purpose." [59] Bruce thinks this interpretation is "the more likely." [60] But Hackett prefers "placed in his mind" [61] and Rackham "set in his spirit." [62] However the latter goes on to say: "In the case of the Christian we need not be careful to distinguish, for his spirit is governed by the Spirit of God which dwells in him." [63] The same ambiguity is found in 18:25 and 20:22.

Dielthōn, **when he had passed through,** is another clear example of this verb as a missionary word (cf. 13:6).

Whether or not Paul made a hurried trip to Corinth at this time is a matter of dispute. Knowling thinks not,[64] as does also Farrar.[65] Rackham deems it "possible." [66]

E. Paul Purposes to Visit Jerusalem (19:21a)

Paul purposed in the spirit . . . to go to Jerusalem (vs. 21a).

While Spain became what Bruce calls Paul's "new Macedonia," [x] yet the Apostle had other more immediate objectives en route. Among these were a revisitation of Macedonia and Achaia, a final visit to Jerusalem, and afterward a voyage to Rome where he prayed and hoped to realize spiritual fruit (cf. Rom. 1:8–15; 15:20, 24, 28). Though Luke but once hints at Paul's purpose in visiting Jerusalem (Acts 24:17), it becomes clear that his final visit to Macedonia and Achaia has as its objective the taking of a collection from the European churches, which he purposed to deliver to the Jerusalem church in person (cf. I Cor. 16:1–5; II Cor. 8:1–15; Rom. 15:25–28).

Paul's expressed intention of personally conveying the collection from the younger Gentile churches to the mother Jewish-Christian church at Jerusalem had a threefold significance. *First*, it indicated the continued poverty of the Jerusalem church, which was evidenced soon after Pentecost and to which the Gentile Christians had ministered from the beginning (Acts 11:29, 30). It appears quite likely that, in addition to the disposal of their property and the pooling of the proceeds in the first communal venture at Jerusalem following Pentecost, many of these Judean Christian Jews had suffered heavy economic losses at the hands of their Jewish contrymen (cf. Heb. 10:32–34). (For further comment on the causes of Jewish–Christian poverty at Jerusalem, see note on Acts 2:44, 45.) *Second*, it reflectep the Christian gratitude and generosity of these Gentile Christians for their Jewish–Christian brethren from whom they had received the Gospel. *Third*, it evidenced Paul's purpose to maintain the spirit of unity and good will between the Jewish and Gentile elements of the Christian Church. Such was the purpose of the General Church Council of Acts 15, and such continued to be Paul's purpose. He, who had so frequently been accused of abrogating the Jewish Law in his Gentile ministry, was careful to allay Jewish–Christian suspicion by demonstrating the charity of the Gentiles toward the Jews.

F. Paul Plans to Visit Rome (19:21b, 22)

I must also see Rome, (vs. 21b).

Ramsay speaks of Paul's "clear conception

---

[58] Page, *op. cit.*, p. 207. [59] *Beginnings*, IV, 244. [60] *Acts*, p. 361.
[61] *Op. cit.*, p. 223. [62] *Op. cit.*, p. 361. [63] *Ibid.* [64] EGT, II, 410.
[65] F. W. Farrar, *The Life and Work of St. Paul* (New York: E. P. Dutton and Co., 1896), pp. 383 f; *Messages of the Books* (New York: Macmillan Co., 1927), p. 211, n. 1.
[66] *Op. cit.*, p. 359.

[x] Bruce, *op. cit.*, p. 394.

22 And having sent into Macedonia two of them that ministered unto him, Timothy and Erastus, he himself stayed in Asia for a while.

23 And about that time there arose no small stir concerning the Way.

24 For a certain man named Demetrius, a silversmith, who made silver shrines of Diana, brought no little business unto the craftsmen;

---

22 **Timothy** had been sent to Corinth (cf. I Cor. 4:17; 16:10). Whether this verse refers to that visit is not certain. Rackham thinks so.[67] Bruce says "probably not."[68] There is no way of deciding the question.

Erastus may or may not be the same one mentioned in Romans 16:23. Again Rackham thinks so.[69] Knowling says the identification is "difficult,"[70] and Bruce that it "is not very likely."[71]

The verb *epechō* **(stayed)** is used in the New Testament only by Luke (three times) and Paul (twice). Literally meaning "hold upon," it has here alone the sense of "stay" or "wait." Moulton and Milligan cite this use in the papyri.[72]

23 *Tarachos*, **stir**, occurs elsewhere in the New Testament only in 12:18.

24 *Argyrokopos*, **silversmith**, occurs only here in the New Testament. It comes from *argyros*, "silver," and *koptō*, "beat." **Shrines** is *naous*, which usually refers to the inner part, or "sanctuary," of the temple. Miniature temples in terra cotta and marble have been found in considerable number near Ephesus.[73] But so far no examples of silver shrines have been discovered. Knowling thinks this was because they were melted down to use the silver.[74] Lake and Cadbury doubt that such were ever made and conclude that the reference here is to silver statuettes of Artemis, which were common. But Knowling's explanation is probably better.

---

of a far-reaching plan"[y] as revealed in this twenty-first verse. Paul's association with Aquila and Priscilla at Corinth, and later at Ephesus, afforded ample opportunity for them to inspire the mind and soul of the Apostle with the challenges to Christianity which that great capital and metropolis, Rome, presently afforded. Only recently had Aquila and Priscilla come from Rome (Acts 18:2), and erelong they evidently returned there (Rom. 16:3). As "all roads led to Rome," so Paul regarded this great capital city as the hub of the ancient world, out from which the Gospel would radiate to all parts of the empire (Rom. 1:8). Indeed, from Rome he purposed to personally convey the Gospel to Spain in the west. Says Ramsay:

> Such an intention implies in the plainest way an idea already existent in Paul's mind of Christianity as the religion of the Roman Empire. Spain was by far the most thoroughly romanized district of the Empire, as was marked soon after by the act of Vespasian in 75, when he made the Latin status universal in Spain. From the centre of the Roman world Paul would go on to the chief seat of Roman civilization in the West, and would thus complete a first survey, the intervals of which should be filled up by assistants, such as Timothy, Titus, etc.[z]

Whether Paul ever reached Spain we cannot be certain. However, Luke's chief interest was with Rome as the terminus of his history, and from henceforth his narrative points to that great capital.

IV. THE APOSTLE'S MALTREATMENT AT EPHESUS

(19:23–41)

Whether Paul personally made a journey to Corinth during his stay at Ephesus, or whether that journey (II Cor. 12:14; 13:1) was made from Troas after his departure from Ephesus, is not clear. In any event before he finally departed from Ephesus, he met with an attack of violent opposition led by one Demetrius, a silversmith.

---

[67] *Op. cit.*, p. 362. [68] *Acts*, p. 361. [69] *Op. cit.*, p. 362.
[70] EGT, II, 410. [71] *Acts*, p. 362.
[72] VGT, p. 232. Paul stayed to take advantage of the great crowds which gathered for the annual Festival of Artemis in May, just before Pentecost (cf. I Cor. 16:8, 9), according to William Furneaux, *The Acts of the Apostles* (Oxford: Clarendon Press, 1912), p. 315.
[73] EGT, II, 411. [74] *Ibid.*

[y] W. M. Ramsay, *St. Paul the Traveller and the Roman Citizen* (Grand Rapids: Baker Book House, rep. 1949), p. 274.
[z] *Ibid* p. 255.

25 whom he gathered together, with the workmen of like occupation, and said, Sirs, ye know that by this business we have our wealth.

26 And ye see and hear, that not alone at Ephesus, but almost throughout all Asia, this Paul hath persuaded and turned away much people, saying that they are no gods, that are made with hands:

Business is *ergasia*, which is used by Luke five out of its six occurrences in the New Testament (cf. Eph. 4:19). Moulton and Milligan cite abundant support in the papyri for the meaning "business" or "trade." [75] It may be doubted whether "gain" (KJV) is a justifiable translation,[76] even though it is found in the American Standard Version in 16:16, 19. **Craftsmen** is *technitais* (cf. technicians).

25 **Gathered together** is the verb *synathroizō*, found only here and in 12:12. **Business** is *ergasia* (cf. vs. 24). *Euporia*, **wealth,** occurs only here in the New Testament. It comes from *euporos*, "well provided for."

26 The genitives *Ephesou* and *pasēs* probably are dependent on *ochlon*, **people.** Ramsay first took **Asia** in its narrowest sense of the cities along the coast.[77] But later he broadened this to include the province of Asia.[78]

A. The Cause of the Opposition (19:23–27)

There arose no small stir concerning the Way . . . this Paul hath persuaded and turned away much people, (vss. 23, 26).

Evidently the fierce opposition which arose against Paul at Ephesus had a twofold basis. First, the Christian **Way** had undermined confidence in the pagan nature worship of Artemis, the great goddess of the Ephesians. (For a description of this influential pagan goddess and her cult, see the note on Acts 19:1a.)

Luke's designation of Christianity as a **Way** occurs six times in the Acts record (cf. 9:2; 19:9; 19:23; 22:4; 24:14; 24:22). The word is clearly designed to indicate the progressive force of the new religion. The author of the Hebrew letter caught the significance of this **Way** and designated it "a new and living Way" (Heb. 10:20a). Thus Christian grace became a spiritual and moral escalator, in contrast with the laborious ladder of Jewish legalism (cf. Rom. 1:16; 8:11; Col. 1:27). Here at Ephesus, as at Thessalonica, these people of the **Way** were turning the world upside down (cf. Acts 17:6). Paganism, however entrenched and influential, must ever crumble and fall before the irresistible impact of the "new and living **Way.**" How significant are Christ's words in this relation: "upon this rock I will build my church; and the gates of Hades shall not prevail against it" (Matt. 16:18b). Weymouth's translation reads: "and the might of Hades shall not triumph over it." Indeed the Apostle had the "keys of the kingdom of heaven" (Matt. 16:19a), and many were they whom he had loosed from their bondage to the pagan cult of Artemis.

In the second place, the Ephesian opposition to Paul arose from an economic motive, caused by the loss of business to the guild of silversmiths who appear to have been led by Demetrius. Bruce holds that they regarded their very craft as falling under the patronage of their goddess, Diana or Artemis, in whose honor many of their wares were made. Ramsay observes that "a certain Demetrius was a leading man in the associated trades, which made in various materials, terracotta, marble, and silver, small shrines (*naoi*) . . . representing the Goddess Artemis sitting in a niche or *naiskos*, with her lions beside her." [a] Bruce remarks:

> Among these wares were miniature silver niches, containing an image of the goddess, which her votaries bought to dedicate in her temple. The sale of these small shrines was a source of considerable profit to the silversmiths, and they were alarmed at the fall in the demand for them which the spread of Christianity was causing.[b]

How like the resentment of the owners of the demon-possessed slave girl at Philippi, when Paul cast the soothsaying demon out of her, with the resultant loss of their nefarious gain (Acts 16:19). And how like

[75] VGT, p. 252. [76] But contra. *Beginnings*, IV, 246—"'Profit' seems here the preferable meaning."
[77] *The Church in the Roman Empire*, p. 166. [78] *St. Paul the Traveller*, p. 278.

[a] *Ibid.*, pp. 277, 278. [b] Bruce, *op. cit.*, p. 398.

27 and not only is there danger that this our trade come into disrepute; but also that the temple of the great goddess Diana be made of no account, and that she should even be deposed from her magnificence whom all Asia and the world worshippeth.
28 And when they heard this they were filled with wrath, and cried out, saying, Great *is* Diana of the Ephesians.

---

27 *Kindyneuei*, **is there danger,** is found elsewhere in the New Testament only in verse 40, Luke 8:23, and I Corinthians 15:30. **Trade** is *meros*, which in the King James Version is translated "part" 24 of the 43 times it occurs in the New Testament. Page holds that here it means "business." [79] Moulton and Milligan cite an example from a third-century (A.D.) papyrus of the meaning "branch or line of business." [80] *Apelegmon*, **disrepute,** has not been found elsewhere in Greek literature. *Thea*, **goddess,** occurs only here in the New Testament. **Deposed** is the strong verb *kathaireō*, "pull down." *Megaleiotētos*, **magnificence,** was sometimes used as a ceremonial title,[81] like "Her Majesty" today.

Demetrius' assertion that **all Asia and the world** *(oikoumenē*, inhabited earth) worshiped Artemis of Ephesus has been fully supported.[82] Lily Ross Taylor writes: "Not only was the cult the most important of the province of Asia: it had a fame throughout the Greek and Roman world that probably no divinity except Apollo of Delphi could surpass." [83] Her temple was one of the seven wonders of the ancient world.

28 After *thymou*, **wrath,** the Western text adds: "They ran to the square" *(amphodon*, cf. Mark 11:4), which probably represents what took place. Ramsay prefers the Western reading "Great Artemis" rather than **Great is Diana** (Artemis), "a common formula of devotion and prayer." [84] But we cannot agree with him that this fits the scene more naturally, and it lacks sufficient manuscript support.

---

the unrestrained opposition of slave-holding Christian clergy and laymen to the activities of the ardent abolitionists of the first half of the nineteenth century in the United States.

Thus the offense of the Gospel to the combined religious devotion and economic gain of these Ephesian silversmiths produced a mob violence from which the Apostle narrowly escaped with his life. Religious fanaticism and greed for monetary gain are two of the greatest enemies to Christ and Christianity. Bruce[c] thinks that the special festival to Artemis which fell at the time of the spring equinox, at the beginning of the month of Artemision, may have coincided with the mob violence against Paul and the Gospel in A.D. 55. Religious patriotism and fanaticism frequently flourish at festivals, as witnesses the uncurbed fervor at the breaking of the Mohammedan fast of Ramadan.

B. The Nature of the Attack (19:28–34)

And the city was filled with the confusion, (vs. 29a).

Paul was no stranger to mob violence and plots laid against his life by enemies of the Gospel which he preached. Luke records ten such attacks in Acts. The *first* was waged by the Jews at Damascus following Paul's conversion (Acts 9:23–25); the *second* by the Grecian Jews at Jerusalem (Acts 9: 29–30); the *third* was instigated by the Jews at Antioch of Pisidia (Acts 13:50); the *fourth* was motivated by the Jews from Antioch and Iconium at Lystra, but executed by the pagan Lyconians (Acts 14:19); the *fifth* occurred at Philippi at the hands of the Philippian officials, who were influenced by the owners of the slave girl from whom Paul expelled the evil spirit (Acts 16:19–24); the *sixth* occurred at Thessalonica at the hands of the jealous Jews and the Gentile rabble (Acts 17:5–9); the *seventh*, at Corinth by the Jews before Gallio (Acts 18:12–17); the *eighth*, at Ephesus by the pagan craftsmen of Diana or Artemis (Acts 19:23–41); the *ninth*, in Greece after Paul left Ephesus (Acts 20:2, 3); and the *tenth* occurred at Jerusalem at the hands of the Jews, on the

[79] *Op. cit.*, p. 207. [80] VGT, p. 399. [81] *Ibid.*, p. 392.
[82] Cf. *Beginnings*, IV, 247—"The archaeological evidence alone . . . shows over thirty places where the reverence for Ephesian Artemis is attested."
[83] Lily Ross Taylor, "Artemis of Ephesus," *Beginnings*, V, 251. [84] *St. Paul the Traveller*, p. 279.

[c] *Ibid.*

29 And the city was filled with the confusion: and they rushed with one accord into the theatre, having seized Gaius and Aristarchus, men of Macedonia, Paul's companions in travel.
30 And when Paul was minded to enter in unto the people, the disciples suffered him not.
31 And certain also of the Asiarchs, being his friends, sent unto him and besought him not to adventure himself into the theatre.

---

29 *Synchyseōs*, **confusion,** is found only here in the New Testament. *Synekdēmous*, **companions in travel,** is found in the New Testament only here and in II Corinthians 8: 19.

30 **People** is the word *dēmos*, which first meant a district or country, then the common people, "especially *the people assembled*."[85] The word occurs again in verse 33 and elsewhere in the New Testament only in Acts 12:22; 17:5. It was "the regular term for the citizenbody of a Greek city-state."[86] But Lake and Cadbury think that here it is "unlikely to mean assembly."[87] Moulton and Milligan agree that in the New Testament "it suggests merely a rabble."[88]

31 **The Asiarchs** were "the chief of Asia" (KJV). Lily Ross Taylor writes: "The Asiarchs were the foremost men of the province of Asia, chosen from the wealthiest and the most aristocratic inhabitants of the province."[89] They held office for one year, and several were appointed each year.[90]

Adventure is literally "give" *(dounai)*. "Venture" (RSV) is rather more accurate today. This is the only passage in the New Testament (out of some 413 times) where *didōmi* carries this meaning. **Theatre** is directly from the Greek *theatron*, which occurs only here (vss. 29, 31) and in I Corinthians 4:9 (metaphorically, "spectacle"). It comes from *theaomai*, "to behold, look upon, contemplate, view."[91] But in Greek cities the theatre was also the meeting place of the citizens.[92]

---

occasion of Paul's last visit to that city (Acts 21:27–32; 23:9, 10, 12–14).

Demetrius, who as Ramsay phrases it, "must have had a good deal of capital sunk in his business"[d] summoned his fellow tradesmen to a meeting in the union hall where he inflamed their minds with propaganda against the Apostle. The Christian propaganda, he charged, devaluated the images and diverted the populace from the purchase of their crafts, as also from the worship of Artemis. Upon this, says Ramsay,

> The tradesmen were roused; they rushed forth into the street; a general scene of confusion arose, and a common impulse carried the excited crowd into the great theatre. The majority of the crowd were ignorant [of] what was the matter; they only knew from the shouts of the first rioters that the worship of Artemis was concerned.[e]

During the two-hour riot that followed they screamed their frenzied loyalty to the goddess, in the repetitious phrase, **Great is Diana of the Ephesians.** Ramsay significantly remarks: "In this scene we cannot mistake the tone of sarcasm and contempt, as Luke tells of this howling mob; they themselves thought they were performing their devotions, as they repeated the sacred name; but to Luke they were merely howling, not praying."[f]

Quite naturally the concourse rushed to the great theater (vs. 29). (For a description of the Ephesian theater, see note on Acts 19:1.) The rioters seized as hostages Gaius and Aristarchus of Macedonia (see Acts 20:4), Paul's fellow travelers. Bruce thinks, without sufficient reason it would seem, that Luke received his story of the Ephesian riot from one of these men.

Apparently Paul was absent when the riot began but appeared when he learned of the peril of his fellow Christians. His self-forgetfulness appears in his endeavor to enter the theater at the risk of his life (vss. 30, 31). Perhaps he sought to protect Gaius and Aristarchus, who had been seized by the mob (vs. 29), by assuming personal responsibility for the movement that had provoked the riot. In any event, the Christian disciples' regard and love for Paul was evidenced by their refusal to allow him to hazard his life in entering the theater (vs. 30).

Luke's reference to **certain . . . Asiarchs** (vs. 31) who were Paul's friends and who

[85] Abbott-Smith, *op. cit.*, p. 104. [86] Bruce, *Acts*, p. 365. [87] *Beginnings*, IV, 248.
[88] VGT, p. 144. [89] "The Asiarchs," *Beginnings*, V, 256. [90] *Ibid.*, p. 258.
[91] Abbott-Smith, *op. cit.*, p. 203. [92] *Beginnings*, IV, 248.

[d] Ramsay, *op. cit.*, p. 278. [e] *Ibid.* [f] *Ibid.*, p. 279.

32 Some therefore cried one thing, and some another: for the assembly was in confusion; and the more part knew not wherefore they were come together.

33 And they brought Alexander out of the multitude, the Jews putting him forward. And Alexander beckoned with the hand, and would have made a defence unto the people.

34 But when they perceived that he was a Jew, all with one voice about the space of two hours cried out, Great *is* Diana of the Ephesians.

---

32 **Assembly** is *ekklēsia*. The word occurs some 115 times in the New Testament. Only here (vss. 31, 39, 41) is it translated **assembly.** In all other instances it is rendered "church." In this chapter we see the original use of the term. Deissmann cites an inscription which shows that the assembly at Ephesus met in the theatre.[93]

33 **They brought** is *synebibasan* (see on 9:22; cf. also 16:10). In its three occurrences in Acts it appears to be used in three different senses, and its exact meaning here is not certain. The Septuagint meaning "instruct" barely fits here. Page calls it "a graphic word accurately describing the way in which a mob, when their attention had been directed to a man, would join in pushing him forward, 'thrust' or 'squeeze' him out." [94]

Kataseisas, **beckoned,** is found only in Acts (four times). **Made a defence** is *apologeisthai*, from which comes "apologize." But the original meaning of 'apology" was "defence."

34 **Cried out** is rendered "howling" by Lake and Cadbury.[95] The cry, **Great is Diana of the Ephesians,** is doubled in Vaticanus, thus emphasizing the repeated shouting of the mob.

---

sought to restrain him from entering the theater, is both interesting and instructive. On this question Ramsay remarks:

> The Asiarchs, or High Priests of Asia, were the heads of the imperial, political-religious organization of the province in the worship of "Rome and the Emperors"; and their friendly attitude is a proof both that the spirit of the imperial policy was not as yet hostile to the new teaching, and that the educated classes did not share the hostility of the superstitious vulgar to Paul.[g]

Ramsay thinks further that some of these **Asiarchs** may have been priests of Artemis, or other deities of the cities, and that evidently the Ephesian priests were not hostile to Paul. It is even possible that they may have regarded the Christian religion with favor as a cultural contribution to the religious electicism of the day, of which Artemis was the center in Asia. Viewed thus, it would appear that the monetary motive dominated the riot, rather than any sincere religious consideration.

Typical of mob violence, the greater part of those participating were totally ignorant of the real purpose of the riot (vs. 32). When emotion dethrones reason, purpose is lost in the fog of confusion.

That the riotous resentment was as strongly anti-Jewish as it was anti-Christian is clear from the fact that when they put forth Alexander to address the mob, he was forthwith rejected and the hysteria was intensified (vss. 33, 34).

Who this Alexander was and who put him forth to speak to the mob, we are not told. Wesley thinks he was a well-known Christian who was forcefully projected into the situation by the artificers and workmen and pushed on by the Jews as a religious scapegoat.[h] However, Bruce[i] holds that Alexander was put forth by the Jews to make clear to the rioters that they were no part of the Christian community responsible for the resentment created. Bruce and Dummelow[j] take the same position. Whether this Alexander is identical with "Alexander the coppersmith" (II Tim. 4:14), or whether he is the same as Alexander the apostate (I Tim. 1:20), is not known for certain. However, both of the latter characterizations appear to fit a Jew such as the Ephesian Alexander, who may have professed faith in Christ and subsequently apostatized to become a bitter enemy of the Christian cause.

[93] *Light from the Ancient East*, pp. 121 f.
[94] Page, *op. cit.*, p. 209. See full discussion in EGT, II, 415 f.
[95] *Beginnings*, IV, 249.

[g] *Ibid.*, p. 281.
[h] Wesley, *op. cit.*, p. 474, n. 33.
[i] Bruce, *op. cit.*, pp. 400, 401.
[j] Dummelow,. *op cit.*, p. 845.

35 And when the town clerk had quieted the multitude, he saith, Ye men of Ephesus, what man is there who knoweth not that the city of the Ephesians is temple-keeper of the great Diana, and of the *image* which fell down from Jupiter?

36 Seeing then that these things cannot be gainsaid, ye ought to be quiet, and to do nothing rash.

---

35 *Grammateus*, **town clerk,** occurs 67 times in the New Testament and aside from this passage is always translated "scribe." Moulton and Milligan write: "The importance of the office at Ephesus . . . is now abundantly confirmed by the inscriptions." [96] **Quieted** is the verb *katastellō*, which in the New Testament is found only here and in verse 36. It means "keep down, restrain." But the usage here is found in II Maccabees (4:31) and Josephus.[97]

Neōkoros, **temple-keeper,** is found only here in the New Testament. Originally applied to individuals, and still used in Greece for the caretaker of an Orthodox church or Jewish synagogue,[98] it later became an honorific title for cities. A coin of A.D. 65, ten years after Paul was there, designates Ephesus as *neōkoros*.[99]

Of the image which fell down from Jupiter is just two words in the Greek—*tou diopetous. Diopetēs*, found only here in the New Testament, means "fallen from the sky" *(dios, piptō)*. There is no reference in the Greek to either **image** or **Jupiter,** which are carried over from the King James Version. The Revised Standard Version gives a correct interpretative translation: "of the sacred stone that fell from the sky." Actually it was probably a meteorite, rather than a man-made image. Although no other ancient writer records this tradition about Artemis of Ephesus, Euripides states that such belief was held concerning Artemis of Tauris.[100]

With regard to the cult of Artemis, Knowling makes this significant observation: "The worship of Diana of the Ephesians was entirely Asian and not Greek, although the Greek colonists attempted to establish an identification with their own Artemis on account of certain analogies between them." [101]

36 *Anantirētōn*, **cannot be gainsaid,** occurs only here in the New Testament. It means "not to be contradicted, undeniable," [102] or "beyond possibility of dispute." [103] *Propetes*, **rash,** occurs only here and in II Timothy 3:4. Literally it means "falling forward or headlong." Metaphorically, as here, it may be translated "reckless."

C. The Arrest of the Attack (35–41)

And when the town clerk had quieted the multitude . . . he dismissed the assembly, (vss. 35a, 41b).

The **town clerk** or secretary of the city, who published the civic assembly decrees, was greatly disturbed by the disorderly conduct of the Ephesians. Bruce designates him "the most important Ephesian official . . . [who] acted as liaison officer between the civil administration and the Roman provincial administration, whose headquarters were also in Ephesus."[k] As such he was responsible to the provincial administration for the conduct of civic affairs and thus was liable for the disorders of the day.

The town-clerk's address to the people was both shrewd and effective. He first appealed to their common sense by citing the universal recognition of Ephesus as the **temple-keeper of the great Diana, and of the image which fell down from Jupiter** (vs. 35b). In the light of such recognition it was folly, he reasoned, for them to madly acclaim that which was taken for granted. Further, this officer seems to imply, Diana will stand or fall on her own merit (vs. 36). He then proceeded to exonerate the accused Christians by citing their unimpeachable character and conduct at Ephesus. Next he indited Demetrius and the craftsmen for their illegal procedures against the Christians. They should have presented their case to the regular court of the proconsul.

If their complaints were such as not to require the decisions of the proconsul, then the town-clerk advised them that the regular meetings of the civic assemblies were open

[96] VGT, p. 132. [97] *Ant.* XX, 8, 8; *War*, II, 21, 5. [98] VGT, p. 425. [99] *Ibid.*
[100] *Beginnings*, IV, 250. See also Page, *op. cit.*, p. 209. [101] EGT, II, 417.
[102] Abbott-Smith, *op. cit.*, p. 32. [103] VGT, p. 36 (in an inscription of about 100 B.C.).

[k] Bruce, *op. cit.*, p. 401.

37 For ye have brought *hither* these men, who are neither robbers of temples nor blasphemers of our goddess.

38 If therefore Demetrius, and the craftsmen that are with him, have a matter against any man, the courts are open, and there are proconsuls: let them accuse one another.

39 But if ye seek anything about other matters, it shall be settled in the regular assembly.

40 For indeed we are in danger to be accused concerning this day's riot, there being no cause *for it*: and as touching it we shall not be able to give account of this concourse.

---

37 **Robbers of temples** (KJV, "robbers of churches") is *hierosylous*, found only here in the New Testament. The corresponding verb, *hierosylēo*, likewise occurs only once (Rom. 2:22). It is from *hieron*, "temple," and *sylaō*, "plunder." So the translation above is literally correct. But Lake and Cadbury say that the term "came to mean 'sacrilege' as being the real crime involved in robbing a temple." [104] So they translate the adjective "sacrilegious" (cf. RSV). Josephus quotes the Egyptian historian Manetho as declaring that the Jews "had been guilty of sacrilege [*hierosylia*] and destroyed the images of the gods." [105] He also quotes Moses as telling the Israelites before they crossed the Jordan: "Let no one blaspheme those gods which other cities esteem such; nor may one steal what belongs to strange temples, nor take away the gifts that are dedicated to any god." [106] It is obvious that these two accusations, of blasphemy and temple-robbing, were leveled against the Jews.

The Greek for **goddess** here (contra. vs. 27) is the odd combination *tēn theon*. Bruce writes: "Magnesian inscriptions show that *hē theos* was the regular term for the great goddess of the city, while the other goddesses were *theai*." [107]

38 **The courts are open** (KJV, "the law is open") is *agoraioi agontai*. The former word occurs elsewhere in the New Testament only in 17:5 (see note there). While in the earlier passage it apparently means "lounging in the agora," here it has the good sense of "proper to the agora"; and so the phrase may be translated "court-days are kept." [108] Lake and Cadbury give numerous examples of this usage without an accompanying noun and suggest "sessions are held." [109]

Accuse is the verb *egkaleō*, which is used six times in Acts and once by Paul (Rom. 8:33). Literally meaning "call in," "demand," in the New Testament it has the technical sense of "bring a charge against" (cf. RSV). This usage is common in the papyri.[110]

39 **About other matters** is the adverb *peraiterō*, "beyond" (cf. RSV, "further"). It is found only here in the New Testament. **Regular assembly** is *ennomō ekklēsia*. The former word, occurring only here and in I Corinthians 9:21, is correctly translated "lawful" in the King James Version. Lake and Cadbury render it "legal."[111] Chrysostom says that the **regular assembly** met three times a month.[112]

40 **Riot** is the noun *stasis*, which literally means "standing" (from *histēmi*). But more commonly in the New Testament it signifies an insurrection (cf. Mark 15:7; Luke 23:19, 25; Acts 24:5). The whole phrase reads literally "accused of riot concerning this

---

to them. According to Chrysostom these assemblies met three times each month. By their riot and irregular assembly they had acted illegally and made both themselves and the city liable to punishment by Rome.

Withal, Luke reflects in his record of this incident the liberal attitude of Rome toward all religions and the consequent legal freedom and protection which Christianity enjoyed under the Roman Empire at that time. Says Ramsay concerning the town-clerk's address:

> His speech is a direct negation of the charges commonly brought against Christianity as flagrantly disrespectful in actions and in language to the established institutions of the State . . .
>
> This address is . . . entirely an *apologia* of the Christians . . . it is included by Luke in his work, not for its mere Ephesian connection, but as bearing on the universal question of the relation in which the church stood to the Empire . . . the basis for the Church's claim to freedom and toleration. [l]

[104] *Beginnings*, IV, 251. [105] *Against Apion*, I, 26. [106] *Ant.* IV, 8, 10. [107] *Acts*, p. 367.
[108] Abbott-Smith, *op. cit.*, p. 7. [109] *Beginnings*, IV, 251. [110] VGT, p. 179.
[111] *Beginnings*, IV, 252. [112] *Homilies*, XLII, 2.

[l] Ramsay, *op. cit.*, pp. 281, 282.

41 And when he had thus spoken, he dismissed the assembly.

---

day." **Concourse** is literally "a twisting together," and so "a gathering together." The noun *systrophē* is found only here and in 23:12. It is used in Polybius (IV, 34, 6) for a seditious meeting or mob [113] (cf. RSV, "commotion").

41 In using **assembly** *(ekklēsia)*, the secretary may have wished to classify the "concourse" as a regular meeting, to avoid getting into trouble with the proconsul for allowing an irregular gathering.[114]

[113] EGT, II, 419.

[114] *Ibid.*

CHAPTER XX

And after the uproar ceased, Paul having sent for the disciples and exhorted them, took leave of them, and departed to go into Macedonia.

EXEGESIS

1 A glance at the King James and Revised versions will show some marked differences of translation. **Having sent for** is *metapempsamenos*,[1] which occurs only in Acts (nine times). "Called unto him" (KJV) is *proskalesamenos*.[2] This verb is found thirty times in the New Testament, including ten times in Acts. *Parakalesas*,[3] **exhorted**, is omitted in the Textus Receptus and so in the King James Version. *Aspasamenos*, **took leave of**, is thus translated in the King James Version in 21:6, but here "embraced." Its most common meaning is "to welcome, greet, salute." [4] But it is used of a parting greeting also.

EXPOSITION

THE APOSTLE'S THIRD MISSIONARY JOURNEY (cont'd.)

VII. The Apostle's Final Mission to Macedonia and Achaia, Acts 20:1–5.
- A. Paul's Mission to Macedonia, vss. 1, 2a, 3b.
- B. Paul's Mission to Greece, vss. 2b, 3a.
- C. Paul's Companions in Travel, vss. 4, 5.

VIII. The Apostle's Ministry at Troas, Acts 20:6–12.
- A. The Message at Troas, vss. 6, 7, 11.
- B. The Miracle at Troas, vss. 8–10, 12.

IX. The Apostle's Meeting at Miletus, Acts 20:13–38.
- A. The Journey to Miletus, vss. 13–16.
- B. The Charge to the Ephesian Elders, vss. 17–35.
- C. The Farewell at Miletus, vss. 36–38.

VII. THE APOSTLE'S FINAL MISSION TO MACEDONIA AND ACHAIA (20:1–5)

It appears likely that the Ephesian riot of Acts 19 shortened Paul's stay there and accounted for an earlier visit to Europe than had been previously planned. In the first Corinthian letter (16:8), which he wrote from Ephesus near the close of his stay there, Paul expressed his intention of remaining in Ephesus until after Pentecost, which he did not do. Correspondence with the Corinthians previous to our first Corinthian letter seems to be indicated in I Corinthians 5:9 and 7:1. Among Paul's verbal informants concerning the Corinthians are mentioned Chloe (I Cor. 1:11) and Stephanas (I Cor. 16:15). The latter was accompanied by Fortunatus and Achaicus, the bearers of a special gift to Paul from the Corinthian church (I Cor. 16:17).

Benjamin Robinson[a] gives an interesting analysis of Paul's correspondence with the Corinthians, as that correspondence is found in our two Corinthian letters, though his analysis may not be acceptable to many conservative readers.

Apparently Paul had personally visited Corinth once during his stay at Ephesus (see II Cor. 12:14; 13:1). He had likely sent Timothy to Corinth from Ephesus twice in the interest of the church there (cf. Acts 19:22; I Cor. 4:17; and 16:10, 11). A crisis had arisen in the Corinthian church, while Paul was at Ephesus, which called forth a lively correspondence and communication between Paul and the Corinthians. Finally he discharged Titus to Corinth on a con-

[1] Aleph B E. [2] A D H L P. [3] Aleph A B E. [4] Abbott-Smith, *op. cit.*, p. 64.

[a] Robinson, *op. cit.*, p. 174.

2 And when he had gone through those parts, and had given them much exhortation, he came into Greece.
3 And when he had spent three months *there*, and a plot was laid against him by the Jews as he was about to set sail for Syria, he determined to return through Macedonia.

2 **When he had gone through** is *dielthōn*, which in Acts suggests a missionary journey (see on 13:6). **Had given them much exhortation** is *parakalesas* [cf. vs. 1] *autous logōi pollōi;* literally, "having exhorted them by much speech." *Hellas* (**Greece**) occurs only here in the New Testament. It is the popular term for Achaia. Luke preferred popular names, Paul Roman provincial names.[5]

3 The **three months** were probably in the winter, when sailing on the Mediterranean was impossible. *Epiboulē* (**plot**) is found only in Acts (four times). *Anagesthai*, **set sail,** is in the middle voice a technical term meaning "put to sea" (see on 13:13). **Syria** should be taken in its larger sense, including Palestine. Here it would mean Caesarea, the seaport of Jerusalem.

ciliatory mission (II Cor. 8:6, 16–18). Paul expected to meet him at Troas upon his return. However, likely because of the hazards of winter sailing, Titus was delayed. Thus Paul, because of his restless anxiety over the Corinthian crisis and his desire to complete the European mission and get on to Jerusalem, and from thence to Rome (Acts 19:21) without further delay, sailed from Troas to Philippi (II Cor. 2:12, 13). There appears to be some evidence that Paul may have suffered a severe illness at about this time, possibly while at Troas waiting for Titus or in Macedonia after having crossed over to Europe. This illness may have been the result of maltreatment at Ephesus (see II Cor. 4:7–5:10).

A. Paul's Mission to Macedonia (20:1, 2a, 3b)

And departed to go into Macedonia, (vs. 1b).

Paul had formerly planned to sail directly from Ephesus to Corinth (II Cor. 1:16), but the acuteness of the Corinthian situation disposed him rather to send Titus with a letter (II Cor. 7:6–8). Titus had previously visited Corinth in the interest of the collection (II Cor. 12:18). Failing to find his messenger Titus at Troas, Paul feared lest the Corinthians had rejected his appeal for the Jerusalem collection (II Cor. 2:13). Probably at Philippi (in February or early March A.D. 56)[b] he met Titus, who brought the good news from Corinth of their restored loyalty, which news revived the spirits of Paul (II Cor. 7:5, 6). Paul then proceeded to revisit the cities of Macedonia where he had established churches on his second missionary journey, giving them **much exortation.**

Chapters eight and nine of II Corinthians indicate that a chief reason for this European visit was the Jerusalem collection. These two chapters, which concern the collection, may have been written while Paul was in Macedonia and following the letter of reconciliation in II Corinthians 1:1–6:13. Paul's purpose to deliver this collection from the younger Gentile churches to the Jerusalem mother church may well reflect the Apostle's sacred regard for the decisions of the General Council of Acts 15 (cf. Gal. 2:10 and see note on Jerusalem Council, Acts 15).

En route from Macedonia to Achaia, Paul may have reached Illyricum (Rom. 15:19–23) as indeed there seems to be no other place in his travels into which this reference fits.[c]

B. Paul's Mission to Greece (20:2b, 3a)

He came into Greece, (vs. 2b).

Paul's purpose in visiting Greece, or Achaia, was twofold. *First*, he wished to revisit and edify the Corinthian church which had been so severely tried. *Second,* he desired to receive a collection for the Jerusalem church.

During his three-month stay at Corinth in the winter of A.D. 55–56 (cf. I Cor. 16:6), Paul may have resided in the home of his old friend and convert, Gaius (I Cor. 1:14), where he penned the letter to the Romans, which he evidently sent to Rome by Phoebe

[5] Bruce, *Acts*, p. 369.

[b] W. M. Ramsay, *St. Paul the Traveller and the Roman Citizen*, p. 390.
[c] *The Interpreter's Bible* (New York: Abingdon-Cokesbury Press, 1954), IX, 264.

4 And there accompanied him as far as Asia, Sopater of Beroea, *the son* of Pyrrhus; and of the Thessalonians, Aristarchus and Secundus; and Gaius of Derbe, and Timothy; and of Asia, Tychicus and Trophimus.

---

4 **Accompanied** is the verb *synepomai*, found only here in the New Testament. **As far as Asia** should probably be omitted, since it is missing in Vaticanus and Sinaiticus.[6] Knowling, however, favors retaining the words.[7]

Gaius of Derbe has often been identified with "Gaius . . . of Macedonia" (19:29),[8] but it is difficult to find an explanation that properly closes the wide gap between Derbe (in Asia Minor) and Macedonia. The Western text substitutes *Douberious* for *Derbaios*. Doberus was a Macedonian town.[9]

(Rom. 16:1, 2). Indeed, Gaius joined Paul in sending words of greetings to the Christians at Rome in that letter (Rom. 16:23; cf. I Cor. 1:14). The Roman letter is the maturest and fullest expression of Paul's religious philosophy that remains. But even here his missionary soul-passion for the unreached regions finds expression (Rom. 15:20–28).

At the close of his Corinthian ministry, Paul thought to sail to Syria and from thence travel to Jerusalem with the collection. However, upon discovery of a Jewish plot to kill him, perhaps aboard a pilgrim ship sailing with Jews to the Jerusalem Passover, he altered those plans and returned through Macedonia (vs. 3), from whence he sailed to Troas (vs. 6). The five days required for the return voyage, as against the earlier two-day voyage, was doubtless occasioned by the inclement weather of the season.

C. Paul's Companions in Travel (20:4, 5)

Luke reveals evident purpose in mentioning Paul's companions at this juncture. The collection was both Paul's principal mission to Europe and the occasion of his intended visit to Jerusalem. Slanderous insinuations of ulterior and even selfish personal motives in the taking of the collection were made by Paul's enemies. This disposed him to exercise scrupulous care in handling the money (II Cor. 8:18–21). His letter to the Corinthians indicates that he wished them to receive and handle the collection quite independent of himself, even to its conveyance to the Jerusalem church by a specially authorized representative of the Corinthian church (I Cor. 16:1–4). Paul intended only to head a delegation of representatives from the various Gentile churches bearing their respective offerings, with a view to closing breaches between the Jerusalem church and the Gentile Christians by this token of Christian charity, loyalty, and unity (cf. Acts 24:17 and Rom. 15:25–27).

Paul's companions representing Macedonia were: *first*, **Sopater of Beroea,** the son of Pyrrhus. Macgregor remarks:

> One Sosipater is mentioned in Rom. 16:21 along with Timothy and Lucius. If the two are identified and Lucius is assumed to be Luke, then . . . Romans and Acts agree that Timothy, Luke, and Sopater were all three with Paul at this point.[d]

Bruce likewise favors identification of Sopater with Sosipater of Rom. 16:21,[e] as does also Clarke.[f] Thus the earlier "nobility" of these, many of whom became Christians (Acts 17:10–12), is reflected in their church loyalty and financial support. *Second*, **Aristarchus and Secundus,** with the doubtful inclusion of Gaius, represented the church of Thessalonica (see exegetical note on Gaius, as also F. F. Bruce).[g] The liberality of the Macedonian and Achaian churches in this instance is highly commended by Paul (cf. 15:26 and II Cor. 8:1–5). Aristarchus is of special interest as Paul's companion in travel at Ephesus (Acts 19:29); his fellow-traveller to Rome (Acts 27:2); his fellow-laborer in Rome (Philemon 24); and his fellow-prisoner at Rome (Col. 4:10, 11). There appears to be no other New Testament reference to Secundus. *Third*, the Achaian, and especially Corinthian, collection which was likely under the charge of Titus, received Paul's special consideration (cf. Rom. 15:26; I Cor. 16:1, 2; II Cor. 8:6; 9:2).

---

[6] It is found in A D E J L P. [7] EGT, II, 422.
[8] Hackett (p. 231) favors identifying this Gaius with the one to whom III John was written.
[9] *Beginnings*, IV, 254.

[d] *Ibid.*, p. 265. [e] Bruce, *op. cit.*, p. 405. [f] Clarke, *op. cit.*, V, 850. [g] Bruce, *op. cit.*, p. 403, n. 5.

5 But these had gone before, and were waiting for us at Troas.

---

5 **Had gone before** is a translation of *proelthontes*, which is the reading of D and the minuscules. But the best manuscripts [10] favor *proselthontes*, "having come to." The Revised Standard Version gives a general rendering, "went on." Ramsay makes **these** refer only to the Asian delegates, Tychicus and Trophimus, and so has: "coming to meet us, awaited us in Troas." This brings out best the literal meaning of *proselthontes* and also eliminates the need for assuming that these men from Asia had first accompanied Paul to Greece and were now returning with him.

Fourth, if the **Gaius** here mentioned is identical with the Gaius of Acts 19:29, where he is designated a *Macedonian*, then he also represented those churches along with Aristarchus and Secundus. Clarke remarks: "Some suppose he was a *native* [of Macedonia], but descended from a family that came from Derbe; but as *Gaius*, or *Caius*, was a very common name, these might have been two distinct persons." [h] It would be a pleasing thought that this Gaius was Paul's Corinthian convert (I Cor. 1:14) and the gracious host of the Apostle while he abode in Corinth (Rom. 16:23), as well as the beloved elder to whom John addressed his third epistle (III John 1:1). If such were true, then Gaius together with Titus may have represented the Corinthian church with its offering, although Luke lists him with the Macedonian delegates. Such would solve the problem of Luke's apparent silence concerning a Corinthian representative. Otherwise, either Titus (II Cor. 8:6, 19) or Paul himself must have been authorized to bear the Corinthian collection. However, in the absence of sufficient evidence we cannot press the point. Ramsay suggests that Luke's apparent silence concerning Titus may be due to the fact that Titus was a close relative of Luke. Ramsay states:

> Thus it may very well have happened that Luke was a relative of one of the early Antiochian Christians; . . . Further, it is possible that this relationship gives the explanation of the omission of Titus from *Acts*, an omission which everyone finds it so difficult to understand. Perhaps Titus was the relative of Luke; and Eusebius found this statement in an old tradition, attached to II Cor. VIII, 18; XII, 18, where Titus and Luke (the latter not named by Paul, but identified by an early tradition) are associated as envoys to Corinth. Luke, as we may suppose, thought it right to omit his relative's name, as he did his own name from his history. [i]

In the *fifth* place, however the foregoing concerning Gaius may fall, we appear to be on safe ground in ascribing to Timothy representation of the Lycaonian churches. Timothy was Paul's convert at Lystra on his first missionary journey (I Tim. 1:1, 2) and became his travelling companion on his second missionary journey (Acts 16:1–3). To this Timothy Paul later wrote the two epistles that bear his name.

Sixth, other representatives of Asia were **Tychicus and Trophimus.** Tychicus is later found with Paul in Rome and is sent by the Apostle with the letter to Ephesus (Eph. 6: 21, 22; II Tim. 4:12). He subsequently bore the Colossian letter from Paul's Roman imprisonment to Colossae (Col. 4:7, 8). It appears that Paul later appointed him to supervise the church at Crete, in Titus' absence from the island (Titus 3:12). He was one of Paul's most intimate and beloved friends.

While Luke does not specifically mention an Ephesian representative as such, it appears reasonable from the prescence of Trophimus, "an Ephesian," with Paul at Jerusalem (Acts 21:29) that he was there to represent the church. Paul later left Trophimus ill at Miletus. Probably he travelled with the Apostle and may have been en route to his home in Ephesus (II Tim. 4:20).

Seventh, it appears most likely that Luke represented the Philippian church, as he rejoined Paul there and sailed with him from Macedonia to Troas. This is inferred from the author's use of the first person plural pronoun (vs. 6), indicating his identification with the Apostle. In fact, judging from the so-called "*We*" sections of Acts, Luke first joined Paul at Troas on his first missionary journey (Acts 16:10) and then dropped out of the picture upon Paul's departure from

[10] Aleph A B E H L P.

[h] Clarke, *loc. cit.*

[i] Ramsay, *op. cit.*, 390.

6 And we sailed away from Philippi after the days of unleavened bread, and came unto them to Troas in five days; where we tarried seven days.

7 And upon the first day of the week, when we were gathered together to break bread, Paul discoursed with them, intending to depart on the morrow; and prolonged his speech until midnight.

---

6 The verb *ekpleō* (**sailed away**) is found here for the third and last time in Acts (cf. 15:39, 18:18). **From Philippi** would actually be from Neapolis, as the former was some ten miles inland. **After the days of unleavened bread** suggests that Paul had observed the Passover at Philippi. The observance of Christian Easter came later.[11]

7 Rackham feels that **the first day of the week** began at sunset Saturday evening following the Jewish reckoning.[12] But Lake and Cadbury say: "It is hard to avoid the conclusion that the meeting in Troas was on Sunday, not Saturday evening"[13] (see also Exposition). **First** is literally "one" *(mia)*, but Hackett notes: "In the New Testament *one (heis)* stands generally for first *(prōtos)* in speaking of the days of the week."[14]

The King James Version has "the disciples" rather than **we**. But the latter is the reading of Aleph A B D E.

Does **break bread** refer to a common meal or to the Lord's Supper? Lake and Cadbury prefer the former.[15] Rackham holds that it was the Eucharist. He outlines the events of the night thus:

> We may conclude then that the Christians at Troas met after sunset and had their evening meal or *Agapē*, and this was prolonged to midnight. Then an interruption occurred, and afterwards S. Paul broke *the bread*, viz. of the Eucharist, and this service lasted till dawn.[16]

The italics in this quotation indicate Rackham's emphasis on *the bread* (vs. 11) as indicating the Lord's Supper.[17] (For a different view of the events see Exposition.)

Instead of **discoursed,** the King James Version has "preached." But this is probably too strong. "Talked" (RSV) is perhaps best. Bruce writes: "A conversation rather than an address is indicated."[18] *Dialegomai* means "to converse with."[19] It occurs in Acts ten out of thirteen times in the New Testament. The verb *exienai* (**depart**) is found only in Acts (four times). It means "to go forth."[20] **Prolonged** is *pareteinen*, found only here in the New Testament.

Philippi (Acts 16:40). Nor does he again appear until he joins Paul on his voyage from Philippi to Jerusalem (Acts 20:6). Hereafter Luke continued with Paul for the most part until the end of his first Roman imprisonment, unless an exception be allowed for the Apostle's two-year imprisonment at Caesarea. The "*We*" sections are hereafter found in the Acts narrative as follows 20:5-15; 21:1–18; 27:1–37; 28:16.

VIII. THE APOSTLE'S MINISTRY AT TROAS

(20:6–12)

After a seven-day stay at Troas, the activities of which time can only be conjectured, Paul and his party assembled in an upper chamber of a private dwelling for worship. Such places were the common assembly rooms of the early Christians (Luke 22:12; Acts 1:13). That this meeting occurred on Sunday evening, rather than our Saturday or the Jewish Sabbath, is indicated by Paul's plans to resume his journey on the following morning. It is likely that he planned Sunday as a day of worship rather than a day of travel. Macgregor remarks: "Almost certainly the latter [Sunday evening], as **the morrow,** when Paul intended to depart, most naturally means the day after the first mentioned, and therefore is presumably Monday."[j] On this problem Bruce observes:

> On Sunday evening, not Saturday evening; Luke is not using the Jewish reckoning from sunset to sunset but the Roman reckoning from midnight to midnight; although it was apparently after sunset that they met, 'break of day' (v. 11) was 'on the morrow' (v. 7).[k]

Two important facts emerge from this meeting at Troas. *First*, it reflects the earliest clear record of Sunday as the Christian day

[11] See *Beginnings*, IV, 254. [12] *Op. cit.*, p. 377. [13] *Beginnings*, IV, 255.
[14] *Op. cit.*, p. 232. Cf. also Moulton, *Grammar*, I, 96. [15] *Beginnings*, IV, 255 f. [16] *Op. cit.*, p. 378.
[17] *Ibid.*, n. 2 (cf. also p. 40). [18] *Acts*, p. 372. [19] Abbott–Smith, *op. cit.*, p. 108. [20] *Ibid.*, p. 159.

[j] *The Interpreter's Bible* IX, 267.,
[k] Bruce, *op. cit.*, p. 408, n. 25.

8 And there were many lights in the upper chamber where we were gathered together.
9 And there sat in the window a certain young man named Eutychus, borne down with deep sleep; and as Paul discoursed yet longer, being borne down by his sleep he fell down from the third story, and was taken up dead.

---

8 *Lampades*, **lights,** is the origin of "lamps." However the common word for lamp in the New Testament is *lychnos*. *Lampas* means "*a torch* (frequently fed, like a lamp, with oil)." [21] Lake and Cadbury translate it here "lamps." They also suggest that the **many lights** are perhaps mentioned because their heat contributed to the drowsiness of Eutychus. *Hyperōion* (**upper chamber**) is found only in Acts (cf. 1:13; 9:37, 39).

9 That **Eutychus . . . sat in the window** probably indicates crowded conditions. *Thyris* (**window**) occurs only here and in II Corinthians 11:33. This was not a glass window but merely a lattice. **Borne down** and **being borne down** are exactly the opposite in Greek: *katapheromenos* (pres.). . . *katenechtheis* (aor.). The first indicates a "being borne down" and the second a state of having been overcome by sleep (cf. RSV). Rackham comments: "The tenses in the Greek exactly paint the continuous struggle and the moment of defeat." [22] Lake and Cadbury maintain that **third story** equals second story in England and third in America.[23]

---

of worship, as opposed to the Jewish Sabbath or our Saturday. Indeed Paul appears to allude to this fact in his Corinthian letter (I Cor. 16:2), but he is not explicit. Likewise there appears to be a strong implication favorable to Sunday as the Christian day of worship in John 20:19, 26. It is worthy of note that the expression, "Lord's day," is first used in Rev. 1:10. *Second,* it depicts the order of a first century Christian worship service. This likely began with a fellowship meal which was followed by the Eucharist or Lord's Supper. Next was a prolonged discourse by Paul, during which time there was probably opportunity for questions and discussions. Finally, there was a later fellowship meal, and then the service came to a close.

A. The Message at Troas (20:6, 7, 11)

Paul discoursed with them (vs. 7).

Luke does not inform us of the nature or content of Paul's message at Troas, though he does indicate its length. That it contained both instruction and exhortation for the Christians may be safely inferred from Paul's recorded addresses, as well as the content of his epistles. Probably slaves and other working people had no free time for religious congregational worship except at night. Since this is likely Paul's third visit to Troas, many would wish to hear the great Apostle.

The length of Paul's address here is most interesting in that it reflects the intensity of interest on the part of his audience. Bruce remarks:

> Church meetings were not regulated by the clock in those days, and the opportunity of listening to Paul was not one to be cut short; what did it matter if he went on conversing with them until midnight.[l]

Clarke reckons that the sun set at Troas at about seven P.M. and rose at five A.M., thus affording a night of eight hours. Then allowing two hours for interruption, he concludes that Paul must have preached a sermon not less than six hours long.[m] Certainly time is a negligible factor when spiritual truth is ministering to recognized spiritual need. Someone has remarked, with a note of sarcasm, that "the modern sermonette is delivered by a preacherette to Christianettes." The briefest religious discourse may be too long in the absence of spiritual content or spiritual interest by the audience, while the longest may seem too brief in the presence of recognized spiritual need. Some justification for the length of Paul's sermon here may be found in the fact that it was his last message to these people. That there was purpose in its length appears from Luke's words [he] **prolonged his speech** (vs. 7b).

B. The Miracle at Troas (8–10, 12)

Was taken up dead . . . And they brought the lad alive, (vss. 9b, 12a).

[21] *Ibid.*, p. 264. [22] *Op. cit.*, p. 380, n. 5. [23] *Beginnings*, IV, 256.

[l] *Ibid.* [m] Clarke, *op. cit.*, p. 851.

10 And Paul went down, and fell on him, and embracing him said, Make ye no ado; for his life is in him.

11 And when he was gone up, and had broken the bread, and eaten, and had talked with them a long while, even till break of day, so he departed.

12 And they brought the lad alive, and were not a little comforted.

---

10 **Embracing** is the double compound *synperilambanō*, found only here in the New Testament. **Make . . . ado** is the verb *thorybeō*, which has already occurred in 17:5. Elsewhere in the New Testament it is found only in Matthew 9:23 and Mark 5:39, in connection with the raising of Jairus' daughter—a close parallel to this incident. The present imperative means: "Stop making a fuss."

11 **Eaten** is literally "tasted," *geusamenos*. It probably means "taken food." [24] **Talked** is *homilēsas* (cf. homily), used only by Luke (cf. 24:26; Luke 24:14, 15). These other passages indicate clearly the idea of informal conversation, and probably that is the meaning here. The verb is from *homilos*, "crowd," and so means: "*to be in company with, consort with*"; hence, "*to converse with.*" [25]

12 **Alive** suggests that **the lad** had really been dead.[26] *Ou metriōs* is a typical litotes. This construction is used sixteen times by Luke in Acts but is rare elsewhere in the New Testament. The adverb, which occurs only here, means "moderately." So the phrase would mean "exceedingly" [27] or "immensely." [28]

Wesley thinks **the many lights in the upper chamber** (vs. 8) were designed "to prevent any possible scandal" [n] against the Christian meeting at night. However, Macgregor[o] depreciates such a suggestion. Indeed it appears likely that the torches consumed so much of the oxygen in the room as to produce a drowsiness on some of the congregation already weary from the day's toil. Such may have been the plight of the young man Eutychus, who sank into a deep sleep while he perched in an open window of the room and tumbled three stories to the ground outside.

Much controversy has raged over the question whether Eutychus was really dead. However, Luke the physician was present and has given us his medical verdict to the effect that he **was taken up dead** (vs. 9b). No such verdict is given by Luke in the case of Paul's "supposed" death at Lystra (Acts 14:19). Nor do Paul's words of comfort to the relatives and friends, **his life is in him** (vs. 10b), abrogate Luke's decision. These words may be regarded as the prophecy of faith. Ramsay[p] credits Luke's verdict, as do Bruce,[q] Robinson,[r] and Dummelow,[s] while the death of Eutychus is discredited by Macgregor.[t]

Paul interrupted his address to mix works with faith and descended to embrace the young man and reassure the Christians that he was restored to life. Parallels are found in Elijah's action in I Kings 17:21 and Elisha's in II Kings 4:34. Whatever the relationship may be, if any, recent medical instances of the restoration of life by "heart massage" reduce the difficulties to faith in this miracle, as also other Bible miracles of resurrection. This miracle finds its moral validation in part in the comfort which it brought to the Christian friends and relatives (vs. 12). True divine miracles are always a source of strength to the faith of Christian believers.

IX. THE APOSTLE'S MEETING AT MILETUS (20:13–38)

A. The Journey to Miletus (20:13–16)

The day after we came to Miletus, (vs. 16b). Why Paul did not sail with his companions on Monday morning but went overland to meet them at Assos, is not certain. Bruce suggests that he wished to remain at Troas until "assured of Eutychus' complete restoration to consciousness and health." [u]

[24] Bruce, *Acts*, p. 374. [25] Abbott–Smith, *op. cit.*, p. 316.
[26] So Knowling, EGT, II, 426. Furneaux thinks the last words of verse 10 "imply a swoon, not death" (*op. cit.*, p. 328).
[27] Abbott–Smith, *op. cit.*, p. 289. [28] *Beginnings*, IV, 257.

[n] Wesley, *op. cit.*, p. 476, n. 8. [o] *The Interpreter's Bible*, IX, 267. [p] Ramsay, *op. cit.*, p. 291.
[q] Bruce, *op. cit.*, p. 408. [r] Robinson, *op. cit.*, p. 182. [s] Dummelow, *op. cit.*, p. 846.
[t] *The Interpreter's Bible* IX, 268. [u] Bruce, *op. cit.*, p. 409; cf. Ramsay, *op. cit.*, p. 291.

13 But we, going before to the ship, set sail for Assos, there intending to take in Paul: for so had he appointed, intending himself to go by land.

14 And when he met us at Assos, we took him in, and came to Mitylene.

15 And sailing from thence, we came the following day over against Chios; and the next day we touched at Samos; and the day after we came to Miletus.

---

13 **Going before** is *proelthontes.* As in verse five, there is a variant reading, *proselthontes,* "going to." But here the evidence is more nearly balanced. The former is found in Aleph C L and 33 ("the queen of the cursives"), the latter in A B E H P. Either word makes good sense here. **To go by land** is literally "to go on foot" (*pezeuein,* only here in N.T.).

14 **Met** is *syneballen.* Ramsay remarks: "Perhaps the imperfect may be used, implying that Paul did not actually enter Assos, but was descried and taken in by boat as he was nearing the city." [29] **Mitylene** was "the cradle of Greek lyric poetry, being the home of Alcaeus and Sappho." [30] It was about 30 miles from Assos.

15 **Over against Chios** evidently means "a point on the mainland opposite Chios," [31] probably near Cape Argennum. The language clearly implies that they did not go to the island (five miles offshore) but anchored near the mainland opposite it. Chios claimed to be the birthplace of Homer. **Touched at** is *parebalomen.* The verb (only here in N.T.) may mean "come near" or "cross over." Probably the latter is better here. Ramsay has "struck across to Samos." [32]

After *Samos* the Western text adds: "and after stopping at Trogyllium." This may very well preserve a true tradition, as it is otherwise difficult to explain the insertion. Ramsay accepts it as authentic, saying: "When the wind fell, they had not got beyond the promontory Trogyllia at the entrance to the gulf, and there ... they spent the evening." [33]

Dummelow[v] thinks rather that Paul wished to avoid the tedious voyage around Cape Lectum en route to Assos. Ramsay offers a more plausible explanation. He observes that at this season the wind in the Aegean Sea generally blows from the north from early morning until sundown, at which time it reaches a dead calm. This is followed by a gentle south wind during the night. The ship would harbor from evening until the change of wind sometime before sunrise. Thus it was necessary for all passengers to be aboard very early in the morning that the ship might "be ready to sail with the first breath of north wind."[w] Since Paul had not completed his service at Troas, he permitted his party to precede him by ship, while he travelled nineteen miles south overland by a road that paralleled the coast, though some miles inland. Thus he crossed the river valley and ascended to the gates of Assos at a half-mile altitude. This city was famed as the home of Cleanthes, the Stoic philosopher, and possessed one of the most imposing and beautiful locations among the Greek cities. It was famous for its excellent wheat which it exported, and here Aristotle taught 348-345 B.C. It is presently marked by an archaeological site and the Turkish village of Behram or Behramkoy. Here Paul boarded the ship and rejoined his Jerusalem-bound party.

The following is a curious though humanly interesting observation on Paul's departure from Troas.

> From II Tim. 4:13 we learn that Paul lost some of his baggage, which presumably his friends omitted to put on the ship; for he asks Timothy to bring on from Troas a cloak—or possibly a case for books—some papyrus volumes, and some parchment rolls.[x]

If the foregoing is intended to refer to a planned visit of Timothy to the Apostle during a later period in his life, then no particular problem is posed.

Probably following a night's anchorage at Assos, they sailed the next day to the port of Mitylene on the mountainous island of Lesbos. The next day found them en route toward the island of Chios and from thence the following day to the island of Samos. The fifth day was spent en route to Miletus where they likely anchored Friday evening.

[29] *St. Paul the Traveller,* p. 293.
[30] Bruce, *Acts,* p. 375.
[31] Ramsay, *St. Paul the Traveller,* p. 292.
[32] *Ibid.*
[33] *Ibid.,* p. 294.

[v] Dummelow, *op. cit.,* p. 846.
[w] Ramsay, *op. cit.,* p. 293.
[x] *The Interpreter's Bible,* IX, 269.

16 For Paul had determined to sail past Ephesus, that he might not have to spend time in Asia; for he was hastening, if it were possible for him, to be at Jerusalem the day of Pentecost.

---

16 The reason why Paul should **sail past** (*parapleusai*, only here in N.T.). **Ephesus** is hard to deduce. Since it took three days to bring the Ephesian elders to Miletus (see Exposition), it would not appear on the surface that he was saving time by stopping there. But with uncertain winds for sailing he may actually have saved time. Lake and Cadbury write: "It is sometimes overlooked that Paul did not sail close by Ephesus: to have gone there would have been to follow two sides of a triangle." [34] That could be slow work, with contrary winds or none at all. Ramsay suggests that Paul chose a faster vessel which was to put in at Miletus rather than a slower one that would turn in to Ephesus.[35] But it would seem that the explanation **that he might not have to spend time in Asia** indicates that if he stopped at Ephesus he would find it difficult to make a short visit; it would be hard to leave. **Asia** probably means Ephesus, since Miletus was also in the province of Asia.

Miletus was second only to Ephesus among the cities of Asia. It was founded by Ionians in the eleventh century B.C., and here Greek philosophy had its origin with Thales, who was born in 625 B.C. Alexander destroyed the city in 334 B.C., but it was soon rebuilt.

Paul's reason for avoiding Ephesus appears to have been a problem of time, as he planned to reach Jerusalem on schedule for Pentecost. It is further possible that he considered his reappearance at Ephesus so soon after his stormy departure (Acts 20:1) might make unnecessary trouble for himself and the Christians there.

He could much more effectively represent and vindicate the Gentile Christians by delivering their offering to the Jerusalem church in the presence of the vast representation of Jews and Jewish Christians attending the feast. Robinson observes: "This day was not only a Jewish celebration, but an anniversary of the outpouring of the Spirit described in Acts, chapter 2. It would be a particularly opportune and appropriate occasion for presenting the contribution of the Gentile churches to the Jewish Christians." [y] Luke does not say that he arrived son time at Jrusalem, but the fact that he epent "some days" (Acts 21:10) at Caesarea in the house of Philip appears to indicate that he was running ahead of schedule. In fact, Ramsay holds that Paul had fully fifteen days to spare when he reached Caesarea.[z]

B. THE CHARGE TO THE EPHESIAN ELDERS (20:17–35)

And when they were come to him, he said unto them, (vs. 18a).

Kraeling[a] reckons that it required three days for messengers to reach Ephesus (Ephesus lay about thirty miles from Miletus) and return with the Ephesian elders to meet Paul. That such a delay argues strongly that Paul's party must have sailed in a chartered ship, which was subject to the Apostle's orders, has been discredited by Ramsay.[b]

The suggestion that these "Ephesian elders" were the twelve disciples whom Paul met upon his arrival in that city has been dealt with earlier (see note on Acts 19:1–7).

Thus far in Acts, Luke has recorded three of Paul's public addresses, ***first***, his message to the Jews in the synagogue at Antioch of Pisidia (Acts 13:16–41); *second*, an address, based upon natural religion, to the pagan Lycaonians at Lystra (Acts 14:14 17) and *third*, an address, based upon natural religion, to the intelligent Athenians (Acts 17:22–31). This account of Paul's final charge to the Ephesian elders is Luke's first and only record of a message by Paul delivered specifically and exclusively to Christian believers. It contains many striking parallels to his epistles. This address is by nature mainly hortatory, though it contains an element of the apologetic.[c] It falls naturally into four principal divisions:

I. *The Apostle's Personal Example and Ministry* (vss. 18a–21).

[34] *Beginnings*, IV, 258. [35] *St. Paul the Traveller*, pp. 295 f.

[y] Robinson, *op. cit.*, p. 183. [z] Ramsay, *op. cit.*, p. 297.
[a] Emil G. Kraeling, *Rand McNally Bible Atlas* (New York: Rand McNally and Company, 1956), pp. 451, 452.
[b] Ramsay, *op. cit.*, 295. Bruce, *op. cit.*, p. 413.

17 And from Miletus he sent to Ephesus, and called to him the elders of the church.
18 And when they were come to him, he said unto them, Ye yourselves know, from the first day that I set foot in Asia, after what manner I was with you all the time,
19 serving the Lord with all lowliness of mind, and with tears, and with trials which befell me by the plots of the Jews;
20 how I shrank not from declaring unto you anything that was profitable, and teaching you publicly, and from house to house,
21 testifying both to Jews and to Greeks repentance toward God, and faith toward our Lord Jesus Christ.

---

18 **Set foot** is *epebēn*. With the exception of Matthew 21:5 (from LXX), this verb is found only in Acts (five times).

19 *Tapeinophrosynē* **(lowliness of mind)** is found only here in Acts, five times in Paul's epistles and once in I Peter. It evidently bulked large in Paul's thinking.

20 Outside of this passage (vss. 20, 27) the verb *hypostellō* **(shrank)** is found (in N.T.) only in Galatians 2:12 and Hebrews 10:38.

II. *The Apostle's Devotion to Duty* (vss. 22–27).

III. *The Apostle's Charge to the Ephesian Elders* (vss. 28–32).

IV. *The Apostle's Personal Vindication* (vss. 33–35).

Paul's appeal to his personal example while he was at Ephesus closely parallels a similar appeal to the Thessalonians (cf. I Thess. 1:9; 2:1–11). Nothing hidden or secretive characterized Paul's conduct at Ephesus or elsewhere. The Jews possessed the Old Testament Scriptures and the instruction and examples they afforded for their directives. Before Paul wrote them, the Gentiles at Ephesus were devoid of any written instruction in Christian righteousness as were the Thessalonians. Hence the importance of Paul's godly example before them, if they were to attain unto correct Christian deportment. Such examples of righteousness in the midst of wickedness either become a blessing unto salvation, or a curse unto damnation, depending on the reaction to the example. Clarke observes, on verse nineteen:

> This relates not only to his zealous and faithful performance of his *apostolic function*, but also to his *private walk* as a Christian; and shows with what carefulness this apostle himself was obliged to walk, in order to have his calling and election, as a Christian, ratified and made firm.[d]

It is noteworthy that Paul gives priority to his service to Christ-**serving the Lord** (vs. 19). Paul is ever and foremost "a servant of Jesus Christ," after which he is "called to be an apostle" (Rom. 1:1. Cf. Phil. 1:1; Titus 1:1). This same humility Paul could later recommend to the Ephesian Christians (Eph. 4:2). Twice he alludes to his tears in this address (vss. 19 and 31. Cf. II Cor. 2:4; Phil. 3:18).

Wesley remarks:

> Holy tears from those who seldom weep on account of natural occurrences, are no mean specimen of the efficacy, and proof of the truth, of Christianity. Yet joy is well consistent therewith (verse 24). The same person may be sorrowful, yet always rejoicing.[e]

Nor does the Apostle omit trials by the Jews from the tool-kit of his effective service for Christ at Ephesus. Even the **plots of the Jews** (a possible allusion to Alexander's attempt to incriminate Paul and the Christians at the Ephesian riot) Paul employed to further the cause of Christ. From his Roman prison, Paul could write of himself as "the prisoner of the Lord" (Eph. 4:1) and not of Nero, as the Jews and Rome thought.

How well did Paul demonstrate at Ephesus his confidence in the Gospel, later expressed in Rom. 1:16! With boldness he executed his ministry both in public and in private (vs. 20). **House to house** dissemination of the Gospel characterized the first-century Christians from the beginning (cf. Acts 2:46; 5:42).

Paul seems to summarize his Ephesian ministry in three words. *First*, his personal witness, **testifying**; *second*, **repentance**; and *third*, encouragement unto **faith.** In the first he is exemplifying the true spirit of early Christianity, the personal witness to Christ. Such Christ commanded (Acts 1:8). Whenever Christians lose their witness they lose Christ. No amount of eloquent preaching or

[d] Clarke, *op. cit.*, p. 853. [e] Wesley, *op. cit.*, p. 477, n. 19.

22 And now, behold, I go bound in the spirit unto Jerusalem, not knowing the things that shall befall me there:
23 save that the Holy Spirit testifieth unto me in every city, saying that bonds and afflictions abide me.
24 But I hold not my life of any account as dear unto myself, so that I may accomplish my course, and the ministry which I received from the Lord Jesus, to testify the gospel of the grace of God.

---

22 Should it be **in the spirit** or "in the Spirit" (RSV)? Lake and Cadbury prefer the latter,[36] as does also Bruce.[37] Hackett,[38] Knowling,[39] and Rackham[40] defend the former. The main argument for Paul's spirit is that the Holy Spirit is specifically mentioned in the next verse.

24 The Greek of the first clause is a bit awkward. Lake and Cadbury suggest the rendering: "I do not regard for myself my life as a thing even worth mentioning."[41]

So that is *hōs* which does not express purpose elsewhere in the New Testament, except in Luke 9:52.[42] It may be that it should be translated "in comparison with" (cf. ASV mg.).

---

profound teaching or convincing argumentation will ever substitute for the humble witness to Jesus Christ. Men are saved only by Christ, and they can know Him only as witness is borne to Him by those who know Him.

Jesus' own words concerning repentance are final: "Except ye repent, ye shall all in like manner perish" (Luke 13:3). Repentance bespeaks a genuine renunciation of one's loyalty to the former way of life with a consequent turning therefrom. Faith, on the other hand, is a new relationship with a new master. **Repentance** is **toward God,** against whom all, both Jew and Gentile, have sinned, whereas **faith** is **toward our Lord Jesus Christ.** There can be no true saving faith in Christ until there has been a genuine repentance toward God. Repentance is heartbreak for sin; saving faith is heartbreak with sin.

The loyal devotion of Paul to the cause of Christ impelled him to move on to Jerusalem for the accomplishment of his mission. Not even the Spirit's warnings of forthcoming **bonds and afflictions** (vs. 23; Acts 21:10–14; Rom. 15:30, 31) could deter Paul from his sense of duty. How like his Master, on a similar occasion, who "stedfastly set his face to go to Jerusalem" (Luke 9:51).

The Apostle regarded his life as expendable for the cause of Christ to **testify the gospel of the grace of God** (vs. 24. Cf. II Tim. 4:7; Col. 4:17).

Paul's prediction, **ye . . . shall see my face no more** (vs. 25b), is to be understood in the light of his devotion to Christ as he faced Jerusalem and the future (vss. 22, 23). In reality, there is strong evidence that he did later visit these parts and probably again saw some of the Ephesian Christians whom he knew (cf. Phil. 1:25–27; 2:24; Philemon 22; I Tim. 1:3). He had thoroughly discharged his responsibility both to Jews and Gentiles at Ephesus, and they were left without excuse if they perished in their sins (cf. Ezek. 33:1–6). In verse twenty-seven Paul returns to the emphasis of verse twenty. Concerning **the whole counsel of God,** Clarke observes: "All that God has *determined* and *revealed* concerning the salvation of man—the doctrine of Christ crucified, with repentance towards God, and faith in Jesus as the Messiah and great atoning priest."[f]

Paul's charge to the Ephesian elders was twofold. *First*, they were exhorted to give diligence to their own lives: **Take heed unto yourselves** (vs. 28a). *Second,* they were admonished to give diligent care to the Church: **to all the flock** (vs. 28). This was their divine appointment made by the Holy Spirit. (For comment on **bishops,** see exegetical note).

Christ has purchased the Church at the expense of His lifeblood (cf. I Pet. 1:18, 19; Eph. 5:25–27; Rev. 5:9). It is the responsibility of the ministry to sustain, edify, and **feed** Christ's treasured possession, **the church** (cf. John 10:12, 13; 21:15–17).

[36] *Beginnings*, IV, 260. [37] *Acts*, p. 378. [38] *Op. cit.*, pp. 238 f.
[39] EGT, II, 431. [40] *Op. cit.*, p. 391. [41] *Beginnings*, IV, 260. [42] *Ibid.*

[f] Clarke, *op. cit.*, p. 854.

25 And now, behold, I know that ye all, among whom I went about preaching the kingdom, shall see my face no more.

26 Wherefore I testify unto you this day, that I am pure from the blood of all men.

27 For I shrank not from declaring unto you the whole counsel of God.

28 Take heed unto yourselves, and to all the flock, in which the Holy Spirit hath made you bishops, to feed the church of the Lord which he purchased with his own blood.

29 I know that after my departing grievous wolves shall enter in among you, not sparing the flock;

30 and from among your own selves shall men arise, speaking perverse things, to draw away the disciples after them.

31 Wherefore watch ye, remembering that by the space of three years I ceased not to admonish every one night and day with tears.

32 And now I commend you to God, and to the word of his grace, which is able to build *you* up, and to give *you* the inheritance among all them that are sanctified.

---

28 **Bishops** is the noun *episkopos* (cf. episcopal), found once each in Acts, Philippians, I Timothy, Titus, and I Peter. Since these same men are called "elders" *(presbyteroi)* in verse 17, it seems apparent that both names apply to the same office. Perhaps the latter term emphasizes the fact that they were older leaders of good standing (as the elders of Israel), while the former indicates their function as "overseers" (KJV), or "guardians" (RSV). *Episcopos* comes from *skopos*, "watcher." It was used in Greek circles for a superintendent or overseer.

Poimainein, **to feed,** literally means "to shepherd." **Of the Lord** is the reading of A C and the Western text, due to the difficulty of "God" (KJV) shedding His blood. But Vaticanus and Sinaiticus both have "of God," and this is the reading of Westcott and Hort, as well as Nestle. Lake and Cadbury accept this reading as the original one but render it "the blood of his Own." [43] That is perhaps the best solution of this problem. **Purchased** is the verb *peripoieō*, which in the middle, as here, means "to keep or save for oneself" (Luke 17:33) or "to get or gain for oneself, get possession of" (here and I Timothy 3:13).[44] Lake and Cadbury translate it "rescued." [45]

29 *Aphixin*, **departing,** is found only here in the New Testament. In classical Greek it usually signifies "arrival." So Chase suggested: "after my long journey is over and I have reached my true home." [46] But Josephus uses it in the sense of "departure" or "removal." [47] **Wolves** is in contrast with true shepherds.

31 The **three years** was Paul's approximate time in Ephesus (cf. 19:8, 10, 22).

32 **Commend,** *paratithemai*, is perhaps more literally "commit." **The word of his grace** is "the revelation of his grace, of his goodness to man revealed in Christ Jesus." [48] **Sanctified** should here be taken in its widest sense as applying to all "saints" (holy ones) as set apart to God.

Verses twenty-nine and thirty clearly indicate Paul's fear of the activities of the ubiquitous Judaizers, whose subtle and damaging work is so clearly and forcefully depicted in the Galatian letter. That this prophecy came true in a measure appears evident from Paul's letter to Timothy while the latter pastored the Ephesian church (see I Tim. 4:1–6; II Tim. 3:1–13), but that the Ephesian elders maintained doctrinal correctness in the church, though having left their "first love," is equally evident from Rev. 2:2.

Paul's benediction in verse thirty-two accords with the purpose of his ministry as set forth in Acts 26:18. Indeed Paul uses a very similar expression in II Thess. 2:13. Salvation is an inheritance which comes only to those who appropriate the sanctifying blood of the redeeming Christ.

In his personal vindication, Paul *first* declared himself innocent of covetousness (a charge so often brought against him by

[43] *Beginnings*, IV, 261 f.
[44] Abbott-Smith, *op. cit.*, pp. 356 f. These are the only occurrences of this word in the New Testament.
[45] *Beginnings*, IV, 261.
[46] F. H. Chase, *The Credibility of the Book of the Acts of the Apostles* (London: Macmillan Co., 1902), pp. 263 f.
[47] *Ant.* II, 2, 4. [48] Rackham, *op. cit.*, p. 395.

33 I coveted no man's silver, or gold, or apparel.

34 Ye yourselves know that these hands ministered unto my necessities, and to them that were with me.

35 In all things I gave you an example, that so laboring ye ought to help the weak, and to remember the words of the Lord Jesus, that he himself said, It is more blessed to give than to receive.

36 And when he had thus spoken, he kneeled down and prayed with them all.

37 And they all wept sore, and fell on Paul's neck and kissed him,

38 sorrowing most of all for the word which he had spoken, that they should behold his face no more. And they brought him on his way unto the ship.

---

35 The expression, **words of the Lord Jesus,** found at the end of this verse does not occur in the Gospels, but this saying is fully in keeping with the spirit of Jesus' teachings (cf. Luke 6:38; 11:9). It also "accords with Luke's interest in giving." [49]

37 **Kissed** is imperfect, *katephiloun*, "were kissing," suggesting a prolonged farewell. The compound verb here means "to kiss fervently, kiss affectionately." [50]

38 **Brought** is also imperfect, *proepempon*. The verb means "to set forward on a journey, escort." [51]

---

his enemies). *Second*, he reminded them that he was not only self-supporting by his craft while he labored at Ephesus, but that he also supported the members of his party (vs. 34). *Third*, he reminded them of his personal example, which they should follow, in sympathetic service and Christian generosity (vs. 35).

C. The Farewell at Miletus (20:36–38)

And they brought him on his way unto the ship (vs. 38b).

Three factors characterize Paul's leave-taking of the Ephesian elders: namely, *first*, his departing prayer **with them all** (vs. 36); *second*, their sorrowful reaction, especially at the prospect of not seeing Paul again (vss. 37, 38a); and *third*, their conveyance of the Apostle to his ship (vs. 38b). The first manifests Paul's concern and care over the Church of Christ (cf. Eph. 3:14–21); the second reveals the Ephesian elders' personal love and regard for the Apostle; and the third reflects their solicitude for Paul.

[49] *Beginnings*, IV, 264. [50] Abbott-Smith, *op. cit.*, p. 240. [51] *Ibid.*, p. 382.

CHAPTER XXI

And when it came to pass that we were parted from them and had set sail, we came with a straight course unto Cos, and the next day unto Rhodes, and from thence unto Patara:

EXEGESIS

1 **Parted** is the verb *apospaō*, found only here and in 20:30, Matthew 26:51, and Luke 22:41. Moulton and Milligan object to the stronger meaning "torn away" here,[1] but most scholars support it.[2] **With a straight course** is the verb *euthydromeō*, found only here and in 16:11. It is a nautical term. Apparently the prevailing wind was northeast, which may explain why Paul called the Ephesian elders to Miletus, rather than trying to sail in (east) to Ephesus. Lake and Cadbury state that the northeast winds usually blow for four or five days, followed by two or three days of calm, and add: "It is not too much to guess that Paul reached Miletus from Troas on one 'wind,' spent the intervening calm with the Ephesians, and then went on with the next wind." [3]

Cos was "about forty nautical miles from Miletus." [4] *Hexēs*, **next**, is used only by Luke (five times). The exact phrase *tēi hexēs*, **the next day**, is found again in 25:17 and 27:18.

After **Patara** the Western text adds "and Myra." This is a tempting reading, since "Myra seems to have been the great port for the direct cross-sea traffic to the coasts of Syria and Egypt." [5] However, Ramsay thinks "and Myra" is "a mere gloss," and that though Paul's ship visited Myra, it actually started its voyage from Patara.[6] But since Myra was fifty miles east of Patara,[7] would it not be natural, if the wind was northeast (see above), to avoid going there?

EXPOSITION

PART I

THE APOSTLE'S THIRD MISSIONARY JOURNEY CONCLUDED

X. THE APOSTLE'S JOURNEY TO JUDEA, Acts 21:1–14.
   A. The Voyage from Miletus to Tyre, vss. 1–6.
   B. The Voyage from Tyre to Caesarea, vss. 7–14.

PART II

THE APOSTLE'S LAST VISIT TO JUDEA

I. PAUL CONFERS WITH THE JERUSALEM ELDERS, Acts 21:15–25.
   A. The Journey from Caesarea to Jerusalem, vss. 15–17a.
   B. The Reception by the Christian Elders, vss. 17b–20a.
   C. The Advice of the Elders, vss. 20b–25.

II. PAUL CONFRONTS JEWISH HOSTILITY, Acts 21:26–36.
   A. Paul Attacked by the Jewish Mob, vss. 26–31a.
   B. Paul Rescued by the Roman Army, vss. 31b–36.

III. PAUL PREPARES TO ADDRESS THE JEWS, Acts 21:37–40.
   A. Paul's Mistaken Identity, vss. 37, 38.
   B. Paul's True Identity, vss. 39, 40.

Paul's parting from the Ephesian elders reminds the reader of the tender relationship between Jonathan and David, of whom it is said, "the soul of Jonathan was 'knit' with the soul of David" (cf. I Sam. 18:1 and Col. 2:2, 19).

At the ship to which these elders escorted Paul (in the rendering of Bruce) "we tore ourselves away from them." [a] Wesley remarks concerning the parting: "Not without doing violence to both ourselves and them."[b]

[1] VGT, p. 68.
[2] E.g., Knowling (EGT, II, 441), Meyer (p. 399), Rackham (p. 398), Ramsay (*St. Paul the Traveller*, p. 297). Hackett (p. 244) prefers simply "departed."
[3] *Beginnings*, IV, 264. [4] EGT, II, 441. [5] Ramsay, *St. Paul the Traveller*, p. 298.
[6] *Ibid.*, p. 299. [7] Rackham, *op. cit.*, p. 398.

[a] Bruce, *op. cit.*, p. 420. [b] Wesley, *op. cit.*, p. 480, n. 1.

2 and having found a ship crossing over unto Phoenicia, we went aboard, and set sail.
3 And when we had come in sight of Cyprus, leaving it on the left hand, we sailed unto Syria, and landed at Tyre; for there the ship was to unlade her burden.
4 And having found the disciples, we tarried there seven days: and these said to Paul through the Spirit, that he should not set foot in Jerusalem.

---

2 **Crossing over** is the verb *diaperaō*. It occurs only here in Acts, but five times in the Gospels, mostly for crossing the Lake of Galilee.

3 *Anaphanantes*, **when we had come in sight of,** is "apparently a nautical term for sighting land."[8] **Landed** is literally "came down" *(katēlthomen)*; that is, from the high seas. It is used with this meaning three times in Acts and nowhere else in the New Testament. *Ekeise*, **there,** is found elsewhere only in 22:5. *Apophortizomenon* (**unlade**) is "probably a nautical term."[9] It occurs only here in the New Testament. *Gomos* (**burden**), a ship's freight or cargo, is found only here and in Revelation 18:11, 12.

4 **Having found** is the verb *aneuriskō* found only here and in Luke 2:16. Ramsay comments: "None of the party seems to have known Tyre, for they had to seek out the Brethren there."[10] But probably Lake and Cadbury write more wisely: "*Aneurontes* means 'to find by search' (cf. Luke ii, 16) and suggests that Paul knew of the existence of these Christians, but had to look for them."[11] Perhaps Rackham goes too far when he suggests that Paul had personal friends at Tyre, since the verb "seems to imply a search for some particular friends."[12]

Paul's farewell parting from his friends at the various locations, as he closes his third missionary journey, is tender and touching in the extreme. Nowhere is the humanity of the Great Apostle more evident than on these occasions (cf. Phil. 4:1).

X. THE APOSTLE'S JOURNEY TO JUDEA (21:1–14)

Certainly Paul must have faced the last lap of his third missionary journey with mixed emotions—sorrow in leaving behind his many converts and friends, eager anticipation of the accomplishment of Christian love and unity between the Gentile-Jewish Christian elements, and thrusts of sharp, apprehensive fear at the threat of Jewish hostility to his plan and person at Jerusalem. But a sense of Christian duty impelled him to accomplish his mission.

A. The Voyage from Miletus to Tyre (21:1–6)

we sailed unto Syria, and landed at Tyre, vs. 3.

A day's voyage brought Paul's party to the island of Cos, one of the Dodecanese, which lay at the entrance to the Ceramian Gulf, where they may have anchored at the city of Cos on the east end of the island. Luke's expression, **we came with a straight course** (vs. 1), probably suggests that they had both the wind and the tide in their favor. Kraeling[c] observes that this island was famous for its production of silk, ointments, wine, and wheat, as well as for its luxurious country life. It was further noted as the home of Hippocrates, the father of medical science, whose "oath" every medical graduate in the western world is required to take. Aesculapius, the god of healing, was the chief deity of Cos. Juno was also an important god here. Apelles, the celebrated painter, is reported to have been born at Cos.

From Cos they sailed a day's voyage to the city of Rhodes (vs. 1b) on the island of the same name. This island was about 20 by 43 miles in size. The city, which was founded in 408 B.C., was situated on the northern tip of the island. The Colossus of Rhodes was one of the "seven wonders of the ancient world." It was a bronze statue of the sun god Apollo which towered 150 feet above the harbor at the entrance to which it stood. It had been erected in 280 B.C. in commemoration of the successful repulsion of an enemy siege, and it stood for 56 years. Clarke remarks that "ships in full sail could

[8] *Beginnings*, IV, 265. [9] *Ibid.* [10] *St. Paul the Traveller*, p. 300.
[11] *Beginnings*, IV, 265; cf. also Knowling, EGT, II, 442. [12] *Op. cit.*, p. 399.

[c] Kraeling, *op. cit.*, p. 452.

5 And when it came to pass that we had accomplished the days, we departed and went on our journey; and they all, with wives and children, brought us on our way till we were out of the city: and kneeling down on the beach, we prayed, and bade each other farewell;
6 and we went on board the ship, but they returned home again.

---

5 *Exartisai*, **accomplished**, is found elsewhere in the New Testament only in II Timothy 3:17. It is used in the papyri in the sense of "completed." [13] **Brought . . . on our way** is *propempontōn*, "escorted" (cf. 20:38; see also on 15:3). *Aligialon*, **beach**, "denotes a smooth shore, as distinguished from one precipitous or rocky." [14] The writer recalls seeing a camel caravan making its way along this beautiful sandy beach. **Bade . . . farewell** is the rare compound *apaspazomai*, found only here in the New Testament.

6 *Embainō* (**went on board**) has regularly in the New Testament the meaning "embark" (16 times in the Gospels and only here in Acts). **The ship** (cf. "a ship," vs. 2) shows that they continued their voyage in the same vessel (cf. vs. 3).

---

pass between its legs. It was the work of Chares, a pupil of Lysippus, who spent 12 years in making it." [d] It was finally destroyed by an earthquake in 224 B.C. Its fragments remained undisturbed until 656 A.D. Kraeling observes that "Strabo, the Greek geographer, calls Rhodes the most splendid city known to him with respect to harbors, streets, walls, and other equipment." [e] This ancient geographer makes further note of its "excellent government" and the "social-mindedness" of its inhabitants toward the unemployed and poor. Rhodes was formerly mistress of Caria and Lycia on the mainland but eventually came under the power of Rome, whose favor it enjoyed as a free city in Paul's day where it remained an important trade city.

From Rhodes Paul's party sailed to Patara on the southwest coast of Lycia and possibly to Myra further east on the coast of Lycia (cf. Acts 27:5). Patara was located on the mouth of the Xanthus River and constituted the chief port of several nearby islands, being itself an important coastal trade center. However, Myra appears to have been more important in this respect, and it may have been here, rather than at Patara, that Paul's party transshipped to Phoenicia (see exegetical note on Acts 21:1).

The ship boarded by Paul's party was likely a large merchant vessel, as it took to open sea rather than following the coast line, as a coastal vessel would have done. This voyage to Tyre covered about 350 miles and likely occupied about five days. En route to Syria their vessel left Cyprus on the left, or "port side," as they struck a direct course from Lycia to Tyre, where its cargo was destined (vs. 3b). Doubtless Paul had revived memories of early missionary experiences at Paphos as their ship sailed within sight of Cyprus (vs. 3).

This was unlikely Paul's first visit to Tyre, as he had doubtless called here during his earlier travels between Palestine and Syria or Cilicia. Tyre had formerly been an island city but was joined to the mainland by Alexander the Great, while it was under siege by this monarch. By ocean accretion, it eventually became an isthmus. Kraeling remarks:

> Here thirty thousand women, children, and slaves were taken and sold into slavery by Alexander; nearly one-third as many men were killed in the defense of the city or executed. The woe of an Ezekiel over Tyre (Ezek. 27–28) was thus completely fulfilled, though later than the prophet expected.[f]

Tyre was annexed by Rome in 65 B.C. and made a free city. The Lord's prediction (Matt. 11:21, 22) suggests something of both the importance and wickedness of this city. It was the accommodative applause of the inhabitants of Tyre to Herod's oration that occasioned that ruler's untimely and horrible death (Acts 12:21–23). Dummelow states that Tyre was,

> the greatest maritime city of the ancient world, claiming to have been founded as early as 2750 B.C. It produced glass and purple dye, but its chief wealth came from the fact that it almost monopolized the carrying-trade of the world. The Tyrian mariners were so skilled in astronomy and constructed such accurate charts, that they sailed by night as well as by day, and made long

[13] VGT, p. 222. [14] Hackett, *op. cit.*, p. 246.

[d] Clarke, *op. cit.*, V, 857. [e] Kraeling, *op. cit.*, p. 452. [f] *Ibid.*

7 And when we had finished the voyage from Tyre, we arrived at Ptolemais; and we saluted the brethren, and abode with them one day.

---

7 **Finished** is the verb *dianyō*, found only here in the New Testament. In later writers it meant "continue,"[15] and that is the rendering preferred here by Lake and Cadbury.[16] But Ramsay remarks: "The emphasis laid on 'finishing the voyage' from Tyre to Ptolemais is due to the fact that it was probably over about 10 A.M."[17] *Ploun*, **voyage,** is found only here and in 27:10. It is from *pleō*, "to sail." Page would apply the reference here to the voyage from Macedonia (cf. 20:6), because the distance from Tyre to Ptolemais was so short.[18]

---

voyages out of sight of land. They are known to have circumnavigated Africa—an extraordinary feat for the small ships of the ancients.[g]

The present city is known as Tyr or Sour (Fr.), Es Sur (Arab), or Zor (Heb.). It has some 7,500 people and is located in southern Lebanon.

At Tyre Paul found a Christian church which had been founded by disciples of the Hellenist dispersion, following the martyrdom of Stephen (Acts 11:19). With these disciples Paul and his party spent a week, probably while they waited for the ship to unload and reload cargo (vs. 3b). Among these disciples were those who appear to have had the spirit of prophecy, in the sense of "foretelling" events. It is, however, quite possible that they spoke in part from actual knowledge of Jewish hostility to Paul and of a plot to kill him, made earlier at Corinth (Acts 20:3), which plot may have been relayed by Jews who had passed through Tyre en route to the Passover in Jerusalem (cf. Acts 23:12–16). In any event, they warned Paul against going on to Jerusalem at this time (vs. 4; cf. Acts 20:23). We are not to suppose that Paul openly disobeyed God in the continuance of his journey to Rome following these warnings. Rather we would agree with Clarke's conclusion:

> *Through the Spirit*, must either refer to their own great *earnestness* to dissuade him from taking a journey which they plainly saw would be injurious to him . . .; or, if it refers to the Holy Spirit, it must mean that if he regarded his personal safety he must not, at this time, go up to Jerusalem.[h]

Indeed the Spirit foretold that Paul would meet persecutions, but it would not appear that he was forbidden of God to go to Jerusalem. Paul was willing to take whatever personal risk was necessary to glorify God in the extension of His cause. The purport of the warning seems to be that if Paul went to Jerusalem, the Jews would persecute and imprison him, and possibly he would be killed. Thus he could go and face the personal consequence for God's glory, or he might desist without losing God's favor. Thus Paul was left to the free exercise of his own personal judgment and conscience, as he was neither commanded of God to go nor to stay. God is always fair in aiding His servants to foresee the consequences of their decisions and actions. Bruce views this incident likewise.

> We should not conclude that his determination to go on was disobedience to the guidance of the Spirit of God; this determination of his was the fruit of an inward spiritual constraint which would not be gainsaid.[i]

In his purpose to fulfill his Jerusalem mission, Paul here again parallels his Master (cf. Luke 9:51).

As at Miletus, the Christian disciples at Tyre, including the women and children, showed their love and respect for Paul by accompanying him to the sandy seashore outside the city where he was to embark for Caesarea. There, unashamed, they knelt together, most likely in the presence of the mariners and other passengers, and offered their prayers to God, possibly concluding with a Christian hymn of praise. The God who fills heaven and earth with His presence can as well be worshiped under the canopy of the open heavens as in the great stone temples (cf. John 4:21–24; Acts 16:13). Open-air services are not without a New Testament precedent. After tender Christian farewells the party boarded the ship, while

[15] E.g., I Clement 25:3. [16] *Beginnings*, IV, 266. [17] *St. Paul the Traveller*, p. 300. [18] *Op. cit.*, p. 220.

[g] Dummelow, *op. cit.*, p. 847. [h] Clarke, *op. cit.*, V, 857, 858 (cf. I Sam. 23:9–13).
[i] Bruce, *op. cit.*, p. 421 (cf. Acts 19:21; 20:22).

8 And on the morrow we departed, and came unto Caesarea: and entering into the house of Philip the evangelist, who was one of the seven, we abode with him.
9 Now this man had four virgin daughters, who prophesied.

---

8 It is not stated whether the party traveled from Ptolemais to Caesarea by land or by sea. It would normally take two days on foot, but less than one by boat. Hackett holds that they traveled by land,[19] as does also Rackham.[20] The added phrase, "that were of Paul's company" (KJV) between *we* and **departed,** is omitted in the earliest manuscripts.[21]

Euangelistēs (**evangelist**; only here, Eph. 4:11, and II Tim. 4:5) reminds one of the use of *euangelizomai* for Philip's preaching in 8:12, 35, 40. Eusebius identified this Philip with Philip the apostle (1:13).[22] But probably no scholar today would think of defending that position. Philip is unequivocally identified as **one of the seven** (cf. 6:5).

9 The four daughters are described as **virgins.** Clement of Alexandria says two of them finally married.[23]

---

the Tyrian disciples returned home, thankful to God for the encouragement and enrichment of their lives by the visit and ministry of the missionary party.

B. The Voyage from Tyre to Caesarea (7–14)

And when we had finished the voyage from Tyre . . . [we] came unto Caesarea, vss. 7a, 8.

The first day's sailing from Tyre brought the ship to Ptolemais, a distance of some twenty miles, which was the most southerly of the Phoenician ports. This city was successor to the Old Testament Acco or Accho (Judg. 1:31) and was of considerable importance. In modern times it is known as Acre or Akka (Fr. Saint'-Jean'-d'A'cre) and has a population of 10,695 (1944 est.). It is now largely superseded by Haifa, just across the bay into which the river Belus empties. Here, as at Tyre, they found Christian believers with whom the party spent a day (vs. 7b), doubtless ministering to their spiritual welfare while the Christians ministered to the material comfort of the party.

It is interesting, if not important, that while Luke designates the Christian believers at Tyre "disciples" (vs. 4a), here at Ptolemais he calls them "brethren" (see notes on names, Acts 11:26).

The following day they departed for Caesarea, a distance of some forty miles, which probably occupied about two days' travel time. (For the method of travel from Ptolemais to Caesarea, see exegetical note). Thus the long voyage "that may have begun about April 15 . . . finally terminated about May 14, two weeks before the Pentecost festival that Paul wanted to spend at Jerusalem."[j]

The fact of this extra time, **some days** (vs. 10), before Pentecost may account for Paul's lack of haste to reach Jerusalem. (For a description of the city of Caesarea, see notes on introduction to Acts 10.)

Quite naturally Paul's missionary party lodged, during their stay in Caesarea, in the home of Philip the evangelist (not Philip the apostle), **who was one of the seven** (vs. 8). Later tradition seems to have tended to confuse **Philip the evangelist** and "Philip the apostle," as also "John the Apostle" and "John the Elder" (See exegetical note on the problem of **Philip the evangelist** and "Philip the Apostle".)

> Evangelists were itinerant officers, whose duty it was to break new ground and establish new churches. They ranked below the prophets and above the presbyters or pastors . . . The N.T. never uses 'evangelist' in the sense of the writer of a Gospel.[k]

Philip has not been mentioned by Luke since his arrival in Caesarea following the conversion of the Ethiopian nobleman (Acts 8:40). From a member of the "seven lay deacons" chosen by the church to look after the temporal affairs of the Grecian widows (Acts 6:1–6), Philip had risen to the position of an effective evangelist, witnessed the conversion of the Samaritans *en masse* (Acts 8:5–8), became God's instrument for the

[19] *Op. cit.*, p. 246. [20] *Op. cit.*, p. 399. [21] Aleph A B C E.
[22] *Ecclesiastical History*, III, 31, 3. [23] *Stromata*, III, 6, 52.

[j] Kraeling, *op. cit.*, p. 453. [k] Dummelow, *op. cit.*, p. 847.

10 And as we tarried there some days, there came down from Judaea a certain prophet, named Agabus.

---

10 *Epimenontōn*, **as we tarried**, is the genitive absolute construction without the usual accompanying substantive, a rare phenomenon in the New Testament.[24] **From Judaea** means from Jerusalem. Caesarea was in the province of Judea, but a Gentile city.

---

conversion of the Ethiopian treasurer (Acts 8:26–39), and evangelized all the coastal cities between Gaza and Caesarea (Acts 8:40). Doubtless Philip had witnessed Paul's (then Saul) part in the martyrdom of his fellow Christian deacon, Stephen (Acts 7:58; 8:1) and had followed with enthusiastic interest and joy Paul's conversion and subsequent Gentile ministry.

Conybeare and Howson observe that Paul's conversion on the Damascus road likely occurred at about the same time that Philip witnessed the Ethiopian nobleman's conversion on the Gaza Road. Further, these authorities remark concerning Caesarea,

> Thenceforth it became his residence if his life was stationary, or it was the centre from which he made other missionary circuits through Judaea . . . The term "evangelist" seems to have been almost synonymous with our word "Missionary." It is applied to Philip and to Timothy.[l]

The introduction of Philip's **four virgin daughters, who prophesied** (vs. 9) is most interesting. This notation indicates, *first*, Philip's godly parental influence in turning their lives into the service of the Lord; and *second*, the place of importance to which women were already attaining within the ministry of the Church (cf. Acts 18:26; Phil. 4:3). It might also be questioned whether Paul's advice concerning celibacy and marriage (see I Cor. 7) may not have reached their ears and influenced their lives in this respect. As prophetesses, Philip's daughters were not without precedent. Miriam (Ex. 15:20), Deborah (Judg. 4:4), Noadiah (Neh. 6:14), Huldah (II Kings 22:14), and the wife of Isaiah (Isa. 8:3) are designated prophetesses in the Old Testament. Indeed Joel's prophecy clearly states that one characteristic of the Pentecostal influence was to be that "your daughters shall prophesy" (Acts 2:17, 18). On the other hand, Clarke simply remarks:

> Probably these were no more than *teachers* in the church: for we have already seen that this is a frequent meaning of the word *prophesy;* and thus is undoubtedly one thing intended by the word prophecy by Joel . . . If Philip's daughters might be *prophetesses* why not *teachers?*[m]

It appears that Philip and his daughters (his wife is not mentioned) with other Judean Christians later settled in the province of Asia. Some or all of the daughters lived to a good old age and became esteemed as historical informants on early Judean Christianity. In fact, several scholars of note think that much of Luke's information for Acts may have been supplied by this family during these few days and later during Paul's two-year imprisonment at Caesarea (Acts 24–27). Is it too fanciful to conjecture that Luke may have resided in Philip's home for two years while Paul was a prisoner at Caesarea? One authority suggests: "It is not improbable that these inspired women gave St. Paul some intimation of the sorrows which were hanging over him." And this authority continues, "Perhaps the force of 'who did prophesy' (vs. 9) is to be found in the fact that they did foretell what was to come."[n]

The prophet Agabus (vs. 10), who came down to Caesarea from Judea, was likely the prophet of the same name earlier met at Antioch of Syria (Acts 11:28), whose first prophecy is declared to have been fulfilled in the days of Claudius, A.D. 46. Agabus was evidently a true prophet in the sense of "foretelling," rather than a preacher or "forthteller" of God's message. The object lesson which he employed to make more vivid and impressive his prophetic warning to Paul was no uncommon practice among the Jews of the Old Testament (cf. I Kings 11:29f; 22:11; Isa. 20:2; Jer. 13:4; 27:2,3; Ezek. 4:1–12). This prophecy was literally fulfilled (Acts 21:27f.).

Agabus indeed claims divine inspiration

[24] Moulton and Howard, *Grammar*, I, 74.

[l] W. J. Conybeare and J. S. Howson, *The Life and Epistles of St. Paul* (Grand Rapids, Eerdmans, repr. ed.), p. 615, n. 2.
[m] Clarke, *op. cit.*, V, 858. [n] Conybeare and Howson, *loc. cit.*

11 And coming to us, and taking Paul's girdle, he bound his own feet and hands, and
said, Thus saith the Holy Spirit, So shall the Jews at Jerusalem bind the man that owneth
this girdle, and shall deliver him into the hands of the Gentiles.
12 And when we heard these things, both we and they of that place besought him not to
go up to Jerusalem.
13 Then Paul answered, What do ye, weeping and breaking my heart? for I am ready
not to be bound only, but also to die at Jerusalem for the name of the Lord Jesus.
14 And when he would not be persuaded, we ceased, saying, The will of the Lord be done.
15 And after these days we took up our baggage and went up to Jerusalem.

---

11 It is not stated that **the Jews** did **bind** Paul. But they were responsible for his being bound (vs. 33).

12 *Entopioi*, **of that place,** is found only here in the New Testament.

13 *Synthryptontes*, **breaking,** is "a rare word meaning to break up, to pound to bits." [25] It is found only here in the New Testament. Knowling comments: "Here *synthryptein* means to weaken the Apostle's purpose rather than to break his heart in sorrow." [26]

14 *Hēsychasamen*, **we ceased,** is used only by Luke (four times) and Paul (I Thess. 4:11). It means to be still or silent.

The words of verses 13 and 14 are strongly reminiscent of Christ's last journey to Jerusalem, when He pressed on, in spite of what He knew awaited Him (Luke 9:51). The last words of verse 14 are of course closely parallel to Jesus' prayer in the Garden of Gethsemane.

15 *Episkeuasamenoi*, **took up our baggage,** occurs only here in the New Testament. The

---

for his prophetic warning to Paul, **Thus saith the Holy Spirit** (vs. 11), but unlike the Tyrian Christians (vs. 4), he does not interpret this warning as a divine prohibition against Paul's intended visit to Jerusalem. A parallel with Christ's own prediction of Himself is found in Mark 10:33. The statement, **shall deliver him into the hands of the Gentiles** (vs. 11b), indicates the restrictions placed upon the Jews by the Romans in the handling of criminal cases in Judea (see note on Acts 7:57, 58). However, this statement also indicates that Agabus placed full responsibility upon the Jews for Paul's arrest (cf. Acts 2:23).

Out of personal love and solicitation, both Paul's party and the Christians at Caesarea earnestly besought Paul to give up his purpose to visit Jerusalem (vs. 12). However, Paul rebuked them for the demoralizing influence which their entreaties were having upon him (vs. 13a) and reasserted his purpose to complete his mission, even at the expense of his life **for the name of the Lord Jesus** (vs. 13b), if need required. Thus Paul reflects the "early Christian martyr spirit," for Christ's sake. Indeed, from Christ's first message to him through Ananias at his conversion experience in Damascus (Acts 9:16), Paul had accepted suffering for Jesus' sake as a part of his heritage. As previously noted, Paul's resolution to visit Jerusalem at this time involved "the collection," with its hoped-for benefits (see comment on Acts 20:4,5). Finally Paul's friends acquiesced, yielding human sentiments to the wisdom and will of God (vs. 14). How often has human sentiment and solicitation, growing out of personal friendships or relationships, served to deter God's servants from His higher will. Bruce regards the Christians' words, **The will of the Lord be done** (vs. 14b), as a prayer which may contain an "echo of the Lord's own prayer in Gethsemane [Luke 22:42]." [o]

Part II

The Apostle's Last Visit to Judea

I. PAUL CONFERS WITH THE JERUSALEM ELDERS (21:15-25)

A. The Journey from Caesarea to Jerusalem (15–17a)

In due time the party packed their baggage (vs. 15)[p] and proceeded to Jerusalem. They

[25] *Beginnings*, IV, 269. [26] EGT, II, 446.

[o] Bruce, *op. cit.*, p. 426.

[p] Ramsay takes this expression to mean that they "equipped horses for the journey." If this is correct then it is the of two instances in Acts where beasts are mentioned in conjunction with Paul's travels. The second was when the n cavalry placed Paul on a beast and spirited him away to Caesarea (Acts 23:24). W. M. Ramsay, *The Cities of* l (London: Hodder and Stoughton, 1907), p. 301.

16 And there went with us also *certain* of the disciples from Caesarea, bringing *with them* one Mnason of Cyprus, an early disciple, with whom we should lodge.

---

verb means "to equip, make ready," and in the middle (as here) "to make one's preparations." [27] Though they find no parallels in the papyri, Moulton and Milligan think the meaning here is "having furnished ourselves for the journey." [28] Ramsay claims that in classical Greek the verb means "to equip or saddle a horse." [29] Lake and Cadbury suggest "having packed up." [30] Hackett thinks the alms being taken to Jerusalem may have consisted in part of clothes and food, involving considerable loading and unloading. [31] But that seems unlikely. The King James rendering, "took up our carriages" is a good example of the changing meaning of words. In old English "carriages" meant something carried; in modern times it means something that carries.

Went up is imperfect, *anebainomen*. Lake and Cadbury translate it "went on up." [32]

16 **Bringing with them** is better translated "bringing us to" (RSV) since **Mnason** is in the dative case. The Western text gives a typical explanatory addition which, as in a number of other instances in Acts, makes very good sense. It reads: "And these brought us to those with whom we should lodge, and we reached a village, and were with Mnason, a Cypriote, an early disciple." The Vulgate places Mnason's house in Jerusalem. But Blass cogently shows that the most reasonable view is that Mnason's house was the stopping place on the way to Jerusalem.[33]

Early is *archaios* (cf. archaic), which means "original, ancient." The implication is that Mnason had been a disciple from the beginning, probably one of the 120 at Pentecost.[34]

---

were accompanied by certain Caesarean disciples. (For the textual problem concerning "Mnason," verse sixteen, see exegetical treatment.) It would be of interest to know whether Philip was in the party. In any event, it appears that **Mnason of Cyprus,** here designated **an early disciple** (vs. 16), was to be their host. Mnason may have been a convert at Pentecost, or even of the Lord Himself. He "may have been one of those Cyprian Jews who first made the Gospel known to the Greeks at Antioch."[q] He was likely a Hellenist, thus accounting for his more liberal outlook in entertaining Paul's missionary party. Mnason may either have been at Caesarea on business when contacted by Paul's party, or he may have been sent for from Jerusalem by Philip to meet Paul at Caesarea. However, Dummelow[r] holds that Mnason's house was probably nearly halfway between Caesarea and Jerusalem and that they lodged with him the first night of the sixty-mile journey. With this position Kraeling agrees (as also Ramsay),[s] supposing that Mnason's town may have been Antipatris, from which they proceeded "to Jerusalem via the Beth-horon Road"[t] (cf. Acts 23:31–33). However, Bruce[u] sees little merit in this latter view but adds that Luke likely gathered valuable data concerning the early days of Christianity from this **early disciple,** Mnason.

Luke records five definite visits of Paul to Jerusalem following his conversion at Damascus, of which this is the last. The *first* was on the occasion of Paul's introduction to the elders by Barnabas (Acts 9:26); the *second*, on the occasion of the delivery of the relief fund from Antioch during the famine (Acts 11:29, 30; 12:25); the *third* was on the occasion of the General Church Council (Acts 15:1,2); the *fourth* was a brief visit at the close of his second missionary journey (Acts 18:22); while the *fifth* and last visit was at the close of his third missionary journey (Acts 21:15, 17). On all but the fourth he encountered stormy opposition from either the Jews or the Judaizers. On the occasion of his fifth visit the Jews, probably incited by the Judaizers, bent every effort to destroy him and put an end to his work.

[27] Abbott-Smith, *op. cit.*, p. 173. [28] VGT, p. 244.
[29] *St. Paul the Traveller*, p. 302. See also Rackham (p. 413) for same view.
[30] *Beginnings*, IV, 269. [31] *Op. cit.*, p. 248. [32] *Beginnings*, IV, 269.
[33] F. Blass, *Philology of the Gospels* (London: Macmillan Co., 1898), p. 130. [34] So Rackham, p. 413.

[q] Conybeare and Howson, *op. cit.*, p. 617. [r] Dummelow, *op. cit.*, p. 847.
[s] Ramsay, *op. cit.*, p. 301. [t] Kraeling, *op. cit.*, p. 453. [u] Bruce, *op. cit.*, pp. 426–427.

17 And when we were come to Jerusalem, the brethren received us gladly.
18 And the day following Paul went in with us unto James; and all the elders were present.
19 And when he had saluted them, he rehearsed one by one the things which God had
wrought among the Gentiles through his ministry.

---

17 **Received** is the verb *apodechomai* (used only by Luke, seven times). It means "to accept gladly, welcome, receive."[35] This with *asmenōs*, **gladly** (only here in N.T.), emphasizes the warm welcome which Paul and his party received.

18 *Eisēiei*, **went in,** is the imperfect of *eiseimi* (three times in Acts, plus Heb. 9:6). Rackham remarks: "The uncommon form of this verb in the Greek marks the solemnity of the occasion."[36] Exactly the same form is found in verse 26.

19 It seems a bit strange that Luke does not mention the presentation of the offering to the Jerusalem church. Rackham explains it as "a silent sign of his modesty, for he was himself one of the bearers."[37]

Conybeare and Howson remark:

> we do find in *the Epistle written to the Romans* . . . a remarkable indication of discouragement, and almost despondency, when he asked the Christians at Rome to pray that, on his arrival in Jerusalem, he might be delivered from the Jews who hated him, and be well received by those Christians who disregarded his authority . . . Rom. XV, 31. We should remember that he had two causes of apprehension,—one arising from the Jews, who persecuted him everywhere; the other from the Judaizing Christians, who sought to depreciate his apostolic authority.[v]

The foregoing authorities further state:

> Now he had much new experience of the insidious progress of error and of the sinfulness even of the converted. Yet his trust in God did not depend on the faithfulness of man; and he went to Jerusalem calmly and resolutely, though doubtful of his reception among the Christian brethren, and not knowing what would happen on the morrow.[w]

B. The Reception by the Christian Elders (21:17b–20a).

The brethren received us gladly, vs. 17b. In verse eighteen is Luke's last identification with Paul, by the use of the plural pronoun, until Acts 27:1 (cf. Acts 16:17). Upon their arrival at Jerusalem, Paul's party was joyously received by the brethren (cf. Acts 28:15). This enthusiastic reception was probably accentuated by the presentation of the gift for the church from the Gentile Christians, though Luke does not mention this matter. Bruce[x] suggests that the Jerusalem church may have regarded these Gentile offerings as a parallel "to the annual half-shekel which proselytes to Judaism (like other Jews) paid into the temple treasury at Jerusalem."[y]

Whether Paul accompanied the party on its first meeting with the brethren at Jerusalem (vs. 17), or whether James was absent from the first meeting seems uncertain. Possibly the latter was the case. In any event, a meeting of the entire party with **James; and all the elders** (vs. 18) was arranged the next day. James was the brother of our Lord and the acknowledged head of the Jerusalem church. He was commonly known as "James the Just." The importance of his role in the Jerusalem church was evident from the beginning (Acts 12:17; 15:13). It appears that all the other "pillar apostles" were gone from Jerusalem by this time. Perhaps they were either dead or engaged in mission work elsewhere, since none are mentioned by name. Bruce remarks:

> But James remained in Jerusalem, exercising wise and judicious leadership over the Nazarene community there, greatly respected not only by the members of that community but by the ordinary Jews of Jerusalem as well.[z]

It appears likely that the Jerusalem church was organizationally patterned after the Jewish temple. James may have had a body of seventy elders, corresponding to the Sanhedrin, to assist him in the administration of the Judean Church. Since "the collection" was for this church, it was fitting that this body of elders should have been present with James to officially receive it. Such an

[35] Abbott-Smith, *op. cit.*, p. 49. [36] *Op. cit.*, p. 414. [37] *Ibid.*

[v] Conybeare and Howson, *op. cit.*, p. 618. [w] *Ibid.*, 619.

[x] Mould holds that "Every Jew, upon reaching the age of twenty, paid an annual tax of one-half shekel into the temple treasury," and he further states that the "gold shekel" was worth about $10.00 at this time, while the "silver shekel" was worth about $.62. Probably the former is to be understood as the temple tax. Mould, *op. cit.*, p. 276.

[y] Bruce, *op. cit.*, p. 429. [z] *Ibid.*

20 And they, when they heard it, glorified God; and they said unto him, Thou seest, brother, how many thousands there are among the Jews of them that have believed; and they are all zealous for the law:
21 and they have been informed concerning thee, that thou teachest all the Jews who are among the Gentiles to forsake Moses, telling them not to circumcise their children, neither to walk after the customs.
22 What is it therefore? they will certainly hear that thou art come.
23 Do therefore this that we say to thee: We have four men that have a vow on them;

---

20 **Thousands** is literally "tens of thousands" (*myriades;* cf. myriads).

21 For *katēchēthēsan,* **informed** (also vs. 24), see on 18:25. **To forsake Moses** is literally "apostasy *(apostasian)* from Moses." **Not to circumcise** is literally "to stop circumcising" *(mē peritemnein)*.

22 **What is it therefore?** is characteristic of Paul's epistles (e.g. Rom. 3:9; I Cor. 14:15, 26). "The multitude must needs come together" (KJV) is omitted by B C, but found in Aleph A D E H L P. Lake and Cadbury "suspect that it is original" and suggest that it may be translated either "there must be a meeting of the whole church," or possibly "a mob will congregate," either one making good sense.[38]

23 *Euchēn,* **vow,** occurs only here, in 18: 18, and in James 5:15 ("prayer"). The prevailing meaning in the papyri is "prayer."[39] Temporary Nazirite vows usually lasted for 30 days.[40]

---

organization appears justified in the light of James' statement that there were **many thousands** (vs. 20) of believers among the Jews, probably meaning Judean believers, but possibly including believers from other parts also who were present for Pentecost.

As on the occasion of Paul's return from his first missionary journey (Acts 14:27) and his address before the Jerusalem Council (Acts 15:4), so now before the Jerusalem elders, he presented his cause in the form of a vivid rehearsal of the mighty works of God among the Gentiles through his ministry (vs. 19b). From the assembly there arose a unaminous chorus, "Glory to God" (vs. 20b). Thus by the presentation of the offering and the recounting of God's visitation to the Gentiles, Paul won the coveted approval and loyalty of the Jerusalem church. However, there is no record of expressed appreciation for the gift, unless verse twenty is to be so understood.

It is of interest to note here that this is the last mention of James in Acts. In fact, Josephus says that he was illegally tried and condemned to death by stoning at the hands of the Sanhedrin under the high priest Ananus, between the Judean governorships of Festus, who died in A.D. 62, and Albinus, who succeeded Festus in the same year. This Ananus was of the Sadducean party, which was noted for its harshness and rigidity in judgment even above the Pharisees. James, with some other Christians, was arraigned before the Sanhedrin and accused of having broken the law, for which they were condemned and stoned to death (for permissions and prohibition of the Jewish Sanhedrin under the Romans, see notes on Acts 4:5, 6; 7:57, 58; 12:1–4). That the whole affair was considered unjust and repellent to the Jewish populace, as well as to the Christians, is evinced by the fact that the Jews protested the action to Albinus, who deposed Ananus.[a]

C. The Advice of the Elders (21:20b–25)

Do therefore this that we say to thee, vs. 23a.

The final victory of the legalistic Judaizing party in the Judean church over the liberals appears evident from Acts 21:20. Though the Jerusalem Council had won liberty from the Jewish law for the Gentile Christians out in the empire (cf. Acts 15; 21:25), such Christian liberty was never accorded Gentile Christians in Judea. The **many thousands** (vs. 20) of Jewish believers in Judea were all extremely **zealous for the law** of Moses (cf. Acts 15:5; Gal. 1:14). It appears very likely that the Hebrew letter was written

---

[38] *Beginnings,* IV, 272. [39] VGT, p. 268. [40] Cf. Josephus, *War,* II, 15, 1.

[a] Josephus, "Antiquities of the Jews," *The Works of Flavius Josephus,* XX, IX, 1.

24 these take, and purify thyself with them, and be at charges for them, that they may shave their heads: and all shall know that there is no truth in the things whereof they have been informed concerning thee; but that thou thyself also walkest orderly, keeping the law.
25 But as touching the Gentiles that have believed, we wrote, giving judgment that they should keep themselves from things sacrificed to idols, and from blood, and from what is strangled, and from fornication.

---

24 The **charges** connected with Nazarite vows formed a prominent phase at this time. Josephus tells how Herod Agrippa I paid the expenses of Nazarites.[41] *Xyrēsontai*, **shave**, is found only here and in I Corinthians 11:5. In 18:18 it is "shorn" *(keiramenos)*. This is an example of the future indicative after *hina*, found several times in the New Testament (e.g., Matt. 13:15; Rev. 6:11; 14:13). **Walkest orderly** is *stoicheis* (cf. *peripatein*, vs. 21). The verb means literally "*to be in rows* [fr. *stoichos*, a row], *to walk in line* (especially of marching in file to battle). Metaphorically, in late writers, *to walk by rule*." [42] Aside from this passage, it is used only by Paul (Rom. 4:12; Gal. 5:25; 6:16; Phil. 3:16).

25 For **we wrote**, see 15:23. *Apesteilamen*,[43] **wrote**, is literally "sent" (cf. RSV—"we have sent a letter").

---

to this very people to show them the superiority of Christ and His grace to Moses and the Law, with a view to saving them from the death-dealing influence of legalism to the Christian spirit and liberty. The final effect of this legalism in the church is evidenced by the fact that Palestinian Jewish Christianity never outlived the first century. Little wonder that Paul wrote to the Corinthian church, which had come under the influence of these Judaizers, "the letter killeth, but the spirit giveth life" (II Cor. 3:6b).

That the slanderous accusations brought against Paul contained in Acts 21:21 were clearly false is seen from Acts 16:1–4. But Dummelow remarks, "it had this amount of truth in it that St. Paul's principle that a man is saved by faith in Christ and not by the works of the law would naturally lead to the abandonment of the ceremonial law even by the Jews." [b] However, for expediency's sake, the elders advised Paul to reassure both the Jews and Jewish Christians by joining **four men that have a vow on them** (vs. 23) in their purification rites. These men were evidently Nazarites (cf. Num. 6:1–21). Paul was advised to associate himself with them in the vow during the week that remained (vs. 27) and to pay for their sacrifices. Thus by taking the Nazarite vow and defraying the sacrificial expenses of these men, Paul could reassure both Jews and Christians of his loyalty to Moses, as well as to Christ (cf. Acts 18:18 with notes). Further, such an act on Paul's part would reflect an acceptable mark of charity toward those of his own race who were unable to pay the expenses of their sacrificial vows. Such appears to have been the intent of Herod Agrippa I, according to Josephus.[c] C. W. Emmet raises the question: "Was Paul's action, as Harnack suggests, a way of expending part of the contribution he had brought?" [d]

In verse twenty-one James appears only to reassure Paul of the position of the Jerusalem church concerning conditions for the admission of Gentile Christians to the church, as decided by the Jerusalem Council.[e] That these conditions had not changed for the Gentile Christians, James here makes clear.

Of verse 26 Dummelow offers the following free translation:

> He entered into the Temple, informing the priests that within seven days (see V, 27) the days of their purification would be accomplished and he purposed to remain with them in the Temple for a whole week until the legal sacrifice had been offered for each of them.[f]

Windisch offers, with considerable reservation and misgiving but by concession, the following considerations of Paul's conduct at this juncture:

[41] *Ant*. XIX, 6, 1. [42] Abbott-Smith, *op. cit.*, p. 418. [43] B D. But Aleph A C have *epesteilamen*.
[b] Dummelow, *op. cit.*, pp. 847, 848. [c] Josephus, *op. cit.*, "Ant", XIX, VI, 1.
[d] F. J. Foakes-Jackson and Kirsopp Lake, *The Beginnings of Christianity* (London: Macmillan and Company, LTD., rep. 1942), Pt. 1, II, 294, n. 2.
[e] For a full discussion of this whole matter, see notes on Acts 15:1–34, but especially vss. 13-21.
[f] Dummelow, *op. cit.*, p. 848.

26 Then Paul took the men, and the next day purifying himself with them went into the temple, declaring the fulfilment of the days of purification, until the offering was offered for every one of them.

---

26 *Diangellōn*, **declaring,** is used only by Luke (here and in Luke 9:60) except in a quotation from the Septuagint (Rom. 9:17). It means "publish abroad, proclaim." Probably it has to do primarily with an announcement to the priests.[44] *Ekplērōsin*, **fulfilment,** (only here in N.T.) is literally "filling out." This apparently refers to "the seven days" (vs. 27). *Hagnismon*, **purification,** is found only here in the New Testament. **Until** evidently means that Paul remained in the temple "until each one's offering was presented."[45] Rackham says: "It seems very likely that he *went into the temple* four days—one day for each one of them."[46] The **offering** (*prosphora*, "a bringing to") for each consisted of one male lamb, one ewe lamb, and one ram, with the accompanying meal and drink offerings (Num. 6:13–15).

---

(1) It is not impossible that Paul, following the principle enunciated in I Cor. IX, 20 (cf. also X, 23, VIII, 1 ff.; Rom. XIV.), made a point of observing the ceremonial Law when he lived among the Jews and especially, when he was at a festival in Jerusalem. (2) Paul may have felt that circumstances, of which we are unaware, justified his concession to Jewish legal scruples on this occasion. (3) Luke may even have related the incident with the special purpose of showing how grievously the Jews had sinned against one so scrupulous to obey the Law as Paul.[g]

Withal it appears most satisfactory to view this incident in the light of the principles which Paul lays down for himself in the Corinthian letter: "I am become all things to all men, that I may by all means save some" (I Cor. 9:22b; see also vss. 19–23). Jackson and Lake remark:

Hence Luke's object was not so much to show that Paul was a strict Jew, but that he was still so far in sympathy with Judaism as to be able to take his part in a religious rite which did not compromise his principles . . . Paul's action does not necessarily imply that he himself had taken a vow, still less that he recognized the ceremonial law as a means of securing salvation.[h]

II. PAUL CONFRONTS JEWISH HOSTILITY

(21:26–36)

It is impossible to state whether Paul was mistaken in accepting the advice of the elders. However, four facts emerge from his compliance with this advice. *First*, Paul's well-intentioned conduct did not accomplish the desired end (vs. 27); *second*, there is no scriptural evidence that either the elders or other Jerusalem Christians supported Paul in his trials here, though a final conclusion cannot be based upon the absence of evidence (see exception in Acts 23:16–22); *third*, the motives of both the elders and Paul remain unquestioned in the light of all available evidence; and *fourth*, the eventuation of the whole affair brought Paul on his way to his desired goal, Rome. Thus if there were well-intended human mistakes, nevertheless God overruled them to the accomplishment of His purpose in the life and ministry of Paul, and thus Paul's philosophy of Romans 8:28 was vindicated. Further, who can say that God was not at this time affording the Judean Jews their last opportunity for repentance and the acceptance of the Messiah before the sharp ax of Roman destruction should fall in A.D. 70.

Rackham has suggested the following parallels between Paul's and Christ's last days in Jerusalem:

The history of the Lord's passion seems to be repeating itself. Like the Lord Jesus, Paul is carried before the Sanhedrin and smitten on the mouth; the multitude of the people cry out, *Away with him;* his fellow countrymen deliver him into the hands of the Gentiles; he is accused before the Roman governor and stands before a Herod; his accusers are the same, the Sadduccean highpriesthood, as also the counts of the indictment which culminate in the charge of treason against Caesar; three times he is pronounced to have done nothing worthy of death, yet he narrowly escapes a scourging, and the governor leaves him bound in order to please the Jews [Lk xxiii, 25.]: incidentally the trial of Jesus resulted in the renewal of friendly relations between Pilate and Herod Antipas, so likewise Paul's case enables Festus to pay a compliment to Herod Agrippa II. Finally, the close of the

---

[44] Cf. Hackett, *op. cit.*, p. 251. [45] *Ibid.* [46] *Op. cit.*, p. 415.

[g] Jackson and Lake, *op. cit.*, II, 321. [h] *Ibid.*, II, 294.

27 And when the seven days were almost completed, the Jews from Asia, when they saw him in the temple, stirred up all the multitude and laid hands on him,

28 crying out, Men of Israel, help: This is the man that teacheth all men everywhere against the people, and the law, and this place; and moreover he brought Greeks also into the temple, and hath defiled this holy place.

29 For they had before seen with him in the city Trophimus the Ephesian, whom they supposed that Paul had brought into the temple.

---

27 For **the seven days,** see Numbers 6:9. This suggests that these men under a Nazirite vow had been defiled, and so after seven days had to be shaved and make their offering of purification.

James had feared the attitude of the Christian Jews toward Paul (vss. 20–22). But it was apparently non-Christian **Jews from Asia** who raised a riot against him. **Stirred up** is the verb *syncheō*, which means "to pour together, confuse"; and so metaphorically, "confound, throw into confusion." [47] It is found only here in the New Testament.

28 **Defiled** is the verb *koinoō*, which literally means "make common." In the Septuagint and New Testament, it means "make ceremonially unclean." Its only other use in Acts is in connection with Peter's vision (10:15; 11:9).

29 **Before seen** is the verb *proorao*, found only here and in 2:25 (from LXX). **Trophimus** is evidently the same one mentioned in 20:4, as a delegate from Asia. Klausner's suggestion that "Paul may actually have brought Trophimus into the Temple" [48] is absolutely unacceptable in the light of the apostle's behavior here.

---

book leaves the apostle in a state of comparative freedom and activity: like S. Peter in ch. xii, he has experienced a deliverance—almost, we might say, a resurrection from the dead. This resemblance is not due to arbitrary invention. It is the natural working out of a law which had been enunciated by the Lord himself: 'as the master, so shall the servant be.' In the Revelation, in a symbolical picture (xi, 1–12), S. John has shown that the experience of the Lord's witnesses must be the same as that of the Lord, the Faithful Witness, himself. How much more certain this will become, when the servant is standing in the same position and on the same spot as the master. Granted the same situation, then the greater the inward likeness of the servant to his master, the greater will be the outward likeness of their experience.[i]

A. Paul Attacked by the Jewish Mob (21:26–31a)

The Jews . . . laid hands on him, vs. 27. Mention of the **Jews from Asia** (vs. 27), who were responsible for the incitement of mob violence against Paul at Jerusalem, appears to give validity to the suggestion that Alexander had been used by these very Jews in an attempt to aggravate the similar riotous situation at Ephesus (see Acts 19:33). In fact, there are certain similarities between the Ephesian and Jerusalem riots; to wit, the multitudinous uproar (vss. 27, 28, 30), the attempted violence (vss. 30, 31), the rescue by the Roman officials (vs. 31–33), and the confused issue of the occasion (vs. 34).[j]

The occasion of the Jerusalem riot against Paul appears to have been due to the presence of Trophimus in Jerusalem. When the Asian orthodox Jews saw Paul in the Temple (vs. 27), they assumed that Trophimus, an Ephesian Gentile Christian whom they knew and who had before been seen with Paul in Jerusalem, was with him in the Temple (vs. 28b, 29). Had their assumption been correct, they would have had legal right to kill Trophimus, who was a Gentile,[k] though not Paul, who was both a Jew and a Roman citizen (see notes on Acts 7:57, 58).

The outer court of the Temple was designated the "Court of the Gentiles." Within this was the "Court of the Women." Between the two was a high wall with doors. An inscription on a stone found in Jerusalem in 1871 and now in the Museum of the Ancient Orient at Istanbul reads: "No foreigner may enter within the balustrade and enclosure around the sanctuary. Whoever is caught will render himself liable to

[47] Abbott-Smith, *op. cit.*, p. 434.

[48] Joseph Klausner, *From Jesus to Paul*, p. 400.

[i] Richard B. Rackham, *The Acts of the Apostles*, Westminster Commentary (London: Methuen and Company LTD., 1922), p. 404.

[j] For comparison, see Acts 19:23–41.

[k] So states Josephus, "Wars," *op. cit.*, VI, II, 4.

30 And all the city was moved, and the people ran together; and they laid hold on Paul, and dragged him out of the temple: and straightway the doors were shut.

31 And as they were seeking to kill him, tidings came up to the chief captain of the band, that all Jerusalem was in confusion.

32 And forthwith he took soldiers and centurions, and ran down upon them: and they, when they saw the chief captain and the soldiers, left off beating Paul.

---

30 **Was moved** is the verb *kinēo* (cf. kinetic). In the New Testament it means "excite, stir up" only here and in 24:5. **The people ran together** is literally "there took place *(egeneto)* a running together (*syndromē*) of the people." *Syndromē* (only here in N.T.) is used by such Greek writers as Aristotle for the "forming of a mob." [49] **Dragged** is the verb *helkō* found in Acts only here and in 16:19. Bruce comments thus on the imperfect here: "With the jostling crowd, dragging Paul out was a slow process; they occupied the time in beating him." [50]

31 Of **band** Lake and Cadbury write: "The garrison of Jerusalem consisted of one cohort of auxiliaries, made up—at least on paper—of 760 infantry with a detachment of 240 cavalry." [51] **Was in confusion** is the verb *synchynnō*, in the New Testament found only in Acts (2:6; 9:22; 19:32, and here). It is the Hellenistic form of *syncheō* (cf. vs. 27).

---

the death penalty which will inevitably follow." [l] Speaking of this wall, Josephus quotes Titus the Roman general as saying to the Jews at the siege of Jerusalem 70 A.D., "Have not you been allowed . . . to engrave in Greek, and in your own letters [Hebrew or Aramaic], this prohibition, that no foreigner should go beyond the wall? Have not we given you leave to kill such as go beyond it, though he were a Roman?" [m] However, there is not a shred of evidence that their assumption was correct. They were guilty of the logical fallacy of "false association." Paul most likely had in mind this temple barrier between Jewish and Gentile Christians when he later wrote of Christ's removal of "the middle wall of partition" (Eph. 2:13–19).

The accusations shouted against Paul by the mob are reminiscent of similar accusations hurled against Stephen, who under like circumstances became the Church's first illegal martyr. The charges consisted of teaching, *first*, **against the people**, or perhaps better, the customs of the Jewish people (cf. Acts 6:14); *second*, against **the law** (cf. Acts 6:13b); *third*, against the Temple, **this place** (cf. Acts 6:13b); and *fourth*, they charged that he **defiled this holy place**, which was equivalent to blasphemy (cf. Acts 6:11). This last accusation was later modified by Paul's enemies before the governor Felix, to the effect that "he assayed to profane the temple" (Acts 24:6; cf. Acts 21:29b). This marks the disposition to greater accuracy in legal procedure where the accuser is held responsible for his statements than when he is under the emotional excitement of irresponsible and unrestrained mob psychology.

Upon the violent eviction of Paul (cf. vs. 32b) from the Temple, the guards hurriedly closed the doors between the "Court of the Jews" and the "Court of the Gentiles" (vs. 30). This measure was likely in part to insure against any other Gentiles entering the inner court, and possibly also to prevent profanation of the Temple by the violence of the mob. Wesley thinks that this action was designed in part "to prevent Paul's taking sanctuary at the horns of the altar." [n] That the Jews' intention was to commit an illegal act of murder on Paul is clear (Acts 21:31a; cf. Acts 7:57–8:1a).

B. Paul Rescued by the Roman Army (21:31b–36)

Then the chief captain came near, and laid hold on him, vs. 33a.

News of the riot quickly reached Claudius Lysias, the chief captain or tribune of the "Italian Band" or "Cohort," which was quartered in the tower of Antonia. The location of this tower where troops were stationed, especially during Jewish feast

[49] Arndt and Gingrich, *op. cit.*, p. 793. [50] *Acts*, p. 396. [51] *Beginnings*, IV, 275.

[l] Finegan, *op. cit.*, p. 246. [m] Josephus, "Wars," *loc. cit.* [n] Wesley, *op. cit.*, p. 484, n. 30.

33 Then the chief captain came near, and laid hold on him, and commanded him to be bound with two chains; and inquired who he was, and what he had done.
34 And some shouted one thing, some another, among the crowd: and when he could not know the certainty for the uproar, he commanded him to be brought into the castle.
35 And when he came upon the stairs, so it was that he was borne of the soldiers for the violence of the crowd;
36 for the multitude of the people followed after, crying out, Away with him.
37 And as Paul was about to be brought into the castle, he saith unto the chief captain, May I say something unto thee? And he said, Dost thou know Greek?
38 Art thou not then the Egyptian, who before these days stirred up to sedition and led out into the wilderness the four thousand men of the Assassins?

---

33 **Who he was** is *tis eiē,* a classical construction with the optative used in the New Testament only by Luke. It is literally "who he might be."

34 **Shouted** is literally "were shouting" *(epephonoun).* In the New Testament it is used only by Luke (four times). **Castle** is *parembolē,* which in Acts (seven times) means "barracks" (cf. RSV).

35 *Anabathmous,* **stairs,** occurs in the New Testament only here and in verse 40. **Violence** is *bian* (cf. 5:26).

36 For **away with him,** see 22:22.

38 "Art thou not"? could be translated "Then you are not?!" The fact that Paul used Greek in speaking to the tribune showed that he was not the Egyptian. Knowling renders it, "'Thou art not then' (as I supposed)." [52] **Four thousand** seems a contradiction of Josephus' figure of 30,000.[53] But perhaps the tribune only reckoned the number of armed **men,** while Josephus mentions 30,000 followers in the revolt.[54]

The Romans had special scorn for an **Egyptian,** as did also the Jews and the Greeks. Cadbury quotes from a papyrus letter written by a Greek, as follows: "You are, my brothers, perhaps considering me a barbarian or an inhuman Egyptian." [55]

---

occasions as a protection against riots, commanded a clear view of the "Court of the Gentiles." [o]

The statement that the captain **took soldiers and centurions** (vs. 32) indicates that at least 200 militia were called out, since a centurion commanded 100 soldiers. Immediately upon the arrival of the soldiers, Paul's assailants ceased beating him (vs. 32b). Both as a measure against the escape of a possible criminal and as a protection against further violence by the Jews, the captain arrested **Paul** and **bound** [him] **with two chains** (vs. 33a). This likely means that Paul was handcuffed to a soldier on either side (cf. Acts 12:6, 7b). The captain neither knew who Paul was, nor what his offense had been (vs. 33b). Nor was the mob of any help in clarifying the issue, since in their emotional confusion **some shouted one thing, some another** (vs. 34). Duty demanded that he know the truth of the matter, as well as afford protection and justice to the accused. Therefore Lysias took Paul to the castle barracks (vs. 34).

Under the violent impulse of a recurrent surge of uncontrolled emotion and hatred the mob bore in on the soldiers as they led Paul to the tower, like a great wave of the turbulent ocean that drives the vessel against the rocky cliff. Here, as on the occasion of Christ's last experience in Jerusalem, the frenzied mob of religious fanatics cried, **Away with him** or "slay him" (vs. 36; cf. Luke 23:18; John 19:15).

III. PAUL PREPARES TO ADDRESS THE JEWS

(21:37–40)

Paul had planned and labored long to bring the collection to the Jerusalem church. He did not propose to lose any opportunity to vindicate his cause, which apparently had so seriously aborted. Thus he requested permission to speak to the captain, evidently

[52] EGT, II, 454. [53] *War* ,II, 13, 4 f. [54] Knowling, EGT, II, 454.
[55] Cadbury, *Book of Acts in History*, p. 33.

[o] For a description of this Roman fortress see Josephus, "Wars," *op. cit.*, V, V, 8.

39 But Paul said, I am a Jew, of Tarsus in Cilicia, a citizen of no mean city: and I beseech thee, give me leave to speak unto the people.
40 And when he had given him leave, Paul, standing on the stairs, beckoned with the hand unto the people; and when there was made a great silence, he spake unto them in the Hebrew language, saying,

---

39 Of **no mean city** Cadbury writes: "Not only is the phrase, 'no mean' in form and application entirely idiomatic but it may be implied from occurrences elsewhere that it is particularly expressive of Greek pride . . . [meaning] pre-eminently Greek." [56]

40 **Hebrew** is *Ebrais*, which occurs only in Acts (cf. 22:2; 26:14). It usually means Aramaic. The cognate adverb is Ebraisti, which means Aramaic, except in Revelation 9:11.[57] Josephus claims he first wrote his *Jewish War* in Aramaic and then translated it into Greek.[58]

---

with the further purpose of gaining permission to address the Jews.

A. Paul's Mistaken Identity (21:37, 38)

Art thou not then the Egyptian, vs. 38a.

The captain's question, **Dost thou know Greek?** (vs. 37b) appears to indicate that he was not familiar with the Latin and hoped to converse with Paul in Greek, with which he evidently was familiar. That Lysias was not a Roman appears further evident from Acts 22:28. It may be observed here that, as a Jew, Paul had a perfect right to be in the Temple worshiping, and that, as a citizen of Tarsus (a free Roman city), he might naturally claim to speak the Greek language.

Immediately upon learning that Paul spoke Greek, the captain jumped to the conclusion that he was the long-sought Egyptian leader of a band of Assassins that had harassed the Romans in Judea (vs. 38; see Exegesis). Such bands of Assassins were common in Judea at this time. They were known as "*Sicarii*" because they hid a knife, "*sica*," in their clothing, and then during religious festivals engaged in "patriotic assassinations." [p] They seem to have been extreme members of the patriotic party of the Zealots. They assassinated influential Jews who were friendly to the Roman rule, as well as Roman officials. They arose during the governorship of Felix (A.D. 52–60), or possibly earlier, and their activities were finally responsible for misleading Judea into revolt and consequent destruction by the Romans in A.D. 70.[q]

According to Josephus,[r] an Egyptian had come to Jerusalem about three years earlier and set himself forth as a prophet, and likely as a purported patriotic deliverer of the Jews from the Romans. He acquired a sizeable following,[s] as such "Messiahs" usually do, from among the disgruntled Jewish populace. He led his band to the Mount of Olives with the promise that the Jerusalem walls would fall at his command (cf. Josh. 6), and they would then easily defeat the Roman garrison and fall into command of the country. However, the governor Felix, sent a contingent of soldiers against them with the result that many were killed, while others were taken prisoners. The leader himself escaped. Thus Lysias reasoned that the sullen resentment of the Jews had at last found expression in their manhandling of this insurrectionist by whom they had been misled and who had now appeared to attempt a second insurrection.

B. Paul's True Identity (21:39, 40)

But Paul said, I am a Jew, of Tarsus in Cilicia, vs. 39a.

Though Lysias seems not to have been unduly impressed with Paul's statement that he was **a Jew, of Tarsus in Cilicia, a citizen of no mean city** (vs. 39), he nevertheless granted him permission to address the Jews who waited below in the outer court of the Temple. Ramsay states:

> The view which we take is that the Jews of Tarsus were, as a body, citizens with full burgess rights. That does not, of course, exclude the possibility that there were some or even many resident stranger Jews in the city. The right of

[56] *Ibid.*, pp. 32 f. [57] Abbott-Smith, *op. cit.*, p. 127. [58] *War*, Preface. 1.

[p] Josephus *op. cit.*, "Wars," II, XIII, 3.
[q] Mould, *op. cit.*, p. 471.
[r] Josephus, *op. cit.*, "*Antiquities*," XX, VIII, 6.
[s] *Ibid.*, "Wars," II, XIII, 5.

citizenship could only be got by inheritance from a citizen father, apart from exceptional cases in which it was bestowed by a formal law on an individual as a reward for services rendered to the city; but such cases were comparatively few in any one city, for the right was jealously guarded.[t]

Customarily, Paul **beckoned with the hand unto the people** (vs. 40) as a gesture for attention (cf. Acts 13:16) and then proceeded to address the Jews in the Hebrew, or possibly Aramaic, language which "was not only the vernacular of Palestinian Jews but was the common speech of all non-Greek speakers in western Asia, as far east as (and including) the Parthian empire beyond the Euphrates."[u] It is noteworthy that Paul's speech here reiterates the exact opening words of Stephen's defense, **Brethren and fathers,** before the Sanhedrin (cf. Acts 7:2). Nor is this the only instance in which Paul's speeches reflect the influence of Stephen's earlier address on his thought, manner, and life.

[t] W. M. Ramsay, *The Cities of St. Paul*, (London: Hodder and Stoughton), p. 174.
[u] Bruce, *op. cit.*, p. 437.

CHAPTER XXII

Brethren and fathers, hear ye the defence which I now make unto you.

2 And when they heard that he spake unto them in the Hebrew language, they were the more quiet: and he saith,

---

EXEGESIS

1 *Andres adelphoi kai pateres,* **brethren and fathers,** is exactly the same as the opening words of Stephen's speech (7:2). **Defence** is *apologia* (cf. apology). In Acts it occurs only here and in 25:16 (five times in Paul).

2 **Language** is *dialektos* (cf. dialect), found (in N.T.) only in Acts (1:19; 2:6, 8; 21:40; 22:2; 26:14). Originally meaning "conversation," "discourse" (from *dialegomai),* in later writers it is used for the language of a people. **They were the more quiet** is literally "they gave more quietness" *(mallon pareschon hēsychian).* The last word is found only here in Acts.

EXPOSITION

THE APOSTLE'S LAST VISIT TO JUDEA (cont'd.)

IV. Paul's Defense before the Jews, Acts 22:1–21.
- A. Paul's Heritage as a Jew, vss. 1–5.
- B. Paul's Encounter with Christ, vss. 6–14.
- C. Paul's Commission from Christ, vss. 15, 16.
- D. Paul's Premonition of Jewish Hostility, vss. 17–21.

V. Paul's Appeal to his Roman Citizenship, Acts 22:22–30.
- A. The Jews Reject Paul, vss. 22, 23.
- B. The Captain Examines Paul, vss. 24, 25a.
- C. The Roman Law Protects Paul, vss. 25b–30.

IV. PAUL'S DEFENSE BEFORE THE JEWS

(22:1–21)

From the steps of the castle Paul stretched forth his hand for attention and spoke forth in the Hebrew (Aramaic) dialect of Judea, though he might have employed the Greek, addressing his assailants as **Brethren and fathers** (vs. 1). Plumptre thinks this was the "received formula"[a] in addressing any assembly of which the scribes and elders were a part. Both the gesture for attention and the employment of his nation's language were designed to identify the speaker with his audience and secure respect and good will. That this purpose was in a measure achieved is evident from their increased interest and attention: **they were the more quiet** (vs. 2b). Their surprise at hearing "the sound of their holy mother-tongue awed them into deeper silence,"[b] occurring as it did at the moment when they expected the renegade to address them in Greek. Lechler[c] observes that Paul's employment of the address **brethren** expressed his love for his own race, while his use of **fathers** conveyed his respect for the eminent rulers of the Jews, some of whom may have been in his audience. Bruce remarks that Paul's speech which follows is both "autobiographical and apologetic."[d]

A. Paul's Heritage as a Jew (22:1–5)

I am a Jew, vs. 3a.

Paul's declaratory statement, **I am a Jew,** seems designed to answer two questions and allay suspicion accordingly. *First,* by this assertion Paul re-emphasized his answer to the captain's question, "Art thou not then the Egyptian?" (Acts 21:38a); and *Second,* he refuted the Jew's accusation that he was

[a] Ellicott, *op. cit.,* VII, 150.
[b] Jamieson, Faussett, and Brown, *Commentary, Critical and Explanatory on the Old and New Testaments* (Grand Rapids: Zondervan Publishing House, n.d.) II, 211.
[c] Lange, *op. cit.,* p. 398. [d] Bruce, *op. cit.,* p. 440.

3 I am a Jew, born in Tarsus of Cilicia, but brought up in this city, at the feet of Gamaliel, instructed according to the strict manner of the law of our fathers, being zealous for God, even as ye all are this day:
4 and I persecuted this Way unto the death, binding and delivering into prisons both men and women.

---

3 **Brought up** is the verb *anatrephō*, which (in N.T.) occurs only here and in 7:20, 21. It may be translated "educated." **Instructed** is the verb *paideuō*, which comes from *pais*, "child." In classical Greek it meant "*to train children*, hence, generally, *to teach, instruct*."[1] *Akribeian*, **strict manner,** is found only here in the New Testament. It means "exactness."[2] It is used thus in the papyri.[3] **Born, brought up,** and **instructed** are all perfect passive participles in the Greek.

4 *Desmeuōn*, **binding,** is found in Acts only here. It means "putting in chains."

---

a renegade Jew. This fundamental statement is supported by the evidence that follows.

First, Paul reminded his hearers that his education had been in the cultural environment of their sacred, religious capital, Jerusalem (vs. 3). This likely began soon after he became "a son of the Law" at twelve years of age (cf. Luke 2:42). Further, he implies that he had benefited from the personal instruction of the single greatest teacher Judaism had ever produced, Gamaliel (vs. 3). Paul's expression, **at the feet of Gamaliel,** reflects the custom of the Jewish rabbinical school where the scholars sat on the floor with the Rabbi on a high chair above them. Thus the expression "sitting at the feet" of a superior instructor persists. Like his Master, Paul had sat "in the midst of the teachers [doctors], both hearing them, and asking them questions" (Luke 2:46).

Paul makes clear that his education under this revered Gamaliel had been thorough and accurate, in accordance with the Jewish educational system (vs. 3). In fact, there appears a subtle suggestion in his defense, to the effect that he had more nearly adhered to Gamaliel's teaching than had his countrymen. One authority points out that "Paul's version of what the rabbis commonly taught concerning the law shows little sign of the influence of Gamaliel, who laid much stress on the importance of repentance rather than on 'works.'[e] The foregoing writer continues: "Indeed one feels that at times Paul's Christian doctrine is nearer to the mind of the great rabbi than is the type of rabbinical doctrine which he attacks."[f]

Second, in consequence of the foregoing exact and rigorous instruction, Paul compares his religious **zeal** to that of his hearers (vs. 3b). Plumptre significantly remarks:

> The Apostle . . . claims their sympathy as having at one time shared all their dearest convictions. There is, perhaps, a touch of higher enthusiasm in the Apostle's language. He was a zealot for God: they were zealots for the law.[g]

As Lechler phrases it, "The Apostle . . . remarks: '*I* was once what *ye* are; ye are still today, indeed, at this very moment, what I too was at a former period.'"[h] In support of the assertion of his former role as a zealot, Paul describes his persecutions of the Christians by a tactfully guarded allusion: **this Way** (cf. Acts 9:2; 19:9, 23; 24:14, 22) **unto the death** (cf. Gal. 1:14; Phil. 3:5,6). In this last statement Paul may well have been assuming responsibility for his part in the martyrdom of Stephen. In a subtle manner Paul appears to set in contrast **the Way** (cf. John 14:6) of eternal life which belongs to the Christian believer, with *the death* which can never extinguish that life in Christ (cf. John 11:25, 26). This fact he discovered for himself as the chief persecutor of the Christians. Paul's testimony here accords with Luke's earlier account (Acts 8:3; 9:2), that he completely disregarded the sanctity of the home as well as sex differences in his vicious onslaughts against the Christians.

Paul's statement, **binding and delivering into prisons** (vs. 4), is more specific than Luke's earlier account of these activities (cf. Acts 9:2). The Millers state that the

[1] Abbott-Smith, *op. cit.*, p. 333. [2] Arndt and Gingrich, *op. cit.*, p. 32. [3] VGT, p. 19.

[e] *The Interpreter's Bible*, IX, 290. [f] *Ibid.* [g] Ellicott, *op. cit.*, p. 151. [h] Lange, *op. cit.*, p. 399.

5 As also the high priest doth bear me witness, and all the estate of the elders: from whom also I received letters unto the brethren, and journeyed to Damascus to bring them also that were there unto Jerusalem in bonds to be punished.

6 And it came to pass, that, as I made my journey, and drew nigh unto Damascus, about noon, suddenly there shone from heaven a great light round about me.

7 And I fell unto the ground, and heard a voice saying unto me, Saul, Saul, why persecutest thou me?

---

5 **Estate of the elders** is *presbyterion* (cf. presbytery). Occurring three times in the New Testament, it is translated three different ways in the King James Version (cf. "elders," Luke 22:66; "presbytery," I Tim. 4:14). Lake and Cadbury write: "Comparison with Luke xxii, 66 shows that *presbyterion* is equivalent to Sanhedrin."[4] *Axōn*, **to bring,** is a future participle expressing purpose.[5] *Ekeise*, **there** (cf. 21:3), is literally "thither." If this strict sense is pressed, the reference will be to Christians who had fled to Damascus from the persecutions in Jerusalem. But probably it is only equivalent to *ekei*. **Punished** is the verb *timōreō*, found in the New Testament only here and in 26:11.

6 *Mesēmbrian*, **noon,** is found only here and in 8:26, where it is translated "the south." **Suddenly,** is *exaiphnēs* (elsewhere in Acts only 9:3). **Shone** is the verb *periastraptō*, which occurs only here and in 9:3 (in the original account of Saul's conversion). It means "flash around."

7 *Edaphos*, **ground,** may mean "pavement."[6] In the papyri it is used for "land."[7]

"prisons of the Near East were sordid"[i] in Bible times. Offenders were incarcerated in *natural* pits or cavelike dungeons where life was eked out by the bread and water "of affliction" (cf. I Kings 22:27). Prisoners were sometimes cast into these pits where their feet were caught in snares (see Jer. 18:22; 48:43). Some were bound with chains (Isa. 61:1), and yet others had their feet fast in stocks (Acts 16:24). Even the dead bodies of the slain were sometimes concealed in these prison pits (Jer. 41:7; cf. 38:11–13, 28; 39:15–18). The punishments alluded to (vs. 5b) would have included scourgings and brutal violence (cf. Acts 9:2; 26:10, 11). The Acts' record gives numerous accounts of the imprisonment of Christians (Acts 4:3; 5:19; 12:1, 4ff.). Paul himself had various occasions to reflect on his treatment of the Christians before his conversion, as he subsequently suffered like fate (see II Cor. 11:23; Eph. 4:1; Acts 16:23ff.; Acts 21:33, 37; 23:35; II Tim. 4:16). Characteristics of jailers and prisoners are depicted in various Bible accounts (see Acts 12:6ff.; 16:25, 27–34; Gen. 40). Something of Christ's tender compassion for prisoners (Matt. 25:36, 39, 43 f.) seems to be indicated in Paul's reflection on his former maltreatment of Christ's followers (vs. 4b).

In support of the truth of his zeal for the law and deadly hatred of Christians, Paul appeals to the testimony of the high priest Ananias, son of Nebaeus, who may have been present and who would have been apprised of the official acts of his predecessors. His further appeal for support to **the estate of the elders** is doubtless an allusion to the Sanhedrin and Senate, if indeed the latter is to be distinguished from the former (see exegetical note on vs. 5). The permanent records of this body would have revealed the official documents issued to Paul for the arrest, return, and punishment of Christians who had likely taken refuge in Damascus following the martyrdom of Stephen (vs. 4b, 5). All of this Paul did as a zealous Jew. **The brethren** (vs. 5) were Jews with whom Paul subtly identified himself in his defense.

B. Paul's Encounter with Christ (22:6–14)

I am Jesus of Nazareth, whom thou persecutest, vs. 8b.

The three accounts of Paul's encounter with Christ on the Damascus road, as recorded by Luke, vary but little in their essen-

[4] *Beginnings*, IV, 279.
[5] Cf. Robertson, *Grammar*, p. 877.
[6] Abbott-Smith, *op. cit.*, p. 129
[7] VGT, p. 180.

[i] Miller, *op. cit.*, p. 580.

8 And I answered, Who art thou, Lord? And he said unto me, I am Jesus of Nazareth, whom thou persecutest.
9 And they that were with me beheld indeed the light, but they heard not the voice of him that spoke to me.
10 And I said, What shall I do, Lord? And the Lord said unto me, Arise, and go into Damascus; and there it shall be told thee of all things which are appointed for thee to do.
11 And when I could not see for the glory of that light, being led by the hand of them that were with me I came into Damascus.

---

9 For the seeming contradiction between this and 9:7, see note on the latter.

11 **For** is literally "from" *(apo)*. But Bruce states: "The causal use of *apo* . . . has parallels both in classical and vernacular Greek." [i]

---

tial elements. The first, in Acts 9:1–19, is recorded in the third person, while the other two accounts in Acts 22:5–21 and Acts 26:12–20, respectively, are recorded in the first person. (For a full treatment of this experience, see notes on Acts 9:1–19.) Only such items of the experience as are recorded in Acts 22, but not in Acts 9, will be discussed here.

Paul's special note of the hour, **about noon** (vs. 6), when his encounter with Christ occurred is not recorded in Acts 9, though a similar expression, **at midday** (26:13a) is employed in Acts 26. Plumptre says that this expression "may fairly be taken as characteristic of a personal recollection of the circumstances of the great event."[j] Nor is it to be supposed that so unusual an experience as Paul had with Christ at this time, with its transforming effects on his whole future, could ever be forgotten, either as to the place or time of its occurrence.

Concerning Paul's introduction of the appellation **Jesus of Nazareth** (vs. 8), not found in Acts 9:5 or 26:15, Lechler observes that "it is very appropriately employed when Paul addresses an assemblage of unconverted Jews, to whom he mentions Jesus for the first time." [k]

Verse nine is found only in this chapter. It seems to signify that while his companions in travel saw the light that blinded Paul, they did not understand the meaning of the voice that spoke to him from heaven (cf. John 12:28, 29). (For further comment on this problem, see exegetical note.)

Verse ten is found in neither of the other accounts of Paul's conversion. It appears clearly to imply that Paul recognized himself to be no longer master of his own fate, but now subject to the will of the divine. The Galilean had conquered, and Paul was ever after "a servant of Jesus Christ" (cf. Rom. 1:1).

Paul takes pains to mention that **Ananias [was] a devout man according to the law, well reported of by all the Jews that dwelt there** (vs. 12). Thus he indicates that this man who is called a **disciple** (a Christian) in Acts 9:10 was also a pious and law-abiding Jew who was highly esteemed by all the Jews at Damascus. Yet it was he who visited Paul and prayed for his recovery (vs. 13). This description was intended as a reconciliatory gesture toward the Jews whom Paul addressed. Such a person as Ananias would not have associated himself with Paul, had he been a renegade blasphemer. Further, this pious Ananias would have required evidence that Paul's conversion was of divine origin.

Three things are recorded of Ananias' message to Paul in this chapter, which are not in chapter 9. *First*, Paul is **to know his will.** It was Paul's final submission to Christ that brought to him a knowledge of God's will (cf. John 7:17). *Second*, Paul was appointed **to see the Righteous One** (cf. Isa. 6:1). *Third*, he was appointed to receive God's message from heaven for communication to **all men** (cf. vss. 14 and 15).

Paul's use of the name **Righteous One** (vs. 14b) for Christ is both striking and instructive. Plumptre remarks:

> The name does not appear to have been one of the received titles of the expected Messiah, but may have been suggested by Isa. XI, 4, 5. It seems to have been accepted by the Church of

[i] *Acts*, p. 402.

[j] Ellicott, *op. cit.*, p. 151.

[k] Lange, *loc. cit.*

12 And one Ananias, a devout man according to the law, well reported of by all the Jews that dwelt there,
13 came unto me, and standing by me said unto me, Brother Saul, receive thy sight. And in that very hour I looked up on him.
14 And he said, The God of our fathers hath appointed thee to know his will, and to see the Righteous One, and to hear a voice from his mouth.
15 For thou shalt be a witness for him unto all men of what thou hast seen and heard.
16 And now why tarriest thou? arise, and be baptized, and wash away thy sins, calling on his name.

---

13 **Receive . . . sight** and **looked up** are the same verb, *anablepō*. In the first the prepositional prefix *ana* has one of its meanings, "again." In the second it has its other meaning "up." One cannot translate the verb "see again" in both clauses (because of **on him**); but Meyer prefers to render it "look up" both times,[9] which is allowable.

14 **Appointed** is the verb *procheirizomai* found only in Acts (cf. 3:20; 26:16). It means "*to take into one's hands*"; hence, metaphorically, "*to propose, to determine, choose.*"[10]

15 Paul had **seen** Christ and **heard** His voice.

16 *Baptisai*, **be baptized,** and *apolousai*, **wash away,** are both middle imperatives. The literal meaning, then, would be: "Get yourself baptized and get your sins washed away."[11] Hackett comments: "One of the uses of the middle is to express an act which a person procures another to perform for him."[12]

Jerusalem, and in I John ii, 1, and, perhaps, in Jas. V, 6 [also Acts 3:14] we find examples of its application. The recent use of it by Pilate's wife (Matt. XXVII, 19) may have helped to give prominence to it. He who had been condemned as a malefactor was emphatically, above all the sons of men, the "righteous," the "Just One."[l]

It is plain at this juncture that Paul is vindicating his "apostleship" above question, against the persistent attacks of the Judaizing party. He claims to have been appointed by **the God of our Fathers,** the God of the Jews, to see Christ, **the Righteous One,** thus fulfilling the requirement of a Christian apostle (cf. I Cor. 15:8) and then to have been appointed a **witness for him unto all men** (vs. 15).

Indeed Bruce holds,

That Paul actually saw the risen Lord outside Damascus in addition to hearing His voice is emphasized more implicitly in the Pauline letters than in Acts . . . Paul himself makes it plain that to him the vision of Christ was the central and all-important feature of his conversion-experience.[m] (cf. I Cor. 9:1; 15:8).

C. Paul's Commission from Christ (22:15, 16)

For thou shalt be a witness for him unto all men, vs. 15.

Luke is careful to record in all three accounts (9:15; 22:15; 26:16) Paul's commission to apostleship by Jesus Christ. The object of his commission in the first account is declared to be "the Gentiles and kings, and the children of Israel" (9:15). In the third account before Agrippa, it is simply stated, "to appoint thee a minister and a witness both of the things wherein thou hast seen me, and of the things wherein I will appear unto thee" (26:16b). However, in the present account Paul tactfully states before this mob-mad Jewish audience that Christ commissioned him to **be a witness for him unto "all men" of what thou hast seen and heard** (vs. 15). Thus Paul avoids further irritation of his Jewish audience by not accentuating his mission to the Gentiles, while at the same time he validates his universal mission to bear the good news of salvation to "all men." Bruce remarks:

henceforth he was to tell forth with confidence what he had seen and heard, with all that implied—that Jesus of Nazareth, crucified by men, exalted by God, was Israel's Messiah, glorified Son of God, and the Saviour of mankind.[n]

The words **arise, and be baptized, and wash**

---

9 *Op. cit.*, p. 418. So also Hackett (p. 257).
10 Thayer, *op. cit.*, p. 554.
11 Robertson, *Grammar*, p. 808.
12 *Op. cit.*, p. 258. Cf. G. B. Winer, *A Grammar of the Idiom of the New Testament* (Andover: Warren F. Draper, 1870), p. 254.
l Ellicott, *op. cit.*, p. 44.
m Bruce, *op. cit.*, p. 442, n. 19.
n *Ibid.*

17 And it came to pass, that, when I had returned to Jerusalem, and while I prayed in the temple, I fell into a trance,

18 and saw him saying unto me, Make haste, and get thee quickly out of Jerusalem; because they will not receive of thee testimony concerning me.

19 And I said, Lord, they themselves know that I imprisoned and beat in every synagogue them that believed on thee:

20 and when the blood of Stephen thy witness was shed, I also was standing by, and consenting, and keeping the garments of them that slew him.

21 And he said unto me, Depart: for I will send thee forth far hence unto the Gentiles.

22 And they gave him audience unto this word; and they lifted up their voice, and said, Away with such a fellow from the earth: for it is not fit that he should live.

---

17 The fact that Paul **prayed in the temple** should have convinced his hearers that he would not have desecrated that place.

22 **It is not fit** is the verb *kathēkō*, which in the New Testament occurs only here and in Romans 1:28. The imperfect form seems odd here. Lake and Cadbury say: "No clear light has ever been thrown on the curious use of the imperfect *kathēken*."[13] Bruce comments: "The imperfect indicative in classical Greek may indicate necessity or possibility when the opposite is taking place; but the usage is extended in the Koine to cover what in classical Greek would be expressed by the present."[14]

---

away thy sins, calling on his name (vs. 16), while not found in either Acts 9 or Acts 26, are of very special significance. They reflect the fact of compliance with Jesus' command (Matt. 28:19), and that for Paul baptism was more than a formal or ceremonial act. Repentance and saving faith are clearly presupposed by the Apostle, which in turn produced the witness of certain forgiveness (cf. Eph. 5:14). Paul's clear concept of the relationship of "the washing of regeneration" to the "renewing of the Holy Spirit" (Titus 3:5) stemmed from his own vital experience in Christ. That this experience was in answer to his prayer to the **Righteous One** (vs. 14) who had appeared to him on the way is evident from Ananias' instruction to call on His name (vs. 16b). Thus Paul's experience in Christ as here recorded involved, *first*, the revelation of Christ to him (vs. 8); *second*, Paul's response to that revelation: **arise**; *third*, baptism, **be baptized**; *fourth*, forgiveness, **wash away thy sins**; and *fifth*, prayer to Christ, **calling on his name.** Without pressing the order, it may be safely assumed that all genuine experience in Christ will embody these elements. (For a fuller treatment of Paul's experience in Christ, see notes on Acts 9:3–19.)

D. Paul's Premonition of Jewish Hostility (22:17–21)

they will not receive of thee testimony concerning me, vs. 18b.

In an effort to reassure the Jews that his Damascus experience in Christ had not divorced him from his national and religious loyalty, Paul relates his subsequent return to Jerusalem and worship in the temple (vs. 17b. Cf. Acts 9:26; Gal. 1:17–19). That this was Paul's first visit to Jerusalem following his conversion appears evident from the fact that he here received his commission to the Gentiles, which would seem quite out of place had he already engaged in that mission in Cilicia and Syria as he did between the first and second visits to Jerusalem.[o]

Paul's **trance** experienced **while [he] prayed in the temple** (vs. 17) at Jerusalem may be identified with the one mentioned in II Cor. 12:1–4.[p] (For a fuller treatment of trances and visions, see notes on Peter's "trance" at Joppa, Acts 10:9–16.)

Paul's statement that he **saw him saying unto me** appears unusual. It may be intended to suggest the soundless communication of Christ's message to him. Christ's command to Paul to leave Jerusalem immediately im-

[13] *Beginnings*, IV, 282.
[14] *Acts*, p. 406. Hackett (p. 259) suggests: "Imperfect, because he had forfeited his life." Cf. Winer, *Grammar*, p. 282—"He ought to have been put to death long ago."

[o] With this position Lechler, Bruce, Macgregor, Plumptre, and others agree.
[p] Dummelow, *op. cit.*, p. 848. Dummelow thinks this identification unlikely for chronological reasons.

23 And as they cried out, and threw off their garments, and cast dust into the air,
24 the chief captain commanded him to be brought into the castle, bidding that he should
be examined by scourging, that he might know for what cause they so shouted against him.

---

23 **As they cried out** is *kraugazontōn.* The verb was first used (as *krazō*) of the inarticulate sounds of animals (e.g. to bay, to croak). So with men it suggests screaming or shouting, often in an unreasonable way. *Rhiptounton,* **threw off,** is from *rhipteō.* Here it probably means "waving," [15] as a manifestation of uncontrollable rage. **Cast dust into the air** is a typical Oriental expression of strong feeling, sometimes adopted in America by ballplayers in disapproval of an umpire's decision.

24 **Examined** is the verb *anetazō,* which occurs only here and in verse 29. It means "to examine judicially." [16] Though found in a papyrus of A.D. 127, the verb is rare.[17] *Mastixin,* **scourging,** is used in the literal sense only here and in Hebrews 11:36. This was "the legal method of examining a slave or alien." [18] It was a far more cruel form of punishment than beating with rods (16:22).

---

plies that the Jews would reject Paul then for the same reasons that they were rejecting him now, namely because of his witness for Christ. Plumptre remarks concerning Paul's reply (vs. 19):

> It was partly an extenuation of the unbelief of the people [Jews]. They were, as he had once been, sinning in ignorance, which was not invincible. Partly it expressed the hope that they too might listen when they saw him whom they had known as a vehement persecutor preaching the faith which he had once destroyed [q]

Paul implies (vs. 20) that in his ignorance and religious zeal, he had participated in Stephen's martyrdom even as they, in their fanatical but ignorant zeal, sought now to take his life. As Paul had sought then to stamp out Christianity by destroying the witness to it, so they sought to do likewise now.

Again, Paul reaffirms the divine origin of his apostleship to the Gentiles: **Depart: for I will send thee forth far hence unto the Gentiles** (vs. 21). Plumptre sees in these words "the promise of a mission rather than the actual mission itself."[r] Thus understood the experience fits better into Paul's first visit to Jerusalem than his second. Nor do these words necessarily imply immediate entry upon that mission. Eventually there was to be a human acceptance and confirmation by the Church of the inner divine conviction that impelled him to go **far hence unto the Gentiles** (see Acts 13:2, 3).

V. PAUL'S APPEAL TO HIS ROMAN CITIZENSHIP

(22:22–30)

The multitude of Jews appears to have given Paul uninterrupted, though perhaps impatient, audience until **this word . . . I will send thee forth far hence unto the Gentiles** (vss. 22a, 21b). That God should turn from the Jews to the Gentiles with the offered hope of redemption was more than the fanatical mob could bear. As when Stephen reached a like juncture in his defense before the Sanhedrin (Acts 7:51–54), so now mob violence was unleashed in all its mad fury against Paul. Only the protective presence of the Roman garrison prevented Paul from suffering a like fate with Stephen at their hands.

A. The Jews Reject Paul (22:22, 23)

Away with such a fellow from the earth, vs. 22.

That the Jews' intention was murder is clear from their own words (vs. 22b). Without trial or legality, they would have slaked their mad thirst with the blood of this blasphemer. These words, **Away with such a fellow from the earth: for it is not fit that he should live,** are but the wild echo of similar demands of the same people against the Christ whom Paul now preached (cf. Luke 23:18; John 19:15).

[15] F. Field, *Notes on the Translation of the New Testament* (Cambridge: University Press, 1899), p. 136. So also *Beginnings,* IV, 282; EGT, II, 461; Hackett, p. 260; Rackham, p. 425. Cadbury calls attention to an apparently similar usage in a recently discovered papyrus (*The Book of Acts in History,* p. 38).
[16] Thayer, *op. cit.,* p. 44.
[17] VGT, p. 42. [18] *Beginnings,* IV, 282.

[q] Ellicott, *op. cit.,* p. 152. [r] *Ibid.*

25 And when they had tied him up with the thongs, Paul said unto the centurion that stood by, Is it lawful for you to scourge a man that is a Roman, and uncondemned?

26 And when the centurion heard it, he went to the chief captain and told him, saying, What art thou about to do? for this man is a Roman.

27 And the chief captain came and said unto him, Tell me, art thou a Roman? And he said, Yea.

---

25 **Tied . . . up** is the verb *proteinō*, which means "stretch out, spread out."[19] It is found only here in the New Testament. **With the thongs,** *tois himasin,*[20] suggests binding to a pillar or post.[21] But many[22] commentators translate the dative as "for," and so make **thongs** refer to the scourge or "whip."[23] *Akatakriton,* **uncondemned,** occurs in the New Testament only here and in 16:37. Moulton and Milligan claim that it has not yet been found elsewhere.[24] **Roman** means "Roman citizen."

The casting off of their garments (vs. 23) is vividly reminiscent of the conduct of the Jews who illegally executed Stephen by stoning him to death (cf. Acts 7:58). Even their casting of **dust into the air** (vs. 23b) may have represented ominous threats of stoning; though Plumptre[s] allows that the reference to the garments and casting of dust may only signify the custom of shaking the dust from the garments against one whom they rejected (cf. Matt. 10:14; Acts 18:6).

B. The Captain Examines Paul (22:24, 25a)

The chief captain commanded . . . that he should be examined, vs. 24.

It would appear that Paul's defense in the Aramaic tongue had been but imperfectly understood by the Roman captain. Consequently the resurgent uproar against Paul by the Jews confirmed his suspicion that they had a valid complaint against the accused. In order to elicit the truth of the offense from Paul's own lips, the captain planned to follow the customary Roman method of scourging (cf. Acts 16:20–23). Thus Paul was stripped to the waist and bound with leather thongs to the whipping post or column in the fortress in preparation for the torture at the hands of the Roman soldiers – all at the command of the captain and not the Jews. Bruce takes a slightly divergent view of the method of Paul's intended punishment. Instead of the "whipping post" he remarks "it is more likely that he was suspended some little distance above the ground."[t] Bruce depicts this mode of Roman punishment most vividly:

> The scourge (Latin *flagellum*) was a fearful instrument of torture, consisting of leather thongs, weighted with rough pieces of metal or bone, and attached to a stout wooden handle. If a man did not actually die under the scourge (which frequently happened), he would certainly be crippled for life. Paul had been beaten with rods on three occasions (presumably at the hands of Roman lictors), and five times he had been sentenced to the disciplinary lash inflicted by Jewish authority, but neither of these penalties had the murderous quality of the *flagellum.*[u]

C. The Roman Law Protects Paul (22:25b–30)

Is it lawful for you to scourge a man that is a Roman, and uncondemned? vs. 25b.

Paul's appeal to his rights as a Roman citizen through the centurion saved him the cruel ordeal of flogging, as also the captain a likely severe penalty for having commanded his punishment.

Bruce[v] holds that Roman citizens were exempt from this penalty, and that under the Empire it could only be inflicted on a citizen after he had been legally convicted by the court. In any event it was not permissible against a citizen as a "third degree" measure, as the captain was about to employ it in the case of Paul.

Plumptre observes concerning the scourging of a Roman citizen:

> It was the heaviest of all the charges brought by Cicero against Verres, the Governor of Sicily, that he had broken this law: "*Facinus est vinciri civem Romanum seclus verberari.*" (Cic. in Verr. V. 57). The words *civis Romanus sum* acted almost like a charm in stopping the violence of provincial magistrates.[w]

[19] Arndt and Gingrich, *op. cit.*, p. 729.
[20] Cf. Mark 1:7; Luke 3:16; John 1:27 (nowhere else in N.T.).
[21] So Knowling, EGT, II, 462.
[22] Lake and Cadbury (*Beginnings*, IV, 282) say "most."
[23] *Ibid.*, see also Rackham, p. 426.
[24] VGT, p. 17.

[s] *Ibid.*, p. 153. [t] Bruce, *op. cit.*, p. 445, n. 35. [u] *Ibid.* [v] *Ibid.* [w] Ellicott, *op. cit.*, p. 109.

28 And the chief captain answered, With a great sum obtained I this citizenship. And Paul said, But I am *a Roman* born.

29 They then that were about to examine him straightway departed from him: and the chief captain also was afraid when he knew that he was a Roman, and because he had bound him.

30 But on the morrow, desiring to know the certainty wherefore he was accused of the Jews, he loosed him, and commanded the chief priests and all the council to come together, and brought Paul down and set him before them.

---

28 **Sum** is *kephalaiou*, which occurs elsewhere in the New Testament only in Hebrews 8:1 ("chief point"). Literally it means "head." But the translation here is amply supported by the papyri.[25] **With a great sum** must be taken in the light of the immense difference in the value of money now and then. Cadbury says that the prices paid by slaves for their liberty ran from about $ 40 to $ 200, although much fancier prices are quoted by Pliny the Elder.[26] **Citizenship** is *politian*, found in the New Testament only here and in Ephesians 2:12 ("commonwealth"). The King James rendering "freedom" is indeed a "free" translation.

In connection with Paul's declaration that he was **born** a Roman citizen might be noted Ramsay's statement that many Jews became citizens of Tarsus as early as 171 B.C. and that some citizens of Tarsus probably received Roman citizenship under Pompey.[27]

Actually Paul had been in an almost identical position once before at Philippi, but there for reasons untold he did not avail himself of his citizenship rights and consequently was beaten and imprisoned, though due apologies were later made by the Roman officials (see Acts 16:36–39).

The captain's question concerning Paul's citizenship (vs. 27) seems to imply that Paul did not present a figure that bespoke such a status. Well may this have been true after the violent treatment given him by the mob.

The captain's citizenship had been purchased at a great price (vs. 28a), possibly during the reign of Claudius (A.D. 41–54) as he bore the name of Claudius Lysias. His last name Lysias, being Greek, indicates that he was of that race, though possessing Roman citizenship and holding a high Roman office.

Paul's reply indicates that his citizenship was by birth (vs. 28b), and thus his father or grandfather may have gained the citizenship as a reward for some superior service to the Roman government in Asia Minor or by other means unknown to us. Citizenship carried with it certain commercial as well as personal advantages.

The discovery of Paul's citizenship status struck fear to the hearts of all who had placed hands on him, but especially so to the captain who had ordered him bound (vs. 29).

The captain's decision to submit the prisoner to a "grand jury" investigation by the Jewish Sanhedrin the next day was made with a view to discovering, through the Jewish court, the information concerning Paul which he had intended to force from him by scourging the day before.

[25] *Ibid*; p. 342. [26] *The Book of Acts in History*, p. 74.
[27] William Ramsay, *The Cities of St. Paul* (New York: A. C. Armstrong and Son, 1908), pp. 174, 180, 198, 205.

CHAPTER XXIII

And Paul, looking stedfastly on the council, said, Brethren, I have lived before God in all good conscience until this day.

2 And the high priest Ananias commanded them that stood by him to smite him on the mouth.

EXEGESIS

1 **Lived** is the verb *politeuomai*, found in the New Testament only here and in Philippians 1:27. It is from *politēs*, "citizen," and so literally means "*to be a citizen, to behave as a citizen.*" [1] The ethical sense, as here, is found in Philo [2] and Josephus,[3] as well as in the Septuagint.[4] **Conscience** is *syneidēsis*, found some 30 times in the New Testament (20 times in Paul's epistles). In Acts it occurs only here and in 24:16. Literally it means "a knowing with." (The English word is from the Latin *con*, "with," and *scio*, "know.") So the original meaning was "consciousness," and that sense is found in Hebrews 10:2 and I Peter 2:19. Apparently Lake and Cadbury would make that meaning universal throughout the New Testament. They write: "The modern connotation of a moral faculty which is a guide for conduct is not included in the term. It is the individual's conscious record of his past acts." [5] But Moulton and Milligan say: "The word would seem, therefore, to have been 'baptized' by Paul into a new and deeper connotation, and to have been used by him as equivalent to *to syneidos*." [6]

2 It is not entirely clear why **Ananias commanded . . . to smite** Paul. Hackett thinks it was because the apostle asserted his innocence.[7] Knowling says it was "because Paul had forgotten that he was before his judges, and ought not to have spoken before being asked." [8] Perhaps it was both.

EXPOSITION

THE APOSTLE'S LAST VISIT TO JUDEA (Concluded)

VI. Paul's Examination before the Sanhedrin, Acts 23:1–11.
- A. Paul Rebukes the High Priest, vss. 1–5.
- B. Paul Divides the Council, vss. 6–9.
- C. Paul Rescued and Reassured, vss. 10, 11.

VII. Paul's Deliverance from the Jews' Plot, Acts 23:12–35.
- A. The Plot to Kill Paul Designed, vss. 12–15.
- B. The Plot to Kill Paul Foiled, vss. 16–22.
- C. The Transfer of Paul Planned, vss. 23, 24.
- D. The Letter concerning Paul Written, vss. 25–30.
- E. The Transfer of Paul Accomplished, vss. 31–35.

VI. PAUL'S EXAMINATION BEFORE THE SANHEDRIN

(23:1–11)

According to Acts 22:30, Lysias' failure to ascertain the real cause for the Jewish hostility against Paul prompted him to arrange a hearing before the Sanhedrin the following day. Whether this assembly was presided over by the high priest or the chief captain is not certain. In either event it was a special, rather than a regular, session of the council.

A. Paul Rebukes the High Priest (23:1–5)

God shall smite thee, thou whited wall, vs. 3.

Luke's statement, **And Paul, looking steadfastly on the council** (vs. 1a), seems clearly designed to indicate that Paul closely scrutinized the personnel and attitude of this sullenly hostile body and then drew his

[1] Thayer, *op. cit.*, p. 528. So in papyri (VGT, p. 526).
[2] Philo, *On the Creation of the World.* 13.
[3] *Life*, 2.
[4] II Maccabees 11:25.
[5] *Beginnings*, IV, 286.
[6] VGT .p. 604.
[7] *Op. cit.*, p. 263. Cf. *Beginnings*, IV, 287.
[8] EGT, II, 466.

3 Then said Paul unto him, God shall smite thee, thou whited wall: and sittest thou to judge me according to the law, and commandest me to be smitten contrary to the law?

---

3 **Whited** is the perfect passive participle of *koniaō*, found in the New Testament only here and in Matthew 23:27. It comes from *konia*, dust or lime, and so means "plaster over, whitewash."[9] **Wall** is *toichos*, found only here in the New Testament. It refers particularly to the wall of a house. **Contrary to the law** is the present particple of *paranomeō*, "transgress the law," found only here in the New Testament.

---

conclusions accordingly. In Acts 6:15 the same expression is used of Stephen before this council. In Acts 7:55 it is used of Stephen as he gazed heavenward when the council unleashed its wrath against him. Again in Acts 14:9 it is used of the cripple at Lystra who was healed by Paul (cf. Acts 3:4; 13:9).

Paul's declaration that he had **lived before God in all good conscience until this day** (vs. 1b) at once posed a problem for scholars and elicited a violent protest from the high priest (cf. Acts 24:16; Rom. 8:5; I Cor. 4:4; I Tim. 1:5; II Tim. 1:3). The very mention of a **good conscience** appears to make Paul self-contradictory. In his letter to Timothy he declared himself to be the chiefest of all sinners saved by the grace of God (I Tim. 1:15). However, here and elsewhere (cf. Acts 24:16; Rom. 2:15; 9:1; 13:5), Paul avows that he lived a perfectly conscientious life. Two things are essential to an understanding of Paul's utterance: namely, what he meant by conscience, and how he applied the term to his life in this instance.

Conscience may be best understood as the moral judging function of the mind or intelligence. It is not something added or separate from the unitary spiritual nature of personality, but it is rather the constitutional intelligence functioning in relation to moral matters. Indeed, conscience may be neglected, educated, perverted, or suppressed. But so may other constitutional functions of human personality. Before any of these things may happen to conscience, its existence is essential. Rackham has well said,

> The conscience is a consciousness which bears testimony with, or to, our personality within; and the subject matter of the testimony is the moral value of actions, the testimony itself being a pronouncement whether they are right or wrong. A good conscience gives a good verdict, and this it can only do if the faculty of judgment is itself clear.[a]

Thus Paul's moral judgment, conditioned as it was by his Pharisaic training, had informed him that his treatment of the Christians was commensurate with the strict requirements of the law as he then understood it (cf. Acts 26:9–11). But Paul had not yet understood, at that time, that "the law is become our tutor to bring us to Christ, that we might be justified by faith" (Gal. 3:24). Williams' translation is graphic: "So the law has been our attendant to lead us to Christ, so that we might through faith obtain right standing with God."[b] The attendant was "usually a slave who cared for the Greek child on the way to and from the teacher."[c]

Paul's great fallacy before his conversion was the common fallacy of confused values. He ascribed intrinsic value to the law, whereas it possessed only extrinsic or instrumental value. He made the law "an end" rather than "a means" to the end, which was Christ. Thus to Paul the law was final, and consequently it was inevitable that it would destroy Christ and His teachings since He purported to supersede the law (Matt. 5:17, 18). Thus as a strict adherent to the law, Paul could rightfully say that he had **lived before God in all good conscience until this day.** He had been conscientious as a Jew, and after his spiritual enlightment he had been conscientious as a Christian. This Jewish conscientiousness was, however, attained by the conformity of his conduct with the requirements of the law. The unsuccessfully attempted reconciliation of his

[9] Thayer, *op. cit.*, p. 354. The meaning of **whited wall** is "a hypocrite who conceals his malice under an outward assumption of piety" (*ibid.*, p. 355).

[a] Rackham, *op. cit.*, pp. 432 f.
[b] Charles B. Williams, *The New Testament n the Language of the People* (Chicago: Moody Press, 1949) p. 418.
[c] *Ibid.*

4 And they that stood by said, Revilest thou God's high priest?

4 The attitude of the bystanders is like that of Josephus, when he writes: "He that does not submit to him [the high priest] shall be subject to the same punishment, as if he had been guilty of impiety towards God himself." [10]

inner motives, desires, and aspirations with the higher ideals and requirements of the law was quite another matter. In this area Paul made no such claims to conscientiousness before God, prior to his Christian conversion (see Rom. 7). His conscientiousness here referred to was in persecuting the Christians and not in attaining to the divine moral ideal.

Paul's argument in verse one implied that as he had been wrong before God in persecuting the Christians, so were the Jews now, but now enlightened he saw Christ as the end of the law, which they if enlightened would likewise see.

The high priest's reaction was immediate and violent in spirit and intent as he ordered Paul to be smitten on the mouth. How similar his reactions, when worsted in reason, to those of the synagogue who "were not able to withstand the wisdom and the Spirit by which [Stephen] spake" (Acts 6:10). There is no better evidence of a defenseless cause than the loss of temper and the employment of violence agianst the victor.

This high priest, Ananias, was the son of Nedebaios. He had succeeded Joseph, son of Camithos, and he was the twentieth high priest in order from the accession of Herod the Great in 40 B.C. He had received his appointment in A.D. 47 or 48 from Herod of Chalcis (A.D. 41–48), a brother to Herod Agrippa I, and held it about a dozen years. Perhaps a more infamous individual never occupied the office. Ananias was a bold, insolent, violent-tempered member of the Sadducean party, noted for its stern and exacting judgment on others. Josephus[d] depicts his infamy. He made himself exceedingly wealthy on the ill-gotten gain of his office, forcibly took the tithes that belonged to the priests, thus leaving some to starve, sheltered a wicked brood of henchmen, and collaborated with the *sicarii* or Assassins of the country. He convened the Sanhedrin in the interim between the governorship of Festus and Albinus and condemned to death by stoning James, the brother of Jesus and pastor of the Jerusalem church, with other Christians, plus innumerable other wicked deeds, according to Josephus.[e] As a member of the Sadducean party he was hated by the extreme nationalistic parties of Judea because of his pro-Roman sympathies and policy. Once five years earlier, he had been ordered to Rome to answer for his conduct on suspicion of involvement in a Judeo-Samaritan incident of violence. However, he was vindicated and restored by the emperor. Eventually, during the war against Rome in A.D. 66, Ananias, with his brother Hezekiah, was slain by the insurrectionists in an aqueduct where they were hiding.[f]

It was to this Ananias that Paul administered his withering rebuke (vs. 3). Paul's analogy, **thou whited wall,** was not without precedent (cf. Matt. 23:27; Luke 11:44). Some have thought they have seen an allusion to Ezekiel's "wall . . . daubed with untempered mortar" (Ezek. 13:10–16) in the words of Paul's rebuke.[g]

Plumptre aptly remarks:

> The whole utterance must be regarded by St. Paul's own confession as the expression of a hasty indignation, recalled after a moment's reflection; but the words so spoken were actually a prophecy, fulfilled some years after, by the death of Ananias by the hands of the *sicarii*.[h]

Paul knew his rights of defense both by Jewish and Roman law, and that until proven guilty he should be considered innocent (cf. Deut. 19:15; John 7:51). Thus the command of Ananias, whether executed or not we are not told, made him a violator of Paul's rights. For this breach of law (cf. Rom. 2:1) and for flagrant hypocrisy, Paul rebuked the high priest. There was no more excuse for the first offense than for the second. In fact, the first may have issued from the

[10] *Against Apion*, II, 24.

[d] Josephus, *op. cit.*, "Antiquities," XX, IX, 1, 2. [e] *Ibid.* [f] *Ibid.*, "Wars," II, XVII, 9.
[g] *The Interpreter's Bible*, IX, 298. [h] Ellicott, *op. cit.*, VII, 154.

5 And Paul said, I knew not, brethren, that he was high priest: for it is written, Thou shalt not speak evil of a ruler of thy people.
6 But when Paul perceived that the one part were Sadducees and the other Pharisees, he cried out in the council, Brethren, I am a Pharisee, a son of Pharisees: touching the hope and resurrection of the dead I am called in question.

---

5 **Brethren** shows Paul's quick resumption of a kind, conciliatory attitude after his strong words of denunciation. On the much discussed question of Paul's declaration here, Edwards writes: "Perhaps the simplest explanation is that Paul meant, 'I did not for the moment bear in mind that I was addressing the high priest.'"[11]

6 **Hope and resurrection** means "hope of the resurrection." Edersheim states that this was one of the fundamental differences between the Pharisees and Sadducees.[12]

---

second. Not infrequently insincerity and hypocrisy are products of censoriousness, unreasonable demands, and severe reprehensions of the legalists. It is a subtle psychological device in which the guilty party, consciously or unconsciously, projects his own perverted spirit or misdemeanor to some other person of his disfavor, with a view to diverting attention from himself to another. It has been suggested that Paul's allusion to the **whited wall** may have signified the precariousness of Ananias' position, like a tottering wall, as well as the veneer of whitewash over corruption and injustice in his life. Of how little worth are priestly garb and office to the production of moral character or its preservation from moral corruption (cf. Matt. 7:15; John 10:12; Acts 20:29).

The rebuke of Paul by the bystanders (vs. 8) closely parallels a similar incident in the experience of Jesus as He stood trial before Caiaphas (John 18:19–22).

Paul's apology (vs. 5) has been variously viewed by Bible interpreters. Possible reasons suggested for his reply, **I knew not, . . . that he was high priest** (vs. 5), include the fact that Ananias had taken the office since Paul had last been associated with the Sanhedrin and thus he was unknown to Paul; that possibly another than Ananias (perchance Lysias) was presiding at this special session; that Paul did not know who had given the order to smite him; that Paul was ironically suggesting that such an order could not have been expected from the high priest; that Paul was afflicted with poor eyesight (cf. Acts 9:18); that he was looking in the opposite direction when the words were spoken and thus did not know who gave the order; and finally, that Paul made an honest mistake. Plumptre[i] favors the view that either Paul's defective eyesight or that Ananias was not presiding, accounts for his mistake. Rackham[j] takes the view that Paul had not sufficiently reflected that the words came from the high priest and that he should have been more deliberate and less vigorous in his reply. Whether Paul should or should not have spoken these words, they were in any event both penetratingly true and prophetically suggestive. Paul's respect for the ceremonial and ethical requirements of the law is reflected in his quotation of Exodus 22:28 (cf. Rom. 13:1–7). Even an apostle's apology should serve as an apt model for the Christian's spirit and deportment in similar circumstances. It has been suggested that Paul apologized to the office, if he did not to the man! As with Elijah who "was a man of like passions with us" (James 5:17a), so Paul the apostle was a fellow human being (cf. Acts 15:37–40).

B. Paul Divides the Council (23:6–9)

He cried out in the council, Brethren, I am a Pharisee . . . touching the hope and resurrection of the dead I am called in question (vs. 6b).

Paul's strategy in dividing the council has been assailed by some as being unworthy of Christian ethics.[k] However, it seems that Christ's words in the parable of the unrighteous steward, "the sons of this world are for their own generation wiser than the sons of the light" (Luke 16:8b), have a bearing on Paul's conduct at this juncture.

11 D. M. Edwards, "Ananias," ISBE, I, 130.
12 *Life and Times*, I, 315.

i *Ibid.* j Rackham, *op. cit.*, p. 433.
k F. W. Farrar, *The Life and Work of St. Paul* (London: Cassell, Petter, Galpin and Co., 1879) pp. 327 f.

7 And when he had so said, there arose a dissension between the Pharisees and Sadducees; and the assembly was divided.

7 **Dissension** is *stasis*, used by Luke in seven of its nine occurrences in the New Testament. Literally it means "a standing." But its late meaning here is supported in the papyri.[13] **Assembly** is *plēthos*, translated "multitude" in 4:32.

Having failed in his attempt at a straightforward, courteous defense before the council, the Apostle counters with a new surprise strategy. He took stock and concluded that the Sanhedrin consisted of a Sadducean majority with a strong, Pharisaic minority party. This situation seems to have changed from Christ's day, if Mould is correct when he states, "But a few members of the Sanhedrin were Sadducees in the time of Jesus."[l] This Sadducean majority in the Sanhedrin in Paul's time may have been due to the influence of Ananias, a Sadducee, as president. Again Mould states:

> The Sadducees, as descendants of the high priestly family, were originally a religious group, but they had long been mixed up in politics by virtue of their civil powers. Since they got and held their wealth and power by virtue of Roman support, their policy was to keep on good terms with Rome. Thus they were diametrically opposed to the Pharisees politically.[m]

Again Mould observes:

> The Pharisees, while not primarily a political party, became such virtually by force of necessity. As Jews loyal to their religious past, they were patriots. They disliked the rule of Rome but considered it a just punishment for the sins of the nation. They believed that when the law should be perfectly kept the Messiah would come and Rome's sway would be miraculously brought to an end.[n]

The Pharisees were the largest and most influential group in Judaism at this time. They were anti-Hellenizing and neutralized the liberalizing influence of Greek and Roman culture on the Jewish religion. They held the model ideal of a life in full accord with God's will, which ideal accounted for their tendency to legalism. They were separatistic and held strictly to orthodox Judaism but became formalistic, narrow, censorious, self-righteous, and conceited. They stifled the spirit while rigorously demanding the letter of the law. Indeed, the party had its exceptions in such noble souls as Gamaliel (Acts 5:33–40) and Nicodemus (John 3:1–15). The Pharisees believed in a coming Messiah, the existence of spirits and angels, and they accepted the doctrine of the resurrection from the dead.

The Sadducees, on the other hand, though the smaller party, were in the main aristocratic and very influential. They favored Hellenization and courted Roman favor. They were worldly in their outlook, accepted only the Torah, rejected the oral law, and hated the doctrine of the resurrection and belief in angels and spirits. Plumptre states: "They were, in fact, carried along by one of the great waves of thought which were then passing over the ancient world and were Epicureans and Materialists without knowing it, just as the Pharisees were . . . the counterpart of the Stoics."[o]

Thus Paul's identification of himself with the Pharisaic party not only placed him in alignment with all that was best in the Judaism of his day, but it also sharply divided the council. Nor was Paul either amiss or dishonest in thus identifying himself, as the following evidence indicates. *First*, before his conversion he had been a conscientious member of the party (Acts 26:4, 5; cf. Phil. 3:4, 5). *Second*, there appears to have been no inconsistency between membership in the Pharisaic party as such and saving faith in, and loyalty to, Jesus Christ (Acts 15:5). *Third*, Paul regarded the Christian faith as the fulfillment and fruition of all that was best in Judaism as conserved by the Pharisaic party (Phil. 3:3).

Thus Paul's citation of three things effectively achieved his purpose to divide the council. *First*, as previously indicated, he identified himself with the Pharisaic party, as against the Sadducees. *Second*, he implied that his preaching had accorded with **the hope** (vs. 6b) of the nation, or the promise of the Messiah, which hope Paul held had

[13] VGT, p. 586.

[l] Mould, *op. cit.*, p. 468. [m] *Ibid.*, p. 471. [n] *Ibid.* [o] Ellicott, *op. cit.*, p. 155

8 For the Sadducees say that there is no resurrection, neither angel, nor spirit; but the Pharisees confess both.

9 And there arose a great clamor: and some of the scribes of the Pharisees' part stood up, and strove, saying, We find no evil in this man: and what if a spirit hath spoken to him, or an angel?

---

8 The Sadducean denial of the Resurrection is stated in the Synoptic Gospels (Matt. 22:23; Mark 12:18; Luke 20:27). Josephus says of the Sadducees: "They also take away the belief of the immortal duration of the soul, and the punishments and rewards in Hades." [14] He also writes: "The doctrine of the Sadducees is this: That souls die with the bodies." [15] The statement that they denied the existence of **angel** or **spirit** has not been confirmed from contemporary sources but is "in keeping with their general attitude." [16] **Both** probably refers to (1) resurrection and (2) angels and spirits. But *amphotera* may be used for more than two (see on 19:16).

The Pharisaic belief in immortality is affirmed thus by Josephus: "They say that all souls of good men only are removed into other bodies,—but that the souls of bad men are subject to eternal punishment." [17] Elsewhere he writes: "They also believe that souls have an immortal vigour in them, and that under the earth there will be rewards or punishments, according as they have lived virtuously or viciously in this life; and the latter are to be detained in an everlasting prison, but that the former shall have power to revive and live again." [18] If Josephus is reporting correctly—and he was in a position to know—the Pharisees believed in the immortality of all souls but in the resurrection of the righteous only.

9 **Clamor** is *kraugē*, "outcry." *Diemachonto*, **strove,** is found only here in the New Testament. "Contended" (RSV) is a good rendering.

---

been fulfilled in Christ (cf. Gal. 4:4). Such a hope the Pharisees held, and those among the party who had believed (Acts 15:5) recognized Christ as the Messiah. Bruce states that "it was not until A.D. 70 or thereby that steps were taken to exclude Jewish Christians from participation in the synagogue worship by the addition of a prayer – the *birkath ha-minim* – that 'the Nazarenes and the heretics might perish as in a moment and be blotted out of the book of life.'"[p] *Third*, Paul held with the Pharisees the doctrine of the resurrection, and for him Christ's resurrection was necessary to the fulfillment of this **hope,** as also for personal salvation (cf. I Cor. 15:12–26).

The resurgence of Jewish orthodoxy in the council greatly agitated the liberal materialistic party of the Sadducees, with the result that **there arose a dissension** so severe that **the assembly was divided** (vs. 7). Josephus[q] once employed this ruse, though of questionable honesty, to escape the violence of a mob. Consequently certain Pharisaic scribes rose to Paul's defense, declaring, **We find no evil in this man** (vs. 9. Cf. Matt. 27:23, 24). Most of the scribes were Pharisees (cf. Mark. 2:16; Luke 5:30), and their allowance that a spirit or angel might have spoken to Paul is reminiscent of Gamaliel's defense of the apostles when they were on trial before the Sanhedrin some twenty-five years earlier (Acts 5:34–39). It has been thought that the scribes' remark was an allusion either to Paul's conversion experience which he had related the previous day (Acts 22:6–11), or to his vision in the Temple upon his first return to Jerusalem (Acts 22:17–21).[r] In any event, in their position, as Plumptre remarks, "After twenty-five years they have not got further than the cautious policy of those who halt between two opinions."[s] How sad that they were unable to come clear over and repose their trust in Him whom they allowed had appeared unto Paul, for such may have been the import of their words, **what if a spirit hath spoken to him, or an angel?** (vs. 9b).

[14] *War*, II, 8, 14.
[15] *Ant.* XVIII, 1, 4. Cf. also Schürer, *op. cit.*, II, ii, 13.
[16] Bruce, *Acts*, p. 412.
[17] *War*, II, 8, 14.
[18] *Ant.* XVIII 1, 3.

[p] Bruce, *op. cit.*, p. 453, n. 14.
[q] Josephus, *op. cit.*, "Life," p. 8.
[r] *The Interpreter's Bible*, IX, 300.
[s] Ellicott, *op. cit.*, p. 155.

10 And when there arose a great dissension, the chief captain, fearing lest Paul should be torn in pieces by them, commanded the soldiers to go down and take him by force from among them, and bring him into the castle.

11 And the night following the Lord stood by him, and said, Be of good cheer: for as thou hast testified concerning me at Jerusalem, so must thou bear witness also at Rome.

12 And when it was day, the Jews banded together, and bound themselves under a curse, saying that they would neither eat nor drink till they had killed Paul.

---

10 For **dissension** see on verse 7. **Torn in pieces** is the verb *diaspaō*. In its only other occurrence in the New Testament (Mark 5:4) it is used of the tearing apart of chains by the Gerasene demoniac. *Strateuma*, **soldiers,** is singular. It means a company or detachment of soldiers; that is, the ones then on duty. **Take . . . by force** is the verb *harpazō*. It means "to seize, carry off by force." [19] Elsewhere in Acts it appears only at 8:39.

11 **The Lord** is evidently Jesus (cf. 9:5). *Tharsei*, **be of good cheer,** is always imperative in the New Testament (seven times). For Paul's purpose to visit **Rome,** see 19:21.

12 **Banded together** is literally "having made a compact" *(poiēsantes systrophēn)*. The latter word occurs elsewhere in the New Testament only in 19:40, where it means a riotous gathering. The verb *anathematizō* (**bound . . . under a curse**) occurs three times in this chapter (vss. 12, 14, 21) and in the rest of the New Testament only in Mark 14:71. In the papyri it has been found three times in a heathen curse.[20]

C. Paul Rescued and Reassured (23:10, 11)

The chief captain . . . commanded the soldiers to go down and take him by force . . . the Lord stood by him, and said, Be of good cheer (vss. 10, 11a).

The Sadducees, incited by an angry, wounded, and vindictive Ananias, threw the full weight of their strength against the Pharisaic defenders of orthodoxy, whose champion Paul had become. Between the contending parties, Paul was in grave danger of being physically dismembered (vs. 10a). Sensing the gravity of the situation with a Roman citizen's life at stake for whom he was personally responsible, the captain forthwith ordered Paul's rescue by the soldiers. Thus Paul was forcibly extricated and returned to the safety of the fortress barracks. Plumptre thinks his prison may have been "the selfsame guard-room as that which had witnessed our Lord's sufferings at the hands of Pilate's soldiers."[t] Luke's words, **And the night following the Lord stood by him** (vs. 11a), seem to imply four things. *First*, Paul felt the keen edge of discouragement in the apparent failure of his whole mission to Jerusalem on this last visit. There is no evidence that his long-planned and carefully executed mission with the offering to his nation had either been appreciated, or that it had accomplished his purpose. *Second*, his attempted personal witness for Christ had apparently miscarried. *Third*, Paul's own personal future stood in uncertainty and jeopardy. *Fourth*, in the darkest hour of Paul's apparent defeat and discouragement, **the Lord stood by him** to comfort and sustain. **Be of good cheer,** says the Lord to Paul, your testimony at Jerusalem has not been in vain as you have supposed. I have yet a greater witness for you to bear for me at Rome (cf. Rom. 1:13; 15:23). Paul must here have learned the lesson concerning temptation about which he wrote to the Corinthians (I Cor. 10:13). On more than one occasion when Paul stood "at wits' end," a special visitation from the Lord succored him, renewing his courage and strength. Such was his case under trial at Corinth (Acts 18:9, 10); such was to be his experience during the storm en route to Rome (Acts 27:23–25); or again when on trial for his life at Rome (II Tim. 4:16–18); and such was this Jerusalem experience. How faithful Christ ever is to His promise, "I am with you always, even unto the end of the world" (Matt. 28:20b), when His servants obey His command to "Go . . ., and make disciples of all the nations" (Matt. 28:19a).

[19] Thayer, *op. cit.*, p. 74.

[t] *Ibid.*

[20] VGT, p. 33; Deissmann, *Light from the Ancient East*, pp. 92 f.

13 And they were more than forty that made this conspiracy.

14 And they came to the chief priests and the elders, and said, We have bound ourselves under a great curse, to taste nothing until we have killed Paul.

15 Now therefore do ye with the council signify to the chief captain that he bring him down unto you, as though ye would judge of his case more exactly: and we, before he comes near, are ready to slay him.

---

13 *Synomosian*, **conspiracy**, is found only here in the New Testament.

14 It is perhaps significant that mention is made of the chief priests and the elders, and not of the Pharisees. Evidently the latter were not consulted for fear they would oppose the plot to kill Paul (cf. vs. 9).

The first part of the quotation (vs. 14b) reads literally, "With an anathema we anathematized ourselves" *(anathemati anethematisamen heautous)*. In Acts the noun is found only here. It first signified something devoted to God, and then a curse. In the rest of the New Testament (Paul, five times), it means "accursed."

15 **Signify** is the verb *emphanizo*, which means "to manifest, exhibit," but in Acts (23:15, 22; 24:1; 25:2, 15) "to declare, make known" [21] (cf. RSV, "give notice"). Concerning "signify" Knowling says: "This rendering apparently conveys a wrong idea, for it implies that the Council had the authority, whereas this lay with the Roman officer." [22] Lake and Cadbury use the legal phrase, "lay information . . . before." [23]

Judge is *diaginōskein*, found in the New Testament only here and in 24:22. Lake and Cadbury write: "It implies decision as well as investigation or inquiry." [24] Abbott–Smith gives "to distinguish, ascertain exactly," and reserves the legal meaning, "to determine," for 24:22.[25] Knowling says: "The word need not be used here in the forensic sense as in xxiv, 22." [26] But the Revised Standard Version has it here. It seems that the judicial sense should be allowed.

Before he comes near was evidently "so that the crime could not be imputed to the priests." [27] Josephus tells of a conspiracy made by ten men to assassinate Herod the Great because of his innovations, and of the terrible punishment meted out to them when their plot was discovered.[28]

VII. PAUL'S DELIVERANCE FROM THE JEWS' PLOT

(23:12–35)

Again foiled and frustrated by the escape of the coveted victim from their net, some forty Jews in desperation committed themselves to a rash oath **saying that they would neither eat nor drink till they had killed Paul** (vs. 12).

A. The Plot to Kill Paul Designed (23:12–15)

And we, before he comes near, are ready to slay him, vs. 15b.

The band of some forty Jews who took the oath to neither **eat nor drink till they had killed Paul** were most likely of the *Sicarii* or Assassins (cf. Acts 21:38), of which there were many in Judea by this time. They were likely of the extreme Zealot party (see Acts 1:13b), and it is more than likely that they were instigated to this plot by Ananias the high priest. Josephus[u] informs us that he (Ananias) regularly employed the *Sicarii* to execute his foul and murderous purposes during his high priesthood. Thus we may well imagine that Ananias was the "master mind" behind the plot. Nor was such a scheme without precedent in Palestine. Plumptre remarks:

> The casuistry of the more fanatical Jews led them to the conclusion that a blasphemer or apostate was an outlaw, and that, in the absence of any judicial condemnation, private persons might take on themselves the execution of the divine sentence.[v]

The technique of their plot seems to imply an intended ambush against Paul. It is an illuminating commentary on the fanatical and frenzied state of their minds that they

[21] Abbott–Smith, *op. cit.*, p. 150. [22] EGT, II, 470.
[23] *Beginnings*, IV, 291. Moulton and Milligan find this meaning in the papyri (VGT, p. 208). Here they would translate it "make an official report."
[24] *Ibid.* Cf. also Arndt and Gingrich, *op. cit.*, p. 181—"to determine his case by thorough investigation."
[25] *Op. cit.*, p. 106. [26] EGT, II, 471. [27] *Ibid.* [28] *Ant.* XV, 8, 1–4.
[u] Josephus, *loc. cit.* [v] Ellicott, *op. cit.*, p. 156.

16 But Paul's sister's son heard of their lying in wait, and he came and entered into the castle and told Paul.

17 And Paul called unto him one of the centurions, and said, Bring this young man unto the chief captain; for he hath something to tell him.

---

16 *Enedran*, **lying in wait,** is found in the New Testament only here and in 25:3. It means "ambush" (RSV). In the papyri it is used in the sense of "treachery." [29] *Paragenomenos*, **he came,** is literally "having been present." But in later Greek the verb often meant "come, come to." It is not certain whether this means that Paul's nephew was present at the conspiracy [30] or that he came to the barracks (**castle**).[31]

---

did not consider the near impossibility of their undertaking and the almost certain heavy loss of life to themselves in an attempt to extricate Paul from the custody of the Roman soldiers en route to the council. In their oath they literally placed themselves under a curse or an *anathema* (cf. Rom. 9:3; I Cor. 16:22; Gal. 1:8, 9). Bruce suggests that it may have taken such a form as, "So may God do to us, and the more also, if we eat or drink until we have killed Paul."[w] Another authority remarks: "Fortunately the rabbis were able to devise means of release from such oaths; so the plot having failed, we need not assume that the plotters starved to death!"[x]

When these Assassins presented their scheme to **the chief priests and the elders** of the Sadducean party, it is noteworthy that **the scribes,** who were mostly Pharisees and who championed Paul's cause in the council the day before, are not mentioned as having been consulted. It appears further that they were proposing to ask of Lysias an opportunity for a verdict against Paul and not simply an inquiry. Thus it would appear that they intended to do by subtle and ruthless violence what they could not hope to do by legal procedure because of their inability to secure a majority in the council.

B. The Plot to Kill Paul Foiled (23:16–22)

Bring this young man unto the chief captain; for he hath something to tell him (vs. 17b).

The appearance of Paul's nephew affords the only reference to Paul's family in the Acts (cf. Rom. 16:7, 11). It has been suggested that possibly Paul's sister had married into a high-priestly family and that Paul's nephew thus inadvertently stumbled onto the plot by having overheard it discussed by the *Sicarii*, after which he secretly reported it to Paul and thence to the chief captain. However, it is not known for certain whether his sister resided in Judea or was there for the Pentecost feast, or possibly for the education of her son in the rabbinical school. Of course, if she were married into a priestly family, the hostility of that caste toward Paul might well account for his not lodging at her home. Nor is it known whether she and her family were Christians. We are on safe ground, however, when we note that this lad had a love and loyalty to his uncle that enabled him to handle privately and judiciously a secret that involved a matter of life and death for Paul. Further, we learn from the incident that Paul was accessible to his friends and acquaintances, even while in custody. This fact may account for Luke's rather full information on the happenings of these days, since he would have been at Jerusalem. Nor is it necessary to suppose that Paul was bound in fetters, even though he is designated **Paul the prisoner** (cf. Eph. 3:1; 4:1; Philemon 1).

Bruce[y] thinks that Paul was likely disinherited from a wealthy father and family in Silicia (cf. Phil. 3:8) upon his having become a Christian.

It appears that the centurions were available to him and complied with his wishes. That the chief captain welcomed the information from Paul's nephew appears evident, and the manner in which he treated the whole affair indicates that he favored Paul's position against the Jews, though of course his responsibility to a Roman citizen might well color his treatment of Paul.

[29] VGT, p. 123. [30] Favored by Bruce (*Acts*, p. 415).
[31] For a discussion of how the nephew may have heard, see Edersheim, *Jewish Social Life*, p. 227.

[w] Bruce, *op. cit.*, p. 457. [x] *The Interpreter's Bible*, IX, 302. [y] Bruce, *loc. cit.*

18 So he took him, and brought him to the chief captain, and saith, Paul the prisoner called me unto him, and asked me to bring this young man unto thee, who hath something to say to thee.
19 And the chief captain took him by the hand, and going aside asked him privately, What is it that thou hast to tell me?
20 And he said, The Jews have agreed to ask thee to bring down Paul tomorrow unto the council, as though thou wouldest inquire somewhat more exactly concerning him.
21 Do not thou therefore yield unto them: for there lie in wait for him of them more than forty men, who have bound themselves under a curse, neither to eat nor to drink till they have slain him: and now are they ready, looking for the promise from thee.
22 So the chief captain let the young man go, charging him, Tell no man that thou hast signified these things to me.
23 And he called unto him two of the centurions, and said, Make ready two hundred soldiers to go as far as Caesarea, and horsemen threescore and ten, and spearmen two hundred, at the third hour of the night:

---

18 *Desmios*, **prisoner,** means "a bound one" (from *deō*, "bind"). It occurs six times in Acts. Paul uses it of himself in his epistles five times.

19 *Anachōrēsas*, **going aside,** is used frequently in the Gospels, but in Acts only here and in 26:31. *Epynthaneto*, **asked,** is used nine times by Luke (three in this chapter) and only three times elsewhere in the New Testament.

20 **Agreed** is the verb *syntithēmi*, which occurs only here in Acts (three times in N.T.). It literally means "to place or put together," and so "to determine, agree, covenant." [32] Moulton and Milligan cite instances of this use in the papyri and suggest "make a compact." [33]

Thou wouldest inquire is "they would enquire" in the King James Version. The former is based on the singular participle *mellōn* found in A B E.[34] The latter follows *mellontes* (plural), the reading of the bulk of the minuscules and versions. Strangely the Revised Standard Version returned to "they." **Thou** suggests the very logical idea that the tribune (chief captain) would normally wish to gain more information about Paul's case.

Akribesteron, **more exactly,** is found in this sense a number of times in the papyri and even with the verb *pynthanesthai*, **inquire,** in a papyrus of the third century B.C.[35]

21 **Yield unto them** is literally "be persuaded by them" *(peisthēis autois)*. *Enedreuousin*, **lie in wait for,** is found in the New Testament only here and in Luke 11:54. For **bound themselves under a curse** see on verse 12. *Prosdechomenoi*, **looking for,** is "expecting, waiting for." In Acts it occurs only here and in 24:15. *Epangelian* is used only here in the New Testament for a human **promise.** Lake and Cadbury say that here it means "consent." [36]

22 *Eklalēsai*, **tell,** occurs only here in the New Testament. It means "to speak out, divulge." [37] For **signified** see on verse 15. This verse has a mixture of indirect and direct speech. Literally the latter part reads: "having charged to tell no one, 'you informed me of this.'"

23 *Hippeis*, **horsemen,** occurs in the New Testament only here and in verse 32. *Dexiolabous*, **spearmen,** has not been found anywhere else in Greek literature until the sixth century, "when its use was probably based on this passage." [38] Lake and Cadbury transliterate rather than translate it.[39] It literally means "taking in the right hand." [40]

C. The Transfer of Paul Planned (23:23, 24)

Make ready . . . to go as far as Caesarea, vs. 23.

The skirmishes of the two previous days in the Sanhedrin, plus information of the plot to kill Paul, sufficiently convinced the chief captain of the gravity and hazards of the situation. From the garrison of about a thousand soldiers he ordered, through two centurions, that two hundred soldiers, seventy cavalrymen and two hundred spear-

[32] Abbott-Smith, *op. cit.*, p. 433. [33] VGT, p. 614. [34] Aleph has *mellon*, also singular. [35] VGT, p. 19. [36] *Beginnings*, IV, 293. [37] Thayer, *op. cit.*, p. 196. [38] *Beginnings*, IV, 293. [39] *Ibid.* [40] Alexandrinus has *dexiobolous*, "throwing with the right hand."

24 and *he bade them* provide beasts, that they might set Paul thereon, and bring him safe unto Felix the governor.

25 And he wrote a letter after this form:

The most logical meaning therefore seems to be **spearmen.**[41] Bruce writes: "The escort was composed of heavy infantry, cavalry, and light-armed troops . . . , the three constituents of the Roman army." [42] The Western text mentions 100 cavalry and 200 infantry, leaving out the strange word *dexiolabous.* But this is probably an emendation of what seemed a difficult passage.[43]

24 **Beasts** is not the best translation, since that term today is usually the equivalent of "brutes" (cf. beastly). We speak of "beasts" of the forest, but not of the farm. *Ktēnos* is from *ktaomai* and so signifies primarily "a possession." [44] In Revelation 18:13 it occurs in close conjunction with sheep and is translated "cattle." It has this meaning in the papyri, as well as that of "pack animal." In Marcus Antoninus it means "domestic animal" in contrast to *thērion*, "wild beast."[45] The "animals" here were either horses or mules.[46]

Epibibazontes, **set . . . thereon,** is found in the New Testament only here and in Luke 10:34; 19:35. **Bring . . . safe** is the verb *diasōzō*, "bring safely through." [47] Aside from I Peter 3:20 (of Noah in the ark) and Matthew 14:36 (of recovery from illness) it is used only by Luke (six times).

Governor is *hēgemōn*. Coming from *hēgeomai*, "lead," it first signified a leader or guide, then a commander. But its most common use in the New Testament is for the procurators of Judea (seven times in Matthew, once in Luke, six times in Acts). This is its first occurrence in Acts.

The Western text adds this explanation: "for he was afraid that the Jews would seize him [Paul] and kill him, and afterwards he would incur the accusation of having taken money"; that is, a bribe to allow Paul to be assassinated. So he furnished a very strong escort for the apostle.

25 **Form** is *typon* (cf. type). This use for the substance of a letter is paralleled in III Maccabees 3:30.

---

men, with special beasts for Paul to ride, be prepared to leave Jerusalem for Caesarea at about nine o'clock at night. It is noteworthy that this affords the only definite instance in Acts, or elsewhere in the New Testament, where Paul ever mounted a beast of transport. Otherwise he walked or sailed, for all we know. Thus safely escorted, both the interests of the chief captain and those of Paul the prisoner would be safeguarded. Lysias could not rest easy with such a plot pending until he knew that Paul was safely in the hands of the chief administrative and executive officer of the colony, Felix. If the *Sicarii* knew of Lysias' plan to spirit Paul out of Jerusalem, there is no evidence that they offered resistance or interference.

D. The Letter Concerning Paul Written (23:25–30)

And he wrote a letter after this form, vs. 25. How Luke knew the content of Lysias' letter to Felix we are not told. Paul may have had a copy of it, but it appears more likely that Luke heard it read in court at Caesarea before Felix. Such was the custom to openly read the charge against the accused.

The practice of letter-writing in the first Christian century afforded the chief means of communication. It was an epistolary age. Much is revealed in the few sentences of this letter preserved for us. Plumptre[z] observes that the epithet, **most excellent,** is the same as that used by Luke of Theophilus (Luke 1:3; cf. Acts 24:3; 26:25), and that the formal salution, **greeting,** is the same as that used in the Jerusalem Council letter by James (Acts 15:23), as well as the Epistle of James (James 1:1). Further, the captain herein reveals his own name, Claudius Lysias, the first being Roman and the last Greek.

Mention of Felix, the governor (more

[41] See Liddell and Scott, *op. cit.*, I, 379. Arndt and Gingrich (*op. cit.*, p. 173) say: "perhaps *bowman* or *slinger*."
[42] *Acts*, p. 416. [43] Cf. *Beginnings*, IV, 293. [44] Abbott-Smith, *op. cit.*, p. 259.
[45] VGT, p. 362. Cf. also Arndt and Gingrich, *op. cit.*, p. 456.
[46] *Beginnings*, IV, 293. [47] Arndt and Gingrich, *op. cit.*, p. 188.

[z] Ellicott, *op. cit.*, p. 157.

26 Claudius Lysias unto the most excellent governor Felix, greeting.
27 This man was seized by the Jews, and was about to be slain of them, when I came upon them with the soldiers and rescued him, having learned that he was a Roman.
28 And desiring to know the cause wherefore they accused him, I brought him down unto their council:
29 whom I found to be accused about questions of their law, but to have nothing laid to his charge worthy of death or of bonds.

---

28 **Cause** is *aitian*, which may be translated "reason, occasion, case, crime." Perhaps the last is best (cf. 13:28; 28:18).

29 **Laid to his charge** is *enklēma*, which occurs in the New Testament only here and in 25:16. It means an accusation.

---

properly *procurator* of an imperial province), throws a painting of varied and conflicting hues on the canvas of Judean administration. Certainly Lysias' address, **most excellent governor Felix** (vs. 26), can be taken as nothing more than a gesture of diplomatic respect, for Felix might be regarded as anything short of **most excellent.** Bruce holds that "The 'most excellent' . . . belongs properly to the equestrian order in Roman history (of which Felix was not a member) and was also given to the governors of subordinate provinces such as Judea who were normally drawn from the equestrian order."[a] He ruled Judea for seven or eight years (A.D. 52–59 or 60), having been preceded by the unhappy Cumanus and succeeded by Festus. The country had been left in a sad and disordered state upon the banishment of the inefficient and corrupt Cumanus by the emperor in A.D. 52. There had been a gruesome massacre of Jews at the Jerusalem Passover because of their riotous activities when a Roman soldier insulted the Temple. There had been a small scale war between the Galileans and the Samaritans when certain Galileans en route to a Jerusalem festival had been attacked, in the unsuccessful settlement of which Cumanus had been accused of accepting bribes to favor the cause of the Samaritans, which accusation effected his downfall. Felix inherited too grave a political situation for his ability. The country was a seething mass of disorder with the "dagger-carrying" *Sicarii* terrorizing the land and pressing the people to revolt against Rome. Assassin and "Messianic" outbreaks were frequent (cf. Acts 21:38). The patronizing high priest, Jonathan, who had helped Felix get his office had been assassinated, either at the instigation of Felix or otherwise.

The Emperor Claudius' mother, Antonia, retained two slave brothers, Antonius Felix and Pallas, who were later made freedmen. Felix became the companion and favored minister of Claudius, and thus he obtained the procuratorship of Judea by the grace of Claudius and the help of Pallas and the high priest Jonathan. Bruce thinks that he may previously "have occupied a subordinate post in Samaria under Cumanus from A.D. 48."[b] It thus appears that he considered the favor of the emperor, his foster brother, immunized him against imperial responsibility for any crime that he might commit. He wielded, in the words of Tacitus, "the power of a tyrant in the temper of a slave."[c] Lust and cruelty characterized his entire rule. He is reported to have married thrice. Plumptre[d] relates that his first wife was Drusilla, the daughter of Selena, who was the wife of Juba king of Mauritania and the daughter of Antonius and Cleopatra. Drusilla, the daughter of Agrippa I and sister of Agrippa II, who had left her husband Azizus, king of Emesa, was his second wife (cf. Acts 24:24).[e] The name of his third wife is unknown. Before such a ruler and judge, Paul the Apostle was to stand trial for his faith in Christ. Though the orator Tertullus, in an effort to curry favor with the Jews, complimented Felix with the words, "Seeing that by thee we enjoy much peace, and that by thy providence evils are corrected for this nation" (Acts 24:2b), it may be doubted if he was either sincere or realistic. Paul's address (Acts 24:10) seems better to suggest Felix's knowledge of Jewish administrative difficulties.

[a] Bruce, *op. cit.*, pp. 459, 460. [b] *Ibid.*, p. 462. [c] Tacitus, *Annals*, XIII, 54; *History*, V, 9.
[d] Ellicott, *op. cit.*, p. 157. [e] Josephus, *op. cit.*, "Ant." XX, 7, 1.

30 And when it was shown to me that there would be a plot against the man, I sent him to thee forthwith, charging his accusers also to speak against him before thee.

31 So the soldiers, as it was commanded them, took Paul and brought him by night to Antipatris.

---

30 **Shown** is the verb *mēnuō*, found four times in the New Testament, only here in Acts. It means "to inform, report."[48] *Katēgorois*, **accusers,** in the New Testament is found only in Acts (23:30, 35; 25:16, 18). In the papyri it is used in the sense of "prosecutor" or "plaintiff."[49]

31 Cadbury thinks the route to **Antipatris** was by way of Gibeon, Beth-horon, and Lydda.[50]

It is noteworthy that Lysias avoids all reference to his binding of Paul and the intended scourging. Nor does he intimate that he had been ignorant of Paul's Roman citizenship at the outset. He ingeniously colors the whole affair to give the impression that he had dutifully rescued, from Jewish mob violence, a victim, whom he knew to be a Roman citizen (vs. 27). He gives a fair and honest account of Paul's examination before the Sanhedrin (vss. 28, 29). This was clearly intended as "a preliminary investigation with a view to preparing a charge to lay before the Roman Court."[f] He states also the Jews' plot to kill Paul and his purpose to place Paul in the safe custody of Felix the governor for fair trial (vs. 30). He gives his judgment that the whole affair is a Jewish doctrinal disputation, not a Roman legal question. Withal, Lysias was a typical office holder who arranged the stage to present himself in the most favorable light before those to whom he owed his position, by taking credit for what did not rightfully belong to him and by taking diligent care to veneer his official mistakes with an appearance of excellence in judgment and service.

E. The Transfer of Paul Accomplished (23:31–35)

And they . . . came to Caesarea and delivered the letter to the governor [and] **presented Paul also before him** (vs. 33).

It appears that the first half, or possibly two-thirds, of the approximately sixty-mile journey from Jerusalem to Caesarea was reached at Antipatris before daybreak (vs. 31). Bruce holds that Antipatris was 35 miles from Jerusalem. And it was, he continues, "at the foot of the Judean hills, on the site of the modern Ral el – 'Ain, built by Herod the Great in the well-watered and well-wooded plain of Kaphar-Saba and called after his father Antipater."[g] Such was quite possible, allowing a distance of some thirty-five miles to Antipatris and remembering that they had left at about nine o'clock in the evening. From Antipatris the foot soldiers returned to Jerusalem leaving the cavalry to escort Paul the remaining 27 miles to Caesarea. This was considered safe as the Jews loathed the use of horses as unclean animals, and thus the *Sicarii* could not have overtaken the party, even if they had learned of Paul's transfer to Caesarea. Also, the remaining journey was through territory that was principally Gentile.

Felix's inquiry concerning Paul's province (vs. 34) was a requirement of Roman jurisprudence. An accused citizen could be tried in either his home province or in the one where the crime was alleged to have been committed (cf. Luke 23:6, 7).

Felix's expressed decision, **I will hear thee fully . . . when thine accusers also are come** (vs. 35a), indicates that upon learning that Paul's home province was Cilicia, he at once knew that he had "jurisdiction over Paul, either as procurator over Judea, in which the "crime" had been committed, or as the deputy of the legate of Syria and Cilicia, Paul's native province, who would rank as his administrative superior."[h] Possibly his immediate decision to try Paul rather than defer to his superior officer (as Pilate had done with Christ, Luke 23:6–12), the Syrian legate, was but a reflection of his characteristic impetuosity and pride of position.

It is apparently at this juncture that Paul assumed an active role in the proceedings.

[48] Thayer, *op. cit.*, p. 412. [49] VGT, p. 337. [50] *Book of Acts in History*, p. 64.

[f] *The Interpreter's Bible*, IX, 305. [g] Bruce, *op. cit.*, p. 461. [h] *The Interpreter's Bible*, IX, 306.

32 But on the morrow they left the horsemen to go with him, and returned to the castle:
33 and they, when they came to Caesarea and delivered the letter to the governor, presented Paul also before him.
34 And when he had read it, he asked of what province he was; and when he understood that he was of Cilicia,
35 I will hear thee fully, said he, when thine accusers also are come: and he commanded him to be kept in Herod's palace.

---

33 **Delivered** is the verb *anadidōmi*, found only here in the New Testament. Moulton and Milligan give several examples from the papyri of its use for delivering an epistle.[51]

35 **Hear . . . fully** is the verb *diakouō*, found only here in the New Testament. It has the technical meaning "to hear judicially."[52] This judicial sense is common in the papyri and inscriptions of the period.[53]

Commanded is the aorist participle, which normally expresses action antecedent to that of the main verb. But here it means simultaneous action.[54] **Palace** is *praitorion*, which occurs only here in Acts. It is from the Latin *praetorium*. First used for the general's quarters in a Roman army camp, it came to designate the official residence of the governor. This is its use in the Gospel (five times).

Thenceforth he seems to have asserted his Roman citizenship rights in a four fold relation. *First*, he did so to escape scourging (Acts 22:25). *Second*, he evidently appealed his right of jurisdiction from the Jewish Sanhedrin to the Roman procurator, in which case his transfer to Caesarea was in compliance with his own expressed rights as a citizen, a demand Lysias would have gladly acceded to, in any event, to relieve his own responsibility. *Third*, he asserted his right of fair trial before the Roman provincial court (Acts 25:10). And *fourth*, Paul asserted his citizenship rights by appeal to the supreme court of Caesarea at Rome (Acts 25:11b, 12b).

With promise of a full and just trial upon the appearance of his accusers, Felix ordered Paul detained under guard in Herod's palace. This was likely the palace built by Herod the Great and later converted into an official residence for the Roman Judean procurator, though it may have served as a fortress and have had a guard room (cf. Mark 15:16; Phil. 1:13). It is not to be supposed that Paul was incarcerated in a common prison such as that into which he and Silas were thrown at Philippi (Acts 16:23, 24).

[51] VGT, p. 32.
[52] Deissmann, *Bible Studies*, p .230.
[53] VGT, p. 150.
[54] Cf. Moulton ,*Grammar*, I, 133.

CHAPTER XXIV

And after five days the high priest Ananias came down with certain elders, and *with* an orator, one Tertullus; and they informed the governor against Paul.

EXEGESIS

1 *Rhētoros,* **orator,** is found only here in the New Testament. At first meaning "public speaker," it came to be used specifically for "a speaker in court, advocate, attorney." [1] Moulton and Milligan cite an example of the latter usage in a papyrus of A.D. 49.[2] **Informed** is the same word *(emphanizō)* which is translated "signify" in 23:15, 22 (see on 23:15).

EXPOSITION

THE APOSTLE ON TRIAL BEFORE FELIX AT CAESAREA

I. Paul's Indictment before Felix, Acts 24:1–9.
   A. The Witnesses against Paul, vs. 1.
   B. The Address to the Judge, vss. 2–4.
   C. The Charges against Paul, vss. 5–9.
II. Paul's Defense before Felix, Acts 24:10–21.
   A. Paul's Address to the Judge, vs. 10.
   B. Paul's Reply to the First Charge, vss. 11–13.
   C. Paul's Reply to the Second Charge, vss. 14–16.
   D. Paul's Reply to the Third Charge, vss. 17–21.
III. Paul's Trial Deferred by Felix, Acts 24:22–27.
   A. Felix's Reason for Deferring the Trial, vs. 22.
   B. Felix's Solicitude for Paul, vs. 23.
   C. Felix's Conferences with Paul, vss. 24–26.
   D. Felix's Disposal of Paul, vs. 27.

I. PAUL'S INDICTMENT BEFORE FELIX

(24:1–9)

Once more, as at Corinth before the Roman governor, the proconsul Gallio (Acts 18:12–17), Paul was arraigned before an official Roman court presided over by Felix, the eleventh procurator of Judea (A.D. 52–59 or 60). Before Felix, as before Gallio, his accusers were the Jews who were enraged because he preached Christ as their Messiah and the Saviour of all men. Before Gallio in Corinth, the capital of a Gentile province where the Jews were a hated minority, he was acquitted, and Christianity was thus given legal status as a form of Judaism. But at Caesarea Paul was being tried by the Roman procurator of Judea, which was predominantly Jewish and where the laws and customs of the Jews were carefully respected by the Roman rulers. Paul was more anxious for the status of Christianity in Judea than he was for his own personal welfare. However, Christianity had ceased to be regarded as a form of Judaism in Judea. A growing hostility of the Jews against the Christians was developing. Erelong James, pastor of the Jerusalem church, with others, was to suffer martyrdom at the hands of the Sanhedrin at the instigation of Ananias (see comment on Acts 23:1–5). Rome did not yet have a hostile attitude toward the Christians, but Jewish pressure on the Roman procurator of Judea was very strong. There was no assurance that Felix would not yield to their demands, even as Pilate had when Christ was on trial before him (cf. Matt. 27:23–26). The cause of Christianity throughout the Roman empire hinged on the outcome of Paul's trial at Caesarea. We may only imagine with what earnestness Paul must have prayed before he went on trial for the defense of Christianity in this most strategically situated Roman provincial court of justice. Nor was the issue to be finally settled until it was carried to the supreme court of Caesar in Rome itself.

[1] Arndt and Gingrich, *op. cit.*, p. 743.

[2] VGT, p. 563.

2 And when he was called, Tertullus began to accuse him, saying, Seeing that by thee we enjoy much peace, and that by thy providence evils are corrected for this nation,
3 we accept it in all ways and in all places, most excellent Felix, with all thankfulness.

---

2 *Pronoias*, **providence,** occurs only here and in Romans 13:14. When used of God it means "providence, forethought"; when used of men, "foresight, care." [3] While both meanings are found in classical and contemporary writings (including the papyri), only the latter occurs in the New Testament.[4]

Evils are corrected is literally "reforms having taken place" *(diorthōmatōn ginomenōn)*. The noun *diorthōma* is found only here in the New Testament.

A. The Witnesses against Paul (24:1)

Ananias . . . with certain elders, and . . . Tertullus . . . informed the governor against Paul (vs. 1).

Plumptre[a] thinks that the **five days'** intervention may have afforded time for the messenger from Felix to go to Jerusalem, summon Paul's accusers, and return. However, he allows that the **five days** may have begun with Paul's departure from Jerusalem, which seems to accord better with verse eleven.

The bloodthirsty persistence of Ananias is eloquently evidenced by his appearance before Felix's court to secure, if possible, either the conviction or custody of Paul. (For the office and character of Ananias, see notes on Acts 23:1–5.) The **certain elders** were his supporting delegation from the Sanhedrin and most certainly such as had participated in the council's attack on Paul at Jerusalem (Acts 23:1–10). Tertullus was evidently a cheap, though "professional, Roman pleader and probably [?] a heathen."[b] Macgregor likewise considers Tertullus as "a Roman professional counsel for the prosecution, a *causidicus* or advocate."[c] However, Bruce regards him as "probably a Hellenistic Jew."[d] From Tertullus' identification of himself with the activities of the Sanhedrin against Paul (**on whom "we" laid hold,** vs. 6), it would appear that he was a Jew or at best a Hellenist. Tertullus is one of two lawyers named in the New Testament, the other Zenos, a Christian convert and worker for whom Paul sent (Titus 3:13). These lawyers are not to be confused with the "scribes and doctors of the law" found in the Gospels. The latter were ecclesiastics and theologians. The lawyers of Tertullus' tribe were many in the first century (see notes on Acts 17:5). If not actually Greeks, they were likely influenced by the Sophist school of philosophy. In any event, Paul had great respect for the law of the nation of which he was a citizen (cf. I Tim. 2:2), as well as for the law of Moses.

Bruce aptly states: "They enlisted the services of an advocate named Tertullus to state it [their case against Paul] in the conventional terms of forensic rhetoric."[e] It sounds very modern when Plumptre remarks:

> Men of this class were to be found in most of the provincial towns of the Roman empire, ready to hold a brief for plaintiff or defendant, and bringing to bear the power of their glib eloquence, as well as their knowledge of Roman laws, on the mind of the judge.[f]

Here is a case where two, yea even three, cultures met in conflict. The Jews were accusing a Christian apostle before a Roman court.

B. The Address to the Judge (24:2–4)

Seeing that by thee we enjoy much peace . . . most excellent Felix, vs. 2.

With flattering eloquence and personal compliments, Tertullus paved the way for his indictment of Paul. Concerning Tertullus' words, **of thy clemency** (vs. 4b), Plumptre remarks: "The epithets of the hired orator stand in striking contrast with the 'righteousness, temperance, and judgment to come,' of which the Apostle afterwards spoke to the same rulers."[g] Clarke analyzes Tertullus' oration thus: "1. The exordium. 2. The proposition. 3. The conclusion."[h] In the first is contained his praise for Felix and his administration of Judea. Clearly his

[3] Arndt and Gingrich, *op. cit.*, p. 715. [4] VGT, p. 543.

[a] Ellicott, *op. cit.*, VII, 158.
[b] A. T. Robertson, *Luke the Historian in the Light of Research* (New York: Charles Scribner's Sons, 1936), p. 190.
[c] *The Interpreter's Bible*, p. 307. [d] Bruce, *op. cit.*, p. 463. [e] *Ibid.* [f] Ellicott, *op. cit.*, VII, 158.
[g] *Ibid.*, p. 159. [h] Clarke, *op. cit.*, V, 873.

4 But, that I be not further tedious unto thee, I entreat thee to hear us of thy clemency a few words.

5 For we have found this man a pestilent fellow, and a mover of insurrections among all the Jews throughout the world, and a ringleader of the sect of the Nazarenes:

---

4 *Enkoptō*, **be . . . tedious,** literally means "cut into," and so "hinder." *Epieikia*, **clemency,** occurs elsewhere in the New Testament only in II Corinthians 10:1. It means "mildness, gentleness, fairness."[5] *Syntomōs*, **a few words,** is found in the New Testament only here. It is an adverb meaning "concisely, briefly"[6] (cf. RSV). The common meaning in the papyri is "at once,"[7] which fits very well here.

5 **We have found** is literally "having found" *(heurontes)*. The same verb introduces a similar threefold accusation against Jesus (Luke 23:2). *Loimos* means "pestilence" (cf. Luke 21:11, its only other occurrence in N.T.). It is used metaphorically in the classics and the Septuagint for "a pest" or **pestilent fellow,** a person dangerous to the public welfare (so in Demosthenes).[8] **Ringleader** is *protostatēs*, found only here in the New Testament. It means literally "one who stands first" and so was used for a soldier in the front rank. Finally it came to signify "a leader." **Sect** is *hairesis*, used of Sadducees (5:17) and Pharisees (15:5).

---

purpose was to curry favor and win the esteem of Felix for his cause.

Obviously Felix had certain accounts to his credit in his Judean administration. In addition to the dispersing of the Egyptian Sicarii's insurrection (Acts 21:38), he had quelled uprisings and banditry under the leadership of one Eliezer[i] and a serious disturbance between the Syrians and the Caesarean Jews. But the other side of the ledger was seriously overbalanced with discredits. He was reprehensible for both bad character and maladministration. His lustful, mercenary, oppressive, unjust, and cruel conduct was all too well known by his Jewish subjects (For a description of Felix's character and conduct, see notes on Acts 23:25–30.)

Tertullus' claim that the Jews graciously and universally accepted Felix's administration (vs. 3) was flagrant hypocrisy. Indeed many of the Sadducees favored him, but there were far more of the loyalists who thirsted for his blood.

Tertullus' reference to Felix's providence (vs. 2) led Plumptre to observe:

> Men spoke then, as now of the "providence of God," and the tendency to clothe the emperors with quasi-divine attributes led to the appearance of this word—"the providence of Caesar"—on their coins and on medals struck in their honor. Tertullus, after this manner, goes one step further, and extends the term to the procurator of Judea.[j]

This tendency to deify Roman rulers was evidenced by the ascription of divinity to Herod Agrippa I by the peoples of Tyre with his resultant divine judgment in death in A.D. 44 (Acts 12:21–23). Robertson sees evidence of Roman emperor worship in Paul's experience at Thessalonica:

> Evidently, Paul, while in Thessalonica, had been stirred up by the worship of the Roman emperor and may have employed language that gave some color to the specious charge of his enemies. Here in Thessalonica Paul began to face the inevitable conflict between Christ and Caesar. The shadow of Rome was cast upon the Cross.[k] (Cf. II Thess. 2:3).

Treason seems to have been the charge that threw both the Thessalonian politarchs and the crowd into pandemonium, and thus Jason was required to give security to insure their good behavior against treason (Acts 17:9).

Concerning Tertullus' words, **that I be not further tedious unto thee,** Bruce remarks:

> It was . . . customary to promise brevity, as Tertullus does here (v. 4), the promise was sometimes kept, sometimes not, but it was calculated to secure good will for the speaker at the outset of his speech.[l]

C. The Charges against Paul (24:5–9)

a pestilent fellow . . . a mover of insurrections . . . a ringleader of the sect of the Nazarenes . . . assayed to profane the temple, vss. 5, 6.

[5] Thayer, *op. cit.*, p. 238. [6] Abbott-Smith, *op. cit.*, pp. 433 f. [7] VGT, p. 614.

[8] Arndt and Gingrich, *op. cit.*, p. 480. They identify the form here and in LXX as the substantive use of the adjective, leaving the noun for Luke 21:11.

[i] Josephus, *op. cit.*, "Antiquities," XX, VIII, 5, and "Wars," XI, XIII, 2.

[j] Ellicott, *op. cit.*, p. 159. [k] Robertson, *op. cit.*, p. 197. [l] Bruce, *op. cit.*, p. 464.

6 who moreover assayed to profane the temple: on whom also we laid hold:
8 from whom thou wilt be able, by examining him thyself, to take knowledge of all these things whereof we accuse him.
9 And the Jews also joined in the charge, affirming that these things were so.

---

6 **Assayed** is the verb *peirazō*. In the earlier writers it means "try" in the sense of "attempt," as here. In the New Testament it usually means "try" in the sense "test" or "tempt." It is translated "tempt" in 29 out of its 39 occurrences in the King James Version. *Bebēloō* (**profane**) is found elsewhere in the New Testament only in Matthew 12:5, of profaning the sabbath. The last clause of the sixth verse, all the seventh, and the first clause of the eighth are omitted from the Revised versions because they are missing in the oldest manuscripts.[9]

9 **Joined in the charge** is the double compound *synepitithēmi*, found only here in the New Testament. In the middle, as here, it means "join in attacking." It has this sense in the Septuagint (Deut. 32:27). *Phaskontes*, **affirming**, occurs also in 25:19 and Romans 1:22.

Though Tertullus advances four general things against Paul, they seem to resolve themselves logically into three specific charges: *First*, he is charged with being a confirmed agitator and promoter of subversive activities: **a pestilent fellow . . . a mover of insurrections.** *Second*, he is charged with being the self-appointed chief of a revolutionary movement: **a ringleader of the sect of the Nazarenes.** And *third*, he is charged with intent to profane the Jewish Temple: **who moreover assayed to profane the temple.**

First, Tertullus shrewdly leveled his charge against Paul before Felix when he alleged that he had been found to be **a pestilent fellow,** or perhaps by implication a deadly, poisonous, pernicious, demoralizing, peace-disturbing, infectious Sicarius at large in the empire who had come to Judea with the purpose of directing a revolt against Rome. It was, as we have seen, in the suppression of these Sicarii of Judea that Felix most prided himself. "Messianic" movements were many and though they began as a religion, they sometimes became political. The charge of Tertullus against Paul seems to imply that he was head of such a movement. Tertullus well knew that if the Jews could secure a verdict against Paul on this first charge, his execution by Felix in the interest of Roman government in Palestine would be assured.

The *second* charge was designed to be cumulative in its import. Herein Paul is depicted as the organizer and director of a subversive, political movement which, under the false guise of the legalized Jewish religion in the empire, had bored its way into every part of the Roman Empire. Tertullus is subtly drawing the lines of demarcation between Judaism and Christianity with the purpose of pushing the latter out into the unfavorable recognition of Rome. Had he succeeded, not only would Paul have suffered execution but the Roman ax would have fallen on the Christians of Judea and perhaps throughout the empire. If he failed, Christianity would come into favorable notice and recognition of Rome and would attain legal status, as indeed it did in A.D. 313 under the emperor Constantine. Tertullus employed no new device in his attempt to set Caesar against Christ. The Jews employed this device against Christ Himself (John 19:12); it was employed against the Christian apostles at Philippi (Acts 16:19–21); and again at Thessalonica (Acts 17:6–8); and at Corinth (Acts 18:12, 13).

Bruce[m] observes that this is the single New Testament employment of the name *Nazarene* in application to the followers of Christ. As such they are designated a party or organization (cf. Acts 5:17). The *third* charge of the attempted profanation of the Temple lacks the detail of the earlier charge against Paul where the Jews actually accused him of doing so by taking the Gentile Trophimus into the Temple. There they accused him of the act, but here Tertullus, perhaps either because of the diffi-

[9] Aleph A B H L P, as well as many minuscules. Bruce comments: "This addition bears the marks of genuineness" (*op. cit.*, p. 422). Lake and Cadbury also favor retaining the addition (*Beginnings*, IV, 299), as does Lumby (CGT, p. 409). Knowling does not (EGT, II, 479).

[m] *Ibid.*, 465.

10 And when the governor had beckoned unto him to speak, Paul answered, Forasmuch as I know that thou hast been of many years a judge unto this nation, I cheerfully make my defence:

11 seeing that thou canst take knowledge that it is not more than twelve days since I went up to worship at Jerusalem:

10 The expression **of many years** has been questioned, since Felix had been procurator of Judea for only about five years. But Tacitus says he had been governor of Samaria for some four years before that.[10] *Euthymōs*, **cheerfully**, occurs only here in the New Testament. **Make my defence** is the verb *apologeomai*, "speak in one's own defense, defend oneself." [11] Moulton and Milligan cite examples of this judicial sense in the papyri.[12]

11 In regard to the problem of the **twelve days** Lake and Cadbury make this suggestion: "It is possible that the phrase means 'I had not been twelve days in Jerusalem when the trouble arose.'" [13] But this alternative is unnecessary. Knowling [14] and Lumby [15] give slightly different reckonings of the twelve days, both of which are fully satisfactory. The latter begins with the day of Paul's arrival in Jerusalem, the former with the day after. The shortness of Paul's stay would give Felix opportunity to check his activities during that period.

Proskynēsōn, **to worship,** may also be translated "on a pilgrimage" [16] (cf. 8:27).

culty of proof or because of the discovery of their mistake, resorts to an accusation against Paul's motives: he **assayed to profane the temple.** Of course if this charge could have been sustained, the Jews would have had the legal right to execute Paul themselves. Perhaps it is this that they most hoped to accomplish in the trial. A verdict here would have been a final victory for them over Paul, if not over Christianity.

Tertullus closed his prosecution by committing the case to the judge with the complimentary assurance that Felix would, by examination, find the charges true as he had presented them (vs. 8). The Jewish delegation gave assent to the charges as presented by Tertullus.

II. PAUL'S DEFENSE BEFORE FELIX (24:10–21)

That both the prosecution and the defense began their addresses at the beckoning of Felix (cf. vss. 2 and 10) makes clear that this was a formal trial.

A. Paul's Address to the Judge (24:10)

I cheerfully make my defence, vs. 10b.

There is a marked difference between the address of the defense (vs. 10) and that of the prosecution (vss. 2–4). Paul is briefer, less ornate, and more direct in his approach. Both are complimentary of the judge, but instead of an enumeration of doubtful achievements ascribed to Felix by Tertullus, Paul, in a straightforward manner, recognizes Felix's knowledge of Jewish affairs, possibly gained in large measure through Drusilla and his experience as administrator and judge of Judea, as favorable criteria for judging the case in question. Plumptre says, "We note at once the difference between St. Paul's frank manliness and the servile flattery of the advocate."[n]

B. Paul's Reply to the First Charge (24:11–13)

Paul replies to the three charges of Tertullus in order (see notes on vss. 5–9). *First*, he denies that he had any seditious intent at Jerusalem. This denial he supports by numerous evidences. Concerning the problem raised by the twelve days (vs. 11), Bruce remarks:

> The notes of time from Paul's arrival in Jerusalem (Ch. 21:17 f.) are given in great detail. But the seven days of Ch. 21:27 and the five days of Ch. 24:1 would in themselves make up twelve days, without taking into consideration the time-notes of Chs. 21:18, 26; 22:30; 28:11 f., 23, 30. We have therefore to suppose (with

[10] *Annals*, XII, 54. [11] Arndt and Gingrich, *op. cit.*, p. 95.
[12] VGT, p. 66. [13] *Beginnings*, IV, 300. [14] EGT, II, 481.
[15] J. Rawson Lumby, *The Acts of the Apostles*, "Cambridge Greek Testament" (Cambridge: University Press, 1885), p. 410. See also F. W. Farrar, *The Life and Work of St. Paul* (New York: E. P. Dutton and Co., 1896), p. 548, n. 7.
[16] *Beginnings*, IV, 301.
[n] Ellicott, *loc. cit.*

12 and neither in the temple did they find me disputing with any man or stirring up a crowd, nor in the synagogues, nor in the city.

13 Neither can they prove to thee the things whereof they now accuse me.

14 But this I confess unto thee, that after the Way which they call a sect, so serve I the God of our fathers, believing all things which are according to the law, and which are written in the prophets;

---

12 **Stirring up** is *epistasin poiounta. Epistasis* (elsewhere in N.T. only in II Cor. 11:28) means "an advancing approach; incursion, onset, press."[17] Arndt and Gingrich think the best meaning of the phrase here is "attack, onset."[18] Moulton and Milligan prefer the latter.[19] The Received Text has *episystasin*, "a gathering, a riotous throng."[20] But *epistasis* has much the better support.[21] Knowling would take it in its weaker sense of "a gathering."[22] Lake and Cadbury have "collecting a crowd."[23] **In the city** is *kata tēn polin*, which has the force of "from one point to another in the city."[24]

13 *Parastēsai*, **prove**, is literally "to place beside." It means "'to put evidence alongside of argument,' as in the Attic orators."[25] Only here in the New Testament does it have this sense.

14 **The Way which they call a sect** is preferable to "the way which they call heresy" (KJV). Christianity was called "the Way" (cf. 9:2). *Hairesis* is translated "sect" in the King James Version in every other place in Acts (5:17; 15:5; 24:5; 26:5; 28:22) and should be rendered thus here.[26]

Latreuō, **serve**, is translated thus in the King James Version in 16 out of its 21 occurrences in the New Testament. But here and in 7:42 (also Phil. 3:3) it is rendered "worship." It comes from *latris*, "servant." But in the New Testament (as in LXX) the word is used only for divine service.[27] **Of our fathers** is *patroō*, found in the New Testament only here, in 22:3, and in 28:17.

The Revised versions follow the Greek of the latter part of this verse more accurately than does the King James Version. It is things **according to the law** and **written in the prophets.**

Rackham . . .) that the five days of Ch. 24:1 are reckoned from Paul's arrest in the temple (which strikes one as most improbable), or that the week prescribed for the four Nazarites' purification was nearly completed when Paul joined them, or that he was arrested early in the week. The last alternative seems to accord with the wording of Ch. 21:27 less well than the second one does.[o]

Concerning the chronological problem, Macgregor simply states: "The truth probably is that Paul is simply speaking in round numbers-as we might say 'about a fortnight.'"[p]

Paul's purpose in going to Jerusalem had not been for political agitation as Tertullus alleged, but rather for religious worship: **I went up to worship** (vs. 11b; cf. vs. 18). Paul's nationality and training supported this claim. As a provincial Jew it was perfectly natural and right that he should have come to Jerusalem to worship at the Pentecostal feast. The brevity of time spent there (12 days) would have been against seditious activities, especially as he accounted for his conduct during that time.

He makes a flat denial that the Jews had found him disputing with any man or gathering and agitating a following, either in the Temple, in a Jerusalem synagogue, or in any other part of the city (vs. 12). Tertullus had generalized in his charges. Paul categorically denied these generalities with their subtle implications. When one has been honest in speech and upright in conduct, it will not be difficult to give a straightforward and satisfactory account of his words and deeds. This categorical denial of seditious activities Paul clinches with a straight-forward challenge to his accusers to offer satisfactory evidence of their accusations (vs. 13).

C. Paul's Reply to the Second Charge (24:14–16)

While ignoring his alleged position as ringleader of the sect of the Nazarenes (vs.

[17] Thayer, *op. cit.*, p. 243. [18] *Op. cit.*, p. 300. [19] VGT, p. 245. [20] Abbott-Smith, *op. cit.*, p. 175.
[21] Aleph A B E against H L P. [22] EGT, II, 482. [23] *Beginnings*, IV, 301. [24] *Ibid.* [25] *Ibid.*
[26] It is rendered "heresy" elsewhere in KJV (I Cor. 11:19; Gal. 5:20; II Peter 2:1). See on 5:17.
[27] Cremer, *op. cit.*, p. 389; Arndt and Gingrich, *op. cit.*, p. 468.
[o] Bruce, *op. cit.*, p. 468, n. 13. [p] *The Interpreter's Bible*, IX, 310.

15 having hope toward God, which these also themselves look for, that there shall be a resurrection both of the just and unjust.

16 Herein I also exercise myself to have a conscience void of offence toward God and men always.

---

15 **Which these . . . look for** implies the presence of some Pharisees among the elders who came down with Ananias. For **resurrection both of the just and unjust** see on 23:8. This is the only place where Paul mentions the resurrection of the unjust.

16 *Askō (askeō)* occurs only here in the New Testament. First used for athletic training, the word became "successively physical, intellectual, ethical, religious." [28] *Aproskopen*, **void of offence,** is used elsewhere in the New Testament only by Paul (I Cor. 10:32; Phil. 1:10). Actively it means "not causing to stumble" and passively "not stumbling, without offence, blameless." [29] In the papyri it has the sense "free from hurt or harm." [30] Arndt and Gingrich would render the phrase here "a clear conscience."[31] They also note that it means "undamaged, blameless." [32] Lake and Cadbury say the phrase here, as in the papyri, "refers to the maintenance of an unspoiled record in one's own self-judgement." [33]

5b), Paul denied Tertullus' allegation that the Christian movement was politically subversive under the cloak of Judaism throughout the empire (vs. 5). Positively, he proudly identified himself with **the Way which they call a sect** (vs. 14). But immediately he defended this sect as a perfectly lawful and orthodox movement within Judaism. In systematic order Paul asserts that he (and these people) of the Way **worship** (vs. 11b) **[and] serve . . . the God of our Fathers** (vs. 14), or the Jehovah of the Jews. Further, he asserts that they believe **all things which are according to the law, and which are written in the prophets** (vs. 14). While not so stated, Paul subtly implies that the Christian faith accepts the essence of Judaism while rejecting the oral additions and accretions of the Jews (cf. Matt. 23:4). Thus Paul places Christianity in direct descent from the law of Moses and implies that it is the fulfillment of the prophets. Christianity is founded upon the teachings of Moses—it rests upon the moral content of the law, and it is the realized fulfillment of what the prophets promised. Further, Paul boldly asserts that his "saving faith" (**hope toward God** vs. 15a) rests upon the very one (the Messiah) to whom the Jews still look forward. Paul seems to say, I repose my faith for salvation in the Messiah who has already come, and in whom the Jews hope to repose their faith when He shall have come. For Paul and the Christians the Messiah was a present saviour; for the Jews He was still a future anticipation. Clearly Paul implies that the object of his hope toward God (Christ) was identical with the Messiah for whom they had long looked and for whom they still looked (cf. John 1:11, 12). Again he asserts his faith, and that of the Christians, in the resurrection, **both of the just and the unjust** (vs. 15b). This latter statement need not be regarded as in conflict with Paul's doctrine of the two resurrections in the Thessalonian letter (cf. I Thess. 4:13–18; I Cor. 15; Rev. 20:13–15).

Macgregor[q] would deny that reference to the resurrection in verse fifteen is Pauline, on the ground that Paul taught two separate resurrections, for the righteous and for the unjust, and that Paul's faith centered in Christ's resurrection which the Jews denied. It seems appropriate to reply, first, that there is no apparent good reason to deny that Paul may have allowed for separate resurrections—**both of the just and the unjust**—in this utterance. It did not fit his purpose to deal with them separately at this time. He is countering Sadducean denial of any resurrection by identifying his belief with that of orthodox Judaism. In the second place, Paul assumed the resurrection of Christ as the condition and the guarantee of the resurrection of the dead (cf. I Cor.

[28] *Beginnings*, IV, 302. [29] Abbott-Smith, *op. cit.*, p. 56. [30] VGT, p. 72.
[31] *Op. cit.*, p. 102. [32] *Loc. cit.* [33] *Beginnings*, IV, 302.

[q] *Ibid.*, p. 311.

17 Now after some years I came to bring alms to my nation, and offerings:
18 amidst which they found me purified in the temple, with no crowd, nor yet with tumult: but *there were* certain Jews from Asia—

---

17 *Pleionōn*, **some,** literally means "more." But in the New Testament the comparative is often used with the superlative force, so that this may be translated "many." [34] Only four or five years had elapsed since Paul's last, brief visit to Jerusalem (18:22), but the reference may be to the Council visit (chap. 15), which was some ten years before this. **After some years** is literally "through many years" *(di' etōn pleionōn)*. Winer translates it: "many years intervening." [35]

To bring alms is "doing alms" *(eleēmosynas poiēson;* cf. Matt. 6:2). Since Paul initiated the collecting of the relief money, he could speak of it in this personal way. **Offerings** evidently does not, as **alms,** refer to the collection for the saints, since the words are carefully separated.[36] Lumby writes: "These were the sacrifices connected with the vow which he had undertaken" [37] (cf. 21:26). This is also the view of Plumptre,[38] Brown,[39] Hackett,[40] and Alexander.[41] Macgregor thinks it "possible." [42] But Lenski [43] and Bruce [44] make **offerings** refer to the same thing as **alms.** Leckler explains **offerings** as meaning the temple sacrifices,[45] while Meyer more specifically identifies them as the festival offerings.[46]

18 **Amidst which** seems to mean in the midst of his offerings in the temple.[47] **But there were certain Jews from Asia** implies that Paul answered the accusation of his having stirred up insurrection (cf. vs. 5) by charging the Asiatic Jews with causing the **tumult,** not he.[48]

15:12–22). Nor did it serve Paul's purpose to assert or argue the resurrection of Christ at this juncture. Continuity of orthodox and Christian theology was Paul's purpose here, with a view to vindicating the Christian cause.

Mention of the resurrection here, as before the Sanhedrin at Jerusalem (Acts 23:6), immediately identified Paul and Christianity with the Pharisees and orthodox Judaism as opposed to the Sadducees, who rejected the doctrine and thus forfeited their right of claim to orthodox Judaism. Most likely the certain elders who accompanied Ananias (vs. 1), who was known to be a Sadducee, were "hand-picked" Sadducees for the occasion, as probably was Tertullus, if indeed he was a Jew (see Exegesis). Thus Paul's assertion of faith in the resurrection placed the Christians in the position of orthodoxy, while leaving his accusers in the position of heterodoxy, a subtile move of defense indeed on Paul's part. Could it have been that Paul knew that Felix's wife Drusilla, who was a Jewess and evidently listened to Paul with great interest, was of the orthodox party and that Felix's religious sympathies would have been with her, rather than with the Sadducees? (cf. vs. 24).

Paul returned (vs. 16) to the reassertion of his strict conscientiousness, a proposition which he had stated before the Sanhedrin at Jerusalem and for which the Jews had attempted to mob him. (See Acts 23:1–5 with notes on "conscience.")

D. Paul's Reply to the Third Charge (24:17–21)

As further evidence of his loyalty to orthodox Judaism, Paul advances the prime purpose of his last visit to Jerusalem: namely, "the collection" (vs. 17). Here however, Paul judiciously refers to it as **alms to my nation, and offerings.** Nor does Paul here differentiate between the Christian and non-Christian Jews in his use of the word "nation." But it must be remembered that in his defense he is attempting to establish that Christianity is the very spiritual essence of orthodox Judaism. Thus there is no shading of truth in his statement here. Concerning the **alms** Plumptre remarks:

[34] Conybeare and Howson say: "'Several,' not so strong as 'many'" (p. 662).
[35] *Grammar*, p. 380. [36] Knowling, EGT, II, 484. [37] *Acts* (CGT), p. 412.
[38] Ellicott, *op. cit.*, VII, 160. [39] JFB, VI, 167. [40] *Op. cit.*, p. 273.
[41] Joseph A. Alexander, *Commentary on the Acts of the Apostles* (Grand Rapids: Zondervan Publishing House, 1956), p. 829.
[42] IB, IX, 311. [43] *Op. cit.*, p. 973. [44] NIC, p. 470. [45] *Op. cit.*, p. 421. [46] *Op. cit.*, p. 446.
[47] *Hais*, the better reading (Aleph A B C E) would refer to the offerings, while *hois*, the inferior reading (H L P) would be more general ("things").
[48] C Hackett, *op. cit.*, p. 274.

19 who ought to have been here before thee, and to make accusation, if they had aught against me.
20 Or else let these men themselves say what wrong-doing they found when I stood before the council,
21 except it be for this one voice, that I cried standing among them, Touching the resurrection of the dead I am called in question before you this day.

---

19 The point of this verse was very pertinent. Foakes-Jackson remarks: "As a lawyer Paul was more than a match for Tertullus. Tarsus, it must be remembered, was a great law school." [49]

20 *Adikēma*, **wrong-doing,** means "a wrong crime, misdeed." [50] It is found elsewhere in the New Testament only in 18:14 and Revelation 18:5.

21 **Except it be** is one letter in the Greek, *ē*, which means "than"; that is, "other than." Did Paul hereby admit that he did wrong in presenting the issue as he did before the Sanhedrin (cf. 23:6)? Farrar thinks so. He takes Paul's remark as "a confession of his error on this occasion." [51] But Lake and Cadbury object strongly to this interpretation. They write: "The meaning is that if the Jews speak the truth they must admit that they had no case against him except theological difference, which in the eyes of Felix would be none at all." [52] Lenski says: "We do not see how anyone can find an admission of wrong in this statement." [53] It was rather a verification of what Lysias wrote to Felix, that Paul was by the Jews "accused about questions of their law" (23:29), which did not concern a Roman court. Paul thus pleads "not guilty," without an exception.

The "alms" were, of course, the large sums of money which St. Paul had been collecting, since his last visit, for the disciples (possibly in part, also, for those who were not disciples) at Jerusalem. It is noticeable that this is the only mention in the Acts of that which occupies so prominent a place in the epistles of this period (See Rom. 15:25; I Cor. 16:1–4; II Cor. 8:1–4).[r]

Plumptre sees a "refined courtesy" in Paul's use of the term **nation** instead of the usual term, "people," for the Jews. "Nation" was commonly used of the heathen, but to have referred to the Jews here as "people" would have "implied a certain assumption of superiority to the magistrate before whom he stood."[s] Such would have weakened his cause with Felix.

Rather than profaning the Temple, Paul declares that he was found **purified in the temple, with no crowd, nor yet with tumult** (vs. 18). The relation between Paul's purification in the Temple (see notes on Acts 21:23, 24) and "the offering" of verse seventeen appears to be inseparable. In fact, it would appear that the Jews discovered him in the Temple presenting his offering during the completion of his Nazarite vow. Plumptre remarks that "he was, as it were, occupied with them [the offerings] when the Jews from Asia found him, not profaning the Temple, but purified with all the completeness which the Nazarite vow required."[t] Macgregor[u] agrees with this position.

The **certain Jews from Asia** (vs. 18b) were evidently those who had seen and recognized Trophimus in the city and then, upon seeing Paul in the Temple, assumed that he had taken Trophimus into the "court of the Jews," and thus started the riot (Acts 21:28, 29). However, these very Asian Jews who were responsible for initiating the whole affair appear to have completely forsaken their cause by evading the consequences of their charges and probably returning to Asia after Pentecost. Thus the Sadducees, forsaken by both their Asian Jewish witnesses and the supporting Pharisaic party of the Sanhedrin, were left to carry on the prosecution of an alleged capital offense without witnesses and with a Sanhedrin divided on the issue involved. Paul assumes the absence of the witnesses as evidence of the untenableness of their cause (vs. 19). He then cleverly turns the burden of proof on the prosecution, which is without witnesses or evidence (vs. 20). Then with a withering blow of irony, Paul

[49] *Acts* (MC), p. 217. [50] Arndt and Gingrich, *op. cit.*, p. 17. [51] *Op. cit.*, p. 543, n. 1.
[52] *Beginnings*, IV, 304. [53] *Op. cit.*, p. 976. See also EGT, II, 467 (on 23:6).

[r] Ellicott, *op. cit.*, p. 160. [s] *Ibid.* [t] *Ibid.* [u] *The Interpreter's Bible*, IX, 311.

22 But Felix, having more exact knowledge concerning the Way, deferred them, saying,
When Lysias the chief captain shall come down, I will determine your matter.
23 And he gave order to the centurion that he should be kept in charge, and should have
indulgence; and not to forbid any of his friends to minister unto him.

---

22 *Akribesteron*, **more exact,** is translated "complete" by Lake and Cadbury, who would take the comparative as a superlative in force.[54] Lenski renders it "rather accurately."[55] Bruce says: "The sense is here elative, 'pretty accurately.'"[56] But Robertson thinks it means that Felix knew "more accurately than one would suppose."[57]

Anebaleto, **deferred,** is found only here in the New Testament. It means "postpone," and as a technical legal term "adjourn" a trial.[58] **Determine** is the verb *diaginōskō*, found (in N.T.) only here and in 2:23. Abbott-Smith says it is used here as an Athenian law term, meaning "to decide."[59] Arndt and Gingrich would treat it so in both passages.[60] Moulton and Milligan agree with Abbott-Smith.[61]

23 **He gave order** is an aorist participle, *diataxamenos*, literally "having charged." It is parallel to *eipas*, "saying," in the previous verse, both words modifying "deferred."

Onesin, **indulgence,** is used four times by Paul[62] in the sense of relief from tribulation. It means, "a loosening, relaxation."[63] The word is used by Josephus for the indulgence granted Agrippa while he was still kept in custody.[64] Hence "liberty" (KJV) is evidently too strong a term, unless it is qualified by "some" (RSV).

Friends is literally "his own" *(tōn idiōn)*, which often means "relatives," but rather obviously not here (cf. 4:23). *Hypēretein*, **to minister,** is found only in Acts (cf. 13:2; 20:34). Literally meaning to serve as an under-rower on a ship, it is used metaphorically as "minister" or "serve." Any of Paul's friends would be permitted to act as a servant to the apostle. Doubtless Luke and others did so.

---

concludes his defense by an allusion to the doctrine of the resurrection which had so sharply divided the council and defeated its cause against him. It was as though he said, "The real issue at stake is the doctrine of the resurrection, on which doctrine the Jews are divided and I stand with the orthodox party." And in this conclusion Paul was not amiss, for the difference between the true Jew as expressed in the Christian faith, and the non-Christian Jew, was the resurrection of the dead—first of Christ and then of His followers (I Cor. 15:20–23).

III. PAUL'S TRIAL DEFERRED BY FELIX

(24:22–27)

Felix was shrewd enough to see that the Jews had no real case against Paul. To have rendered a verdict against the apostle in the light of the evidence would have been a violation of his sense of Roman justice and might have involved him in serious trouble with Rome. To have acquitted Paul would have incurred for Felix the violent disfavor of the Sadducean majority in the Sanhedrin. Thus his position was almost identical to that of Pilate at the trial of Jesus (Matt. 27:20–24), but Felix appears to have been shrewder than Pilate in that he escaped between the horns of the dilemma by deferring the trial rather than accepting either of the alternatives of acquittal or condemnation of Paul.

A. Felix's Reason for Deferring the Trial (24:22)

Felix, having more exact knowledge concerning the Way, deferred them, vs. 22a.

Felix's deference of Paul's trial seems to have been the result of his **more exact knowledge concerning the Way,** or concerning Christianity. "The comparative, **[more exact]** implies a reference to an average standard,"[v] Plumptre thinks. From whence did he obtain his knowledge of Christianity? There are several possible answers. *First*, he had ruled Judea for some years and had had opportunity to observe Christianity there. *Second*, he may have contacted the Christians in

[54] *Beginnings*, IV, 304. [55] *Op. cit.*, pp. 976 f. [56] *Acts*, p. 426. [57] *Grammar*, p. 665.
[58] Arndt and Gingrich, *op. cit.*, p. 50. [59] *Op. cit.*, p. 106. [60] *Op. cit.*, p. 181. [61] VGT. p. 147.
[62] II Cor. 2:13; 7:5; 8:13; II Thess. 1:7 (not elsewhere in N.T.). [63] Abbott-Smith, *op. cit.*, p. 36. [64] *Ant.* XVIII, 6, 10.

[v] Ellicott, *op. cit.*, p. 161.

24 But after certain days, Felix came with Drusilla, his wife, who was a Jewess, and sent for Paul, and heard him concerning the faith in Christ Jesus.

---

24 **His wife** is literally "his own wife." But *idios* had lost much of its original force and had become "exhausted." [65] So the common translation is correct. **Drusilla** had married Felix when she was about 16 years of age.[66]

Rome before coming to Judea as procurator. *Third*, he may well have observed Christianity at Jerusalem, especially during the annual feasts which he quite naturally had visited, at least in the interests of his wife who was a Jewess. *Fourth*, he doubtless contacted and observed the Christians in Caesarea where Christianity had invaded the Roman army itself through the conversion of Cornelius and his household under Peter some twenty-five years earlier (Acts 10). Likewise Philip had lived here for a quarter of a century evangelizing and had doubtless founded and developed a Christian community. *Fifth*, he may have acquired considerable knowledge of Christianity from his present wife Drusilla, who was a Jewess and may have been informed of Christianity. In any event, Felix's knowledge of Christianity appears to have been favorable.

The conflicting accounts of Tertullus and Paul made it imperative that Felix gain further information on the whole matter from Lysias who had arrested Paul and sent him to Felix for trial (vs. 22b).

B. Felix's Solicitude for Paul (24:23)

And he gave order . . . that . . . [he] **should have indulgence** (vs. 23).

Felix's charge concerning Paul following the trial was threefold. *First*, he ordered a centurion to keep Paul **in charge.** In other words, Paul was to be kept in custody. Macgregor says of Paul's detention: "The **custody** would be military confinement, which would safeguard the accused pending trial without subjecting him to the discomfort of a public jail."[w] *Second*, Paul was to **have indulgence.** This seems to imply such consideration as would be fitting a Roman citizen who had not been proven guilty of any crime. *Third*, he was to have free intercourse with his friends or relatives who might wish to visit him and minister to his comfort and needs (cf. Acts 23:16).

C. Felix's Conferences with Paul (24:24–26)

He sent for him the oftener, and communed with him, vs. 26b.

That Paul's defense before Felix had definitely awakened an interest in his mind in the Christian religion is evident from the fact that Felix and Drusilla subsequently **sent for Paul and heard him concerning the faith in Christ Jesus** (vs. 24b). Felix's second wife, Drusilla, was the daughter of Herod Agrippa I and sister of Herod Agrippa II. (For Drusilla's life, see notes on Acts 24:24–26.) Drusilla was but six years old when her father died in A.D. 44 (Acts 12:21–23). Thus Drusilla must have had some, possibly much, acquaintance with the history and development of Christianity in Judea. She would have known of her father's execution of James the brother of John and of his imprisonment and planned execution of Peter (Acts 12:1–4). Plumptre thinks that "She may have connected her father's tragic end at Caesarea with the part he had taken in persecuting the faith, of which one of the chief preachers was now brought before her."[x] Thus her evident renewed interest in Christianity appears to have influenced her husband, and together they sought opportunity to learn more of this Way by private interviews with Paul. Here, as later at Rome, Paul's prison became his parish. Little wonder that Paul came to consider himself the "prisoner of Christ" (Eph. 3:1; 4:1; II Tim. 1:8; Philemon 1, 9). We would concur with Plumptre that "The procurator and his wife were apparently in the first stage of an earnest inquiry which might have led to a conversion."[y]

Paul took advantage of the awakened interest in Christianity in Felix and Drusilla and proceeded to deliver a carefully reasoned evangelistic *message* to their minds and consciences. Three elements constitute that *message*: namely, **righteousness** or justice,

[65] Deissman, *Bible Studies*, p. 124. [66] *Beginnings*, IV, 304.

[w] *The Interpreter's Bible*, *op. cit.*, IX 312. [x] Ellicott, *loc. cit.* [y] *Ibid.*

25 And as he reasoned of righteousness, and self-control, and the judgment to come, Felix was terrified, and answered, Go thy way for this time; and when I have a convenient season, I will call thee unto me.

---

25 *Engkrateias*, **self-control,** is found elsewhere in the New Testament only in Galatians 5:23 and II Peter 1:6. Burton says that the word means "mastery of one's own desires and impulses."[67] **Was terrified,** *emphobos genomenos*, is better than "trembled" (KJV). *Emphobos*,[68] literally "in fear," means "afraid, startled, terrified."[69]

To nyn echon, **for this time,** and *kairon metalabōn*, **when I have a convenient season,** are both found only here in the New Testament, though good idiomatic Greek. Of the latter Lake and Cadbury write: "That *kairon metalabōn* means a 'convenient season' (A.V., R.V.), or as is usually now misquoted 'more convenient,' is rather an inference from the context than a deduction from the words."[70] They translate it "when I have spare time."

---

self-control or moderation, and **judgment to come** or man's final and personal accountability to God for his life and conduct on earth. A more fitting approach and application to the pair before him could not have been made. Paul's address may be analyzed thus:

1. **Righteousness,** *God's ideal for man.*
2. **Self Control,** *God's requirement for man.*
3. **Judgment to come,** *God's assessment of man.*

First, righteousness, as Paul used the term, may be fairly equated with justice. Paul is reasoning with a Gentile ruler who had been influenced by Greek and Roman philosophical thought more than Jewish. To the Greek philosophers' ideal of justice, neither Paul nor Felix, himself of Greek nationality, would have been strangers. Plato had defined *justice* as *having and doing what is one's own.* This was understood at once as a *responsibility*, a *privilege*, and a *prohibition*. As a responsibility it meant that man was obligated to acquire and to do those things that were expected of him as a member of society, whether possessions, position, or performance. As a privilege, it granted to man permissions of possession and performance that made life rich and meaningful. But as a prohibition, it forbade man to infringe upon the rights of his fellows, either as to the acquisition of their property or position. Such became the Greek concept of justice or righteousness. This ideal will accord with the Jewish and Christian ethical requirements. Thus Paul used the known to lead his hearers to the unknown. But Felix, like Herod (Mark 6:17, 18), had taken another man's wife (see notes on Acts 24:24–26) and thus he stood condemned by the Greek ethical ideal, as also by the Christian. *Second*, the Greek ethical ideal of **self-control** had received its highest treatment in Aristotle's *summum bonum* or the *via media — the golden mean.* This noble concept of moderation in the use of all things struck directly at the sensuous and emotional nature of Felix. Thus it established the principle that "things" can only have instrumental or utilitarian value and must be used only as means to worthy ends, unless they are to destroy their own users. Noble manliness is thus the end, while things are but means (cf. Matt. 6:19–34 and Phil. 4:5). With the Christian ideal and requirement this again fully accorded, and thus Paul brought to bear on the conscience of Felix and Drusilla both the requirements of the Greek philosophy and the Christian religious ideal. *Third*, Paul did not end as a philosopher by simply presenting the ideal, but he proceeded to bring to bear upon their moral judgment and their emotional sense the fact that as these noble ideals were inherent in the very nature of a righteous God, so God would ultimately bring man to account for his use of the ideals. **Judgment to come** was to be the final measurement of man's earthly life and conduct (cf. Psa. 51:4). Felix and Drusilla had been weighed in the balances and were found wanting. Little wonder that **Felix was terrified** (vs. 25). Sinful man will always be terrified when thus arraigned

[67] Ernest De Witt Burton, *A Critical and Exegetical Commentary on the Epistle to the Galatians* [ICC] (Edinburgh: T. & T. Clark, 1921), p. 318.
[68] Used four times by Luke and in Rev. 11:13.
[69] Arndt and Gingrich, *op. cit.*, p. 257. [70] *Beginnings*, IV, 305.

26 He hoped withal that money would be given him of Paul: wherefore also he sent for him the oftener, and communed with him.

26 **The oftener,** *pyknoteron,* may be translated "very often" (elative). **Communed** is the verb *homileō* (see on 20:11). A better translation is "conversed" (RSV).

before the bar of divine justice by such faithful preaching.

Felix, unable to bear more of Paul's message, bade him retire until such future time as would be conveniently suited to hear more of this **Way.** His conscience was rudely awakened, but in Plumptre's words, "Its voice was silenced by the will which would not listen."[z] Felix with Paul, and Herod Antipas with John the Baptist, are striking parallels at this juncture (cf. Mark 6:20). There is no evidence that for Felix the **convenient season** ever bore fruit in repentance and saving faith. Like so many since, Felix played for time to rationalize himself out of the severe conviction which had gripped his soul. Procrastination became the enemy that robbed his soul of its prize of salvation.

But Felix was plainly a man of mixed motives in relation to his interest in Paul. **He hoped withal that money would be given him of Paul** (vs. 26). Ramsay makes much of Paul's supposed wealth.[a]

A worthy counter suggestion to Ramsay's hypothesis might be that Paul was not a wealthy man, but that Luke was likely a man of means and that, as the missionary companion and friend of the apostle, he generously expended his resources on Paul's imprisonments and trials.

After discrediting the theory that Paul may have used any of the "collection" for his personal expense, Ramsay states: "There seems no alternative except that Paul's hereditary property was used . . . we must regard Paul as a man of some wealth during these years."[b] Whether or not Ramsay's hypothesis concerning Paul's wealth merits respect (it does appear quite strained), Paul was nevertheless, for some reason which Luke does not tell us, regarded by Felix as a favorable prospect for a substantial bribe. Possibly Paul's allusion to **alms . . .** and **offerings** (vs. 17), which he had brought to his nation, led Felix to the mistaken notion that these were Paul's personal contributions and thus that he was a man of financial means.

Felix's hopes for a bribe from Paul were but the natural outflow of his perverted character and conduct. Plumptre remarks: "This greed of gain in the very act of administering justice was the root-evil of the weak and wicked character."[c]

Felix's subsequent interviews with Paul are aptly suggested by Plumptre as follows:

> It is not difficult to represent to ourselves the character of these interviews, the suggestive hints—half promises and half threats of the procurator, the steadfast refusal of the prisoner to purchase the freedom which he claimed as a right, his fruitless attempt to bring about a change for the better in his judge's character.[d]

Again there is a striking parallel between Paul and the philosopher Socrates at this juncture. Socrates refused to allow his disciples to bribe the judge or guards for his release when he was condemned to die by the hemlock cup for the principles which he taught in Athens.

We should like to know the effect of Paul's life and ministry on Drusilla, but Luke passes this over.

D. Felix's Disposal of Paul (24:27)

Felix left Paul in bonds.

What Paul did during his two years of Caesarean imprisonment is left untold by Luke, and we can do no more than conjecture. That he was afforded comfortable circumstances and possibly a considerable degree of liberty appears likely from the circumstances of the case. Some have conjectured that he wrote the Epistle to the Hebrews during this period (if indeed it was written by Paul); others that the Ephesian, Colossian and Philippian epistles, with perhaps Philemon, were written here. However, evidence is lacking for any of these hypotheses. It seems most probable that he had contact and encouraging fellowship with Luke, Philip, and the other Christians at

[z] *Ibid.*, p. 162.
[a] See Additional Note I, "Paul's Supposed Wealth" at end of chapter XXIV.
[b] W. M. Ramsay, *St. Paul the Traveller and the Roman Citizen*, p. 312.
[c] Ellicott, *op. cit.*, p. 162.
[d] *Ibid.*

27 But when two years were fulfilled, Felix was succeeded by Porcius Festus; and desiring to gain favor with the Jews, Felix left Paul in bonds.

---

27 **Was succeeded** is *elaben diadochon*, "received as successor." *Diadochon*, found only here in the New Testament, is from *diadechomai* (only in 7:45 in N.T.), which means "receive in turn." **Felix** received **Festus** as the one who received his office in turn. *Katathesthai*, **to gain favor,** is found in the New Testament only here, in 25:9, and in Mark 15:46. It means "to lay up for oneself." [71] With *charis* it suggests: "lay up a store of gratitude." [72]

The mention of **two years** creates a chronological difficulty. Most naturally this would be taken as referring to the length of Paul's detention by Felix at Caesarea, and that interpretation is preferred by Bruce, who thinks Festus became procurator in A.D. 58 or 59.[73] That would put Paul's arrival at Rome in the early spring of A.D. 60.[74] Kirsopp Lake prefers to refer the **two years** to Felix, making the accession of Festus correspond to the year of, or the year after, Paul's arrival in Jerusalem (A.D. 55 or 56).[75] This would bring Paul to Rome in A.D. 56 or 57.[76]

The complexity of the problem can only be appreciated by those who have read C. H. Turner's article on "Chronology of the New Testament" in Hasting's *Dictionary of the Bible*,[77] or some similarly comprehensive treatment. Turner makes Paul arrive at Rome early in A.D. 59,[78] which is probably the best conclusion that can be reached. Ramsay's date, A.D. 60,[79] is probably a year too late. Armstrong's preference for A.D. 60 as the year when Festus succeeded Felix [80] is definitely too late to be acceptable.

Caesarea. Doubtless they ministered to his material, as also to his spiritual, comfort. It seems possible that Luke may have utilized the time and opportunity in association with Paul for further collection of materials for his histories. It would have been here, at least in part, that Paul learned the secret of patient resignation to God's will (Phil. 4:11).

The Jews multiplied complaints against the abuses of Felix's government, and finally he was recalled by Nero. His brother Pallas' influence with the emperor saved him from more serious punishment. Porcius Festus succeeded Felix as procurator of Judea and died in the second year of his administration. Josephus[e] gives Festus credit with suppressing the ravaging Sicarii activities of the country and maintaining peace while he lived.

Characteristically patronizing, Felix, on the occasion of his recall, left Paul in prison at Caesarea as a favor to the Jews who might have added this to their charges against him before Caesar had he released Paul. Too cowardly to condemn Paul to death or release him to the Sanhedrin, which would have done so, and too deferent to Jewish pressure groups to acquit and release him, Felix committed the logical fallacy of "decision by indecision" and left Paul to be disposed of by his successor. Plumptre remarks of Luke's words, **desiring to gain favor with the Jews, Felix left Paul in bonds** (vs. 27b), "It was, so to speak, an investment in iniquity."[f] How often do people leave their personal and official responsibilities for others to execute while they thus attempt to evade the consequences of their own acts!

Additional Note I

PAUL'S SUPPOSED WEALTH

"But several other factors show clearly that, during the following four years, Paul had considerable command of money. Imprisonments and a long lawsuit are expensive. Now, it is clear that Paul during the following four years did not appear before the world as a penniless wanderer, living by the work of his hands. A person in that position will not, either at the present day or in the first century, be treated with such marked respect as was certainly paid to Paul, at

[71] Abbott-Smith, *op. cit.*, p. 239. [72] Arndt and Gingrich, *op. cit.*, p. 420.
[73] *Acts*, pp. 428 f. [74] *Ibid.*, p. 56. [75] *Beginnings*, V, 471.
[76] *Ibid.*, pp. 466 f. Harnack, although he would also put Paul's arrival in Rome at A.D. 57, strongly objects to applying the two years to Felix's tenure of office (*Acts of the Apostles*, p. 7, n. 1).
[77] HDB, I, 403–425. This problem is discussed on pp. 417–419. [78] *Ibid.*, p. 424.
[79] Cf. *St. Paul the Traveller*, p. 322 (sailing A.D. 59). [80] ISBE, I, 649.

[e] Josephus, *op. cit.*, "Wars," II, XIV, 1. [f] Ellicott, *loc. cit.*

Caesarea, on the voyage, and in Rome. The governor Felix and his wife, the Princess Drusilla, accorded him an interview and private conversation. King Agrippa and his Queen Bernice also desired to see him. A poor man never receives such attentions or rouses such interest. Moreover, Felix hoped for a bribe from him; and a rich Roman official did not look for a small gift. Paul, therefore, wore the outward appearance of a man of means, like one in a position to bribe a Roman procurator. The minimum in the way of personal attendants that was allowable for a man of respectable position was two slaves; and, as we shall see, Paul was believed to be attended by two slaves to serve him. At Caesarea he was confined in the palace of Herod; but he had to live, to maintain two attendants, and to keep up a respectable appearance. Many comforts, which are almost necessities, would be given by the guards, so long as they were kept in good humor, and it is expensive to keep guards in good humor. In Rome he was able to hire a lodging for himself and to live there, maintaining, of course, the soldier who guarded him.

An appeal to the supreme court could not be made by everybody that chose. Such an appeal had to be permitted and sent forward by the provincial governor; and only a serious case would be entertained. But the case of a very poor man is never esteemed as serious; and there is little doubt that the citizen's right of appeal to the Emperor was hedged in by fees and pledges. There is also one law for the rich man and another for the poor: at least, to this extent, that many claims can be successfully pushed by a rich man in which a poor man would have no chance of success. In appealing to the Emperor, Paul was choosing undoubtedly an expensive line of trial. All this had certainly been estimated before the decisive step was taken. Paul had weighed the cost; he had reckoned the gain which would accrue to the Church if the supreme court pronounced in his favor; and his past experience gave him every reason to hope for a favorable issue before a purely Roman tribunal, where Jewish influence would have little or no power. The importance of the case, as described in the preceding section, makes the appeal more intelligible."[g]

[g] Ramsay, *op. cit.*, pp. 310–312.

CHAPTER XXV

Festus therefore, having come into the province, after three days went up to Jerusalem from Caesarea.

2 And the chief priests and the principal men of the Jews informed him against Paul; and they besought him,

3 asking a favor against him, that he would send for him to Jerusalem; laying a plot to kill him on the way.

EXEGESIS

1 *Epibas,* **having come into,** is literally "having entered upon" or "having gone on to." The verb occurs only in Acts (five times), with the exception of Matthew 21:5 (in a quotation from LXX). Moe would place the beginning of Festus' procuratorship in A.D. 58.[1] *Eparcheia,*[2] **province,** was "strictly either the office of a prefect *(eparchos)* or the district governed by a prefect," but it was "used more widely in the sense of a Province of any sort."[3] The word occurs in the New Testament only here and in 23:34.

3 *Enedran,* **plot,** is the same word as is used in 23:16, where it is translated "lying in wait." The margin of the Harclean Syriac says the plotters were the same as those mentioned in 23:12, 13. But that is probably mere conjecture.

EXPOSITION

THE APOSTLE'S DEFENSE BEFORE FESTUS AND AGRIPPA II

I. Paul's Case Revived before Festus, Acts 25:1–12.
II. Paul's Case Referred to Agrippa II, Acts 25:13–21.
III. Paul's Case Reviewed by Agrippa II, Acts 25:22–27.

In the year of Felix's recall by Nero (or possibly a little later), Porcius Festus came into the office of procurator of Judea where he lived but two years and then died in office. Little is known concerning the life or character of this man, apart from a brief account by Josephus. He appears to have been an honorable and prudent man, for the most part. Had the circumstances of his reign been more favorable, his success might have been greater. However, the impossibility of his situation was brought about by the corruption and maladministration of his predecessor, Felix. Violence, intrigue, sedition, and extreme loyalist bigotry made of the Jews an impossible people for this Roman procurator. Josephus describes the beginning of his rule thus: "Festus succeeded Felix as procurator, and made it his business to correct those that made disturbances in the country. So he caught the greatest part of the robbers, and destroyed a great many of them."[a] Josephus[b] describes somewhat in detail the nature of these disorders and the measures employed by Festus to correct them. Withal his task proved impossible and the situation grew worse, a condition which may have contributed to his early death.

I. PAUL'S CASE REVIVED BEFORE FESTUS

(25:1–12)

And the chief priests and the principal men of the Jews informed . . . [Festus] **against Paul,** vs. 2a.

Three days after taking his office Festus went up from Caesarea, the Roman seat of government, to Jerusalem (vs. 1), the religious capital of the Jews whom he was to rule. It was a conciliatory visit to the capital and court of this troublesome people,

[1] Olaf Moe, *The Apostle Paul.* Trans. L. A. Vigness (Minneapolis: Augsburg Publishing House, 1950), p. 18.
[2] So Vaticanus. Sinaiticus has *eparcheiō.*
[3] *Beginnings,* IV, 306.
[a] Josephus, *op. cit.,* "Wars," XIV, 1.
[b] *Ibid.,* "Antiquities," XX, VIII, 9, 10.

4 Howbeit Festus answered, that Paul was kept in charge at Caesarea, and that he himself was about to depart *thither* shortly.

5 Let them therefore, saith he, that are of power among you go down with me, and if there is anything amiss in the man, let them accuse him.

6 And when he had tarried among them not more than eight or ten days, he went down unto Caesarea; and on the morrow he sat on the judgment-seat, and commanded Paul to be brought.

---

4 "Was being kept" (RSV) is more accurate for *tēreisthai* than either **was kept** or "should be kept" (KJV).

5 *Dynatoi*, **that are of power,** is used by Josephus for the "principal men" of the Jews.[4] "Which . . . are able" (KJV) wrongly suggests physical ability to make the trip. *Synkatabantes*, **go down with me,** is found only here in the New Testament. *Atopon*, **amiss,** is literally "out of place." In the papyri and inscriptions it has the ethical connotation "improper," [5] as here.

6 Festus **sat on the judgment-seat.** Schürer says: "The judge's sitting upon the *sella* was a necessary formality, without which the decision would have no legal effect." [6] This is illustrated by what Josephus tells about the custom of Philip, son of Herod the Great. He writes: "He used to make his progress with a few chosen friends; his tribunal also, on which he sat in judgment, followed him in his progress; and when anyone met him who wanted his assistance, he made no delay, but had his tribunal set down immediately, wheresoever he happened to be, and sat down upon it, and heard his complaint: he there ordered the guilty that were convicted to be punished, and absolved those that had been accused unjustly." [7]

---

as well as an informative visit for Festus. Early acquaintance with the ruling Jews of Judea was both desirable and wise on Festus' part.

Though Ananias had been replaced by a new high priest, Ishmael ben Phabi, there had been no change in the policy of the Sanhedrin.[c]

The chief priests and the principal men of the Jews (vs. 2a), the same Sadducean element that had not ceased to thirst for Paul's blood, made a quick move to prejudice the mind of the new ruler (cf. vs. 24) against the prisoner left by Felix, by renewing their indictment of Paul. Bruce states, "They lost no time in exploiting the favor which Felix had done them in leaving Paul in prison in Caesarea."[d] Rackham identifies **the principle men of the Jews** (vs. 2), or "leaders of the Sanhedrin" with "the First Ten [who] were a board of magistrates in the Greek cities of the East. In Roman colonies in Italy the name had been given to the ten who ranked first on the roll of the senate."[e] It appears that they sought to take advantage of Festus' recent arrival and lack of experience in Judea by requesting as an official favor that he would grant the Sanhedrin custody of the prisoner whose offense concerned Jewish law and jurisdiction. Macgregor states, "The point would be that the Jews asked Festus to issue an official 'order' handing over Paul to their own jurisdiction at Jerusalem."[f] It is further probable that they sought to intimidate Festus by impressing him with their influence in having effected the recall of Felix.

Luke's statement concerning the Jews' **plot to kill him** [Paul] **on the way** (vs. 3b) may indicate that this was either a revival of the foiled plot that the "more than forty men" (Acts 23:12ff.) had earlier made, or it was a new plot laid by others quite as zealous for revenge, who hoped for greater success in waylaying Paul en route to Jerusalem from Caesarea. These assassination plots reveal how intricately related the Jewish religious leaders of this time were with the Sicarii or Assassins of the land. Festus' refusal to allow Paul to fall into their trap may have been due to knowledge which he had of their previous plot.

Festus informed the Sanhedrin that Paul was legally a charge of the Roman govern-

[4] *War*, I, 12, 5. See also Schürer, *op. cit.*, II, i, 178.
[5] VGT, p. 90. [6] *Op. cit.*, I, ii, 14, n. 8. [7] *Ant.* XVIII, 4, 6.

[c] Rackham, *op. cit.*, p. 454. [d] Bruce, *op. cit.*, p. 475.
[e] Rackham, *op. cit.*, p. 222, n. 5. [f] *The Interpreter's Bible* IX, 317.

7 And when he was come, the Jews that had come down from Jerusalem stood round
about him, bringing against him many and grievous charges which they could not prove;
8 while Paul said in his defence, Neither against the law of the Jews, nor against the
temple, nor against Caesar, have I sinned at all.
9 But Festus, desiring to gain favor with the Jews, answered Paul and said, Wilt thou
go up to Jerusalem, and there be judged of these things before me?

---

7 **The Jews . . . stood round about him;** that is, Paul. *Auton*, **him,** is missing in the late manuscripts (cf. KJV), but occurs in the oldest ones.[8] It makes the scene a bit more vivid. *Barea*, **grievous,** is literally "heavy." Perhaps the best translation here is "weighty." *Aitiōmata*, **charges,** is described by Knowling as "a word which does not occur elsewhere." [9] But recently it has been found in a Fayum papyrus of A.D. 95–96.[10] *Apodeixai*, **prove,** is literally "to show forth, exhibit." This is the only place in the New Testament where it means "demonstrate" or "prove." The latter is its *(apodeichnō's)* meaning in modern Greek.[11]

9 For **desiring to gain favor with the Jews** compare 24:27. Arndt and Gingrich say that the Greek phrase in both places means "do someone a favor" (cf. KJV, RSV).[12] The emphatic position of **before me** "seems to imply that Festus undertakes not to give up Paul to Jewish jurisdiction." [13]

---

ment at Caesarea and could not be transferred to their court (vs. 4a). He himself was soon to return to Caesarea (vs. 4b) in anticipation of an official visit from Agrippa II and other official provincial dignitaries who appear to have customarily staged an official welcome for a new procurator of Judea (cf. vss. 13, 23). Therefore, if they thought they had a case against Paul they should select a delegation of responsible and influential men (Cf. I Cor. 1:26) to proffer the charges and produce substantial evidence (vs. 5), and not send some hired "rhetorician" and "pleader" such as Tertullus had been before Felix (Cf. Acts 17:5; 24:1).

Within eight or ten days Festus returned to Caesarea, where the following day he opened a formal trial of Paul (vs. 6). Bruce remarks: "The whole case against Paul was now opened afresh, thanks to Felix's neglect to pronounce his acquittal and discharge him." [g]

The many and grevious charges (vs. 7) which were brought against Paul by the Jews before Festus were likely a reiteration of the earlier charges brought against him by Tertullus before Felix, with certain variations and additions (see Acts 24:5, 6 with notes). However, they were all totally without support (vs. 7b). Rackham significantly remarks: "The prosecutors **from Jerusalem surrounded him** and made up for their want of evidence by the violence of their *outcries*, declaring that *he was unfit to live*" [h] (Cf. Luke 23:10). Plumptre observes:

> The line of St. Paul's defense indicates the three counts of the indictment. He had broken, it was alleged, the law of Israel, which Rome recognized as the religion of the province, and was therefore subject to the spiritual jurisdiction of the Sanhedrin; he had profaned the Temple; he was a disturber of the peace of the empire, and taught that there was another king than Nero.[i]

The last charge was quite clearly a revival of the second charge brought against Paul by Tertullus (Cf. Acts 21:27, 28; 24:5, 6).

Paul proceeded to deny categorically all three of the charges in order: **Neither against the law of the Jews, nor against the temple, nor against Caesar, have I sinned at all** (vs. 8). As there was no supporting evidence for the charges, (vs. 7b) there could be no verdict of guilt.

Festus, anxious to improve his position and influence with his Jewish subjects, as Felix had been (Acts 24:27), offered a counter proposition to Paul's outright acquittal. **"Wilt thou [Paul] go up to Jerusalem and there be judged of these things before me?** (vs. 9b). The whole proposition appeared perfectly reasonable. Festus, not having Felix's "more exact knowledge concerning

[8] Aleph A B C L. [9] EGT, II, 492, critical note. [10] VGT, p. 15.
[11] *Ibid.*, p. 60. [12] *Op. cit.*, p. 420. [13] *Beginnings*, IV, 308.

[g] Bruce, *op. cit.*, p. 476. [h] Rackham, *op. cit.*, p. 454.
[i] Charles J. Ellicott, ed., *Ellicott's Commentary on the Whole Bible* (Grand Rapids: Zondervan Publishing House, n.d.). VII, 163.

10 But Paul said, I am standing before Caesar's judgment-seat, where I ought to be judged: to the Jews have I done no wrong, as thou also very well knowest.

11 If then I am a wrong-doer, and have committed anything worthy of death, I refuse not to die; but if none of those things is *true* whereof these accuse me, no man can give me up unto them. I appeal unto Caesar.

---

10 Codex Sinaiticus has *hestōs*, **standing,** at the beginning of Paul's declaration. Alexandrinus, Ephraemi, and all the later manuscripts have it just before *eimi*, **I am.** Vaticanus has it in both places. So Lake and Cadbury render the clause: "Standing before Caesar's Bench, I am standing where I must be tried." [14]

Kallion, **very well,** is the comparative of *kalōs*, "well." So it literally means "better." Robertson writes: "Paul hints that Festus knows his innocence better than he is willing to admit." [15] But Bruce says: "Here the comparative is definitely elative, 'very well.'" [16] Lake and Cadbury agree that it "is the 'intensive' comparative," but add that it might possibly be "the comparative of politely qualified expression." [17]

11 *Adikō*, **I am a wrong-doer,** means "I am in the wrong." [18] or "I am guilty." [19] *Paraitoumai*, **I refuse,** means "beg off, ask to be excused." [20] Arndt and Gingrich would translate the phrase here: "I am not trying to escape death" [21] (cf. RSV). *Charisasthai*, **give . . . up,** means "to give freely" (cf. Rom. 8:32; I Cor. 2:12). It is used in the same way in verse 16.

---

the Way" (Acts 24:22), was at a loss to understand the case between the allegations of the Jews and the denials of Paul. The principal charge that concerned the Sanhedrin was the profanation of the Temple. Any violation of Caesar's rights was no concern of the Jews and should be dealt with by the Roman court. Therefore an investigation before the Sanhedrin at Jerusalem with Festus presiding seemed the logical method of resolving the whole problem. And thus Festus would favor the Jews and gain their favor in return, so he hoped. Festus certainly was unaware of the similar abortive attempt made by Lysias (Acts 22:30 — 23:10).

Although Festus seemed to assure Paul that the Jerusalem investigation would still be under the control of the Roman court, Paul had a wholesome distrust of the Jews and thus replied: "**I am standing before Caesar's judgment-seat, where I ought to be judged** (vs. 10a). Macgregor states: "The provincial tribunal, before which he is already standing, derives its power by delegation from Caesar himself, and as a Roman citizen he *ought to be tried* by Caesar's representative and none other."[j] Rackham states: "But Paul was a Roman citizen, and his case could not be submitted to a provincial tribunal without his own consent. This he refused to give."[k]

Paul made a final appeal to Festus' sense of justice when he stated, **to the Jews have I done no wrong, as thou very well knowest** (vs. 10b). This being the case, why submit the case to the Sanhedrin, with the personal perils involved?

Paul was quite willing to pay the supreme penalty if he could be proven guilty of anything worthy of death (vs. 11). However, in the absence of such proof and faced with a choice between two alternatives, trial before the treacherous religious Sanhedrin or the supreme secular court of Caesar at Rome, he accepted the latter and declared, **I appeal unto Caesar** (vs. 11b). Bruce thinks that Paul "may even have hoped to secure recognition for Christianity as a *religio licita* distinct from Judaism"[l] in his appeal to Caesar.

Rackham remarks:

> He [Paul] refused as a confessedly innocent man, *to be made a present* of to the Jews [as had been the case with the Lord—Acts 3:13-15] This he once for all made *impossible* by uttering the two words, *Caesarem appello, I appeal unto Caesar.*[m]

Rackham further states:

[14] *Beginnings*, IV, 308. [15] *Grammar*, p. 665. [16] *Acts*, p. 431. [17] *Beginnings*, IV. 308.
[18] Arndt and Gingrich, *op. cit.*, p. 17. [19] Bruce, *Acts*, p. 431.
[20] Abbott-Smith, *op. cit.*, p. 340. [21] *Op. cit.*, p. 622.

[j] *The Interpreter's Bible*, *op. cit.*, IX, 318. [k] Rackham, *op. cit.*, p. 455.
[l] Bruce, *op. cit.*, p. 478, n. 7. [m] Rackham, *loc. cit.*

12 Then Festus, when he had conferred with the council, answered, Thou hast appealed unto Caesar: unto Caesar shalt thou go.

---

12 *Synlalēsas*, **when he had conferred,** is literally "having talked with." The verb is found only here in Acts (plus five times in the Gospels). *Symbouliou*, **council,** occurs elsewhere in the New Testament seven times in the Gospels, where it always means "counsel." Only here does it have the unusual meaning, **council.** It refers to "the governor's assessors, of whose advice he might avail himself, though the decision lay in his hands alone." [22] Apparently it represents the Latin *consilium*.[23] This usage is well illustrated by a papyrus document of the first half of the second century.[24] *Epikeklēsai*, **thou hast appealed,** is literaly "thou hast called upon."

> . . . it was with great reluctance that S. Paul made his appeal. It was the final and complete assertion of his Roman citizenship and acceptance of Caesar as his king: to the Jews it meant repudiation of the theocracy and apostasy from Moses. But the apostle in the past two years must have thoroughly weighed the question. The Lord himself in the vision at Jerusalem (XIII, 11) might almost be said to have suggested it; for it seemed at the time the only possible method of reaching Rome.[n]

Concerning Paul's appeal to Caesar, Bruce remarks:

> The right of appeal to the emperor (*prouocatio ad Caesarem*) took the place of the earlier right of appeal to the sovereign people of Rome (*prouocatio ad populum*), which Roman citizens had enjoyed from time immemorial. It was usually exercised by appealing against the verdict of a lower court, but might be exercised at any stage in the proceedings, the defendant claiming that the case be tried at Rome and the verdict pronounced by the emperor. Ordinary provincial subjects of the Roman Empire had no such privilege.[o]

Paul's appeal to Caesar must have elicited from Festus mixed emotional reactions. *First*, his personal and official pride would likely have been wounded in having had the first (known) court trial of his new administration appealed from his court to that of Caesar's. Rackham sees an indication of this displeasure in Festus' reply, **Thou hast appealed unto Caesar: unto Caesar shalt thou go** (vs. 12b) and remarks: "The interrogative translation . . . gives it a ring of annoyance, as if Festus was not pleased with being appealed against in his first trial"[p] (cf. I Cor: 1:13; 7:18, 21, 27).

Second, upon reflection Paul's appeal to Caesar must have come as something of a relief to Festus as it delivered him from the unwelcome and vexing responsibility of deciding Paul's case at either the expense of the Jews' favor or Roman justice. Consequently, after a brief conference with his council he acceded Paul's appeal. This appeal forever took the case out of the Sanhedrin's reach. Rackham graphically puts it: "By these solemn and decisive words the Jews, who had been thronging Paul like hungry wolves, were balked of their prey."[q] Thenceforth Paul was bound for Rome.[r]

According to Macgregor[s] the right of a Roman citizen to appeal against a magistrate's verdict dated from an early time and was ratified by the *Lex Valeria* of 509 B.C. The appeal had originally been to the people and then to the "tribunes of the people" and from thence to the emperor himself who by reason of his tribunitial power constituted the highest and final court of appeal. Thus from the instant of appeal, all lower court proceedings were arrested. Though such right of appeal had at first been limited to the city and immediate environs (within a mile of the walls), by Paul's day it appears to have extended to all citizens throughout the empire.

The foregoing authority holds that Paul's motive in appealing to Caesar was primarily to escape the unjust jurisdiction of the Sanhedrin to which Festus seemed disposed to deliver him. Indeed, it is allowed, Paul likely considered it providential that he should have this opportunity of reaching his coveted destination, Rome (cf. Acts 19:21; 23:11; Rom. 1:7–16). However, in this view, Paul is motivated by the evidence that Festus is inclining toward an unfavorable

[22] Bruce, *Acts*, p. 432. See also Schürer, *op. cit.*, I, ii, 60.
[23] Deissmann, *Bible Studies*, p. 238. [24] VGT, p. 597.

[n] *Ibid.*, p. 452. [o] Bruce, *loc. cit.* [p] Rackham, *op. cit.*, p. 455. [q] *Ibid.*
[r] Rackham, *ibid.*, pp. 408, 409, significantly treats Paul's appeal.
[s] *The Interpreter's Bible*, IX, 314, 315.

13 Now when certain days were passed, Agrippa the king and Bernice arrived at Caesarea, and saluted Festus.

14 And as they tarried there many days, Festus laid Paul's case before the king, saying, There is a certain man left a prisoner by Felix;

15 about whom, when I was at Jerusalem, the chief priests and the elders of the Jews informed *me*, asking for sentence against him.

---

13 **Passed** is the verb *diaginomai*, found (in N.T.) only here and in 27:9, Mark 16:1. *Aspasamenoi*, **saluted,** has in Josephus and two second-century papyri the meaning "pay one's respects."[25] The aorist participle[26] instead of the future participle of purpose *(aspasomenoi)*[27] has raised a question. But Lake and Cadbury assert "the probability that the aorist participle was used occasionally to express purpose."[28]

14 *Anetheto*, **laid,** means "set forth, declared." Moulton and Milligan give the meaning "impart" or "communicate."[29] The word occurs elsewhere in the New Testament only in Galatians 2:2. Knowling says: "In the middle voice the idea is that of relating with a view to consulting."[30] **Left** is literally "left behind" *(kataleleimmenos)*.

15 *Katadikē*, **sentence,** means a "condemnation." The word is found only here in the New Testament.

---

view of his case, possibly influenced in part by derogatory reports left by Felix in deference to the Jews whose accusations he sought to mitigate in view of his recall and trial in Rome. Should Paul be condemned on the religious charges by the Sanhedrin, which was inevitable, then his chances of acquittal before Festus on the political charges, reserved for judgment by Rome, would be slim indeed, since to acquit Paul on the second charge would be tantamount to vetoing the Sanhedrin's guilty verdict on the first charge. Thus Festus would lose favor with the Jews. Paul's only alternative was appeal to Caesar.

II. PAUL'S CASE REFERRED TO AGRIPPA II

(25:13-21)

Festus laid Paul's case before the king, vs. 14.

This is not the first, though it is the last, known appearance of a Christian before a member of the Herodian dynasty. Rackham significantly remarks of this occasion:

> And now Paul the apostle is brought into contact with this wordly and philo-Roman family of the Herods. It is striking how the fortunes of that family were bound up with the origins of the church, but it was an ill-starred connection for the Herods. Their founder, Herod the Great, had tried to destroy the infant Jesus. His son Antipas, the tetrarch of Galilee, beheaded John the Baptist, and won from the Lord the title of 'fox.' His grandson Agrippa I slew James the son of Zebedee with the sword. Now we see Paul brought before Agrippa's son. As the Lord before Herod Antipas, so Paul stands before Herod Agrippa II; and on each occasion the trial served to cement the friendship between the Herodian prince and the Roman governor. S. Peter also had the honour of being arrested by a Herod: and the pomp of this scene is an evident counter-picture to the ostentatious display made at Caesarea by the first Agrippa [Matt. 2; 14:1-12; Luke 3:19, 20; 9:9; 13:32; 23:7-12; Acts 4:27; 12:21-23]. Of all these Herods, Agrippa II comes out the best. The Lord would not open his lips before Antipas; nor would Paul give an exposition of his faith before Drusilla. But before Agrippa II the apostle makes his most elaborate 'apologia pro vitâ suâ'; he bears witness to the king's Jewish faith; he had even hopes of winning him to Christianity. It is true that Agrippa somewhat cynically warded off S. Paul's advances, but had he been as morally worthless as the other Herods, we feel sure that the apostle would have adopted a different tone.[t]

Herod Agrippa II was the son of Herod Agrippa I who died under divine judgment at Caesarea in A.D. 44 (Acts 12:23). At that time Agrippa II was at Rome in the court of Claudius Caesar in training for future Palestinian governmental service. Agrippa II was but seventeen years old at his father's death and because of his youth and the governmental problems inherent in Judea he was some years later given the

[25] Deissmann, *Bible Studies*, p. 257. [26] So Aleph A B E H L P. [27] Textus Receptus (cf. KJV). [28] *Beginnings* IV, 310. [29] VGT, p. 38. [30] EGT, II, 496.

[t] Rackham, *op. cit.*, pp. 457, 458.

16 To whom I answered, that it is not the custom of the Romans to give up any man, before that the accused have the accusers face to face, and have had opportunity to make his defence concerning the matter laid against him.

17 When therefore they were come together here, I made no delay, but on the next day sat on the judgment-seat, and commanded the man to be brought.

18 Concerning whom, when the accusers stood up, they brought no charge of such evil things as I supposed;

---

16 The optatives here *(echoi, laboi,* and *bouloito* in vs. 20) reflect "the educated Greek of the Governor." [31] For *katēgorous,* **accusers,** see on 23:30. **Opportunity** is *topon,* "place." But the translation here is supported by Josephus.[32] Literally the Greek reads "might receive a place of defence concerning the accusation." **Matter laid against him** is all one word, *egklēma,* "accusation, charge." It is found only here and in 23:29. "To die" (KJV) after "man" is omitted in the earliest manuscripts.[33]

17 *Anabolēn,* **delay,** is found only here in the New Testament. In an early papyrus it is used the same way as here.[34]

18 *Aitian,* **charge,** means "cause, reason." Only here and in verse 27 does it have in the New Testament the forensic sense of "accusation." [35] Supposed is *hypenooun,* "suspected, conjectured." The verb occurs (in N.T.) only in Acts (cf. 13:25; 27:27).

---

former tetrarchies of Philip and Lysanias, which later included certain towns in Galilee and Perea,[u] rather than his father's kingdom. He was given the responsibility for the temple treasury and the appointment of the Jewish high priest, as well as the custody of the high priestly ceremonial vestments which were worn on the Great Day of Atonement. Thus he was something of a co-ruler of the Jews, with Festus as procurator of Judea. His greater knowledge and experience in Jewish affairs (himself being part Jew) disposed Festus to refer Paul's exasperating case to Agrippa II upon his arrival in Caesarea. Rackham[v] holds that Agrippa II was first given the small kingdom of Chalcis upon the death of his father's brother, Herod King of Chalcis (A.D. 48) four years after his father's death, and then in A.D. 53 Claudius exchanged Chalcis for the larger realms before referred to, at which time Agrippa II was given the *title of King.* For these favors Agrippa II renamed Caesarea Philippi, the capital of Philip's tetrarchy from 4 B.C. to A.D. 34, Neronias in honor of Nero. This Agrippa remained loyal to Rome to the last, lived to see the destruction of Jerusalem in A.D. 70, but died childless in A.D. 100 at 73 years of age in the reign of Trajan. Thus ended the Herod dynasty.[w]

Agrippa I also had three daughters: namely, Berenice or Bernice, a year younger than Agrippa II, Mariamne, and Drusilla. The last named was the wife of Felix whose sordid story has already been related (see notes on Acts 24:24). Bernice had married her father's brother, Herod of Chalcis and was left a widow upon his death. She then went to live with her brother, Herod Agrippa II. Macgregor says of her:

> She was a fascinating but utterly profligate woman, and eventually became the mistress of the Emperor Titus. Yet once she displayed real magnanimity by appearing as a suppliant with bare feet to intercede for the Jews, and narrowly escaped with her life from the brutal procurator Gessius Florus.[x]

Scandalous reports of criminal incestuous relations between Bernice and Herod II spread, and she left Herod to marry a Cilician potentate by the name of Polemo who professed the Jewish religion and was circumcised for her sake. But she soon forsook him (and he forthwith forsook the Jewish religion) and she returned to her brother with whom she appeared on the occasion of Paul's trial.[y]

[31] *Beginnings,* IV, 311. [32] *Ant.* XVI, 8, 5. [33] Aleph A B C E.
[34] VGT, p. 30. [35] Abbott–Smith, *op. cit.,* p. 14.

[u] Josephus, *op. cit.,* "Ant.", XIX, IX, 1; XX, I, 3; VIII, 5.
[v] Rackham, *op. cit.,* pp. 455, 456.
[w] For further accounts of Agrippa II see Josephus, *op. cit.,* "Wars," II, XII, 1, 7; XV, 1; XVI, 4; VII, V, 1; "Ant.", XIX, IX, 2; XX, V, 2; VI, 3; VII, 1; VIII, 4; IX, 6.
[x] *The Interpreter's Bible, op. cit.,* IX, 319.
[y] For further accounts of Bernice see Josephus, *op. cit.,* "Wars," II, XI, 6; XVII, 6; "Ant.," XIX, V, 1; IX, 1; XX, VII, 3.

19 but had certain questions against him of their own religion, and of one Jesus, who was dead, whom Paul affirmed to be alive.

20 And I, being perplexed how to inquire concerning these things, asked whether he would go to Jerusalem and there be judged of these matters.

21 But when Paul had appealed to be kept for the decision of the emperor, I commanded him to be kept till I should send him to Caesar.

---

19 *Zētēmata*, **questions,** is found only in Acts (five times). *Deisidaimonias*, **religion,** is found only here in the New Testament (see on 17:22, the only place where the cognate adjective occurs). It first meant "fear of the gods." [36] Whether it here means **religion** or "superstition" is a matter of perennial debate. Lake and Cadbury prefer the latter.[37] But Knowling writes: "In addressing a Jewish king, Felix would not have used the term offensively, especially when we consider the official relation of Agrippa to the Jewish religion" [38] (see Exposition). Bruce agrees.[39]

20 *Egō*, **I,** is emphatic. The Greek reads: "And I being in doubt about the debate concerning these things."

21 **Decision** is the noun *diagnōsis*, which has been taken over bodily in to English.[40] As now, it was a medical term with the Greeks.[41] But it also was a law term, as here. Deissmann writes: "*Diagnōsis* is a technical expression for the Latin *cognitio*, but is not found elsewhere until 144 A.D." [42] However, Moulton and Milligan cite an example from a papyrus of about 250 B.C.[43] **The emperor** is "the Augustus" *(tou Sebastou)*. **Send** is literally "send up" *(anapempsō)*. Deissmann notes that in Philo, Josephus, Plutarch, and the papyri it means "send up to a higher authority."[44] It could be translated "refer." [45]

Agrippa's arrival at Caesarea was exceedingly fortunate for Festus since Agrippa was a Jew, an authoritative administrator, and thoroughly conversant with Jewish custom and administration, as well as religion. However, in culture and loyalty he was thoroughly Roman. He seems to have been out of favor with the Jewish rulers at this time, due perhaps to the fact that he had deposed Ananias. (Incidentally it was Agrippa II who later deposed the high priest Ananus after he had illegally put to death James, the pastor of the Jerusalem church.) He had also built a tower in his Jerusalem palace which overlooked the temple courts, but which view was obstructed by a counter wall constructed by the high priests. The quarrel which ensued was settled at Rome. All of this may have accounted for Agrippa's interest in, and likely sympathies with, Paul's case (cf. vs. 22). Festus' relating of Paul's case to Agrippa II adds little to our knowledge of the whole affair. Festus appears especially concerned to obtain Agrippa's aid in composing intelligible charges against Paul to send with him to Rome (cf. vss. 14, 20, 26).

Festus relates his inheritance of Paul's case from Felix (vs. 14b); the demand of the Sanhedrin at Jerusalem for custody of Paul that they might pass sentence on him (vs. 15); his refusal to accede to their demand, with the explanation that the Roman policy is fair trial for everyone (vs. 16); his subsequent arraignment of trial for Paul at Caesarea (vs. 17); the Jews' failure to produce any charges of concern to the Roman government (vs. 18); and their introduction of certain religious questions which focused on **one Jesus who was dead, whom Paul affirmed to be alive** (vs. 19). Festus then admits his personal and official perplexity as to how to obtain clear and correct evidence in the case that he might justly judge the man. Thinking, as Lysias had earlier done, that such evidence might be obtained through a grand jury investigation of the whole matter before the Jerusalem Sanhedrin, Festus had proposed to Paul that the matter be referred to that court (vs. 20). He concluded his narration to Agrippa II with the information that Paul had appealed to Caeser rather than return to Jerusalem, and that he had ordered him held in custody

[36] *Ibid.*, p. 100. [37] *Beginnings*, IV, 311. [38] EGT, II, 496 f. [39] *Acts*, p. 436.
[40] The cognate verb, *diaginōskō*, occurs only in 23:15; 24:22.
[41] Abbott-Smith, *op. cit.*, p. 106. [42] *Light from the Ancient East*, p. 342, n. 3.
[43] VGT, p. 147. [44] *Bible Studies*, p. 229. [45] VGT, p. 37.

22 And Agrippa *said* unto Festus, I also could wish to hear the man myself. To-morrow, saith he, thou shalt hear him.

23 So on the morrow, when Agrippa was come, and Bernice, with great pomp, and they were entered into the place of hearing with the chief captains and the principal men of the city, at the command of Festus Paul was brought in.

24 And Festus saith, King Agrippa, and all men who are here present with us, ye behold this man, about whom all the multitude of the Jews made suit to me, both at Jerusalem and here, crying that he ought not to live any longer.

25 But I found that he had committed nothing worthy of death: and as he himself appealed to the emperor I determined to send him.

---

22 **I . . . could wish** is "I was wishing" *(eboulomēn)*. Whether or not this indicates a previous desire is a matter of dispute. Perhaps it simply indicates a polite form of request: "I should like."[46] Lake and Cadbury prefer "I had wished."[47]

23 **Pomp** is the word *phantasia* (cf. fantasy), found only here in the New Testament. It means "show, display." *Akroatērion*, **place of hearing,** occurs only here in the New Testament. Obviously it means "auditorium." This was evidently some room in Herod's palace.

24 The double compound *synpareimi* (**are here present**) is found only here in the New Testament. It means "be beside together." **Made suit** is the verb *entygchanō*, which in Acts occurs only here. It means "appeal, petition."[48]

25 **Found** is the verb *katalambanō*, which in the middle may mean "grasp, find, understand."[49]

---

until he could be sent to Rome (vs. 21). Thus the case is summarized for Agrippa II. Agrippa with his greater knowledge of Judaism, and probably Christianity as well, read much between the lines in the case which was not evident to Festus. His curiosity was aroused and his appetite whetted to know more of this unusual case and the unusual man involved in it.

III. PAUL'S CASE REVIEWED BY AGRIPPA II

(25:22–27)

And Agrippa said unto Festus, I also could wish to hear the man myself, vs. 22a.

Plumptre remarks that this expressed desire of Agrippa implies "that the wish was not now formed for the first time."[z] Macgregor observes concerning Agrippa's words: "If, more literally, we translate 'I had a desire,' we shall have an interesting parallel with another Herod who 'had long desired to see [Jesus]' "[a] (Luke 23:8). Agrippa, like his sister Drusilla, the wife of Felix, doubtless had vivid memories of his father's execution of James, the Lord's brother (Acts 12:1, 2), and the general persecution of the Christians some fifteen years earlier. Too, he had likely known something of the disturbance between the Jews and Christians in Rome while resident there under Claudius (cf. Acts 18:2). There were, of course, many Christians in his realm to the north. He had likely heard much of Paul and his missionary activities, but such knowledge as he possessed was flamed into anxious desire at the opportunity that presented itself for him to see and hear Paul in person.

Luke's description of the pompous court procession and array in preparation for Paul's hearing on the following day (vs. 23) strongly suggests that he was an eyewitness. Bruce remarks of the **chief captains** who attended the hearings; "The 'chief captains' . . . would be five in number, as there were five auxiliary cohorts stationed at Caesarea."[b] Macgregor states of the chief captains and the principal men of the city: "These play much the same part as the 'council' or 'assessors' in vs. 12. They are called in 26:30 'Those who were sitting with them.' "[c]

The contrast between the humble, shack-

[46] Cf. EGT, II, 498.
[47] *Beginnings*, IV, 312. See also Robertson, *Grammar*, p. 919—"the courteous or polite use of the imperfect indicative."
[48] Arndt and Gingrich, *op. cit.*, p. 269. [49] *Ibid.*, p. 414.

[z] Ellicott, *op. cit.*, VII, 165. [a] *The Interpreter's Bible*, IX, 320.
[b] Bruce, *op. cit.*, p. 484, n. 23. See also Josephus, *op. cit.*, "Ant.," XIX, IX, 2.
[c] *The Interpreter's Bible*, IX, 321.

26 Of whom I have no certain thing to write unto my lord. Wherefore I have brought him forth before you, and specially before thee, King Agrippa, that, after examination had, I may have somewhat to write.

27 For it seemeth to me unreasonable, in sending a prisoner, not withal to signify the charges against him.

---

26 *Anakrisis* (**examination**) is found only here in the New Testament. Strictly speaking it means "a preliminary examination,"[50] but perhaps its meaning here is more general.[51]

27 *Alogon*, **unreasonable**, occurs elsewhere in the New Testament only in II Peter 2:12 and Jude 10, in both of which places it is used of creatures "without reason." Moulton and Milligan find the meanings "senseless" and "unreasonable" in the papyri.[52]

Signify is the verb *sēmainō*, which aside from John's Gospel (12:33; 18:32; 21:19) and Revelation 1:1, occurs only here and in 11:28. It comes from *sēma*, "sign," and means "make known, report, communicate."[53] In the papyri it denotes "indicate" or "signify."[54]

---

led, missionary prisoner before the bar and the richly robed formal procession of Roman royalty that assembled to hear his defense was most striking. Comparisons were then impossible, but native greatness will eventually assert itself, while the sham and show will disappear before the ravages of time as the proverbial mist before the rising sun. The tables have turned, and Paul marches on down the way of time touching and animating the lives of men wherever his life and works are read or heard. He has become the moral and spiritual giant of the ages, while **Felix** and **Drusilla** and **Festus** and **Agrippa** and **Bernice** and **the chief captains** and **the principal men** before whom he once made his defense are but the forgotten ghosts of a pretentious past. And so must it ever be when true greatness meets superficial show and sham.

Rackham remarks: "The solemnity of the occasion is marked by its elaborate setting and the repetitions which it involves. Three times over we read the account of Festus' dealings with the Jews; and thereby three times is the apostle's innocence insinuated"[d] (vss. 10, 18, 25).

With due official dignity, Festus introduced Paul to the court and briefly summarized the previous proceedings against him, both by the Sanhedrin and by his own Roman court, and then announced the fact of Paul's appeal to Caesar (vss. 24, 25).

Festus concluded his remarks in opening the case with a frank acknowledgement of his complete bewilderment concerning charges to accompany Paul before Caesar (vs. 26a) and humbly deferred to the superior knowledge and experience of Agrippa for this needed information which he hoped Agrippa would obtain by his personal examination of Paul and his review of the case (vs. 26, 27).

Dummelow summarizes Festus' purpose in Agrippa's review of the case thus: "As Agrippa was expert in all matters of the Jewish law, Festus hoped that he would help him to compose a letter to the Emperor, which would make it clear what the charges against Paul really were."[e] "According to the Digest (XLIX. b) such written reports, called *litterae dimissoriae*, had to be sent when cases were remanded to the supreme court."[f]

The recurrence of emperor deification is in evidence in Festus' reference to Nero as **my lord** (vs. 26). Bruce remarks:

> The title "lord" (*kyrios*) with a divine connotation was given to Roman emperors in the eastern provinces as it had been given to the Ptolemies and other dynasts; Deissmann notes that there is a remarkable rise in the frequency of such inscriptions in the time of Nero and his successors (Light from the Ancient East [Eng. tr., London, 1927], pp. 353 ff.).[g]

Macgregor remarks:

> Caligula was the first to style himself *Dominus*, and Domitian improved on this with the title *Dominus deus*. The papyri show that in Egypt from the middle of the first century B.C. *kyrios* is more and more frequently used of the emperor.[h]

[50] VGT, p. 35. [51] Cf. EGT, II, 500; *Beginnings*, IV, 313. [52] VGT, p. 24.
[53] Arndt and Gingrich, *op. cit.*, p. 755. [54] VGT, p. 572.

[d] Rackham, *op. cit.*, p. 456. [e] Dummelow, *op. cit.*, p. 850. [f] *The Interpreter's Bible*, *loc. cit.*
[g] Bruce, *op. cit.*, p. 485, n. 24. [h] *The Interpreter's Bible*, *loc. cit.*

CHAPTER XXVI

And Agrippa said unto Paul, Thou art permitted to speak for thyself. Then Paul stretched forth his hand, and made his defence:
2 I think myself happy, king Agrippa, that I am to make my defence before thee this day touching all the things whereof I am accused by the Jews:
3 especially because thou art expert in all customs and questions which are among the Jews: wherefore I beseech thee to hear me patiently.

EXEGESIS

1 *Epitrepetai soi*, **thou art permitted,** is literally "it is permitted to thee." This meaning is well illustrated in the papyri.[1] *Hyper*, **for,** is "on behalf of." **Made his defence** shows that while this was not an official trial, Paul felt the need of defending himself.

2 *Makarion*, **happy,** is the same word as that used in the Beatitudes (Matt. 5:3–12) and there translated "blessed." The high literary quality of this speech, reflecting Paul's superior educational background, has often been noted.[2] It is evidenced in both the vocabulary and the style of this verse.

3 *Malista*, **especially,** is "most of all" or "above all." *Gnōstēn*, **expert,** is literally "one who knows." The word is found only here in the New Testament. Rabbinical writers say that Agrippa excelled in a knowledge of the Mosaic law.[3] *Makrothymos*, **patiently,** also occurs only here. It means "with forbearance."

EXPOSITION

THE APOSTLE'S DEFENSE BEFORE FESTUS AND AGRIPPA II (Cont'd)

- IV. Paul's Formal Introduction, Acts 26:1–3.
- V. Paul's Former Life, Acts 26:4, 5.
- VI. Paul's Version of the Issue, Acts 26:6–8.
- VII. Paul's Persecution of the Christians, Acts 26:9–11.
- VIII. Paul's Encounter with Christ, Acts 26:12–15.
- IX. Paul's Commission from Christ, Acts 26:16–18.
- X. Paul's Faithfulness to Christ, Acts 26:19–23.
- XI. Paul's Impact on Festus and Agrippa, Acts 26:24–29.
- XII. Paul's Innocence Affirmed, Acts 26:30–32.

Whether Paul knew the words of the Master as recorded by Mark (Mark 13:9–11) we cannot say, but that he felt the assurance of the divine wisdom and strength for this occasion, as promised in those words, appears evident from his confident manner. This was not only to be his last opportunity to declare his innocence of the charges which the Jews had brought against him, but it was also a challenging opportunity to witness for Christ before Roman royalty and officialdom (cf. Acts 25:23 and 26:30).

IV. PAUL'S FORMAL INTRODUCTION

(26:1–3)

Paul's introduction consisted of two phases. *First*, Festus introduced the prisoner to the august assembly with official permission to deliver an address in his self-defense. There is no evidence of Jewish enemies or accusers at this hearing, and therefore we are left free to assume that Paul was addressing a private assembly of Roman officials (see Acts 25:23; 26:1). *Second*, Paul made his formal introduction to the assembly. Luke's statement that he **stretched forth his hand** (vs. 1) is evidently a gesture of greeting to the king, as perhaps also to his company. Bruce holds that "the expression is different from that in Acts 13:16 and 21:40 ... [where it is intended] to denote a gesture

[1] VGT, p. 249. [2] Cf. Moulton, *Grammar*, I, 148. [3] Hackett, *op. cit.*, p. 282.

4 My manner of life then from my youth up, which was from the beginning among mine own nation and at Jerusalem, know all the Jews;

5 having knowledge of me from the first, if they be willing to testify, that after the straitest sect of our religion I lived a Pharisee.

---

4 *Biōsin*, **manner of life,** is also a (N.T.) *hapax legomenon* (said once for all). *Neotētos*, **youth,** is used of Timothy in I Timothy 4:12. So it does not necessarily imply childhood. *Isasi* (third person plural of *oida*), **know,** is "perhaps a conscious classicism." [4] The form is found only here in the New Testament.

5 *Proginōskontes*, **having knowledge,** is literally "who knew beforehand." *Anōthen*, **from the first,** is used thus (in N.T.) only here and in Luke 1:3. Since the preface to Luke's Gospel was written in classical style, it may be assumed the word means the same there as here.[5] *Akribestatēn*, **straitest,** is a true superlative—not elative, as are most of the superlatives in the New Testament. Moulton says there is "only one example of the -tatos superlative" in the New Testament.[6] But Robertson finds three: this one, *hagiōtatos* (Jude 20), and *timiōtatos* (Rev. 18:12; 21:11).[7] For **sect,** ***hairesin*,** see on 5:17. Josephus gives ample testimony to the strictness of the Pharisees. He says of them: "These are a certain sect of the Jews that appear more religious than others, and seem to interpret the laws more accurately." [8] *Thrēskeias*, **religion,** means "religion in its external aspect," and so "worship." [9] The word is found elsewhere in the New Testament only in Colossians 2:18 and James 1:26, 27.

---

inviting silence and attention."[a] Plumptre remarks: "Here it acquires a fresh pictorial vividness from the fact that St. Paul now stood before the court as a prisoner, with one arm, probably the left, chained to the soldier who kept guard over him. (Comp. verse 29.)"[b]

It would appear that Paul intended something more than a formal compliment in his address to Agrippa (vs. 2). In faithfulness to the Herodian dynasty, Agrippa II remained loyal to Rome to the end, even during the subsequent Jewish War with Rome. However, he bore his national Jewish interest at heart and strove earnestly to avert the catastrophe. As a Jew he knew well their customs and was sympathetic with their interests. Thus Paul's knowledge of Agrippa's Judeo-Roman character and sympathies made him the more ready to answer before him. Bruce remarks: "He, at least, might appreciate the strength of Paul's argument that the message which he proclaimed was the proper consummation of Israel's ancestral faith."[c] However, Paul's address was both frank and courteous. He would not flatter a ruler whose character he knew to be corrupt (cf. Acts 24:2–4), but he recognized his advantages in making his defense before a ruler who knew well the doctrinal distinctions between Pharisees and Sadducees, especially on the question of the "resurrection" and their common anticipation of the Messiah, plus the fact that the hopes of some, at least of the Pharisees if not also of the Sadducees, had found fulfillment in Christ (Acts 6:7; 15:5; 21:20).

Paul expresses no such intent of brevity as was promised Felix by Tertullus (cf. Acts 24:4), but rather recognizing the necessity of time to present adequately his case and the cause of Christ he simply and courteously requested patience of his audience while he made a fair presentment. Perhaps the difference between Tertullus' brevity and Paul's more extended address was due to the fact that Tertullus had little of import to say while Paul was about to narrate the most important story ever told.

Macgregor observes concerning the word **especially** (vs. 3a) that it might possibly be placed in the sentence in three different ways: "(a) **Because you are especially familiar;** (b) Especially because you are familiar. (c) That is especially before you which would be in line with the use of the word in 25:26."[d]

V. PAUL'S FORMER LIFE

(26:4, 5)

My manner of life . . . from my youth up . . . know all the Jews, vs. 4.

---

[4] EGT, II, 501; cf. Bruce, *Acts*, p. 441.
[5] Not "from above" (cf. John 3:31), as some have claimed.
[6] *Grammar*, I. 78.
[7] *Grammar*, p. 280.
[8] *War*, I, 5, 2.
[9] Abbott-Smith, *op. cit.*, p. 208.

[a] Bruce, *op. cit.*, p. 488, n. 9.
[b] Ellicott, *op. cit.*, VII, 165.
[c] Bruce, *loc. cit.*
[d] *The Interpreter's Bible*, IX, 323.

6 And now I stand *here* to be judged for the hope of the promise made of God unto our fathers;
7 unto which *promise* our twelve tribes, earnestly serving *God* night and day, hope to attain. And concerning this hope I am accused by the Jews, O king!
8 Why is it judged incredible with you, if God doth raise the dead?

---

7 The compound *dōdekaphylos*, **twelve tribes**, is found only here in the New Testament. **Earnestly** is *en ekteneia*. The noun occurs here alone in the New Testament. It means "zeal, intenseness, earnestness." [10]

8 *Apiston*, **incredible**, is used in this impersonal sense only here in the New Testament. Elsewhere (22 times) it is used of persons and means "unbelieving." Here it is "unbelievable."

It appears evident that Luke records only a brief summary outline of Paul's address before Agrippa II. Dummelow remarks: "This speech, though in form of a defense to the Jews, is really intended by St. Luke to be Paul's defense to the world — an apology for his whole life and work."[e] Bruce notes that Paul's address largely covers the ground of the speech delivered before the Jews from the steps of the fortress of Antonia (Acts 21:40–22:22):

> but the general tone and atmosphere of the two speeches are different, each being adapted to its very distinctive audience. Here, in the calm and dignified setting of the governor's audience-chamber at Caesarea, he delivered the speech which, above all his other speeches recorded in Acts, may worthily claim to be his *Apologia Pro Vita Sua*.[f]

The dignity and literary style of this address is somewhat reminiscent of Paul's earlier address before the Areopagus at Athens (Acts 17:22–31), though the content is quite different.

Paul's words, **mine own nation and at Jerusalem** (vs. 4), seem to imply that his former life was common knowledge to the Jews, both in his youth among the Jews at Tarsus in Cilicia and during his subsequent education and activities at Jerusalem. Here, as before Felix (Acts 24:10), Paul's employment of the term "nation," instead of the usual term "people" used of the Jews, seems designed to soften the common harsh distinction between Jews and heathen, likely in courtesy to Festus and the chief captains present (see note on Acts 24:10). Macgregor states: "Alternatively it is just possible that *ethnos* was technically used to mean a "province" — here Judea, in 26:4, Cilicia."[g] In any event he is making his accusers, the Judean Jews, responsible for knowledge of his Jewish upbringing at Tarsus and his Pharisaic training and activities at Jerusalem (cf. Gal. 1:13ff.; Phil. 3:5, 6). It is clear that Paul intended to establish before Agrippa the fact of his strict orthodox education and life, to which his accusers, if honest, would be forced to admit (vs. 5). Macgregor[h] observes that Paul here places greater emphasis on his practice and form of worship than the Jewish creed or system of beliefs, as was commensurate with the custom of the better Jewish teachers (cf. James 1:26, 27).

VI. PAUL'S VERSION OF THE ISSUE (26:6–8)

And concerning this hope I am accused by the Jews, O King, vs. 7b.

Having historically and logically established his claim to Jewish orthodoxy in belief and practice, Paul next proceeded to set before Agrippa **the hope of** [in] **the promise** (vs. 6) in relation to the "resurrection of the dead" (vs. 8), which is the real issue at stake between Paul and his accusers. Weymouth aptly renders the passage thus: "And now I stand here impeached because of my hope in the promise made by God to our fathers,"[i] while the RSV reads: "And now I stand here on trial for hope in the promise made by God to our fathers." Wesley remarks that Paul's claim shows "that what the Pharisees rightly taught concerning the resurrection Paul likewise asserted at this day."[j]

Paul proceeded to indicate that it was but

[10] *Ibid.*, p. 142.

[e] Dummelow, *op. cit.*, p. 850.
[f] Bruce, *op. cit.*
[g] *The Interpreter's Bible*, IX, 308.
[h] *Ibid.*, p. 323.
[i] Weymouth, *op. cit.*, p. 339.
[j] Wesley, *op. cit.*, pp. 499–500.

a matter of fact that a good Pharisee believed in the resurrection from the dead, and that he rested his faith on the resurrection for the fulfillment of Israel's ancient hope, **the hope in the promise.** This may appear to allude to the "Messianic hope," but when considered in relation to Acts 23:6; 24:15, and 26:8, it becomes quite clear that it was the resurrection which Paul had ultimately in mind. On the other hand, Paul implicitly reasoned that the hope of the resurrection rested upon God's fulfillment of His promise of the Messiah, and that without the Messiah the hope in the resurrection was in vain. But again Christ's claim to be God's fulfillment of the Messianic hope rested for its validation on Christ's own resurrection from the dead. However, both the fulfillment of the Messianic hope and Christ's resurrection from the dead which validated that hope, were requisite to the forgiveness of our sins and the ultimate hope of our resurrection from the dead (cf. I Cor. 15:12–23). Bruce remarks: "It was the hope which gave life and meaning and purpose to the ordinances of divine worship, faithfully maintained by all twelve tribes of Israel."[k]

It has been suggested that Paul's words, **our twelve tribes** (vs. 7), imply "that in their hope the twelve tribes are one single community."[l] Bruce significantly observes: "Neither Paul nor any other NT writer knows anything of the fiction of the ten 'lost' tribes. (Cf. Matt. 19:28; Luke 22:30; Jas. 1:1; Rev. 7:4 ff.; 21:12."[m] And again the same authority remarks on the Jews gathered from the Diaspora for the Jerusalem Pentecost of Acts 2:

> "Parthians and Medes and Elamites, and the dwellers in Mesopotamia" lived to the east of Judea . . . These were the lands of the earliest dispersion, to which exiles from the ten northern tribes of Israel had been carried by the Assyrians. They did not lose their identity so completely as is commonly supposed.[n]

Thus Paul agrees with James (James 1:1), and perhaps also with Peter in part (I Pet. 1:1), in his view that the **twelve tribes** (vs. 7) were sharers alike in the common hope of Israel. How devastating Paul's utterance is to the ancient and oft revived legend, that following Shalmaneser's conquest of the ten Northern Tribes they lost themselves in remote regions of the earth. This legend seems to have made its first appearance in the apocryphal literature[o] where they are represented as having gone to an uninhabited country where they might keep the laws of Jehovah which they had failed to keep in their native land. This unfounded legend played a large role in the origin and development of the American Mormon movement. The American aboriginal Indians have likewise been identified with the supposed "ten lost tribes," and some have tried to identify them with the gypsies.

Paul returned to his thesis with the words: **And concerning this hope I am accused by the Jews, O King** (vs. 7b). Having sufficiently demonstrated that his position was identical with that of the orthodox Jews on the question of the resurrection, Paul then proceeded to assert that it was for his faith in, and advocacy of, this very blessed hope of orthodox Judaism that he was indicted by the Jews. It is implicit in this argument that Paul is still driving the sharp edge of doctrinal division through the center of the Sanhedrin, thus separating the orthodox Pharisees from the liberal, materialistic Sadducees, and then identifying himself with the former and placing the blame for his indictment on the latter. In fact, it would appear that Paul was implying that the real controversy was one of the liberal Sadducean Jewish party against the orthodox Pharisaic party, rather than the Jews against him personally. Having clearly defined the issue and drawn the line of demarcation, Paul then directly appealed to Agrippa by a direct question for a personal verdict (vs. 8; cf. I Kings 17:17–23; II Kings 4:18–37). One could almost suspect that Paul regarded Agrippa's religious sympathies and beliefs to be Pharisaic rather than Sadducean, though according to Plumptre, "the rest of his kindred had been [allied] with the Sadducean high priest, not a few of whom he had himself nominated."[p] It has been observed that Paul's question to Agrippa (vs. 8) was general, but that he had in mind specifically the resurrection of Jesus Christ, since for Paul the resurrection of the dead in general was dependent upon Christ's resurrection (cf. I Cor. 15:12–23).[q]

[k] Bruce, *op. cit.*, p. 489.
[l] *The Interpreter's Bible*, IX, 324.
[m] Bruce, *loc. cit.*, n. 13.
[n] *Ibid.*, p. 61.
[o] II Esdras 13:40–46.
[p] Ellicott, *op. cit.*, VII, 166.
[q] *The Interpreter's Bible*, *loc. cit.*

9 I verily thought with myself that I ought to do many things contrary to the name of Jesus of Nazareth.

10 And this I also did in Jerusalem: and I both shut up many of the saints in prisons, having received authority from the chief priests, and when they were put to death, I gave my vote against them.

11 And punishing them oftentimes in all the synagogues, I strove to make them blaspheme; and being exceedingly mad against them, I persecuted them even unto foreign cities.

---

10 **When they were put to death** suggests that a number of Christians had been killed, though only the deaths of Stephen and James are recorded. *Psēphon*, **vote,** means "a small smooth stone, a pebble" [11] (cf. Rev. 2:17, the only other place in the N.T. where it occurs). From the use of pebbles in voting, it came to mean **vote.** A black stone meant conviction, a white one acquittal. The subscription to the Epistle to Philemon has the interesting phrase *hē psēphos tou martyriou*, which may be translated "condemnation to martyrdom." [12]

11 *Timoron*, **punishing,** first meant "helping," then "avenging." Here, though active, it has the middle sense of "avenging oneself, punishing." The word occurs (in N.T.) only here and in 22:5. **I strove to make them** is *ēnangkazon*. Robertson labels this the "conative" imperfect and says it should be represented in English by "tried." [13] The King James Version wrongly gives the impression that he succeeded,—as he "compelled" them. *Blasphēmein*, **blaspheme,** probably refers to cursing the name of Jesus. **Being . . . mad** is the verb *emmainomai*, "rage against," found only here in the New Testament.

The import of Paul's argument, Bruce thinks, was

> that this belief had now been validated in that God had already raised up one man from the dead, and had by that very fact demonstrated that man to be Israel's long-expected Messiah and Deliverer, the one in whom the age-old hope was realized. Why should those who believed in the resurrection of the dead refuse to believe that God had in fact raised up Jesus, and so declared Him to be the Son of God? If God did not raise up Jesus, why believe that he raised up the dead at all.[r]

VII. PAUL'S PERSECUTION OF THE CHRISTIANS

(26:9–11)

I gave my vote against them . . . I persecuted them even unto foreign cities (vss. 10b, 11b).

Paul's words in these verses are an illuminating commentary on the persecution that followed the martyrdom of Stephen (cf. Acts 8:1–4; 9:1, 2). In fact, they seem to suggest even a much more extensive and ferocious persecution of the Church than do the earlier records. Paul's part in that persecution receives special emphasis here, likely as an indication of his fanatical devotion to Judaism. Thus Paul shows his sympathetic understanding of the present Jewish opposition to the doctrine of Christ's Messiahship and resurrection. This sympathetic understanding appears to give birth to a degree of hope for Israel's salvation, in the heart of the Apostle. He had passed from unbelief in Christ and persecution of the Christians to saving faith in Christ as the resurrected Messiah. He could not despair of hope for Israel, and even for Agrippa himself (cf. Rom. 9:1–8; I Tim. 1:12–17).

Paul again called the Jews to witness his pre-Christian conduct **in Jerusalem** (vs. 10a). In contrast he now made bold, even before Agrippa whose father had beheaded James and sought to execute Peter (Acts 12:1–6), to call the Christians **saints,** or the "holy ones" of Israel.[s]

While the Scriptures record Paul's direct implication in the death of but one Christian, Stephen, it appears from the apostle's words here that he may have participated in many other martyrdoms also (cf. Acts 9:1, 2; I Thess. 2: 14–16; Heb. 10:32).

Paul's assertion, **I gave my vote against them** (vs. 10b), has been the subject of much controversy among scholars, some holding

[11] *Ibid.*, p. 488. [12] Arndt and Gingrich, *op. cit.*, p. 901. [13] *Grammar*, p. 885.

[r] Bruce, *op. cit.*, pp. 489, 490. [s] See I Maccabees 7:13 and II Maccabees 14:6.

that it identifies him as a member of the Sanhedrin, but others denying this meaning of the expression. Macgregor states: "This does not necessarily prove that Paul had been an official member of the Sanhedrin, for the expression is often used metaphorically. It may mean little more than 22:20. 'I also was standing by and approving' " (cf. 8:1).[t] Plumptre remarks: "The words show that St. Paul, though a 'young man'... must have been a member either of the Sanhedrin itself or of some tribunal with delegated authority."[u] Bruce remarks: "The expression 'was consenting' (ch. 8:1; it recurs in ch. 22:20) need not be taken to mean that Saul was actually a member of the Sanhedrin."[v]

However, Conybeare and Howson state:

> There are strong grounds for believing that if he was not a member of the Sanhedrin at the time of St. Stephen's death, he was elected into that powerful senate soon after; possibly as a reward for the zeal he had shown against the heretics. He himself says that in Jerusalem he not only exercised the power of imprisonment by commission from the High Priests, but also, when the Christians were put to death, gave his vote against them. From this expression it is natural to infer that he was a member of the supreme court of judicature.[w]

The foregoing authority notes that membership in the Sanhedrin was restricted to fathers with children, since such would dispose them to mercy. Since it was customary for Jews to marry young, Paul may well have qualified, though it is not known what became of his wife and family.[x] Dummelow is specific when he says, "The Gk. means 'the vote of a judge' and establishes the fact that at the time of the death of Stephen, Paul, though so young a man, was a member of the Sanhedrin."[y] Thus we must be content to conclude that Paul was either a member of the Sanhedrin, or if he was not, then he was invested with very special authority by that body, before his conversion.

Paul's allusion to his punishment of the Christians, **oftentimes in all the synagogues** (vs. 11a), indicates the wide-spread activities of his persecutions. There are reported to have been several hundred Jewish synagogues in Jerusalem at this time. Paul's trip to far away Damascus suggests the wide range of his activities. Bruce notes that "the ruling body of each synagogue constituted a minor law-court or *beth din*."[z]

Paul does not claim to have succeeded in forcing any of the Christians to blaspheme, but that such was his purpose is evident: **I strove to make them blaspheme** (vs. 11). He evidently considered it more profitable to his cause to secure apostates from the Christian faith than to have killed the Christians. Pliny observes that renegade Christians could be made to curse Christ (*maledicere Christo*), but that the true Christians could not be compelled to do so.[a] Empty profession under persecution has no sustaining power, but the true Christian is fortified against external pressures by an inward power that is greater than the outer (I John 4:4).

Paul's statement that he was **exceedingly mad against them** (vs. 11) expresses "with a wonderful vividness, . . . [his] retrospective analysis of his former state. It was not only that he acted in ignorance (I Tim. 1:13); he might plead also the temporary insanity of fanaticism."[b]

Nor was Paul the last instance of this "religious insanity of fanaticism" which made of him the mad murderer of the saints. The "Spanish Inquisition," the "New England Witch-burning Craze," and many other more modern instances of the merciless persecution of non-conformist Christians by the established church have effectively testified to a violent insanity produced by religious fanaticism. It would appear that Paul had in mind the distinction between this "insanity of fanaticism" and the "sobriety" that grace works in the heart when he wrote, "For the spirit which God has given us is not a spirit of cowardice, but one of power and of love and of sound judgment" (II Tim. 1:7; Weymouth).

Paul's words, **I persecuted them even unto foreign cities** (vs. 11b), indicate that Damascus was not the only instance of such activities, but that Samaria, Phoenicia, Galilee, Perea, Decapolis, and other regions likely felt the fury of his mad rage.

t *The Interpreter's Bible*, IX, 325.
u Ellicott, *loc. cit.*
v Bruce, *op. cit.*, pp. 172, 173.
w Conybeare and Howson, *op. cit.*, p. 12.
x *Ibid.*, p. 67, n. 2 and p. 72, n. 3.
y Dummelow, *op. cit.*, p. 851.
z Bruce, *op. cit.*, p. 490, n. 15.
a Pliny, *Letters*, X, 96.
b Ellicott, *op. cit.*, VII, 167

12 Whereupon as I journeyed to Damascus with the authority and commission of the chief priests,
13 at midday, O king, I saw on the way a light from heaven, above the brightness of the sun, shining round about me and them that journeyed with me.
14 And when we were all fallen to the earth, I heard a voice saying unto me in the Hebrew language, Saul, Saul, why persecutest thou me? it is hard for thee to kick against the goad.
15 And I said, Who art thou, Lord? And the Lord said, I am Jesus whom thou persecutest.

---

12 *Epitropēs*, **commission,** occurs only here in the New Testament. It means "full power."[14]

13 *Lamprotēta*, **brightness,** is found only here in the New Testament. *Perilampsan*, **shining round,** occurs elsewhere only in Luke 2:9.

14 **Hebrew language** *(dialektōi)* probably means Aramaic. Dalman illustrates from the rabbinical writings the idea that the voice from heaven preferred Aramaic to Hebrew and liked to use the double vocative, as here.[15] *Laktizein*, **to kick,** occurs only here in the New Testament. *Kentra*, **the goad,** is plural.

VIII. PAUL'S ENCOUNTER WITH CHRIST (26:12–15)

And I said, who art thou, Lord? And the Lord said, I am Jesus whom thou persecutest (vs. 15).

We are again confronted, for the third time in Acts, with Luke's account of Paul's Damascus road experience.[c] Here, however, it is characterized by certain variants evidently designed for the special occasion. With those variants we are especially concerned in this section.

Concerning Paul's **authority and commission** (vs. 12), Plumptre observes: "The former word [**authority**] implies the general power delegated to him, the latter [**commission**] the specific work assigned to him, and for the execution of which he was responsible."[d] (On Luke's notation that Christ spoke to Paul in the Hebrew language, vs. 14, see exegetical note.)

In this account only, of the three, Luke records Christ's words to Paul, **it is hard for thee to kick against the goad** (vs. 14b). It is doubtless designed especially for his Gentile hearers, as also for the Hellenistic Agrippa on this occasion. Macgregor observes that the expression was

> A proverbial saying, found both in Greek and Latin, usually with reference to fighting against the will of the gods, but not yet paralleled from any Semitic source. The word . . . means, in this context, not "difficult" but "painful," hence RSV, It hurts you to kick . . ."[e]

Another remarks of the expression: "It supplies an apt figure for resistance to God; and here it conveys an important intimation that Saul's zeal for Judaism had not been according to knowledge, but rather against the driving of the divine will."[f] Withal it is apparent from the figure employed that Paul was already subconsciously convinced of the truth of Christianity. This conviction probably arose in part from the unanswerable "wisdom and . . . spirit" (Acts 6:10) with which Stephen worsted his Jewish contestants of the synagogues (Acts 6:9), and likely in part from the noble example of Stephen in his life and death (Acts 6:8, 15; 7:54–8:1a), as well as that of other Christians whom he unsuccessfully attempted to force to blaspheme the name of Christ (vs. 11). It would be revealing to discover how many communists have been convinced of the truth of Christianity behind the "Iron and Bamboo Curtains" by the faithful witness of Christians who under persecutions and "brainwashings" have refused to recant their faith in Christ or become "turncoats." The deeper the conviction of the truth of Christianity in the mind of Paul the more ferociously did he fight against that conviction. Bruce states:

> It was probably in large measure to stifle this conviction and impression that Paul threw himself so furiously into the campaign of repression. But the goad kept on pricking his conscience, until at last the truth that Jesus was risen indeed burst forth into full realization and acknowledgement as He appeared to Paul in person and

[14] Arndt and Gingrich, *op. cit.*, p. 303.
[15] G. H. Dalman, *Jesus–Jeshua*. Trans. (London: 1929), pp. 17 ff.

[c] For the most part Paul's experience as here related has been treated in Acts 9:1–6 and 22:5–10, to which the reader is referred for the exposition.
[d] Ellicott, *loc. cit.*
[e] *The Interpreter's Bible*, IX, 326.
[f] Rackham, *op. cit.*, p. 468.

16 But arise, and stand upon thy feet: for to this end have I appeared unto thee, to appoint thee a minister and a witness both of the things wherein thou hast seen me, and of the things wherein I will appear unto thee;
17 delivering thee from the people, and from the Gentiles, unto whom I send thee,

---

16 *Procheirisasthai*, **to appoint,** is the same word as that used by Ananias in 22:14 (elsewhere in N.T. only in 3:20). *Hypēretēn*, **minister,** is perhaps better rendered "servant" (see on 5:22).

17 *Exairoumenos*, **delivering,** literally means "taking out for oneself." Thayer here prefers "choosing out."[16] Arndt and Gingrich list the reference under this meaning, then go on to say: "But in this passage the meaning *deliver*, *save* is also possible and probably to be preferred."[17] Lake and Cadbury note that "rescuing" is the meaning "everywhere else in Luke's work and usually in the LXX and similar Greek."[18]

---

spoke to him by name outside the walls of Damascus.[g]

Many of Christianity's greatest victories and accomplishments have occurred under the most severe circumstances, and Christian faithfulness under extreme opposition and suffering has always been productive of spiritual prosperity and progress in the Church.

IX. PAUL'S COMMISSION FROM CHRIST

(26:16–18)

I appeared unto thee, to appoint thee a minister and a witness, vs. 16.

In blunt language, Paul the determined opponent and persecutor of Christianity had to be "knocked down" by God before he could qualify to **arise, and stand upon ... [his] feet** (vs. 16) for Christ.

Like certain prophets of old, Paul is commanded of Christ to stand upon his feet and receive the divine commission (see Ezek. 2:1, 3; cf. Acts 22:14, 18; Isa. 6:6–13; 42:1–4; Jer. 1:7–10). No mention is made of the mission of Ananias in relation to Paul's commission, perhaps for the obvious reason that it would not have been important to his purpose before his largely Gentile audience, and the fact that he was compressing the whole experience into such brief compass. Plumptre[h] thinks that Paul's summary of his commission as given here was designed to embody the substance of the "visions and revelations of the Lord" (II Cor. 12:1–7), in which his future had been charted for him and he had received the revelation of the Gospel which he was to preach to the world. In any event, Paul's commission to the Gentiles was evidently first delivered to him through Ananias (Acts 22:12–15) and then was subsequently directly and definitely revealed to him in the temple at Jerusalem in a vision by the Lord Himself (Acts 22:17–21). Thus Paul apparently summarized the contents of more than one vision.

Christ's purpose **to appoint ... [Paul] a minister and a witness** (vs. 16) makes evident the fact that his divine commission was twofold. He was to be a herald of the Gospel to the nations, of which Gospel he was, through encounter with Christ, a personal witness. No man can be an effective minister (John 15:16; Eph. 6:19–20; cf. I Cor. 4:1) until he has had a saving encounter with Christ (cf. Isa. 6:5–8; II Cor. 5:17–20; II Tim. 2:6). Thus the true gospel ministry is inseparable from the personal witness to the saving efficacy of Christ.

While on the one hand, **the things wherein thou hast seen me** (vs. 16) may relate to both the revelation of Christ to Paul on the Damascus road and to the revelation of Christ in the lives of the Christians Paul had formerly persecuted, on the other hand, **the things wherein I will appear unto thee** (vs. 16) related to Christ's subsequent revelations to Paul (Acts 18:9, 10; 22:17–21; 23: 11).

Christ's promise to Paul in relation to the execution of his commission was twofold: **delivering thee from the people, and from the Gentiles, unto whom I send thee** (vs. 17). Indeed the protective power of Christ over His servant Paul while he was under attack

[16] *Op. cit.*, p. 221. [17] *Op. cit.*, p. 271. [18] *Beginnings*, IV, 319.

[g] Bruce, *op. cit.*, p. 491. [h] Ellicott, *op. cit.*, VII, 167.

both from **the people** (the Jews) and **the Gentiles** has been in evidence frequently in the Acts record, and without doubt this interpretation of Christ's promise has validity. However, Macgregor offers a challenging variant to the foregoing interpretation.[i]

It was doubtless this last qualification that especially recommended Paul to Barnabas for the ministry of the mixed Greco-Jewish Christian congregation at Antioch (see Acts 11:25, 26).

Paul's Gentile ministry is specifically delineated in verse eighteen. In outline form it might appear as follows:

1. *A Ministry of Spiritual Illumination*: **to open their eyes.**
2. *A Ministry of Spiritual Conversion*: **that they may turn from darkness to light.**
3. *A Ministry of Spiritual Deliverance*: **from the power of Satan unto God.**
4. *A Ministry of Spiritual Remission*: **that they may receive remission of sins.**
5. *A Ministry of Spiritual Inheritance*: **that they may receive . . . an inheritance among them that are sanctified by faith in me.**

First, the apostle likely thought of his own recovery from physical (and spiritual) blindness when he had met Christ (cf. 9:8, 9, 17, 18; 22:11–15), as he uttered these words of his commission. Indeed light became one of Paul's prime symbols for Christian conversion and life (cf. Rom. 13:12; II Cor. 4:6; Eph. 5:8–14; Col. 1:12–14; I Thess. 5:4–8; see also Isa. 2:5; 9:2; 35:5; 42:6; 49:6; 60:1, 19, 20).

Second, Paul is equally clear in his emphasis on man's moral freedom and responsibility in responding to the initiative of God and His offered mercies in Christ. Nowhere does the apostle represent God as imposing Christ and His salvation upon man (cf. Eph. 5:14; I Thess. 1:9b, 10). While the KJV reads "to turn them from darkness to light," the ASV conveys the better sense of the passage: **that they may turn from darkness to light**; thus representing the non-Christian as responding to the divine appeal.

Third, it is evident that Paul clearly recognized the personality and dominance of Satan over the lives of unconverted men. Here it is not simply a decision on man's part to accept and follow Christ, but it involves a demonstration of divine power by which man is extricated from Satan's authority over his life and placed under the Lordship of Jesus Christ (cf. Rom. 1:16; 12:1, 2). The universal Lordship of Jesus Christ, as opposed to the dominance of Satan over the lives of men, is the burden of the first-century Christian message (cf. Matt. 28:18–20; Acts 1:8).

Fourth, the remission of sins is the gateway to the Kingdom of God, through which all who would enter must pass. That repentance, as a condition of remission of sins is implied, becomes evident both from Paul's previous statement (vs. 20), and from Christ's own words: "I tell you, Nay: but, except ye repent, ye shall all in like manner perish" (Luke 13:3, 5). It was an orthodox Jewish doctrine that the power to forgive sins rested exclusively with God (Luke 5:21). However, Christ offered a miracle of healing before the skeptical scribes and Pharisees as evidence of His divine authority to forgive sins (Luke 5:24–26). Divine forgiveness is likewise assured by the apostle John (I John 1:9).

Fifth and finally, Paul declares that the ultimate aim of Christ's Gospel is to offer converted man an assured holy heritage through faith in Christ (cf. I Cor. 1: 30; Eph. 5:25–27; I Thess. 4; 3, 4; 5:23; II Thess. 2:13; Heb. 13:12; I Peter 1:2). Phillips' translation of the passage is graphic: ". . . that they may . . . take their place with all those who are made holy by their faith in Me."[j] This great divine provision was the principal import of Christ's high priestly prayer (John 17:15, 17, 19).

In summary it may be noted that Paul's commission implies a series of spiritual transferences for the converted man: (1) *from blindness to sight*; (2) *from darkness to light*; (3) *from the kingdom and dominion of Satan to the kingdom and dominion of Christ* (cf. Rom. 1:18–32); (4) *from condemnation unto death to remission of sins unto eternal life*; and (5) *from spiritual poverty and moral pollution to a heavenly inheritance and moral purity.*

[i] *The Interpreter's Bible*, IX, 327.

[j] J. B. Phillips, *The Young Church in Action* (New York: Macmillan Company, 1955), p. 68. (Cf. Rom. 1:7; 6:22; II Cor. 7:1; Eph. 4:24; I Thess. 3:13; 4:7).

18 to open their eyes, that they may turn from darkness to light and from the power of Satan unto God, that they may receive remission of sins and an inheritance among them that are sanctified by faith in me.
19 Wherefore, O king Agrippa, I was not disobedient unto the heavenly vision:
20 but declared both to them of Damascus first, and at Jerusalem, and throughout all the country of Judaea, and also to the Gentiles, that they should repent and turn to God, doing works worthy of repentance.
21 For this cause the Jews seized me in the temple, and assayed to kill me.

---

19 *Optasia*, **vision,** is used only by Luke (cf. Luke 1:22; 24:23) and Paul (II Cor. 12:1). It has this meaning in modern Greek.

20 The Greek for **throughout all the country of Judaea** is admittedly awkward and difficult to translate. Also some have claimed a contradiction between this statement and Galatians 1:22. But Paul may here be referring to a later ministry in Palestine.[19]

21 **Assayed** is the verb *peiraomai*, "try, attempt." It is found only here in the New Testament. For *diacheirisasthai*, **to kill,** see on 5:30.

X. PAUL'S FAITHFULNESS TO CHRIST

(26:19–23)

I was not disobedient unto the heavenly vision, vs. 19b.

Plumptre remarks:

> The language of the Apostle is significant in its bearing on the relations of God's grace and man's freedom. Even here, with the "vessel of election" (chap. IX, 15) "constrained" by the love of Christ (2 Cor. V, 14), there was the possibility of disobedience. There was an act of will in passing from the previous state of rebellion to that of obedience.[k]

Paul's experience had been definitely a vision, as contrasted with a dream or trance (cf. Luke 1:22; II Cor. 12:1; see also expositional notes on Peter's trance, Acts 10:10–17).

From his conversion Paul had but one supreme object of affection, Christ, and but one ultimate purpose, the fulfillment of Christ's purpose for his life (cf. Phil. 3:13, 14).

In verse twenty the apostle reviews his witness to Christ at **Damascus, Jerusalem, Judea,** and **to the Gentiles** (possibly his Cilician ministry before going to Antioch) following his conversion. However, this may be a general summary of Paul's entire ministry from his conversion until his arrest at Jerusalem, as verse twenty seems to suggest (see exegetical note for further comment). Paul's ministry was designed to produce a threefold effect in the lives of his hearers: *first*, repentance: **that they should repent;** *second*, conversion: **that they should . . . turn to God;** and *third*, good works: **that they should . . .** [do] **works worthy of repentance** (cf. Matt. 3:8). Nowhere does Paul ever recognize works as the grounds of man's justification, either before conversion or after, but everywhere, as here, Paul requires good works as the criterion of salvation. The order set forth here is logical and Scriptural. Nor should anyone, not even the Jews or Agrippa himself, object to the preaching of a doctrine that made good men out of bad ones by way of repentance and by the forsaking of wicked ways to follow the righteousness of God in Christ. However, Paul concluded that it was for this very reason that the Jews had seized him in the Temple and had attempted to kill him (vs. 21). Thus Paul indicts his accusers for attempting to destroy the very righteousness which they professed to stand for and teach. But it is clear (here Paul appeals to Agrippa's sympathies with Rome, as well as to the Gentile members of his audience) that Paul's unpardonable sin in the sight of the Jews was that he taught the Gentiles that they were fellow-heirs of the promise made to the Jews. For this same cause Stephen had become the first Christian martyr, and Paul had consented unto his death (cf. Acts 13:46; Eph. 3:6, 7).

His deliverance from the murderous intent of the Jews Paul attributed to the very God they profess to serve (vs. 22a). He then

[19] *Ibid.*, p. 320.

[k] Ellicott, *op. cit.*, VII, 167.

22 Having therefore obtained the help that is from God, I stand unto this day testifying both to small and great, saying nothing but what the prophets and Moses did say should come;
23 how that the Christ must suffer, *and* how that he first by the resurrection of the dead should proclaim light both to the people and to the Gentiles.
24 And as he thus made his defence, Festus saith with a loud voice, Paul, thou art mad; thy much learning is turning thee mad.

---

22 *Epikourias*, **help,** occurs only here in the New Testament. It comes from *epikoureō*, "be an ally," and so means "aid" or "assistance" arising from an alliance.

23 *Pathētos*, **must suffer,** is found only here in the New Testament. It is an adjective meaning "subject to suffering" (ASV margin) or "destined to suffer." Arndt and Gingrich give only the former definition.[20] Moulton and Milligan agree that it means "capable of suffering."[21] Robertson also insists on this connotation.[22]

Ei, **how that** (twice), is literally "whether." But Lake and Cadbury write: "In this and in the next clause *ei* is best rendered by 'that,' but there is in *ei* a stronger implication that the proposition which follows is denied and must be argued out, than would be made by the simple *hoti*."[23]

24 *Mainē*, **thou art mad,** meant first "to rage, be furious," then "to rave, be mad."[24] It was often connected with demonic influence (cf. John 10:20). Here it perhaps means that Paul's "enthusiasm seems to have overcome his better judgment."[25] **Much learning** is *polla grammata*, literally "many letters." But the meaning here seems supported in John 7:15. It may be that Festus had been impressed with Paul's very studious habits while a prisoner. **Mad** is literally "to madness" *(eis manian)*. The latter word is found only here in the New Testament.

---

declared that his message was but the message of orthodox Judaism based upon a correct interpretation of the Messianic predictions of the Jewish prophets and the law which God gave to Moses (vs. 22b). Plumptre states: "The name of Moses was added by an instantaneous afterthought to meet the case of those among the hearers who, like the Sadducees, placed the Pentateuch on a higher level of authority than the prophets."[l] That message, more specifically, concerned the sufferings and death of Christ (cf. Isa. 35), His resurrection from the dead, and the proclamation of the good news of salvation for all men thus procured, first to the Jews and then to the Gentiles (vs. 23).

But the concept of a suffering Messiah had always been a stumbling block to the Jews, as also foolishness to the Greeks (I Cor. 1:23). Though the Jews had conceived of, and emphasized only, the glories of the coming Messiah's kingdom, thus missing the import of the Cross, Paul's principal emphasis was ever on Christ crucified and resurrected (cf. Acts 13:27–35). Even Christ's Jewish disciples were exceedingly dull of understanding in this respect (cf. Matt. 16:22). It was not until after His death and resurrection that the truth of His sufferings began to dawn upon them (see Luke 24:25, 26, 44). In fact, not until Pentecost were they completely disillusioned of their materialistic concepts of His Kingdom (see Acts 1:6–8).

It is noteworthy that it was by the preaching of the resurrection of Christ that **light** (vs. 23b) should come to Jew and Gentile alike. Christ's resurrection then, as now, was the hope of the world.

XI. PAUL'S IMPACT ON FESTUS AND AGRIPPA

(26:24–29)

And Agrippa said unto Paul, with but little persuasion thou wouldest fain make me a Christian, vs. 28.

Under the impact of Paul's inescapable logic and undeniable evidence for the truth of Christianity, Festus momentarily forgot the dignity of his position and unrestrainedly exclaimed, **Paul, thou art mad; thy much learning is turning thee mad** (vs. 24b). Macgregor remarks, "Paul had deliberately been

[20] *Op. cit.*, p. 607. [21] VGT, p. 473. [22] *Grammar*, p. 1097.
[23] *Beginnings*, IV, 321. [24] Abbott-Smith, *op. cit.*, p. 275. [25] Arndt and Gingrich, *op. cit.*, p. 487.

[l] *Ibid.*, p. 168.

25 But Paul saith, I am not mad, most excellent Festus; but speak forth words of truth and soberness.

26 For the king knoweth of these things, unto whom also I speak freely: for I am persuaded that none of these things is hidden from him; for this hath not been done in a corner.

27 King Agrippa, believest thou the prophets? I know that thou believest.

28 And Agrippa *said* unto Paul, With but little persuasion thou wouldest fain make me a Christian.

---

25 *Sophrosynēs*, **soberness**, occurs (in N.T.) only here and in I Timothy 2:9, 15. It means "soundness of mind, good sense, sanity." [26]

26 The last clause is a common proverb, found in such writers as Plato and Epictetus. It is another evidence of the classical character of Paul's speech.[27]

28 The exact meaning of Agrippa's reply is uncertain. Lake and Cadbury contend that "'Christian' in the mouth of Agrippa can only be interpreted as a sneer." [28] Since the Greek literally means, "In a little you are persuading me to make (or do) a Christian," they offer these possible translations: "You rapidly persuade me to make a Christian"—that is, you want me to help you convert Festus—or, "You rapidly persuade me to play the Christian." [29] The latter would be a colloquial meaning of *poiēsai* ("to do"). Hackett expresses his opinion thus: "Agrippa appears to have been moved by the apostle's earnest manner, but attempts to conceal his emotion under the form of a jest." [30] With regard to "almost" (KJV), he writes: "It is held, at present, to be unphilological to translate in little, almost."[31] Lechler takes a similar view of Agrippa's attitude. He says: "It is indeed possible that for a moment a serious impression was made on the king; still, he immediately replies in derisive terms." [32]

Alford takes a somewhat more negative view of Agrippa's seriousness. He declares: "Most of the ancient commentators take the words as implying some effect on Agrippa's mind, and as spoken in earnest: but this I think is hardly possible, philologically or exegetically." [33] Brown supposes that Agrippa's reply was "a high compliment to the persuasiveness of the speaker." [34]

It does not appear that the question as to whether Agrippa was serious or sarcastic can be settled on the basis of the Greek text. The best that can be said is that the Greek of this verse seems to favor an insincere or cynical attitude on his part.

---

using language which while intelligible to Agrippa the Jew, to whom the defense is chiefly directed, might well appear to the sophisticated Roman as the ravings of a demented apocalyptist!"[m] Whether Festus spoke in scorn, unrestrained sincerity, or utter amazement, it is equally evident that Paul's defense had made a tremendous impact upon him.

Paul's protest (vs. 25) reflects his self-control and the courtesy due Festus' position (cf. Acts 24:3). In contrast to Festus' accusation of "madness," Paul asserts that he has spoken **words of truth and soberness** (vs. 25b). Excesses, of which Festus accused Paul, are denied by the apostle in his claim to **soberness,** or a harmony of the reason and impulses. Aristotle[n] made much of the virtue of this state of mind to which Paul laid claim, a fact of Greek philosophy with which Paul may have been well acquainted. In support of his claim to **truth and soberness,** which to Festus' Greek mind appeared to be madness, Paul appealed to the Greco-Jewish judgment of Agrippa (vs. 26). That appeal appears to have been, *first*, to Agrippa's knowledge that the Law and the Prophets had predicted a coming Messiah who was known to the Jews as the Christ. *Second*, Agrippa knew that from the days of Jesus of Nazareth there had been communities of Jews throughout Palestine, Syria, Asia Minor, Europe, and even in Rome (cf. Acts 9:31), who believed that the Christ had come, suffered, died, and had risen again. These congregations of Nazarenes,

[26] Abbott-Smith, *op. cit.*, p. 438. [27] EGT, II, 512. [28] *Beginnings*, IV, 322.
[29] *Ibid.*, p. 323. [30] *Op. cit.*, p. 289. [31] *Ibid.*
[32] Lange *op. cit.*, p. 444. [33] Henry Alford, *op. cit.*, II, 283. [34] JFB, VI, 175.

[m] *The Interpreter's Bible*, IX, 329.

[n] Aristotle, "Nicomschean Ethics," *On Man in the Universe* (New York: D. Van Nostrand Company, Inc., 1943), III, 10.

29 And Paul *said,* I would to God, that whether with little or with much, not thou only, but also all that hear me this day, might become such as I am, except these bonds.

30 And the king rose up, and the governor, and Bernice, and they that sat with them:

31 and when they had withdrawn, they spake one to another, saying, This man doeth nothing worthy of death or of bonds.

32 And Agrippa said unto Festus, This man might have been set at liberty, if he had not appealed unto Caesar.

---

29 The main argument for thinking that Agrippa was serious is the language of Paul's reply. But this may simply reflect his courtesy and his concern for Agrippa's salvation.

Euxaimēn is the classical use of the optative for a softened assertion. Bruce comments: "The whole sentence is very elegantly expressed." [35] Literally the expression, *euxaimēn an tōi theōi,* **I would to God,** means "I could pray to God."

---

as they were commonly known to the Jews, were not by now an obscure people, nor were their doctrines unknown to Agrippa (vs. 26b).

Paul evidently sought to establish a more satisfactory point of contact with Agrippa and thus afford a basis for discussion in his question directed to the king (vs. 27). As a Jew, Agrippa could not deny faith in the prophets, but he was not to be forced into an admission of unwelcome truth. Whether Agrippa's reply (vs. 28) is to be understood as an evasive cynical sneer, as many scholars hold, or whether Agrippa spoke in sincerity, it is equally evident that he had been forced by Paul's logic into a position where he could offer no counter argument to Paul's conclusions concerning Christianity. Conybeare and Howson remark concerning Agrippa's reply:

> The words were doubtless spoken ironically and in contempt: but Paul took them as though they had been spoken in earnest, and made that noble answer, which expresses, as no other words ever expressed them, that union of enthusiastic zeal with genuine courtesy, which is the true characteristic of a Christian.[o]

Paul made one last appeal (vs. 29) to Agrippa, and perhaps Bernice as well as the Gentile members of his audience, for a realistic facing of truth. Bruce paraphrases Paul's reply thus: " 'In short or at length,' said Paul, 'I could pray that not only Your Majesty, but all who are here today listening to me were Christian like myself-except for these chains' (holding up his shackled wrists)."[p] Thus Paul stood before this august assembly of Roman rulers, himself a prisoner in chains, wishing that they might be as he was:

> . . . pardoned and at peace with God and man, with a hope stretching beyond the grave, and an actual present participation in the powers of the eternal world—this was what he was desiring for them. If that could be effected, he would be content to remain in bonds, and to leave them upon their thrones.[q]

The lingering effect of Paul's defense on the minds of Paul's audience we cannot know. That he had been a faithful witness for Christ before a court of Roman officials is evident and sufficient.

XII. PAUL'S INNOCENCE AFFIRMED (26:30–32)

This man doeth nothing worthy of death or bonds, vs. 31b.

Paul's defense before Agrippa was at an end. It had not been a trial but simply a review of the case by Agrippa that he might aid Festus in the formulation of charges to accompany Paul to Rome. The company withdrew and conferred. Whatever their personal opinion of Paul, the unanimous verdict was, **This man doeth nothing worthy of death or of bonds** (vs. 31b). Not guilty, they said, but there is nothing that can be done for him short of Caesar's court. Agrippa said unto Festus **this man might have been set at liberty, if he had not appealed unto Caesar** (vs. 32). The case had passed to the highest court of appeal, and thus it was forever removed from provincial jurisdiction.

[35] *Acts,* p. 449.

[o] Coneybeare and Howson, *op. cit.,* p. 675.
[p] Bruce, *op. cit.,* p. 496.
[q] Ellicott, *op. cit.,* VII, 169.

CHAPTER XXVII

And when it was determined that we should sail for Italy, they delivered Paul and certain other prisoners to a centurion named Julius, of the Augustan band.

EXEGESIS

1 *Apoplein*, **sail**, occurs only in Acts (four times). Literally it means "to sail away." *Desmōtas*, **prisoners**, is found (in N.T.) only here and in verse 42. The common New Testament word for prisoner is the adjective *desmios*. Both come from *deō*, "bind." With regard to *Sebastēs*, **Augustan**, Schürer says: "Sebastē is . . . an exact translation of *Augusta*, a title of honour very frequently bestowed upon auxiliary troops." [1]

EXPOSITION

THE APOSTLE'S VOYAGE TO ROME

I. The Voyage from Caesarea to Crete, Acts 27:1–8.
   A. The Ship's Personnel, vss. 1–2.
   B. The Officer's Treatment of Paul at Sidon, vs. 3.
   C. The Ship's Course from Sidon to Myra, vss. 4, 5.
   D. The Ship's Course from Myra to Fair Havens, vss. 6–8.

II. The Voyage from Crete to Malta, Acts 27:9–26.
   A. The Decision to Sail from Crete, vss. 9–12.
   B. The Storm at Sea, vss. 13–20.
   C. The Reassurance of Paul, vss. 21–26.

III. The Shipwreck at Malta, Acts 27: 27–44.
   A. The Surmise of Land, vss. 27, 28.
   B. The Sailors' Plan of Escape, vss. 29–32.
   C. The Seamen's Fast Broken, vss. 33–38.
   D. The Ship's Wreckage, vss. 39–41.
   E. The Passengers' Escape, vss. 42–44.

The presence of Luke with Paul at this juncture is evidenced by the author's resumption of the plural pronoun "we" (vs. 1). The last "We" section had dropped off upon the party's arrival at Jerusalem (cf. Acts 21: 18; Acts 16:10–17; 20:6–21:18 for other "We sections"). From that point to the present we have been left to conjecture the whereabouts of Luke and the other members of Paul's party, except for a single note concerning Trophimus (Acts 21:29).

I. THE VOYAGE FROM CAESAREA TO CRETE (27:1–8)

Here begins the most dramatic section of the entire Acts record. The account that follows is of special interest and importance for the light that it sheds upon ancient nautical terms and methods. The impression is received that the account of the entire voyage was written by an eyewitness, which impression is supported by the author's identification of himself with the party and the events by his use of the personal plural pronoun "we" almost throughout.

Bruce's comment is both interesting and instructive:

> Luke . . . viewed the sea through Greek eyes and tells us what he saw in unforgettable word-pictures. He could also draw upon a well-established literary tradition for the description of a storm and wreck at sea—not that this in any way depreciates the factual worth of his narrative. From Homer's *Odyssey* onwards, the account of a Mediterranean voyage in antiquity almost invariably included a storm or shipwreck. Homer, in fact, set the fashion in which such accounts continued to be related for many centuries. Luke himself has in this chapter one or two unmistakable Homeric reminiscences.[a]

Bruce[b] further suggests that Luke appears to have been influenced by the OT narrative of Jonah's "storm experience" on the Mediterranean. He notes that this voyage has

[1] *Op. cit.*, I, ii, 53.

[a] Bruce, *op. cit.*, p. 498. [b] *Ibid.*, pp. 498, 499.

2 And embarking in a ship of Adramyttium, which was about to sail unto the places on the coast of Asia, we put to sea, Aristarchus, a Macedonian of Thessalonica, being with us.

---

2 For *anēchthēmen*, **put to sea,** see on 13:13. The word occurs six times in connection with this voyage to Rome (27:2, 4, 12, 21; 28:10, 11). James Smith writes: "St. Luke, by his accurate use of nautical terms, gives great precision to his language, and expresses by a single word what would otherwise require several." [a]

---

afforded a rich source for the allegorical interpretation of the experiences, all the way from a comparison of life to a storm-wrought sea voyage to the figurative prediction of the course of church history through the ages. While there are dangerous pitfalls in such allegorical interpretation of the Scriptures, at the same time there are valid moral and spiritual lessons of great worth to be found in the account. Perhaps the example of Paul under the stress of adverse circumstances affords the greatest single source of instruction and encouragement to the Christian. Bruce states:

> . . . we have seen Paul in many rôles but here he stands erect as the practical man in a critical emergency. Not once or twice the world has had to thank the great saints and mystics for providing timely help in moments of crisis when realistic, practical men of affairs were unable to supply it.[c]

It has been noted that:

> The important features in the account are: first, the light it throws on the dominating personality of Paul who, prisoner though he is, exerts his influence at every crisis; and second, the sobriety of the narrative in spite of all its vividness.[d]

A. The Ship's Personnel (27:1, 2)

they delivered Paul and certain other prisoners to a centurion named Julius . . . Aristarchus . . . being with us. vss. 1, 2.

Both Ramsay[e] and Bruce[f] acknowledge heavy indebtedness to the work of James Smith[g] for "seafaring technicalities" in their treatment of Paul's voyage to Rome.

Presumably the Roman officials took the first opportunity to place Paul aboard a ship en route to Italy, along with **certain other prisoners** (vs. 1) who evidently were of a different class than Paul. Though they too may have appealed to Caesar, as Paul had,[h] Rackham regards them "not as appellants but criminals, condemned it may be to suffer their penalty in the games of the amphitheater . . . The word for *prisoner* is peculiar to this passage in the N.T.S. Paul was in bonds but not a (convicted) prisoner"[i] (cf. Luke 23:32 where "two 'other, malefactors' [were] led with him to be put to death"). Ramsay agrees with Rackham on the position of these **certain other prisoners.**

> He [Paul], of course, occupied a very different position from the other prisoners. He was a man of distinction, a Roman citizen who had appealed for trial to the supreme court in Rome. The others had been, in all probability, already condemned to death and were going to supply the perpetual demand which Rome made on the provinces for human victims to amuse the populace by their death in the arena.[j]

Reference to **the centurion named Julius, of the Augustan band** (vs. 1b), to whom Paul and the other prisoners were delivered, has long puzzled Bible scholars. Ramsay's conclusion appears to be the most satisfactory:

> It would naturally be a legionary centurion on detached service for communication between the Emperor and his armies in the provinces . . . That the centurion [Julius] to whom Luke alludes was one of this body is confirmed by the fact that, when he reached Rome, he handed Paul over to his chief. We conclude, then, that the "troops of the Emperor" was a popular colloquial way of describing the corps of officer couriers; and we thus gather from Acts an interesting fact, elsewhere unattested but in perfect conformity with the known facts.[k]

Macgregor cautiously concludes:

> Possibly the name was given to a body of imperial couriers, elsewhere called *frumentarii,* who were detailed for such duties as keeping open communications between the emperor and his provincial armies, controlling the commissariat, and conducting prisoners to Rome. It seems likely that one entrusted with such responsible duties as was Julius would belong rather to such a select corps than to a Syrian auxiliary cohort.[l]

[a] James Smith, *The Voyage and Shipwreck of St. Paul* (4th ed.; London: Longmans, Green, and Co., 1880), p. 61, n. 1.

[c] *Ibid.*, p. 499. [d] *The Interpreter's Bible*, IX, 331, 332.
[e] Ramsay, *Saint Paul the Traveller and the Roman Citizen*, p. 314. [f] Bruce, *loc. cit.*
[g] James Smith, *The Voyage and Shipwreck of St. Paul* (London: 1880, o.p.)
[h] Ellicott, *op. cit.*, VII, 170. [i] Rackham, *op. cit.*, 480. [j] Ramsay, *loc. cit.*
[k] *Ibid.*, p. 315. With this position, Rackham, *op. cit.*, p. 408; Bruce, *op. cit.*, 500; Ellicott, *loc. cit.*, and others agree.
[l] *The Interpreter's Bible*, IX, 332.

3 And the next day we touched at Sidon: and Julius treated Paul kindly, and gave him leave to go unto his friends and refresh himself.

---

3 *Katēchthēmen*, **touched,** is used alone by Luke as a nautical term, meaning "bring to land" (cf. 28:12; Luke 5:11). **Sidon** is 67 miles from Caesarea, which means that they made good time to arrive there **the next day.** Probably they were favored by the prevailing westerly winds of that season. **Sidon** had one of the best harbors on the Syrian coast.[3] It still has a good harbor, well protected by a breakwater.

Plumptre[m] interestingly suggests that possibly Julius and his band may have escorted Festus to his Judean province and that this was their return voyage to Rome. Could this have been a detachment of the 3,000 man bodyguard of the equestrian order recently formed by Nero and named Augustiani, which was assigned to accompany the emperor to the games and to applaud his public performances in the theater?

The port of embarkation is assumed to have been Caesarea. The ship which they boarded belonged to, and was bound for, Adramyttium, an important seaport of Mysia across the bay northeast of the island of Lebos and southeast of Troas. Adramyttium was situated on the old Roman road that passed from Assos and Troas to Pergamus, Ephesus, and Miletus. The gulf (Adramytti) still bears its ancient name. En route the ship was booked to call at certain **places on the coast of Asia** (vs. 2). Due to the difficulty of securing direct passage to Rome at that season, it may have been the original intention of Julius to sail to Adramyttium and from thence to Greece or more likely Macedonia, after which they would have proceeded overland, probably via the *Egnatian Way* to the Adriatic Sea.

The presence of Aristarchus of Macedonia (vs. 2; cf. Acts 19:29; 20:4; Col. 4:10; Philemon 24) as also of Luke, with Paul en route to Rome poses a problem which Ramsay holds can only be solved by allowing that they were permitted to accompany Paul as his personal slaves, "not merely performing the duties of slaves . . ., but actually passing as slaves."[n] Ramsay regards this as having greatly enhanced Paul's position with the Roman officer Julius. Bruce remarks that "Ramsay's argument merits the respect due to his great knowledge of social history in the Roman Empire of the first century A.D."[o] However, it might be suspected that Ramsay unconsciously read into the narrative more of the aristocratic cultural influence of the British society of his day than the known facts of the case would warrant. Aristarchus, who had accompanied Paul to Jerusalem from Macedonia (Acts 20:4), may have remained with Paul during the two years of his imprisonment at Caesarea and was now intending to return home, but due to changed plans in the sailing (vs. 6), went to Rome with Paul where he is later found sharing Paul's imprisonment, possibly still serving his comforts (Col. 4:10). Kraeling regards Aristarchus as "the diarist whose journal [was] used by Luke."[p] The total passenger complement of the ship is given later by Luke as 276 persons (vs. 37).

B. The Officer's Treatment of Paul at Sidon (27:3)

Julius treated Paul kindly, and gave him leave to go unto his friends and refresh himself.

The day following their embarkation the ship came to Sidon, some 20 miles north of Tyre. Here 40,000 people had perished in the flames of the city when it was destroyed by the Persian monarch Artaxerxes III in 351 B.C.

n the third century B.C. a new Hellenistic city had arisen under the Seleucids. By Paul's time it was a free city with its own municipal government and magistrates. It had become noted for its artists and scholars, especially in mathematics and astronomy. It was a chief center of wealth and trade, as well as of skilled workmen in glass and purple dyes. Thus it afforded a challenging opportunity for Christian evangelism and the development of a church. That the Christians had taken advantage of this

[3] *Ibid.*, p. 64, n. 3.

[m] Ellicott, *loc. cit.* [n] Ramsay, *op. cit.*, p. 316. [o] Bruce, *op. cit.*, p. 501. [p] Kraeling, *op. cit.*, p. 454.

4 And putting to sea from thence, we sailed under the lee of Cyprus, because the winds were contrary.

5 And when we had sailed across the sea which is off Cilicia and Pamphylia, we came to Myra, *a city* of Lycia.

Treated is the verb *chraomai*, which has this meaning only here in the New Testament. But Moulton and Milligan give several examples of this use in the papyri.[4] *Philanthrōpōs*, **kindly**, occurs only here in the New Testament. **Refresh himself** is literally "to obtain care" *(epimeleias*, only here in N.T.).

4 *Hypepleusamen*, **we sailed under the lee of**, is found (in N.T.) only here and in verse seven. They passed east of Cyprus,[5] though the direct route would have been west of that island.

5 **Off Cilicia and Pamphylia** they evidently zigzagged along the coast, tacking against the wind.[6] *Pelagos*, **sea**, is literally "the depth" (cf. Matt. 18:6, the only other place where it occurs in N.T.). *Diapleusantes* (only here in N.T.), **sailed across** is literally "sailed through." The Western text adds "for fifteen days," which Ropes favors as genuine.[7]

---

opportunity is evidenced by the Christian **friends** whom Paul visited in the city, and who were likely the fruit of the Gospel planted there more than a quarter of a century earlier (Acts 11:19). Sidon has a present population of about 10,000 people and is known by the French as Saidan but to Arabs as Saïda. Its ancient spacious harbor has been largely silted up.

Paul appears to have favorably impressed Julius (cf. Acts 18:14–16; 19:31, 37) who treated him philanthropically, though he was in custody.

The friends to whom Paul went at Sidon were, according to Harnack,[q] Christian believers. Harnack thinks **friends** may have been one of the current names by which Christians greeted one another in Paul's day (cf. John 15:14, 15; III John 14). The church at Sidon likely originated with the witness of the scattered disciples following the martyrdom of Stephen (Acts 11:19). In addition to the mutual spiritual edification and encouragement shared by Paul and the Sidon Christians, they likely contributed to his personal comfort in food and clothing for the voyage, which would have been welcomed by Paul after a two-year imprisonment. He was most likely in the custody of a soldier while ashore.

C. The Ship's Course from Sidon to Myra (27:4, 5)

And putting to sea from thence . . . we came to Myra, a city of Lycia, vss. 4a, 5b.

En route from Patara to Tyre two years earlier, the vessel on which Paul and his companions sailed passed by a direct course across the eastern Mediterranean (Acts 21:1–3). Ramsay[r] holds that while it was common for vessels to follow this course eastward it was hardly possible for them to return thus, for there was seldom a steady easterly wind that could be trusted for such a voyage. The westerly breezes were constant throughout the summer months, and consequently the westward-bound vessels sailed northward east of Cyprus and from thence westward along the coast of Asia Minor leaving Cyprus on the south. Since Luke explains the reason for the course followed (vs. 4b), Ramsay[s] considers it evident that he was a stranger to the sea and had expected that the vessel should have followed the direct course taken from Myra to Sidon two years earlier. However, it may be legitimately questioned whether Luke may not have made his explanation, **because the winds were contrary** (vs. 4b), in the interest of his uninformed readers, rather than as an expression of his personal surprise. The ship moved along the coasts of Cilicia and Pamphylia, aided by the local offshore breezes and a steady westward coastal current. "The Adramyttian ship," says Ramsay, "crept on from point to point up the coast, taking advantage of every opportunity to make a few miles, and lying at anchor in the shelter of the winding coast, when the westerly wind made progress impossible."[t]

[4] VGT, p. 690. [5] James Smith, *op. cit.*, pp. 66–68.
[6] See the map in James Smith, *op. cit.*, opposite p. 61. [7] *Beginnings*, III, 241.

[q] Adolph Harnack, *op. cit.*, I, 419 f. [r] Ramsay, *op. cit.*, pp. 316, 317.
[s] *Ibid.*, 316, 317. [t] *Ibid.*, p. 317.

6 And there the centurion found a ship of Alexandria sailing for Italy; and he put us therein.

---

6 Ramsay, in his very comprehensive article "Roads and Travel (in N.T.)," says that ships of that day would never attempt to go straight across from Egypt to Italy. Instead they would work their way to Myra, which was due north of **Alexandria.** Then a northerly wind would take them to Sicily, and by manipulating carefully in a west wind, they could reach the west coast of Italy.[8]

Enebibasen, **he put,** is found only here in the New Testament. It is one of Luke's many nautical terms.

One authority notes that Luke's expression, **sailed across** (vs. 5), "seems to imply that after a time they ceased to hug the coast and cut across from point to point presumably from the southwest point of **Cilicia** to the promontory of Lycia just east of **Myra,** across the great bay made by the coast of **Pamphylia.**"[u]

After fifteen days[v] of sailing they reached the harbor of Myra, which was the great port for Syrian and Egyptian commerce. The city of Myra, a port of Lycia, on the most southerly point of Asia, was located some two miles inland from the harbor. Ramsay states that Myra was "the seat of the sailors' god."[w]

The site of the ancient city is marked by ruins of the theater, an aqueduct, rock tombs and other buildings.

Conybeare and Howson relate concerning Myra: "In the seclusion of the deep gorge of Dembra is a magnificent Byzantine church, - probably the cathedral of the diocese, when Myra was the ecclesiastical and political metropolis of Lycia."[x] Thus it would appear that eventually Christianity made its impact upon the city whose honor had been stolen from Paul and the Gospel by St. Nicholas, the patron saint of the Greek sailors, who had been born at Patara and was buried at Myra.

D. The Ship's Course from Myra to Fair Havens (27:6–8)

If Julius' plan had originally been to sail to Macedonia and from there to take the overland route to the Adriatic, then his plans were changed at Myra in favor of a continued sea voyage direct to Italy. What may have changed his plans can only be conjectured. Plumptre thinks it may have been the presence of an Alexandrian grain ship bound for Rome, in the harbor of Myra upon their arrival, that offered:

> An easier and more expeditious route to go straight to Rome, instead of landing at Myra, and then taking another ship to Macedonia in order to journey by land to the coast of the Adriatic. A local inscription describes Myra as a "horrea," or store-house of corn . . . and the Alexandrian ship may therefore have gone thither to discharge part of its cargo.[y]

Plumptre thinks that this ship had been driven out of its course by a strong westerly wind (an argument that does not seem consistent with his account otherwise) en route from Alexandria to Rome. Ramsay considers such a conclusion both "unnecessary and incorrect."[z] He holds rather that it was on its "regular and ordinary course" and had likely experienced favorable sailing. The colossal city of Rome had by this time become largely dependent upon foreign markets, of which Egypt was chief, for her corn (wheat) supply, and consequently such government grain vessels were common on the sea and in the ports between Alexandria and Rome by this time. If this was a government-owned grainship, then it is quite understandable that Julius should have requisitioned passage to Rome for himself, his troops, and the prisoners. These vessels which carried grain "were of a specially large build,"[a] and consequently such a ship could have accommodated so large a passenger complement as 276 people (vs. 38).[b]

Troubles began when the Alexandrian

[8] HDB, V, 379–381.

[u] *The Interpreter's Bible,* IX, 333.
[v] Rackham, *op. cit.,* p. 481.
[w] Ramsay, *op. cit.,* p. 298. For further description of eastern Mediterranean sailing in relation to Myra, see *Ibid.,* pp. 298, 316–319, 399.
[x] Conybeare and Howson, *op. cit.,* p. 691.
[y] Ellicott *op. cit.,* VII, 171.
[z] Ramsay, *op. cit.,* p. 319—For an interesting description of a wind-driven ship by Lucian in his dialogue *The Ship,* see *Ibid.,* pp. 319, 320.
[a] Rackham, *op. cit.,* p. 482.
[b] One of these ships, that of Lucian, has been described as 180 feet by 45 feet with a calculated tonnage of about 1200. James Hastings, ed., *Dictionary of the Bible,* p. 851.

7 And when we had sailed slowly many days, and were come with difficulty over against Cnidus, the wind not further suffering us, we sailed under the lee of Crete, over against Salmone;

---

7 *Bradyplоountes*, **when we had sailed slowly**, is likewise a (N.T.) *hapax legomenon*. James Smith lists seven compounds of *pleō*,[9] all of them used as nautical terms only by Luke.[10] The verb *proseaō* is another *hapax legomenon*. It means "permit further."

---

ship set sail from Myra for Cnidus. The difficulties encountered were occasioned by the strong northwesterly Etesian gales which prevail in those regions during late July and throughout August. The **many days** (vs. 7) of slow sailing consumed about 25 days, for the distance of about 130 miles,[c] which with favorable weather could have been done in a day. The lateness of the season likely accounted for their not having put in port at Cnidus to wait for better weather. Though Cnidus appears to have been too far north for their course, it is evident that the coast afforded them protection from the northerly wind and enabled the ship to sail more southerly toward Crete than otherwise possible, while at the same time keeping clear of the treacherous northern coast of Rhodes.

Cnidus was located on a peninsula on the southwest coast of Asia Minor with a harbor on either side. Since the coast of Asia Minor bends away northward here, they were exposed to the full force of the Etesian (periodical or annual Mediterranean) winds. Thus the impossibility of "heading" these winds disposed the ship's captain to take the only course open and sail southward with a view to coming under the lee of the coast of Crete, which is modernly known as Candia. From Cape Salmone at the eastern tip of the island they sailed with difficulty, but with some protection, westward under the lee of the coast until they came to the harbor known as Fair Havens, near the city of Lasia where they remained for some time. Fair Havens was a small bay lying east of Cape Matalda. It is still known by this name.

Concerning the island of Crete, Souther remarks:

> Crete, the modern Candia, is an island 60 miles S. of Greece proper, about 150 miles long, and varying in breadth from 30 to 7 miles, with mountains as high as 8000 feet. It is about equidistant from Europe, Asia, and Africa, and was inhabited from the earliest times of which we have any knowledge.
>
> . . . The epithets which a native of the island, the poet Epimenides (flourished B.C. 600), flung at the Cretans, are quoted in a somewhat unapostolic manner in the Epistle to Titus (1:12). Epimenides styled them 'always liars, evil beasts of prey, lazy gluttons.'[d]

The record of Christianity in Crete is somewhat obscure. We know that there were Cretan Jews present at Pentecost (Acts 2:11), and it is likely that some of them were converted (Acts 2:37–42) and carried the Christian faith back to their island with them. In any event, Christianity seems to have been well established in the island in the first century. That Titus was placed here by Paul to superintend the churches of the island, we learn from Paul's letter to Titus (Titus 1:4–9). Further, the considerable extent of Christianity by the time of this epistle (*ca.* A.D. 65) is indicated by Paul's instructions, "ordain elders in every city, as I had appointed thee" (Titus 1:5b). How many cities there were we are not told, but Hurlbut[e] lists eighteen towns in all on the island, three of which are on the west end, eight on the north side, five on the south side, and two in the interior. So if Paul's words to Titus (1:5) are to be taken literally, the Christian community on Crete must have been considerable. Both the influence of Judaizing Christianity on the native Cretans and the influence of pagan Cretan culture on the Christians becomes apparent from Paul's letter to Titus. That there were Christians here when Paul was en route to Rome seems evident, but there is no indication that Paul made contact with them at Fair Havens, as he did at Tyre (Acts 21:4) and Sidon (vs. 3).

There is no evidence that Paul founded

[9] Besides *pleo* itself. [10] *Op. cit.*, p. 28.

[c] Kraeling, *op. cit.*, p. 455. [d] Hastings, *op. cit.*, p. 166.
[e] Jesse L. Hurlbut, *Bible Atlas* (Chicago: Rand McNally Publishers, rev. ed., 1910), "map," p. 132.

8 and with difficulty coasting along it we came unto a certain place called Fair Havens: nigh whereunto was the city of Lasea.

8 **Coasting,** *paralegomenoi,* suggests "going along the coast." The verb literally means "lie beside." It occurs (in N.T.) only here and in verse 13, where it is translated "sailed along." **Fair Havens** is not mentioned by any other ancient writer.[11]

the church on Crete, although he may have reorganized it. At all events, it is evident that he visited the island at a time other than on his voyage to Rome, that he was acquainted with the Christian community there (Titus 1:5), and that Titus was with him, whom he left in charge of the churches of Crete, not as a bishop but as a superintendent (Titus 1:5). From A.D. 54 or 55 (see II Cor. 7:5–16; 8:16–24), nothing is known of Titus until following Paul's release from his first Roman imprisonment, or perhaps until after Paul had written I Timothy in about A.D. 64 or 65. It appears to have been at this time that he accompanied Paul to visit the Christians of Crete. Paul subsequently promised to send Artemas or Tychicus to Crete to relieve Titus, at which time Titus was instructed to join Paul to winter at Nicopolis (Titus 3:12). Further, it seems evident that Titus was with Paul in his second Roman imprisonment and that Paul sent him to Dalmatia on an errand (II Tim. 4:10).

Regarding the epistle to Titus as a commentary on the church in Crete, three things become evident. *First,* false teachers, especially a branch of Judaizers, were doing a damaging work. They stressed Jewish ceremonials such as circumcision, taught Jewish fables, laid down the commandments of men, raised and discussed foolish questions, contended about genealogies, and strove about technical points of the Jewish law. *Second,* Paul wrote to instruct Titus concerning the organization and direction of the church and to offer his personal encouragement for his difficult task. *Third,* Paul sent his letter to Titus by the hands of Zenas and Apollos who had evidently planned a missionary journey to Crete, possibly as Apollos had gone from Ephesus to Corinth to edify the church there (Acts 18:24–28).

There appears a slight indication that Paul may have joined Apollos at Corinth on his third missionary journey and there have sent the Epistle to Titus by Apollos and Zenas (cf. I Cor. 16:12), in which event Paul would have visited Crete with Titus, at an earlier date, possibly from Corinth on his second missionary journey. In that case Paul might have had one of his three previous shipwrecks en route to, or returning from, Crete (cf. II Cor. 11:25). Such an hypothesis could account for Paul's apparent knowledge of the hazards of sailing in the region of Crete (see Acts 27:9, 10). However, scholars have generally noted the similarity of the style of Titus to I Timothy and have dated the epistle at about A.D. 65. Theissen summarizes Paul's purpose and plan in the writing of Titus.[f]

II. THE VOYAGE FROM CRETE TO MALTA (27:9–26)

Luke's notation that the **Fast was now already gone by** (vs. 9) is a chronological landmark for Paul's voyage to Rome. Kraeling[g] and Bruce[h] agree with Ramsay (as also many other scholars) that this **Fast** or "The Great Day of Atonement," fell on October 5 in 59 A.D., and that as Paul and Aristarchus observed this occasion, Luke used it as a mark of time. Ramsay[i] further notes that September 14 to November 11 was a dangerous season for navigation, and from November 11 to March 15 it appears that all open-sea sailing was discontinued. Ramsay thinks the ship reached Fair Havens in late September and did not leave until after October 5.

Bruce succinctly treats this chronological problem thus:

> By the 'Fast' he [Luke] means, of course, the Great Day of Atonement, which falls on Tishri

[11] *Beginnings,* IV, 328.

[f] Henry Clarence Thiessen, *Introduction to the New Testament* (Grand Rapids: Wm. B. Eerdmans Publishing Company, 1943), pp. 266, 267.

[g] Kraeling, *op. cit.,* p. 455. [h] Bruce, *op. cit.,* p. 506. [i] Ramsay, *op. cit.,* p. 322.

9 And when much time was spent, and the voyage was now dangerous, because the Fast was now already gone by, Paul admonished them,
10 and said unto them, Sirs, I perceive that the voyage will be with injury and much loss, not only of the lading and the ship, but also of our lives.

---

9 *Episphalous*, **dangerous**, is found only here in the New Testament. It literally means "prone to fall." [12] **Admonished** is the verb *paraineō*, which occurs only here and in verse 22 ("exhort"). The meaning ranges from "advise, recommend" to "exhort, urge."

10 **Injury** is the word *hybris*, found only here, in verse 21, and in II Corinthians 12:10. *Phortiou*, **lading**, is literally "burden, load," from *pherō*, "bear, carry." [13] **Lives** is *psychōn*, the primary meaning of which is "souls." But, as in English, "souls" often means "persons."

---

10. Luke's remark has point only if that date fell rather late in the solar calendar that year. In A.D. 59 it fell on October 5, but in all the neighbouring years from A.D. 57 to 63 it fell earlier. A late date for the Day of Atonement is required also by the subsequent time notes of the journey to Italy. When they set sail from Fair Havens, fifty or sixty miles brought them under the lee of Candia (v. 16): on the fourteenth night from Candia (V. 27) they drew near land, and the following day (V. 39) they landed on Malta, where they spent three months (Ch. 28:11). The seas were closed to sailing until the beginning of February at the earliest; the three months spent in Malta must therefore have corresponded roughly to November, December and January; they must have left Fair Havens not much earlier than mid-October. The solar date of the Day of Atonement in A.D. 59 thus accords well with Luke's implication that the Fast took place while they were at Fair Havens.[j]

A. The Decision to Sail from Crete (27:9-12)

The more part advised to put to sea from thence, vs. 12.

Paul's experience in ocean travel was more extensive than may appear on the surface of the Acts record (cf. II Cor. 11:25, 26). Thus he felt confident and made bold to offer advice against sailing from Fair Havens (vs. 9b). However, Julius, who appears to have made the decision (vs. 11), took the advice of the ship's master who wished to proceed to the more commodious harbor of Phoenix near the western end of Crete for wintering quarters (vs. 12). Ramsay[k] suggests that a council was held to consider the advisability of sailing and that Paul was consulted as a man of rank and travel experience. Ramsay[l] goes on to argue that the evidence is conclusive that there was an "official council" at which Julius presided and that this fact, plus his final and official decision to sail, indicates that they were sailing on a government ship on which a high-ranking military officer such as Julius, rather than the master of the ship, would have had the final decision to make. Rome's absolute dependence upon grain from the foreign ports to feed and passify the urban masses made it imperative that the government own and control these merchant vessels. Further, Ramsay thinks, this naturally placed matters of decisions for movement and directions of such grain ships under military or naval officers (which were not at that time distinct) rather than the sea captains, though such authority did not extend to navigation as such. This vessel, Ramsay believes, belonged to the "Alexandrian fleet in the Imperial service." The problem of **the owner of the ship** (vs. 11) Ramsay[m] resolves by rejecting the rendering as incorrect, both in the KJV and the RV. Indeed Williams' translation would allow Ramsay's position where it reads, "But the colonel was influenced by the pilot and the captain of the ship rather than by what Paul said"[n] (vs. 11). Similarly Phillip's version reads: "But Julius paid more attention to the helmsman and the captain than to Paul's words of warning."[o]

"The harbor of Phoenix or Phenice," says Kraeling, "was forty geographical miles farther up the Cretan coast. It was better protected and in every way more attractive, and there was reasonable hope of being able to make it in a few hours under favourable circumstances."[p] A southerly breeze

[12] Abbott-Smith, *op. cit.*, p. 175.
[13] The Received Text has *phortos*, not found elsewhere in the New Testament.

[j] Bruce, *op. cit.*, p. 506. [k] Ramsay, *op. cit.*, 323. [l] *Ibid.*, pp. 323–326. [m] *Ibid.*, p. 324.
[n] Williams, *op. cit.*, p. 323. [o] Phillips, *op. cit.*, p. 70. [p] Kraeling, *op. cit.*, p. 455.

11 But the centurion gave more heed to the master and to the owner of the ship, than to those things which were spoken by Paul.

12 And because the haven was not commodious to winter in, the more part advised to put to sea from thence, if by any means they could reach Phoenix, and winter *there; which is* a haven of Crete, looking north-east and south-east.

---

11 **Master** is the word *kybernētēs*, which means "steersman, pilot" [14] and is used figuratively by Philo for God as Pilot.[15] The word occurs (in N.T.) only here and in Revelation 18:17. **Owner of the ship** is *nauklēros*, found only here in the New Testament. Although Arndt and Gingrich give the meaning "ship-owner" they add: "But it can also mean *captain*, since the sailing-master of a ship engaged in state service was called a *nauklēros*." [16] Moulton and Milligan insist on the latter rendering.[17]

12 *Limenos*, **haven**, occurs (in N.T.) only in this verse and in the eighth (as part of the name Fair Havens). *Aneuthetou*, **not commodious** (only here in N.T.) literally means "not well placed." **Phoenix** is "one of the many place-names showing the extent of Phoenician influence in ancient times." [18]

The expression **looking north-east and south-east** has caused a great deal of discussion. The Greek literally means "down the southwest wind and down the northwest wind" (ASV margin; cf. KJV). The confusion of interpretation is well illustrated in the Revised Standard Version, which in the text reads "northeast and southeast" but in the margin "southwest and northwest." Obviously the correct meaning is uncertain.

Thayer notes that *lips* (only here in N.T.) is used for southwest wind in Herodotus and Polybius.[19] But Deissmann calls attention to the fact that in the Septuagint *lips* three times means *west* and elsewhere *south*.[20] The former meaning is found clearly in the Egyptian papyri, probably due to the fact that Libya lies west of Egypt.[21] But since Libya is *southwest* of Greece, the word carries that sense in Greek writers. *Chōros* (from Latin *corus)*, meaning "northwest wind," "appears not to be found elsewhere in Greek." [22]

The reason for the Revised rendering is apparently to be found in James Smith's explanation of *kata liba kai kata chōron*. With regard to *kata* he says: "I apprehend it means '*in the same direction as*'; if I am right, *bleponta kata liba* does not mean, as is generally supposed, that it is open to the point *from* which that wind blows, but to the point *towards* which it blows—that is, it is not open to the south-west but to the north-east." [23] For this reason he prefers Lutro, on the east side of the promontory Muros, rather than Phineka on the west side.[24]

---

bade fair for their voyage, and so they set sail, with difficulty rounding Cape Matala, which cape projects south six miles, and then entered the Gulf of Messara.

Concerning Julius' acceptance of the master's advice rather than Paul's, Wesley remarks: "And indeed it is a general rule, Believe an artificer in his own art. Yet when there is the greatest need, a real Christian will often advise even better than him."[q] How well advised would governmental administrators often be if they consulted the judgment of experienced God-fearing missionaries, though their training might not have been in the technicalities of administration. Here is a case in which "the wish became the father of the deed." Though the decision of **the more part** (vs. 12) or the majority carried, subsequent events proved the minority judgment and advice to have been right. There is hardly sufficient historical evidence that majority decisions have always been right and minorities wrong. Especially are majority decisions dangerous when they have been motivated by selfish desires, as is so often the case. Plumptre sees in Paul's admonition (vs. 9), "The tone . . . of a man who speaks more from the foresight gained by observation than from a direct, supernatural prediction."[r] In fact,

[14] Frequently so in the papyri (VGT, p. 363). [15] Arndt and Gingrich, *op. cit.*, p. 457.
[16] *Ibid.*, p. 536. [17] VGT, p. 422. [18] Bruce, *Acts*, p. 457. [19] *Op. cit.*, pp. 378 f.
[20] *Bible Studies*, pp. 141 f. [21] VGT, p. 377. So it may be that the harbor looked west and northwest (*ibid.*).
[22] *Beginnings*, V, 343. [23] *Op. cit.*, p. 88. [24] See map, *op. cit.*, opposite p. 97.

[q] Wesley, *op. cit.*, p. 405, n. 11. [r] Ellicott, *op. cit.*, VII, 172.

13 And when the south wind blew softly, supposing that they had obtained their purpose, they weighed anchor and sailed along Crete, close in shore.

Lake and Cadbury take issue with this interpretation. They write: "Thus in Acts xxvii, 12 *kata liba* either means west or west with a tendency to south, and *kata chōron* ought to mean west with a tendency to north."[25] They add that this "suits the harbour of Phineka in Crete fairly well."[26] In their commentary note, however, they leave the question more open.[27]

Hackett argues strongly for a haven facing west and notes that **looking** "implies, certainly, that the wind and the harbor confronted each other, and not that they were turned from each other."[28] It seems best to accept Phineka as the most likely identification, in spite of the fact that the three Revised versions have all followed James Smith.

13 *Hypopneusantos*, **blew softly,** is another compound of *pneō*, found only here in the New Testament. Literally the verb means "blow underneath," and so "blow gently." *Arantes*, **weighed anchor,** is simply "having taken up." Thayer,[29] Arndt and Gingrich,[30] Ramsay,[31] and others support the Revised rendering. James Smith would translate it either "weighed" or "set sail."[32] But Lake and Cadbury write: "An apparently intransitive or absolute use is well attested in contemporary and earlier Greek with the meaning of starting out on journeys by land . . . as well as those by sea."[33] So Bruce translates it, "having set out"[34] (cf. KJV). *Asson*, **close in shore,** is a literary form found only here in the New Testament.

Bruce quotes James Smith as saying, "the prudence of the advice given by the masters and owners was extremely questionable and that the advice given by St. Paul may probably be supported even on nautical grounds."[s] Beside his previous sea and shipwreck experiences, Paul evidenced an acquaintance with Crete itself in his Epistle to Titus, though it is not known for certain when he acquired that knowledge, as the epistle was written at a later date. Paul speaks in warning of the loss of the precious cargo of grain, as also of the more precious lives of the passengers. The former prediction was fulfilled, but by divine intervention the latter was averted (see vs. 20).

On the problem of **A haven of Crete, looking northeast and southeast** (vs. 1), Bruce remarks:

> But it is not necessary to suppose that any mistake was made. A short distance west of Lutro, on the other side of the peninsula of Muros, lies Phineka, which evidently preserves the ancient name Phoenix. Phineka lies open to the westerly wind and may have had quite a good harbour in the first century; the two streams shown as entering the bay in its vicinity may have silted up in the course of the centuries.[t]

Dummelow's explanation is both clear and simple: "The bay or harbour formed a semicircle, of which one half looked SW. and the other half NW."[u]

B. The Storm at Sea (27:13-20)

no small tempest lay upon us, all hope that we should be saved was now taken away, vs. 20b.

Luke makes a sharp distinction between the opinionated decision of Julius and the seamen to sail from Fair Havens, and the studied sober judgment of Paul that safety required them to remain in port. Such is suggested by his placement of responsibility for sailing upon "them": **supposing that "they" had obtained "their" purpose, "they" weighed anchor and sailed** (vs. 13). Previously, as later, Luke identifies Paul and his party with the movements of the ship by the use of the pronouns **we** and **us** (see vss. 1-5, 7, 8). Here however, the picture has changed and "**they**" venture forth against the sober advice and warnings of the man of God and the lessons that nature itself should have taught them. Such presumptiveness is always dangerous and is certain to carry its own

[25] "The Winds," *Beginnings*, V, 343. [26] *Ibid.*, p. 343. [27] *Beginnings*, IV, 330.
[28] *Op. cit.*, p. 297. [29] *Op. cit.*, p. 16. [30] *Op. cit.*, p. 23.
[31] *St. Paul the Traveller*, p. 326. [32] *Op. cit.*, p. 97.
[33] *Beginnings*, IV, 330. Both meanings are illustrated in Josephus (Ant. II, 1, 3; XIII, 4, 3).
[34] *Acts*, p. 458.

[s] James Smith, *op. cit.*, p. 85 n., as quoted by Bruce, *op. cit.*, p. 507.
[t] Bruce, *op. cit.*, p. 508. [u] Dummelow, *op. cit.*, p. 852.

14 But after no long time there beat down from it a tempestuous wind, which is called Euraquilo:

15 and when the ship was caught, and could not face the wind, we gave way *to it*, and were driven.

---

14 **Tempestuous** is *typhōnikos* (only here in N.T.). It comes from *typhōn*, "typhoon, hurricane." *Eurakylōn*, **Euraquilo,** has better support than *euroklydōn*, "Euroclydon" (KJV).[35] The former has not been found elsewhere, but it is evidently a compound of the Greek *euros*, east wind, and the Latin *aquilo*, north wind. Both this and *chōros* (vs. 12) are Latinisms that may have been due to the influence of the Italian soldiers on board.

15 **Caught** is a strong compound, *synarpazō*, meaning "to seize and carry away." [36] *Antophthalmein* is found only here in the New Testament. It means "to look in the face," and so metaphorically "to face, withstand." As one of Luke's many nautical terms it means "to beat up against," [37] or "head up." [38] *Epidontes*, **gave way,** has this sense only here in the New Testament. *Epherometha*, **were driven,** is literally "were borne or carried."

---

reward. Nor would Paul bear responsibility for conduct which was against his own best judgment and advice. The necessity of circumstances demanded that he accompany the ship on its ill-fated course, but he could not commit himself to a course of action which he foresaw would be disastrous.

They found slight circumstantial confirmation for their decision in a gentle south wind which arose and promised to bring them safely on to their desired haven at Phoenix. However, this temporary breeze proved only to be as the miraged lake on the burning desert sands that lures the thirst-mad traveller on, only to vanish, leaving him in disillusionment and deeper despair of hopelessness. Luke's statement that they **sailed along Crete, close in shore** (vs. 13b) suggests how little they trusted the out-of-season **south wind** which promised to take them to their destination. The rounding of Cape Matala threatened to be their greatest danger. However, this was accomplished without incident, and from thence they hopefully charted a course across the gulf of Messara to Phoenix. Erelong their rising hopes of reaching Phoenix some seventeen miles across the bay were dashed to pieces by the sudden conversion of the promising south wind into the **tempestuous Euraquilo** or "Levanter," (vs. 14) which **beat down** upon them from the 7000-foot Mount Ida of legendary fame. Ramsay calls it "a sudden eddying squall,"[v] but Luke describes it as a "typhonic wind" suggesting "the whirling motion of the clouds and sea caused by the meeting of contrary currents of air. From this derives our English typhoon."[w]

"The sailors recognized this wind as an old enemy and had a name for it – Euraquilo."[x] Having passed Cape Matala, they lost the further protection of the coast line which they had thus far closely followed (vs. 13b). Consequently as **the ship was caught, and could not face the wind, we gave way to it and were driven** (vs. 15b). Kraeling vividly describes the incident that followed thus:

> The ship with a single large sail which could not be slackened quickly was in great peril. They drifted with starboard toward the wind until they got into calmer water under the shelter of an island named Gauda or Clauda (Gozzo), [or the modern Gavdho] some twenty-three miles to the south. Here they were able to take refuge. The waterlogged lifeboat or the "dinghy" which they had been towing, was got aboard, a hard job ['with difficulty', says Luke, probably remembering his blisters] in which the diarist seems to have helped. [There were certain jobs which only trained members of the crew could carry out, but any landlubber could haul on a rope and some of the passengers were pressed into service]. The ship was then undergirded with ropes to reinforce her, lest she break apart from the strain caused by shifting cargo. This could be done by lowering a cable under the hull in U-shaped manner, drawing it along both sides to the center and fastening it there.[y]

35 Aleph A B against H L P. See further James Smith, *op. cit.*, pp. 159–161.
36 Abbott-Smith, *op. cit.*, p. 426. 37 *Ibid.*, p. 42. 38 *Beginnings*, IV, 331.

v Ramsay, *op. cit.*, p. 327.
w Pliny the Elder describes this as the chief plague of sailors, "not only breaking up the spars but the hull itself." Pliny, *Natural History*, II, 132. x Bruce, *op. cit.*, p. 509. y Kraeling, *op. cit.*, p. 456.

16 And running under the lee of a small island called Cauda, we were able, with difficulty, to secure the boat:

17 and when they had hoisted it up, they used helps, under-girding the ship; and, fearing lest they should be cast upon the Syrtis, they lowered the gear, and so were driven.

---

16 *Hypodramontes*, **running under the lee of,** occurs only here in the New Testament, as does *nēsion*, **a small island. Cauda** is the reading of Vaticanus, whereas Sinaiticus originally had *Klauda*. Lake and Cadbury think that "*Kauda* may be the Latin and *Klauda* the Alexandrian form." [39] The name of the island today is *Gaudo* in Greek and Gozzo in Italian. **To secure** is *perikrateis genesthai*. The former word is found only here in the New Testament and means "having full command of."

Schaphēs, **boat,** occurs (in N.T.) only in this chapter (cf. vss. 30, 32). It literally means "something scooped out," and so signifies a light boat or skiff.

17 *Boētheiais*, **helps,** found elsewhere in the New Testament only in Hebrews 4:16, is here a technical nautical term meaning "frapping." [40] Hobart quotes a passage from Aristotle *(Rhetorica* II, 5) in which this noun signifies gear used on board ship during storms at sea.[41] *Hypozōnnyntes*, **undergirding,** (only here in N.T.) may also be translated "frapping." Cadbury has a long, detailed note on the meaning of the cognate noun, *hypozōmata*.[42] He thinks it probably referred to vertical exterior bands. He writes: "The planks ran lengthwise of the ship's hull, and a rope passed under the keel and fastened either at the gunwale on opposite sides, or joined on deck and pulled tight by twisting, or by a windlass, would hold the planks as the hoops hold the staves of a barrel." [43]

Chalasantes, **lowering,** is used of lowering Paul from the wall at Damascus (9:25). It occurs again in verse 30, of lowering the lifeboat. As to the meaning here, Smith says: "Every ship situated as this one was, when preparing for a storm, sends down upon the deck the 'top-hamper,' or gear connected with the fair-weather sails, such as the . . . top-sails.[44]

Vivid as is Kraeling's description, there remains some doubt as to the exact nature of the operation suggested by Luke in verse seventeen. Macgregor offers the following possible explanations. This authority questions the afore-described operation and then asks:

> Or (b), [were they] undergirders of ropes or chains stretched across the ship's hold under the deck and made fast to one of the stout ribs on each side? Or (c), as shown in ancient pictures of Egyptian ship rope trusses, 'stretched above decks from stern to stem intended to prevent the boat from breaking its back amid-ship by binding the stern and stem together'? . . . The last suggestion is attractive because such trusses were kept taut by being raised from the deck by props—which might well be the function of the **helps.**[z]

Kraeling's view appears the more likely as his description of **the helps** accords with Bruce's[a] identification of **the helps** with the "undergirders," or "frapping cables," nautical terms attested by Aristotle, Philo, and Josephus. The practice is sometimes followed by modern seamen and is called "frapping."[b] Plumptre sees an allusion to this practice in the lines of Horace (Od. 1:14), which he translates thus "['And scarcely can our keels keep sound, e'en with the ropes that gird them round and against the imperious wave']."[c]

Why the ship did not attempt to find refuge at Cauda Luke does not say, but it is assumed that there may have been no harbor available there.

A new fear arose with the seamen lest the **Euraquilo** should drive them on the Syrtis (vs. 17b). The Syrtis was a great stretch of sand-banks along the coast of Cyrene and Carthage, Africa, the major one to the southwest of Cauda, and directly toward which the wind was blowing. Kraeling remarks: "The Syrtes were two areas on the coast of Africa – the westerly one being the Syrtis Minor and the easterly one the

[39] *Ibid.*, p. 332. [40] Abbott-Smith, *op. cit.*, p. 83. [41] *Op. cit.*, p. 274.
[42] *Beginnings*, V, 345-354. [43] *Ibid.*, p. 348. [44] James Smith, *op. cit.*, p. 111.

[z] *The Interpreter's Bible*, IX, 336. See also H. J. Cadbury, *The Beginnings of Christianity* (New York: Macmillan and Company, 1920), pt. II, vol. V, 351.
[a] Bruce, *op. cit.*, p. 509, n. 38. [b] Dummelow, *loc. cit.* [c] Ellicott, *op. cit.*, VII, 173.

18 And as we labored exceedingly with the storm, the next day they began to throw *the freight* overboard;
19 and the third day they cast out with their own hands the tackling of the ship.
20 And when neither sun nor stars shone upon *us* for many days, and no small tempest lay on *us*, all hope that we should be saved was now taken away.

---

18 *Cheimazomenon*, **labored . . . with the storm,** and *sphodrōs*, **exceedingly,** are both found only here in the New Testament. The former is from *cheima*, "winter cold," and so literally means "to expose to winter cold," but here "to be driven with storm."[45] The phrase might be translated "as we were exceedingly tempest-tossed" (cf. RSV, "violently storm-tossed"). **They began to throw the freight overboard** is literally "they were doing a throwing out" *(ekbolēn epoiounto)*. The former word (fr. *ekballō)* is found only here in the New Testament.

19 *Autocheires*, **with their own hands,** and *skeuēn*, **tackling,** both occur only here in the New Testament. The latter is closely akin to *skeuos*, "gear" (vs. 17).

20 *Cheimōnos*, **tempest,** is literally "winter" (see on vs. 18). It then came to mean a winter storm and finally any storm or tempest. **Taken away** is the verb *periaireō*, which here means "to take away entirely."[46]

Syrtis Major; both were greatly feared by ancient navigators."[d] And Dummelow cites Farrar as authority that "The 'Greater Syrtis,' 'the Goodwin Sands of the Mediterranean' . . . lay to the SW of Cauda."[e]

Luke's expression, **they lowered the gear, and so were driven** (vs. 17b), may be best understood in Dummelow's words, "They probably lowered the main sail more than halfway, but left the sail 'artemon' or storm sail extended."[f] Phillips renders the passage, "so they shortened sail and lay to drifting,"[g] and Williams says, "they lowered the sail and let her drift."[h] According to Ramsay, the ship drifted with her bow to the north, held on course by a low sail "making leeway proportionate to the power of the wind and waves on her broadside."[i] Kraeling describes the operations at this point in vivid, nautical terminology:

> Precautions were taken to reduce the hazards by 'straking sail,' or 'lowering the gear.' This meaning getting flat on the deck every bit of fair-weather sailing equipment such as spars, rigging, sails, etc. But this precaution was not enough to keep Paul's ship from being blown southward. A ship in this situation had either to scud or heave to. The former was out of the question, since that would have taken them to the Syrtis. They had to heave to with some storm-sail set. This was necessary to keep her on the starboard track in order to hold a course west of north.[j]

Ramsay cites James Smith as authority that the resultant speed would vary, depending upon the size of the vessel and the velocity of the wind, from three-fourths to two miles per hour, with a likely mean rate of about one and one-half miles per hour. The direction, he thinks, would have been eight degrees north of west. Thus he calculates that by leaving Cauda at evening, the ship would have neared Malta by the fourteenth night, having covered roughly five hundred miles of ocean. It appears that their greatest danger was foundering the ship because of leakage due to the sail and heavy winds at the starboard side, for which excessive strain ancient vessels were not constructed. This fact seems to account for the conduct of the fearful seamen in lightening the ship by throwing the cargo overboard the following day (vs. 18; cf. Jonah 1:5).

On the third day desperation demanded that even the equipment be cast into the sea to save the ship. This they began to do, which seems to have been progressively carried out (cf. vs. 38). Thus they made the supreme sacrifice which, says Ramsay, "makes a striking picture of growing panic."[k] The tackling of the ship (vs. 19), which may have included spars, ("including the mainyard . . ., an immense spar, probably as long as the ship, which would require the united efforts of passengers and crew to launch overboard"),[l] the ropes, the ship's furniture, such as tables, benches, chests, boxes, beds,

[45] Abbott-Smith, *op. cit.*, p. 480.
[46] *Ibid.*, p. 354.

[d] Kraeling, *op. cit.*, p. 456.
[e] Dummelow, *loc. cit.*
[f] *Ibid.*
[g] Phillips, *op. cit.*, p. 71.
[h] Williams, *op. cit.*, p. 323.
[i] Ramsay, *op. cit.*, pp. 330, 331.
[j] Kraeling, *loc. cit.*
[k] Ramsay, *op. cit.*, p. 332.
[l] James Smith, *op. cit.*, p. 116, as quoted by Bruce *op. cit.*, p. 511.

21 And when they had been long without food, then Paul stood forth in the midst of
them, and said, Sirs, ye should have hearkened unto me, and not have set sail from Crete,
and have gotten this injury and loss.
22 And now I exhort you to be of good cheer; for there shall be no loss of life among you,
but *only* of the ship.
23 For there stood by me this night an angel of the God whose I am, whom also I serve,

---

21 **When they had been long without food** is *pollēs asitias hyparchousēs*, "when there had been much fasting." *Asitia* (only here in N.T.) means "without wheat." **Hearkened** is a rather mild translation. The verb *peitharcheō* means "*to obey* one in authority, *be obedient*." [47] It is used in 5:29, 32 of obeying God.[48] The literal meaning of *kerdēsai*, **gotten**, is "to gain." All they had "gained" by their disobedience was **injury** and **loss.**

22 **Exhort** is the same word, *paraineō*, which is translated "admonished" in verse nine. *Euthymein*, **to be of good cheer,** occurs (in N.T.) only here, in verse 25, and in James 5:13. *Apobolē*, **loss,** is found only here and in Romans 11:15. It literally means "a throwing away."

---

and such like were heaved overboard. It is amazing how easily expendable material possessions become when life itself is at stake. Satan's words to God concerning Job are near the truth when taken from their setting and applied to material possessions: "all that a man hath will he give for his life" (Job 2:4b).

Luke does not fail to depict the progressiveness of their dawning despair. Caught in the storm, driven out of course, personal possessions and the ship's equipment plus most of the cargo overboard, and now for eleven more weary days and nights they were driven blindly on with the raging tempest hiding the sun by day and the stars by night. Thus they were robbed of direction or distance as no astronomical bearings could be taken. They were doubtless hard pressed to bail a leaking ship and stay it from foundering. All hope of driving the vessel ashore to elude a watery interment seemed to be lost. For fourteen days they had been too sick or distraught to eat. The bad had come to the worst. There remained no alternative. They were helpless victims trapped in the death grasp of a mad and raging sea! How utterly helpless! Luke, perhaps expressing the pagan mariner's perspective, seems almost to personalize their fate in his words, **All hope that we should be saved was now taken away** (vs. 20b). Perhaps Paul had looked upon his pagan travelling companions in this extreme hour and learned from them what he later wrote from his Roman prison: "having no hope, and without God in the world" (Eph. 2:12b). It would seem that God allowed them to be utterly robbed of every human or material source of dependence or hope that He might "show himself strong in the behalf of them whose heart is perfect toward him" (II Chron. 16:9). Or in the words of the author of Hebrews, "He taketh away the first, that he may establish the second" (Heb. 10:9).

C. The Reassurance of Paul (27:21–26)

wherefore sirs, be of good cheer: for I believe God that it shall be even as it hath been spoken unto me, vs. 25.

We may well imagine that while panic and frustration reigned in the pagan minds of these men, Paul, perhaps with his Christian companions, was hidden away somewhere in the dark hold of the ship keeping his prayer vigil with God. The hymn writer so aptly expressed what we may well imagine characterized the content of Paul's prayer on this occasion, when she wrote,

Master, the tempest is raging!
  The billows are tossing high!
The sky is o'er-shadowed with blackness,
  No shelter or help is nigh:
Carest Thou not that we perish?
  How canst Thou lie asleep,
When each moment so madly is threatening
  A grave in the angry deep?

Then out of the darkness of despair came the answer of God through an angel who **stood by** (vs. 23) Paul this night and said **Fear not, Paul** (vs. 24).

---

[47] *Ibid.*, p. 350.
[48] The only other N.T. occurrence is Titus 3:1—"be obedient."

24 saying, Fear not, Paul; thou must stand before Caesar: and lo, God hath granted thee all them that sail with thee.

25 Wherefore, sirs, be of good cheer: for I believe God, that it shall be even so as it hath been spoken unto me.

26 But we must be cast upon a certain island.

---

24 **Fear not** is "stop being afraid" *(phobou)*.

26 **Be cast** is literally "fall out" *(ekpiptō)*.

The winds and the waves shall obey My will,
  Peace, be still!
Whether the wrath of the storm-tossed sea,
  Or demons, or men, or whatever it be,
No water can swallow the ship where lies
  The Master of ocean and earth and skies;
They all shall sweetly obey My will;
  Peace, be still! Peace, be still!
They all shall sweetly obey My will;
  Peace, peace, be still![m]

Then suddenly out of the midnight darkness there shone a light, not the light of the sun that had broken through the storm clouds, but the light of God's glory that had illumined with new rays of hope, out of the midst of despair, the countenance of the "man of God" aboard.

Their abstinence from food (vs. 21) does not imply that their provisions were exhausted, (vss. 35, 38), but probably suggests that extreme seasickness had largely deprived them of appetite (vs. 33), and the uncertainties ahead may have placed them on slim rations. Added to this was the likely fact that the violent storm had prevented them from preparing food.

Julius, the captain, and the seamen had rejected Paul's counsel in their self-sufficiency at Fair Havens (vs. 11), but now, however, with all hope gone (vs. 20), they were glad to listen to his advice (vs. 21). Bruce remarks: "It warms our hearts to see . . . that in some human respects he was so like ourselves; he would not resist the temptation to say, 'I told you so,' to those who had despised his good advice at Fair Havens."[n]

It appears that Luke's narrative implies that the pagan mariners and passengers had turned in vain to wailing to their gods (cf. Jonah 1:5), while Paul prayed faithfully on in confidence until he had God's answer (vs. 22–25).

Paul had received from God, and was now prepared to deliver to his fellows what the situation most needed, a message of good cheer and hope. His very manner and message reflected the confidence born of divine assurance (cf. Acts 3:6, 7). At Fair Havens Paul had spoken out of experience and human judgment and his prediction had been fulfilled, except for the loss of life (vss. 9, 10). However, now as Bruce phrases it:

> No amount of experience or shrewd calculation could have given him this assurance; he ascribes his new confidence to a supernatural revelation made to him during the past night by an angel of God. Not only would he himself survive to stand before the emperor; the lives of his shipmates were also to be spared for his sake. The world has no idea how much it owes, in the mercy of God, to the presence in it of righteous men.[o]

It would be interesting to know if the **angel of God** that **stood by** Paul (vs. 23) on this dark night and reassured him that he should **stand before Caesar** (vs. 23) was the same messenger that appeared to him earlier with assurance that he should **bear witness also at Rome** (Acts 23:11; cf. Gen. 18:26ff.).

The angel of the Lord had dispelled Paul's doubts and fears, **Fear not, Paul** (vs. 24a), and now Paul was prepared to encourage his fellows: **Wherefore sirs, be of good cheer** (vs. 25a). Before he could offer encouragement to others, Paul had to experience their depression and be divinely lifted from it (cf. Heb. 2:18).

Of Paul's statement **whose I am, whom also I serve** (vs. 23), Plumptre remarks: "The service implied is that of worship rather than labour. The word and thought were eminently characteristic of St. Paul"[p] (cf. Rom. 1:9; II Tim. 1:3).

Paul assumed the role of a prophet and shared the divine revelation which had been made to him: **But we must be cast upon a certain island** (vs. 26). Nor is it necessary to suppose that Luke added these words after the occurrence.

[m] Written by Mary A. Baker, quoted from *Power and Praise* (Nashville: John T. Benson Pub. Co., n.d.), p. 165.
[n] Bruce, *op. cit.*, pp. 511, 512. [o] *Ibid.*, p. 512. [p] Ellicott, *op. cit.*, VII, 174.

27 But when the fourteenth night was come, as we were driven to and fro in the *sea of* Adria, about midnight the sailors surmised that they were drawing near to some country:
28 and they sounded, and found twenty fathoms; and after a little space, they sounded again, and found fifteen fathoms.
29 And fearing lest haply we should be cast ashore on rocky ground, they let go four anchors from the stern, and wished for the day.

---

27 *Diapheromenōn*, **driven to and fro** (cf. KJV, "driven up and down"), is more accurately rendered "carried along" or "drifted across." **Sea of Adria** is the Adriatic. For *hypenooun*, **surmised**, see on 25:18. **They were drawing near to some country** is literally "some land was approaching." Smith comments: "St. Luke here uses the graphic language of seamen, to whom the ship is the principal object, whilst the land . . . nears and recedes."[49] Of *chōran* he says: "The word chōran evidently means the land as distinguished from the sea."[50]

28 *Bolisantes*, **sounded**, and *orguias*, **fathoms**, are both found only here in the New Testament. The former literally means "heaving the lead" and the latter "lengths of the outstretched arms."

29 **Rocky** is literally "rough" *(trachys,* in N.T. only here and Luke 3:5). *Angkyras*, **anchors**, occurs again in verses 30, 40 (elsewhere in N.T. only in Heb. 6:19). *Prymnēs*, **stern**, is in verse 41 (plus Mark 4:38). Ships then, as now, usually anchored by the bow. But Smith points out that a stern anchoring was safer in this situation.[51] **Wished** is "prayed" *(euchomai)*.

III. THE SHIPWRECK AT MALTA (27:27–44)

The detailed accuracy with which God's revelation to Paul was fulfilled in the events that follow is most amazing.

A. The Surmise of Land (27:27, 28)

About midnight the sailors surmised that they were drawing near to some country, vs. 27b.

The fourteenth night (vs. 27) seems to have been calculated from the time of their departure from Fair Havens (cf. vss. 18, 19, 33), as based upon James Smith's calculations referred to earlier in this chapter. Bruce states that "The soundings recorded in vs. 28 indicate that the ship was passing the Point of Koura located on the east coast of Malta, at the east extremity of St. Paul's Bay."[q]

It is quite possible that the sound of breakers against the rocky shore and a dim line of sea foam alerted the seamen to approaching land. When they sounded (measured the depth of the sea) they first found it to be 20 fathoms or about 120 feet, but a second sounding indicated only 15 fathoms or about 90 feet. Thus their suspicions that they were approaching land were confirmed. These soundings have been found to agree with modern measurements taken among the breakers of Cape Koura.

Reference to the **sea of Adria** (vs. 27) may be best understood as a name which was commonly applied to the whole of the eastern Mediterranean, though in a more technical sense it belonged to the waters lying to the northeast between Sicily and Achaia.

B. The Sailors' Plan of Escape (27: 29–32).

The sailors were seeking to flee out of the ship, vs. 30a.

Cognizance was taken of approaching dangerous rocks. The sailors cast out four anchors from the stern of the ship and wished for the day (vs. 29). Ancient ships were equipped for stern anchors as well as bow anchors. This appears to indicate that they were anchored off the north shore of Malta, and thus, with a heavy northeasterly wind blowing, the bow of the ship would be aimed at the shore in readiness to run aground at such time as the anchors should be lifted or severed from the ship.

Once the ship was thus anchored the sailors sought to insure their own safety at the expense of the other passengers by escaping to land (vs. 30). Thus they lowered

[49] James Smith, *op. cit.*, p. 120, n. 1.
[50] *Ibid.*
[51] *Ibid.*, p. 133.
[q] Bruce, *op. cit.*, p. 514.

30 And as the sailors were seeking to flee out of the ship, and had lowered the boat into
the sea, under color as though they would lay out anchors from the foreship,
31 Paul said to the centurion and to the soldiers, Except these abide in the ship, ye cannot
be saved.
32 Then the soldiers cut away the ropes of the boat, and let her fall off.
33 And while the day was coming on, Paul besought them all to take some food, saying,
This day is the fourteenth day that ye wait and continue fasting, having taken nothing.
34 Wherefore I beseech you to take some food: for this is for your safety: for there shall
not a hair perish from the head of any of you.
35 And when he had said this, and had taken bread, he gave thanks to God, in the presence
of all; and he brake it, and began to eat.
36 Then were they all of good cheer, and themselves also took food.

---

30 **Sailors** is *nautōn* (cf. nautical), found (in N.T.) only here and in Revelation 18:17. *Prophasei*, **color,** is "pretense" or "pretext." *Prōirēs*, **foreship** (only here and vs. 41), is "bow" or "prow."

32 *Schoinia*, **ropes,** occurs (in N.T.) only here and in John 2:15 ("cords").

33 *Achri*, **while,** is literally "until." But that meaning will not fit here. **Besought** is literally "was beseeching" *(parekalei*, imperfect). *Diateleite*, **continue,** is found only here in the New Testament. Literally it means "accomplish."

34 **Safety** is "salvation" *(sōtērias)*.

36 **Took** is the verb *proslambanō*, the same as in the last part of verse 33. In the first part of verse 33 and in verse 34 *metalambanō* is used for "take." In verse 35 it is the simple verb *lambanō*. Apparently they are used interchangeably, for variety. *Trophēs*, **food,** generally has the old English rendering "meat" in the King James Version.

---

the lifeboat under pretense of laying out anchors from the bow of the ship. Paul immediately detected their scheme and divulged to Julius and his soldiers the plot, with the warning that their escape would preclude the salvation of the remainder of the ship's passenger complement. Obviously the sailors were necessary for the management and maneuvering of the ship as occasion should arise. At Julius' command the soldiers cut away the ropes and let the dinghy drop into the sea. This appears to have been a rash move on the part of the soldiers as the dinghy might have been used in getting passengers to shore after daybreak, and thus it is possible that the ship itself might have been saved from wreckage by beaching. However, it may have been considered by Julius as a necessary precautionary move against the sailors' further attempt to escape.

C. The Seamen's Fast Broken (27:33–38).

he gave thanks to God in the presence of all; and he brake it, and began to eat, vs. 35b.

Paul's advice, as day dawned, that they **take some food: for this is for your safety** (vs. 34), reflects its own merit. For fourteen days they had taken little if any food. They would naturally have become very weak and unfit for the difficult task that lay ahead in beaching the ship and getting ashore. The food, though simple and quickly prepared, would afford renewed physical strength and moral courage. Though Paul **gave thanks to God in the presence of all** (an act of piety; cf. I Tim. 4:4–6), **and broke the bread and began to eat,** (vs. 35), this is not to be confused with the Eucharist (cf. Luke 24:30).

The number of passengers aboard need not surprise us as Josephus[r] relates a voyage to Rome in A.D. 63 where there were 600 passengers aboard, which ship likewise went down in the Adriatic Sea. It has been suggested that the enumeration may have been with a view to the distribution of the food supplies.

The operation of lightening the ship by jettisoning the wheat cargo, begun at verse eighteen, was completed here perhaps in order that the ship might better run aground well up the beach.

[r] Josephus, *op. cit.*, "Life," p. 3.

37 And we were in all in the ship two hundred threescore and sixteen souls.
38 And when they had eaten enough, they lightened the ship, throwing out the wheat into the sea.
39 And when it was day, they knew not the land: but they perceived a certain bay with a beach, and they took counsel whether they could drive the ship upon it.
40 And casting off the anchors, they left them in the sea, at the same time loosing the bands of the rudders; and hoisting up the foresail to the wind, they made for the beach.

---

37 Instead of 276 **souls** Westcott and Hort adopt the reading of Vaticanus and the Sahidic version, "about 76." Lake and Cadbury also prefer this.[52] But Bruce says it is "probably to be rejected."[53] Lumby observes that a ship with four anchors astern must have been sizable.[54]

38 **Eaten enough** is the verb *korennymi*, "satisfy." It is used metaphorically in I Corinthians 4:8 (not elsewhere in N.T.). *Ekouphizon*, **lightened**, occurs only here in the New Testament.

39 For **drive** Westcott and Hort read[55] *eksōsai* (only here in N.T.), "to bring safe." But Nestle has[56] *exōsai* (only here and 7:45), "to drive on shore" *(exōtheō)*. Bruce prefers the latter, "as a more natural expression for running a ship ashore."[57]

40 **Casting off** is the same verb *(periaireō)* as in verse 20 ("taken away"), but here it is a nautical term meaning to weigh anchor. *Eiōn* (imperfect of *eaō)* here alone (in N.T.) means **left.** But it has this sense in the papyri.[58] *Zeuktērias*, **bands,** has not been found anywhere else.[59] It means "*the cross-bar* of a double rudder."[60] *Pēdaliōn*, **rudders,** occurs (in N.T.) only here and in James 3:4. Ancient ships were steered by two large paddles, one on each side of the stern. The exact meaning of *artemōna*, **foresail,** is not certain. Lake and Cadbury write: "The word is not known elsewhere in Greek, except in lexicographers probably dependent on this passage."[61]

D. The Ship's Wreckage (27:39–41).

the stern began to break up by the violence of the storm, vs. 41b.

When day dawned they saw land, but they were unable to identify it. Bruce[s] thinks they may have been familiar with the main harbor of Valletta where the other Alexandrian ships anchored (Acts 28:11) some eight miles distance from St. Paul's Bay, which itself lay some five miles from Melita the capital, located in the heart of the island. However, from St. Paul's Bay where they were shipwrecked, and with which location they were not familiar, they were unable to identify the island. When they saw a certain bay with a beach they (probably the ship's officers, Julius, and Paul) held consultations and decided in favor of beaching the ship at this spot (vs. 39). Kraeling states:

> Tradition has localized the shipwreck on the eastern side of the bay and here was built a church of St. Paul *ad Mare;* that church was rebuilt in 1610, at which time the Tower of St. Paul was also erected nearby.[t]

In the operation that followed (vs. 40), **casting off the anchors,** for which they had no further use, **loosing the bands of the rudders,** or steering paddles, that they might drop into position and guide the ship, and **hoisting up the foresail** used only to direct the ship, they let her drive for the beach. Bruce vividly describes the bay and what happened to the ship thus:

> But there was something which they had not noticed, because it could not be seen until they had entered into the bay. "From the entrance of the bay, where the ship must have been anchored, they could not possibly have suspected that at the bottom of it there should be a communication with the sea outside" (Smith, *Voyage*, p. 143). St Paul's Bay is sheltered on the north-west by the island of Salmonetta, which is separated from the Maltese mainland by a narrow channel about a hundred yards wide. This channel is the "place where two seas met."[u]

Ramsay[v] suggests that the ship probably drew about eighteen feet of water. When it struck the muddy bottom, it plowed on into tenacious clay which held the forepart of the ship fast and exposed the stern to the

[52] *Beginnings*, IV, 336. [53] *Acts*, p. 466. [54] *Acts* (CGT), p. 444.
[55] With B C, many minuscules, and versions. [56] With Aleph A and the Vulgate.
[57] *Acts*, p. 467. [58] VGT, p. 178.
[59] Abbott-Smith, *op. cit.*, p. 195. But cf. *Beginnings*, IV, 337 f., for discussion of a similar form in the papyri.
[60] *Ibid.*, p. 195. [61] *Beginnings*, IV, 338.
[s] Bruce, *op. cit.*, p. 518. [t] Kraeling, *op. cit.*, p. 457. [u] Bruce, *loc. cit.* [v] Ramsay, *op. cit.*, p. 341.

41 But lighting upon a place where two seas met, they ran the vessel aground; and the foreship struck and remained unmoveable, but the stern began to break up by the violence *of the waves.*

42 And the soldiers' counsel was to kill the prisoners, lest any *of them* should swim out, and escape.

43 But the centurion, desiring to save Paul, stayed them from their purpose; and commanded that they who could swim should cast themselves overboard, and get first to the land;

44 and the rest, some on planks, and some on *other* things from the ship. And so it came to pass, that they all escaped safe to the land.

---

41 **Lighting upon** is the verb *peripiptō*, "fall around," and so "fall in with." It is used in James 1:2 of falling into manifold temptations. *Dithalasson*, **where two seas met,** is found only here in the New Testament. It means "with the sea on both sides" and "is probably a *sandbank* at some distance from the shore, with rather deep water on both sides of it, a reef." [62] James Smith suggests rather the mud at the entrance to the creek.[63] *Epekeilan*, **ran . . . aground,** *naun*, **vessel,** and the verb *ereidō*, **struck,** are all found only here in the New Testament. Since *epikellō* and *naus* are both poetical words from the oldest classics, Blass insists that Luke had read Homer.[64] Lake and Cadbury remark: "The cumulation of classical words not found elsewhere in the N.T. is remarkable." [65]

42 *Ekkolymbēsas*, **swim out,** and the verb *diapheugō*, **escape,** occur only here in the New Testament.

43 *Aporipsantas*, **cast themselves,** is likewise found only here.

44 The same is true of *sanisin*, **planks. On other things from the ship** may rather be "on other persons from the ship"; that is, on the back of sailors.[66]

---

violence of the waves. Though the ship's stern began to break up under the impact, the bow was held together until every passenger safely escaped to shore.

E. The Passengers' Escape (27:42–44)

and so it came to pass that they all escaped safe to land (vs. 44b).

The soldiers' counsel . . . to kill the prisoners (vs. 42) may be best understood by the fact that Rome's rigid laws demanded that capital punishment be inflicted upon those in charge of prisoners if they allowed them to escape, especially in the case of capital crimes (cf. Acts 12:19; 16:27). The suggestion to slaughter the prisoners seems to have come from the soldiers, possibly some under-officer, and not from Julius himself.

Julius' admiration for, and confidence in, Paul by this time was such (vs. 1) that he at once countermanded the order or intention of the soldiers (vs. 43a). Thus we again see "the man of God" as the instrument of the salvation of those who otherwise would have perished.

Julius evidenced his disciplinary command of the situation and followed a plan, which Paul may have suggested, in which those able were to swim ashore and then give assistance to the non-swimmers as they attempted to get ashore on pieces of wreckage (vs. 43). Paul may have been among the former, judging from his previous shipwreck experiences (cf. II Cor. 11:25).

The non-swimmers made for shore on planks and such other pieces of wreckage as were available from the disintegrating ship (vs. 44). They all made it safely to shore with no loss of life, though the ship and its cargo were a total loss (vs. 22).

Additional Note I

SOME LESSONS FROM PAUL'S VOYAGE AND SHIPWRECK

A. The beneficent influence of a godly life among the ungodly.

B. The spiritual and moral transcendence of physical handicap and limitation. Paul sets sail a prisoner bound for Caesar's court under a Roman centurion but ends in command of the army and the ship.

C. The advice of one sober experienced man of God may be safer than that of many motivated by selfish desires.

62 Arndt and Gingrich, *op. cit.*, p. 194. 63 *Op. cit.*, p. 144.
64 *Op. cit.*, p. 186. 65 *Beginnings*, IV, 339. 66 *Ibid.*, pp. 339 f.

D. Prayer and divine aid may avail when all other hope is lost.

E. Man's extremity often becomes God's special opportunity.

F. The darkest hour of human despair is often just before the breaking of spiritual dawn and new hope.

G. All things temporal and material can profitably be sacrificed for life itself.

H. Things often turn out much better than a threatening situation promises.

I. The example of moral courage under extreme stress and strain when others have fallen into confusion and despair.

CHAPTER XXVIII

And when we were escaped, then we knew that the island was called Melita.

2 And the barbarians showed us no common kindness: for they kindled a fire, and received us all, because of the present rain, and because of the cold.

EXEGESIS

1 *Melitē*,[1] **Melita,** is probably the preferred reading rather than *Melitēnē*,[2] "Melitene," even though Westcott and Hort adopt the latter.

2 Because the Greeks could not understand the language of foreigners they called them *barbaroi*, **barbarians;** that is, those who say "bar-bar-bar." The word is used three times by Paul (Rom. 1:14; I Cor. 14:11;

EXPOSITION

THE APOSTLE'S VOYAGE TO ROME
Concluded

IV. The Winter on Malta, Acts 28:1–10.
  A. The Incident of the Viper, vss. 1–6.
  B. The Healing of Publius' Father, vss. 7–10.
V. The Arrival at Rome, Acts 28:11–16.
  A. The Voyage from Malta to Puteoli, vss. 11–13.
  B. The Journey from Puteoli to Rome, vss. 14–16.
VI. The Conferences with the Jews of Rome, Acts 28:17–29.
  A. The First Conference, vss. 17–22.
  B. The Second Conference, vss. 23–28.
VII. The Ambassador in Bonds, Acts 28:30–31.

IV. THE WINTER ON MALTA

(28:1–10)

There seems to be no reasonable doubt that the island of Malta (or Melita) was the place of Paul's shipwreck and three months' stay en route to Rome. The name Melita, later Malta, means "refuge," and it was given to the island by the Phoenicians. The island is 17½ miles long and has 95 square miles of land surface. It is located about 60 miles south of Sicily. It has a present population of approximately 235,000. The present capital is its chief city Valletta. Its harbors are excellent, the finest of which is Valletta, which is reported to be one of the strongest naval bases of Great Britain. It was the most bombed spot of the world during World War II, having undergone over 1,200 air raids. Originally a Phoenician and Carthaginian colony, it was captured by Rome in 218 B.C. It was taken by the British from Napoleon in 1800 and given dominion status in 1921, but it reverted to a crown colony in 1933 following a church-state controversy in 1930–32. Though treeless, it has a thin layer of fertile soil over a limestone formation which is agriculturally productive. It originally had a wealthy temple dedicated to Juno.

The Christian faith planted by Paul on Malta continues to the present. Traditional landmarks associated with Paul and Publius live on to the present. Publius' home is said to have become a Christian church. A Christian bishop represented Malta at the Council of Chalcedon in A.D. 451.

A. The Incident of the Viper (28:1–6)

A viper came out by reason of the heat, and fastened on his hand . . . Howbeit he shook off the creature into the fire, and took no harm, vss. 3b, 5.

The Maltese were regarded as barbarians both by the Romans and the Greeks. The word does not signify that they were an uncivilized people, but rather that they were neither Greeks nor Romans, perhaps the equivalent of the modern word "native," or those who speak a foreign language, a somewhat patronizing term. Plumptre remarks that "The language of Malta at the

[1] Aleph A C. [2] B.

3 But when Paul had gathered a bundle of sticks and laid them on the fire, a viper came out by reason of the heat, and fastened on his hand.

Col. 3:11), but only here (cf. vs. 4) in Acts. **Kindness** is *philanthrōpian* (only here and Titus 3:4).

3 *Systrepsantos*, **gathered**, is literally "twisted together." **Bundle** is *ālēthos*, "a great number" or "multitude." **Sticks** is the word *phryganon* (only here in N.T.). It is from *phrygō*, "to parch," and so means "a dry stick," In the plural it "comprises all dry sticks, brush-wood, fire-wood, or similar material used as fuel." [3] It is used in the Septuagint for straw or stubble (Isa. 40:24, etc.) and brambles (Job 30:7). *Echidna*, **viper**, occurs only here in Acts.[4] **By reason of the heat** is literally "from the heat" *(thermēs*, only here in N.T.). **Fastened** is the verb *kathapto* (only here). It is common in medical writers.[5]

---

time, if not absolutely Punic, was probably a very bastard Greek."[a]

Luke must have understood their dialect, for upon landing he learned that the island was called Malta (vs. 1).

The hospitality of the Maltese was most heartening to the shipwrecked men. They quickly built a large bonfire and warmly brought the drenched and cold victims of the merciless sea to the inviting heat, or as one authority says, "gave us first aid."[b] In fact Plumptre[c] sees an implication of both hospitality and shelter in Luke's words. They made no difference between soldiers, sailors, and prisoners, but received and treated them all alike (vs. 2) as brothers in need (cf. Rom. 14:1, 3). It is amazing how considerate and compassionate the heart of even pagan peoples may be in the presence of human suffering or calamity. Even a mongrel Samaritan had compassion on a helpless, suffering, wayside victim of heartless robbers, while Jewish religionists "passed by on the other side" (Luke 10:30–35). The cold of the late autumn intensified by the heavy rain that followed the windstorm greatly added to the discomfort of the wretched sea victims.

The unbounded energy of Paul was, as usual, in evidence as he gathered wood to feed the flames. Perhaps by the chain on his wrist, the Maltese recognized him as one of the prisoners. Thus, when under duress of the heat, a viper slithered out of the burning wood and fastened itself upon Paul's hand (vs. 3b), the natives at once judged him to be a murderer (cf. Luke 13:1-5; John 9:1, 2) pursued by the inescapable law of fate or **Justice,** what the Hindus call Karma (vs. 4).

Two objections to Luke's account of the events immediately following the landing have been offered. First, it is held that no trees grow on Malta and therefore there could have been no wood to gather. There are two possible answers to this objection. The Maltese required fire for comfort and cooking. They did not have coal on the island. There may have been trees on the island in Paul's day, though there are not now, or wood may have been one of the items of trade by sea with other peoples to supply their need. Or, more likely, the reply of Plumptre may be adequate: "The Greek word, however, is applied to the dry stalks of herbaceous plants rather than to the branches of trees, and, as such exactly describes the stout, thorny heather that still grows near the bay."[d]

The second objection is that there are no poisonous serpents on the island of Malta. Here again, however, this is hardly sufficient evidence that there were not such creatures there in Paul's day. They may well have become extinct under the heavy population of so small an island in subsequent centuries. It has been observed[e] that wolves were still existent in England for many centuries after Paul visited Malta, though they are now extinct, as also with poisonous snakes in Ireland.

Whether the serpent was actually poisonous or just thought by Luke to be so, and whether it actually bit Paul's hand or just fastened itself on his hand by some manner,

[3] Thayer, *op. cit.*, p. 659.
[4] Elsewhere in N.T. only by John the Baptist and Jesus (Matt. 3:7; 12:34; 23:33; Luke 3:7).
[5] Hobart *op. cit.*, p. 288.

[a] Ellicott, *op. cit.*, p. 178. [b] *The Interpreter's Bible*, IX, 342.
[c] Ellicott, *loc. cit.* [d] *Ibid.* [e] Rackham, *op. cit.*, p. 492, n. 7.

4 And when the barbarians saw the *venomous* creature hanging from his hand, they said one to another, No doubt this man is a murderer, whom, though he hath escaped from the sea, yet Justice hath not suffered to live.

5 Howbeit he shook off the creature into the fire, and took no harm.

6 But they expected that he would have swollen, or fallen down dead suddenly: but when they were long in expectation and beheld nothing amiss come to him, they changed their minds, and said that he was a god.

---

4 *Thērion*, **venomous creature,** is "still commonly used in modern Greek for a snake." [6] Its ordinary use in the New Testament is for "wild beast" (cf. 11:6). **Justice** is capitalized, probably because of the definite article *(hē dikē)*, and thus "personified as a goddess" in this passage.[7] But the article is often used with abstract nouns without any idea of personification (cf. RSV), so that one cannot be sure which is preferable here.

5 **Shook off** is the verb *apotinassō*, found (in N.T.) only here and in Luke 9:5.

6 **Swollen** is the verb *pimprēmi* (only here in N.T.). **Amiss** is *atopon*. Hobart writes: "*Atopos* was employed in medical language to denote . . . something out of the way [see on 25:5]—deadly—fatal—as in this

---

is in considerable dispute. Macgregor suggests that the serpent may have been "the *Coronella Austriaka*, which bites though it has no poison fangs. In any case Luke, and certainly the onlookers, thought that the snake was poisonous and that it had struck Paul, and not merely coiled around his hand."[f] Certainly a trained medical man in ancient times would have been well informed about serpents, to which great respect was paid in ancient medicine and custom.[g]

Luke likely saw a relationship between this incident and Mark 16:18; Luke 10:19, if indeed he was acquainted with the former.

The pagan concept of **Justice,** while it may have been derived from the Greeks, clearly carried the connotation of retribution rather than the Platonic concept of equity. Plato had defined justice as having and doing what is one's own. The would-be comforters of Job reflected the idea of the inescapable mechanical law of justice. In the absence of any clear concepts of divine providence, primitive people have usually been disposed to consider nature as divine in something of the Greek hylozoistic, or cruder pagan, animistic sense. Though there may be a disposition to semi-personalize natural objects or manifestations and think of them as quasi-gods, this view usually involves a fatalistic concept of the universe. Thus there arises the idea that all beneficent conduct procures its own good reward while all malevolent conduct likewise procures its own evil rewards. The philosophy is the result of reasoning from effect to cause. Macgregor states, concerning *Justice* (vs. 4), that "Probably the word should be understood in a personal sense as the name of *Dike*, the goddess of justice and vengance."[h] This authority further states: "There is extant an interesting epitaph (quoted by Wettstein from *Anthol. Pal.* VII. 290) to a man [a murderer] who, though he came safely through a shipwreck on the sandy shores of Libya, was immediately afterward killed in his sleep by the bite of a viper."[i]

As the natives watched in wonderment, they beheld Paul dispatch the serpent into the flames with no personal harm. They supposed that either **he would have swollen** rapidly or that he would have **fallen down dead suddenly** (vs. 6). Lucan is reported to have written the following lines concerning the effect of the bite of a venomous African serpent known as the Prestes (or inflamer): "The Prestes bit him, and a fiery flush lit up his face, and set the skin a-stretch, and all its comely grace had passed away" (Lucan, IX. 790).[j]

How like the pagans at Lystra (cf. Acts 14:11–19), however set in reverse, as the former first acclaimed Paul and Barnabas gods and then stoned Paul and left him for

[6] *Beginnings*, IV, 342.
[7] Arndt and Gingrich, *op. cit.*, p. 197. Cf. also Samuel Green, *Handbook to the Grammar of the Greek Testament.* (rev. ed.: New York: Fleming H. Revell Co., 1912), p. 184.

[f] *The Interpreter's Bible, loc. cit.*
[g] See Dummelow, *op. cit.*, p. 852.
[h] *The Interpreter's Bible*, IX, 343.
[i] *Ibid.*
[j] Quoted in Ellicott, *loc. cit.*

7 Now in the neighborhood of that place were lands belonging to the chief man of the island, named Publius; who received us, and entertained us three days courteously.
8 And it was so, that the father of Publius lay sick of fever and dysentery: unto whom Paul entered in, and prayed, and laying his hands on him healed him.

---

passage."[8] Harnack comments: "The whole section XXVIII. 3–6 is tinged with medical colouring."[9] *Metabalomenoi*, **changed their minds,** is found only here in the New Testament. It literally means "turn oneself about."

7 The adverb *philophthronōs*, **courteously,** is found only here in the New Testament. The **three days** may refer to the time they were entertained at the seashore, following which they were taken to a city in the interior.

8 **Dysentery** comes directly from the Greek *(dysenterion*, only here in N.T.). **Healed** is the verb *iaomai.*

---

dead, perhaps as a devil, while the Maltese first judged Paul to be a murderer and then changed their minds and said that he was a god (vs. 6b). How easily swayed are the minds of primitive peoples controlled by superstitions. Plumptre thinks that "their thoughts may have travelled quickly to the attributes of the deities who, like Apollo or Aesculapius, were depicted as subduing serpents."[k] Bruce states, "It is not difficult to detect Luke's quiet humor in his account of this remarkable change of mind."[l]

B. The Healing of Publius' Father (28:7–10)

Paul entered in, and prayed, and laying his hands on him healed him (vs. 8b).

It appears that Publius owned an estate near the location of the shipwreck. Such is not surprising when it is considered that the Maltese of this time were reported to be a wealthy and even somewhat luxurious people in their manner of life. Publius is correctly designated **the chief man of the island** (vs. 7). Macgregor remarks: "The exact word (protos) has been found in two inscriptions as a title of an official in Malta, so that we may list this with the use of the title 'politarch' of the Thessalonian officials (17:6) as an illustration of Luke's accuracy in small details of local color."[m]

It does not appear to be quite clear whether Publius was a representative of the Roman government or a native official on Malta. The island was evidently attached to the province of Sicily in Paul's day, in which case Publius may have been the legate of the proconsul of Sicily, with which his Latin name would agree. Kraeling remarks:

> One would expect the official [Publius] to have resided at the capital (Citta Vecchia). And indeed tradition, which would make him the first bishop of Malta, seeks his residence where the cathedral of that town now stands; but he may have had a country estate near the seashore. A prominent villa, found near the church of St. Paul at Mare, but covered up again for protection, is a candidate for identification with the country house of Publius, if one favors the traditional landing place . . . Whether a Christian group was created through his efforts is, however, unknown . . . There are believed to be traces of Christian influence in second-century art on the island, but the first reference to a churchman from Malta dates from the fifth century.[n]

It is interesting that there seems to be neither Biblical nor historical evidence of any Jews on Malta.

It seems unlikely that Publius' three days of courteous hospitality was extended to the entire group of 276 persons. Luke's omission of the word **all** (vs. 7b) seems to imply that only a select number of the party, possibly including Paul, Julius, the ship's captain, and Luke, were entertained in Publius' home, though he may have contributed toward the comforts of the other members.

Publius' courtesy and kindness to the shipwrecked men was richly rewarded in the healing of his seriously ill father for whom Paul prayed the prayer of faith (vs. 8).

The cause of Publius' father's illness is given by Luke as **fever and dysentery** (vs. 8). Luke's medical knowledge supports his diagnosis of this particular case (cf. Luke

[8] *Op. cit.*, p. 289.
[9] Adolph Harnack, *Luke the Physician*. Trans. J. R. Wilkinson; ed. W. D. Morrison (New York: G. P. Putnam's Sons, 1907), p. 179.

[k] *Ibid.*, p. 178. [l] Bruce, *op. cit.*, p. 523.
[m] *The Interpreter's Bible, op. cit.*, IX,343. [n] Kraeling, *op. cit.*, p. 458.

9 And when this was done, the rest also that had diseases in the island came, and were cured:

10 who also honored us with many honors; and when we sailed, they put on board such things as we needed.

11 And after three months we set sail in a ship of Alexandria which had wintered in the island, whose sign was The Twin Brothers.

---

9 *Astheneias* (only here in Acts), **diseases,** literally means "weaknesses" or "frailties," and so "sicknesses." **Cured** is the verb *therapeuō*. It comes from *therapōn*, "servant," and suggests the idea of an attending physician "treating" his patients. So Harnack thinks the word here indicates that Luke gave medical care to the sick.[10]

10 *Epethonto*, **put on board,** may mean simply "provided."

11 *Parasēmos*, **sign,** occurs only here in the New Testament. It is an adjective, "marked with a sign" (so in LXX), here used as a substantive, "figurehead." *Dioskouroi* (only here), **The Twin Brothers,** is from *dios* (gen. of Zeus) and *koros*, "son."

4:38-40). Bruce designates his condition as "intermittent attacks of gastric fever and dysentery."[o] The same authority states that "Malta has long had a peculiar unpleasant fever of its own 'Malta fever,' due to a microbe in goat's milk."[p] From the character of the disease it may be suspected that Publius' father was afflicted with amoebic dysentery in combination with the fever, a disease not uncommon in such countries. Hyppocrates (Hyppocrates, Aph. VI. 3) lends support to Luke's diagnosis.

Luke's statement that Paul **prayed, and laying his hands on him healed him** (vs. 8b), suggests the combination of the two acts recommended by James (James 5:14, 15). Again the relation of the viper's bite to this healing suggests the juxtaposition of Christ's promises in Mark 16:18, though this passage is of doubtful authority. It should be observed that in Luke we have a firsthand medical witness to the miraculous character of the healing of Publius' father.

The many healings that followed may well have received "medical treatment" at Luke's hands, as there appears to have been a distinction between the healing of Publius' father in answer to Paul's prayers and the others who were cured (vs. 9b). Indeed, Luke's statement that the Maltese **honored us with many honors** (vs. 10) is taken by some to mean that they paid him liberal fees or gave him an honorarium for his services (cf. Acts 3:7, 16; 4:34; 5:2, 19:19; I Tim. 5:17, and especially Ecclus. 38:1, which says, "Honor a physician according to thy need of him with the honor due unto him").

As the party departed the island the Maltese, out of their appreciation, lavished on them such things as they would need for their journey to Rome. Luke does not name the articles donated, but we may well imagine that they included provisions and clothing of which they had been deprived in the storm and shipwreck.

V. THE ARRIVAL AT ROME

(28:11-16)

Beyond the aforementioned incidents of the serpent and the healings, Luke does not tell us of the activities of Paul's party or of the other shipwrecked men during their three winter months' stay on Malta. We may well imagine, however, that Paul busied himself evangelizing among the natives while Luke ministered to the physical welfare of the people.

A. The Voyage from Malta to Puteoli (28:11-13)

And after three months we set sail in a ship of Alexandria . . . and on the second day we came to Puteoli; vss. 11a-13b.

The three-months' stay on Malta were made necessary because of the winter weather which forbade sailing on the open sea. They left Crete sometime after October (see note on Acts 27:9) and two weeks later arrived at Malta. Thus a three-months' stay on Malta would have placed their

[10] *Luke the Physician*, p. 16.

[o] Bruce, *loc. cit.* [p] *Ibid.*, n. 17.

12 And touching at Syracuse, we tarried there three days.
13 And from thence we made a circuit, and arrived at Rhegium: and after one day a south wind sprang up, and on the second day we came to Puteoli;

13 **Made a circuit** is based on the reading *perielthontes* (in A). The better supported text has *perielontes*[11] (cf. 27:40). Of the latter Bruce says: "This seems to be a technical nautical term whose meaning we cannot determine."[12]

departure in late January or early February. This departure would have been before the safe sailing season opened about March 5, according to Vegetius (Vegetius *De Re Militari* IV. 39). Pliny the Elder (Pliny *Natural History* II. 47, 122) placed the reopening date nearly a month earlier, February 8. Vegetius may refer to longer voyages on the open sea than Pliny. It is evidently nearer the latter date that they sailed, and that probably because of unseasonably favorable weather. They boarded another grain ship from Alexandria which had wintered at Malta, probably in the harbor of Valletta. This ship, as was customary, took its name from its figurehead, **The Twin Brothers,**" or "Castor and Pollux" (KJV), or the "Dioscuri," the two sons of Zeus and Lida. They were regarded as patron deities of the sailors. Bruce remarks: "Their constellation, Gemini, was considered a sign of good fortune in a storm."[q] Ramsay[r] suggests that Luke's reason for giving the name of this vessel, but no others, lies in the fact that he heard the name of this ship before he saw it, and thus it was fixed in his mind. To Luke, a non-sailor, ships were only means of conveyance. Ramsay thinks that Paul's party may have learned that **The Twin Brothers** of the Alexandrian Imperial fleet was lying in the great harbor of Valletta while they were entertained by Publius shortly after the shipwreck (vs. 7).

After about a day's sailing, they arrived at the great port of Syracuse on the east coast of the island of Sicily some eighty miles from Malta. Sicily was divided into two parts and the whole was under a *praetor*, with a *quaestor* over each half. Syracuse was the capital and principal city of the eastern half. It had been a very prosperous Greek state but had suffered decline under the Rome rule in the second century B.C. It had only begun to recover from the days of Augustus Caesar.

Perhaps due to either a lull or adverse winds, their vessel harbored at Syracuse for three days. With the appearance of favorable weather, the ship made a circuit (the KJV reads "we fetched a compass," or followed a circuitous route (cf. II Sam. 5:23; II Kings 3:9) and arrived at Rhegium (vs. 13) on the southwest coast of Italy, where they evidently remained in harbor for one day, again because of adverse weather.

Rhegium (now Reggio) was situated close by the narrow straits of Messina, where the famed Scylla and Charybdis were situated. Scylla was a great rock to the north of the cape and Charybdis was a dangerous whirlpool near the Strait of Messina. Thus **The Twin Brothers,** like many other ships that called at Rhegium, had to lie in harbor awaiting a favorable wind to avoid the dangerous currents and the whirlpool. **The Twin Brothers** appear on the coins of Rhegium, indicating perhaps both that they were invoked here for the safety of the ship as it passed through the straits and that the ship was a frequent caller at this port. Josephus[s] records that Caligula undertook the construction of a harbor for Egyptian corn-ships at Rhegium, "A great and kindly undertaking," but he never completed the enterprise.

With the appearance of a south wind, they set sail and a day later entered the port of Puteoli (now Pozzuoli) on the coast of Italy to the north (vs. 13). Since the distance from Rhegium to Puteoli was approximately 180 miles, the wind evidently favored their voyage. Puteoli, which lay at the northern part of the bay of Naples was the chief port of Rome in Paul's day. Here the ocean voyage for the passengers ended. En route they had sailed past Pompeii framed against

[11] Aleph B. [12] *Acts*, p. 474 Cf. also *Beginnings*, IV, 344.

[q] Bruce, *op. cit.*, p. 525, 526. [r] Ramsay, *St. Paul the Traveller*, p. 346.
[s] Josephus, *op. cit.*, "Antiquities," XIX, II, 5.

14 where we found brethren, and were entreated to tarry with them seven days: and so we came to Rome.

15 And from thence the brethren, when they heard of us, came to meet us as far as The Market of Appius and The Three Taverns; whom when Paul saw, he thanked God, and took courage.

---

15 Of *apantēsis*, **meet** (literally "a meeting"), Moulton and Milligan write: "The word seems to have been a kind of technical term for the official welcome of a newly arrived dignitary—a usage which accords excellently with its NT usage." [13]

Vesuvius and on past Neapolis (now Naples). Puteoli was probably the principal cargo depot for Rome. The ruins of the mole where Paul landed are said to be still visible at Puteoli. Only the ruins of the amphitheater, where Nero once performed, and the Serapeum remain to mark the site of the ancient city.

B. The Journey from Puteoli to Rome (28:14–16)

And so we came to Rome, vs. 14.

At Puteoli Paul's heart was gladdened by the presence of Christians, with whom he and his party were permitted to tarry and fellowship for a full week. Paul's last known contact with any Christians, apart from the members of his party and converts he may have made en route, had been at Sidon some six months earlier. It is possible that Julius awaited further orders here from his superior officer before proceeding to Rome with his troops and the prisoners.

The presence of Christians at Puteoli is significant in that it indicates the wide spread of Christian faith in the absence of any distinct record of these parts (cf. Rom. 1:8; Col. 1:6). It is possible that here, even as likely at Rome, the Christian faith was carried back from Pentecost by Jews and proselytes converted there (Acts 2:10). Then, as Plumptre remarks, "a city which was *en rapport*, like Puteoli, with both Alexandria and Rome, may have received it from either."[t] Plumptre[u] further advances the hypothesis that the *Epistle to the Hebrews* was written from Puteoli by Apollos (Acts 18:24) to Hebrew Christians of the ascetic class in the Nile Delta. He argues that the salutation, "They of [or from] Italy salute you" (Heb. 13:24), was not a natural way of speaking of Christians at Rome, and since there was no other known Christian church in Italy, it must have reference to these Christian disciples at Puteoli. Thus, according to this hypothesis, Apollos would have been at some later date associated with these Christians at Puteoli, possibly as their pastor, and from here wrote the Hebrew letter to Egyptian Hebrew-Christians. While the hypothesis seems to have certain merits, it lacks sufficient evidence for unqualified acceptance. That there were Jews at Puteoli is attested by Josephus.[v]

It appears that Paul's **seven days** (vs. 14) with the Christians at Puteoli, as also at Troas (Acts 20:6) and at Tyre (Acts 21:4), were designed to enable him to fellowship with and minister to them on the Lord's day. Julius' courtesy in granting Paul this privilege would have been but the repetition of an earlier like incident at Sidon (vs. 3).

Luke's statement, **and so we came to Rome** (vs. 14), simply indicates that the city of Rome was the next stage of their journey. En route Christian disciples from Rome who had heard of his arrival, perhaps by messengers during the week Paul was at Puteoli, came out to officially greet and welcome the Great Apostle of their faith to the city. In fact, they appear to have constituted an official delegation from the church at Rome. It seems that some came as far as the **Market of Appius** (about 40 miles from Rome), while others met him at **The Three Taverns** (about 30 miles from Rome). Possibly Luke intends to indicate that there were two different delegations that came to welcome him, one having received the word of his arrival earlier than the other. From his letter written to Christians of Rome from Corinth nearly three

[13] VGT, p. 53.

[t] Ellicott, *op. cit.*, VII, 180. [u] *Ibid.*

[v] Josephus, *op. cit.*, "Antiquities,", XVII, XII, 1, and "Wars," II, VII, 1.

16 And when we entered into Rome, Paul was suffered to abide by himself with the soldier that guarded him.

17 And it came to pass, that after three days he called together those that were the chief of the Jews: and when they were come together, he said unto them, I, brethren, though I had done nothing against the people, or the customs of our fathers, yet was delivered prisoner from Jerusalem into the hands of the Romans:

---

16 Between **Rome** and **Paul** the Western text inserts: "the centurion delivered the prisoners to the military commander *(stratopedarchos)*, but." Ropes thinks this is just a "paraphrastic expansion." [14]

17 **Delivered** is the verb *paradidōmi*, which is used frequently in the Gospels for Judas' betrayal of Jesus. Lake and Cadbury say: "*Paradidōmi* seems, when used in this sense [given over], always to carry the suggestion of treachery, or at least injustice." [15]

---

years earlier, they knew of his plans to visit Rome, though they probably had little idea of when he might arrive. Over the "Appian Way" Paul travelled with the company of soldiers and his fellow prisoners. Plumptre[w] thinks that the reason Paul's Christian friends had not come farther than **Appii Forum** was because they did not know whether he would come thence by road or canal. As quoted by Plumptre "Horace (Sat. i. 5, 1. 4), had condemned the town to a perpetual infamy, as . . . [with sailors filled, and scoundrel publicans!]".[x] However, as Paul met here with the Christians from Rome, it may well be imagined that they conducted together a service of prayer and thanksgiving to God that would have given a moral complexion to the place not before experienced.

The next mentioned place on their Romeward journey was **The Three Taverns** (vs. 15) where the second contingent of Christians met them. Little wonder that **Paul . . . thanked God and took courage** (vs. 15) as he met these Christians. He had long desired to visit Rome (cf. Acts 19:21; Rom. 1:9ff.; 15:23f.), and at last he had realized his desire. If he had been apprehensive about his reception by the Christians at Rome (as his words in vs. 15 seem to imply), this warm welcome more than allayed any fears he may have had. Many questions may have plagued his mind since his departure from Caesarea such as: Would there be friends to welcome him or would he enter Rome unescorted as a common criminal? Were the Christians, to whom he wrote his Roman letter nearly three years earlier and who were so much in his mind (Rom. 1:10–12), still safe, or had they been killed or driven from Rome by persecution? Had they been deflected from the faith or poisoned against him by the deadly work of the Judaizers? All of these fears were dispelled in an instant by the welcome accorded him by his Christian friends from Rome. Thus reassured and re-animated, Paul entered Rome, perhaps by the "Porta Capena," like a victor returning from the defeat of a powerful enemy. His goal, Rome, was at last realized, and Luke triumphantly announces: **and . . . we entered into Rome** (vs. 16a).

Luke's notation that **Paul was suffered to abide by himself with the soldiers that guarded him** (vs. 16) indicates the special privilege accorded him by the Romans. This was unquestionably due to the favorable recommendation of Julius and may also have possibly been augmented by a favorable report on his case by Festus. Concerning the officer to whom Paul was delivered, Macgregor states:

> This official was either the *princeps peregrinorum*, an officer of the praetorian guard in command of the courier troops or *frumentarii* . . . , or, perhaps more probably, the *praefectus praetorii*, commander of the praetorian guard, who took prisoners into custody on their arrival at Rome. Paul himself was granted the privilege of *custodia libera* and would be permitted to **stay by himself** in his own quarters under the supervision of **the soldier that guarded him.**[y]

VI. THE CONFERENCES WITH THE JEWS OF ROME (28:17–29)

As was Paul's policy throughout his ministry, he desired at the earliest possible

[14] *Beginnings*, III, 253. [15] *Beginnings*, IV, 346.

[w] Ellicott, *op. cit.*, VII, 181. [x] *Ibid.* [y] *The Interpreter's Bible*, IX, 346.

18 who, when they had examined me, desired to set me at liberty, because there was no cause of death in me.

19 But when the Jews spake against it, I was constrained to appeal unto Caesar; not that I had aught whereof to accuse my nation.

20 For this cause therefore did I entreat you to see and to speak with *me*: for because of the hope of Israel I am bound with this chain.

---

20 The marginal reading "Call for you, to see and to speak with you" (cf. RSV) is perhaps the preferable translation. The first meaning of *parakaleō* is "to call to one's side, call for." [16]

---

opportunity to meet with the Jews at Rome. However, his confinement prevented him from going to their synagogue for a meeting where he might preach Christ. There appear to have been a number of synagogues in Rome at this time, and the Jews were a well-known community to the Romans, though sometimes a very troublesome one (cf. Acts 18:2).

A. The First Conference (28:17–22)

after three days he called together those that were the chief of the Jews, vs. 17.

Paul invited the Jewish leaders at Rome to a conference at his residence. After brief introductions he summarized the events that had brought him to Rome, from his arrest at Jerusalem to the present. He declared his innocence of any adverse activities against the Jewish people or their customs, thus implying his loyalty to Judaism (vs. 17b). Nevertheless, he related, his own people had brought accusations against him and delivered him to the Roman officials for trial (vs. 17c). He asserted that the Romans had carefully examined the accusations brought against him by the Jews at Jerusalem and found them groundless and had desired to set him free (vs. 18). However, when the Jews insisted upon his punishment, he had found that his only recourse was appeal to Caesar. He assures them that he has no accusations to bring against his own nation before Caesar (vs. 19). Since Rome had been so greatly plagued by the troublesome Jews in the city, as elsewhere, and had at one time expelled them from Rome (Acts 18:2), it must have been a relief to these leaders to learn that Paul was not there to make further trouble for them.

Having carefully avoided placing undue responsibility upon the Jewish authorities at Jerusalem for his arrest and appeal, Paul then proceeded to bear his ever faithful witness to Christ: **Because of the hope of Israel I am bound with this chain** (vs. 20b). "He is a prisoner because as a Christian he believes that in Jesus Christ **the hope of Israel** had been fulfilled."[z] Bruce states, "In Rome as in Jerusalem he emphasized that the Christian message which he proclaimed far from undermining the religion of Israel, was its divinely appointed fulfillment"[a] (cf. Acts 23:6; 24:14–15; 26:6ff.).

The reply of the Jewish leaders was to the effect that they had no adverse reports on Paul, either by letter from the Jerusalem Jews or by personal communication from travelling Jews (vs. 21). Bruce[b] thinks that the failure of the Jerusalem Jews to succeed in prosecuting Paul before the provincial magistrates may have discouraged them from attempting further prosecution before Caesar. It should be noted, however, that Paul's appeal to Caesar was made very soon before his actual sailing and that due to the lateness of the season, with the soon closing of the seas to sailing, they may not have had opportunity to send complaints to Rome against him. If, as Bruce[c] thinks, it had been a bit later when Nero married Poppaia Sabina in A.D. 62, who was friendly to the Jews and as Josephus[d] asserts was a God-fearing proselyte to the faith, their chances to influence the emperor against Paul might have been better.

Whether the Jews knew more about Paul than they admitted, we cannot be certain. However, they planned to keep themselves clear of any involvement with the Roman

[16] Thayer, *op. cit.*, p. 482.

[z] *Ibid.* [a] Bruce, *op. cit.*, p. 530. [b] *Ibid.* [c] *Ibid.*
[d] Josephus, *op. cit.*, "Life," 3.

21 And they said unto him, We neither received letters from Judaea concerning thee, nor did any of the brethren come hither and report or speak any harm of thee.

22 But we desire to hear of thee what thou thinkest: for as concerning this sect, it is known to us that everywhere it is spoken against.

23 And when they had appointed him a day, they came to him into his lodging in great number; to whom he expounded *the matter*, testifying the kingdom of God, and persuading them concerning Jesus, both from the law of Moses and from the prophets, from morning till evening.

---

21 **Letters** is not *epistolai* (cf. 9:2; 22:5; I Cor. 5:9; 16:3; II Cor. 3:1) but *grammata*, which primarily refers to letters of the alphabet. This is the only place in the New Testament where the latter is used for epistles. But Moulton and Milligan give several examples of this usage in the papyri and offer the comment: "When *gramma* becomes collective, its primary meaning is 'a letter,' just as Latin *littera* produced *litterae*."[17] **Harm,** is *ponēron*, "evil."

23 *Xenian*, **lodging,** occurs only one other place in the New Testament, Philemon 22. Thayer notes that from Homer down it means "hospitality," but thinks that in the New Testament it signifies "lodging-place."[18] Arndt and Gingrich agree that this is "perhaps more probable."[19] But Moulton and Milligan assert that the common meaning "hospitality" in the papyri "seems to make it practically certain that the word is best understood in the same sense in Acts 28:23, Philemon 22, rather than a *place* of lodging."[20] Commentators are divided in their opinion. Bruce[21] and Lake and Cadbury[22] prefer "hospitality." For *exetitheto*, **expounded,** see on 11:4. It literally means "exposed." **Testifying** is the verb *diamartyromai*, which originally meant "testify under oath."[23]

---

authorities against a Roman citizen. They cautiously reflected their suspicions of Paul by admitting their knowledge of Christianity as a **sect** which was, they said, in ill repute everywhere (vs. 22). Just when and how the Christian church came into being at Rome is not certain, but it is clear that when Paul wrote his letter to Rome from Corinth in about A.D. 57, it was then a well-established Christian community widely and favorably renowned (cf. Rom. 1:8). The unfavorable attitude of the Jews toward Christianity may even have been influenced by the Roman suppression of riots by dispersing the Jews from Rome under Claudius (Acts 18:2), which riots may have been characterized by Jewish attacks upon the Christians. In any event the Jews, while noncommittal, were willing to hear Paul further on the subject of Christianity. Their professed ignorance of firsthand knowledge of Christianity may be due to the fact that the synagogue and the church here were already separated, the church having started mainly as a non-Jewish body. Indeed, the number of Latin names found in the sixteenth chapter of Romans would seem to lend weight to this theory.

B. The Second Conference (28:23–28)

and when they had appointed him a day, they came to him into his lodging in great number, vs. 23a.

Paul's method of approach on this occasion was as always when preaching to the Jews: namely, exposition and witness (vs. 23). From both the law of Moses and the prophets, Paul reasoned throughout the entire day that Jesus was the Messiah and that His Kingdom was the Church. Bruce states that "His text was the whole volume of Hebrew scripture, interpreted by the events of the advent, passion, and triumph of Jesus of Nazareth, 'declared to be the Son of God with power, according to the spirit of holiness, by the resurrection from the dead' (Rom. 1:4)."[e] Without question there was much debate and possibly no little contention over the meaning and application of certain Messianic prophecies throughout the day, as Paul earnestly labored to convince these leading Jews of Rome that

[17] VGT, p. 131. [18] *Op. cit.*, p. 431. [19] *Op. cit.*, p. 549. [20] VGT, p. 433.
[21] *Acts*, p. 478. [22] *Beginnings*, IV, 346. [23] Arndt and Gingrich, *op. cit.*, p. 185.

[e] Bruce, *op. cit.*, p. 532.

24 And some believed the things which were spoken, and some disbelieved.
25 And when they agreed not among themselves, they departed after that Paul had spoken
one word, Well spake the Holy Spirit through Isaiah the prophet unto your fathers,
26 saying,
Go thou unto this people, and say,
By hearing ye shall hear, and shall in no wise understand;
And seeing ye shall see, and shall in no wise perceive:
27 For this people's heart is waxed gross,
And their ears are dull of hearing,
And their eyes they have closed;
Lest haply they should perceive with their eyes,
And hear with their ears,
And understand with their heart,
And should turn again,
And I should heal them.

---

25 **Agreed not** is the adjective *asymphōnos* (only here in N.T.), which is composed of alpha-privative and *symphōnos*[24] (cf. symphony), "agreeing in sound" (*syn*, "with" and *phōnē*, "sound"). So it means "discordant" or "at variance."

26, 27 This long quotation is taken almost verbatim from the Septuagint.

Jesus Christ was the fulfillment of Israel's age old hope.

That the Apostle's efforts were not in vain is clear from the fact that **some believed** (vs. 24). However, others disbelieved, with whom Paul renounced fellowship, with the inevitable result that, as usual, strife arose among them (vs. 25). Paul, as so often before, rebuked the unbelieving Jews with the words of their own prophets (Isa. 6:9, 10). Then he declared to them the universal import of the **salvation of God** in Christ, with his personal confidence that the Gentiles in Rome as elsewhere would hear and believe the message concerning Christ (vs. 28).

VII. THE AMBASSADOR IN BONDS (28:30–31)

And he abode two whole years in his own hired dwelling . . . preaching the kingdom of God, and teaching the things concerning the Lord Jesus Christ, vss. 30, 31.

Paul was evidently accorded the utmost leniency while a prisoner at Rome. He was permitted to dwell in his own rented house or apartment in the city at his personal convenience (and evidently at his personal expense) under the surveillance of a soldier-guard who was responsible to give account of his charge. A light chain, presumably fastened by the wrist, evidently secured Paul to his guard, which guard would naturally have been changed regularly. He was at liberty to invite his friends to his quarters and to preach or minister to all who came to him, though he was not permitted to go out at liberty. He doubtless found ample opportunity to rest and recuperate after the rigorous and trying experiences of the sea. His spirits would have been revived from the ordeals of the past two years and more, as he enjoyed the fellowship and encouragement of his visiting friends at Rome, and especially as he engaged in a profitable and victorious ministry for Christ to those who came to him for help (cf. Philemon 9–12). He carried on correspondence with his friends and former converts at such places as Phillippi, Colossae, and Ephesus.

At Rome Paul did not regard himself as a prisoner of Caesar, but rather as "the prisoner of Jesus Christ in behalf of . . . [the] Gentiles" (Eph. 3:1; also cf. Eph. 4:1; Philemon 1, 9). In fact, he was a prisoner of Christ by divine appointment that he might be God's special ambassador to the Gentiles at Rome (Eph. 6:20). To the end that he might execute well this divine appointment at Rome, Paul earnestly requested the prayers of his Christian friends in other parts (see Eph. 6:18–20). Withal, Paul was not without his severe spiritual

[24] Found in N.T. only in I Cor. 7:5.

28 Be it known therefore unto you, that this salvation of God is sent unto the Gentiles: they will also hear.

30 And he abode two whole years in his own hired dwelling, and received all that went in unto him,

31 preaching the kingdom of God, and teaching the things concerning the Lord Jesus Christ with all boldness, none forbidding him.

---

29 This entire verse is missing in the oldest manuscripts.[25]

30 **In his own hired dwelling** should rather be "at his own expense" (RSV). Lake and Cadbury say: "There is no evidence that *misthōma* ever meant 'a hired house' (KJV)." [26] The word (not elsewhere in N.T.) in the classics and the Septuagint always means "price, hire." [27]

31 **None forbidding him** is all one word, *akōlytōs* (only here in N.T.). Moulton and Milligan note that in the papyri the term occurs constantly in legal documents with the meaning "without hindrance." They assert, "The word is legal to the last," and refer to "the triumphant note on which it brings the Acts of the Apostles to a close." [28]

---

conflicts and temptations to discouragement during his Roman imprisonment, which he likens to a warfare against a subtle and powerful enemy, the victories over which he uses to encourage his Christian friends (see Eph. 6:10–20). Well did Paul set the example of Christian courage and fortitude, while in prison, for such subsequent saints as Madame Guyon and John Bunyan.

That Paul wrote Ephesians, Colossians, Philippians, and Philemon from his Roman imprisonment has been held by most scholars. The exact order and dates of the writing have less agreement among scholars. These letters likely dated from the middle of the two-year imprisonment at about A.D. 61. That Philippians was written last, and at a time when it seems that Paul's trial was in progress and he felt confident of acquittal, appears fairly evident from the tone of the Philippian letter.

The character of Paul's ministry in Rome, **with all boldness** (vs. 31), and the liberty and favor that he enjoyed at the hands of the Roman officials as he carried on his preaching ministry, is suggested by Luke's statement: **none forbidding him** (vs. 31b). Though delays of justice were not uncommon at Rome, the two-year delay in Paul's trial (vs. 30), Dummelow thinks, was caused "(1) by the loss of the official papers in the wreck, (2) by the non-appearance of the accusers, (3) by the difficulty of getting together the witnesses."[f]

Luke drops out of the picture at verse sixteen, though we learn from Paul's epistles that he was with him there during his imprisonment (cf. Col. 4:14; II Tim. 4:11). He closes his record with Paul actively engaged in the ministry he loved so well. What better conclusion could he have given to this great record than to present the great Apostle as an ambassador of Jesus Christ, the Lord and King of the universe, to the court of the most ungodly of all earthly rulers, Nero? (Eph. 6:19, 20).

That he was not unsuccessful in his ambassadorship, even within the household of Nero Caesar, we seem to have evidence in his epistles to the Philippians, where he says, "All the saints salute you, especially they that are of Caesar's household" (Phil. 4:22).

Only a few times in the Acts does Luke use the full title for Christ, as here, **the Lord Jesus Christ** (vs. 31; cf. Acts 11:17; 15:11; 16:31; 20:21). As earlier noted, the title **Lord** is the most often repeated important word in Acts (110 times) and constitutes the burden of the apostolic message.

That Christ was redemptively the Lord of the universe gave validity to Paul's universal concept and proclamation of the Gospel of Jesus Christ. Thus Luke closes this great record of the life and ministry of the greatest of all Christian apostles in a triumphant display of (1) the transcendence of the Christian faith over all obstacles: Paul the ambassador of Christ in wicked Nero's prison (Eph. 6:19, 20); (2) the free-

[25] Aleph A B E. [26] *Beginnings*, IV, 348. [27] Abbott-Smith, *op. cit.*, p. 294. [28] VGT, p. 20.

[f] Dummelow, *op. cit.*, p. 853.

dom and independence of Paul, even as Nero's prisoner: **in his own hired dwelling** (cf. II Tim. 2:9); (3) the universal reach of the Gospel: **"All" that went in into him** (cf. Acts 1:8; 2:38, 39); (4) the universal spiritual kingdom of Christ over men: **preaching the kingdom of God** (cf. Acts 1:3; 8:12; 19:8; 20:25; 28:23); (5) the exposition of Christ's teachings and work for man's salvation and edification: **teaching the things concerning the Lord Jesus Christ** (cf. Matt. 9:35; 28:18–20); (6) the Christian confidence and boldness commensurate with the proclamation of Christ's salvation for man: **with all boldness** (cf. Acts 4:13, 29, 31; Eph. 6:18, 19); and (7) the favor accorded the Gospel proclamation by the ruling authorities: **none forbidding him.**

Luke brought his Acts account to a conclusion, having accomplished his historical purpose. That his purpose was several-fold became evident in the course and culmination of the record. *First*, in accordance with his thesis implied at the outset of the book (Acts 1:1–5), Luke traced the continuance of Christ's work, begun while He was in the flesh, from Pentecost throughout the Roman empire. *Second*, he traced the spread of the Gospel and the development of the Church according to the plan which he laid down in the first chapter of the book (Acts 1:8). *Third*, he demonstrated the power of the Christian faith to invade the non-Christian world and establish itself wherever it went. *Fourth*, he revealed the inherent and relentless animosity and opposition of the Jewish church to Jesus Christ and His gospel of salvation, while at the same time demonstrating the victory of the new faith over the old religion. *Fifth*, he portrayed in succession the leading characters in the gospel drama of the first Christian century: Peter, Stephen, Philip, Barnabas, and the greatest of all, Paul. *Sixth*, he traced the break of the new Christian faith with the old Jewish system, beginning at Jerusalem at Pentecost with the Christian disciples worshipping in the Temple and ending with Christianity established in the capital of the empire as a religion distinct from Judaism (Acts 28:22). *Seventh*, Luke demonstrated the ability of the Christian faith to win the favor of, and legal status in, the pagan Roman Empire (Acts 28:30, 31), though it required to await the Emperor Constantine's Edict of Toleration (A.D. 313) for final governmental confirmation.

Whether Paul was acquitted or convicted in the court of Nero at the end of his two-year imprisonment seems not to have been in the purpose of Luke to relate. Evidence from Paul's *Pastoral Epistles*, plus the testimony of tradition, seems to point favorably toward his acquittal, a fourth missionary journey in which he may have gone to Spain, Crete, Nicopolis, and other regions, then to have been again arrested, tried at Rome, condemned, and executed by beheading in about A.D. 67. Whether Paul suffered martyrdom at the close of his first or a second imprisonment at Rome, he left his clear testimony to a finished life work, his readiness to meet God by way of Nero's beheading-block, and a clear assurance of a heavenly coronation in righteousness by the Lord of the universe whom he served and whose lordship he proclaimed across the ancient world, and who is the "righteous judge," in distinction from the unrighteous Nero (II Tim. 4:6–8).

BIBLIOGRAPHY

BIBLIOGRAPHY

I. Archaeology

Albright, W. F. "The Old Testament and Archaeology." *Old Testament Commentary.* Edited by H. C. Alleman and E. E. Flack. Philadelphia: Muhlenberg Press, 1948.

Caiger, Stephen L. *Archaeology and the New Testament.* London: Cassell and Co., 1939.

Cobern, Camden M. *The New Archaeological Discoveries* (6th ed.). New York: Funk & Wagnalls, 1922.

Deissmann, Adolph. *Bible Studies.* Translated by Alexander Grieve. Edinburgh: T. & T. Clark, 1901.

———. *Light from the Ancient East.* Translated by Lionel R. M. Strachan. New revised ed. New York: George H. Doran Co., 1927.

Finegan, Jack. *Light from the Ancient Past.* Princeton: University Press, 1946.

Free, Joseph, P. *Archaeology and Bible History.* Wheaton: Van Kampen Press, 1950.

Wright, G. Ernest. *Biblical Archaeology.* Philadelphia: Westminster Press, 1957.

II. Bible Atlases

Grollenberg, L. H. *Atlas of the Bible.* Translated and edited by Joyce M. H. Reid and H. H. Rowley. New York: Nelson, 1956.

Hurlbut, Jesse L. *Bible Atlas* (rev. ed.). Chicago: Rand McNally & Co., 1910.

Kraeling, Emil G. *Rand McNally Bible Atlas.* Chicago: Rand McNally & Co., 1956.

Stirling, John. *An Atlas of the Acts of the Apostles and the Epistles.* London: George Philip and Son, Ltd., 1939.

Wright, G. E. and Filson, F. V. (eds.). *The Westminster Historical Atlas* (rev. ed.). Philadelphia: Westminster Press, 1945, 1956.

III. Bible Dictionaries

Davis, John D. *Dictionary of the Bible.* (4th rev. ed.) Grand Rapids: Baker Book House (reprint) 1956.

———. *The Westminster Dictionary of the Bible.* Revised and rewritten by Henry S. Gehman. Philadelphia: Westminster Press, 1944.

Jacobus, M. W., Nourse, E. E., and Zenos, A. C. (eds.). *A Standard Bible Dictionary.* New York: Funk & Wagnalls Co., 1909.

Hastings, James (ed.). *Dictionary of the Apostolic Church.* 2 vols. New York: Charles Scribner's Sons, 1916 (rep. 1921).

———. *A Dictionary of the Bible.* 5 vols. New York: Charles Scribner's Sons, 1898.

———. *A Dictionary of Christ and the Gospels.* 2 vols. New York: Charles Scribner's Sons, 1906.

Miller, M. S. and Miller, J. L. *Harper's Bible Dictionary.* New York: Harper & Brothers, 1952.

Orr, James (ed.). *The International Standard Bible Encyclopedia.* Revised by Melvin Grove Kyle. Chicago: Howard–Severance Co., 1929.

IV. Commentaries

Aberly, John. "The Acts," *New Testament Commentary* (rev. ed.). Edited by H. C. Alleman. Philadelphia: Muhlenberg Press, 1936.

Alexander, Joseph Addison. *Commentary on the Acts of the Apostles.* 2 vols. in 1. Grand Rapids: Zondervan Publishing House, 1956 (reprint).

Alford, Henry. *The Greek Testament,* 6th ed. Vol. II. London: Rivingtons, 1871 (Moody Press, 1958, reprint).

———. *The New Testament for English Readers* (3rd ed.). 2 vols. (each bound in two parts). Boston: Lee and Shepard, 1872 (Moody Press, 1955, reprint).

Barclay, William. *The Acts of the Apostles.* Philadelphia: Westminster Press, 1955.

Barnes, Albert. *Notes on the New Testament: Acts of the Apostles.* Edited by Robert Frew. Grand Rapids: Baker Book House, 1949 (reprint).

Bartlet, J. V. *The Acts.* "The Century Bible." Edinburgh: T. C. & E. C. Jack, n.d.

Bengel, John Albert. *Gnomon of the New Testament.* Translated by C. T. Lewis and M. R. Vincent. 2 vols. Philadelphia: Perkinpine & Higgins, 1860.

Benson, Joseph. *The New Testament of Our Lord and Saviour Jesus Christ.* Vol. I. New York: Carlton & Phillips, 1856.

Bloomfield, S. T. *The Greek Testament, with English Notes, Critical, Philological, and Exegetical* (5th Am. ed.). Vol. I. Philadelphia: H. C. Peck & Theo. Bliss, 1836.

Blunt, A. W. F. *The Acts of the Apostles*. "The Clarendon Bible." Oxford: Clarendon Press, 1923.
Bruce, F. F. *The Acts of the Apostles*. The Greek text with Introduction and Commentary. Grand Rapids: Wm. B. Eerdmans Publishing Co., 1952.
———. "The Acts of the Apostles," *The New Bible Commentary*. Edited by F. Davidson. Grand Rapids: Wm. B. Eerdmans Publishing Co., 1953.
———. *Commentary on the Book of the Acts*. "The New International Commentary on the New Testament." Grand Rapids: Wm. B. Eerdmans Publishing Co., 1954.
Burch, Ernest W. "Acts of the Apostles," *The Abingdon Bible Commentary*. Edited by F. C. Eiselen *et al.* New York: Abingdon–Cokesbury Press, 1929.

Calvin, John. *Commentary upon the Acts of the Apostles*. Edited by Henry Beveridge. 2 vols. Grand Rapids: Wm. B. Eerdmans Publishing Co., 1949 (reprint).
Carroll, B. H. *The Acts*, "An Interpretation of the English Bible." Edited by J. B. Cranfill. Nashville: Broadman Press, 1942 (1st ed., 1916).
Carver, William Owen. *The Acts of the Apostles*. Nashville: Broadman Press, 1916.
Clarke, Adam. *The New Testament of Our Lord and Saviour Jesus Christ*. New York: Methodist Book Concern, n.d. Also Nashville: Abingdon–Cokesbury Press, n.d.
Clarke, W. K. L. *Concise Bible Commentary*. New York: Macmillan Co., 1953.
Cook, F. C. (ed.). *The Holy Bible*. Commentary . . . by Bishops and Other Clergy of the Anglican Church. New Testament, Vol. II. New York: Charles Scribner's Sons, 1907.
Cowles, Henry. *Acts of the Apostles*. New York: D. Appleton and Co., 1883.
Cox, Lilian E. "The Acts of the Apostles," *The Twentieth Century Bible Commentary* (rev.). Edited by G. H. Davies *et al.* New York: Harper & Brothers, 1955 (1st ed., 1932).

Davidson, F., (ed.). *The New Bible Commentary*. Grand Rapids: Wm. B. Eerdmans Publishing Company, 1954.
Dummelow, J. R. (ed.). *A Commentary on the Holy Bible*. London: Macmillan Co., 1909. Also New York: Macmillan Co., 1936 (rep. 1951).

Ellicott, Charles John (ed.). *Ellicott's Commentary on the Whole Bible*. Grand Rapids: Zondervan Publishing House. n.d. Acts, E. H. Plumptre, Vol. VII.
Erdman, Charles R. *The Acts: An Exposition*. Philadelphia: Westminster Press, 1919.
Exell, Joseph S. *The Biblical Illustrator: The Acts*. 3 vols. Grand Rapids: Baker Book House, 1954 (reprint).

Furneaux, William M. *The Acts of the Apostles*. Oxford: Clarendon Press, 1912.

Gaebelein, A. C. *The Acts of the Apostles: An Exposition*. New York: "Our Hope," 1912.
Gloag, Paton J. *A Critical and Exegetical Commentary on the Acts of the Apostles*. 2 vols. Edinburgh: T. & T. Clark, 1870.
Godbey, W. B. *Commentary on the New Testament*. Vol. V. Cincinnati: Revivalist Press, 1899.
Gore, Charles, Goudge, H. L., and Guillaume, Alfred. *A New Commentary on Holy Scripture*. New York: Macmillan Co., 1928.
Gould, Ezra P. *A Critical and Exegetical Commentary*. New York: Charles Scribner's Sons, 1896.

Hackett, H. B. *A Commentary on the Acts of the Apostles* (rev. ed.). Edited by Alvah Hovey. Philadelphia: American Baptist Publication Society, 1882.
Hastings, Edward (ed.). *The Speaker's Bible: The Acts of the Apostles*. 2 vols. Aberdeen: "The Speaker's Bible" Office, 1927.
Henry, Matthew. *Commentary on the Whole Bible*. Vol. VI. New York: Fleming H. Revell Co., n.d.
Hervey, A. C. and others. "The Acts of the Apostles," *The Pulpit Commentary*. Edited by H. D. M. Spence and J. S. Exell. Grand Rapids: Wm. B. Eerdmans Publishing Co., 1950 (reprint).

Jackson, F. J. Foakes. *The Acts of the Apostles*. "The Moffatt New Testament Commentary." New York: Harper and Brothers, 1931.
Jackson, F. J. Foakes, and Lake, Kirsopp (eds.). *The Beginnings of Christianity*. Part I, "The Acts of the Apostles." 5 vols. London: Macmillan & Co., Ltd., 1920–33. Also 1942 (reprint).
Jamieson, Robert, Fausset, A. R., and Brown, David. *A Commentary Critical Experimental and Practical on the Old and New Testaments*. 6 Vols. (Am. ed.) Grand Rapids: Wm. B. Eerdmans Publishing Co., 1948. Also Grand Rapids: Zondervan Publishing House, n.d. (1 vol.).

Knowling, R. J. "The Acts of the Apostles," *The Expositor's Greek Testament*. Edited by W. R. Nicoll. Grand Rapids: Wm. B. Eerdmans Publishing Co., n.d.
Knox, Ronald A. *A New Testament Commentary*. Vol. II. New York: Sheed & Ward, 1954.

Lange, John Peter. *Commentary on the Holy Scriptures* (Critical, Doctrinal, and Homiletical-Trans. from Ger. and ed. by Philip Schaff) "Acts." Grand Rapids: Zondervan Publishing House, (reprint).
Lechler, G. V., and Gerok, Charles. "The Acts of the Apostles," *A Commentary on the Holy Scriptures*. Edited by John Peter Lange. Translated and edited by Philip Schaff. Grand Rapids: Zondervan Publishing House, n.d.

Lenski, R. C. H. *The Interpretation of the Acts of the Apostles*. Columbus, O.: Wartburg Press, 1944.

Lumby, J. R. *The Acts of the Apostles*. "The Cambridge Bible." Edited by J. J. S. Perowne. Cambridge: University Press, 1890.

———. *The Acts of the Apostles*. "Cambridge Greek Testament." Cambridge: University Press, 1885.

Macaulay, J. C. *A Devotional Commentary on the Acts of the Apostles*. Grand Rapids: Wm. B. Eerdmans Publishing Co., 1946.

McGarvey, J. W. *New Commentary on the Acts of the Apostles*. 2 vols. in 1. Cincinnati: Standard Publishing Co., 1892.

Macgregor, G. H. C. "The Acts of the Apostles" (Exegesis), *Interpreter's Bible*. Edited by G. A. Buttrick *et al.* Vol. IX. New York: Abingdon–Cokesbury Press, 1954.

Maclaren, Alexander. *Exposition of Holy Scripture: The Acts*. Grand Rapids: Wm. B. Eerdmans Publishing Co., 1932 (rep. 1944).

Menzies, Allan. "The Acts of the Apostles," *A Commentary on the Bible*. Edited by A. S. Peake. London: Thomas Nelson and Sons, 1919.

Meyer, H. A. W. *Critical and Exegetical Handbook to the Acts of the Apostles*. Translated from the 4th German ed. by Paton Gloag. Revised and edited by W. P. Dickson. Am. ed. by William Ormiston. New York: Funk & Wagnalls, 1883.

Moorehead, William G. *Outline Studies* (Acts, Romans, I & II Corinthians, Galatians). London & Eden.: Fleming H. Revell, 1902.

Morgan, G. Campbell. *The Acts of the Apostles*. New York: Fleming H. Revell Co., 1924.

Nicoll, W. Robertson, (ed.). *The Expositor's Greek Testament*. Grand Rapids: Wm. B. Eerdmans Publishing Company, n.d. Vol. II.

Olshausen, Hermann. *Biblical Commentary on the New Testament*. 1st Am. ed. by A. C. Kendrick. Vol. III. New York: Sheldon, Blakeman & Co., 1857.

Page, T. E. *Acts of the Apostles*. London: Macmillan and Co., 1886.

Parker, Joseph. *Apostolic Life*. 3 vols. New York: Funk & Wagnalls, 1883–85.

———. *The People's Bible* (Discourses upon the Holy Scriptures), Vols. XXIII–XXV. New York: Funk and Wagnalls Company, 1883.

Plumptre, E. H. "The Acts of the Apostles," *Commentary on the Whole Bible*. Edited by C. J. Ellicott. Vol. VII. Grand Rapids: Zondervan Publishing House, n.d.

Rackham, R. B. *The Acts of the Apostles*. "Westminster Commentaries" (8th ed.). London: Methuen & Co., Ltd., 1919 (1st ed., 1901).

Robertson, A. T. *Word Pictures in the New Testament*. Vol. III. New York: Richard R. Smith, 1930.

Sadler, M. F. *The Acts of the Apostles*. London: G. Bell and Sons, 1887.

Scott, Thomas. *The Holy Bible* (5th ed.). Boston: Crocker and Brewster, 1849.

Simpson, A. B. *The Acts of the Apostles*. "Christ in the Bible Series." Harrisburg, Pa.: Christian Publications, n.d.

Spence, H. D. M. (ed.). *Pulpit Commentary, Acts and Romans*. Grand Rapids: Wm. B. Eerdmans Publishing Company, 1950 (rep.).

Stellhorn, F. W. "Annotations on the Acts of the Apostles." *The Lutheran Commentary*. Edited by H. E. Jacobs. Vol. VI. New York: Christian Literature Co., 1896.

Stokes, G. T. "The Acts of the Apostles." 2 vols. *The Expositor's Bible*. New York: A. C. Armstrong and Son, 1892.

Thomas, David. *Acts of the Apostles: A Homiletic Commentary*. Grand Rapids: Baker Book House, 1955 (reprint of 1870 edition).

Vincent, Marvin R. *Word Studies in the New Testament*. Vol. I. Grand Rapids: Wm. B. Eerdmans Publishing Co., 1946 (1st ed., 1887).

Weiss, Bernhard. *A Commentary on the New Testament*. Translated by G. H. Schodde and E. Wilson. Vol. II. New York: Funk & Wagnalls, 1906.

Wesley, John. *Explanatory Notes upon the New Testament*. London: Epworth Press, 1954

Whedon, D. D. *Commentary on the New Testament*. Vol. III. New York: Hunt & Eaton, 1871.

Whitby, Daniel. "A Commentary on the Gospels and Epistles of the New Testament," *A Critical Commentary and Paraphrase on the Old and New Testament and the Apocrypha*. Edited by Patrick, *et al.* Vol. IV. Philadelphia: Carey and Hart, 1848.

Whitelaw, Thomas. "A Homiletical Commentary on the Acts of the Apostles." *The Preacher's Complete Homiletical Commentary on the New Testament*. New York: Funk & Wagnalls, 1896.

Williams, George. *The Student's Commentary on the Holy Scriptures* (4th ed.). Grand Rapids: Kregel Publications, 1949 (reprint).

Williams, R. R. *The Acts of the Apostles*. "Torch Bible Commentaries." Edited by John Marsh, *et al.* London: SCM Press, 1953.

V. Concordances

Cruden, Alexander. *Cruden's Unabridged Concordance.* Grand Rapids: Baker Book House, 1953.

Ellison, J. W. (ed.). *Nelson's Complete Concordance of the Revised Standard Version.* New York: Thomas Nelson & Sons, 1957.

Englishman's Greek Concordance (9th ed.). London: Samuel Bagster and Sons, 1903.

Hazard, M. C. *A Complete Concordance to the American Standard Version of the Holy Bible.* New York: Thomas Nelson & Sons, 1922.

Moffatt Bible Concordance. New York: Harper & Brothers, 1950.

Moulton, W. F., and Geden, A. S. *A Concordance to the Greek Testament* (3rd ed.). Edinburgh: T. & T. Clark, 1950.

Smith, J. B. *Greek-English Concordance to the New Testament.* Scottdale, Pa.: Herald Press, 1955.

Strong, James. *The Exhaustive Concordance of the Bible.* New York: Abingdon-Cokesbury Press, 1890.

Walker, J. B. R. *The Comprehensive Concordance to the Holy Scriptures.* New York: Macmillan Co., [1929], 1936.

Young, Robert. *Analytical Concordance to the Bible* (22nd Am. ed., revised by W. B. Stevenson). New York: Funk & Wagnalls Co., n.d.

VI. Grammars

Dana, H. E., and Mantey, J. R. *A Manual Grammar of the Greek New Testament.* New York: Macmillan Co., 1927.

Green, Samuel G. *Handbook to the Grammar of the Greek Testament* (rev. ed.). New York: Fleming H. Revell Co., 1912.

Moulton, James H. *A Grammar of New Testament Greek.* Vol. I. Edinburgh: T. & T. Clark, 1906.

Robertson, A. T. *A Grammar of the Greek New Testament in the Light of Historical Research* (5th ed.). New York: Harper & Brothers, 1931 (1st ed., 1914).

Winer, G. B. *A Grammar of the Idiom of the New Testament* (7th ed. by G. Lunemann). Am. ed., J. H. Thayer. Andover: Warren F. Draper, 1870 (1st ed., 1822).

VII. Lexicons

Abbott-Smith, G. *A Manual Greek Lexicon of the New Testament* (2nd ed.). Edinburgh: T. & T. Clark, 1923.

Arndt, W. F., and Gingrich, F. W. *A Greek-English Lexicon of the New Testament and Other Early Christian Literature.* Chicago: University of Chicago Press, 1957.

Cremer, Hermann. *Biblico-Theological Lexicon of New Testament Greek.* Translated from the German of the 2nd edition by William Urwick. Edinburgh: T. & T. Clark, 1878.

Liddell, H. G., and Scott, Robert. *A Greek–English Lexicon.* New edition revised and augmented throughout by Henry S. Jones. Oxford: Clarendon Press, 1940.

Moulton, J. H., and Milligan, George. *The Vocabulary of the Greek Testament Illustrated from the Papyri and Other Non-literary Sources.* Grand Rapids: Wm. B. Eerdmans Publishing Co., 1949.

Thayer, J. H. *A Greek–English Lexicon of the New Testament.* Grimm's Wilke's Clavis Novi Testamenti translated, revised, and enlarged. New York: American Book Co., n.d. (Copyright, 1886, by Harper & Brothers; corrected edition, 1889).

VIII. New Testament Versions

Confraternity Edition of the New Testament. New York: P. J. Kenedy & Sons, 1950.

English Revised Version of *The New Testament.* Oxford: University Press, 1881.

Goodspeed, Edgar J. *The New Testament: An American Translation.* Chicago: University of Chicago Press, 1923.

Holy Bible-Old and New Testaments (ASV). New York: Thomas Nelson and Sons, 1901.

King James Version of *The Holy Bible.* 1611 (1st ed.).

Knox, Ronald. *The New Testament of Our Lord and Saviour Jesus Christ: A New Translation.* New York: Sheed & Ward, 1944.

Moffatt, James. *The New Testament: A New Translation* (rev. ed.). New York: George H. Doran, 1922.

Phillips, J. B. *The Young Church in Action: A Translation of The Acts of the Apostles.* New York: Macmillan Co., 1955.

Revised Standard Version of The New Testament. New York: Thomas Nelson & Sons, 1946.

Spencer, F. A. *The New Testament of Our Lord and Saviour Jesus Christ.* New York: Macmillan Co., 1937.

Verkuyl, Gerrit. *Berkeley Version of The New Testament.* Grand Rapids: Zondervan Publishing Co., n.d.

Wesley, John. *The New Testament.* Introduction by George C. Cell. Philadelphia: John C. Winston Co., 1938 (1st ed., 1755).

Weymouth, R. F. *The New Testament in Modern Speech* (5th ed.). Newly revised by J. A. Robertson. Boston: Pilgrim Press, 1929 (1st ed., 1902).
Williams, Charles B. *The New Testament: A Translation in the Language of the People.* Chicago: Moody Press, 1950 (original edition, 1937).

IX. Other Works Cited

Aberly, John. *An Outline of Missions.* Philadelphia: Muhlenburg Press, 1945.
Andrews, Samuel. *The Life of Our Lord upon the Earth.* Grand Rapids: Zondervan Publishing House, 1954 (reprint).
Angus, S. *The Environment of Early Christianity.* New York: Charles Scribner's Sons, 1915.
Archer, J. K. *Faiths Men Live By.* New York: Thomas Nelson & Sons, 1934.
Aristotle. *On Man in the Universe.* New York: D. van Nostrand Co., Inc., 1943.

Barnett, Albert E. *The New Testament.* New York: Abingdon–Cokesbury Press, 1946.
Blass, Frederick. *Philology of the Gospels.* London: Macmillan Co., 1898.
Bowen, C. R. *Studies in the New Testament.* Edited by R. J. Hutcheon. Chicago: University of Chicago Press, 1936.
Brightman, Edgar Sheffield. *A Philosophy of Religion.* New York: Prentice-Hall, Inc., rep. 1947.
Bringle, F. J., and Grubb, Kenneth G. *World Christian Handbook.* London: World Dominion Press (rev. ed.).
Bruce, F. F. *The Acts of the Apostles.* Chicago: Inter-Varsity Christian Fellowship, 1952.
———. *Second Thoughts on the Dead Sea Scrolls.* Grand Rapids: Wm. B. Eerdmans Publishing Co., 1956.
Burrell, David James and Joseph Dunn. *The Early Church* (Studies in the Acts of the Apostles). New York: American Tract Society, 1897.
Burrows, Millar. *The Dead Sea Scrolls.* New York: Viking Press, 1955.
Burton, Ernest De Witt. *A Critical and Exegetical Commentary on the Epistle to the Galatians.* "International Critical Commentary." Edinburgh: T. & T. Clark, 1921.

Cadbury, Henry J. *The Book of Acts in History.* New York: Harper & Brothers, 1955.
———. *The Making of Luke-Acts.* New York: Macmillan Co., 1927.
Carver, William Owen. *The Bible a Missionary Message.* New York: Fleming H. Revell and Company, 1921.
———. *Missions in the Plan of the Ages.* Nashville: Broadman Press, 1951.
Chadwick, Samuel. *The Way to Pentecost.* Berne, Ind.: Light and Hope Publications, 1937 (reprint).
Chase, Frederick H. *The Credibility of the Book of the Acts of the Apostles.* London: Macmillan Co., 1902.
Clarke, A. C. *The Acts of the Apostles.* Oxford: University Press, 1933.
Clogg, F. B. *An Introduction to the New Testament.* New York: Charles Scribner's Sons, 1937.
Coates, J. R. (ed. and trans.). *Bible Key Words.* New York: Harper & Brothers, 1951.
Conybeare, W. J., and Howson, J. S. *The Life and Epistles of St. Paul.* Hartford, Conn.: S. S. Scranton and Co., 1899.
Cowles, Henry. *The Date of the Acts and the Synoptic Gospels.* New York: Williams and Norgate, J. P. Putman's Sons, 1911.
Creed, J. M. *The Gospel according to St. Luke.* London: Macmillan and Co., 1930.
Cushman, Herbert Ernest. *A Beginner's History of Philosophy.* New York: Houghton Mifflin Company, 1946.

Dalman, G. H. *Jesus-Jeshua.* New York: Macmillan Co., 1929.
———. *The Words of Jesus.* Edinburgh: T. & T. Clark, 1909.
Davies, J. G. *Daily Life of Early Christians.* New York: Duell, Sloan and Pearce, 1953.
Davies, W. D., and Daube, D. (eds.). *The Background of the New Testament and Its Eschatology.* Cambridge: University Press, 1956.
Dibelius, Martin. *A Fresh Approach to the New Testament and Early Christian Literature.* New York: Charles Scribner's Sons, 1936.
———. *Studies in the Acts of the Apostles.* Edited by H. Greenen. New York: Charles Scribner's Sons, 1956.
Dodd, C. H. *According to the Scriptures.* New York: Charles Scribner's Sons, 1953.
Dods, Marcus. *An Introduction to the New Testament.* New York: Thomas Whittaker, 1902.

Earle, Ralph. *The Gospel according to Mark.* Grand Rapids: Zondervan Publishing House, 1957.
Edersheim, Alfred. *The Life and Times of Jesus the Messiah* (8th ed.). 2 vols. New York: Longmans, Green, & Co., 1903.
———. *Sketches of Jewish Social Life in the Days of Christ.* London: Religious Tract Society, 1876.
Eusebius, Pamphilus. *Ecclesiastical History.* Translated by Frederick Cruse. Grand Rapids: Baker Book House, 1955 (reprint).
Exell, Joseph S. *The Biblical Illustrator.* Acts Vol. I. New York: Fleming H. Revell Company, n.d.

Farmer, William R. *Maccabees, Zealots, and Josephus.* New York: Columbia University Press, 1956.
Farrar, F. W. *The Life and Work of St. Paul.* New York: E. P. Dutton & Co., 1896 (Exegesis). London: Cassell, Petter, Galpin and Co., 1879 (Exposition).
———. *Messages of the Books.* New York: Macmillan Co., 1927.
Ferm, Vergilius (ed.). *An Encyclopedia of Religion.* New York: The Philosophical Library, 1943.
Field, F. *Notes on the Translation of the New Testament.* Cambridge: University Press, 1899.

Glover, Robert Hall. *The Bible Basis of Missions.* Los Angeles: Bible House of Los Angeles, 1946.
———. *The Progress of World Wide Missions.* New York: Harper and Brothers, Publishers, 1939.
Goodspeed, Edgar, J. *An Introduction to the New Testament.* Chicago: University of Chicago Press, 1937.
Goodwin, Frank J. *A Harmony and Commentary on the Life of St. Paul.* Grand Rapids: Baker Book House, 1951.
Green, Bryan. *The Practice of Evangelism.* New York: Charles Scribner's Sons, 1955.
Groves, C. P. *The Planting of Christianity in Africa.* Vol. I. London: Lutterworth Press, 1948 (1st ed. 1840).

Harnack, Adolph von. *The Acts of the Apostles.* Translated by J. R. Wilkinson. New York: G. P. Putnam's Sons, 1909.
———. *The Date of the Acts and of the Synoptic Gospels.* Translated by J. R. Wilkinson. New York: G. P. Putnam's Sons, 1911.
———. *Luke the Physician.* Translated by J. R. Wilkinson. Edited by W. D. Morrison. London: Williams & Norgate. New York: G. P. Putnam's Sons, 1907.
———. *The Mission and Expansion of Christianity.* Vol. I, II. New York: G. P. Putnam's Sons, 1908.
Hayes, D. A. *Paul and His Epistles.* New York: Methodist Book Concern, 1915.
Henshaw, T. *New Testament Literature.* London: George Allen and Unwin, 1952.
Higdon, E. K. *New Missionaries for New Days.* St. Louis: The Bethany Press, 1956.
Hobart, W. K. *The Medical Language of St. Luke.* Grand Rapids: Baker Book House, 1954 (original ed., 1882).
Hocking, William Earnest. *Living Religions and a World Faith.* New York: Macmillan Company, 1940.
Huffman, Jasper A. *Golden Treasures from the Greek New Testament for English Readers.* Winona Lake: Standard Press, 1951.

Josephus, Flavius. *Works.* Translated by William Whiston. Philadelphia: Henry T. Coates & Co., n.d. (also Exposition, Philadelphia: David McKay, n.d.)

Kent, Charles F. *The Work and Teachings of the Apostles.* New York: Charles Scribner's Sons, 1916.
Kilgour, R. *The Bible throughout the World.* London: World Dominion Press, 1939.
Klausner, Joseph. *From Jesus to Paul.* Translated from the Hebrew by W. F. Stinespring. New York: Macmillan Co., 1943.
Knox, John. *Marcion and the New Testament.* Chicago: University of Chicago Press, 1942.
Knox, Wilfred L. *The Acts of the Apostles.* Cambridge: University Press, 1948.
Kraemer, Hendrick. *The Christian Message in a Non-Chtistian World.* London: The Edinburg House Press, 1938.

Lake, Kirsopp. *The Earlier Epistles of St. Paul.* London: Rivingtons, 1911.
Lake, Kirsopp, and Lake, Silva. *An Introduction to the New Testament.* New York: Harper & Brothers, 1937.
Latourette, Kenneth Scott. *A History of the Expansion of Christianity,* Vol. I. New York: Harper and Brothers, 1937.
Lewis, C. S. *The Screwtape Letters.* New York: Macmillan Co., 1948.
Lewis, Edwin. *The Creator and the Adversary.* New York: Abingdon–Cokesbury Press, 1948.
Lietzmann, Hans. *The Beginnings of the Christian Church,* Vol. I. New York: Charles Scribner's Sons, 1949.
Lightfoot, J. B. *St. Paul's Epistle to the Galatians.* Grand Rapids: Zondervan Publishing House, n.d.
———. *St. Paul's Epistle to the Philippians.* London: Macmillan Co., 1894.
Love, Julian Price. *The Missionary Message of the Bible.* New York: Macmillan Company, 1941.
Luckock, H. M. *Footprints of the Apostles as Traced by St. Luke in the Acts.* London, 1897.

Mackie, G. M. *Bible Manners and Customs.* London: A. and C. Black, Ltd., 1936.
Major, H. D. A., Manson, T. W., and Wright, C. J. *The Mission and Message of Jesus.* New York: E. P. Dutton and Co., 1938.
Mathews, Basil. *Forward through the Ages.* New York: Friendship Press, 1951.
Mayor, J. B. *The Epistle of St. James.* Grand Rapids: Zondervan Publishing House, 1954 (reprint).
Moe, Olaf. *The Apostle Paul.* Translated by L. A. Vigness. Minneapolis: Augsburg Publishing House, 1950.

Moffatt, James. *An Introduction to the Literature of the New Testament* (3rd ed.). New York: Charles Scribner's Sons, 1918.
Morgan, G. Campbell. *The Missionary Manifesto*. New York: Fleming H. Revell Co., 1909.
Morton, H. V. *In the Steps of St. Paul*. New York: Dodd, Mead & Co., 1936.
Mould, Elmer W. K. *Essentials of Bible History* (rev. ed.). New York: T. Nelson & Sons, 1951.
Mowinckel, S. *He That Cometh*. Translated by G. W. Anderson. New York: Abingdon Press, 1954.

Neighbour, R. E. *The Baptism in the Holy Ghost, or, Before and after Pentecost*. Cleveland: The Union Gospel Press, 1930.

Peake, Arthur S. *A Critical Introduction to the New Testament*. New York: Charles Scribner's Sons, 1911.
———. *The People and the Book*. Oxford: Clarendon Press, 1925.
Pierson, Arthur T. *The Acts of the Holy Spirit*. New York: Fleming H. Revell Company, 1898.
Plummer, Alfred. *A Critical and Exegetical Commentary on the Gospel According to St. Luke*. "International Critical Commentary." New York: Charles Scribner's Sons, 1896.

Ramsay, W. M. *The Bearing of Recent Discovery on the Trustworthiness of the New Testament*. Grand Rapids: Baker Book House, 1953 (reprint).
———. *The Church in the Roman Empire, before A.D.* 170. Grand Rapids: Baker Book House, 1954 (1st ed. 1897).
———. *The Cities of St. Paul*. Grand Rapids: Baker Book House, 1949 (reprint).
———. *St. Paul the Traveller and the Roman Citizen*. Grand Rapids: Baker Book House, 1949 (1st ed., 1895).
———. *Was Christ Born at Bethlehem?* New York: G. P. Putnam's Sons, 1898.
Robertson, A. T. *A Harmony of the Gospels*. New York: George Doran Co., 1922.
———. *Luke the Historian in the Light of Research*. New York: Charles Scribner's Sons, 1920.
Robinson, Benjamin Willard. *The Life of Paul*. Chicago: University of Chicago Press, 1928 (rep. 1946).
Rowlingson, Donald. *Introduction to New Testament Study*. New York: Macmillan Co., 1956.

Sabatier, A. *The Apostle Paul*. London: Hodder and Stoughton, Ltd., 1903.
Saltau, T. Stanley. *Missions at the Crossroads*. Grand Rapids: Baker Book House, 1954.
Schaff, Philip. *The Nicene and Post-Nicene Fathers of the Christian Church*. Grand Rapids: Wm. B. Eerdmans Publishing Company, (rep. 1956).
Schmidt, Wilhelm. *High Gods in North America*. Oxford: University Press, 1933.
———. *The Origin and Growth of Religion: Facts and Theories*. Trans. H. J. Rose, New York: Dial, 1935.
Schürer, Emil. *A History of the Jewish People in the Time of Jesus Christ*. 2 vols. Edinburgh: T. & T. Clark, 1885.
Schweitzer, Albert. *The Mysticism of Paul the Apostle*. Translated by W. Montgomery. New York: Henry Holt and Co., 1931.
Scott, E. F. *The Literature of the New Testament*. New York: Columbia University Press, 1936.
Scroggie, W. Graham. *Know Your Bible*. Vol. II. London: Pickering and Inglis, Ltd., 1940, and New York: Loizeaux Bros., n.d.
Selwyn, E. G. *The First Epistle of Peter* (2nd ed.). London: Macmillan & Co., Ltd., 1947.
Smith, George Adam. *The Historical Geography of the Holy Land* (16th ed.). New York: George H. Doran, 1919.
Smith, James. *The Voyage and Shipwreck of St. Paul* (4th ed.). London. Longmans, Green, and Co., 1880.
Soper, Edmund Davison. *The Philosophy of the Christian World Mission*. New York: Abingdon–Cokesbury Press, 1943.
Stendahl, Krister (ed.). *The Scrolls and the New Testament*. New York: Harper & Brothers, 1957.
Stonehouse, N. B. *Paul before the Areopagus*. Grand Rapids: Wm. B. Eerdmans Publishing Co., 1957.
Streeter, B. H. *The Four Gospels*. London: Macmillan and Co., 1936.

Taylor, William M. *Paul the Missionary*. New York: Richard R. Smith, Inc. 1930.
Thiessen, Henry C. *Introduction to the New Testament*. Grand Rapids: Wm. B. Eerdmans Publishing Co., 1943.
Torrey, C. C. *The Composition and Date of Acts*. Cambridge: Harvard University Press, 1916.
Trench, Richard Chenevix. *Notes on the Parables of Our Lord*. Philadelphia: William Sychelmoore, n.d.
———. *Synonyms of the New Testament*. Grand Rapids: Wm. B. Eerdmans Publishing Co., 1947.
Turnbull, Grace H. *Tongues of Fire: A Bible of Sacred Scriptures of the Pagan World*. New York: Macmillan Co., 1929.

Van Baalen, J. K. *The Chaos of Cults*. Grand Rapids: Wm. B. Eerdmans Publishing Co., 1949.

Walker, James. *Philosophy of the Plan of Salvation.* New York: Chautauqua Press, 1887.
Wright, J. Stafford. *Man in the Process of Time.* Grand Rapids: Wm. B. Eerdmans Publishing Co., 1956.
Zahn, Theodor. *Introduction to the New Testament.* Translated by John Trout, *et al.* Grand Rapids: Kregel Publications, 1953 (reprint).
Zeller, Eduard. *The Contents and Origin of the Acts of the Apostles.* Translated by Joseph Dare. London: Williams & Norgate, 1875.
Zwemer, Samuel. *Into All the World.* Grand Rapids: Zondervan Publishing House, 1943.
———. *The Origin of Religion.* New York: Loizeaux Brothers, 1945.

ACKNOWLEDGMENTS

Grateful acknowledgment is made to the following authors and publishers for permission granted to quote from their publications:

Bruce, F. F. *A Commentary on the Book of the Acts.* "The New International Commentary on the New Testament." Grand Rapids: Wm. B. Eerdmans Publishing Co., 1954.

Cushman, Herbert Ernest. *A Beginner's History of Philosophy.* New York: Houghton Mifflin Company, 1946.

Dummelow, J. R. *A Commentary on the Holy Bible.* New York: Macmillan Co., 1936 (rep. 1951).

Finegan, Jack. *Light From the Ancient Past.* Princeton: University Press, 1946.

Greenlee, Harold. "Christian Communism in the Book of Acts." *The Asbury Seminarian.* Wilmore, Ky.: Fall & Winter, 1950.

C. P. Groves. *The Planting of Christianity in Africa,* Lutterworth Press, London, U.S. Distributor, Allenson, Naperville, Illinois.

Hastings, James (ed.). *A Dictionary of the Bible.* New York: Charles Scribner's Sons, 1898.

Huffman, Jasper A. *Golden Treasures from the Greek New Testament for English Readers.* Winona Lake: Standard Press, 1951.

Jackson, F. J. Foakes, and Lake, Kirsopp (eds.). *The Beginnings of Christianity.* Part I, "The Acts of the Apostles." New York: Macmillan Company.

Kraeling, Emil G. *Rand McNally Bible Atlas.* Chicago: Rand McNally & Co., 1956.

Lietzman, Hans. *The Beginnings of the Christian Church,* Vol. I. New York: Charles Scribner's Sons, 1949.

Macgregor, G. H. C. "The Acts of the Apostles" (Exegesis) in *The Interpreter's Bible,* Vol. IX. New York: Abingdon Press, 1954.

Miller, Madeline S. and J. Lane. From: *Harper's Bible Dictionary,* Copyright 1952, 1954, 1955, 1956, 1958 by Harper & Brothers. Used by permission.

Morgan, G. Campbell. *The Missionary Manifesto.* New York: Fleming H. Revell Co., 1909.

———. *The Acts of the Apostles.* New York: Fleming H. Revell Co., 1924.

Mould, Elmer W. K. *Essentials of Bible History* (rev. ed.). New York: Ronald Press, 1951.

Phillips, J. B. *The Young Church in Action: A Translation of The Acts of the Apostles.* New York: Macmillan Co., 1955.

Rackham, R. B. *The Acts of the Apostles.* "Westminster Commentaries" (8th ed.). London: Methuen & Co., Ltd., 1919.

Robertson, A. T. *Luke the Historian in the Light of Research.* New York: Charles Scribner's Sons, 1920.

Robinson, Benjamin Willard. *The Life of Paul.* Chicago: University of Chicago Press, 1928 (rep. 1946).

Schmidt, Wilhelm. *High Gods in North America.* Oxford: University Press, 1933.

Weymouth, R. F. From: *Weymouth's New Testament in Modern Speech.* Harper & Brothers. Used by permission.

Williams, Charles B. *The New Testament: A Translation in the Language of the People.* Chicago: Moody Press, 1950.

Wright, J. Stafford. *Man in the Process of Time.* Grand Rapids: Wm. B. Eerdmans Publishing Co., 1956.

Zwemer, Samuel. *The Origin of Religion.* New York: Loizeaux Brothers, 1945.

CPSIA information can be obtained at www.ICGtesting.com
Printed in the USA
LVOW10s2000230716

497492LV00007BA/19/P

9 780880 190503